The Encyclopedia of
IRELAND

The Encyclopedia of
IRELAND

An A–Z guide to its people, places, history, and culture

Ciaran Brady

General Editor

OXFORD
UNIVERSITY PRESS

OXFORD
UNIVERSITY PRESS

Published in the United States of America and Canada by
Oxford University Press, Inc.
198 Madison Avenue
New York, NY 10016
www.oup.com

Library of Congress Cataloging-in-Publication Data available upon request
ISBN: 0-19-521685-7

Typesetting by Tradespools Ltd, Frome, Somerset

Printed and bound in Slovenia by
DELO-Tiskarna

Editorial Director
Hilary McGlynn

Managing Editor
Elena Softley

Project Manager
Barbara Fraser

Text editors and proofreaders
Andrew Bacon
Clare Collinson
Katie Emblen
Elizabeth Martyn
Sue Purkis
Edith Summerhayes
Catherine Thompson

Technical editors
Tracey Auden
Claire Lishman

Picture research
Elizabeth Loving

Cartography
Olive Pearson

Page design
Paul Saunders

Production Manager
John Normansell

Design Manager
Lenn Darroux

PREFACE

Mention Ireland and, for many, an immediate image springs to mind, a montage made up of rolling green hills, rain, Guinness, Dublin, city of James Joyce, and the native people who effortlessly blend philosophy and passion with a wicked sense of humour. Such images are not in themselves wrong, but they are often misleading and, more importantly, they obscure complex forces underlying the character of modern Ireland.

Though academic works of reference specializing in Irish history and literature have been produced recently, there has been as yet no up-to-date, single-volume reference work that provides an authoritative and informative guide to Irish cultural, intellectual, and public life. The aim of this book is to answer that need. Compiled and written almost exclusively by experts living and working in Ireland, supported by a number of North American academics specializing in Irish studies, it serves as an introduction and presents a considered evaluation of the most important people, topics, and themes that have contributed to Irish culture.

While detailed attention has been paid to contemporary Ireland, a large part of the encyclopedia is properly concerned with the island's complex and troubled history. Every effort has been made to supply our readers – whether they are strangers to Irish history or already acquainted with its debates and controversies – with the most balanced account possible. To this end we have sought to provide some secure scaffolding to enable readers to find their way around the subject with confidence. The extensive chronology at the back of the book, with cross-references to main entries, aims to put events into perspective in the most straightforward and objective way. In the A to Z entries themselves, every effort has been made to indicate areas of dispute and debate, where they exist. Additional material is provided in a wide range of feature essays – on topics from sport and music to Irish republicanism and Ireland's economic revival – and in a selection of telling quotations both by and about the Irish.

In keeping to the confines of a single volume, difficult decisions have had to be made. Generally, only the most significant figures who have contributed to Ireland's historical and cultural development have been included as separate entries. To have earned a main entry, a person must either have been Irish-born, and been significant in Ireland or on the world stage, or made their mark on Ireland, having been born elsewhere. Some of the emigrants included left at a young age, but their Irish origins are judged to have had a deep influence on how they lived their lives. In several areas, general entries include mention of a range of people and their activities and in each case we have sought to supply the basic facts concerning their careers. For places of contemporary importance, a threshold population of 3,000 has been applied, but many smaller settlements with special historical or cultural importance feature too, as do archaeological sites and outstanding natural features. Institutions have also been included but, given the constraints of space, selection has been made only from amongst those which play or have played a unique role in Irish life and culture.

In the last decade, the face of Ireland has changed to the extent of being well nigh unrecognizable. Taking into account those changes, this new encyclopedia aims to be both timely and useful not just for those coming to Ireland for the first time, but also for those more familiar with the country, for whom recent developments are possibly even more astonishing. It is our hope that *The Encyclopedia of Ireland* enables readers to look afresh at this rich, diverse, and infinitely surprising island.

CB
July 2000

CONTENTS

CONTRIBUTORS

General editor
Ciaran Brady, Department of Modern History, Trinity College, Dublin

Subject editors and contributors
Dick Ahlstrom, *Irish Times*
Catherine Bates, Limerick School of Art
Allan Blackstock, Queen's University of Belfast
Ciaran Brady, Department of Modern History, Trinity College, Dublin
Tim Campbell, architectural consultant
Dennis Carroll, Trinity College, Dublin
Ian Chilvers, freelance writer
Jim Clancy, freelance journalist
Charles Doherty, University College, Dublin
Sean Dorren, freelance journalist
Seán Duffy, Department of Medieval History, Trinity College, Dublin
Danine Farquharson, Department of English, Memorial University of Newfoundland, Canada
Catherine E Foley, The Irish World Music Centre, University of Limerick
Patrick Geoghegan, Department of Modern History, Trinity College, Dublin
Angie Gleason, Department of Medieval History, Trinity College, Dublin
John Horgan, Department of Communications, Dublin City University
Sandra Joyce, Irish World Music Centre, University of Limerick
Niall Keegan, Irish World Music Centre, University of Limerick
Tom Kelley, Department of Modern History, Trinity College, Dublin
Rory Kerr, freelance journalist
Carla King, Department of History, St Patrick's College, Drumcondra, Dublin
Brigid Laffan, Dublin European Institute, University College Dublin
Michael Marsh, Department of Political Science, Trinity College, Dublin
Tony McCarthy, owner-editor of *Irish Roots* magazine
Fearghal McGarry, Department of Modern History, Trinity College, Dublin
Stuart Marshall, British Council, Manchester
Rebecca Minch, National College of Art and Design, Dublin
Janet Nolan, Department of History, Loyola University, Chicago, USA
Alan O'Day, University of North London
Thomas O'Connor, National University of Ireland, Maynooth
Dáithí Ó hÓgáin, Department of Irish Folklore, University College, Dublin
Susan M Parkes, Department of Education, Trinity College, Dublin
Oliver P Rafferty SJ, St Patrick's College, Maynooth
Ben Ramos, freelance writer
Kevin Rockett, Trinity College, Dublin
Stephen Royle, School of Geography, Queen's University of Belfast
Laura Smethurst, formerly of University of Cork
Bruce Stewart, School of Languages and Literature, University of Ulster at Coleraine
Cliff Taylor, *Irish Times*
Karen Vandevelde, National University of Ireland, Galway
Mark Walker, Chester College of Higher Education, UK
Emer Williams, National College of Art and Design, Dublin

IRELAND – PHYSICAL

▲ peak (height in metres)
━━ national boundary

ATLANTIC
OCEAN

Malin Head
Giant's Causeway
Rathlin I.
Cardonagh
Coleraine
NORTHERN IRELAND
Ballymoney
Errigal ▲752
L. Foyle
Letterkenny
Derry
Sperrin Mts.
Bann
Antrim Hills
Larne
U L S T E R
Glenties
Lifford
Strabane
Magherafelt
Ballymena
Carrickfergus
Blue Stack Mts.
Antrim
Donegal
Foyle
Omagh
Lough Neagh
Belfast
Bangor
Belfast Lough
Donegal Bay
Lower Lough Erne
Lurgan
Lagan
Lisburn
Ards Peninsula
Blackwater
Portadown
Enniskillen
Armagh
Ardglass
Strangford Lough
Erris Head
Sligo Bay
Sligo
Upper Lough Erne
Monaghan
Newry
Mourne Mts.
852 ▲ Slieve Donard
Belmullet
Erne
Cavan
Dundalk
Blacksod Bay
Lough Conn
Ballina
Charlestown
Carrick-on-Shannon
Dundalk Bay
Nephin ▲806
Castlebar
R E P U B L I C
Longford
Kells
Drogheda
Irish Sea
Achill I.
Clew Bay
Westport
C O N N A U G H T
Shannon
Roscommon
Lough Ree
Navan
Lough Mask
Tuam
Suck
Mullingar
Swords
Connemara
Lough Corrib
O F
Athlone
Boyne
Leixlip
Slyne Head
Clifden
Ballinasloe
Brosna
Tullamore
Dublin
Dublin Bay
Galway
Loughrea
Liffey
Naas
Dún Laoghaire
Aran Islands
Galway Bay
Bray
Burren
Lough Derg
L E I N S T E R
Portlaoise
Wicklow Mts.
926
Wicklow
Cliffs of Moher
Roscrea
Lugnaquilla Mountain
Ennis
Nenagh
Barrow
Carlow
Arklow
Kilkee
Limerick
I R E L A N D
Kilkenny
Mt. Leinster ▲795
Loop Head
Slaney
Mouth of the Shannon
Listowel
Tipperary
Cashel
Nore
Enniscorthy
Tralee Bay
M U N S T E R
Clonmel
Suir
New Ross
Great Blasket I.
Tralee
Galtee Mts.
Waterford
Wexford
Dingle Bay
Blackwater
Comeragh Mts.
Tramore
Rosslare
Carnsore Point
Carrantuohill ▲1041
Killarney
Boggeragh Mts.
Youghal
Dungarvan
Valencia I.
Macgillycuddy's Reeks
Kenmare
Macroom
Lee
Cork
Cobh
Caha Mts.
Bandon
Kinsale
Bantry
Dursey Head
Bantry Bay
Skibbereen
Cape Clear

| 0 | 30 mi |
| 0 | 60 km |

IRELAND – COUNTIES

national boundary
county boundary

0   30 mi
0   60 km

NORTHERN IRELAND

DONEGAL

DERRY

ANTRIM

TYRONE

Belfast

DOWN

FERMANAGH

ARMAGH

MONAGHAN

SLIGO

LEITRIM

CAVAN

LOUTH

MAYO

ROSCOMMON

LONGFORD

WESTMEATH

MEATH

GALWAY

OFFALY

KILDARE

Dublin

REPUBLIC OF IRELAND

CLARE

LAOIS

WICKLOW

TIPPERARY

CARLOW

LIMERICK

KILKENNY

WEXFORD

KERRY

CORK

WATERFORD

ABBEY THEATRE

Playhouse in Dublin, associated with the literary revival of the early 1900s, that was part of a general cultural revival in Ireland. The theatre opened in 1904 and staged the works of a number of Irish dramatists, including Lady Gregory, W B Yeats, J M Synge, and Seán O'Casey. Burned down in 1951, the Abbey Theatre was rebuilt in 1966.

Financed by Annie Horniman, the theatre was built to house the Irish National Theatre Society, formed in 1901 by W G Fay, Yeats, and Lady Gregory to perform the plays of the new Irish dramatists. The theatre's licence was held by Lady Gregory and for most of the early years she and Yeats were its only directors. It soon became self-supporting and made a name for itself as a specialized repertory theatre with well-acted plays of fine quality. Among its early authors, apart from Yeats and Lady Gregory, were J M Synge, Padraic Colum, George Fitzmaurice, and George Bernard Shaw.

The company toured in England and the USA, where its excellence in production and acting had a profound influence in the years before 1914. The theatre survived the troubles of World War I, and in later years produced the early plays of Seán O'Casey. A number of actors graduated from its ranks, including Sara Allgood and Arthur Sinclair. An influx of young dramatists in the 1920s and 1930s deflected the Abbey from poetic to realistic drama, but standards remained high in spite of the loss of the theatre building in 1951 from fire. The company played at the Queen's Theatre until the new Abbey Theatre opened in 1966.

ABBEY THEATRE *Lady Gregory, an energetic administrator, fund-raiser, and dramatist, managed the Abbey Theatre with W B Yeats for almost 30 years. Her own plays ranged from comedies based on rural Irish life to tragedies dealing with moments that proved decisive to Irish history.*

From the 1960s onwards, the Abbey Theatre made a series of highly innovative departures as it embraced the new Irish drama created by Tom Murphy, Thomas Kilroy, Frank McGuinness, Sebastian Barry, Marina Carr, and others, without abandoning its hold on the established repertoire associated with playwrights such as Seán O'Casey and T C Murray. Actors such as Donal McCann and Fiona Shaw succeeded Cyril Cusack, Siobhan McKenna, and F J McCormick from previous generations. The Abbey continues to tour successfully with plays by Brian Friel, Conor MacPherson, and others. (See ⇨theatre, 20th century.)

ABSENTEEISM

The widespread practice of Irish landowners residing abroad, which became an enduring political and social problem. As early as 1360, King Edward III of England was petitioned with a complaint that five-sixths of the land was in absentee hands. Despite frequent attempts to persuade landlords to reside in Ireland, the demands of politics and other concerns prevented any resolution of the problem until the 19th century.

The absentee landlords were usually portrayed in a negative light, the popular perception being that they lived prosperously in England off their income from Ireland. This was challenged by the Irish politician Edmund Burke and others in the 18th century, when a tax on absentee landlords was proposed. Burke argued that landlords should be free to reside wherever they wanted to and look after the greater interests of empire. Nevertheless, absenteeism remained a major perceived grievance in Ireland well into the 19th century when a series of Land Acts allowed the tenants to buy the land, thus resolving the centuries-old problem.

Although absenteeism was usually equated with bad management, this was often not the case, and many estates prospered despite the irregular presence of the landowner.

ACHILL ISLAND (or EAGLE ISLAND)

Largest of the Irish islands, off County Mayo; area 148 sq km/57 sq mi; population (1996) 976. It has mountain peaks rising to over 610 m/2,000 ft, moorland, and fine cliffs and beaches. It has been connected to the mainland by a bridge since 1888.

ADAIR, JAMES (c. 1709–c. 1783)

Trader and historian of the American Indians, who emigrated from County Antrim to South Carolina in 1735. His intensive dealings with the Cherokees, Chickasaws, and other American Indian tribes, among whom he lived for 40 years, formed the subject of his *History of the American Indians* (1755). Though his work, which includes the theory that American

ACHILL ISLAND *Magically peaceful and unspoilt, the moorland beauty of Achill Island has exerted a strong pull over writers and poets. Nobel prize-winner Heinrich Böll had a cottage at the foot of Mount Slievemore, while J M Synge, Louis MacNiece, and Graham Greene have all sought inspiration here.*

Indians came from ten lost tribes, was inaccurate and misleading, it remains a valuable source for the relations between American Indians and Southern colonists in the 18th century.

ADAMS, GERRY (GERARD) (1948–)

Northern Irish politician, president of ⇨Sinn Féin (the political wing of the Irish Republican Army, IRA) from 1978. Adams was born in Belfast, the son of an IRA activist. He was elected member of parliament for Belfast West in 1983 but declined to take up his Westminster seat, as he refused to take an oath of allegiance to the British queen. He lost his seat in 1992 but regained it in 1997, still refusing to sit in the Westminster parliament. He has been a key figure in Irish peace negotiations. In 1994 he was the main

Sinn Féin believe the violence we have seen must be for all of us now a thing of the past – over, done with and gone.

GERRY ADAMS A statement – approved by the British, Irish, and US governments – issued on the eve of President Clinton's visit to Ireland, September 1998.

~

architect of the IRA ceasefire and in 1997 Adams entered into multiparty talks with the British government which, on Good Friday, 10 April 1998, resulted in an agreement accepted by all parties and subsequently endorsed in referenda held simultaneously in Northern Ireland and in the Irish Republic.

Adams became involved with Northern Ireland politics from an early age. In 1971 he was allegedly given his first IRA command, the 2nd Battalion, Belfast brigade. From 1994 he travelled widely, particularly to the USA, to promote the cause of Sinn Féin and all-Ireland integration.

ADARE MANOR

Large house in the Tudor style at Adare, County Limerick. The original house was probably built in the 1720s for the 1st Earl of Dunraven, Valentine Quinn. It was enlarged from 1832 by the 2nd Earl of Dunraven in the Tudor style with assistance from the architect James Pain. Later the English architect A W N Pugin was employed to design interior details and, following his death in 1852, P C Hardwick continued the work. Adare boasts some of the most impressive interiors in Ireland, including a Great Gallery which contains a fine stained-glass window by Thomas Willement and an imposing timbered roof. The house was finally completed by 1862 and is now a hotel.

AGRICULTURE

See feature essay on Irish agriculture, page 4.

AHERN, BERTIE (1951–)

Politician, Taoiseach (prime minister) from 1997, leader of Fianna Fáil from 1994. Born in Dublin, Ahern practised as an accountant before becoming active in politics. After the May 1997 election he formed a minority government as Ireland's youngest Taoiseach. His promotion of peace negotiations culminated in the 1998 Good Friday Agreement between Northern Ireland's contending parties, which received 94% backing in a referendum in the Republic of Ireland in May 1998. Following the devolution of Northern Ireland government from Westminster on 2 December 1999, he rescinded those articles of the 1937 Irish constitution that staked a territorial claim to the north, and led the Irish delegation to the first north-south ministerial council.

After entering the Dáil (parliament) in 1977,

Ahern became chief whip in Charles Haughey's short-lived minority government of 1982. When Fianna Fáil returned to power, he was minister for labour 1987–91 and minister for finance 1991–94. Meanwhile, Albert Reynolds had taken over the Fianna Fáil leadership and formed successive coalitions with the Progressive Democrats and Labour. In 1994 Reynolds lost Labour support and was forced to resign. He also surrendered the Fianna Fáil leadership and Ahern was elected as his successor.

Ahern was educated at the Rathmines College of Commerce and University College, Dublin, before qualifying as an accountant. In 1979 he started serving on Dublin City Council, becoming lord mayor 1986–87.

AIKEN, FRANK (1898–1983)

Activist, politician, and founder member of Fianna Fáil, see ⇨Anglo-Irish Treaty. He was a major force in the development of Irish foreign policy in the 1950s and 1960s.

AIKENHEAD, MARY (1787–1858)

Catholic nun, founder of the Irish Sisters of Charity in 1816. She was appointed superior general of the order, a position she held for the remainder of her life. She supervised the foundation of eight convents in Ireland, St Vincent's Hospital, and an asylum, despite being confined to bed in her later years.

Born in County Cork and raised a Protestant, Aikenhead converted to Catholicism after the death of her father when she was 16. Following the death of her mother, she was invited by Archbishop Daniel Murray to form a congregation of Sisters of Charity in Ireland, the first of its kind in the country. After training to be a nun in York, England, for three years, she returned to Ireland and founded the order at North William Street in Dublin.

ALEXANDER, CECIL FRANCES

(born Humphreys) (1818–1895)

Poet and hymn writer, born in County Wicklow. She published *Verses for Holy Seasons* (1846) and the popular *Hymns for Little Children* (1848), which included such well-known works as 'All Things Bright and Beautiful', 'Once in Royal David's City', and 'There is a Green Hill Far Away'. She also wrote a number of ballads on Irish historical themes. She was married to Bishop William Alexander (1824–1911).

AGRICULTURE – SHAPED BY CLIMATE, TENANCY, AND MARKET NEEDS

by Carla King

The pattern of agriculture in Ireland has been shaped by the interaction of three main factors: physical conditions, particularly soil and climate, which have tended to predispose the island to grass production; land tenure arrangements; and market trends.

pastoral to plantation models

In early times, Irish agriculture was predominantly pastoral and landholding remained communal for longer than on mainland Europe, where ploughing for crop production became established. Prior to the Elizabethan conquest the country maintained this traditional pastoral pattern, apart from pockets of ploughing-based agriculture on land in the south and east, where Anglo-Norman influence was strong. The effects of Elizabethan and subsequent plantations, coupled with expanding markets, led to the emergence of a landlord–tenant system and a more mixed pattern of agriculture.

expanding markets

With the growth of trans-Atlantic migration in the 17th and 18th centuries, a provisioning trade to the North American colonies emerged, particularly in Munster, that encouraged the production of salted meat and butter; this activity, along with trade to Europe, was fuelled by the Cattle Acts (1663, 1671) which prohibited livestock imports to Britain until 1758–59, when domestic supply fell behind demand. At this time industrialization and urbanization in Britain stimulated production for the British market, so that Ireland became a producer of agricultural raw materials for the British consumer. Buoyant prices in the late 18th and early 19th centuries, coupled with a very rapid population rise in Ireland offering cheap and abundant labour, caused a switch to concentration on grain production as a cash crop and potato cultivation for subsistence. With the population at its peak, a good deal of marginal land was brought into cultivation. Whereas Irish land was owned in often quite large estates, tenant holdings remained very small by European standards.

Moreover, owing to the effects of plantation and the operation of the anti-Catholic penal laws of the 18th century, there was a wider social and cultural distance between landlords and their tenants and sub-tenants, with frequent absenteeism on the part of landlords. This meant that landlord investment in agricultural improvement on Irish estates was much more limited than in Britain.

famine and post-famine years

The crisis of the Great Famine (historically dated 1845–49, though recently considered as lasting until 1852), that occurred when the potato harvest was destroyed by potato blight, brought about a dramatic fall in population from 8.18 million in 1841 to 6.55 million a

The agricultural show, like this one at Killadysert, County Clare, is still a significant feature of Irish rural life. With the transformation of farming brought about by technological change, these familiar sights may become less common in future.

decade later. That contraction, which continued through prolonged high levels of emigration, allowed the consolidation of farms into larger units. This occurred almost simultaneously with a shift in market conditions against tillage. The repeal of the Corn Laws in 1846, which removed tariffs on imported grain, resulted in lower grain prices on the British market. In addition, generally rising living standards among the British working class allowed a greater consumption of meat and therefore an increase in opportunities for meat producers. For these reasons, post-famine agriculture showed a marked trend from tillage to pasture, with a pattern emerging in which the younger stock was raised in the west and midlands and sold on to the richer land of Meath and Kildare for fattening, following which cattle were shipped live to British markets. Recent research has tended to suggest that productivity levels of Irish agriculture were higher and market orientation greater than was once thought.

agricultural unrest

From the mid-18th century rural society was characterized by sporadic violence, much of it carried out by agrarian secret organizations, often referred to as Whiteboys or Ribbon societies. They engaged in acts such as sending threatening notices, maiming cattle, burning hay, and making personal assaults against landlords, their agents, and larger tenant farmers in an effort to prevent eviction, discourage tenants from occupying holdings from which other tenants had been evicted, and keep down rents.

A more public and peaceful effort emerged in the years following the Great Famine, when the better-off farmers formed tenant associations, aimed at reforming the law to provide more protection for tenants. Various associations came together in 1850 to form the Tenant League, which worked with the Irish Independent Party at Westminster to express farmers' grievances. However, the party and league split in 1859.

the land wars

With the onset of the agricultural depression of the late 1870s, a new type of organization emerged with the establishment of the Irish National Land League in 1879. This was a mass movement of farmers led by Michael Davitt, Charles Stewart Parnell, and others, set up in order to put peaceful pressure on landlords to reduce rents and refrain from evicting tenants for non-payment of rent. It grew very rapidly, Davitt estimating that by 1881 it had about 200,000 members in 1,000 branches, although this may have been an overestimate. Using the tactic of the boycott (a form of economic ostracism first applied to Captain Boycott, a Mayo land agent), the league aimed to put moral pressure on landlords and their agents. It also maintained close links with the Irish Parliamentary Party at Westminster, led by Parnell. The first phase of the land wars that ensued lasted from 1879 to 1882, and resulted in the granting of reform that recognized a dual interest in the land on the part of both landlord and tenant. The next period of confrontation occurred with the Plan of Campaign to achieve fair rents, launched in 1886. This continued until the dispute over Parnell's divorce case in 1890 and shortage of funds led to its abandonment. A third phase of militancy followed in 1898, lasting until 1903. It was initiated by William O'Brien among small farmers in the disadvantaged regions of the west of Ireland and was directed both against landlords and in opposition to large cattle graziers, whose efforts to obtain tracts of land cut across the interests of smaller and economically weaker tenants.

the 20th century

Ultimately, the land wars of the late 19th century resulted in the introduction of peasant proprietorship. This change in tenure did not, however, bring about any major alterations in production; rather it tended to reinforce a pattern of conservative practices and an immobile land market. Despite the efforts of various bodies such as the cooperative movement and the Department of Agriculture and Technical Instruction to encourage farmers to diversify, Irish agriculture remained heavily dependent on cattle and dairy farming in the 20th century.

European Union

Ireland's entry into the European Economic Community, now the European Union (EU), in January 1973 provided greater agricultural investment and subsidies and has brought much wider markets for produce. Irish farmers have responded, some modernizing their production, others diversifying into areas such as market gardening, agri-tourism (notably accommodation), forestry, and fish and oyster farming. Sheep farming has also expanded.

There remain, however, quite a number of small farms that face difficulty and marginalization, particularly given the impending reduction or removal of subsidies to farmers for growing certain crops, under the winding down of the EU Common Agricultural Policy.

This, combined with increased competition arising from the accession to the EU of countries in central and eastern Europe, suggests an uncertain future for Irish agriculture and the likely continuation of a pattern of population drift from the land and consolidation of farms.

ALLEN, LOUGH

Lake in County Leitrim, on the upper course of the River Shannon. It is 11 km/7 mi long and 5 km/3 mi wide.

The lough is surrounded by mountains, of which Slieve Anierin (586 m/1,922 ft) is the highest. On Inismagrath Island are the remains of a church reputedly founded by St Beoy. The area surrounding Lough Allen has some reserves of coal and iron ores.

Drumshanbo, a small town on the southern shores of the lake, is an angling resort and also hosts *An Tostal*, an annual Irish music festival.

ALLGOOD, SARAH (1883–1950)

Irish-born US actor. She appeared at the opening night of the ⇨Abbey Theatre, Dublin, in 1904 in Lady Gregory's *Spreading the News*, and played the Widow Quinn in J M Synge's *The Playboy of the Western World*. She was on stage with Annie Horniman's company in Manchester in 1908 and later toured Australia with *Peg O'My Heart* (1915). In 1914 Allgood became a member of the Liverpool Repertory Theatre, but occasionally returned to the Abbey to perform in successful plays such as Seán O'Casey's *Juno and the Paycock* and *The Plough and the Stars*. Her performance of Juno in the Hitchcock film of Casey's play in 1930 gives a glimpse of the dignity and realism she brought to the part.

Allgood was born in Dublin. In 1940 she settled in Hollywood, USA, and became a US citizen in 1945. She appeared in over 30 films there, including haunting appearances in *Jane Eyre* (1943), *The Lodger* (1944), and *Between Two Worlds* (1944). She was seldom offered parts commensurate with her talent, however, and died penniless.

She made the film *Just Peggy* while on tour in Australia in 1918 and her first British feature was Alfred Hitchcock's *Blackmail* (1929), Britain's first film with synchronous sound.

ALTAN

Traditional music band. Developed by the husband-and-wife team Frankie Kennedy (1955–1994; flute) and Máireád Ní Mhaonaigh (1959– ; fiddle and vocals), Altan are one of the few contemporary bands to be adopted by a mainstream record company, Virgin Records, whilst remaining in the mould of the traditional music ensemble. Their music is rooted in Máireád's local fiddle and song tradition of Gweedore, west Donegal.

The line-up includes Máiréad Ní Mhaonaigh, Ciarán Tourish (fiddle), Ciarán Curran (bouzouki), Dermot Byrne (accordion, who replaced Frankie Kennedy), and Mark Kelly (guitar). Important recordings include *Island Angel* (1993) and *Runaway Sunday* (1997).

AMORY, THOMAS (1691–1788)

Novelist, born in Dublin. Amory studied medicine at Trinity College, before moving to London, where he lived as a recluse, devoting all his time to writing. His main works are *Memoirs of Several Ladies of Great Britain* (1755), concerned with learned women living in remote and scenic retreats, and the *Life of John Buncle, Esq., Containing various Observations and Reflections, Made in Several Parts of the World* (1756–66). Written in the form of a first-person narrative, the *Life of John Buncle* blends theology and utopian fantasy with a sentimental account of eight marriages to intellectual women, and includes much discussion of Anglo-Irish society and native Irish culture.

Amory also wrote a manuscript on *The Ancient and Present State of Great Britain*, which was accidently burned.

ANCESTORS, TRACING IRISH

See feature essay on how to go about tracing Irish ancestors, opposite.

ANCIENT ORDER OF HIBERNIANS (AOH)

Irish-American Catholic fraternal society, founded in New York in 1836 to aid recently arrived Irish emigrants, and maintain contacts within the Irish diaspora and with Ireland. Politically radicalized in the 1860s and 1870s through its association with the revolutionary ⇨Fenian organization Clan-Na-Gael, it became more moderate in the 1880s. After 1900 the AOH gained influence in Ireland as the political machine of Belfast nationalist Joseph ⇨Devlin, and its conservative brand of nationalism was confirmed after the foundation of Northern Ireland. Concentrating now on voluntary community and charitable work, it also functions as a useful network for the Catholic business community.

AN COIMISIÚN LE RINCÍ GAELACHA

(The Irish Dancing Commission)
First Irish step dance organization. Established in

THE DREAM AND AMBITION OF MANY – TRACING IRISH ANCESTORS

by Tony McCarthy

'It was a cold drizzly afternoon when we stopped the car on the road outside and walked into the yard. I cannot describe my feelings as I stepped over the threshold into the cottage. To think that my great grandparents had left here.' That was how one man described the end of a 20-year search for his Irish ancestors.

It is the dream of a million others: to find the homestead, to walk the fields, to bring home a stone from the old cottage. It is a dream that can come true; but jumping on a plane and coming to Ireland is not the way to start.

initial research

Early research must be geared towards finding, or narrowing down, the place in Ireland from which an ancestor came, and getting other vital information such as dates of birth, marriage, or death. This kind of preliminary research can be carried out in your own country. Helpful documents include family papers, birth, marriage and death records, census returns, church and cemetery records, passenger lists, and naturalization papers. Needless to say, if there are elderly relatives alive, they should be the first port of call.

Unless you know at least the county from which an ancestor came, your job will be very difficult. Family history research is one of the most popular hobbies in the world, so there may be a genealogical society in your locality. Many such societies have Irish interest sections that can offer good guidance.

professional genealogists

Following your preliminary research, you should know enough about your Irish ancestor to identify his or her name in Irish records. At this point you need to decide whether to do the research yourself or pay a professional genealogist to do the work for you. If you opt for the latter course, it is worth remembering Oscar Wilde's definition of a genealogist as 'one who will trace your ancestors back as far as your money will go.' There are two organizations for professional genealogists: the Association of Professional Genealogists in Ireland (APGI), based at National Archives, Bishop Street, Dublin 8; and the Association of Ulster Genealogists and Record Agents (AUGRA), who may be contacted c/o Glen Cottage, Glenmachan Road, Belfast, BT4 2NP. Though neither of the associations publishes a list of recommended charges –

and fees can vary considerably – both associations require high standards from their members. It should also be noted that some independent genealogists provide a very good professional service.

heritage centres

Each of the 32 counties of Ireland has a heritage centre that offers genealogical research services. Most of the centres confine their services to the area within their own borders, though some of the larger ones, particularly those in Northern Ireland, are able to offer a countrywide service. These centres are part of the Irish Genealogical Project (IGP), an all-Ireland effort to index and computerize all genealogically relevant records, such as census returns, church registers, and taxation records. For a fee, which again can vary widely from county to county, the database will be searched for information relevant to the names submitted and the results forwarded. A list of the centres is available from the Irish Family History Foundation, c/o Yola Farmstead, Tagoat, County Wexford; and at the IGP website: **http://www.irishroots.net**.

research tools

Those who would like to carry out research personally should familiarize themselves with Irish records by reading some of the standard Irish genealogy books, such as *The Irish Roots Guide* by Tony McCarthy, published by Lilliput Press, *Tracing Your Irish Ancestors* by John Grenham, published by Gill and Macmillan, and the Collins Pocket Reference *Tracing Irish Ancestors* by Máire MacConghail and Paul Gorry. Detailed up-to-date information can be found in the quarterly heritage magazine *Irish Roots*, available by subscription worldwide from *Irish Roots*, Belgrave Publications, Belgrave Avenue, Cork, Ireland. A course on Irish genealogy could also be considered, either in your own country or in Ireland; the University of Limerick holds week-long courses.

the Web

The most comprehensive listing of genealogy sites on the World Wide Web is the internationally renowned Cyndi's List. Most Irish sites are grouped there and constantly updated. The Irish section of Cyndi's List may be accessed directly at: **http://www.CyndisList.com/ireland.htm**.

1929 under the auspices of the ⇨Gaelic League, it controlled the formal aspects of Irish step dance, including examinations for teachers, registration of teachers and competitions, and the gradual establishment of rules concerning the teaching, performance, and adjudication of the genre.

In 1999 there were approximately 400 teachers registered with An Coimisiún in Ireland alone. The organization has a monopoly on Irish step dance from a global perspective, its main competitions being the world championships. Dancers from the USA, Canada, Australia, New Zealand, England, Scotland, Wales, Holland, and Africa may attempt to qualify for the World Irish Dancing Championships, held annually in Ireland since 1969.

ANDREWS, 'TODD' (CHRISTOPHER STEPHEN) (1901–1985)

Revolutionary and public servant, born in Dublin. Andrews was active in the Anglo–Irish War. He took the anti-Treaty side in the Civil War but followed De Valera's return to constitutional politics and was an early member of Fianna Fáil. Refusing invitations to enter political life, Andrews rapidly developed a career in the Irish public service, working with the Irish Tourist Board, the Electricity Supply Board and was especially successful as chief executive of the Irish Turf Board (Bord na Móna). In 1958 he was appointed chairman of the Irish public transport corporation (Córas Iompar Eireann), where he set about a radical programme of modernization and cost-cutting. His closure of several rail lines remains the most controversial aspect of his career. Andrews's memoirs *Dublin Made Me* (1979) and *Man of No Property* (1982) are useful sources for the history of the early Irish State.

ANDREWS, THOMAS (1813–1885)

Physical chemist, born in Belfast and educated at five universities, including Edinburgh, from the age of 15. Andrews experimented on the liquefaction of gases, postulating the idea that the process is governed by critical temperature and pressure. He initially investigated the liquefaction of carbon dioxide, and by 1869 had concluded that it has a critical temperature (or critical point) of 30.9°C/87.6°F, above which it cannot be condensed into a liquid by any pressure. He then applied his methods to the liquefaction of hydrogen, nitrogen, and air.

Andrews was the first to establish the composition of ozone, proving it to be a form of the element oxygen, and was professor of chemistry at Queen's College, Belfast, 1849–79. His work brought a sense of order to what had previously been a chaotic branch of physical chemistry.

ANGLO-IRISH AGREEMENT

Agreement signed by the Irish and British governments in November 1985, to consult formally on North Ireland policy; see ⇨Northern Ireland.

ANGLO-IRISH TREATY

Articles of agreement between Britain and southern Ireland signed in London in December 1921, which confirmed the end of the ⇨Anglo–Irish War (1919–21) but then precipitated the ⇨Irish Civil War (1922–23). The settlement created the ⇨Irish Free

ANCIENT ORDER OF HIBERNIANS

Members parade along the seafront in the County Antrim resort of Carnlough, in 1979. In 1900 this Irish-American benevolent society was 100,000 strong, but membership has fallen dramatically since the early 1970s.

State within the British Commonwealth and endorsed the creation of Northern Ireland. (Previously, the 1920 Government of Ireland Act had provided for partition of Ireland and two home rule parliaments.) Republicans split into pro-Treaty and anti-Treaty factions, opposition mainly centring on the subjugation of the Irish to the British monarchy, by the appointment of a British governor-general, and an oath of allegiance to Britain required by members of the parliament of the Irish Free State. Civil war was initiated by the provisional government of the Free State in 1922 to crush the anti-Treaty movement.

Í have seen the stars, and I am not going to follow a flickering will o' the wisp.

CONSTANCE MARKIEVICZ Politician speaking in the Dáil (Irish parliament) in 1921, against the Anglo-Irish Treaty.

≈

Following the truce between the ⇨Irish Republican Army (IRA) and British government forces in July 1921, five Irish delegates including Michael ⇨Collins and Arthur ⇨Griffith travelled to London to negotiate a peace settlement with the Liberal government of British prime minister David Lloyd George (1863–1945). Controversially, the president of Dáil Éireann (parliament) and leader of the nationalist movement, Éamon ⇨de Valera, chose not to accompany them.

The subsequent settlement, reluctantly signed by the delegates on 6 December under Lloyd George's threat of 'immediate and terrible war', granted dominion status to the southern 26 counties but confirmed the partition of Ireland to create Northern Ireland (six of the nine counties of Ulster), established by the Government of Ireland Act (1920). The Treaty granted a substantial degree of political and economic autonomy. It allowed for the creation of an army but significantly limited Irish sovereignty by retaining control of a number of strategic ports.

republican hostility

The agreement was generally popular throughout southern Ireland, particularly among business interests, farmers, and the Catholic church, but proved less so amongst the Sinn Féin politicians and Irish Republican Army (IRA) volunteers who had led the campaign against British rule. Many IRA volunteers who had sworn an oath to 'the Republic' were unwilling to accept any compromise that fell short of a fully independent republic. The symbolic aspects of Irish subordination to the British crown, such as the oath of fidelity, rather than partition and other practical limitations on sovereignty, provoked most republican hostility towards the treaty.

The Treaty's most influential opponent, de Valera, insisted that the delegates should have sought the decision of the Dáil before signing the agreement. His alternative compromise proposal, external association with Britain, was rejected by Treaty supporters on the basis that it had been refused by the British government during the negotiations and generated little enthusiasm among the anti-Treaty IRA leadership who felt it was little different from the Treaty. Republican supporters of the Treaty, led by Griffith and the charismatic Collins, argued that compromise had been inevitable once the decision was made to negotiate with Britain and maintained that the Treaty provided sufficient freedom to enable future constitutional evolution towards full sovereignty.

After the Treaty was passed by a narrow majority of the Dáil on 7 January, the political and military wings of the nationalist movement fragmented into pro- and anti-Treaty factions. The latter, divided between uncompromising militants such as Cathal Brugha (1874–1922) and Liam Lynch (1890–1923), and less belligerent republicans such as Frank Aiken (1898–1983), refused to accept the authority of the pro-Treaty Provisional Government and the clear mandate for the Treaty demonstrated by the general election of June 1922. After the failure of negotiations between the opposing IRA factions and in the atmosphere of increasing political violence, the Provisional Government attacked the anti-Treaty garrison in Dublin's Four Courts on 28 June 1922; this led to the Irish Civil War. Lynch, as Chief of Staff of the Irregulars, refused to consider defeat and an end to the hostilities was achieved only after his death in action in April 1923. See 'Ireland after Independence' on page 182.

ANGLO–IRISH WAR (also known as the War of Independence)

Conflict in Ireland 1919–21, between the ⇨Irish Republican Army (IRA), the paramilitary wing of ⇨Sinn Féin, and British government forces, reinforced by the ex-service Auxiliaries and ⇨Black and Tans. Its outbreak is usually dated to the IRA's killing of two policemen in Soloheadbeg, County Tipperary, on 21 January 1919. Following a war of guerrilla tactics, ambushes, assassinations, and reprisals, a truce negotiated in July 1921 led to the ⇨Anglo-Irish Treaty, which established the ⇨Irish Free State. Over 550 soldiers and police and over 750 volunteers and civilians died during the conflict.

Despite the Soloheadbeg incident, which coincided with the day of the first meeting of the Dáil, the illegal republican parliament in Dublin, IRA attacks against the Royal Irish Constabulary (RIC) and other targets had begun in 1918 against the wishes of Sinn Féin, the political wing of the republican movement. The IRA was nominally controlled by the Dáil minister for defence Cathal Brugha (1874–1922) and IRA headquarters under Michael ⇨Collins and Chief of Staff Richard Mulcahy (1886–1971), but little effective control was exercised over local IRA units. Collins's network of spies and assassins effectively disrupted British intelligence in Dublin. The fighting was unevenly distributed and concentrated in central Munster and the border regions of Ulster. IRA volunteers were predominantly drawn from the lower middle-class youths of rural and small-town Ireland.

The conflict escalated in 1920 when the RIC was strengthened with two forces of ex-servicemen known as the Auxiliaries and Black and Tans, which both earned unsavoury reputations. The harsh tactics adopted by government forces and condoned in London, including murder, looting, and arson, undermined the credibility of British rule in Ireland. By the spring of 1920 British forces had withdrawn from hundreds of garrisons in rural Ireland while flying columns, full-time mobile units of 'on the run' IRA personnel, engaged in guerrilla tactics. When both sides had fought to near-exhaustion with no clear victor in sight, a truce was called in July 1921 to allow peace talks to begin.

ANNALS

The practice of compiling annals (historical records usually comprising a narrative of events arranged in years) has a long and rich history in Ireland. Records were kept from just after the introduction of Christianity in the 5th century to the middle of the 17th century. The annals generally represent a limited geographical area and were written in monastic scriptoria (writing-rooms) by clerical scribes, though the practice

was later continued by hereditary secular families. The principal Irish annals are the *Annals of Tigernach*, compiled in Latin and Irish at the monastery of Clonmacnoise in County Offaly until 1178; the *Annála Uladh/Annals of Ulster*, not limited to the geographical Ulster, compiled by the dean of Lough Erne, Cathal Mac Maghnusa (Maguire), until his death in 1498, and other scribes until 1604; the *Annals of Clonmacnoise*, surviving only in an English translation from Irish by a scribe in Lismoyne, County Westmeath, in 1627; and the *Annals of Inisfallen*, a rich source for the history of Munster, compiled in a monastery on Lough Lene in Killarney from the late 11th century until 1326. The *Annals of the Four Masters* (1632–1636), properly titled *Annála Ríoghachta Éireann/Annals of the Kingdom of Ireland*, was a compilation of Ireland's annals by the 17th-century scribe Mícheál Ó Cléirigh and three assistants; their task was an attempt to preserve, copy, and condense the existing annalistic material into a standard edition.

Other works include the *Annals of Connacht* and the *Annals of Loch Cé* (both compiled in the 15th and 16th centuries); the *Annals of Boyle*; and the *Chronicum Scotorum* (around 1643), a record from the earliest times to 1135, copied by the Sligo historian and genealogist Dubhaltach Mac Fhir Bhisigh (*c.* 1600–1671).

AN TAIBHDHEARC ('place of magical appearances')

Irish-language theatre based in Galway. It was founded in 1928 by Liam O Bríain, professor of French at University College, Galway. For the opening production, Mícheál ⇨MacLiammóir played the lead role in his own play *Diarmaid agus Gráinne*.

Minister for finance Ernest Blythe was responsible for granting the theatre government support from its early years. Despite its claims to be a truly national theatre, the theatre survived mainly on a diet of translations into Irish rather than original productions. Though mainly amateur-based, the theatre attracted some extraordinary Irish actors and directors such as Siobhán McKenna, Mick Lally, and Maelíosa Stafford. In 1978 the group bought the hall in Middle Street that it had formerly rented.

ANTRIM

County of Northern Ireland; population (1981) 642,000; area 2,830 sq km/1,092 sq mi. It occupies the northeastern corner of Northern Ireland, with a coastal eastern boundary. The principal towns and cities are ⇨Belfast (county town), Larne (port), Antrim, Ballymena, Lisburn, and Carrickfergus.

physical

Antrim borders Lough Neagh, and is separated from Scotland by the North Channel, which is only 21 km/13 mi wide at Torr Head, the narrowest point. The Antrim Mountains (highest point Trostan 554 m/1,817 ft) run parallel to the coastline. The main rivers are the Bann and the Lagan, and there are peat bogs.

features

The Giant's Causeway, a World Heritage Site, consists of natural hexagonal and pentagonal basalt columns on the coast; other notable natural features include the Glen of Antrim and Kebble National Nature Reserve, on Rathlin Island, off the coast near Ballycastle. Bushmills Distillery, in the village of Bushmills, has the oldest known licence for distilling whiskey. There are a number of early fortifications, castles (including the 12th-century Carrickfergus Castle and romantic ruins of the 16th-century Dunluce Castle), and medieval ecclesiastical remains in the county. The village of Cushendun was built by Clough Williams-Ellis. Gobbins Cliff Path (19th century) is being restored as a millennium project. The traditional Ould

Lammas Fair at Ballycastle takes place in August.

economy

Agriculture is important in the county (the Bann Valley is particularly fertile). There is also shipbuilding and whisky distilling. Traditional linen production has largely been replaced by the manufacture of man-made fibres.

ANTRIM

Town in County Antrim; population (1991) 23,500. It is situated on the Six Mile Water where it enters the northeast corner of Lough Neagh, 28 km/17 mi northwest of Belfast. Antrim is a manufacturing and market town with engineering, electronics, and construction industries as well as computer-software development. The Round Tower (28 m/92 ft high) is all that remains of the 10th-century Aentrebh monastery after which the town is named.

In 1643 Antrim was burnt by Scottish Covenanters, Scottish Presbyterians who swore to uphold their own form of worship, as opposed to an English form, in a National Covenant signed in February 1638; in 1798 it was the site of the Battle of Antrim, at which the ⇨United Irishmen were defeated by English troops.

On the outskirts of the town, the formal ⇨Antrim Castle Gardens date from the 17th century. Clotworthy House, an arts centre and theatre, is located in the

COUNTY ANTRIM *A long and winding road follows the coastline and affords marvellous views of the Irish Sea as it pounds the red sandstone rocks typical of this area. The cliffs are formed of white chalk, and offer rich pickings to fossil-hunters.*

grounds of the former castle, as is a golf course.

Castle Upton, designed in the late 18th century by Robert Adam, is 9 km/5.5 mi east of Antrim at Templepatrick. Shane's Castle Park and deer park are 8 km/5 mi west of Antrim, and Randalstown Forest wildlife reserve is nearby.

A number of archaeological sites are located near Antrim: 3 km/2 mi to the east are the ring forts of Rathmore and Rathbeg (the possible seat of the kings of Dál nAraide during the 6th and 7th centuries); 5 km/3 mi to the east on Donegore Hill is a Neolithic enclosed settlement; and at nearby Ballywee, ring fort excavations show evidence of house foundations and souterrains (underground dwellings).

ANTRIM CASTLE GARDENS

Gardens on the outskirts of Antrim in County Antrim. Antrim Castle, which was noted for its Caroline doorway and contents, including the Speaker's chair from the Dublin parliament, was severely damaged by fire in 1922 and not rebuilt. The extensive gardens remain, however, and are one of only two main examples of a Dutch-style garden in Ireland, the other being Kilruddery, County Wicklow. Antrim Castle and gardens were formerly in the possession of Sir Hugh Clotworthy who was an ancestor of the Earls of Massereene.

AN TÚR GLOINE (The Tower of Glass)

Stained-glass studio set up by Sarah Purser (1848–1943) in Dublin in 1903, that operated until 1944. Its stained glass can be found all over the world.

Artists from the studio produced windows for the two most important new church buildings at the time, Loughrea Cathedral, County Galway (1901), and the 1915 Honan College Chapel, Cork, among their many commissions, both religious and secular. Michael Healy (1873–1941) was the first artist to join the studio, and his early work, inspired by Renaissance painting, evolved into a more richly textured style, as he experimented with acid etching. Another notable studio member was Wilhelmina Geddes (1887–1955), whose strong, bold expressionist windows have parallels in her powerful illustration work. She continued to produce windows after her departure from An Túr Gloine in 1922.

Irish painter Evie ⇨Hone was the last to join the studio, in 1935, and her devout, medieval-inspired glass is well known. Having made its mark on the international glass scene, the studio closed in 1944, the year after Purser's death. See also ⇨Arts and Crafts Movement.

ARAN ISLANDS

Group of three limestone islands in the mouth of Galway Bay, which is about 32 km/20 mi wide. They lie 48 km/30 mi from Galway, on the west coast of the Republic of Ireland; the principal town is Kilronan on Inishmore. The islands form a natural breakwater, and comprise Inishmore (Irish Inis Mór), area 3,092 ha /7,637 acres, population (1996) 838; Inishmaan (Irish Inis Meáin), area 912 ha/2,253 acres, population (1996) 191; and Inisheer (Irish Inid Oírr), area 567 ha/1,400 acres, population (1996) 274. The chief industries are tourism, fishing, and agriculture. J M ⇨Synge wrote about the customs and life of the islanders in his plays and book *The Aran Islands* (1907).

Another island of the same name is situated off the county of Donegal, but it is usually called Aranmore to avoid confusion.

history

The earliest architectural remains on the islands may date back to the late Bronze Age (*c.* 700 BC). There are ruins of a number of early churches, of which Teaghlach Einne, 'the house of St Enda', near Killeany on Inishmore, was the most important religious centre on the islands. The ruins are now largely submerged under sand. Killeany is also the site of the remains of Teampall Bheanain, reputed to be one of the smallest churches in the world

The Aran Islands are also noted for a number of well-preserved early fortifications, of which the largest is ⇨Dún Aengus on Inishmore (a semicircular stone fort on the clifftop, possibly dating from the Bronze Age). Inishmore is also the site of one of the best-preserved clochans, Aocan na Carraige.

traditions

Since the 19th century great interest has been shown in the islands because of their continued use of the Irish language, the preservation of cultural traditions, and the wealth of folklore passed down orally through the generations orally in songs and stories. The islanders' way of life was portrayed in the 1934 documentary film by Robert Flaherty, *Man of Aran*.

The islands are now to a large extent economically dependent on tourism. Tarred, canvas-covered *currachs* (wickerwork fishing boats) are still used by a few fishermen. The traditional *crios* (woollen belt), *báinín* (knitted sweaters, originally an undyed woollen coat, the intricate patterns for which were passed down through family lines), and pampootie, or *brógaí urleathair* (a heeless hide shoe) are produced for the tourist market.

ÁRAS AN UACHTARÁIN

Residence of the president of the Republic of Ireland, in Phoenix Park, Dublin. Formerly known as Phoenix Lodge and later Viceregal Lodge, this large house dates from 1751 and was designed and built by Nathaniel Clements, a member of parliament. It was bought by the government in 1782 and subsequently altered and enlarged several times, although the central portion of the house remains much the same as in the 1750s. The library contains an ornate plaster ceiling of Jupiter and the Four Elements brought from Mespil House in Dublin (which no longer exists). The ballroom of 1802 is now the State reception room where foreign dignitaries are received.

ARDAGH

Village in County Limerick, 5 km/3 mi north of Newcastle West. The enamelled Celtic Ardagh chalice, of gold, silver, and bronze, and brooches dating from the 8th century, now in the National Museum, Dublin, were discovered in Reevassta ring fort in 1868. Ballylin, one of the largest ring forts in Ireland, is 2 km/1 mi northwest of Ardagh.

ARDEE

Market town in County Louth, on the River Dee, halfway between Drogheda and Dundalk; population (1996) 3,400. It has several medieval buildings, including Ardee Castle (built by Roger de Peppard in 1207, now the courthouse) and Hatch's Castle, which also dates from the 13th century. Ardee is a centre for golf, and salmon and trout fishing in the River Dee.

Ardee has always been an important crossing point of the Dee. It was occupied by the English during the 15th century and continued to be a strategic outpost in the Pale (the territories under the rule of the English crown from the 14th to the 16th century). In 1689 Ardee was the headquarters for James II in Ireland. Cappock's Gate is the only remaining section of the medieval town walls.

ARDFERT

Small town in County Kerry, 10 km/6 mi north west of Tralee; population (1996) 600. Ardfert was first established as a missionary site in the 5th century; its ruined cathedral was constructed in the 13th century, and is now a national monument.

There is a stone inscribed in the Celtic ogham alphabet in the graveyard. Nearby are the ruins of the Franciscan Ardfert friary; 2 km/1 mi west of Ardfert is Casement's Fort, an earthen fort where the nationalist Roger Casement was arrested in 1916 after supplying arms for the Easter Rising.

Ardfert was a former see of the bishop of Ardfert and Aghadoe, now incorporated into the diocese of Kerry.

ARDMORE STUDIOS

Film studios based in County Wicklow, established in 1958. Its early policy of adapting Abbey Theatre plays as films gave way to seeking to encourage foreign producers to make films at the studios. Productions based there have included *Shake Hands With the Devil* (1959), *A Terrible Beauty* (1960), and *Excalibur* (1981), the latter made during the time that English director John Boorman (1933–   ) was the studios' chairman. The use of state funding to subsidize Ardmore while it was under state ownership from 1975 to 1982 was a major point of contention for independent film-makers in their campaign for an indigenous Irish cinema, and helped lead to the setting up of the ⇨Irish Film Board/Bord Scannán na héireann. Today the studios service Irish and foreign productions.

ARDRESS HOUSE

Seventeenth-century manor house at Charlemont, 14 km/9 mi north of Armagh, County Armagh. It is a five-bay gabled property, built about 1662, with slight projections enlarged for his own use by the Dublin architect George Ensor (brother of the more famous Irish architect John Ensor), who married the Ardress heiress in 1760. Some of the original, more intimate house remains unaltered, including an original oak staircase, but it is better known for a drawing room with elaborate Adamesque plasterwork and plaques, thought to have been created by the Dublin stuccodore Michael Stapleton. It is now owned by the National Trust.

ARMAGH (Irish *Ard Mhacha* 'the height of Mhacha' a legendary queen)

County of Northern Ireland; population (1981) 119,000; area 1,250 sq km/483 sq mi. It borders Lough Neagh to the north and the Republic of Ireland to the south. Its principal towns and cities are ⇨Armagh (county town), ⇨Craigavon (created by merging Lurgan and Portadown), and Keady.

history
Emain Macha, west of Armagh city, was the seat of the kings of Ulster until AD 332, and, dominated by the O'Neills in the late middle ages, the territory was resettled in the plantation of Ulster. The county of Armagh has been significant in many conflicts over territory, including battles over Ulster between the British and Irish in the 17th–19th centuries.

physical
Armagh is the smallest county of Northern Ireland. It is flat in the north, with many bogs and mounds formed from glacial deposits, and has low hills in the south, the highest of which is Slieve Gullion (577 m/1,893 ft). The principal rivers are the Bann, the Blackwater, and its tributary, the Callan.

features
Armagh is noted for its rich archaeological remains, including those at ⇨Emain Macha, a large earthwork 3 km/2 mi west of the city of Armagh, reputed to have been built by Queen Mhacha in 300 BC. Other features include Blackwater River Park, the 17th-century manor Ardress House, and Camagh Forest.

economy
The county has good farmland, apart from the marshy areas by Lough Neagh. The north of the county is a fruit-growing and market gardening area, while to the south livestock rearing is important. From the end of the 17th century Lurgan, and subsequently Portadown, were the centres of the linen industry, and linen is still manufactured there.

ARMAGH

City and county town of County ⇨Armagh; population (1991) 14,300. Industries include textiles (Armagh's chief product), including linen; the manufacture of shoes, optical instruments, and chemicals; and engineering and food processing. The city became the religious centre of Ireland in the 5th century when St Patrick was made archbishop. Armagh was also a noted seat of learning; St Patrick founded a monastic school here, and in 1169 Rory O'Connor, the last high king of Ireland, founded a 'professorship'. The city was the seat of the kings of Ulster for 700 years, and is now the seat of both the Roman Catholic and Protestant archbishops of Ireland, each of whom bears the title 'Archbishop of Armagh and Primate of All Ireland'.

*a*rmagh: where two cathedrals sit upon opposing hills like the horns of a dilemma.

SAM HANNA BELL Scottish-born writer and broadcaster *In Praise of Ulster*, radio broadcast, 1960.

The Church of Ireland cathedral occupies the traditional site of the church built by St Patrick. The Protestant cathedral houses several fine monuments, including pre-Christian stone statues (one of which is reputed to be of the legendary queen, Mhacha), and a statue of Thomas Molyneaux by Roubiliac; in the library is an annotated handwritten copy of Jonathan Swift's *Gulliver's Travels* (1726).

Emain Macha, 3 km/2 mi to the west of Armagh, is a large earthwork and tumulus reputed to be the burial site of Queen Mhacha; it was also the seat of the Ulster kings until AD 332. At Béal an Átha Buidhe, 3 km/2 mi to the north of Armagh, is the site of a battle where English troops under Henry Bagenal were defeated by Hugh O'Neill's army in 1598.

There are a number of fine Georgian houses lining the Mall, and the 18th-century Protestant Archbishop's Palace now contain council offices. ⇨Ardress House, a 17th-century mansion, is 14 km/9 mi north of the city. The ruins of a 13th-century Franciscan friary have been restored to form an equestrian heritage centre. The Gothic revival Catholic cathedral was constructed 1840–73. There is an observatory, founded in 1791, a planetarium, and a number of museums.

ARMS CRISIS

Crisis of May 1970 when Taoiseach Jack ⇨Lynch dismissed ministers Charles ⇨Haughey and Neil Blaney for allegedly using government money to purchase weapons for the IRA; minister Kevin Boland resigned in protest.

ART COLLECTING

Significant art collecting in Ireland began in the early 18th century with the Protestant ascendancy (Anglo-Irish landed gentry), who focused their attentions on Old Masters and antiquities. In the 19th century the Catholic church was an important patron of the arts, and towards the end of that century private collections of contemporary Irish art, with a particular taste for the art of the ⇨Irish revival, began to develop. The National Gallery of Ireland, the first major public collection in Ireland, opened in 1864, containing important donated collections. It was followed by other municipal and specialist galleries, with the state becoming involved in art collecting in 1951. In the latter half of the 20th century increased private and corporate wealth once again led to important new collections being formed, often specializing in historical and modern Irish art.

18th-century private collections

With the consolidation of their power in the early 18th century, the Protestant ascendancy gave a new impetus to the arts in Ireland, especially in the areas of portraiture and landscape painting. At the same time they made the Grand Tour to Italy which, coupled with stronger links with London and its art market, resulted in the making of a number of notable collections in Ireland. Great country houses such as ⇨Castletown House near Celbridge, County Kildare, and ⇨Russborough House near Blessington, County Wicklow, with their elaborate stuccowork, provided the setting for these collections. The scale of one such collection, that of the Earls of Milltown, may still be appreciated today as the bulk of it was donated to the National Gallery of Ireland in 1902. Significant collections were also amassed in this period by a number of Irish artists such as Charles Jervas (c. 1675–1739), Jonathan Fisher (1763–1809), and Philip Hussey (1713–1783), while the painter James Dowling Herbert (1762/3–1837) operated as one of a number of art dealers in Dublin.

19th-century

The Act of Union (1801), which dissolved the Irish parliament, saw the loss of Dublin's status as a leading cultural centre. The wealthy rising Catholic middle class did not on the whole collect art. The single biggest collector and patron of art was the resurgent Catholic church, which was engaged in a huge building programme after ⇨Catholic emancipation (1829). Private collections of contemporary Irish art developed towards the end of the century.

Ít is a symbol of Irish art. The cracked looking-glass of a servant.

JAMES JOYCE Writer *Ulysses* (1922).

〜

19th- and 20th-century public collections

The National Gallery of Ireland opened in 1864 to display Ireland's first major public collection. It has benefited from a number of important gifts including that of Sir Alfred Beit (1903–1994), which in international terms was one of the most important museum donations of the 1980s. The collector Sir Hugh ⇨Lane initiated the public collecting of modern art in Ireland. His gift of paintings formed the nucleus of the collection in Dublin's Municipal Gallery of Modern Art, which is named after him. Collecting and exhibiting contemporary art is the rationale behind the Irish Museum of Modern Art in Dublin, where innovative educational policies seek to bring pieces from the collection to audiences throughout the country. When the Arts Council was established in 1951, the state became involved in collecting.

20th-century private and corporate collections

Private collecting remained limited until the 1960s. Since then a greater awareness of international cultural developments, increased wealth, and the growth of private galleries has led to major private and corporate collections being formed. This is reversing the trend whereby, until recently, objects of Irish fine and decorative art were exported in huge quantities.

ART, PREHISTORIC AND PRE-CHRISTIAN

Craftsmanship reached high standards in the Neolithic, Bronze, and Iron ages, and Celtic period, particularly in gold and other metals.

early decoration

Pottery was one of the first crafts to reach Ireland. Both funerary and domestic vessels were produced from at least 4000 BC. Early Neolithic pots are simple, round-bottomed with a neck and rim, and decorated with patterns of incised lines. Personal adornment took the form of beads and bracelets. An unusual object from this time is the Knowth mace-head, a small flint object skilfully carved with diamond patterns and spirals. Large, carved passage grave stones display the most impressive art of this period (see ⇨Newgrange).

Pottery continued to be made in the Bronze Age (*c.* 2000–500 BC), but in different forms. Beaker pottery from the very early Bronze Age was flat-bottomed, with gently curving sides, and horizontal bands of incised decoration. Later pottery consisted of food vessels, which were used in settlements and for burials and cremations, and urns, which were solely funerary. These vessels were bowls or vases with horizontal decorative bands, incised and applied.

Bronze Age metalwork

The major developments of the Bronze Age in Ireland were in metalwork. In the early Bronze Age (*c.* 2000–1500 BC), gold was worked in flat sheets with simple incised linear decoration. Lunulae (crescent moon-shaped collars) were the main type of jewellery produced. Simple moulds were used to cast bronze axe-heads and daggers. In the middle Bronze Age (*c.* 1500–1000 BC) metalwork became more three-dimensional, with twin-valve moulds enabling the casting of more sophisticated daggers, spearheads, and rapiers in bronze. Repoussé (relief patterns hammered into the reverse of the metal) was used to decorate gold jewellery. From around 1200 BC, bars of twisted gold were bent into torcs, which could be worn on the wrist, ankle, or waist, or as earrings.

Late Bronze Age (*c.* 1000–500 BC) metalwork skills developed even further. Horns, swords, shields, and cauldrons were cast or made from sheet bronze. Gold jewellery included bracelets, dress-fasteners, and hair ornaments, but the highlight of this period was the gorget, or neck-piece. This evolved from the lunula into a form unique to Ireland, the best example of which is the Gleninsheen Gorget (8th century BC). This is a ribbed crescent-shaped collar, ending in two round terminals finely decorated in patterns of concentric circles.

Iron Age

The Celts brought the Iron Age (*c.* 300 BC–AD 450) to Ireland and the Celtic artistic style most widely found is called La Tène, named after a prehistoric settlement at the east end of Lake Neuchâtel, Switzerland. It is based on abstracted and stylized nature-inspired forms, and is recognized by its flowing curves, in spirals, triskeles, trumpet-shapes, scrolls,

and stylized bird-heads. Trumpets, shields, swords, and objects associated with horses, such as bits, have been found in Ireland bearing these designs, as has jewellery. The gold Broighter torc (1st century BC), with rhythmic, curving repoussé and inscribed decoration, shows the style at its best. A small number of figure sculptures from this period are the first recorded in Irish history, such as the austere three-faced stone head from Corleck, County Cavan.
See also ⇨metalwork.

ARTS AND CRAFTS MOVEMENT

Flowering of Irish crafts in the late 19th and early 20th centuries, and a revival of pre-colonial Irish designs.

beginnings

Concern about rural poverty in the second half of the 19th century, combined with a feeling that traditional crafts could provide employment, led to the foundation of many associations, studios, and classes to promote and teach craft and design skills. This coincided with a growing sense of nationalism and a search for a native Irish design style, inspired by recently discovered artefacts such as the Ardagh Chalice and Tara Brooch (both 8th century; see ⇨metalwork).

The initial impetus came from convents and patrons from the landowning classes who set up craft classes in various disciplines, but the movement solidified with the establishment of Irish branches of key British Arts and Crafts organizations in the 1880s and 1890s. Crafts taught and promoted included embroidery, lacemaking, weaving, porcelain painting, illustration, handprinting, woodwork, metalwork, leatherwork, and stained glass, the latter arguably the finest work of the period.

main studios

Three key Irish studios stand out from the rest. The Irish Decorative Arts Association in Belfast was set up in 1894 by Mina Robinson (active *c.* 1890–1905) and Eta Lowry (active *c.* 1894–1905), specializing in needlework and in pokerwork decoration of wooden ⇨furniture. They rapidly turned to highly individual interpretations of Celtic designs, which became very popular. The association continued into the 1930s. ⇨An Tur Gloine (The Tower of Glass) was set up by the artist Sarah Purser (1848–1943) in Dublin in 1903. The Dun Emer Guild was established in 1902 in County Dublin by Evelyn Gleeson (1855–1944) with sisters Lily (1866–1949) and Lolly (1868–1940)

Yeats; the sisters later left to form their own workshop, Cuala Industries. Production was initially divided into weaving and tapestry, embroidery, and hand-printing, although other crafts were later included. Their stated aim was to make beautiful things by Irish hands in Irish materials and an Irish style. The guild lasted into the 1960s. Individuals working outside the guilds who produced high quality work included Oswald Reeves (1870–1967) and Mia Cranwill (1880–1972) in metalwork, Wilhelmina Geddes (1887–1955), originally associated with An Túr Gloine, but subsequently an independent, highly original illustrator and glass artist, and Harry ⇨Clarke, whose stained glass is world renowned.

decline

The Arts and Crafts movement declined in the late 1920s, owing to the death or retirement of many of its central figures, and, ironically, to the great popularity of the crafts, which led to an emphasis on quantity over quality in production.

ASHFORD CASTLE

Victorian baronial castle at Cong, County Mayo. It was built mostly in 1870 by Sir Arthur Guinness on the rump of a house bought by his father in 1855. The designers were James Franklin Fuller and George Ashlin. Ashford Castle is approached by a magnificent castellated six-arch bridge and impressive gateway. It was converted into a hotel in 1939 and has accommodated many famous visitors, including US presidents.

ATHLONE

Town in County Westmeath; population (1996) 7,700. Situated on the River Shannon, Athlone is an important road, rail, and canal junction, and is known as the 'capital of the midlands'. Its principal industries are pharmaceuticals and medical supplies, engineering, electronics, and manufacture of machine components. There is a large military barracks here. The town is also a centre for game fishing and sailing events.

From the time of ⇨Brian Bóruma in 1001, Athlone has been the scene of constant struggles for possession. The castle, founded in the 13th century,

AVONDALE HOUSE *The birthplace and home of Charles Stewart Parnell, the elegant, neoclassical Avondale House contains a museum of Parnell memorabilia. The house is now also the base for a forestry school, and its surrounding estate is planted with specimens from all over the world.*

was of major strategic importance in the conflicts of the Tudor period. It was besieged by William III in 1688, and finally captured by Gen Godart Ginkell (later Earl of Athlone) in 1691. Parts of the 13th-century town walls and later 16th- and 17th-century defences still remain.

The modern Shannon bridge is a fine example of bowstring and lattice ironwork.

AVONDALE HOUSE

Eighteenth-century house, 2 km/1 mi south of Rathdrum, County Wicklow. It was built in 1779 for Samuel Hayes and possibly designed by James Watt, although Hayes himself was an amateur architect. Avondale contains some superb plasterwork, especially in the drawing room, which some attribute to James Wyatt, and has a fine two-storey hall with a gallery. It was the birthplace of Charles Stewart ⇨Parnell, the Irish nationalist leader. The house is now a museum.

BACON, FRANCIS (1909–1992)

Painter, one of the greatest painters of the human figure in the period since 1945. He created surreal, often disturbing images where the figure is subject to violent distortion. He was one of the earliest artists to make overt homosexual references in his work.

Born in Dublin to an Anglo-Irish family, Bacon grew up in Ireland and London. He lived in Berlin and Paris 1927–29 before settling in London where he worked briefly as a furniture designer. Eschewing formal training, Bacon was self-taught as an artist. As

> **I**t's an attempt to bring the figurative thing up onto the nervous system more violently and more poignantly.
>
> FRANCIS BACON Quoted in David Sylvester, *The Brutality of Fact: Interviews with Francis Bacon* (1975).

~

he later destroyed much of his early work, little is known of this period. He himself saw *Three Studies for Figures at the Base of a Crucifixion* (1944; Tate Gallery, London) as his first mature work. Preferring to work from photographs, his subjects, handled in a highly expressive and painterly style, are deliberately obscure. The contents of his studio are in the Hugh Lane Municipal Gallery of Modern Art, Dublin.

BALBRIGGAN

Seaside resort in County Dublin, 35 km/22 mi north of the capital; population (1996) 5,700. The main

FRANCIS BACON *The exhibition of* Three Studies for Figures at the Base of a Crucifixion *in 1944 established Bacon as one of the most controversial post-war painters. His idiosyncratic use of paint produced smudged and twisted figures, often in isolated or despairing poses.*

industries are the manufacture of CD-ROMs and audio CDs and, on a smaller scale, clothing and plastics. Near Naul, 8 km/5 mi west of Balbriggan, is Fourknocks Hill, an important early Bronze Age site containing a large passage-grave, part of the ⇨Boyne Valley necropolis.

BALE, JOHN (1495–1563)

English radical Protestant bishop of Ossory (mostly in County Kilkenny) 1552–53. He was among the earliest of the vocal native English Protestants. A reputation for radicalism deprived him of high ecclesiastical office in England, but in 1552 he was appointed to the important diocese of Ossory where enthusiastic advancement of doctrinal change coupled with his insensitivity to local feeling aroused strong reaction among the clergy and laity. Upon the accession of Queen Mary, Bale abandoned his diocese and left Ireland altogether.

The account of his Irish experience in *The Vocacyon of John Bale* (1553) provides a unique if strongly polemical source for the early history of the Irish Reformation and offers some glimpse of the ecclesiastical and pastoral problems encountered by reforming clerics in 16th-century Ireland.

Bale, his book, and his traumatic experiences were the subject of a novel, *The Book of Bale* (1988) by John Arden.

BALFE, MICHAEL WILLAM (1808–1870)

Composer and singer, born in Dublin. Balfe was a violinist and baritone at Drury Lane, London, when only 16. In 1825 he went to Italy where he met Rossini, and in 1827 appeared as Figaro in his opera *The Barber of Seville* at the Théâtre Italien. Balfe also sang at Palermo and at La Scala, Milan. In 1842 he went to live in Paris for some years and worked there with great success, though in 1843 he returned to London for a time to produce The Bohemian Girl, for which he is most famous today. Triumphant visits to Berlin in 1849 and St Petersburg in 1852 followed, and in 1854 he produced *Pittore e Duca* at Trieste.

Balfe's 29 operas include: *Un avvertimento ai gelosi* (Pavia, 1830), *The Siege of Rochelle* (1835), *Joan of Arc* (1837), *Falstaff* (1838), *Le Puits d'Amour*, *The Bohemian Girl* (1843), *Les Quatre Fils Aymon* (Paris, 1844), *Satanella* (1858), and *The Armourer of Nantes* (1863).

BALL, ROBERT STAWELL (1840–1913)

Astronomer who refined observational methods at the Birr Observatory, County Offaly. A gifted public lecturer, he published 13 volumes of his popular works on astronomy and was appointed Astronomer Royal for Ireland in 1874. He also conducted mathematical research into screw motions.

Born in Dublin, Ball was educated in Dublin and Chester before entering Trinity College, Dublin, in 1857 where he enjoyed a distinguished career. He accepted a post as tutor to the sons of the Earl of Rosse on the understanding that he would be given access to the Leviathan, a 183-cm/72-in reflector at Birr Castle built by William ⇨Parsons, 3rd Earl of Rosse, which was then the largest telescope in the world. There he improved the techniques for capturing observational data on faint nebulae.

Ball became Andrews professor of astronomy at the University of Dublin. In 1892 he was appointed Lowndean professor of astronomy and geometry at the Cambridge Observatory, England, but deteriorating eyesight forced him to abandon astronomical observations.

Ball wrote several popular books on astronomy, of which the best known are *The Story of the Heavens* (1885), *In Starry Realms* (1892), and *In the High Heavens* (1893).

BALLET

Ireland's classical ballet has not achieved the same stature or wide appeal as Irish traditional dance, and suffered setback with closure of the Irish National Ballet in 1989; most Irish students of classical ballet train and work abroad. Evolving from the Cork Ballet Company (founded in 1934), the Irish National Ballet had flourished in the 1970s under the leadership of Joan Denise Moriarty, creator of over 100 original works on themes of Irish mythology and legend. Moriarty departed in 1985, and in 1989 the Arts Council decided to remove funding due to poor audiences and rising costs, forcing the company's closure.

There are currently three main classical ballet companies: the Cork City Ballet, directed by Alan Foley; the Irish National Youth Ballet Company; and Ballet Ireland.

The Irish National Youth Ballet Company (formerly the Irish Junior Ballet Company) was established by Anne Campbell-Crawford in 1996 to provide tuition for young Irish ballet dancers aged 10 to 21. Using internationally trained teachers and choreographers, the students train as a company and conduct an annual season of performances in professional theatres.

Ballet Ireland is a full-time company established in 1977 by Anne Maher and Günther Falusy. Talented and glamorous, its mission is to revitalize classical ballet in Ireland. Maher, a Dubliner, was principal ballerina at the Wiener Ballett Theatre, Munich, where Falusy was artistic director. The company aims to retrieve Irish dancers working abroad and reestablish Ireland in the international ballet scene.

BALLINA

Seaport and large market town in County Mayo, 60 km/37 mi southwest of Sligo; population (1996) 6,900. Ballina is built on both banks of the River Moy; the eastern part of the town is called Ardnaree. Ballina has manufacturing and small light engineering industries. The Ballina salmon fishery is one of the most important in Ireland. Mary Robinson, president of the Republic of Ireland 1990–97, was born in the town in 1944.

Two US multinationals manufacturing car components and medical products are major employers in Ballina. The River Moy and nearby Lough Conn are popular fishing resorts, and Ballina is also a centre for golf and hunting.

At Ardnaree are the ruins of an Augustinian friary, dating from the 14th and 15th centuries. To the north are the remains of the 15th-century Franciscan Tertiary friary, Rosserk Abbey, including an imposing tower and well-preserved cloisters. Ballina is the cathedral town for the Catholic diocese of Killala.

BALLINASLOE

Market town in Galway, on the River Suck, a tributary of the Shannon; population (1996) 5,600. Industries include limestone quarrying, footwear, bonemeal, and electrical equipment. The annual horse, cattle, and sheep fair, founded in the 17th century, is held in the week of the second Tuesday of October, and is the largest in Ireland.

Some 14 km/9 mi west of Ballinasloe is the site of the Battle of Aughrim (1691) fought between the Catholic supporters of James II and the troops of William of Orange, following the Battle of the ⇨Boyne. The well-preserved Gothic remains of the Franciscan Kilconnell Abbey (founded in 1400 by Liam O'Kelly) are 11 km/7 mi from the town. At Clontuskert, 6 km/4 mi to the south, are the ruins of a 15th-century Augustinian abbey. Garbally Castle, former seat of the Earl of Clancarty, is now St Joseph's College.

BALLYCASTLE

Market town and seaside resort in the north of County Antrim; population (1991) 3,300. It is the port from which Rathlin Island is reached. Ballycastle's large Lammas Fair has been held since 1606 on the last Monday and Tuesday in August; a feature of the fair is to eat dulse, a dried seaweed.

There are a number of medieval ruins around Ballycastle, including Bonamargy friary (1 km east), an 11-m/35-ft round tower (8 km/5 mi south near Armoy), and Dunaneanie Castle (1 km west). Knocklayd Mountain (517 m/1,695 ft) is to the south, as is Ballycastle Forest; the sheer columnar basalt cliffs of Fairhead (190 m/626 ft) are 10 km/6 mi to the east, and impressive basaltic columns are also found at Grace Staples Cave to the west of Ballycastle.

The Italian inventor Guglielmo Marconi made the first successful wireless transmissions over water from Ballycastle to Rathlin Island in 1898.

BALLYMENA

Town in County Antrim, on the River Braid, 45 km/28 mi north west of Belfast; population (1991) 28,700. The town has a range of textile, food-processing, and light engineering industries, and there are fish farms nearby. It was created as a Lowland Scots plantation in the 17th century.

Harryville motte and bailey, the remains of a 12th-century fortification comprising an earthen castle mound (motte) and protected courtyard (bailey) below, is located on the southern outskirts of the town. Some 2 km/1 mi to the southwest is Galgorm Castle, built at the time of the plantation (1618–19), and Gracehill, a settlement established in 1746 by the Moravian Brethren sect of Protestants. Linen manufacture was introduced in Ballymena in 1733.

BALLYMOTE

Market town in County Sligo; population (1996) 1,400. The town takes its name from a 13th-century motte (earthen castle mound) located 2 km/1 mi to the west. In 1300 Richard de Burgh built a castle in Ballymote, extensive remains of which are still standing. There are also the remains of a 13th-century Franciscan friary here.

Ballymote Castle was an important defensive structure, which changed hands frequently in conflicts between the Irish and the English during the late 16th and 17th centuries.

The *Book of Ballymote* (Royal Irish Academy) is a manuscript collection of prose, verse, and stories of historic events, compiled about 1391 in Gaelic; it is also a key to understanding early inscriptions in ogham characters found on many standing stones.

Animal remains and evidence of early human occupation have been found in caves on the slopes of Keshcorran Mountain (362 m/1,188 ft) 6 km/4 mi to the southeast. The caves and the surrounding district are the sites of many legends and myths found in early Irish texts.

BALLYNAHINCH

Village in County Galway, 11 km/7 mi southeast of Clifden. It lies beneath the Twelve Bens (or Twelve Pins), a series of conical mountains that dominate the landscape. Ballynahinch Lake is popular for salmon and sea-trout fishing.

Ballynahinch Castle Hotel is a converted 18th-century house, and was once the home of Richard ('Humanity Dick') Martin, a founder of the UK's Royal Society for the Prevention of Cruelty to Animals.

BANBRIDGE

Town in County Down, on the River Lower Bann, 35 km/22 mi southwest of Belfast; population (1991) 9,700. It is a shopping and service centre with a small textile industry and shoe manufacturing. In the past, the main industry in Banbridge was the manufacture of linen.

Lisnagade ring fort, 5 km/3 mi southwest of Banbridge, is the largest of the forts that marked the boundary of the ancient kingdoms of Ulaidh and Oriel. Scarva, 6 km/4 mi southwest of Banbridge, was the site where William III's armies gathered before marching to the Battle of the ⇨Boyne in 1690, and is therefore an important focus in the annual celebrations of Protestant Orangemen.

BANDON

Town in County Cork; population (1996) 1,700. It is situated 27 km/17 mi southwest of the city of Cork on both banks of the River Bandon. It has telecommunications industries, and is a centre for salmon and trout fishing. Bandon was one of the towns founded by Richard Boyle (1566–1643), 1st Earl of Cork, on the forfeited lands he acquired for the plantation of English and Scottish settlers during the early 17th century.

BANGOR

Belfast commuter town in County Down, on the shore of Belfast Lough, 20 km/12 mi northeast of Belfast; population (1991) 52,400. It is the site of a famous missionary abbey of the Celtic church, founded by St Comgall in AD 555 and sacked by the Danes in the 9th century. The abbey was the home of St Columbanus and St Gall. A Protestant church, the Abbey Church, was built on the site in 1617 by Thomas Hamilton (later Viscount Clandeboye). Bangor Castle, built by Robert Ward in 1852, is now the town hall and a heritage centre. Bangor has the largest marina in Ireland, and the Royal Ulster Yacht Club is based here.

A 7th-century prayer book, *The Antiphonary of Bangor*, one of the oldest ecclesiastical manuscripts in the world, was created in Bangor; the original manuscript is now housed in Milan, but a facsimile is housed in the museum of the Bangor Heritage Centre. The lands of Bangor were granted by James I to Thomas Hamilton in the 17th century, and planted with Scottish settlers. The tower house, now a tourist information centre, was built in 1637 as a customs house, in the Scottish baronial style. The lands were inherited by the Wards in the 18th century, the descendants of whom were responsible for promoting the textile industry in the area during the early 19th century.

Crawfordsburn Country Park, the former estate of the Crawford family, is situated 11 km/7 mi west of Bangor; it was originally planted in the 17th century, and has now been developed into a series of walks; the Park Centre is a museum that illustrates the natural history in the Country Park. Grey Point Fort, a restored coastal gun site, is situated within the bounds of the park; it was built in 1907 to protect the entrance to Belfast Lough. The Somme Heritage Centre, 5 km/3 mi to the south of Bangor, commemorates the men from Irish regiments killed in the Battle of the Somme in 1916.

BANIM, JOHN (1798–1842) AND MICHAEL (1796–1874)

Brothers, joint writers, born in Kilkenny, sons of a small farmer and shopkeeper. Their *Tales by the O'Hara Family* were the first to chronicle Irish peasant life, agrarian unrest, and the violence to which it led. Written somewhat in the manner of Walter Scott's *Waverley* novels, they mirror the views of the Irish Catholic peasantry and emerging middle class in the period leading up to Catholic emancipation. Begun in 1822, they include the trilogy *Crohoore of the Bill-*

hook, *The Fetches*, and *John Doe*, published in 1825; and *The Nowlans* and *Peter at the Castle*, published in 1826.

John studied art at the academy of the Royal Dublin Society and taught drawing in Kilkenny before moving to Dublin in 1820, where he published *The Celts' Paradise* (1821), a long poem based on Irish folklore. His drama *Turgesius*, set in Viking Dublin, could not find a patron, but the great success of his tragedy *Damon and Pythias* (1828) at Covent Garden encouraged the brothers to move for a time to London. His other works include *The Boyne Water* (1826), a story of the Williamite War and its political consequence, and *The Anglo-Irish of the Nineteenth Century* (1828), a satirical novel comparing the Protestant ascendancy in decline, with the rising Catholic democracy led by Daniel ⇨O'Connell.

John Banim's youth was blighted when the Protestant girl he loved was denied permission to see him and died soon after. The advancing symptoms of spinal tuberculosis caused him great suffering in later life, and in 1829 he travelled to France to seek a cure, but returned to Ireland an invalid before the end of the year. Back in Kilkenny, he settled at Windgap Cottage, where he died. His last novel, *Father Connell* (1845), a portrait of a lovable priest, was completed with his brother's help.

Michael abandoned legal studies in order to save his father's failing business, but responded energetically to John's suggested collaboration over *Tales by the O'Hara Family* in 1822. He also conducted research for his brother's historical novels; his own historical works include *The Croppy* (1828), which deals with the ⇨Rebellion of 1798. Later novels include *Clough Finn* (1852) and *Town of the Cascades* (1864). In 1865 he published the collected works of *Tales by the O'Hara Family*, an edition produced by the Dublin publisher James Duffy. He was appointed Kilkenny postmaster in 1853, and in 1873 he retired to Booterstown, County Dublin. His youngest daughter, Mary Banim (died 1939), was also a writer.

BANN

Name of two rivers in Northern Ireland: the Upper and Lower Bann. The Upper Bann rises in the Mourne Mountains and flows 65 km/40 mi northwest into Lough ⇨Neagh on its southern side. The Lower Bann runs northwards from the northwest corner of Lough Neagh, flowing through Lough Beg and entering the Atlantic 8 km/5 mi south of Coleraine. For most of its 64 km/40 mi length it forms the boundary between counties Antrim and Derry.

There is much fishing in the Bann, particularly for roach, bream, pike, and sea trout, with salmon and eel fisheries on the Lower Bann. It is also a habitat for a variety of wildlife, with nature reserves and bird sanctuaries at Lough Neagh and Coleraine.

BANSHEE (Irish *bean sí*, 'fairy woman')

In Gaelic folklore, an otherworld female spirit whose crying portends the death of a person of old Irish stock. She is rarely seen, and descriptions of her can vary from a beautiful young woman to an old crone. She derives from the ancient land-goddess, and her role echoes the notion that a nobleman is ritually married to his territory. Belief in the banshee is still very common in Ireland, and her cry is even heard among Irish emigrants abroad.

BANTRY HOUSE

Country house at Bantry, County Cork. The original square house, which dates from 1710 and was built by the Hutchinson family, has had many alterations. A wing was built about 1770, under the ownership of Richard White. In 1845 the house was considerably enlarged by a later Richard White, the 2nd Earl of Bantry, who added two more wings; the present house is largely his creation. The 2nd Earl was also responsible for assembling a fine collection of paintings and furniture, which are a notable feature of the house.

BANTRY HOUSE *Built in a commanding position overlooking Bantry Bay, the house attracts around 50,000 visitors each year, who come to view the collections of paintings and furniture and the Italian-style gardens, which were laid out in the mid-19th century.*

BANVILLE, JOHN (1945–)

Writer and literary editor. Born in Wexford town, he worked for the *Irish Press* and became literary editor of the *Irish Times* in 1988. His first publication was the 1970 collection of short stories, *Long Larkin*, but he is best known for his novels, such as *The Book of Evidence* (1989), shortlisted for the Booker Prize and winner of the Guinness Peat Aviation Award. *Birchwood* (1973) establishes an interest in the Irish big house theme which, in combination with the history of science, philosophy, and art, operates in many of his novels.

The Book of Evidence, *Ghosts* (1993), and *Athena* (1995) comprise a trilogy centered on the main character Freddie Montgomery and examine, often with self-conscious ironic humour, notions of beauty, love, art, and writing. He has also written books about scientists: *Doctor Copernicus* (1976), *Kepler* (1981), *Newton Letter* (1982), and *Mefisto* (1986).

BARCROFT, JOSEPH (1872–1947)

Physiologist who was renowned for his research into the properties of blood, especially blood gases and the oxygen-carrying function of haemoglobin.

Barcroft was born in Newry, County Down, and was educated at the University of York and at Cambridge where he graduated in 1893. He was a lecturer and demonstrator at Cambridge for many years and was appointed professor of physiology 1926–37.

He evolved the theory of the division of the blood into circulating blood and depot blood, and studied the physiology of the fetus, especially in sheep. In 1941 he became director of the unit of animal physiology at the Agricultural Research Council, a post he held until his death.

His works include *The Respiratory Function of the Blood* (1914), *Features in the Architecture of Physiological Function* (1934), and *Researches on Pre-Natal Life* (1946). He was knighted in 1935.

BARONS COURT

Seat of the Hamilton family, Dukes of Abercorn, in County Tyrone, 5 km/3 mi southwest of Newtownstewart. The early 18th-century Georgian house was remodelled by the architect George Steuart from 1779. It was subsequently enlarged by Sir James Sloan (1791–1792) for the 1st Marquess of Abercorn. The interior, designed by William Vitruvius ⇨Morrison, is of a Neo-Classical style, dates from the early 19th century, and includes a superb rotunda at the heart of the house.

BARRINGTON, JONAH (c. 1760–1834)

Lawyer and historian, best remembered for *Personal Sketches of His Own Times* (3 volumes, 1827–32) containing comical historical portraits of political and legal figures. Born at Knapton in County Laois, Barrington was educated at Trinity College, Dublin. He was called to the bar in 1788, became Admiralty Court judge in 1798, and was knighted in 1807. In 1830, after he was removed from office for embezzlement, he lived in exile, where he wrote *The Rise and Fall of the Irish Nation* (1833). He died in France, having fled there in 1815 to escape creditors.

BARROW

River in the Republic of Ireland; length 190 km/ 118 mi. It rises on the northeast side of the Slieve Bloom mountains in County Laois, and flows east to the border of County Kildare, then south. With the River Suir, which it joins 48 km/30 mi from the sea, and the River Nore, which flows into it 3 km/2 mi above New Ross, the Barrow forms the estuary of Waterford harbour.

BARRY, GERALD (1952–)

Composer from Newmarket-on-Fergus, County Clare. His major influences are the composers with whom he has studied: Peter Schat in the Netherlands, Stockhausen and Mauricio Kagel in Germany, and Friedrich Cerha in Austria. His *Cheveux-de-frise* caused a stir at the 1988 London Promenade Concerts. His opera *The Intelligence Park* (1987), commissioned by the Institute of Contemporary Arts in London, was first performed at the 1990 Almeida Festival and a second opera, *The Triumph of Beauty and Deceit* (1993), was written for Channel 4 Television.

BARRY, JAMES (1741–1806)

Neo-Classical painter, regarded as the most important Irish artist of the 18th century. His paintings for the Royal Society of Arts in London, *The Progress of Human Culture* (1777–83), comprise the greatest cycle of history paintings of the period in Britain.

Born in Cork, Barry had high artistic ambitions from an early age. With the support of the British politician Edmund Burke, he went to London and travelled to Rome. His self-portrait (c.1780; National Gallery of Ireland, Dublin) encapsulates his self-image of the artist as an embattled hero and is rich in symbolism relating to his understanding of his role as an artist. His belief in the artist's duty to morally instruct the viewer lies behind works such as *King Lear Weeping over the Body of Cordelia* (1787; Tate, London).

Barry's difficult temperament made many enemies in the artistic establishment, and he was the first and only artist to be expelled from the Royal Academy. His belief in religious and social equality was also a defining feature of his art and many of his prints contain references to the Irish political situation.

BARRY, JOHN ('the Father of the American Navy') (1745–1803)

Naval officer, born in Wexford. Barry settled in Philadelphia around 1760. An ardent American patriot, he joined the Continental navy at the outbreak of the American Revolution (1775–83) and commanded many ships to victory. As captain of the *Lexington*, he captured the *Edward*, the first ship taken by the Continental navy. He became a commodore in 1794 and the senior captain in the US navy in 1798, commanding all US ships in the West Indies.

BARRY, SEBASTIAN (1955–)

Novelist, poet, and dramatist, born in Dublin and educated at Trinity College, Dublin. His material is set in Ireland and America and deals with themes of isolation and abandonment against the backdrop of recent history. Barry's novels include *Macker's Garden* (1982) and *The Engine by Owl-Light* (1987), while his poems include the collections *The Water-Colourist* (1983) and *The Rhetorical Town* (1985). As a dramatist he has had work produced in Dublin (*Boss Grady's Boys*, 1988) and New York (*The Steward of Christendom*, 1995).

BARRY, SPRANGER (1719–1777)

Actor and theatre manager. He joined David Garrick's company at Drury Lane, London, in 1746 and was a successful actor on the stages of Covent Garden, London, and Smock Alley Theatre, Dublin. He founded the Crow Street Theatre in Dublin in 1758 as a rival to the Smock Alley Theatre, then the only licensed theatre in Dublin.

BARRY, TOM (THOMAS BERNARDINE) (1897–1980)

Revolutionary, who was a policeman's son from a prosperous family in Bandon, County Cork. He became leader of the West Cork flying column, the most notorious of the ⇨Irish Republican Army's (IRA) mobile units in the ⇨Anglo–Irish War (1919–21). A tough and ruthless commander, Barry's daring ambushes, most notably the killing of 17 British Auxiliaries at Kilmichael in November 1920, made him a household name throughout nationalist Ireland. He opposed the Anglo-Irish Treaty (1921), which established the Irish Free State, and fought with anti-Treaty republicans in the Irish Civil War (1922–23). He remained within the IRA and became its chief of staff for a brief period in 1937, but broke with the organization over its policy of bombing in mainland Britain.

Barry initially joined the British army, serving in France and Mesopotamia during World War I. After demobilization, his first attempts to join the Bandon IRA were rejected due to his suspect background, but after the escalation of guerrilla warfare in the summer of 1920, Barry was given the post of brigade training officer and subsequently flying column leader. His memoirs *Guerilla Days in Ireland* (1949) remain of historical value.

BASKETBALL

Basketball in Ireland dates back to the early 1920s when Sgt-Maj Doogan first introduced the sport into the army. In 1945 the first club was formed at University College, Dublin, and the first intervarsity competition was held the following year. In 1948 Ireland sent a basketball team to the Olympics for the first – and only – time.

The highlight of the basketball calendar is the Sprite National Cup, with over 100 teams competing for the event in 1999. The games are held at the National Arena in Tallaght, Dublin, to capacity crowds. Currently there are over 150,000 playing the sport, making it the second most popular team sport after Gaelic football in Ireland.

BEATTY, ALFRED CHESTER (1875–1968)

US art collector and philanthropist. Born in New York city, Beatty made his fortune as a mining engineer, specializing in copper. He then travelled the world accumulating the largest private collection of oriental manuscripts and books, numbering over 13,000 items. On settling in Ireland in 1953 he built a library to house his collection, which on his death he left in trust to the state. The Chester Beatty Library, now in Dublin Castle, remains one of the most important archives of oriental materials in the West. In addition, Beatty donated several paintings to the National Gallery of Ireland. He was made the first honorary citizen of Ireland in 1963.

BEAUFORT, FRANCIS (1774–1857)

Irish-born admiral of the Royal Navy, who ranked as its greatest hydrographer and chartmaker. He is best remembered for the Beaufort scale, a system of recording wind velocity at sea.

Beaufort was born in Navan, County Meath, the second son of the Rev Daniel Beaufort, rector of Collon and Navan and himself a distinguished cartographer. He joined the Royal Navy in 1790 and did major charting and surveying work, particularly around the Turkish coast in 1812. He was shipwrecked at the age of 15 due to a lack of accurate navigational charts, an occurrence which encouraged his life-long devotion to the preparation of detailed charts.

He devised the Beaufort wind scale in 1805, a system based on the effect of wind at sea on a full-rigged man-of-war, which specified the amount of sail appropriate to various wind conditions. By 1835 it had become mandatory for Royal Navy log entries to include Beaufort scale records, and the practice was adopted in 1874 by the International Meteorological Committee for international use.

Beaufort participated in many naval battles and was wounded in action. In 1829 he was appointed hydrographer of the Admiralty, a post he held for 26 years. He rose to the rank of rear admiral before he retired and was knighted in 1848. The Beaufort Sea, north of Canada and Alaska, is named after him.

BECKETT, SAMUEL BARCLAY (1906–1989)

Dramatist, novelist, and poet, who wrote in both French and English. His play *En attendant Godot* – first performed in Paris 1952, and then in his own translation as *Waiting for Godot* in London in 1955 and New York in 1956 – and his later dramas, such as *Fin de partie/Endgame* (1957–58) and *Happy Days* (1961), won him international acclaim. He was awarded the Nobel Prize for Literature in 1969.

As well as paring character to the grimmest essentials, Beckett honed his prose with meticulous precision to a painful articulateness, scrupulously cautious of redundancy. Composition in French, before trans-

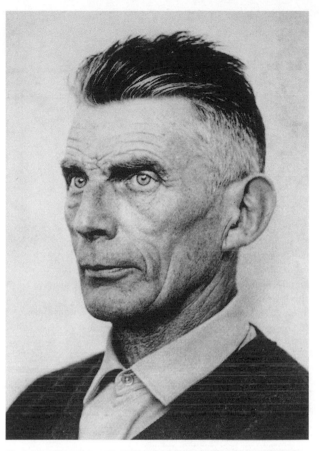

SAMUEL BECKETT *Beckett could have had a conventional academic career, but after teaching in Belfast, Paris, and at Trinity College, Dublin, where he had been a student, he settled in France and, living off a small annuity, began his life as a writer.*

lating into English, helped towards this distillation of style.

Beckett was born in Foxrock, near Dublin, and educated at Trinity College, Dublin. He lectured in English in Paris, where he became a member of James Joyce's circle. He briefly lectured in French at Trinity College 1930–31, but abandoned his academic career. After several years of European travel, in 1937 he settled in Paris, where he spent most of the rest of his life. He was awarded the Croix de Guerre for his service in the French Resistance.

Beckett's earliest work included criticism on Joyce and Proust, witty and allusive poetry – notably *Whoroscope* (1931) – and an unfinished novel, *Dream of Fair to Middling Women* (posthumously published in 1992). His published fiction began with the short stories of *More Pricks than Kicks* (1934), which, with grim humour, plot the slow peregrinations of their hero Belacqua among the Dublin streets; his work at this period was heavily indebted to Joyce. With *Murphy* (1938), *Molloy* (1951), *Malone meurt/ Malone Dies* (1951/1958), *Watt* (1953), *L'Innommable/The Unnamable* (1953/1960), and *Comment c'est/How It Is* (1961/1964), the protagonist's mobility decreases, being reduced in *How It Is* to a cyclic crawl in the mud. Beckett's increasingly spare and cadenced prose becomes extraordinarily concentrated in his later short fiction, which includes *Imagination Dead Imagine* (1965), *Ill Seen Ill Said* (1982), and his last prose work, *Stirrings Still* (1988).

*T*he expression that there is nothing to express, nothing with which to express, nothing from which to express, no power to express, no desire to express, together with the obligation to express.

SAMUEL BECKETT Explaining the paradox he faced as a writer.

~

The preoccupations of Beckett's fiction are repeated in his drama. His characters are trapped in various states of incapacity and near-immobility: two tramps waiting in vain for a mysterious figure; an old couple confined to dustbins; a woman buried to the waist in sand. In his later short 'dramaticules' he developed an even more minimalist conception of theatre: the illuminated mouth declaiming in *Not I* (1973), for example, or the solitary sigh over a rubbish-strewn stage of *Breath* (1969). Beckett also experimented with scripts for radio, television, and a short film.

Early critics associated Beckett's drama with the Theatre of the Absurd, and his fiction with the French vogue for the *anti-romain*, but his work was shaped by a far wider set of influences drawn from his extensive reading in European literature and philosophy. Grappling with fundamental problems of identity, volition, knowledge, and narration, his characters evince a distinctively Beckettian compound of despair, endurance, and wit in the face of an implacable universe.

BECTIVE ABBEY

Cistercian foundation near Kells, County Meath. The first daughter house of ⇨Mellifont Abbey, it dates from 1147 and was founded by Murchad O'Meaglin, King of Meath. It was extensively rebuilt in the 15th century and the triple cloister arcades date from this period. Nothing remains of the 12th-century construction; the earliest surviving structure is the square chapter house from the 13th century. After the dissolution of the monasteries in the 16th century, Bective Abbey was turned into a fortified Tudor mansion. Bective is associated with the short-story writer Mary ⇨Lavin, whose collection *Tales from Bective Bridge* (1942) won the James Tait Black Memorial Prize.

BEDELL, WILLIAM (1571–1642)

English cleric who became Church of Ireland bishop of Kilmore 1629–42. He was responsible for the first translation of the Old Testament into the Irish language. As provost of Trinity College, Dublin, 1621–29, he was an energetic reformer and enthusiastic advocate of teaching his clerical students the Gaelic language as a means of spreading the gospel among the native Irish. His zeal as a reformer of clerical conduct and practices as well as his respect for Irish culture provoked hostility and suspicion among his fellow clergymen, but rendered him uniquely respected among Irish Catholics.

In the native uprising in Ulster in 1641, Bedell was treated with remarkable leniency and respect. Allowed to take refuge in a protected home, he died of natural causes and was the subject of a tribute by one of the leaders of the rebellion. His Old Testament, known as 'Bedell's Bible', was first printed in 1685.

BEERE, THEKLA (1901–1991)

Civil servant, the first woman to head a department in the civil service in the Republic of Ireland. Beere served as secretary of the Department of Transport and Power 1959–66. She also sat on the boards of the *Irish Times* and the Rotunda Hospital, Dublin. In 1970 she chaired the Commission for the Status of Women.

BEHAN, BRENDAN FRANCIS (1923–1964)

Writer and dramatist, born in Dublin and educated by the Christian Brothers until the age of 14. Behan's extended family included many talented musicians and writers as well as Republican activists. An important figure of both controversy and literary brilliance, Behan is best known for his autobiography *Borstal Boy* (1958), based on his experiences of prison and knowledge of the workings of the ⇨IRA. These themes are revisited in his play *The Quare Fellow* (1954), and tragicomedy *The Hostage* (1958), first written in Gaelic as *An Giall*. Behan's other output included poetry in Gaelic, radio plays, and some late volumes of reminiscence and anecdote, notably *Brendan Behan's New York* (1964).

the ordinariness of people is what is often extraordinary.

> BRENDAN BEHAN *Weekend* (1968).

Behan's plays are imbued with black humour and a grim realism; it was largely Joan Littlewood's adaptation of *The Hostage* for the London stage which imparted to it a strong music-hall sensibility, which includes song and dance. After living a hard life of drinking and being a famous figure of the Dublin literary and pub scene, Behan died young and, many believe, before his best work could be produced.

there's no such thing as bad publicity except your own obituary.

> BRENDAN BEHAN Remark quoted in Dominic Behan, *My Brother Brendan*.

BRENDAN BEHAN *Always the maverick, when asked what was the message of his play,* The Hostage, *about a kidnapped English soldier, Behan replied: 'Message? Message? What the hell do you think I am, a b****y postman?'*

BELFAST (Irish *Beal Feirste*, 'the mouth of the Farset')

City and industrial port in County Antrim and County Down, at the mouth of the River Lagan on Belfast Lough; county town of County ⇨Antrim, and capital of Northern Ireland since 1920; population (1994 est) 290,000 (Protestants form the majority in east Belfast, Catholics in the west). The city's industries inclue aircraft components, engineering, electronics, fertilizers, food processing, textiles; linen production and shipbuilding have declined in importance since the 19th century though the Harland and Wolff shipyard is still active. The city is currently undergoing major redevelopment, both in terms of physical infrastructure (particularly along the River Lagan) and industrial investment, which is partly funded by the EU. The *Titanic* was built here in 1912.

main features

City Hall (1906); Stormont (the former parliament buildings and from 1998 the seat of the Northern Ireland Assembly); Waterfront Hall, opened in 1997; the Linen Hall Library (1788); ⇨Belfast Castle (built 1870; former home of the Donegall family); Queen's University (1849, 1909); Botanic Gardens; Cave Hill Country Park; Ulster Museum.

location and public buildings

On the landward side Belfast is dominated by the basalt hills of County Antrim. The city centre is built on marshy land (sleech), the larger buildings being supported on piles sunk deep into alluvial deposits, and the shipyards were built on reclaimed land.

Most of its major public buildings have been built since the late 19th century: the royal courts of justice

(1933), the museum and art gallery (1929), the public library (1888), the harbour office (1896), St Anne's Cathedral (1904), and the parliament buildings, Stormont (1932). The Customs House dates from 1857.

Queen's University was founded as Queen's College in 1849. It was associated with the other Queen's Colleges at Cork and Galway until it received its royal charter as an independent university in 1909. In addition to the public and university libraries, the Linen Hall Library, founded in 1788, still flourishes as a subscription library. It has an important collection of publications on the linen trade and concerning the political life of Northern Ireland since 1966. The grounds of the 19th-century Belfast Castle, presented to the city by Lord Shaftesbury in 1934, lie on the slopes of Cave Hill, as do the public parks of Hazelwood and Bellevue, where there is a public zoo.

regeneration in the 1990s

The city underwent extensive redevelopment in the 1990s, especially along the River Lagan, including the building of the Waterfront Hall and Conference Centre, which includes a major concert hall opened in 1997. Industrial development and regeneration also took place during the 1990s, particularly in the service and quaternary industries.

Belfast harbour

The harbour of Belfast is under the management of the Belfast Harbour Commissioners, established by the Belfast Harbour Act in 1847. Extensive land reclamation has been carried out; Belfast City airport, formerly the airstrip of the planemakers Shorts, was opened on reclaimed land in 1937. The harbour area covers 668 ha/1,650 acres and includes a shipyard and an aircraft components factory as well as 102 ha/252 acres of commercial docks.

architecture

City Hall, designed by the London architect Alfred Brumwell Thomas and completed in 1906, is one of Ireland's most impressive buildings and considered one of the finest examples of Baroque Revival architecture in the British Isles. It is quadrangular in form, with a copper dome, and is faced with Portland stone. The interior is lavishly decorated, with extensive use of Greek and Italian marble, and there is a striking black-and-white paved floor in the grand entrance hall. The workmanship and materials are of the highest quality throughout the building.

BELFAST *The dome of City Hall, a vast Baroque Revival building, which dominates Donegall Square, was inspired by St Paul's Cathedral, and even contains a whispering gallery. A statue of Queen Victoria stands in front of the building, looking down Royal Avenue.*

The Crown Bar public house in Great Victoria Street, described above the door as a 'Liquor Saloon', is considered by many the finest example of a bar of the late Victorian period in the British Isles. The building was originally the Ulster Railway Hotel, dating from 1839, but the Crown Bar, on the ground floor, is of a later date and was completed in two stages from 1885. It was designed by E & J Byrne and the interior is lavishly decorated in the late Victorian style, with brightly coloured glass, mosaic, art nouveau ceramics, and beautiful woodwork. The later faience front was built in 1898. The property is owned by the National Trust.

The Lanyon Building, Queen's University, in University Road, is the most significant High Victorian building in Ulster, built by Charles ⇨Lanyon between 1846 and 1849 as one of three Queen's Colleges established in Ireland (the others being in Cork and Galway). It is constructed in a charming red-brick Tudor style, reproducing parts of the 15th-century Founder's Tower at Magdalen College, Oxford, England. There are extensions by W H Lynn (1911–12), W A Forsyth (1933), and John MacGeagh (1951).

The Grand Opera House, Great Victoria Street, was built between 1894 and 1895 and was designed by Frank Matcham of London, considered the foremost theatre architect of his day. It is one of Belfast's best-known buildings and its lavish interior includes elephant head brackets and other Indian motifs. It was restored between 1976 and 1980 by Robert McKinstry and has survived numerous bombings.

transport

Belfast is 180 km/112 mi north of Dublin, and is the centre of the Northern Ireland's road and rail network. It is a terminus for ferries from Liverpool and Heysham in England, the Isle of Man, and Scotland, and has an international airport at Aldergrove, 31 km/19 mi to the west. The port of Larne 32 km/20 mi to the north is a terminus for ferries to Scotland.

early history

Belfast grew up around a castle built in 1177 by John de Courcy. After the invasion of Ulster in 1177 de Courcy built his castle on the site of an earlier fort at the ford over the River Lagan as a stronghold to command the crossing-point. This was destroyed by the troops of Edward Bruce in 1316, but later rebuilt. Throughout medieval times Belfast was a small settlement, much less important than the neighbouring port of Carrickfergus, which was the main Anglo-Norman stronghold in the north of Ireland. For about 300 years the Lagan valley was controlled by the O'Neill family. The castle and surrounding settlement were subject to frequent dispute between the O'Neills and English forces, changing hands several times until 1574 when the lands were captured by the Earl of Essex.

The modern Belfast Castle, a victorian Scottish-style baronial castle was built in 1870 for the 3rd Marquess of Donegall and stands on a different site to the original.

Ít's starting to rain. The boys will go in now. Let the Brits lie out in it and get saturated. A man's army. It's spoiled the garden, all this running in and out through it with guns and army-issue boots.

MARY COSTELLO Writer *Titanic Town* (1992).

17th-century history

In 1603 the settlement at Belfast came under the control of Arthur Chichester, as part of the ⇨plantation of Ireland. Under Chichester, Belfast received a charter in 1613, and it grew to be the market town for the Lagan valley. Belfast was settled by Protestant families from Devon and Scotland and became a centre of Irish Protestantism. Real growth came with the establishment of linen manufacture after an influx of Huguenots in 1685. Belfast also became an important trading port with Scotland.

18th-century history

The shipbuilding industry was established in Belfast by William Hugh Ritchie in 1791. Also in 1791 the Society of the United Irishmen was founded in Belfast to fight the repression of the Penal Laws. This united both Catholic and Presbyterian inhabitants of the city in a bid for independence. Henry Joy McCracken (1767–1798), a member of the United Irishmen who led the Irish troops at the Battle of Antrim in 1798, was later executed in the city.

19th and 20th-century history

The 1800 Act of Union with England resulted in the promotion of Belfast as an industrial centre, and the shipbuilding industry developed throughout the 19th century. Between 1831 and 1901 Belfast's population grew from 30,000 to 350,000. Belfast was incorporated into a borough in 1842, created a city in 1888, with a lord mayor from 1892. During World War II Belfast was bombed in 1941, and nearly 100 people were killed. Since 1968 Belfast has been at the centre of 'the Troubles' in ⇨Northern Ireland.

the parliament of Northern Ireland

The first Northern Ireland parliament sat in the City Hall in Belfast, the state opening being performed in 1921 by King George V. The parliament buildings at Stormont were opened by the Prince of Wales in 1932, and were used until the parliament's suspension in 1972. The multi-party peace talks of 1997–98, leading up to the agreement of 10 April 1998, were held at Stormont, which since summer 1998 has been the official seat of the Northern Ireland Assembly.

BELFAST LOUGH

Inlet on the east coast of Northern Ireland, between the counties of Antrim and Down. It is an estuary of the River Lagan, and is 11 km/7 mi wide at its mouth. Belfast Lough extends 24 km/15 mi inland, and has the towns of Belfast, Carrickfergus, Holywood, and Bangor on its shores. The area adjacent to the port of Belfast is heavily industrialized.

BELL, SAM HANNA (1909–1990)

Scottish-born writer and broadcaster. Bell moved to Strangford Lough, County Down, as a child and then to Belfast in 1921. Opposed to traditional Unionism, he co-founded the socialist journal *Lagan* (1943) with the Belfast playwright John Boyd (1912–   ) and Bob Davison. He worked extensively with BBC Northern Ireland as a documentary script writer and producer. Much of Bell's radio work dealt with folklore and folk music, and he also wrote about Ulster culture. His short stories and novels include *December Bride* (1951), subsequently made into a film; and *Across the Narrow Sea* (1987), a study of the effects of ⇨plantation in 17th-century Ulster.

BELL-BURNELL, (SUSAN) JOCELYN (1943–   )

Astronomer who built a radio telescope and discovered the first pulsar with fellow astronomer, Antony Hewish (1924–   ), at the Mullard Radio Astronomy Observatory, Cambridge, England. She also made significant contributions in the fields of X-ray and gamma-ray astronomy.

Born in Belfast, Bell-Burnell spent much time as a child at the nearby Armagh Observatory. She studied at Glasgow University and then later at Cambridge, where as a student she built a radio telescope specifically designed to track quasars, very distant sources of intense radio waves.

While using the device in 1967, she noticed an unusual radio wave signal composed of a series of rapid pulses that repeated every 1.337 seconds. The source was likened to an interstellar beacon so the phenomenon was originally nicknamed LGM for Little Green Men. Within a few months however Bell-Burnell had located three other similar sources with slightly differing pulse times and in different parts of the sky. These rapidly flashing stars were named pulsars.

Bell-Burnell did research in gamma-ray astronomy at the University of Southampton, England 1968–82 and in X-ray astronomy at the Mullard Space Science laboratory at University College, London. She then worked on infrared and optical astronomy at the Royal Observatory, Edinburgh, Scotland. In 1991 she was appointed professor of physics at the Open University, Milton Keynes, England.

BELVEDERE HOUSE

Villa dating from about 1740, near Mullingar, County Westmeath. It was designed by Richard Castle for Robert Rochfield, afterwards the 1st Earl of Belvedere. It contains Rococo plasterwork thought to be by Bartholomew Cramillion, whose work is also in the Rotunda Hospital in Dublin. In the grounds is the largest Gothic sham ruin in Ireland, known as the Jealous Wall. It was built about 1760 by Lord Belvedere and was supposedly intended to obscure the view of the property belonging to his brother, whom he suspected was his wife's lover.

BENBULBEN

Mountain in County Sligo, rising to 497 m/1,730 ft. A prominent flat-topped limestone buttress, scored by erosion, it forms part of the Dartry range and dominates the surrounding landscape. The peak is celebrated in 'Under Ben Bulben' by the poet W B Yeats, who chose to be buried at nearby Drumcliff.

According to the legend of the hero Fionn Mac Cumhaill (Finn McCool), the young warrior Diarmuid was killed on Belbulben by a wild boar after being left alone during a hunt with Fionn and his men. Diarmuid had angered Finn by eloping with Grainne, daughter of the king of Tara, during their betrothal feast.

BERESFORD, CHARLES WILLIAM DE LA POER (1st Baron) (1846–1919)

Naval commander and politician, born in Philipstown, County Offaly. The son of the 4th Marquis of Waterford, he joined the navy in 1859 and was a popular and flamboyant officer. In 1882 he won his first command, for distinguished service at the bombardment of Alexandria, which also earned him great public acclaim and the affectionate nickname 'Charlie B'. He subsequently served in the Nile expedition of 1884. His political career began in 1874, when he was elected as the Conservative member of parliament for Waterford; he later represented York and Portsmouth in parliament. He held appointments as Fourth Lord of the Admiralty 1886–88 and commander of the Mediterranean Fleet 1905–07 and Channel Fleet 1907–09.

Beresford's service career came to an end after bitter public disagreements with the First Sea Lord, Admiral Sir John Fisher, over naval policy and reforms. He was raised to the peerage in 1916 as 1st Baron Beresford of Curraghmore.

BERGIN, PATRICK (1953–)

Actor, born in Dublin, who achieved commercial success with the film *Sleeping with the Enemy* (1991). Before starring in the Irish gangster feature *The Courier* (1988), Bergin, from a theatrical family, had acted, directed, and produced plays in London. He then appeared in the television film *Act of Betrayal* (1989) as a terrorist who had abandoned the 'Cause'. He then appeared in the epic *Mountains of the Moon* (1990) in which he played the 19th-century English explorer Sir Richard Burton.

Other films include *Robin Hood* (1991), *The Real Charlotte* (1991), *Highway to Hell* (1992), *Love Crimes* (1992), *Frankenstein* (1993), *Map of the Human Heart* (1993), *They* (1993), and *Lawnmower Man 2* (1996).

BERKELEY, GEORGE (1685–1753)

Philosopher and Church of Ireland bishop of Cloyne. A central figure in 18th-century philosophy, he denied the existence of a reality independent of the mind and believed that the all-seeing mind of God made possible the continued apparent existence of things.

Truth is the cry of all, but the game of few.

GEORGE BERKELEY *Siris* 368.

~

Born at Dysart Castle in County Kilkenny, Berkeley was educated at Kilkenny College and Trinity College, Dublin. A contemporary of the great 18th-century philosophers Emmanuel Kant, John Locke, and David Hume, Berkeley's theory is considered a key philosophical argument. He believed everyday objects to be collections of ideas or sensations, hence the dictum *esse est percipi*, 'to exist is to be perceived'. With Locke and Hume he is considered to be one of the British empiricists (believing that all knowledge is derived from sense experience), but his philosophy – that nothing exists except in the mind – is also described as subjective idealism.

Berkeley's major philosophical works were *An Essay towards a New Theory of Vision* (1709) and *The Principles of Human Knowledge* (1710). He also wrote extensively on Ireland's economic problems, which he felt required both government intervention and a church-directed moral and social response. The publication of his philosophical tracts contributed to the growth and increasing success of the Irish publishing industry in the 18th century.

In 1713 Berkeley travelled to London, where he became acquainted with the poet and satirist Alexander Pope and the Irish essayist Richard Steele. He later visited Rhode Island 1729–31, where he made an unsuccessful attempt to establish a missionary college. In 1734 he was appointed bishop of Cloyne and took up residence in County Cork, where he pursued his work on social and economic reform.

BERMINGHAM

Anglo-Norman family granted Irish lands in Offaly by Richard de ➪Clare (Strongbow), soon after his arrival in Ireland in 1170. They took part in the conquest of Connacht, the Offaly branch being known as the de Berminghams of Tethmoy, while those of Connacht being based in Athenry. Like many such families, the de Berminghams were ultimately absorbed into Gaelic society, some adopting the name Mac Fheorais (son of Piers), now Corish. Despite their Gaelicization, they are best remembered for the massacre of 30 of the O'Connors in 1305, carried out by Piers (Peter) de Bermingham of Tethmoy (died 1308) while they feasted at his castle in Carbury; the deed was applauded by the English and lamented by their Irish counterparts.

BERNAL, JOHN DESMOND ('SAGE')

(1901–1971)

Physicist and X-ray crystallographer. He helped pioneer the field of molecular biology and carried out extensive studies of solid compounds using methods of crystallography that he developed.

Bernal was born in Nenagh, County Tipperary, and educated by Jesuits at Stonyhurst College, Lancashire, and later Emmanuel College, Cambridge. He lectured there for a time before moving to Birkbeck College, University of London, where he was professor of physics 1938–63 and professor of crystallography 1963–68. He was a committed communist, and supported the pseudoscientific theories of the Soviet biologist Trofim Denisovich Lysenko, who believed in the inheritance of 'acquired characteristics' in opposition to the science of genetics.

During World War II Bernal was a scientific advisor to Lord Mountbatten, undertaking research on munitions and in support of the D-Day landings. He also worked on an unsuccessful scheme to create artificial icebergs for use as aircraft carriers.

He advanced the science of crystallography and used it to study a wide range of compounds. In particular he helped in the development of molecular biology with his work on the structure of water and his studies into the origins of life. He also completed research on the structure and composition of the Earth's crust.

BEST, GEORGE (1946–)

Footballer, born in Belfast. One of football's greatest talents, he was a vital member of the Manchester United side that won the league championship in 1965 and 1967, and the European Cup in 1968, when he was voted both English and European footballer of the year.

Best joined Manchester United as a youth and made his full debut when only 17 years old. Just seven months later he won his first international cap. He scored 134 goals in his 349 appearances for Manchester United between 1963 and 1973. For Northern Ireland, he scored nine goals in 37 appearances between 1964 and 1978. Alcohol-related problems and trouble with managers, fellow players, and the media meant that when he left Manchester United his career was already in decline. He subsequently made a series of short-lived comebacks with teams in England, the USA, and Scotland, but without recapturing the form on which he had built his reputation.

BIANCONI, CHARLES (CARLO)

(1786–1875)

Transport entrepreneur, born in Lombardy, Italy. Bianconi came to Ireland as a travelling salesman specializing in prints and small artworks. On opening a craft shop in Carrick-on-Suir, County Tipperary, in 1806, he became aware of the acute transportation difficulties of the region and in 1815 initiated his own horse-drawn carriage service, carrying passengers and goods around Tipperary. Rising demand enabled him to expand both the extent of his operation and the size of his carriages; by the mid-1840s a large fleet of 'Bians' covered a road network of over 5,000 km/ 3,000 mi. His coaches remained popular until challenged by the expansion of the railway system in the later 19th century.

BINCHY, MAEVE (1940–)

Journalist and author. Born in Dublin and educated at University College, Dublin, the city and its environs often form a backdrop to her work. She has written a number of plays, but is best known as a writer of short stories and novels. Among her collections of short stories are *Victoria Line, Central Line* (1987) and *Dublin 4* (1982), while her novels include *Light a Penny Candle* (1982), *Firefly Summer* (1987), *Circle of Friends* (1990; filmed 1995), *The Copper Beech* (1992), *The Glass Lake* (1994), *Evening Class* (1996), and *Tara Road* (1998).

Binchy worked as a teacher and part-time travel writer before joining the *Irish Times* in 1969, later becoming the paper's London correspondent. Several of her plays have been staged in Dublin, and she won awards both at home and abroad for her television play *Deeply Regretted By* (1979).

BIRMINGHAM, GEORGE A

Pseudonym of Irish novelist James ⇨Hannay.

MAEVE BINCHY *A shrewd analyser of society, Binchy has charted changes in the lives of Irish women over more than 20 years in hugely successful popular novels such as* Light a Penny Candle *and* Circle of Friends.

BIRMINGHAM SIX

Victims of a miscarriage of justice who spent nearly 17 years in British prisons convicted of an IRA terrorist bombing in Birmingham in 1974. They were released in 1991 when the Court of Appeal quashed their convictions. The methods of the police and prosecution were called into question. The highly acclaimed film *In the Name of the Father* (1993), directed by Jim Sheridan, was based on the case.

BIRR (formerly Parsonstown)

Market town in County Offaly; population (1996) 3,400. Cable is manufactured here. Birr was formerly a garrison town; its streets and public buildings are a fine example of 18th-century town planning. ⇨Birr Castle, built in 1620, was the residence of the Earls of ⇨Rosse who were scientists and astronomers in the 19th century.

BIRR CASTLE

Seat of the Parsons family, the Earls of Rosse, since 1620, at Birr, County Offaly. The present Birr Castle is the work of several periods – it was burnt in 1643, besieged in 1690, and largely altered in the Gothic style by the 2nd Earl of Rosse in the early 1800s. The interior boasts a magnificent Gothic ballroom and an original yew staircase, which dates from the 17th century and has been described as the finest example of its kind in Ireland. The gardens are picturesque and well maintained.

In the grounds of the demesne are the walls and barrel of the Rosse Telescope, built by the 3rd Earl in 1845, which was the largest in the world until 1915. The remains of the observatory can still be seen, together with astronomical artefacts and a scale model of the telescope.

BLACK, CATHAL (1952–)

Film director and writer. Although Black has made only a few films, they are noted for their visual richness. His film *Our Boys* (1981) combines actuality material, documentary interviews, and drama sequences in the first critical examination of Irish Catholic education. The television station RTÉ, despite being one of the film's sponsors, held off broadcasting the film for a decade because of the sensitivity of the material. Similarly challenging was Black's *Pigs* (1984) which featured, amongst its disparate group of social outcasts, the first representation of a gay man in an Irish film.

Black's first film *Wheels* (1976), an adaptation of a short story by Irish novelist John ⇨McGahern, explores the relationship between a son and his father who remains on the family farm after the son migrates to the city. His more recent films include *Korea* (1995) and *Love and Rage* (1999), which received mixed reactions from critics and audiences.

BLACK, DONALD TAYLOR (1951–)

Film-maker; formerly a theatre director. One of Ireland's leading documentary film-makers, Black's debut documentary, *At the Cinema Palace* (1983), was about the actor, director, and archivist Liam ⇨O'Leary, and he returned to the cinema in *Irish Cinema: Ourselves Alone?* (1995). The wide range of subjects he has treated also includes Gaelic sports and soccer, prisons in *The Joy* (1997), the divorce referendum in *Hearts and Souls* (1995), Ireland's leading forensic pathologist in *Dead Man's Doctor* (1995), tourism, and archaeology. His films on the arts have looked at Jimmy O'Dea (1985), Sam Thompson (1986), Oliver St John Gogarty (1987), then Brian Friel (1993), and, most recently, Micheál Mac Liammóir (1999).

BLACK AND TANS

Nickname of a special auxiliary force of the Royal Irish Constabulary formed from British ex-soldiers on 2 January 1920 and in action in Ireland from March 1920. They were employed by the British government to combat the killing of policemen by the Irish Republican Army (IRA) during the ⇨Anglo–Irish War (1919–21). The name derives from the colours of their improvised khaki and black uniforms, and was also the name of a famous pack of hounds.

The Black and Tans acquired a reputation for violent reprisals against the civilian population after IRA attacks. The peak of Black and Tan retribution is traditionally 21 November 1920, known as ⇨'Bloody Sunday'. After the IRA assassinated 13 men in Dublin, mainly British intelligence officers, later that day the Black and Tans fired on a crowd at a Gaelic football match in Croke Park, killing 12 onlookers.

BLACKBURN, HELEN (1842–1903)

Social reformer and campaigner for women's suffrage, born in Knightstown, County Kerry. Having moved to London in 1859, she was secretary of the National Society for Women's Suffrage 1874–95 and editor of *The Englishwoman's Review* 1881–90. In 1899 she joined with the journal's proprietor, Jessie Boucherett, to found the Freedom of Labour Defence League, to block anti-women factory legislation. Forced to retire from public life in 1895, due to her father's illness, her main contribution to the suffrage movement was her political writing. *Women's Suffrage: A Record of the Movement in the British Isles* (1902) was an important history of the movement, and she also edited Lydia Becker's speeches (1897).

Although she was shy in public, Blackburn's writing was passionate and her numerous works included *A Handbook for Women Engaged in Social and Political Work* (1881), *A Handy Book of Reference for Irishwomen* (1888), and *Women under the Factory Acts* (1903), with Nora Vynne.

BLACK DEATH

Massive epidemic of bubonic plague that coursed through Europe in the 1340s; it was first reported to have reached Ireland in 1348. Both the magnitude and character of its effects on the country were disputed at the time and thereafter. Contemporary accounts claimed that the English population suffered greater losses than the native Irish, but while, as else-where, town dwellers were more vulnerable than the rural population, there is evidence that most parts of the island suffered severely. Modern estimates of rural population loss have settled on a range of between 33% and 50% of the total population. However, the major contribution of the plague to the economic decline and political shrinkage of the English colony as a whole is undisputed.

BLACKWATER

River in Northern Ireland; length 80 km/50 mi. It rises in the southeast of County Tyrone, flowing into Lough Neagh at its southwestern corner. It forms the boundary between counties Tyrone and Armagh.

BLACKWATER

River in the Republic of Ireland; length 165 km/ 102 mi. It rises in County Kerry, forms the boundary between Kerry and County Cork, and then flows east through Cork and County Waterford. At Cappoquin it becomes navigable and turns south to reach the sea at Youghal, County Cork. The Blackwater offers roach, dace, and salmon fishing.

BLANCHFLOWER, DANNY (ROBERT DENNIS) (1926–1993)

Footballer, born in Belfast. A right-half renowned for the subtlety and inventiveness of his play, he made 56 international appearances for Northern Ireland between 1949 and 1963. In 1958, under his captaincy, Northern Ireland reached the quarter-finals of the World Cup.

S port is a wonderfully democratic thing, one of the few honourable battle-fields left. It is a conflict between good and bad, winning and losing, praise and criticism. Its true values should be treasured and protected.

DANNY BLANCHFLOWER (1968).

Blanchflower began his career at Glentoran in 1945, moving to Barnsley in 1948, Aston Villa in 1951, and then finally to Tottenham Hotspur in

1954. In 1960–61, with Blanchflower as captain, Tottenham famously became the first club since the 19th century to win the league championship and FA Cup 'double'. Blanchflower was voted English Footballer of the Year in 1958 and 1961. He retired in 1964 and became a noted sports journalist. He later managed Northern Ireland 1976–79 and, briefly, Chelsea 1978–79.

BLARNEY

Town in County Cork, 8 km/5 mi northwest of the city of Cork; population (1996) 2,000. Tourism is the principal industry, and there is woollen manufacturing. The Blarney Stone, which is supposed to confer the power of persuasive eloquence on all who kiss it, is situated at the top of the battlements of ⇨Blarney Castle, and is a major tourist attraction.

The 19th-century Blarney Castle mansion house is also open to visitors, and the grounds of the house and castle are an example of 18th-century gardening.

BLARNEY CASTLE

Castle at Blarney, County Cork. It consists mainly of a massive square keep with a battlemented parapet, built by Cormac MacCarthy about 1446. The castle is internationally known for the Blarney Stone, which is built into its battlements; the stone is supposed to endow anyone who kisses it with eloquence. The origin of this practice may be associated with a former MacCarthy who, although known for his eloquence, failed to impress Queen Elizabeth I who described his rhetoric as 'All Blarney'.

BLASKETS

Group of seven islands off the west coast of County Kerry, near Slea Head. Great Blasket is 6 km/4 mi by 1 km/0.6 mi; other islands include Inishtooskert, Inishnabro, and Inishvickillane. The Blaskets have been uninhabited since 1953, and are an important breeding ground for sea birds such as gannets, puffins, and Manx shearwaters.

Inishvickillane contains the ruins of St Brendan's Oratory. An interpretive centre, which recalls the history and culture of the islands, has been established on the mainland at Dunquin.

The Blaskets produced several important Gaelic writers in the 20th century, including Maurice O'Sullivan, Peig ⇨Sayers, and Tomas Ó Criomhthainn.

Two ships from the Spanish Armada, the *Santa Maria de la Rosa* and the *San Juan de Ragusa*, sank near the Blaskets in 1588.

BLIGH, WILLIAM (1754–1817)

English Royal Navy officer, chartmaker, and hydrographic surveyor who completed the Dublin Bay Survey, a highly detailed chart on which Dublin's port

BLARNEY CASTLE *This Georgian manor house was built on to the keep of Blarney Castle in the early 18th century, by James St John Jefferyes. His descendants lived in the 19th-century mansion, known as Blarney House, which is also found in the castle grounds.*

BLARNEY STONE *A good head for heights is needed at this popular attraction, since to kiss the stone, tourists must hang their head backwards, beneath the battlements. In legend, the stone was given by a witch to a king of Munster who had saved her from drowning.*

facilities were later based. He is more widely known as the captain of *HMS Bounty*, which he commanded until the notorious mutiny of its crew in 1789.

Bligh was born in Cornwall, England. He was one of a number of marine experts and harbour engineers brought to Dublin to consider how to improve port access. His task was to complete a detailed survey of Dublin Bay, which would include information about tides, currents, local winds, and their effects on navigation, and where ships might safely shelter while awaiting tides.

He completed his commission over three months during the difficult winter of 1800–01 and his charts were used in the development of Dublin's port for a century afterwards.

BLOOD'S PLOT

A Protestant conspiracy of 1663, led by Captain Thomas Blood (*c.* 1618–1680), to seize Dublin Castle and kidnap the Duke of Ormond (1610–1688), lord lieutenant of Ireland. Provoked by Ormond's attempts to reclaim some of the confiscated Irish lands granted to Blood and other former parliamentary soldiers in the 1650s, the plot was discovered before it matured; seven conspirators were arrested and one executed, but Blood escaped into exile.

In 1670 Blood attempted to assassinate Ormond in London; he escaped again but was arrested while attempting to steal the English crown jewels in 1671. His pardon and subsequent grant of Irish lands worth £500 strengthen the contemporary rumour that he had been acting as a government *agent provocateur* all along.

BLOODY SUNDAY

One of two shootings of unarmed civilians. The first occurred in Dublin on 21 November 1920 after Irish Republican Army (IRA) agents killed 13 men, most of whom were British intelligence officers. Three IRA leaders were killed in retaliation, including Peadar Clancy and Richard McKee, and later that day a government force of Black and Tans opened fire on a crowd at a Gaelic football match in Croke Park, killing 12 onlookers.

The second incident refers to the shooting dead of 13 unarmed demonstrators in Derry by soldiers of the British army's 1st Parachute Regiment on 30 January 1972. The demonstrators were taking part in a banned march to protest against the introduction of internment without trial to Northern Ireland on 9 August 1971. The event led to an escalation of violence in Northern Ireland. The British government-appointed Widgery Tribunal found that the paratroopers were not guilty of shooting dead the 13 civilians in cold blood. A new inquiry into the 1972 incident opened in Derry in March 2000.

BLOUNT, CHARLES (1st Earl of Devonshire, 8th Baron Mountjoy) (1563–1606)

English courtier and soldier; lord deputy of Ireland 1600–03 and lord lieutenant of Ireland 1603–06. A client of Robert Devereux, 2nd Earl of ⇨Essex, with whom he sailed on an expedition to the Azores in 1597, he succeeded Essex as lord deputy in 1600 following the latter's disastrous term. He immediately abandoned the cautious strategies of previous governors and adopted a ruthless scorched earth policy, which paid dividends after the failure of Hugh ⇨O'Neill and the Ulster Irish to relieve besieged Spanish forces at Kinsale in December 1601. Upon O'Neill's surrender at Mellifont in March 1603, Mountjoy offered surprisingly generous terms, requiring no compensation and restoring much of O'Neill's lands and titles.

Made Earl of Devonshire in 1603 as reward for his victory, Blount continued to be a quiet defender of O'Neill's interest at court. His sudden fall from grace following his marriage to Penelope Rich and his early death have been seen by some historians as important contributions to O'Neill's decision to go into exile.

BLUESHIRTS

Fascistic movement established by the Army Comrades Association (ACA), supporters of the ⇨Anglo-Irish Treaty of 1921, in response to the election of Éamon de Valera's republican Fianna Fáil in 1932. Under the leadership of Eoin ⇨O'Duffy from 1933, it became known as the National Guard. At its peak the Blueshirts recruited over 40,000 members, predominantly rural supporters opposed to the Irish government's ⇨Economic War with Britain.

The Army Comrades Association (ACA) was established by Ned Cronin in February 1932 to promote the rights of ex-servicemen and honour Irish Volunteers who had died in the Anglo–Irish War (1919–21). After T F O'Higgins became president, the ACA became more politicized, adopting a fascist-style shirted uniform and raised-arm salute.

In July 1933, following the appointment of O'Duffy, recently dismissed as commissioner of the Garda Síochána (civic guard), the Blueshirts, now known as the National Guard, developed into a mass movement with corporatist objectives. Violent clashes with the Irish Republican Army (IRA) and de Valera's supporters occurred frequently during the following year. After the banning of the organization, the National Guard merged with ⇨Cumann na nGaedheal and the Centre Party to form a united opposition party, ⇨Fine Gael, in September 1933. O'Duffy's fascist rhetoric and political ineptitude resulted in his resignation from the presidency in 1934, and the fragmented Blueshirt movement had declined into obscurity by 1935.

BOARD OF WORKS (now the Office of Public Works)

Body established in 1831 by the British government to develop the economy and improve social conditions in Ireland. Led by three salaried commissioners, and with a large staff, the Board of Works was made responsible for a number of key areas that had previously been controlled by other bodies. One of its major successes was in the area of inland navigation. Kingstown (Dun Laoghaire) harbour and Dunmore harbour were completed, and loans were made for the construction and redevelopment of roads and bridges. Soon the Board had responsibility for a wide range of areas including new railways, fisheries, supervision of public buildings, and construction of labourers' cottages.

However, the Great Famine (historically dated 1845–49, but now believed to have lasted until 1852) was a crisis that the Board failed to cope with, despite having responsibility for directing relief, and its influence subsequently declined. Under the control of the Department of Finance after Irish independence, the main function now of the renamed Office of Public Works is the protection and maintenance of public buildings. A national monuments heritage division, Dúchas, has completed a number of ambitious projects restoring and developing heritage sites, with funding by the ⇨European Union (EU).

BOG

See ⇨peat bog.

BOLAND, EAVAN (AISLING) (1944–)

Poet and academic. Born in Dublin and educated in London, New York, and Trinity College, Dublin, Boland has lectured and taught creative writing in Ireland and the USA. Most significantly she helped open Irish poetry to the female voice and experience as in *In Her Own Image* (1980) and *The Journey and Other Poems* (1986). With the 1975 publication of *The War Horse*, Boland turned her attention to 'the Troubles' in Northern Ireland, but always with a clear and poignant attention to how the home environment and community are affected by political violence. She addressed this tension between domesticity and disruption again in *In a Time of Violence* (1994). In 1980 she co-founded Arlen House, a feminist press.

Boland's first collection of poetry, *New Territory* (1967), included a retelling of the Ulster cycle saga

'Tochmarc Étaíne/Wooing of Étain' and a contemplation of Irish history. Her later pamphlet 'A Kind of Scar' (1988) analyzed the position of women poets in the Irish literary tradition and the lasting impact of the personification of sovereignty as a woman in ancient Gaelic culture. Her autobiography *Object Lessons* was published in 1996.

BOOLE, GEORGE (1815–1864)

English mathematician whose work in algebraic logic, known as Boolean algebra, formed the basis for the circuitry found in modern digital computers. His *The Mathematical Analysis of Logic* (1847) helped to establish modern symbolic logic, and argued that logic was more closely allied to mathematics than to philosophy.

Boole was born in Lincoln, but developed strong associations with Ireland where he lived and worked for many years in County Cork. Although his father first tutored him in mathematics, Boole was largely self-taught and developed a remarkable skill in the discipline without studying for a university degree. He began writing papers on mathematics in 1839 and discussed new methods of algebra and calculus. He argued not only that there was a close analogy between algebraic symbols and those that represented logical forms, but also that symbols of quantity could be separated from symbols of operation. These ideas received fuller treatment in *An Investigation of the Laws of Thought on which are Founded the Mathematical Theories of Logic and Probabilities* (1854).

In 1849 Boole was appointed professor of mathematics at Queen's College, Cork, and developed his new algebra of logic, now called Boolean algebra. He remained in Ireland until his death in 1864 at Ballintemple, County Cork.

BORD SCANNÁN NA HÉIREANN

See ⇨Irish Film Board.

BOTANIC GARDENS, DUBLIN

See ⇨National Botanic Gardens.

BOTANIC GARDENS, BELFAST

Gardens dating from 1829 in Belfast, County Antrim. They are noted for a splendid and almost unique Palm House designed by Charles ⇨Lanyon and constructed in two phases between 1839 and 1851. The wings date from 1839 and were built by Richard Turner of Dublin; they are the earliest known work by Turner who also built the Great Palm House at Kew Gardens, London, England. The central dome was built in 1852 by Young of Edinburgh. Also located in the gardens is the Tropical Ravine House built in 1886 and extended in 1900, which contains a sunken ravine surrounded by a balcony walk. Both the Palm House and Tropical Ravine House were renovated in the 1980s. The Ulster Museum is situated within the Botanic Gardens.

BOTHY BAND, THE

Traditional Irish band of the 1970s that could be claimed to have set the mould for traditional bands right up to the present day. It was formed in Dublin in 1974 and, after a few initial personnel changes, the line-up quickly settled as Matt Molloy (flute; later a member of the Chieftains), Donal Lunny (bouzouki, guitar, bodhran), Micheál Ó Domhnaill (guitar, vocals), Tríona Ní Domhnaill (clarinet, vocals), Paddy Keenan (uilleann pipes, whistle), and Tommy Peoples (fiddle, later to be replaced by Kevin Burke). The band recorded their eponymously named first album in 1975 for Mulligan Records and went on to record three more. They also toured extensively, especially in Europe, before disbanding in 1979.

The Bothy Band was perhaps most notable for its energetic and powerful arrangements of dance tunes, featuring a driving harmonic and rhythmical accompaniment on guitar, bouzouki, bodhran, and clarinet. This arguably owed more to popular than traditional music. They also placed the performance of dance music into popular music settings, such as festivals and clubs, for the first time. Most significantly, their style of arrangement – developing textures by combining and recombining instruments that played the melody or chordal accompaniment with the occasional use of simple contrapuntal harmony lines – is that followed by the majority of traditional bands to this day.

Their most important albums are *The Bothy Band* (1976), *Old Hag You Have Killed Me* (1976), and *After Hours – Live in Paris* (1979).

BOUCICAULT, DION(YSUS) LARNER (1822–1890)

Playwright and actor. He established himself in London as an actor and made his name as a playwright with the social comedy *London Assurance* (1841). During his career he wrote or adapted some 200 plays, many of them melodramas, including *The Corsican*

*M*en talk of killing time, while time quietly kills them.

DION LARNER BOUCICAULT *London Assurance* (1841).

❧

Brothers (1852), *Louis XI* (1855), *Arragh na Pogue* (1864), and *The Shaughraun* (1874). He moved to the USA in 1872 where *The Poor of New York* (1857), *The Octoroon* (1859), and *The Colleen Bawn* (1860) were extraordinary successes amongst Irish expatriates. The popularity of his drama had profound influence on the playwrights J M Synge, George Bernard Shaw, and Seán O'Casey.

BOUNDARY COMMISSION

A group set up under the terms of the ⇨Anglo-Irish Treaty (1921) to establish the boundary between the Irish Free State and Northern Ireland, both created by the treaty (see also ⇨partition). The commission collapsed in 1925 and the boundary was settled by the Irish Free State, and the UK government.

The commission had started work only the year before, in 1924, with Eoin ⇨MacNeill as the Irish Free State representative, and Richard Feetham of South Africa as chair. The treaty stipulated that economic and geographic considerations should be taken into account as well as local views, and MacNeill resigned when it became evident that certain areas, including Londonderry and Newry, would go to Northern Ireland.

BOWEN, ELIZABETH (DOROTHEA COLE)

(1899–1973)

Novelist, born in Dublin of Anglo-Irish descent, but taken to England as a child. She inherited the family home in County Cork in 1930, and her account of the house and the family, *Bowen's Court* (1942) remains a classic of its kind.

Bowen's novels and short stories deal with a

*Í*f you begin in Ireland, Ireland remains the norm; like it or not.

ELIZABETH BOWEN *Pictures and Conversations* (1975).

❧

number of subjects including the loss of innocence and essential human fears and frailties. She published her first volume of short stories, *Encounters* in 1923. Her novels include *The Death of the Heart* (1938) and *The Heat of the Day* (1949), considered her finest achievements.

Other works include the short story collection *The Demon Lover* (1946), which has elements of Gothic horror; a study of Anthony Trollope (1946); and a book of essays, *Collected Impressions* (1950).

BOYCOTT, CHARLES CUNNINGHAM

(1832–1897)

English ex-serviceman and land agent in County Mayo, Ireland, 1873–86. He strongly opposed the demands for agrarian reform by the Irish Land League 1879–81, with the result that the peasants refused to work for him; hence the word boycott, meaning to isolate an individual, organization, or country, socially or commercially.

In response to his ostracism Boycott hired 50 Protestant ⇨Orangemen for the autumn harvest of 1880, but 1,000 troops were needed to protect them at a cost of £10,000 to the government. In 1886 he left Ireland permanently.

BOYDELL, BRIAN (1917–)

Composer, teacher, and conductor. His works include *In Memoriam Mahatma Gandhi*, Op. 30 (1948), and *Masai Mara*, Op. 87 (1988), both first performed by the Republic of Ireland's National Symphony Orchestra.

Boydell was born in Dublin, and studied at University College Dublin, Cambridge University, England, and the University of Heidelberg, Germany. He was professor of music at Trinity College, Dublin, from 1962 to 1982, and a founder of the Music Association of Ireland and the Dowland consort. As a conductor, he worked with the Dublin Orchestral Players and the RTÉ Symphony Orchestra (now the National Symphony Orchestra). For many years he was a member of the Arts Council and he was one of the founders of Aosdána, a state-supported academy of creative artists from a variety of disciplines and fields.

BOYLE, RICHARD (1st Earl of Cork)

(1566–1643)

Anglo-Irish administrator and Munster planter. Appointed deputy escheator general in 1588, an office responsible for the discovery of concealed crown lands and defective leases, Boyle exploited his position to defraud both the Crown and its tenants in his own interests. Purchase of Sir Walter Raleigh's Munster estates at bargain prices and marriage to a daughter of the Irish Secretary of State established his fortune. He became a privy councillor, held several lucrative offices, and was created earl of Cork in 1620. In the 1630s the English viceroy, Sir Thomas Wentworth (1593–1641) sought to reduce Boyle's wealth and influence but Boyle successfully resisted the challenge and played a major role in the viceroy's impeachment and ruin.

BOYLE, ROBERT (1627–1691)

Chemist and natural philosopher; one of the influential Boyle dynasty. He conducted extensive experiments on the properties of gases and formulated Boyle's law to describe his findings. He pioneered the use of experimentation and the application of the scientific method.

Boyle was born in Lismore, County Waterford, the 14th child of Richard Boyle, 1st Earl of Cork, and began his early experimental work in Dorset, England, at the age of 18. He questioned the alchemical basis for the chemical theory of his day and taught that the proper object of chemistry was to determine the compositions of substances. He coined the term 'analysis', introduced the use of litmus to indicate acids and bases, and was the first chemist to collect a sample of gas.

He studied at Oxford University 1654–68 and

Father of Chemistry and Uncle of the Earl of Cork.

ROBERT BOYLE On his tombstone in Dublin, quoted in R L Weber *More Random Walks in Science* (1973).

≈

joined with the English scientist Robert Hooke to develop and build an air pump, a device that would become central to many of Boyle's experiments. He used the device to demonstrate the characteristics of air and the role of air in combustion, respiration, and sound transmission. He presented a report to the Royal Society about his findings that at a constant temperature the volume of a gas is inversely propor-

ROBERT BOYLE *A religious man as well as a scientist, Boyle believed that his new approach, of demanding empirical proof for scientific phenomena rather than relying on speculation, provided independent evidence of the work of a divine creator.*

tional to the pressure, now known as Boyle's law.

In 1661 he released his seminal book *The Sceptical Chymist*, in which he proposed that chemical substances were composed of corpuscles, capable of arranging themselves into groups, a theory close to the modern understanding of atoms. He rejected the Aristotelian theory of four elements (earth, air, fire, and water) as the basis for matter, and the three elements (salt, sulphur, and mercury) favoured by Swiss scientist Paracelsus (1493–1541), theories that were strongly held at that time by the scientific community. In 1667 he was the first to study the phenomenon of bioluminescence, and he can also be credited with the invention of the first match in 1680.

Boyle was also a strongly religious man, bequeathing the Boyle Lectures for the defence of Christianity, which continue to this day. He funded activities such as the translation of the Bible into Turkish, and its distribution in that country. He retained contact with Ireland through his estates in County Waterford, which required periodic attention.

BOYLE ABBEY

One of the largest Cistercian abbeys in Ireland, at Boyle, County Roscommon. It was founded in 1161 but took almost 60 years to build. Despite damage suffered in the reign of Elizabeth I and then in the Cromwellian era, it remains in remarkably well preserved condition. The chief feature is the cruciform church with the lower portions of the crossing tower dating from the time of original construction. It was closely associated with ⇨Mellifont Abbey in County Louth.

BOYNE

River in the Republic of Ireland, rising in the Bog of Allen in County Kildare, and flowing 110 km/69 mi northeastwards through Trim, Navan, and Drogheda to the Irish Sea. An obelisk marks the site of the Battle of the ⇨Boyne, fought at Oldbridge near the mouth of the river on 1 July 1690.

BOYNE, BATTLE OF THE

A major confrontation fought on 1 July 1690 between ⇨Jacobite and Williamite forces and the most commemorated battle in modern Irish history.

Following William III's arrival at Belfast in June 1690, the Jacobites sought to obstruct his progress to Dublin at the major natural barrier of the River Boyne. An initial stand-off was broken by a Williamite diversionary tactic which drew the bulk of Jacobite forces under James II upstream, and left the small force under ⇨Tyrconnell to resist the main army at Oldbridge. After initial valiant resistance the Jacobite forces broke and were scattered, while the main army under James failed to arrive in support and James precipitately took ship for France. Though the initial forces engaged were large, (36,000 Williamites; 25,000 Jacobites) actual losses were small and the strategic significance of the result were not dramatic. The crucial confrontation took place at Aughrim, County Galway, a year later on 12 July 1691, when the Williamite general Ginkel faced the Jacobite St Ruth with forces of 20,000 each, and the Jacobites were routed with losses so severe (over 7,000 Jacobite dead) that surrender at ⇨Limerick was virtually inevitable.

Although it was not initially celebrated, the victory of the Boyne became a symbol of the Protestant cause in the 1790s, when a miscalculation gave the date under the New Style Gregorian calendar as the 12th, though it was properly the 11th, while ironically the actual date (Old Style) of the decisive battle at Aughrim was 12 July.

BOYNE VALLEY (Irish *Brú na Bóinne*, 'palace of the Boyne')

Vast necropolis of the Neolithic and Bronze Age Boyne Valley culture in County Meath. One of Europe's most remarkable prehistoric sites, the remains of four massive tumuli (burial mounds) containing passage-graves and burial chambers have been excavated at Newgrange, Knowth, and Dowth on the River Boyne between Slane and Drogheda, and at Fourknocks Hill, 20 km/32 mi to the southeast. The structures, dating from 3100 BC to 1800 BC, exhibit outstanding examples of megalithic abstract engraving and have yielded numerous Bronze Age and Early Christian artefacts. Their original purpose, as a centre of ritual or royal burial, is unclear but their precise alignment with the winter solstice suggests possible use as a calendar.

Newgrange, dating from 3100 BC, incorporates the world's oldest known astronomical observatory. Its tumulus, 80 m/278 ft in diameter and 9 m/30 ft high, is faced with sparkling white quartzite embossed with granite pebbles. The mound is bounded by 97 kerbstones and was once ringed by 38 monoliths, of which 12 remain. From the entrance, a 20 m/66 ft-long passage leads to a corbelled central chamber, 6 m/20 ft high; a narrow aperture allows the rising sun to enter only at the winter solstice. Three smaller recesses contain hollowed stones for cremated human bones and offerings. Geometric symbols decorate the kerbstones and other surfaces, including a unique triple spirals motif on the threshold stone.

Knowth has the greatest concentration of megalithic art in Europe, including lozenges, squares, sun symbols, triangles, zizags, and concentric arcs – also a feature of Breton sites. An unusual dotted pattern is similar to engraving found on Malta. The tumulus contains two extensive passage-graves, 34 m/118 ft and 40 m/140 ft in length, and is surrounded by 17 satellite tombs. Evidence of continuous occupation has been found from its construction around 3000–2500 BC until the 14th century.

Dowth tumulus encloses two passage-graves, but has suffered from Viking raids and pillaging for stones. The west passage opens into a cruciform chamber which contains a recess leading to a series of small compartments, a feature unique to the site.

Fourknocks Hill contains a huge passage-grave established 2200–1800 BC. Three niches in the burial chamber bear zizag motifs, and a human face is carved on one of the stones.

BOYZONE

See ⇨pop and rock music.

BRADY, LIAM (WILLIAM) (1956–)

Footballer, born in Dublin, who won 72 caps for the Republic of Ireland between 1974 and 1990, a national record until surpassed by Paul ⇨McGrath. An elegant midfield player, who at his peak in the late 1970s and early 1980s was one of the best playmakers in European football, he joined Arsenal at the age of 17 and spent seven years at the London club before joining Juventus in 1980. After winning two championship winner's medals he moved to Sampdoria. He later played for Internazionale, Ascoli, and West Ham. In retirement Brady managed Celtic and Brighton, before returning to Arsenal as youth team coach.

BRADY, PAUL (1947–)

Rock singer/songwriter, from Londonderry. He first came to prominence as a traditional singer and accompanist of dance music in the folk revival of the late 1960s and 1970s. He was a member of one of the first bands of the Irish folk revival, the Johnstons, and later joined ⇨Planxty. During this period he made a number of notable recordings, culminating in his 1978 solo recording *Welcome Here Kind Stranger* and his 1979 album with Andy Irvine. His next recording, *Hard Station* (1981), marked a notable departure with self-penned songs and a rock style. Since then he has continued as a contemporary songwriter and performer with a further five albums to his name.

A good introduction to Paul Brady's music is *Nobody Knows – The Best of Paul Brady* (1999). Many of his songs have been covered by other artists such as Delores Keane and Tina Turner.

BRANAGH, KENNETH CHARLES (1960–)

Stage and film actor, director, and producer, born in Belfast. He co-founded the Renaissance Theatre Company in 1987 and gained international recognition with his first film as both actor and director,

KENNETH BRANAGH *Branagh's adaptation for cinema of Shakespeare's courtship comedy,* Love's Labour's Lost, *(2000), put a new spin on the traditional play by turning it into a 1930s musical version, featuring songs by Cole Porter.*

Henry V (1989). He returned to Shakespeare, again performing a dual role, with lavish film versions of *Much Ado About Nothing* (1993), *Hamlet* (1996), and *Love's Labour's Lost* (2000).

Branagh trained at the Royal Academy of Dramatic Art, London, and began his career with the Royal Shakespeare Company. He came to wider attention in 1987 in a television series based on Olivia Manning's *Fortunes of War*, in which he played opposite his regular co-star, English actor Emma Thompson whom he married in 1989 (they separated in 1995). Having co-founded the Renaissance Theatre Company, with David Parfitt, he earned comparisons with Laurence Olivier for his performances, notably in *Hamlet* and *Much Ado About Nothing*. He also staged his own play *Public Enemy* (1988).

Branagh's first Hollywood film as director and actor was *Dead Again* (1992), a stylish film noir thriller. He also demonstrated a deft comic touch with *Peter's Friends* (1992) and *In the Bleak Midwinter* (1995), which he directed and for whom he wrote the original script, although his extravagant interpretation of Mary Shelley's *Frankenstein* (1994) was coolly received.

Branagh has also appeared in the films *High Season* (1987), *A Month in the Country* (1987), *Swing Kids* (1993), *Othello* (1995), *The Gingerbread Man* (1998), Woody Allen's *Celebrity* (1998), and Glatter's *The Proposition* (1998), and in *Wild Wild West* (1999).

BRAY

Coastal resort in County Wicklow; population (1996) 25,300. Bray is the gateway to Wicklow and the surrounding area; there is a fine view from Bray Head (241 m/790 ft). The National Aquarium is located at Bray and there are golf courses near the town.

One of the oldest seaside resorts in Ireland, Bray was largely developed under William Dargan, a railway entrepreneur, during the 19th century. Since the 1960s the town has expanded rapidly, partly as a result of commuter pressure from Dublin.

Leopardstown racecourse is 10 km/6 mi from Bray. Also nearby is the wooded Glen of Dargle, a valley traversed by an aqueduct carrying water from Vartry Reservoir.

BREATHNACH, PADDY (1964   )

Film director, born in Dublin. Although also directing documentaries, Breathnach made his mark as one of the most interesting of the younger generation of film-makers with his first two feature films *Ailsa* (1994) and *I Went Down* (1997). A sombre study of sexual obsession and psychosis, *Ailsa*'s European art cinema sensibility is very different from the US genre resonances of *I Went Down*, written by playwright Conor McPherson, which depicts low-lifers and crime in contemporary Ireland and achieved considerable success at the Irish box office.

BRIAN BÓRUMA (or BRIAN BORU) (941–1014)

King of Munster from 976 and high king of Ireland from 1001 until his death in 1014. He was the first Irish king to gain control over the majority of the island. Starting his meteoric rise to power in 976,

Brian defeated his chief rival, the king of Tara, in 1001 after a long series of campaigns, whereupon he was recognized as Ireland's high king. By 1011 he had received the submission of all the kings of Ireland, which he held until his death. He was killed in victory at the Battle of Clontarf on Good Friday, 23 April, 1014, where he and his son defeated a large faction of Leinstermen and Dublin Norse (see Battle of ⇒Clontarf). His body is reported to have been ceremoniously marched from Clontarf to his burial at Armagh. An Irish national hero whose legend has often obscured his actual achievements, Brian is also known as a builder of churches and forts, as well as a patron of the arts.

BRIGID, ST (*c.* 5th–6th centuries)

A patron saint of Ireland who represents the important role of both women and monasteries in early Irish Christianity. Her feast day is 1 February.

Very little is known about Brigid with historical certainty; indeed, many scholars view her as a mythical personification of the Celtic goddess Brid. She probably did exist as the first abbess of the women's (later mixed) monastery at Kildare (founded around AD 500). She appears to have held episcopal-like authority and therefore hints that the monastic dominance of the Irish church, from the 7th century onwards, developed from an originally female church structure.

BRINKLEY, JOHN (1763–1835)

English astronomer who spent most of his career working in Ireland, from 1790 as the first Andrews professor of astronomy at Dublin University and from 1826 as the Church of Ireland bishop of Cloyne in County Cork.

Born in Woodbridge, Suffolk, Brinkley studied at Cambridge and worked with English astronomer Nevil Maskelyne at Greenwich before taking up the post of professor of astronomy at Dublin University in 1790. Shortly afterwards he became the first Astronomer Royal for Ireland.

Brinkley conducted all his astronomical work at Dunsink Observatory, just outside Dublin, where he attempted to overcome the observational problem of refraction in the atmosphere. He studied numerous methods to defeat the problem, measuring the constants of aberration due to the motion of the Earth. He made it his life's work to measure the trigonometric parallax of bright stars, but he was unsuccessful due to problems with his instruments.

SAINT BRIGID *In the mid-7th century there was a major church at Kildare with a shrine to Brigid. Devotion to her became widespread, and by the 9th century she was the most revered saint after Saint Patrick.*

While working as an astronomer, Brinkley also became an authority in ecclesiastical law in the Church of Ireland and he was eventually made bishop of Cloyne in 1826. He was the only Irish resident to serve as president of the Royal Astronomical Society and was also president of the Royal Irish Academy.

BROOKE, CHARLOTTE (*c.* 1740–1793)

Translator and anthologist. Her *Reliques of Irish Poetry* (1789) is a primary anthology, with extensive notes and introductory comments, of poems and songs that she translated from Irish into English. Her work included the first translations of songs by ⇨Carolan. Born in Rantavan, County Cavan, she was educated by her father, the novelist Henry Brooke (1703–1783), and published an edition of his poetry in 1792. Brooke is now seen as a major force in the development of cultural nationalism.

BROOKEBOROUGH, BASIL STANLAKE BROOKE (Viscount Brookeborough) (1888–1973)

Unionist politician and prime minister of Northern Ireland 1943–63. He was born in Colebrook, County Fermanagh, and educated at Winchester and Sandhurst. A conservative unionist and staunch advocate of strong links with Britain, he entered the Northern Ireland House of Commons in 1929 and held ministerial posts 1933–45. His regime saw moderate improvements in economic prosperity but maintained an illiberal stance towards Northern Ireland's Catholic minority, and made no real attempt at significant political or economic reform.

C atholics are out to destroy Ulster with all their might and power. They want to nullify the Protestant vote, take all they can out of Ulster and then see it go to hell.

VISCOUNT BROOKEBOROUGH Speech at Mulladuff, Newtownbutler, 12 July 1933.

Brooke served in the Hussars during World War I, winning the Military Cross. He resigned his commission in 1920 to run his large estates in Fermanagh; he became viscount in 1952. He was elected to the Northern Ireland senate in 1921 but resigned to play a leading role in the establishment of the Ulster Special Constabulary. Elected Unionist MP for County Fermanagh in 1929, he was appointed minister of agriculture 1933–41, and minister of commerce and production 1941–45. Following the death of Lord Craigavon in 1940, and the failure of his successor John Andrews (1871–1956), Brooke emerged as prime minister in 1943.

His views on Northern Ireland's Catholics were notoriously bigoted. He advocated discrimination in private as well as public employment, and in 1959 supported the section of the Unionist Council which rejected the notion of allowing Catholics to join the Unionist Party. Following increasing political discontent led by the Northern Ireland Labour Party and dissension within his own party, Brookeborough resigned at the age of 75 on 23 March 1963. He retired from politics in 1968.

BROSNAN, PIERCE (1953–   )

Actor, born in Drogheda, who has become an international star through his role as James Bond, in the films *GoldenEye* (1995), *Tomorrow Never Dies* (1997), and *The World is Not Enough* (1999). Beginning his career as a theatre actor with London's Oval House Theatre Company, Brosnan later studied at the Drama Centre there. More interested in film acting, he gained his first break as Irish horse trainer Eddie O'Grady in the television drama-documentary *Murphy's Stroke*. Following his role in the television series *The Mannions of America*, he moved to the USA to star, for five years, in the series *Remmington Steele* (1982–87).

Brosnan's feature film debut was in 1979 when he played an IRA hitman in *The Long Good Friday*. His Hollywood debut was in the thriller *Nomads* (1986), which was followed by the superior spy thriller, *The Fourth Protocol* (1987). In the 1990s his career took off with more inspiring roles in films as various as *Mister Johnson* (1991), *The Lawnmower Man* (1992), *Live Wire* (1992), *Mrs Doubtfire* (1993), *Love Affair* (1994), *Mars Attack* (1996), *Dante's Peak* (1997), *The Nephew* (1997), and *The Thomas Crown Affair* (1999). He was offered the role of James Bond in 1986 but owing to contractual obligations he was unable to take it until 1995.

BROUGHAM, JOHN (1810–1880)

Irish-born US actor, playwright, and manager who moved to the USA in 1842. A popular comedian, specializing in the stock character of the 'stage Irishman', he went on to write over 100 plays, including spoofs such as *Much Ado about the Merchant of Venice* (1869). His adaptation of *Dombey and Son* in 1848 was a considerable success.

Born in Dublin, Brougham began his acting career in London. As a theatre manager for the Lyceum Theatre, he was less successful, and moved to New York. He wrote and produced burlesques and musical comedies, and in a legal suit claimed to have co-written *London Assurance* (1841) with Dion Boucicault. His memoirs and a selection of his writing were published as *Life, Stories and Poems of J. B.* in 1881.

BROUNCKER, WILLIAM (2nd Viscount Brouncker of Castle Lyons) (1620–1684)

Mathematician who was a founder-member and first president of the Royal Society 1662–77. One of the most brilliant mathematicians of his time, Brouncker was the first to express pi as a continuing fraction, and calculated logarithms by infinite series. Together with the English mathematician John Wallis, he solved Pierre de Fermat's questions about Pell's equation, giving a general method for their solution.

Brouncker was born at Castle Lyons, County Cork, and educated at Oxford, graduating in 1647. He was president of Gresham College, London, 1664–67. He was a friend of the English diarist Samuel Pepys, appearing frequently in his *Diary* (1616–69), and had a keen amateur interest in music.

BROWN, WILLIAM (1777–1857)

Sea captain and admiral in the Argentine navy, born in Foxford, County Mayo. Moving to South America in 1811, he lived in Buenos Aires, Argentina, becoming a government privateer during the war with Spain 1812–14. Arrested for piracy in 1816, he was forced out of the navy, and attempted suicide in 1819. The outbreak of war with Brazil saw him restored to full rank in 1825 and he was given command of the navy. Although facing a vastly superior fleet, he won a number of crucial victories, especially the Battle of Juncal in 1827. He helped sign the peace in 1828, and retired that year.

Brown was briefly governor of Buenos Aires 1828–29. Recalled to protect Argentina in the 1830s and 1840s, he successfully fought against Uruguay until his fleet was captured in 1845. He visited Ireland in 1847 and was shocked by the Great Famine.

BROWNE, NOEL (1915–1997)

Radical politician. Born into poverty. Browne was adopted by a wealthy medical family, the Chances, on the death of both of his parents from tuberculosis. Trained as a doctor, he entered politics with the principal ambition of improving the public provision of health care. On the success of his party, Clann na Poblachta, in 1948 he was made minister for health in the coalition government formed by John A Costello and immediately launched an ambitious programme to eradicate tuberculosis. The programme enjoyed great success. An equally ambitious scheme to improve care for mothers and children aroused the opposition of the Catholic church, which regarded it as a threat to the sanctity of the family. Abandoned by his cabinet colleagues, Browne resigned in April 1951 and though he remained active in politics until the 1970s, never again regained his early influence in government.

BRUCE, EDWARD (died 1316)

Scottish earl, brother of Robert the Bruce, King of Scotland. He invaded Ireland in May 1315 with a series of successful and damaging raids, predominantly in the north. With the support of several Irish lords, notably Domhnall Ó Néill (died 1325), King of Cenél nEógain (in modern County Donegal), he was proclaimed king of Ireland. In the winter of 1316–17 he was joined by his brother Robert, and after striking many areas up to and surrounding Dublin, he marched to Munster in the vain hope of joining forces with the Irish of that province. The decision not to attack Dublin marked the turning-point in the Bruce invasion, Edward's smaller victories in 1317 never posing a genuine threat. He died in battle in May 1318 at Fochart (Faughart), just north of Dundalk, County Louth.

BRUGHA, CATHAL

Republican activist, see ⇨Anglo–Irish War (1919–21).

BRUTON, JOHN (1947–)

Irish politician, leader of Fine Gael (United Ireland Party) from 1990 and prime minister 1994–97. The collapse of Albert ⇨Reynolds's Fianna Fáil–Labour government in November 1994 thrust Bruton, as a leader of a new coalition with Labour, into the prime ministerial vacancy. He pledged himself to the continuation of the Anglo-Irish peace process as pursued by his predecessor; in 1995 he pressed for greater urgency in negotiations for a permanent peace agreement. However, his alleged over-willingness to support the British government's cautious approach to the peace process produced strong criticism in April 1995 from the Sinn Féin leader, Gerry Adams.

A Dublin-trained lawyer and previously a working farmer, Bruton entered parliament in 1969. He served as a junior minister in the departments of agriculture and education, and became minister for finance 1981–82 and 1986–87, and minister for industry and commerce 1983–86 under the premiership of Garret ⇨FitzGerald. His budget in 1982 briefly brought down FitzGerald's government when defeated in the Dáil. He succeeded Alan Dukes as party leader in 1990.

BUNCRANA

Seaside resort in County Donegal; population (1996) 3,300. It is situated on the eastern shore of Lough Swilly, about 23 km/14 mi northwest of the city of Londonderry. Industries include the manufacture of clothing and textiles, and the town has museums of knitting and textiles, the latter in a restored mill. There is a vintage-car museum and, at nearby Fort Dunree, a coastal-defence battery has been restored as a naval and military museum.

At Fahan, 7 km/5 mi from Buncrana, is the site of a 7th-century monastery containing St Mura's Cross, embellished with Celtic art and now a national monument; other remains from the monastery, including a bell and a staff, are in museum collections in Dublin and London. On Greenan Mountain (245 m/803 ft) 18 km/11 mi south of Buncrana is Grianán of Aileach, a circular stone fort 23 m/77 ft in diameter and 5 m/17 ft high; built about 1700 BC and restored in 1870, it was the stronghold of the O'Neills, former kings of Ulster.

BUNRATTY CASTLE

Fifteenth-century castle at Bunratty, County Clare. Considered one of the finest castles of its period in Ireland, it stands on the site of earlier fortifications from about 1250 and 1355. The castle is really a late medieval tower house. It was purchased by Lord Gort in 1956 and restored by John Hunt and Percy Le Clerc who described it as 'the most important civil building that has come down to us from the period'. It is furnished with Lord Gort's collection of medieval and 16th-century pieces and was bequeathed to the nation on his death. A 19th-century reconstructed Irish village in the castle grounds is a major tourist attraction.

BUNTING, EDWARD (1773–1843)

Collector of traditional music. Born in Armagh, he lived in Drogheda from 1782 and eventually settled in Dublin in 1819. A trained organist, Bunting made a

BUNRATTY CASTLE *The MacNamaras were the original builders of this magnificent castle. Inside the keep, there is rare 17th-century stuccowork in the chapel and banqueting hall, where tapestry hangings and medieval French furniture are also on display.*

major contribution to the survival of Irish music with his *General Collection of The Ancient Music of Ireland* (1796); subsequent editions in 1809 and 1840 added hundreds of new pieces. Much of the material was gathered during his travels across Ireland. His collections inspired writers and Irish nationalists alike, and continue to serve as the foundational texts for research into traditional Irish music, in particular airs for the harp.

BURGH, THOMAS (1670–1730)

Military engineer and architect. Burgh was born in Drumkeen, County Limerick, the son of the Rev Ulysses Burgh. In 1700 he was appointed surveyor general in Ireland, a post he held until his death. As well as remodelling numerous fortifications all over Ireland, including Dublin Castle, he provided 18th-century Dublin with the original Customs House (1707); Trinity College Library (1712–32); Dr Steeven's Hospital (founded 1717); the Linen Hall; the Royal Barracks (1701), now Collins Barracks; and numerous other smaller public buildings.

Burgh's architectural style was more sober than that of his contemporaries in England, such as the Baroque architects William Talman and John Vanbrugh. In particular, he favoured the arcading of ground floors and the provision of central blocks with five bays, crowned by a large pediment.

BURKE, EDMUND (1729–1797)

Politician and political theorist, born in Dublin and educated at Trinity College. After studying law in London, he embarked on a major career in politics that would span over three decades, and numerous controversies. As private secretary to Lord Rockingham he was the leading theorist and writer of the Whig party, and enumerated various arguments in favour of Catholic emanicaption, and against the government's attempts to coerce the American colonists.

A vehement opponent of official corruption, Burke led a lengthy crusade against English colonial administrator Warren Hastings in the 1780s over mismanagement in India. In 1789 the French revolution had a profound affect on his character and he soon came to see it as both a threat to society and a dangerous menace to political order.

a state without the means of some change is without the means of its conservation.

EDMUND BURKE *Reflections on the Revolution in France.*

In his famous *Reflections on the Revolution in France* (1790), Burke set out the principles of modern conservatism and followed this with other trenchant attacks on revolutionary France. He broke with his ally and friend, Charles James Fox, in 1790 over the revolution and later supported the breakaway Whig coalition with the government. Devastated by the death in 1796 of his son, Richard, a former agent of the Catholic Committee, he withdrew from political life and died in 1797.

BURKE, ROBERT O'HARA (1821–1861)

Explorer who in 1860–61 made the first south–north crossing of Australia (from Victoria to the Gulf of Carpentaria), with William Wills (1834–1861). Both died on the return journey, and only one of their party survived.

Burke was born in County Galway, Ireland, but had a cosmopolitan upbringing in Europe. After being educated in Belgium, he entered the Austrian army in 1840. Returning to Ireland, he joined the Royal Irish Constabulary in 1848, and in 1853 emigrated to Melbourne, Australia, where he served as a police inspector in the goldfields of Victoria.

BURREN, THE (Irish *bhoireann*, 'stony place')

Barren limestone plateau with caves and subterranean waterways in northwest County Clare; the most extensive limestone region in the British Isles. Bounded to the west by the Atlantic Ocean and to the north by Galway Bay, it stretches over an area of 300 sq km/115 sq mi, and is a national park. The Cliffs of ⇨Moher rise dramatically on the southwest coast, overlooking the Aran Islands. The region's unique ecological environment shelters an extraordinary mixture of ground-hugging Arctic, Mediterranean, and Alpine plants. Numerous ruined castles, monasteries, lost villages, and prehistoric sites dot the treeless landscape, including Poulnabrone Dolmen, a Neolithic portal-grave whose majestic silhouette has become the symbol of the Burren.

In March 2000, following four years of proceedings, the High Court found in favour of a Burren action group for the conservation of the region, and declared that a partially built visitor centre at Mullaghmore, supported by the minister for the arts and heritage, was unauthorized. It said that completion of the centre would lead to an unacceptable degradation of the environment; the building is expected to be dismantled.

physical

Limestone pavements with deep crevices or grykes give way in the south to the black shale and sandstone of the Cliffs of Moher. Ice Age glaciers have scoured and rounded the hills, and deposited enormous boulders. The highest point is Slieve Elva, 318 m/ 1,109 ft, in an area capped with mud and shale. The Caher is the only permanent river, but turloughs (seasonal lakes) ebb and fill with the changing water table. Rainwater has gouged out vast underground systems, including Pollinagollum, the longest cave known in Ireland, which extends for over 12 km/7 mi. Ailwee Cave, 3 km/2 mi south of Ballyvaughan, is the only system open to the public. The region was once lightly wooded, but erosion occurred after the uplands were cleared for grazing by early inhabitants.

towns

The main coastal settlements are Doolin (or Fisherstreet), a ferry port for the Aran Islands renowned for its traditional music; and Ballyvaughan, a tourist and fishing village on Galway Bay. Inland lies Lisdoonvarna, a Victorian spa town notable for its month-long Matchmaking Festival in September. Kilfenora, a tourist centre on the southern edge of the Burren, is the seat of the smallest Catholic diocese in Ireland, and has the Pope for its bishop.

features

Over 65 megalithic tombs, 500 ringforts, and numerous Christian churches, monasteries, round towers, and high ⇨crosses are found in the region. Prehistoric monuments include Gleninsheen Wedge Tomb and Poulnabrone Dolmen, dating from 3800 BC. The spectacular 9th-century cliff fort of Cahercommaun, 3 km/2 mi south of Carron, includes souterrains (underground dwellings) opening on to the cliff face. Kilfenora contains 12th-century St Fachan's Cathedral with several high crosses, and the Burren Centre.

fauna and flora

Rich, limey soils in the warm limestone crevices nurture a wide variety of plants, including mountain avens, Irish saxifrage, maidenhair ferns, and orchids; low-growing holly and hawthorn are the only trees. The pearl-bordered fritillary, unique to the Burren in Ireland, and the endemic Burren green are two of the 28 species of butterfly found here. Among the native birds are razorbill, guillemot, puffin, and the hooded crow, while overwintering species include the Icelandic whooper swan. Wild goats and the Irish hare are commonly found, while pinemartens, badgers, and stoats are more elusive; otters and seals inhabit the coast.

BUTLER, ELEANOR (Countess of Desmond)
(died *c.* 1613)

One of the few women of substantial political importance in 16th-century Ireland for whom an adequate record survives. The daughter of Edmund Butler, Baron of Dunboyne, her marriage to Gerald Fitzgerald, 14th Earl of Desmond (*c.*1533–1583), in 1565 was intended to cool traditional rivalries between the two families. These efforts were rendered futile when Desmond and his rival 'Black' Tom Butler, Earl of Ormond, were summoned to London to answer charges connected with Affane, a feudal battle they had held in 1565. Following Desmond's arrest and subsequent imprisonment, during which his captain general James Fitzmaurice Fitzgerald led the first Desmond rebellion (1569–73) against the crown, Eleanor joined her husband in the Tower of London. Her assurances to the crown were held to be crucial in securing his release and reinstatement in 1573.

Back in Ireland, Desmond supported the Elizabethan government in its attempts to introduce ⇨composition, a controversial reform of feudal military dues. However, this imposed strains on the Desmond lordship which the earl was unable to contain, finally forcing him into rebellion (1579–83). Eleanor continued to mediate with the crown until 1582 when it became clear that her husband was not to be pardoned, and she sued independently for mercy. This being granted, she spent years of hardship seeking unsuccessfully for a partial restoration of Desmond lands, which became part of the crown's Munster plantation. She entered another politically-motivated marriage in 1596 with O'Connor Sligo (died 1609), and played a significant role in reconciling her second husband, and his tenants and vassals, to English law.

BUTLERS OF ORMOND (or ORMONDE)

A principal Anglo-Irish dynasty established in Munster in 1171 by the Anglo-Norman Theobald Fitzwalter, who was created chief butler of Ireland by Henry II in 1177. James Butler, his seventh direct descendant, was made 1st Earl of Ormond by Edward III in 1328.

Over the next century and a half the Ormond family extended and consolidated its influence in Leinster and east Munster, and removed the family seat from Gowran in north Kilkenny to the magnificent castle at Kilkenny city established in 1391. Both the 2nd Earl of Ormond (earl 1338–82) and James, 3rd Earl of Ormond (earl 1382–1405) served as chief governors of Ireland. However, it was under the 'White Earl', James, 4th Earl of Ormond (*c.* 1390–1452), that Butler influence was at its highest in Ireland in the later middle ages; he established increasing influence over the Gaelic lordships while successfully resisting interference from England.

After his death the family was eclipsed by the rise of their neighbours and rivals the Fitzgeralds of Kildare but, in the 16th century, Piers, 8th Earl of Ormond (earl 1515–39) and James, 9th Earl of Ormond (earl 1539–46), exploited the suppression of the house of Kildare to re-establish their national importance. Under 'Black' Tom, 10th Earl of Ormond (1532–1614), the house enjoyed unprecedented influence at the English court due to his special relationship with Elizabeth I, but the hostility of the New English planters combined with his failure to produce a male heir plunged the family into crisis in the early years of the 17th century.

The house recovered under James, 12th Earl and 1st Duke of Ormond (1610–1688), whose unswerving loyalty to the house of Stuart in the civil wars led to his creation as 1st Duke of Ormond at the Restoration in 1660. Butler loyalty rendered them suspect as Jacobites after 1688 and in 1715 James, 2nd Duke of Ormond was accused of treason and forced into exile in France. The house was restored by George II in 1755 but, while the family recovered its estates and has survived to the present, it never again enjoyed such high political influence.

BUTT, ISAAC (1813–1879)

Protestant lawyer who founded the idea of home rule for Ireland, born in Glenfin, County Donegal. Educated at Trinity College, Dublin, Butt initially defended the Act of Union. Appointed professor of political economy at Trinity (1836), Butt subsequently became a lawyer in 1838 and Tory member of parliament for Youghal in 1851. He set up the weekly *Protestant Guardian* and came to national prominence when he defended Fenian prisoners, 1865–69. Converting to nationalism, he was president of the Amnesty Association which wanted the release of Irish Republican Brotherhood prisoners. He popularized the slogan 'home rule', and founded the Home Government (Rule) Association (Home Rule League) in 1870, which he led until 1878, when he lost out to followers of Charles Stewart Parnell.

BYRNE, EDDIE (1911–1981)

Actor, born in Dublin. Following experience as a variety theatre performer at Dublin's premier venue, the Theatre Royal, Byrne appeared in the film *I See A Dark Stranger* (1946) and went on to act in more than 20 films. He usually played Irish character roles in British films, having the lead in only one film, *Time Gentlemen Please!* (1952), in which he played a tramp who disturbs the equanimity of a sedate English village. His later career included roles in *The Mutiny on the Bounty* (1962) and *Star Wars* (1977), his last film. Byrne's other films include *Captain Boycott* (1947), *The Gentle Gunman* (1952), *Happy Ever After* (1954), and *Rooney* (1958).

BYRNE, GABRIEL (1950–   )

Actor, born in Dublin, who became an international star through memorable performances as an investigative journalist in *Defence of the Realm* (1985), as an

Irish-American gangster in *Miller's Crossing* (1990), and as a traveller/gypsy in *Into the West* (1992).

Byrne began his career at the Dublin Shakespeare Society in 1974, and thereafter worked at the Focus, Project, and Abbey theatres. His first television appearances were in *The Riordans*, a rural soap, and its successor, *Bracken*. His first film role was in Thaddeus ⇨O'Sullivan's *On a Paving Stone Mounted* (1978), while his debut commercial cinema roles were in *The Outsider* (1979) and *Excalibur* (1981).

Other roles include *All Things Bright and Beautiful* (1994), *Little Women* (1994), the highly acclaimed *Usual Suspects* (1995), *Last of the High Kings* (1996), *Mad Dog Time* (1996), *Smilla's Sense of Snow* (1997), *The Man in the Iron Mask* (1998), *Enemy of the State* (1998), *End of Days* (1999), and in 2000, an acclaimed live theatre role in New York, in *A Moon for the Misbegotten*.

BYRNE, GAY (1934–   )

Radio and television presenter, born in Dublin. Prior to becoming RTÉ's and Ireland's most influential television presenter he had worked with Radio Éireann, Granada Television, and the British Broadcasting Corporation (BBC). His major break came in the early 1960s when he hosted what became the successful and innovative chat show, RTÉ's long-running *The Late Late Show*. Likewise, his morning radio show, which was often in dialogue with *The Late Late Show*, helped set national agendas and showed how opinion in Ireland was shifting, especially in the 1980s and 1990s. Through the use of the phone-in and by reading listeners' letters he addressed public, particularly women's, concerns. He retired in 1998 from his radio

GAY BYRNE *His long and successful career as Radio Telefís Éireann's best-known presenter took off when he hosted* The Late Late Show, *a 1960s discussion programme notorious for its lighthearted approach to topics and personalities that had previously been treated with reverence. It ran for over 30 years.*

programme and in 1999 from *The Late Late Show*. In 1999 he presented a series *Make 'Em Laugh*, which looked back over 40 years of comedy on RTÉ. He also has hosted many other shows including *The Rose of Tralee*.

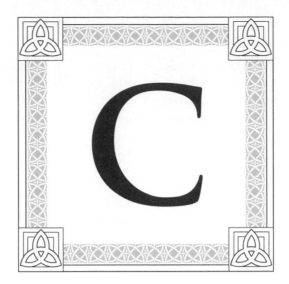

C

CAHIR

Town in County Tipperary, 23 km/14 mi southeast of Tipperary town; population (1996) 2,200. It is situated on the River Suir, at the foot of the Galtee Mountains. Cahir's main industries are tourism and engineering.

Just southwest of Cahir is the 19th-century ⇨Swiss Cottage. It has been restored and is, like Cahir Castle, open to the public. The Motte of Knockgraffon, 6 km/4 mi north of Cahir, is reputed to have been the coronation site for Munster kings before this was transferred to Cashel. Adjacent to the motte are the ruins of Butler Castle, built in the 16th century. The Glen of Aherlow in the Galtee Mountains near Cahir was the site of many ancient battles. There is now a fish farm, open to the public, here. At the head of the glen are the ruins of Moor Abbey, near the village of Galbally; this Franciscan monastery was used as a fortress in the 16th century during the Elizabethan wars.

CAHIR CASTLE

Castle in County Tipperary, 23 km/14 mi southeast of Tipperary town. The largest and best preserved castle of the 15th and 16th centuries in Ireland, it was the seat of the Butler family, Barons Cahir. A few parts survive from the earlier Norman castle, which was possibly built by William de Braose, who had been granted the lands by King John. Cannonballs from the siege of 1599 by Robert Devereux, 2nd Earl of Essex, remain embedded in the outer walls, and in 1650 the castle was besieged by

CAHIR CASTLE *The huge keep has three storeys and was built around a fortified gateway dating back to the 13th century, a remnant of Conor O'Brien's original castle, which was swallowed up in the massive construction works of the 15th century.*

Oliver Cromwell when it was taken without resistance. Although the castle never fell into ruin, it was not lived in after the 18th century, and was partially restored in 1840. It has a massive keep and a great hall, reroofed in the 19th century.

CALLAN, NICHOLAS (1799–1864)

Roman Catholic priest and physicist who was a pioneer in the study of electricity. He was one of the first to build an induction coil, and in 1837 produced his 'giant coil', which generated the highest artificial voltage available at the time. He also developed electromagnets, working electric motors, and batteries, including, in 1848, the world's most powerful battery.

Callan was born in Dromiskin, near Adree, County Louth. He was ordained in 1823 and appointed the professor of natural philosophy at the seminary at Maynooth, County Dublin, in 1826, where he conducted pioneering experiments in electromagnetism. His most important work was in the induction coil, a step-up transformer which converted low voltages to high voltages, central to the modern use of electricity. His giant coil was wound with about 46 km/29 mi of fine iron wire and generated up to 600,000 volts. Callan's inventions are exhibited at the Maynooth Museum.

CALLANAN, JEREMIAH J(OSEPH) (1795–1829)

Poet who was born in Cork and educated at Trinity College, Dublin. He is notable for a handful of poems, most of them very free variations of Gaelic originals. His 'Outlaw of Loch Lene' (1828) is the best known and most haunting.

After college, Callanan returned to Cork and led a life of almost total indolence. Occasionally he made excursions into western Cork with a view to gathering Gaelic material and translating it, but whatever he may have gathered has disappeared. He died in Lisbon while working there as tutor.

CAMOGIE

Ireland's native field sport for women, a 12-a-side stick-and-ball game. It is a modified form of ⇨hurling, and the rules are very similar except that unnecessary physical contact and shouldering, or body-charging, are expressly forbidden.

The game was established at the start of the 20th century when some branches of the Gaelic League (the Irish language movement) evolved their own game from men's hurling which they called 'camogie'. The Cumann na CamUgaíochta Na Gael (Camogie Association of Ireland) was founded in 1904, but the game did not develop until the first intervarsity competition, the Ashbourne Cup, was established in 1915. The first national championship was held in 1932, when Dublin beat Galway. The All-Ireland Championship is now held annually with the final being played at Croke Park, Dublin, the principle Gaelic games venue in the country.

Other differences from hurling are the size of the field, which is marginally smaller; the duration of play, 25 minutes a side for championship games; and the use of a 'camóg' rather than the larger 'cáman'. The camóg is about 91 cm/3 ft long in the handle and used to strike a ball, or 'sliotar', of about 23 cm/9 in circumference.

CAMPBELL, AGNES (c. 1540–c. 1590)

Scottish noblewoman, one of the most important figures in Scottish-Ulster politics in the 16th century. She was daughter of the 4th and sister of the 5th earl of Argyle, wife to James MacDonald of the Isles (d. 1565) and later (1569) to Turlough Luineach O'Neill (c. 1530–1595) chief of the O'Neills. A key figure in the negotiation for the supply and control of Scots mercenaries in Ulster and Connacht, she had the power to advance or destroy the fortunes of several of the major Irish lordships and was largely responsible for the maintenance of the power of O'Neill. She also played a key role in brokering truces between the Macdonalds and the Campells in Scotland. Regarded in general as a restraining force on O'Neill and a figure of great shrewdness, she appears, by the silence of the record, to have predeceased Turlough Luineach by about five years.

CAMPBELL, JOSEPH (1879–1944)

Poet, born in Belfast. Campbell emigrated to New York after the Irish Civil War (1922–23), but returned in 1935 to live in County Wicklow. Under the influence of Douglas ⇨Hyde and the Irish literary revival he began collecting folk songs, being strongly attracted to the Ulster folk tradition. Among his publications are *The Gilly of Christ* (1907), *Irishry* (1913), *Earth of Cualann* (1917), and *Complete Poems* (1963).

CAMPBELL, OLIVER (SEAMUS) (1954–)

Rugby player, born in Dublin. A controversial replacement for the fans' favourite Tony Ward during the Irish tour to Australia in 1979, in his first game he demolished Ward's record of 19 points as Ireland beat the Australians 27–12 in the first Test in Brisbane. For the next four years Campbell remained first-choice out-half for his county. His seven penalties against Scotland helped Ireland capture the Triple Crown in 1982, their first since 1951. In all, Campbell kicked 217 points for his country before an illness forced him out of the international game in 1984. He also toured with the British and Irish Lions.

CANTWELL, NOEL (1932–)

Footballer, born in Cork. He signed for West Ham in 1952 from the League of Ireland club Cork Athletic and spent seven seasons with West Ham before signing for Manchester United in 1959. He led United to victory in the FA Cup in 1963 and made 123 league appearances for the club in his seven seasons there. After a short stint as chair of the Professional Footballers Association, he turned his attention to management in 1967 and had spells with Coventry City and Peterborough United. He captained the Republic of Ireland team 23 times, scoring 14 goals in his 36 internationals.

CAREY, D(ENIS) J(OSEPH) (1971–)

Hurler, born in Kilkenny. He emerged from the Young Ireland's Club to make an immediate impact on the game when he made his intercounty debut in 1989. Operating at corner forward, he played in three successive All-Ireland finals between 1989 and 1991, his tally of 3–23 in 1991 helping Kilkenny to win back-to-back titles. His legendary pace and fielding made it very difficult for opponents to mark him. He has also won numerous All-Ireland handball titles.

CAREY, JAMES (1845–1883)

Activist; see ⇨Phoenix Park Murders.

CAREY, JOHN (1919–1995)

Footballer, born in Dublin. He signed from the League of Ireland side St James Gate for Manchester United in 1936 at the age of 17 and spent 17 years with the club. As captain, he lifted the FA Cup in 1948 in United's 4–2 win over Blackpool. Playing at fullback under manager Matt Busby, he was a versatile team member, filling in at nine different positions. Having collected four runner-up medals between 1947 and 1951, he finally won his first league championship medal in the 1951–52 season. In all, Carey won 306 league appearances and was 'Footballer of the Year' in 1949. He was capped 29 times for the Republic of Ireland.

CAREY, PATRICK (1917–1999)

Director and cameraman, who was born in London but grew up in Ireland. From a theatrical family, Carey worked for several years on the Dublin stage, but from 1945 he began working in films in Britain, shooting his first film, a documentary, in 1947. During the following six years, he worked mainly in Asia and was one of the crew that filmed the 1953 ascent of Mount Everest. Continuing to work in Britain, and for the National Film Board of Canada, he specialized in 'nature documentaries'. He won an Academy Award in 1967 for his photography on *Wild Wings* (1966). He also received nominations for three earlier films, including his most admired film *Yeats Country* (1965), which drew on the Sligo landscape to evoke W B Yeats's poetry. Carey rarely worked in feature production, but one exception was as second unit director-cameraman on *A Man for All Seasons* (1966).

CARLETON, WILLIAM (1794–1869)

Novelist, born into a Gaelic-speaking family in Prillisk, County Tyrone, and educated in hedge-schools (informal and clandestine Catholic schools held out of doors in good weather). *The Black Prophet* (1846) is based on his personal experience of the 1817 and 1822 famines. Among his other novels are *Fardorougha the Miser* (1837), *Rody the Rover* (1845), *Valentine MacClutchy* (1845), and *The Tithe Procter* (1849).

His contributions to the *Christian Examiner* were published as *Traits and Stories of the Irish Peasantry* (1830–33). Critical of Catholic fundamentalism, the stories capture the energy and gloom, humour and violence of pre-famine rural Ireland. The collection was published by the Dublin publisher Curry & Company, and marked a revival of Irish publishing; the book was powerful evidence that an Irish writer did not necessarily require a British-backed publisher.

In his early career Carleton led a picaresque life, recounted in his *Autobiography*, wandering about the countryside and observing the colourful life that later appeared in his books. Eventually he settled in Dublin, married a Protestant, and changed his religion.

He is at his best with simple, vigorous character and lively, peasant dialogue, but is less successful with plots, particularly in his novels, which rely on sensationalism and incredible coincidence.

CARLINGFORD LOUGH

Inlet of the Irish Sea at the mouth of the River Newry, between County Louth in the Republic of Ireland and County Down in Northern Ireland. It is 16 km/10 mi long and 3 km/2 mi wide, with rich wildlife and a shingle shore. It is a popular centre for sea angling and sailing.

CARLOW

Second-smallest county in the Republic of Ireland, in the province of Leinster; county town ⇨Carlow; area 900 sq km/347 sq mi; population (1996) 41,600. The land is mostly flat except for the Blackstairs mountains in the south (rising to 796 m/2,612 ft in Mount Leinster). The land in the west is fertile and well suited to dairy farming. Products include barley, wheat, and sugar beet.

CARLOW

County town of County ⇨Carlow; population (1996) 11,700. It is situated on the River Barrow, about 80 km/50 mi southwest of Dublin. The sugar refinery is in the centre of an extensive sugar beet-growing

CARLINGFORD LOUGH *The lighthouse in the lough is set just off the easternmost tip of the Cooley Peninsula, and on the opposite shore the Mourne Mountains slope gently down to the lough's edge. The little town of Carlingford nearby once boasted 32 castles, but only ruins remain.*

area. There are also electrical and engineering industries and tool and appliance manufacturing here. Carlow was a strategic stronghold of the Anglo-Normans and was the site of many conflicts in the 14th–18th centuries.

Ruins of an Anglo-Norman keep dating from the 13th century are still visible. A Neolithic stone tomb 3 km/2 mi east of Carlow, Mount Browne Dolmen, has the largest capstone in Ireland, weighing over 100 tonnes.

Carlow is the seat of the Roman Catholic bishop of Kildare and Leighlin. St Patrick's College, a seminary, was founded here in 1793. Carlow is also the location of a major regional technical college.

CAROLAN, TURLOUGH (1670–1738)

Harpist, born near Nobber, County Meath; one of the last representatives of a long tradition of harping in Ireland. A composer and performer, he travelled around Connaught, north Leinster, and south Ulster over a period of about 40 years. Despite the fact that he was blind and itinerant, his music had qualities that crossed the cultural boundaries between Gaelic Ireland, Anglo-Ireland, and Britain and reached far beyond his own time. The reason for this has often been put down to the 'duality' of his compositions, which on the one hand represented the native, oral, art-music tradition of his Irish harping predecessors, and on the other hand the more modern elements commonly described as the 'Italian baroque' influence (namely Corelli, Vivaldi, and Francesco Geminiani).

The man and his music are often regarded as different from the 'mainstream' Irish dance music tradition, even though there is considerable knowledge of his music among the traditional music community. The Irish harping tradition, a Gaelic art music patronized by the nobility, died out at the beginning of the 19th century. A major contributor to the popularity of Carolan's music is the fact that his pieces were published in a variety of contexts in Ireland and Britain throughout the 18th, 19th, and 20th centuries – from ballad opera to antiquarian-inspired collections. Over 200 pieces attributed to him survive today.

CARRAGHEEN (or CARRAGEEN) (also

known as Irish, sea, pearl, curly, or jelly moss)

Species of edible red seaweed or algae, *Chondrus crispus*, which grows on rocky shorelines on both sides of the North Atlantic. It is named after Carragheen,

County Waterford. A deeply branched seaweed, it grows to 5–25 cm/2–10 in and has many commercial and industrial uses.

Carragheen loses its deep reddish-brown colour when dried to become shades of green-yellow to dark purple. When boiled it yields carrageenin, a product that is used to cure leather, and as an emulsifying and suspending agent (E407) in pharmaceuticals and foods such as ice cream, soups, jellies, and confectionery. It is sometimes eaten dried in Ireland and has been used as both cattle feed and to enrich poor agricultural soils.

A small industry has grown up around seaweed harvesting, particularly along the west coast of Ireland. About 500 people are employed full- and part-time in harvesting and processing more than 35,000 tonnes of seaweed annually.

CARRANTUOHILL

The highest mountain in Ireland, at 1,004 m/ 3,414 ft. It is one of the ⇨Macgillycuddy's Reeks range in County Kerry. Its ascent can be made from Gortbue School or Lough Acoose. It has some very steep and dangerous crags.

CARRICKFERGUS

Seaport on Belfast Lough, County Antrim; population (1991) 32,800. There is some light industry, and the town was formerly a major centre for the artificial fibre industry. The well-preserved ⇨Carrickfergus Castle now houses a museum. The church of St Nicholas dates partly from the 12th century. The port has a large marina and a sailing school. Carrickfergus was the main port of medieval Ulster but declined from the 17th century onwards, with the development of Belfast.

Carrickfergus is reputedly named after Fergus McErc, ruler of the former kingdom of Dalriada, and a king of Scotland during the 6th century. The town was the site of a number of conflicts between English and Irish troops from the 14th–17th centuries, and was briefly held by the French army under Thurot in 1760.

Parts of the Protestant Church of St Nicholas date from the end of the 12th century, but the church is largely a 17th- and 18th-century construction with some modern additions. The church contains a monument to Arthur Chichester (1563–1625), a former governor of Carrickfergus. The father of the poet Louis MacNeice (1907–1963) was a rector of this parish.

Some remains of the town walls, dating from the 17th century, can still be seen, and there is a statue at the harbour commemorating the landing of William III (William of Orange) here in 1690. There is an historical theme park in the centre of the town. 3 km/ 2 mi north of Carrickfergus is the Andrew Jackson Centre, a restored 17th-century cottage housing a museum commemorating the life of Andrew Jackson (1767–1845), 7th president of the USA, whose father emigrated from Carrickfergus in 1765. The ruins of Kilroot church, where Jonathan Swift was minister between 1694 and 1696, are 3 km/2 mi northeast of the town.

CARRICKFERGUS CASTLE

Castle in Carrickfergus, County Antrim, situated on a basalt promontory guarding the entrance to Belfast Lough. It is one of the largest Anglo-Norman castles in Ireland, and the most complete. It was built between 1180 and about 1205 by either John de Courcy or Hugh de Lacy around a central 27-m/ 88-ft tall square keep or donjon with curtain wall. Further defensive walls and two massive bastions were added to the northern side from about 1220. Carrick-

CARRICKFERGUS CASTLE

For centuries this mighty stronghold, the best-defended in Ulster, controlled traffic going in and out of Belfast Lough. The keep, seen towering above the ramparts, houses the Great Chamber, used by high-ranking castle occupants.

fergus Castle dominates the the town, as it has done for the last 800 years. Medieval banquets and the Lughnasa Festival, a harvest celebration, are held annually in the castle grounds.

CARRICK-ON-SHANNON

River port and county town of County ⇨Leitrim; population (1996) 1,900. Situated on the River Shannon, 60 km/37 mi southeast of Sligo town, it is an angling centre and has a marina for cruisers. In 1994 the Ballyconnell–Ballinamore Canal was reopened here, the final link in the Shannon–Erne Waterway (navigable length 382 km/239 mi).

On the main street is Costello Chapel (built in 1877), which is reputed to be the second-smallest chapel in the world.

CARRICK-ON-SUIR

Town in County Tipperary; population (1996) 5,200. It is connected with Carrickbeg, in County Waterford, by two bridges over the River Suir. Tipperary crystal is manufactured here. The town has a fortified Elizabethan mansion (built by Thomas Butler, 10th Earl of Ormond), which adjoins the ruins of the 15th-century ⇨Carrick-on-Suir Castle The town is a centre for fishing on the River Suir and for climbing and hill-walking in the Comeragh Mountains.

CARRICK-ON-SUIR CASTLE

Castle of the Earls of Ormond at Carrick-on-Suir, County Tipperary, dating from 1450. It is unique in Ireland in having a manor house added to it in 1568 by Thomas Butler ('Black Tom'), 10th Earl of Ormond and cousin of Elizabeth I. The house is noted for its Elizabethan design with curved-headed mullioned windows, ornate plasterwork, long gallery, and piano nobile.

CARROWKEEL

Neolithic and Bronze Age cemetery set on a hilltop of the Bricklieve Mountains overlooking Lough Arrow, in County Sligo. An impressive group of 14 round cairns contain megalithic passage-graves, cruciform in layout with corbelled vaults; one chamber is lit by the setting Sun of the summer solstice. Neolithic pottery discovered here dates from 2500 to 2000 BC. During the Bronze Age a number of wedge dolmens were constructed for individual burials, until about 1500 BC. The remains of a Neolithic settlement of clocháns

or beehive huts lie nearby on the northern slopes of the mountain.

CARROWMORE

Extensive Neolithic cemetery in County Sligo, 5 km/3 mi southwest of Sligo; the largest group of megalithic monuments in the British Isles and the second largest in Europe after Carnac in Brittany, France. The site has suffered severe depredation and damage, particularly due to gravel quarrying, but over 60 partially complete circles, standing stones, passage-graves, and portal tombs survive. An 1839 survey listed a further 23 tombs, now vanished, and the original necropolis may have numbered more than a hundred. Excavated burial chambers contain cremated remains dating from 3000 BC.

CARRUTH, MICHAEL (1967–)

Boxer, born in Dublin. Originally coached by his father, Carruth trained at the Drimnagh boxing club in Dublin where as a lightweight he won local and provincial titles. Between 1987 and 1990 he won four senior national titles at three different weights, the last in 1992 when he captured the welterweight crown. Having represented Ireland in the 1987 and 1989 European Championships and the 1988 Seoul Olympics, the pinnacle of his career came four years later when he defeated Juan Hernández of Cuba to win the gold medal in the welterweight category. It was Ireland's first gold in the sport. A year later Carruth turned professional, and in 1998 he beat Scott Dixon to capture the World Athletic Association welterweight crown.

CARSON, EDWARD HENRY (Baron Carson of Duncairn) (1854–1935)

Anglo-Irish lawyer and Unionist politician. He played a decisive part in the trial of the writer Oscar ⇨Wilde and, in the years before World War I, led the movement in Ulster to resist Irish ⇨home rule by force of arms if need be.

Born in Dublin and educated at Portarlington School and Trinity College, Dublin, Carson was called to the Irish bar in 1877. He became an Irish queen's counsel (QC) in 1889, and rapidly built up a lucrative legal practice. His success as a crown prosecutor in the 1880s, during the nationalist Plan of Campaign for tenant rights, led to his appointment as solicitor general for Ireland in 1892. In the same year he was elected to Westminster as Unionist member of parliament for Trinity College, Dublin, continuing to hold that seat until 1918 when he was returned for Duncairn, Belfast. In 1893 he was called to the English bar, and in 1894 became an English QC. His representation of the Marquis of Queensberry in 1895 ruined the career of the writer Oscar Wilde and gave Carson wide public acclaim. He was knighted in 1900 and appointed solicitor general for England 1900–06.

As leader of the Irish Unionist Parliamentary Party from 1910, he mobilized the resistance of Protestant Ulster to home rule; the threat of armed rebellion against the Liberal government by his 'Ulster Volunteers' effectively wrecked the scheme before the beginning of World War I. In cooperation with the Ulster Unionist politician James ⇨Craig, he became the primary orator and charismatic leader of Ulster Unionism, and his strategy of publicly encouraging popular disorder while privately seeking a constitutional agreement brought Ireland near to civil war by late 1914.

After 1914 Carson's career moved away from controversy. In 1915 he became attorney general in the coalition government and was a member of the war cabinet 1917–18, briefly serving as 1st lord of the admiralty during 1917. In 1921 he resigned as Unionist leader and was appointed lord of appeal 1921–29. He was created a life peer as Baron Carson of Duncairn in 1921. Although he failed in his goal of preventing self-government for any part of Ireland, Carson is credited with securing the exclusion of the 'six counties' of Ulster from control by a Dublin parliament.

CARTON HOUSE

Large Palladian-style seat of the Fitzgeralds, later Dukes of Leinster, at Maynooth, County Kildare. Built on the site of a previous winged manor house, it was remodelled by Richard Castle in 1739 with several notable 18th-century rooms, including a saloon with a Baroque ceiling (1739) by the Lafranchini brothers. Richard ⇨Morrison was engaged by the 3rd Duke of Leinster in 1815 to make alterations which included new rooms on either side of the central block and a southern entrance which gave views over the most picturesque part of the demesne. The Chinese bedroom in which Queen Victoria slept remains as originally decorated. In the grounds is a shell house, a type of summer pavilion, the interior of which is highly decorated with seashells.

CARY, (ARTHUR) JOYCE (LUNEL)
(1888–1957)

Writer, born in Londonderry and educated at Oxford and in Edinburgh and Paris. He used his experiences gained in the Nigerian political service, which he entered in 1913, as a backdrop to such novels as *Mister Johnson* (1939), and he used the trilogy form to look at a subject from different viewpoints. The first and best known of his trilogies was about the life of an artist, Gulley Jimson, and comprised the novels *Herself Surprised* (1941), *To Be a Pilgrim* (1942), and *The Horse's Mouth* (1944).

Cary's fiction is influenced by the work of Tolstoy and Joyce and reflects similar thematic interests in violence and the nature of good and evil. Other works include *Castle Corner* (1938), *A House of Children* (1941), and *The Captive and the Free* (1959).

CASEMENT, ROGER DAVID (1864–1916)

Diplomat and revolutionary, who was hanged for treason by the British in 1916. Born in County Dublin, Casement joined the British colonial service in Africa in 1892, and exposed the ruthless exploitation of plantation workers in the Belgian Congo and Peru, for which he was knighted in 1911 (degraded 1916).

> It is a cruel thing to die with all men misunderstanding.
>
> ROGER CASEMENT From his last letter to his sister before being hanged as a spy (1916).

❧

Always an Irish nationalist, Casement joined the ⇨Gaelic League in 1904 and contributed to the nationalist press. In 1913 he joined the ⇨Irish Volunteers and in 1915, following the outbreak of World War I, he went to Berlin to seek German aid for an Irish rising, and tried to recruit for an Irish Brigade among British prisoners in Germany. In 1916 he was captured in Ireland, having returned aboard the German submarine the *Aud* in the hope of postponing a rebellion. Tried for treason, he was executed on 3 August 1916, despite appeals for clemency. British government agents circulated details of his diaries, which revealed an active homosexual private life, in the attempt to discredit him. His remains were returned to the Republic of Ireland in 1965.

Cashel

Town in County Tipperary; population (1996) 2,300. Cashel is one of the most important historic sites in Ireland. The town is dominated by the Rock of ⇨Cashel. Ecclesiastical remains in the town include the 15th-century ruins of a Dominican friary founded in 1243, at the base of the rock, and the Cistercian Hole Abbey, founded in 1266. Quirke's Castle, a 15th-century tower, is located on Main Street. The 18th-century Protestant deanery on the main street is now a hotel. The G P A Bolton Library contains a fine collection of manuscripts and books. There is also a heritage centre and rural folk museum.

Leaders of the 1848 Young Ireland rebellion are

ROGER CASEMENT *Despite having been knighted for his work as a British diplomat, Casement was hanged for attempting to muster German support for the Easter Rising in 1916. Arrested on the coast of Kerry, Casement claimed he was trying to avert the rising because he felt the rebels would be inadequately armed.*

said to have frequently met in a house known as Alla Eileen off the Main Street.

Cashel, Rock of (also known as St Patrick's Rock)

Limestone outcrop rising 60 m/200 ft above the surrounding Golden Vale at Cashel, County Tipperary. It is the site of the most impressive group of medieval structures in Ireland. The Rock of Cashel was the seat of the kings of Munster in the 5th century, when it was supposedly visited by St Patrick, and remained so until the 12th century. St Patrick is said to have baptized King Aengus here in 450, and Cashel was the site of a number of coronations.

The buildings on the rock include the 13th-century roofless Gothic St Patrick's Cathedral (adjacent to the site of the original cathedral founded in 1169, of which nothing remains); the 12th-century Cormac's Chapel (the largest and most complete Romanesque building in Ireland); the 15th-century Hall of the Vicars Choral; the 15th-century Bishop's Castle; the 11th-century round tower (28 m/92 ft high); and the Cross of St Patrick, a decorated Irish cross. The buildings were burnt by Murrough O'Brien in 1647. The site has been restored by the Board of Works with funding from the European Union (EU).

Casino Marino

The 'little house by the sea', near Dublin, on what was formerly the Marino estate, is one of the most elegant small buildings in Europe. A garden pavilion, it was designed from 1758 by the Scottish architect Sir William Chambers for the 1st Earl of Charlemont. Originally the design had been included in plans for a wing of Harewood House in England, but these were rejected. Simon Vierpyl, a sculptor and builder from Rome, worked on the construction using the best materials. The pavilion contains many fine examples of 18th-century architecture and was given protection under the National Monument Act in 1930, the only post-medieval building to gain this status. Major restoration work has been carried out by the Office of Public Works.

Castlebar

County town of County ⇨Mayo; population (1996) 6,600. It is the service centre of a large farming area, and has extensive sales of agricultural produce. Its principal industries are health-care products and pharmaceuticals; there are also manufacturers of clothing and electric cable. The district is a centre for fishing, shooting, and tourism. From 2001 Turlough Park House, Castlebar, will be home to the National Museum of Folklife, a new addition to the National Museum of Ireland.

Castlebar was captured by the Confederate Irish in 1641, and in the ⇨Rebellion of 1798 the French general Humbert defeated an English force here, in a battle known as the Races of Castlebar.

CASTLE COOLE

The finest Neo-Classical country house in Ireland, situated southeast of Enniskillen, County Fermanagh. It was built 1790–96, in dressed Portland stone, for Armar Lowry-Corry, 1st Baron Belmore, on the site of an earlier plantation castle. The first designs for the property are basement plans by Richard Johnston, brother of Francis Johnston, which were added to by the fashionable English architect James Wyatt. The house contains plasterwork by John Rose and statuary by the English sculptor Richard Westmacott. There is a notable ballroom, state bedroom, and outbuildings by Richard ⇨Morrison. The 32-ha/79-acre estate was given to the National Trust by the Ulster Land Fund in 1951.

CASTLEDERMOT

Historic town in County Kildare, 10 km/6 mi northeast of Carlow; population (1996) 1,200. Originally the site of a monastery founded by Saint Dermot in 812, it became a walled town, and gained great military significance following the construction of a castle in 1182. Edward Bruce was defeated here in 1316 by Edmund Butler, and a parliament was held in 1499. Oliver Cromwell sacked the town in 1649, but traces of its medieval walls and Carlow Gate still stand. Significant monastic remains include two 9th-century high crosses with scripture panels, a Romanesque doorway, and a 10th-century round tower, 22 m/76 ft high.

Other local remains include a 14th-century Franciscan friary and Pigeon House, the square tower of a house of Crutched Friars, founded around 1200.

Kilkea Castle, built in 1180 by Hugh de Lacy and now a hotel and leisure centre, lies 4 km/2 mi northwest of the town. Formerly the seat of the Fitzgerald family, Earls of Kildare, it is the oldest inhabited castle in Ireland. It was the birthplace of the Antarctic explorer Ernest Shackleton in 1874.

CASTLETOWN HOUSE

Country house near Celbridge, County Kildare. Begun in 1722, it is the first and greatest Palladian house in Ireland built to correct Classical proportions by a professional architect, and its design was a significant influence on later 18th-century works. Castletown was built for William Conolly, Speaker of the Irish House of Commons, to the designs of the Italian architect Alessandro Galilei. The hall was designed by Edward Lovett Pearce in 1724. Other notable features are the plasterwork (1759) on the staircase by the Lafranchini brothers, and the Long Room and unique surviving Print Room (about 1765). The Irish Georgian Society is based here.

CASTLE WARD HOUSE

18th-century three-storey country house in County Down, 11 km/7 mi northeast of Downpatrick. It was built for Bernard Ward, later 1st Viscount Bangor, between 1760 and 1773, probably by an unknown English architect. Ward faced the house with Bath stone brought from Bristol in his own ships. He could not agree with his wife, Lady Anne, daughter of the 1st Earl of Darnley, on a style for the frontage and interior. As a result the entrance front and interiors were created in the Classical style, which he favoured, and the rear in her 'whimsical' choice of Strawberry Hill Gothic (so named after a house at Richmond, Surrey, in England, designed by Horace Walpole), with battlemented parapets, pinnacles, and pointed windows.

CATHOLIC ASSOCIATION

See Daniel ⇨O'Connell.

CATHOLIC COMMITTEE

Committee founded in 1760 by the Catholic activists Charles O'Conor and John Curry, aiming for Catholic equality before the law. It had greatest impact during the late 18th century. Seeking repeal of penal laws, its strategy was reformist rather than revolutionary. Its middle-class and aristocratic leadership distanced it from the American Revolution of 1775.

During the 1790s the Catholic Committee appointed Wolfe ⇨Tone as executive secretary. Its move towards the United Irishmen in 1795 incurred displeasure from conservative prelates such as Arch-bishop John Troy. After the Act of Union (1801), it joined ⇨Daniel O'Connell in promoting Catholic interests, particularly emancipation which was enacted in 1829.

CATHOLIC EMANCIPATION

Progressive removal of restrictions on Catholics, who had been prevented from holding positions govern-ment and the judiciary, which was completed in 1829; see ⇨Catholicism.

CATHOLICISM

Three-quarters of people living in Ireland describe themselves as Roman Catholic. Catholics account for over 90% of the population of the Republic of Ireland and 75% of the island's total. They are served by nearly 4,000 diocesan clergy, over 4,000 regular clergy, over 12,000 religious sisters, and about 1,000 religious brothers. The church is organized into 26 dioceses, overseen by bishops, and into four provinces, presided over by archbishops. The archdio-cese of Armagh enjoys the primacy but it is mostly honorific as Dublin is the most important in terms of population and influence. Weekly attendance at reli-gious service is estimated to be about 70% in the country as a whole but considerably lower in urban areas.

CATHOLICISM *Historically a key figure in the Irish community, the local priest is still a familiar sight on the streets of small country towns. Away from the urban centres, around three-quarters of the population are regular churchgoers.*

***t**he time has long since gone when Irishmen and Irish women could be kept from thinking, by hurling priestly thun-der at their heads.*

JAMES CONNOLLY Socialist and patriot *Labour, Nationality and Religion*, 18 April 1914.

~

history since the Reformation

Catholicism has been one of the shaping forces of Irish life since the Reformation in the 16th century divided Western Christianity into Catholic and Protestant communities. In the 16th and 17th cen-turies most Irish people did not accept Protestantism. Catholicism at the time was a mix of traditional reli-gion and new influences from Europe, the latter inspired by the Council of Trent (1545–63). Despite

severe persecution, Catholicism succeeded in gradu-ally modernizing itself. Parish structures were re-established, the authority of bishops was enhanced, religious doctrines were clarified, and superstition was condemned.

17th century: conflict of loyalties

The main political problem for Irish Catholics in the 17th century was reconciling religious loyalty to Rome with political loyalty to a Protestant king. Adversity helped forge a distinct Irish Catholic iden-tity which was well established when Oliver Cromwell's campaign in the late 1640s and 1650s undid a half-century of religious reform. Large-scale persecution of Catholics followed. With the defeat of the Catholic king James II at the Battle of the Boyne in 1690, a penal code was put in place to exclude Irish Catholics from land ownership and political power. This was highly successful, and by the early decades of the 18th century Catholics owned only 5% of the land in the country.

***a**mong the best traitors Ireland has ever had, Mother Church ranks at the very top, a massive obstacle in the path to equality and freedom.*

BERNADETTE DEVLIN (McALISKEY) Politician *The Price of My Soul* (1969).

~

18th century: reform and repression

Despite this exclusion from power and property, 18th-century Catholics continued the process of reform begun by the Council of Trent. The network of ⇨Irish Colleges in Europe helped the Catholic community maintain its links with the larger world, a system of primary education was established, diocesan and parochial structures were streamlined, and efforts were made to assist the poor. Relations with the Irish Protestant State improved as the memory of the religious wars faded and the government began to listen to Catholic requests for readmission to political life and property ownership. The radicalization of Irish politics in the 1790s, however, was a major setback to the normalization of the position of Catholics in Ireland. Severe repression followed the ⇨Rebellion of 1798 and Catholic Emancipation was delayed until 1829. It was achieved mainly thanks to the political organization of Catholics under Daniel ⇨O'Connell, aided by the clergy.

19th century: after Emancipation

Catholics gradually entered political life. In a protracted legal and political conflict they won back possession of the land. The Great Famine (historically dated 1845–49, but now believed to have lasted until 1852) decimated the poorer sections of the Catholic community in particular and drove many abroad. Especially after 1850, Irish Catholicism became an international phenomenon. The Irish built up strong Catholic communities in the USA, Canada, Australia, New Zealand, and elsewhere. They played a pivotal role in the political, cultural, and economic development of their host countries. Back home, missionary activity in Africa and Asia was encouraged.

Love is never defeated, and I could add, the history of Ireland proves that.

JOHN PAUL II Pope, Speech in Galway, 30 September 1979.

20th century: political involvement

Always closely associated with those who favoured separation from Britain by peaceful means, the bond between the church and constitutional nationalists was consolidated by the late 19th century. When the Irish State was founded in 1922 the Catholic church

Religion dies hard in the Irish.

KATHARINE TYNAN Poet and novelist *The Middle Years* (1917).

acted as a stabilizing force and left its mark on the new state's identity, especially in education and health care. The 1937 constitution granted the Catholic church a 'special position' in the state and promoted various aspects of Catholic morality, but the close relationship between the Catholic church and the Irish state came under pressure after the 1950s. The far-reaching changes wrought by the Second Vatican Council, economic development, and the political turmoil of the Northern Irish conflict pose an important challenge to contemporary Irish Catholicism.

CATTLE ACTS

Protectionist legislation passed by the English parliament in 1663, 1667, 1671, and 1681, giving effect to a total prohibition of imports of Irish cattle, beef, pork, and bacon into England. Once interpreted as part of a deliberate English policy to destroy the Irish economy, the legislation is now seen as a reflection of the influence of specific agricultural and commercial interest groups within the English parliament. The legislation damaged the Irish economy but not fatally, encouraging greater development in the Irish butter and salted meat export market to Europe and the British colonies. The acts were repealed 1758–59.

CAVAN

County of the Republic of Ireland, in the province of Ulster; county town ⇨Cavan; area 1,890 sq km/730 sq mi; population (1996) 52,900. The chief rivers are the Woodford, the Shannon (rising on the south slopes of Cuilcagh mountain; 667 m/2,188 ft), and the Erne, which divides Cavan into two parts: a narrow, mostly low-lying peninsula, 30 km/19 mi long, between Leitrim and Fermanagh; and an eastern section of wild and bare hill country. The chief towns are Cavan, population (1996) 3,500, and Kilmore, seat of Roman Catholic and Protestant bishoprics. The soil is generally poor and the climate moist and cold.

Much of the county is covered in bog and forest. The chief lakes, noted for their scenery and coarse fishing, include the tortuously shaped Lough

Oughter, and Loughs Ramor, Sheelin, Sillan, and Brackley. Other towns include Bailieborough, Ballyjamesduff, Belturbet, Cootehill, Kingscourt, and Virginia.

CAVAN

Market and county town in County ⇨Cavan; population (1996) 3,500. It is situated on a tributary of the River Annalee, near Lough Oughter, 8 km/5 mi west of Killykeen Forest Park. Cavan crystal is handblown and cut here in the traditional manner. Cavan was the seat of the O'Reillys, rulers of the ancient territory of east Breifne. It has a modern Roman Catholic cathedral, built in 1942.

The belfry tower of a Franciscan friary founded in 1300 can be seen in the town. St Fethlimidh's Protestant cathedral, 5 km/3.5 mi soutwest of Cavan in Kilmore, is a Gothic revival structure which incorporates a Romanesque doorway from a monastery founded on Trinity Island in Lough Oughter; the tomb of Bishop Bedell (1571–1642), who first translated the Old Testament into Irish, is in the graveyard. Some 10 km/6 mi northwest of Cavan on an island in Lough Oughter are the ruins of the 13th-century Cloghoughter Castle, a round fortress which was the stronghold of the O'Reillys and was destroyed in 1653 by Cromwellian forces.

At Cornafean, 11 km/7 mi from Cavan, is a museum of folk and rural life called the Pighouse Collection.

CAVENDISH, LORD FREDERICK CHARLES

British administrator, appointed chief secretary for Ireland in 1882. He was a victim of the ⇨Phoenix Park Murders.

CÉITINN, SEATHRÚN

Gaelic name of Irish Gaelic poet and historian Geoffrey ⇨Keating.

CELBRIDGE

Town in the northeast of County Kildare; population (1996) 12,300. It is situated on the River Liffey, 19 km/12 mi west of Dublin. Nearby is ⇨Castletown House, a mansion in the style of Andrea Palladio, built in 1722.

Celbridge Abbey was the home of Esther Vanhom-

righ (1690–1723), the 'Vanessa' of Jonathan Swift's poem *Cadenus and Vanessa*.

On the Lyons estate (now owned by University College Dublin), 5 km/3 mi south of Celbridge, is Lyons Hill (197 m/645 ft), an Iron Age hill fort and once a seat of the kings of Leinster. Lyons House was built in 1797 and was once the home of Valentine Lawless, 2nd Lord Cloncurry (1773–1853), an active member of the United Irishmen. Later it was home to the historian, poet, and novelist Emily Lawless (1845–1913).

CELT

Member of an Indo-European tribal people that originated in Alpine Europe about 1200 BC and spread throughout Europe and beyond, settling in Ireland from about 300 BC. The Celts had a distinctive religion, led by Druids, and were renowned for their horsemanship, ferocity in battle, and their ritual savagery. While Celts in other areas were subjugated by the invading Romans after AD 43, those in Ireland survived unopposed.

See feature essay on the Celtic influence on Ireland, opposite.

CEOLTÓIRÍ CUALANN

Innovative Irish traditional music ensemble directed by the musician, composer, and academic, Seán Ó Riada. It emerged out of the ensembles gathered together by Ó Riada while he was musical director at the Abbey Theatre, Dublin, at the end of the 1950s. The ensemble made their first radio broadcast in 1961 and in the same year performed the score for the film *The Playboy of the Western World*. The group disbanded in 1969 after its final performance in Cork City Hall. Their most important recording is the live album *Ó Riada sa Gaiety* (1969).

Ceoltóirí Cualann was revolutionary because of the motivation of Ó Riada. He intended to create, through this ensemble, a form of Irish art music. The band's arrangements were heavily influenced by classical music and, particularly, jazz, especially in the way that timbre and colour were changed by combining instruments into different groups and concentrating on solos within pieces. Ó Riada's aims were also evident in the presentation of the band in formal music settings – they played in venues associated with classical music and theatre, attired in dress suits. Ceoltóirí Cualann in essence marked the first major move away from a dance music aesthetic and towards a concert,

HOW THE CELTS INFLUENCED IRELAND

by Charles Doherty

The word 'Celts' comes from the Latin *Celtae*, which in turn derives from *Keltoi*, a name used by the ancient Greeks to describe a barbarian people on the northern fringes of their world. The term *Keltoi* or Celts was eventually applied to a great variety of peoples or tribal groups who spoke closely related languages (with evidence of distinct dialects), and who shared a similar material culture. It has been suggested that their language goes back to the Bronze Age in the second millennium BC. These ancestors of the Celts can be distinguished clearly during the 7th–6th centuries BC from the cultural mix of central Europe. By 600 BC they are associated with the Hallstatt culture of Austria. By the 5th century BC their material culture had evolved into what archaeologists have named La Tène, 'the shallows', after an Iron Age site at Lake Neuchâtel in Switzerland. Here magnificent artefacts were discovered in princely graves – weapons, vehicles, rich personal ornaments, and highly decorated utensils. There was evidence of trade with, and influence from, the Mediterranean world and even further afield. La Tène art is regarded as the first definitive Celtic art. Initially its fantastic imagery often included interpretations of Classical and Oriental forms, but later its distinctive styles were more reminiscent of plant forms. The La Tène culture reached its flowering in the 3rd century BC.

controlling land from Ireland to Spain and Hungary

The first written historical reference to the Celts is around 450 BC when the Greek historian Herodotus (*c.*484–*c.*424 BC) tells of Celtic settlements near the source of the Danube. From this point on, the migration of the Celts is recorded all over Europe. They sacked Rome 387–86 BC and Delphi in 279 BC. Their migrations took them as far west as Spain and north into Britain and Ireland. At their greatest extent they controlled lands from Ireland and Spain to the plains of Hungary. At no point did the Celts form an empire, their territory consisting of independent kingdoms or groups of kingdoms.

The most important descriptions of the Celts come from the Greek philosopher Posidonios (*c.*153–*c.*51 BC) and the Roman statesman Julius Caesar (100–44 BC), who depicted them as war-loving and vainglorious. Champions fought naked, engaged in single combat, were driven into battle on chariots, and took the heads of their enemies. Their priests were the Druids. By the time of Julius Caesar their kingships were giving way to magistracies; they had towns engaged in international trade, used coinage, and some Celtic peoples were using writing. The Roman conquest of Europe and the later barbarian invasions obscured the Celtic past in these regions, but in non-Romanized Ireland a Celtic world survived.

In sagas written by monks in 7th and 8th century Ireland there are remarkable parallels for the descriptions of the continental Celts. Irish society is Celtic but has traces of earlier peoples. When the Celts arrived in Ireland is a matter of continuing debate, but traces of La Tène culture are found in the 3rd century BC and probably represent groups migrating into an island that had been Celtic for a long time previously.

a rich cultural fusion

The coming of Christianity brought with it 'Romanitas', the culture of Rome. Native Celtic tradition now fused with these new ideas to create an extremely rich cultural environment. Ireland produced some of the greatest works of Celtic art in each of the media, including epic hero-tales, illuminated manuscripts such as the Book of Durrow and Book of Kells, and the Celtic high crosses that were distinctive features of Celtic Christianity.

Irish missionaries and scholars were major contributors to the Christianization and civilization of Europe in the early Middle Ages. Ireland was also a harbinger of developments in law, both native Breton and Christian canon law, and a Christian form of kingship derived from earlier Celtic models. In its Gaelic language, a mixture of Celtic and pre-Celtic languages, Ireland inherited the earliest vernacular language of medieval Europe, with a unique literature; Gaelic was introduced to Scotland by Irish settlement. Another branch of the Celtic language continues in the native languages of Wales and Brittany.

Although Gaelic identity was stimulated by the coming of the Vikings, native Gaelic society and culture was profoundly changed following the Anglo-Norman invasion of the 12th century. It continued to survive independently in the Gaelic lordships, and saw revival in the later Middle Ages when the Anglo-Irish colony declined, but the Reformation in Ireland and renewal of English crown power finally led to the collapse of traditonal Gaelic society in the 17th century as the English Protestant conquest and colonization was completed.

listening music aesthetic. Some of the members of Ceoltóirí Cualann formed the ⇨Chieftains.

CERAMICS

Ceramics have been produced in Ireland since before the Bronze Age. The earliest Irish pots were hand-made, and this remained the universal method of ceramics production until the introduction of the potter's wheel into Ireland, around the 12th century.

demand in the 17th and 18th centuries

Imports of Chinese porcelain in the 17th century, along with new customs such as coffee, tea, and chocolate drinking, caused a new demand for delft – earthenware with a tin glaze. Factories were set up in Belfast in the late 17th century, and in Dublin around 1735, the latter becoming the centre of production. Blue and white ware was the main type produced, in Chinese, Dutch, and English styles. In the 1750s and 1760s Henry Delamain's (died 1757) Dublin factory produced particularly high quality work, excelling in the painting of fine landscape scenes on tableware. One distinctively Irish form was the octagonal plate. The invention of printing onto ceramic around this time meant that decoration could be faster and more standardized.

Irish production was forced to specialize later in the 18th century, in the face of English competition

CERAMICS *This delicate porcelain basket is a typical design from the Belleek Pottery, set up in 1857 by John Caldwell Bloomfield. The finely detailed decoration and light glaze have brought the pottery's products international recognition.*

and the ready availability of Eastern ceramics. By 1771 delft production in Dublin had completely died out, and the industry focused instead on painting, printing, and gilding ceramic wares.

expression of national identity

Growing nationalism in the second half of the 19th century found expression in ceramics, particularly at the Belleek Pottery, a company set up in 1857 in Belleek in County Fermanagh, which used local clay, and local turf and water to power the pottery. Its main lines were domestic and industrial earthenware and stoneware, but it was, and is, best known for its fine porcelain. The Victorian style was evident in its glazed busts and tableware decorated with foliage, shells, and basketwork designs.

Irish revival designs can also be seen in the ceramics of Frederick Vodrey, who set up what was probably Ireland's first art pottery studio in Dublin in the 1880s. The ⇨Arts and Crafts movement in Ireland towards the end of the 19th century assisted the small-scale production of ceramics. Industrial potteries were set up with the encouragement of the Free State government, such as Carrigaline in County Cork (1928), Arklow in County Wicklow (1934), and the Royal Tara company in County Galway (1953). With a growth in the number of independent ceramic studio artists in the middle of the 20th century, public interest in art ceramics increased, and the Craft Potters Society of Ireland was set up in 1977.

CHARLES FORT

Large, star-shaped fort named after King Charles II, at Kinsale, County Cork. It was designed by William Robinson and built from 1678 for Roger Boyle, Earl of Orrery. It is probably the finest example of surviving military architecture in Ireland. The only time it was besieged was in 1690, when it held out for 13 days before being was captured by John Churchill, Earl of Marlborough. It became a scheduled national monument in 1973.

CHARLTON, JACK (JOHN) (1935–)

English football player and coach under whose guidance the Republic of Ireland team enjoyed the most successful phase of its history, qualifying for the European Championship finals in 1988, and the World Cup finals in 1990 (when they reached the quarter-finals) and 1994. During Charlton's reign as manager from 1986 to 1995, the team gained 46 victories, 30 draws, and suffered only 17 defeats. In 1995, as a mark of gratitude for his contribution to Irish football, he was made an honorary Irish citizen.

CHICHESTER, ARTHUR (1563–1625)

English soldier and viceroy of Ireland 1605–15. He arrived in Ireland as part of the expedition under Robert Devereux, 2nd Earl of Essex, and was appointed constable of the castle of Carrickfergus, County Antrim, in succession to his brother John who had been killed in action. He conducted a ruthless campaign against the Gaelic rebels in Ulster, which hastened the surrender of Hugh O'Neill, Earl of Tyrone, and Rory O'Donnell, Earl of Tyrconnell, in March 1603. He was rewarded with a grant of Belfast Castle and its lands, to which he added substantially by private purchase.

Having served as Lord Justice in the absence of the viceroy, Charles ⇨Blount, Baron Mountjoy, Chichester was appointed Lord Deputy in 1605. The ⇨Flight of the Earls and the revolt of Sir Cahir O'Doherty (1587–1608) enabled him to lay plans for the ⇨Ulster plantation. Though an advocate of plantation and an avid pursuer of confiscated lands, Chichester soon became critical of the overambitious royal project, particularly in relation to the terms imposed on the undertakers (English and Scottish settlers granted allotments of land) and the treatment of the loyal native Irish. His strongly anti-Catholic policies, especially his use of fines for the enforcement of conformity, alienated the majority of the island's native inhabitants and provoked serious opposition in the parliament he summoned 1613–15.

His impressively decorated tomb remains intact in Carrickfergus Cathedral.

CHIEFTAINS, THE

Traditional Irish band, formed from members of Seán Ó Riada's ground-breaking band ⇨Ceoltóirí Cualann in 1963. Their performances are notable for their instrumental dance music, airs, harp music, and, most recently, their recordings with musicians from other musical genres. These include *The Chieftains in China* (1984), which featured Chinese repertoire and musicians; *Another Country* (1992), recorded in Nashville, USA; and *The Long Black Veil* (1995), featuring popular artists such as Van Morrison and Sting. However the distinctive sound of the Chieftains remains the same, reminiscent of Seán Ó Riada and his innovative presentation of traditional music.

THE CHIEFTAINS *The group was responsible, with other bands, for the 1960s revival in popularity of Irish folk music. By adapting traditional melodies to appeal to modern audiences, they found success in both Europe and America.*

The band has gone through many personnel changes, but has been led consistently by the piper Paddy Moloney. It became fully professional in 1975 after a successful period of international touring promoted by the impresario Jo Lustig and culminating in a successful concert in the Royal Albert Hall, London. The current line-up is Paddy Moloney (uilleann pipes), Matt Molloy (flute), Martin Fay, Seán Keane (fiddles), Kevin Conneff (bodhrán, vocals), and Derek Bell (harp). The Chieftains have attained spectacular international success with their later fusion recordings and since 1993 they have won many international awards, including Grammy awards in 1994, 1996, and 1997.

CHILDERS, (ROBERT) ERSKINE

English-born Irish republican; see ⇨Irish Volunteers.

CHILDERS, ERSKINE H(AMILTON)

Fianna Fáil politician, president 1973–74. He was the son of Erskine Childers; see ⇨Irish Volunteers.

CHRISTIAN BROTHERS

Confirmed by papal brief in 1820 as the 'Institute of the Brothers of the Christian Schools of Ireland', this lay Catholic teaching order was founded by philanthropist and educator Edmund Rice. Rice had originally opened a school for poor boys in Waterford in 1803. Similar schools were opened in other towns in Ireland, and by the time of his death more than 22 schools had been established in Ireland and England, and the order expanded in Australia. The schools, which provided cheap and free education to large numbers, were founded on religious doctrine and observance but were also strongly nationalist. Many of the leaders of the independence movement and of post-independence Ireland were educated in Christian Brothers' schools, including Patrick ⇨Pearse and Éamon de ⇨Valera. Recent scandals of sexual and physical abuse in Christian Brothers' schools have exacerbated a general decline in the numbers entering the order.

CHRISTIANIZATION OF IRELAND

Later tradition ascribes the Christianization of all Ireland to St Patrick, but historical evidence suggests that Patrick led a British church mission to Ulster and Connaught, while the Gaulish church evangelized Leinster and Munster. Indeed, Ireland was not fully Christianized until some time in the 6th century, long after Patrick's death.

Gaulish and British missions

The history of Ireland's Christianization is very vague because later historiographers rewrote the tradition to exalt Patrick's (and Armagh's) role. Patrick was not the first missionary bishop to visit Ireland; he was preceded by Palladius in the 5th century, who was sent by the Gaulish church at the request of Christians in Ireland. As this request came while he was in Britain, it is likely that these first Irish Christians were mostly, like Patrick, British slaves. Little is known of Palladius' mission. Tradition claims that he left (or died) soon after arriving in Ireland and that Patrick was sent as his successor, but this is probably another Patrician revision. Palladius came from the Gaulish church, as did other important figures such as Secundius (Dunshaughlin, County Meath), Auxilius (Killashee, County Kildare), and Isernius (Kilcullen, County Kildare). Later tradition views these three as Patrick's subordinates, but they worked in Leinster, whereas Patrick's writings show that he remained in Ulster (and possibly Connaught). This suggests that they were in continuity with Palladius' Gaulish mission, while Patrick spearheaded a British mission in Ulster

and Connaught. Other 5th-century figures (about whom we know relatively little) are Ibar (Wexford), Ailbe (Emly, County Tipperary), Mel (Ardagh, County Limerick), and Mac Cuilinn (Lusk, County Dublin).

development of Irish Christianity

Gradually, the British and Gaulish missions declined in importance as a distinctively Irish Christianity developed that emphasized monastic abbots/abbesses rather than bishops. This was largely a result of the radical changes in Irish power structures during the 5th century. The old provinces were gradually being replaced by a less static dynastic structure that did not favour an episcopal system based around the traditional centres of power (such as ⇨Tara Hill). The monasteries gained such control that some episcopal settlements, such as Armagh, became monastic centres.

CINEMA

See feature essays on the history of Irish cinema, opposite, and on recent developments in Irish cinema, page 68.

CIVIL WAR

A conflict, 1922–23, that followed the signing of the ⇨Anglo-Irish Treaty, which established the ⇨partition of Ireland into the Irish Free State and Northern Ireland. In June 1922 the Irish government, led by Michael ⇨Collins, attacked the headquarters of the anti-treaty faction (mostly from the Irish Republican Army) at the Four Courts in Dublin. Fighting continued until April 1923, when the IRA gave up the fight. There were over 900 casualties. See the feature essay on post-independence Ireland, page 182.

CLANCY BROTHERS AND TOMMY MAKEM, THE

Seminal Irish ballad group whose influence has been central to the folk revival and the huge revival of interest in and performance of traditional Irish music throughout the world. The original group, formed in New York in the 1950s, consisted of the brothers Pat (1923–1998), Tom (1923–1990), and Liam Clancy (1936–   ), and Tommy Makem (1932–   ) from Carrick-on-Suir, County Tipperary. Their style of performance was grounded in straightforward unison singing with guitar and tin whistle accompaniment. An important part of their appeal was their relaxed,

THE EARLY FILM INDUSTRY, HAMPERED BY CENSORSHIP AND A LACK OF CASH

by Kevin Rockett

The indigenous Irish film industry has had an intermittent history. Although Irish-Canadian Sidney Olcott made the first fiction film in Ireland in 1910, an emigration story called *The Lad From Old Ireland*, it was not until 1916 that the first Irish film outfit, the Film Company of Ireland, began production. They made comedies and dramas, including the feature films *Knocknagow* (1918) and *Willy Reilly and His Colleen Bawn* (1920). After independence, the Anglo–Irish War (1919–21) was a frequent theme of films, as in *Irish Destiny* (1926), the British *Ourselves Alone* (1936), John Ford's *The Informer* (1935) and *The Plough and the Stars* (1936), and the hugely popular Irish feature, *The Dawn* (1936). Despite this activity, the Irish government did not offer encouragement, financial or other, to indigenous film production, so Irish films remained small in scale and poor in budget. Instead, the government favoured foreign film producers and supported the establishment of Ardmore Studios as a film factory in 1958.

Ireland on camera

Better known than many Irish productions are the numerous films that have been made about the Irish by the American and (to a lesser extent) British film industries. Hugely popular films, such as John Ford's *The Quiet Man* (1952) and David Lean's *Ryan's Daughter* (1971), have in their different ways reinforced a stereotypical view of Ireland in which feckless, work-shy, and drinking Irish live in a bucolic vision of west coast life. Rather more sinisterly, some films dealing with Irish history and politics have portrayed the Irish as prone to irrational political violence, without any critique being offered of the English colonial power.

The type of film that could be shown in an Irish cinema was also constrained. Through the Censorship of Films

Neil Jordan's commercially successful films have given Irish film-making a new impetus. He grew up in the 1960s, when Ireland was, '...very grey. The only bits of colour were in churches, with gaudy religious vestments...but there was a sweet irrationality to the whole place.'

Act (1923), the Irish government imposed severe moral criteria, targeting Hollywood films in particular. The censors determined that any representation of non-traditional, or non-Christian, sexuality was banned or cut, so films featuring extra-marital affairs, divorce, illegitimacy, birth control, or abortion were restricted, while scantily-clad singers and dancers were regularly cut from musicals. Some 2,500 films have been banned and 10,000 cut since 1923.

flowering of the Irish film industry

As film censorship began to loosen in the 1970s (to become now more or less in line with its British counterpart), so, too, did the stranglehold by foreign film-makers on images of Ireland. Beginning with pioneers Bob Quinn, Cathal Black, Joe Comerford, Kieran Hickey, Thaddeus O'Sullivan, and Pat Murphy, a new generation of film-makers began to produce politically and culturally challenging and formally innovative films. Simultaneously, the statutory Irish Film Board, established in 1981, began to support indigenous film-makers and, although it withdrew such funding between 1987 and 1993, in the 1990s the Film Board, together with generous tax breaks for investors in film, has underpinned a huge expansion of Irish film production.

As a result, the 1990s saw already established international commercial film-makers such as Neil Jordan and Jim Sheridan produce some of their most interesting films, while a new generation of directors, including Paddy Breathnach, Gerry Stembridge, and Damien O'Donnell, came to prominence.

CINEMA IN THE 1990S – NEW TALENT THAT IS CELEBRATING IRISHNESS

by Emer Williams

In the 1990s Irish cinema underwent a rapid and sustained expansion, facilitated by government tax breaks, subsidies, and loans. With few exceptions the new films, which are marked by high production values, move away from the non-linear narratives and the thematic concerns of the independent film-makers of the late 1970s and 1980s, and speak, in the first instance, to the international rather than the local audience.

Films such as *The Commitments* (1991), *Spaghetti Slow* (1997), *This is My Father* (1998), and *Angela's Ashes* (1999), celebrate 'Irishness', but in a way that draws on, and plays into, an outsider's preconceived ideas about the nation and its people, while Paddy Breathnach's gangster film, *I Went Down* (1997), filters the narrative through an American genre. In becoming less obviously Irish and more self-consciously universal in appeal, Irish cinema has in some cases looked specifically to Europe – as in Breathnach's *Alisa* (1994), and the breakthrough *November Afternoon* (1996) directed by John Carney and Tom Hall.

new directors

Amongst the new directors are Damian O'Donnell, whose company ClingFilms, established with producer Paul Fitzgerald, cameraman Harry Purdue, and director John Moore, made *35-Aside* (1995), generally regarded as the funniest short of the decade. O'Donnell's feature debut, *East is East* (1999), a Pakistani comedy set in Manchester, was greeted with great acclaim and won the *Evening Standard* Film of the Year award.

Northern Ireland film-maker Enda Hughes set about demisting the po-faced representations of politics in the province in his action-packed feature *The Eliminator* (1996), while his short, *Flying Saucer Rock 'n' Roll* (1997), with its cast of angst-ridden teenagers and aliens, cast an irreverent eye over the rural north. David Caffrey, another Northern Ireland film-maker, progressed from making shorts (*The Connivers, I Shudder, Bolt*) to make *Divorcing Jack* (1998), a satire on contemporary politics in the north from the novel by Colin Bateman.

new film actors

While there are many fine Irish performers, unfortunately, given the nature of commercial film production, they have not always been given the chance to play leading roles, even when the director is Irish. Examples of lead roles given to big box-office, but non-Irish, names are the casting of Julia Roberts in *Michael Collins* (1996) and Meryl Streep in *Dancing at Lughnasa* (1998), which also featured Brid Brennan, who had played the eponymous Anne Devlin in Pat Murphy's 1984 film. Therefore, the potential of actors such as Angeline Ball, Andrew Connolly, Tina Kellegher, Emer McCourt, Ruth McCabe, Donal McCann, Sean McGinely, Gerald McSorely, or Ger Ryan, has not been seriously tested in the cinema, with many doing most of their screen work on television.

Ruggedly handsome Liam Cunningham's real breakthrough was as the male lead in the RTÉ series based on Deirdre Purcell's novel *Falling for a Dancer* (1998). He then starred, to critical acclaim, in the real-life dramatic love story of a couple torn by religious bigotry in Syd McCarty's *A Love Divided* (1999). His other films include: *Into the West* (1992), *War of the Buttons* (1994), *Undercurrents* (1995), *First Knight* (1995), *Jude* (1996), *A Little Princess* (1995), and *Sweety Barrett* (1999).

Adrian Dunbar, whose films include *My Left Foot* (1989), *The Playboys* (1992), *The Crying Game* (1992), *Force of Duty* (1992), and *Widow's Peak* (1994), was powerful as the lead in *Hear My Song* (1991).

Susan Lynch came to prominence more in Britain than in Ireland when she played in the BBC's *Ivanhoe* and as Rosalind in its *As You Like It*. Her main Irish television appearance was in the RTÉ series *Amongst Women*, which featured Tony Doyle in a powerful performance as the father. She also played small roles in *Interview With a Vampire* (1994) and *The Secret of Roan Inish* (1994), before going on to play the female lead in the thriller *Downtime*, Maggie in *Waking Ned Devine* (1998), and as James Joyce's wife in Pat Murphy's *Nora* (2000).

Lorraine Pilkington has also been developing her career. Her films include *The Miracle* (1991), *All Things Bright and Beautiful* (1994), *The Disappearance of Finbar* (1996), *The Last of the High Kings* (1996), *Gold in the Streets* (1997), and *Human Traffic* (1999).

Finally, both Moya Farrelly, who had played a minor role in *Spaghetti Slow* (1996), and Gina Moxley, whose previous work includes lead roles in *The Sun, The Moon, and the Stars*, and *Snakes and Ladders* (both 1996), were impressive in *This is My Father* (1998).

informal style and slightly irreverent approach.

Their first major exposure to a large US audience came when they appeared on the Ed Sullivan television show in 1961, which led to widespread acclaim in the USA. The band continued to perform through the 1970s, 1980s, and 1990s with several changes in personnel, although the original members did occasionally regroup for special performances.

Their songs were a break from the Irish-American standards that preceded them, but have since become the core of the traditional ballad repertoire. Songs such as 'The Leaving of Liverpool' and 'The Jug of Punch' were brought to the attention of millions through their performances and recordings.

CLAN-NA-GAEL

Irish-American revolutionary society; see ⇨Fenian movement.

CLANN NA POBLACHTA ('Children of the Republic')

Former Irish political party founded by Sean ⇨MacBride in 1946. Its aims included the reintegration of the whole of Ireland as an independent republic and the restoration of the Irish language. It ceased to exist in 1969.

CLARE

County on the west coast of the Republic of Ireland, in the province of Munster, situated between Galway Bay in the north and the Shannon estuary in the south; county town ⇨Ennis; area 3,190 sq km/1,231 sq mi; population (1996) 94,000. Other towns include Kilrush, Kilkee, and Shannon, an important 'new' town noted for its light industry, and electronics and aerospace industries. Dairying and cattle rearing are the principal farming activities; there are also important salmon fisheries and extensive oyster beds. Slate and black marble are quarried and worked; lead is also found. The Shannon is a source of hydroelectricity: there is a power station at Ardnacrusha, 5 km/3 mi north of Limerick.

County Clare has a reputation as the centre of Irish traditional music. It is said to be named after Thomas de Clare, an Anglo-Norman settler, to whom this area was granted in 1276.

physical

The coastline is rocky and dangerous; in the north are the Cliffs of ⇨Moher (213 m/700 ft). Inland Clare is an undulating plain, with mountains in the east, west, and northwest: the chief ranges are the Slieve Bernagh mountains in the southeast, rising to over 518 m/1,700 ft; and the Slieve Boughta mountains, which lie partly in county Galway. The principal rivers are the Shannon, which forms the southern border, and its tributary the Fergus. Much of the spring water contains iron salts, and there are over 100 lakes in the county, including Lough Derg on the eastern border, which is 67 mi/108 km long and 21 mi/34 km wide (on average); at its widest point it is 43 mi/69 km across. In the northwest is the ⇨Burren, a barren limestone area, with caves and underground waterways, which shelters a wide variety of rare animals and plants; the area is now a national park.

CLARE, RICHARD DE ('STRONGBOW')

(Earl of Pembroke and Strigoil) (died 1176)

Anglo-Norman soldier. The son of Gilbert FitzGilbert de Clare, Earl of Pembroke and Strigoil (in southern Wales), he succeeded to the earldom in 1148. At the request of the exiled king of Leinster, Dermot ⇨MacMurrough, he invaded Ireland in August 1170 to support MacMurrough's reinstatement, sparking a full-scale Anglo-Norman invasion under the English king Henry II in September of the following year.

After capturing Waterford, de Clare led a victorious attack on Dublin in the autumn of 1170, and furthered his hold on Dublin in 1171 following the fail

RICHARD DE CLARE *This black marble effigy in Christ Church Cathedral, Dublin, is said to be the likeness of Richard de Clare. However, although this celebrated knight, known as Strongbow, died in 1176, the remains within the tomb date from the 14th century.*

ure of a siege led by Rory ⇨O'Connor, High King of Ireland. Having restored MacMurrough, de Clare married his daughter Aoife and inherited the kingship of Leinster on MacMurrough's death in 1171. His success attracted the intervention of Henry II, who was fearful of the establishment of an independent Norman power on his western shores, and de Clare was forced to hand over his conquests to the crown.

After supporting Henry II's campaigns in Normandy in 1173, de Clare returned to find his possessions in Ireland and Wales in open rebellion. Quelling the revolts he continued his kingship of Leinster, as well as receiving the towns of Wexford, Waterford, and Dublin for his service to the crown. He died in 1176 and is buried in Christchurch Cathedral, Dublin.

CLARKE, AUSTIN (1896–1974)

Poet, born in Dublin and educated at University College, Dublin. Clarke worked in London for 15 years as a reviewer and critic, but returned to Ireland, settling in Templeogue, near Dublin. A leading member of the 'second wave' of the Irish literary revival, he found an alternative to the vague sensuousness of the Celtic twilight in the literature and art of medieval Ireland. From the mid-1950s he became a voice of modern Ireland's conscience, despising things false, unnatural, and life-denying.

Following publication of *The Vengeance of Fionn* (1917), he was acclaimed as the 'new Yeats'. However, he shook off the early influence of W B Yeats and Irish mythology, his volume of poems *Pilgrimage* (1929) showing medieval influence. Between 1929 and 1955 Clarke wrote mostly plays and three beautifully worked novels, *The Bright Temptation* (1932), *The Singing Men at Cashel* (1936), and *The Sun Dances at Easter* (1952). In 1955 he published *Ancient Lights*, poems and satires. *Twice Around the Black Church* (1962) and *A Penny in the Clouds* (1968) are autobiographical.

CLARKE, HARRY (1889–1931)

Stained-glass artist and illustrator. His style, both in glass and in his illustration work, is a personal interpretation of the stylized naturalism of Art Nouveau. His glass is minutely detailed, with jewel-like colours and patterns, obtained through painstaking acid etching of coloured glass. Major glass commissions included the Honan College Chapel, Cork

(1914–16), and the secular Eve of Saint Agnes (1923–24), now in the Hugh Lane Municipal Gallery of Modern Art, Dublin. His illustration was initially similar in style to Aubrey Beardsley, but rapidly became far more individual, with the same precise detail and feel for pattern and composition as his glass.

Born in Dublin, Clarke studied stained glass with the English artist A E Child (1875–1939). Among the books he illustrated were *Fairytales of Hans Christian Andersen* (1916) and *Edgar Allan Poe's Tales of Mystery and Imagination* (1919). His glass work, *The Geneva Window* (1929; Mitchell Wolfson Jr Collection, Miami, USA), which depicts scenes from 20th-century Irish literature, was commissioned by the Irish government but was not accepted on its completion due to the originality with which he dealt with the subject. His work may also be seen in Bewley's Café, Grafton Street, Dublin.

CLARKE, MARY FRANCIS (1803–1887)

Irish-American religious foundress, born in Dublin, who emigrated to the USA in 1833. She overcame financial woes to found a school in Philadelphia. She also formed a teaching community, the Sisters of Charity of the Blessed Virgin Mary, which she relocated to Iowa in 1843.

CLERKE, AGNES MARY (1842–1907)

Astronomer and writer who had a particular talent for collecting and summarizing results of astronomical research. Born in Skibbereen, County Cork, she showed an early interest in astronomy and began writing a history of the science at the age of 15. Her book, *A Popular History of Astronomy during the Nineteenth Century* (1885), received international recognition.

Clerke moved to Dublin in 1861, to Queenstown (now Cobh), County Cork in 1863, and then lived in Italy 1863–77 before settling in London where most of her important writing was done. Her first major article, 'Copernicus in Italy', was published in the *Edinburgh Review* in October 1877. Other notable works included *Problems in Astrophysics* (1903), and *Modern Cosmogonies* (1905). Although not a practical astronomer she spent three months at the Royal Observatory, Cape Town, South Africa. She was a member of the British Astronomical Association and was elected an honorary member of the Royal Astronomical Society in 1903, at the time one of only four women to have been elected.

CLIFDEN

Market town and port in County Galway; population (1996) 900. It is situated 64 km/40 mi southwest of Westport, near the Twelve Bens mountain range. Clifden is a major tourist centre for Connemara, with fishing, boating, golf, and riding. Connemara ponies are bred around Clifden and the town hosts an annual pony show. The town was founded by entrepreneur John D'Arcy.

Near Clifden are the remains of the first transatlantic wireless telegraph station in Europe, built for the Italian inventor Guglielmo Marconi. It was destroyed during the Anglo–Irish War of Independence 1919–21. Nearby, a monument marks the spot where John William Alcock and Arthur Whitten Brown landed on their first nonstop flight across the Atlantic, from Newfoundland, in 1919. The Connemara marble quarries are also nearby.

CLONMACNOISE

Monastic site in County Offaly, 6 km/4 mi north of Shannonbridge. It is one of the most historically important monastic sites in Ireland. St Ciaran founded the monastic city, which flourished from 548 until its destruction by the English garrison of Athlone in 1552. The remains of the site are in excellent condition, and are the focus of an annual pilgrimage on 9 September (the feast of St Ciaran).

The extensive ruins at Clonmacnoise consist of eight churches, one of which, the Ciaran Temple, dates from the 9th century; a cathedral built in 904; two round towers; five high crosses (notably the Cross of the Scriptures); over 200 slabs from graves, some highly decorated, dating from the 6th to the 11th centuries; and the remains of a fortified tower constructed in 1214. The Crosier of Clonmacnoise is now in the Royal Irish Academy in Dublin.

CLONMEL

Market town in County Tipperary, on the River Suir; population (1996) 15,200. Clonmel is the administrative centre for the South Riding of Tipperary. Its principal industries are pharmaceuticals, computer hardware, and construction engineering; there is also a meat-processing and tanning industry and the production of mineral water and cider. A 13th-century choir and a 15th-century tower are all that remain of the friary founded here in 1269.

During the plantation of Ireland by English settlers, Clonmel was purchased first by the Earl of Desmond in 1338, and later taken by the Earls of Ormond; Clonmel remained loyal to the English crown until the mid-17th century. The Mainguard in Sarsfield Street was built in 1674 as the seat of the counts of the palatinate of Ormond and was reputedly designed by Christopher Wren. The 19th-century Protestant church of St Mary, which has an octagonal tower, incorporates parts of a 15th-century church.

Clonmel was the birthplace of the novelist Laurence Sterne. Charles ⇨Bianconi (1786–1875) was mayor here and Hearn's Hotel was the first staging post in his pioneering system of public transport. The town was a notorious centre of nationalism, and several notable figures were imprisoned and tried here, among them Father Nicholas ⇨Sheehy (1766).

CLONTARF, BATTLE OF

Perhaps the best-known battle in the history of Ireland. It took place on Good Friday, 23 April, 1014 to the north of Dublin, and represented the culmination of an earlier revolt of the Leinstermen and Dublin

CLONMACNOISE *This wealthy monastic settlement was subject to frequent attack over the centuries – the Vikings plundered it 35 times over 300 years. The round towers may have been used to store treasure when the monastery was under threat.*

Norse against Ireland's high king ⇨Brian Bóruma. Brian and his son Murchad were victorious on the day, though both sides suffered heavy losses; according to one report, the Norse lost some 6,000 men. The most significant casualty of the battle was Brian himself, who was killed in his tent by a retreating Norseman.

While considered an important and symbolic victory over the Leinstermen and their allied Vikings/Ostmen, Brian's death once again created a division in which there was no recognized high king of Ireland.

Cobh (formerly Queenstown, 1849–1922)

Town and port in County Cork, 24 km/15 mi southeast of the city of Cork; population (1996) 6,500. The town is built on a series of terraces overlooking the harbour, and is dominated by St Colman's Cathedral, built 1868–1918, a blue granite structure. Cobh was the departure point for many emigrants to America during the 19th century and the heritage centre on the quayside has a permanent exhibition on the Irish diaspora.

Cobh has a number of fine Georgian and 19th-century residential houses. The cathedral has a carillon (a set of bells played on a keyboard) of 42 bells – the largest in Ireland; and Cobh's Royal Yacht Club, founded in 1720, is the oldest in the world.

A memorial to the victims of the ocean liner *Lusitania*, which was sunk by a German submarine off the Irish coast on 7 May 1915, stands on the quay. It was designed by Jerome Connor, and completed after his death by Donal Murphy. Near Cobh is the Fota Estate, now owned by University College Cork and developed as a wildlife park and arboretum. Adjacent is a large private golf course. Spike Island, a former prison, is now an army coastal defence station.

Cobh was known as Queenstown in commemoration of a visit by Queen Victoria.

Coffey, Brian (1905–1995)

Modernist poet, born in Dublin and educated at Clongowes Wood College and in France. His experiments with form, rhythm, and syntax indicate a distrust of the ability of language to communicate clearly and precisely, and his poetry is often interrupted by illustrations and cartoons, which challenge the reader to think beyond conventional modes of expression. He first published *Poems* (1930) with Denis ⇨Devlin and, after some time away from writing, published steadily in the 1970s and 1980s. His collections include *Selected Poems* (1971), *Advent* (1975), *Death of Hektor* (1980), and *Chanterelles* (1985).

Coffey initially worked as a researcher in physical chemistry in Paris but transferred into the study of philosophy at the Institut Catholique in 1933. He worked in London as a teacher during World War II, taught philosophy in the USA at St Louis, Missouri, 1947–52, and returned to London as a maths teacher in 1954.

Coleraine

Town in County Derry, on the River Bann, 6 km/ 4 mi from the sea; population (1991) 16,100. It is a market town with textile and food-processing industries and salmon fisheries. Coleraine is the site of the University of Ulster, which opened in 1968.

Coleraine was originally the site of a monastery dedicated to St Patrick, of which nothing remains. The present town owes its origins to the granting of lands to the London companies as part of the Derry plantation in the early 17th century.

The Mesolithic site at Mount Sandel, 2 km/1 mi to the south, has yielded much archaeological information. It was also the site of the stronghold of Fintan, who ruled Derry in the 1st century AD. During the 13th century a castle was built here by the historical prince of Ulster John de ⇨Courcy.

Colgan, John (Seán Mac Colgáin) (1592–c. 1657)

Writer, born near Carndonagh, County Donegal, Colgan travelled to Spain and joined a Franciscan order in 1618. He is remembered for two works that chronicle the lives of saints: *Acta Sanctorum Hiberniae* (1645), concerning saints with feast days between 1 January and 30 March; and *Triadis Thaumaturgae* (1647), which describes saints Patrick, Brigid, and Columba (Colum Cille).

Colles, Abraham (1773–1843)

Surgeon who helped develop the use of splints to stabilize bone fractures. He also described a common fracture of the wrist known today as Colles fracture.

Born in County Kilkenny, Colles was educated in Dublin and Edinburgh, and in 1797 he set up a practice in Dublin. He began to teach anatomy and surgery, and at the age of 29 he became president of the Royal College of Surgeons, where he was a professor 1804–36.

MICHAEL COLLINS *A charismatic military figure, Collins's leadership of the IRA during the Anglo–Irish War gave him heroic status in Ireland. In 1922 Collins briefly became Ireland's head of state.*

Colles advocated the use of tin splints to stabilize the wrist after closed reduction of a fracture. His use of splints performed exactly the same function as today's plaster of Paris casts. In 1814 he observed and described what was later known as the Colles fracture, a common wrist fracture often misdiagnosed. It involves breakage at the distal or carpel end of the radius bone in the forearm and causes deformity and swelling of the wrist. The fracture is easily treated once diagnosed and Colles's work helped doctors to recognize the break.

COLLINS, MICHAEL (1890–1922)

Nationalist who was a ⇨Sinn Féin leader. Collins was a founder and director of intelligence of the ⇨Irish Republican Army (IRA) in 1919, a minister in the provisional government of the ⇨Irish Free State in 1922, commander of the Free State forces in the civil war, and for ten days head of state before being killed by Irish republicans opposed to the ⇨Anglo-Irish

*Th*ink what I have got for Ireland? Something which she has wanted these past seven hundred years. Will anyone be satisfied at the bargain? Will anyone? I tell you this – early this morning I signed my death warrant.

MICHAEL COLLINS On signing the treaty establishing the Irish Free State. From a letter dated 6 December 1921.

❧

Treaty (1921) which endorsed partition.

Born in County Cork, the son of a small farmer, Collins was educated at Clonakilty national school. At 16 he went to London where he worked as a clerk in the Post Office and joined the Irish Republican Brotherhood. He returned to Ireland to take part in the ⇨Easter Rising of 1916. Following his release in December 1916, the charismatic Collins became a leading republican organizer. In 1918 he was elected to the Dáil (then the illegal republican parliament), and became consecutively minister of home affairs and finance in the first Dáil government

Collins combined his political career with the key position of director of organization and intelligence in the Irish Volunteers (later the IRA). During the ⇨Anglo–Irish War he exhibited considerable energy, skill, and cunning in his role as IRA leader, most notably in his infiltration of the British intelligence system in Ireland and his ruthless assassination of its operatives.

In 1921 Collins, along with vice-president Arthur ⇨Griffith and three other delegates, negotiated the Anglo-Irish Treaty signed on 6 December 1921. His support for the treaty persuaded key IRA figures to back it. He became chairman of the pro-Treaty provisional government. During the ensuing civil war Collins was commander-in-chief of the National Army, which crushed the opposition in Dublin and the large towns within a few months. He became head of state after Griffith's death on 12 August 1922 but was ambushed and killed in his native County Cork by anti-Treaty republicans on 22 August.

COLLINS, STEVEN (1964–   )

Boxer, born in Cabra, County Dublin. The winner of 36 professional fights, Collins's durability in the ring made him an extremely tough opponent. As an amateur, he won titles at three different divisions before electing to box at middleweight when turning professional in 1986. Although winning 16 straight fights, Collins also suffered marginal defeats in 1990 and 1992 against the Americans Mike McCallum and Reggie Johnson respectively. On 11 May 1994, he defeated Chris Pyatt to take the WBO Middleweight crown. The chance to fight Chris Eubank from England saw Collins vacate his crown and on 18 March 1995 in Millstreet, County Cork, he created an upset when he defeated Eubank on points to take the WBO Super Middleweight Championship of the world. He retired in May 1999.

May I never leave this world / Until my ill-luck is gone; / Till I have cows and sheep, / And the lad that I love for my own.

PADRAIC COLUM 'The Poor Girl's Meditation'.

~

COLUM, PADRAIC (1881–1972)

Writer, born in Longford and educated at Glasthule and University College, Dublin. Colum joined the 'Irish Renaissance' group of writers, which included W B Yeats, J M Synge, and Lady Gregory. He was associated with the foundation of the ⇨Abbey Theatre, Dublin, where his plays *The Land* (1905) and *Thomas Muskerry* (1910) brought realism into the Abbey's repertoire. His lyric poetry is best represented in *Wild Earth* (1907), *The Story of Lowry Maen* (1937), and *The Poets Circuit* (1960). With James Stephens and Thomas MacDonagh, he founded the *Irish Review*, editing it 1912–13. In 1914 he visited the USA and eventually settled in

She stepped away from me and she moved through the fair, / And fondly I watched her go here and go there, / Then she went her way homeward with one star awake, / As the swan in the evening moves over the lake.

PADRAIC COLUM 'She Moved Through the Fair'.

Manet in meo corde Dei amoris flamma, / ut in argenti vase auri ponitur gemma.
The fire of God's love stays in my heart, / As a jewel set in gold in a silver vessel.

COLUM CILLE Christian abbot and missionary 'Noli, pater' ('Do not, Father').

~

Connecticut, but towards the end of his life he moved back to Dublin.

COLUMBA, ST

See ⇨Colum Cille.

COLUM CILLE, (ST COLUMBA) (521–597)

(Latin *Colum-cille*, 'Colum of the cell')

Christian abbot, founder of the monastery of Iona, and missionary to the Picts of northwest Scotland. Born of royal descent in Gartan, County Donegal, Columba was educated by St Finnian of Movilla. He founded monasteries and churches in Ireland, most notably Durrow, near Ballycowan in County Meath, and Londonderry, in Northern Ireland. For historically uncertain reasons, Columba was excommunicated and went into exile (along with 12 companions) to establish the monastery on the island of Iona, off the Scottish coast, in 563. Iona was instrumental in the Christianization of Britain, with Columba responsible for the first conversions of Picts. He wielded great political influence over both Irish and Pictish rulers, and crowned Aidan, an Irish king of Argyll, on Iona.

He numbered the stars of Heaven, / this teacher of all things, / this Dove, this Colum Cille.

DALLÁN FORGAILL Writer From 'Amrá Colum Cille', about Colum Cille, the earliest poem in the Irish tradition (dated about 597), quoted in *The New Oxford Book of Irish Verse*, edited by Thomas Kinsella.

It was probably later craftsmen from the Iona community who devised the Celtic or high ⇨cross and produced one of the finest illuminated Gospels, the

9th-century Book of ⇨Kells, on view at Trinity College, Dublin. Since 1938 there has been an ecumenical Christian community on Iona, keeping Columba's heritage alive. His feast day is 9 June, which commemorates his death.

COMERAGH MOUNTAINS

Mountain range in County Waterford. There are nine peaks of over 610 m/2,000 ft, rising to the highest, Fauscoum, at 792 m/2,598 ft. There is good rock climbing on the eastern slopes of the range.

COMERFORD, JOE (1949–)

Film director and writer, one of the main contributors to recent developments in Irish cinema. His films have brought to the screen previously ignored or excluded marginal social groups: drug addicts in *Withdrawal* (1974); working-class teenagers in *Down the Corner* (1978); travellers in *Traveller* (1982); and IRA renegades in *Reefer and the Model* (1988), a film which won the Europa prize for best film in 1988; and the disturbed Benny in the Irish Border story, *High Boot Benny* (1993). Comerford's films are often informed by a gloomy, dark image of the Irish, with the inarticulate incest victim, Angela, in *Traveller* an extreme example.

COMHALTAS CEOLTÓIRÍ ÉIREANN

(Traditional Music Society)

Major Irish organization for the promotion of traditional Irish music, song, and dance, founded in 1951. It organizes a series of fleadhanna, or competitions, throughout the world every year, culminating in the All Ireland Fleadh Cheoil, possibly the largest music festival in Ireland. It also organizes concert tours around the world and is involved in traditional music education. It has its head office in Dublin, and there are some 400 branches of the organization throughout Ireland, Britain, Europe, North America, Australia, and the Far East.

The All Ireland Fleadh Cheoil is held in a different venue each year. Alongside the competitions, the informal music performances (sessions) that take place on the streets or in public houses are a major feature of the festival. Comhaltas undertakes important work in the field of education, with local branches organizing instrumental classes for children outside of existing educational structures where, in the past,

traditional music culture has been largely ignored or marginalized. Young musicians feature predominantly in the concert tours.

Comhaltas is politically associated with the Fianna Fáil party and promotes a brand of Devalerian cultural nationalism associated with it, in which an idealized, virtuous past features strongly.

COMPOSITION

A key Elizabethan reform policy first instituted by Lord Deputy Henry Sidney (1529–1586) in the mid-1570s, which commuted the feudal practice of ⇨coyne and livery (military billeting exacted on tenants and subjects) into a fixed tax collected by English government officials for a commission. The scheme aimed to demilitarize the lordships and settle relations between great lords and lesser families, while securing revenue for the crown.

Composition was devised by Sidney, in collaboration with his personal adviser Edmund Tremayne. After a favourable reception in Munster and Connacht, Sidney attempted to secure a similar permanent tax from the gentry of the English Pale in place of cess (the traditional maintenance of government troops), but his efforts provoked a constitutional crisis which resulted in his dismissal in 1578; the proposed tax was commuted to an agreed one-year sum. His successor, Lord Deputy John Perrot (c. 1527–1592), promoted composition successfully in Connacht and Ulster in the mid-1580s, but this revival ended with his sudden recall in 1588. However, the expected reintroduction of composition caused increasing dissension between the Irish lordships.

CONCHOBAR

In Celtic mythology, king of Ulster whose intended bride, Deirdre, eloped with Noísi. She died of sorrow when Conchobar killed her husband and his brothers.

CONFEDERATION OF KILKENNY (or CONFEDERATE CATHOLICS OF IRELAND)

Title given to the series of assemblies of Old English and Gaelic Irish Catholics held 1642–48. The confederation was organized by the Catholic clergy after the Old English joined the Gaelic Irish rebellion against government forces begun in 1641. However, fundamental divisions between the groups, and between secular and clerical leaders, paralyzed its ability to conduct war, and dissension increased from 1646 after conservative elements within the Old English sought peace with the Marquis of Ormond (1610–1688), commander of the royalist forces. Failure to form a united front proved fatal as the English parliament, victorious in the English Civil War (1642–51), turned its attention to Ireland, and Oliver ⇨Cromwell's campaign of 1649–51 crushed all opposition.

The confederation originally intended to administer Catholic areas of Ireland until a settlement could be agreed, asserting their rights as subjects of Charles I; their motto was *Pro Deo, Rege et Patria Hibernia Unanimis*, 'For God, King and Ireland United'.

CONGESTED DISTRICTS BOARD

British government initiative established in 1890 by the chief secretary for Ireland, Arthur Balfour, to develop agriculture and industry in Ireland. The Board's area of control soon extended to a third of the country, stretching from County Donegal to County Cork. Part of 'constructive unionism', the attempt to 'kill home rule with kindness', the Board had an immediate popular success but few long-term benefits.

Harbour construction was promoted, the mackerel fishing and curing industry was developed, and land drainage schemes were introduced. Despite the large budget at its disposal (a quarter of a million pounds in 1909), the Board lacked genuine ideas and often wasted money in fruitless schemes. Seven members (later 14) presided over the Board, with experts drawn from the worlds of business, farming, and religion, but very often ideas were sacrificed for unanimity. It is difficult to gauge the Board's achievements, but its work did little to lessen the growing political desire for home rule.

CONNACHT (or CONNAUGHT)

Historic province of the Republic of Ireland, comprising the counties of Galway, Leitrim, Mayo, Roscommon, and Sligo; area 17,130 sq km/6,612 sq mi; population (1996) 433,200. The chief towns are Galway, Roscommon, Castlebar, Sligo, and Carrick-on-Shannon. Mainly lowland, it is agricultural and stock-raising country, with poor land in the west.

The chief rivers are the Shannon, Moy, and Suck, and there are a number of lakes which include Loughs Corrib, Mask, Arrow, and Ree. The Connacht dialect is the national standard.

CONNAUGHTON, SHANE (1946–)

Writer of stage and television plays, films, and prose, born in County Cavan. He came to international prominence when he was nominated, with Jim ⇨Sheridan, for Best Adapted Screenplay for the Academy Award-winning *My Left Foot* (1989). Though unsuccessful on that occasion, he had already collected an Academy Award in 1981 for writing the short film *The Bottom Dollar*. The linked stories published as *A Border Station* (1989) and his original screenplay for *The Playboys* (1992) centre on his own childhood, especially his relationship to his policeman father and are set in and near the village of his childhood, Redhills, County Cavan, which was where *The Playboys* was shot. *The Run of the Country* (1995), adapted by the writer from his own novel, revisited terrain familiar from his other work.

CONNEMARA *Drystone walls divide the land into a patchwork of tiny plots. On the islands fringing the coast the local soil is supplemented with earth brought from the mainland, and fertilized with rotted seaweed.*

CONNEMARA (Irish *Comnhaicne Mara*, 'the tribe of the sea')

Northwestern part of County Galway, an area of rocky coastline and glaciated, quartzite, mountainous scenery, dominated by the Twelve Bens, the highest of which is Benbaun (730 m/2,395 ft). The principal town is Clifden. Connemara is noted for its quarries of green marble. There is fishing and tourism, and Connemara ponies are bred; kelp gathering and weaving were also once important, and continue as minor cottage industries.

Connemara is 48 km/30 mi long (north–south) and varies in breadth from 24 km/15 mi to 32 km/20 mi. It is subdivided into Joyce's Country in the north, (named after the Welsh Joyce family who settled lands here in the 13th century), which stretches from Leenane to Lough Corrib; Connemara proper (the ancient barony of Ballynahinch) in the west, a wild area of moors, hills, lakes, and bogs; and Iar Connacht in the south. There is a large Gaeltacht (Irish-speaking area) in Connemara.

Connemara National Park (2,000 ha/4,942 acres) includes part of the Twelve Bens mountain range and is noted for its alpine flora, red deer, and the Connemara pony. There is a visitor centre which houses an archaeological and natural history museum, and interpretative centre.

CONNOLLY, JAMES (1870–1916)

Socialist and revolutionary. Born in Edinburgh of immigrant Irish parents, Connolly combined a Marx-inspired socialism with a Fenian-inspired republicanism. He helped found the Irish Socialist Republican Party in Dublin in 1896, and organized a strike of transport workers in 1913 with the Irish Labour leader James ⇨Larkin. His Irish Citizen Army took part in the ⇨Easter Rising against British rule in 1916, for which he was executed by the British.

After establishing the Irish Socialist Republican Party and founding *The Workers' Republic*, the first Irish socialist paper, Connolly grew disillusioned with his political progress and moved to the USA in 1903, where he was active in the International Workers of the World. Returning to Ireland in 1910, he became involved in trade-union, industrial, and political affairs in Belfast and Dublin and played a key role in the establishment the Irish ⇨Labour Party.

Connolly the international socialist opposed World War I, but Connolly the Irish republican hoped to

JAMES CONNOLLY *One of the leaders of the Easter Uprising of 1916, Connolly was a follower of Lenin and wanted to take part in what the Russian political leader described as, 'the European revolt of the proletariat' in protest at World War I.*

take advantage of it to begin an anti-British rebellion. Consequently he committed his small Irish Citizen Army to a joint operation with the Irish Republican Brotherhood that resulted in the Easter Rising. Connolly was a signatory of the declaration of the Irish Republic, and was responsible for its more socially radical sentiments. He was commandant general of the Dublin Division in the rising and was wounded in the fighting. News of his execution while sitting propped-up in a chair was said to have fuelled the indignation of Irish nationalists at the government's treatment of the rebels.

His books *Irish History* (1910) and *The Reconquest of Ireland* (1915), exercised profound influence on Irish socialist thought long after his death.

CONNOLLY, SYBIL (1921–1998)

Welsh-born fashion designer who through her innovative use of traditional Irish textiles brought Irish fashion to international attention in the 1950s and 1960s.

After an apprenticeship in London, Connolly moved to Dublin in 1940 to work in the fashion firm,

Richard Alan. By 1952 she was its house designer, and came to the attention of the US press and fashion buyers. In 1957 she set up her own business in Dublin, and continued to design clothes until her death. Her distinctiveness lay in her contemporary tailoring of traditional Irish fabrics such as linen, lace, crochet, poplin, tweed, and flannel, as in her 'Irish washerwoman' outfit (1952), a quilted skirt in red flannel like the petticoats worn in the west of Ireland, with a white cambric blouse and black shawl. Connolly's greatest innovation was pleated linen, made creaseproof by a secret process.

CONOLLY, WILLIAM (1662–1729)

Politician and landowner, whose origins are unknown. Apparently a Catholic who converted to Protestantism, he trained as a barrister in Dublin. Through marriage to Katherine Conyngham he acquired a considerable fortune, which he used to build a power base in the country. Buying his way into office, he first became a revenue commissioner before reluctantly accepting the office of speaker of the Irish House of Commons in 1714. He was soon appointed a lord justice (1717), deputizing for the lord lieutenant and thus wielding considerable power. Although supportive of the English regime, in the 1720s he was obliged to join with native Irish opposition over the 'Wood's Halfpence' dispute, when Ireland was threatened to be flooded with potentially useless copper coinage. He resigned as speaker in 1729 and died soon afterwards.

Conolly was one of the richest and most important commoners in the period 1714–29, a key figure whose support was carefully cultivated by successive administrations.

CONSTITUTION OF IRELAND

Constitution of 1937, devised by prime minister Éamon de Valera to replace the 1922 constitution of the Irish Free State and change the name of the state to Eire. It removed many of the unpopular constitutional links with Britain and weakened, but did not end, Irish membership of the British Commonwealth. Controversially, it asserted that the territory of Northern Ireland formed part of the 'national territory', a claim which provoked unionist anger. The constitution also granted the Catholic church a 'special position' in the state and promoted various aspects of Catholic morality.

De Valera's essentially republican constitution emphasized the importance of popular sovereignty. The British monarch's representative in Ireland, the governor-general, was replaced by a popularly elected president. Valera's constitution has recently been amended in several crucial areas, including the removal of the special position of the Catholic church, the lifting of the ban on divorce, the removal of the absolute ban on abortion, and most notably, in 1998, the abandonment of articles two and three, the claim of sovereignty over Northern Ireland.

CONTEMPORARY DANCE

Ireland's chief centres of contemporary dance are Dublin, Cork, and Limerick. The Irish Modern Dance Theatre, founded in Dublin in 1991 and directed by John Scott, is Ireland's premier experimental dance theatre company, noted for its integration of dance with theatre, music, literature, and the visual arts, and for choreography inspired by such varied sources as Latin plainsong and silent film.

Also Dublin-based are the Dance Theatre of Ireland, directed by Robert Connor and choreographer Loretta Yurick, and the dynamic young CoisCéim Dance Theatre, established in 1995 and directed by David Bulger. CoisCéim, named after the Irish word for 'footstep', celebrates the spirit and energy of Ireland's youth; integrated workshops on its tours feature styles ranging from neo-classical to break-dancing.

The Firkin Crane Dance Development Agency based at Shandon, Cork, is Ireland's only dedicated dance venue. Directed by Mary Brady, Firkin Crane is a choreographic research centre with studio facilities and a 240-seat theatre for the presentation of new pieces, as well as the work of national and international dance companies. Cork's most avant-garde dance company, the half/angel, uses interactive technology to create new dance movements. In *The Secret Project* (1999), by half/angel's co-directors Richard Povall and Jools Gilson-Ellis, motion sensors and video cameras sense the movement of the dancers to trigger sound or video.

The Daghdha Dance Company, established at the University of Limerick in 1988, focuses on the production of original choreographic works by its founder and artistic director Mary Nunan.

CONTINUITY IRA

Extremist Irish republican terrorist group which split from the Provisional IRA (formerly the ⇨Irish

Republican Army) in 1995. Although its membership was estimated to be below 50, from September 1998 it, together with the ⇨Real IRA, were the only republican terrorist bodies to remain officially active.

COOKSTOWN

Market town in County Tyrone, 21 km/13 mi north of Dungannon; population (1991) 7,700. Cookstown is named after Alan Cook, who founded the town in 1609 during the plantation of Protestant settlers, and mainly consists of one high street, 3 km/2 mi long, which was laid out in the 18th century by its subsequent owner, William Stewart. Wellbrook Beetling Mill, Cookstown's 18th-century water-powered linen beetling mill, has been restored to full working order by the National Trust. The beetling process, powered by its great wheel, hammered the cloth and gave the world-famous Irish linen its final sheen. The process of manufacturing linen from flax is explained on placards on the walls.

Adjacent to Cookstown is Killymoon Castle, now a golf club. It was designed by John Nash for William Stewart.

COOPERATIVE MOVEMENT

Catering more to the needs of producers than consumers, the cooperative movement in Ireland was closer to the pattern in continental Europe than the more consumer-based societies of Britain.

While there had been a few isolated cooperative efforts in Ireland from the mid-19th century, the effective origins of the Irish movement began in 1889, when Horace ⇨Plunkett, a member of the Anglo-Irish aristocracy and manager of the family estate at Dunsany, began a concerted effort to persuade the rural population to form farming cooperatives. His initial attempts to establish retail cooperatives were quickly abandoned in favour of cooperative creameries to address a crisis facing butter production. This became the most successful field of cooperatives, although they were adopted in other areas such as poultry and flax. Other forms of cooperative were also tried, such as the agricultural societies in which farmers jointly purchased goods. In the 1890s cooperative credit societies spread in the poorer western counties where joint-stock banking was underdeveloped.

In 1893 the Irish Cooperative Agency Society (later the Irish Agricultural Wholesale Society) was founded, and in 1894 a central organizing structure, the Irish Agricultural Organization Society, took shape. Pioneers of the cooperative movement viewed their efforts as social as well as economic, encompassing a radical reformation of rural society, summarized in Plunkett's phrase, 'better farming, better business, better living'.

Leaders of the Irish ⇨home rule movement were divided in attitude to the cooperative movement, some seeing it as an attempt to distract attention from the national question. Others, however, valued its benefits. By 1914 there were some 839 societies in operation, with a combined membership of almost 104,000, and Plunkett's ideas attracted international interest. However, after World War I the movement fell into decline. Although creamery cooperatives continue to play an important role in agricultural production and processing, the movement's commitment to social reform, characteristic of its earlier era, has disappeared.

COOTE, EYRE (1726–1783)

General in British India, born at Ash Hill, County Limerick. Joining the army at an early age, Coote first served in Scotland in 1745. Promoted to captain, he was sent to India in 1854, the beginning of a distinguished military career. He was a key advisor of Capt Robert Clive in the successful Bengal expedition of 1756, and he won praise for his pursuit of the French after the Battle of Plassey in 1757. He was promoted to lieutenant colonel in 1759. Given the Madras presidency in 1760, he won an important victory against the French at Pondicherry in 1761, removing their influence from India.

Moving to England in 1770, Coote was knighted in 1771 and served as member of parliament for Poole 1774–80. He returned to India in 1777 as commander-in-chief, but steered clear of political affairs.

As a military general his leadership was decisive, and his victories against the rebel sultan of Mysore, Hyder Ali, were instrumental in maintaining British control in India. He retired in 1782 because of ill health and died in Madras in 1783. A monument was erected in his honour in Westminster Abbey, London.

CORK

Largest county of the Republic of Ireland, in the province of Munster; county town ⇨Cork; area 7,460 sq km/2,880 sq mi; population (1996) 420,500. Cork is mainly agricultural, but there is some copper and manganese mining, marble quarrying, salmon farming, and river and sea fishing; industries include chemical, and computer hardware and software. There are natural gas and oil fields off the south coast at Kinsale. Angling is a popular sport, and tourism is concentrated in Kinsale, Bantry, Glengarriff, and Youghal; one of the most popular visitor attractions is ⇨Charles Fort, Kinsale. Cork is rich in Christian and pre-Christian antiquities.

The coastline off County Cork in the west is composed of a number of rocky and mountainous peninsulas and deep bays; Sheep's Head, Mizen Head, and the Beara Peninsula (which forms the boundary with County Kerry) are particularly noted for their dramatic scenery. Cork's largest coastal inlet is Bantry Bay, where there was an important oil terminal (no longer in use), and its towns include Blarney, Cobh, Fermoy, Mallow, Youghal, Macroom, Bandon, Skibbereen, and Clonakilty. The west is mountainous, and there are also two mountain ranges running across the centre of the county, separating its two main rivers, the Blackwater and the Lee.

physical

Geologically, the county is formed of limestone and brownstone, a type of sandstone. Its coast is irregular and deeply indented, especially in the west. There are many harbours (including Youghal, Kinsale, Courtmacsherry, Cork, and Glandore) and bays (including Clonakilty, Ballycotton, Rosscarbery, Roaring Water, and Dunmanus); the bays in the west are particularly rocky. Islands off the coast include Sherkin, Clear, Dursey, and Bear Islands, and there are many more in Cork Harbour, including Great, Little, Haulbowline, and Spike Islands.

The Rivers Blackwater and Lee rise near the Cork–Kerry border and constitute the natural drainage for most of the county. Close to the source of the River Lee near Inchigeela is Lough Allua, a large freshwater lake. As well as mountains in the west, there are the Slieve Mikish, the Caha, and the Shehy Mountains in the southwest on the Cork–Kerry border. One of the two mountain ranges that run across Cork separates the Rivers Bandon and Lee, the other the Rivers Lee and Blackwater. In the west of the first of these two ranges, in the Derrynasaggart and Boggeragh Mountains, is Caherbarnagh, (682 m/2,238 ft), the highest point in Cork. Fastnet Rock, off the southwest coast near Baltimore, is the most southerly point in Ireland.

The climate is mild, the prevailing winds from the

COUNTY CORK *Although milk and butter production have always been important industries, Ireland does not have a long tradition of cheese-making. In recent years however, varieties such as this Gubbeen cheese, made near Skull, County Cork, have begun to gain a reputation in Ireland and beyond.*

southwest and west making the atmosphere warm and generally moist.

agriculture

Cork is a rich agricultural county, with several agricultural colleges. There is a great variety of soil types, such that different districts employ different agricultural systems, and grow different crops. The main crops are sugar beet, wheat, barley, potatoes, and oats. The meat and dairy industries are the principal ones in the county; cattle are raised extensively, and pigs, sheep, and poultry are also important.

historical features

There are round towers at Cloyne and Kinneigh, and Cork has over 40 ecclesiastical foundations and over 300 castles. Among the more ancient remains are forts, megalithic tombs, stone circles, and stones inscribed in ogham characters, the ancient Irish alphabet.

In 1602 an Irish lord and clan chief of South Munster, Cormac MacDermot MacCarthy, was asked to recognize the crown as the legitimate granter of lands, rather than the clan chief system of tenure; he sent flattering messages to the English commander, Lord President Carew, appearing to agree; it became evident that he had no real intention of agreeing to the demands, and Carew became the laughing stock of the royal court in London. According to legend 'Blarney' thus came to refer to flattering talk intended to deceive; the Blarney Stone, set in the wall of the 15th-century Blarney Castle, 8 km/5 mi west of Cork city, is traditionally believed to give powers of persuasion to anyone who kisses it.

Edmund ⇨Spenser composed the first half of his *Faerie Queen* at Kilcolman Castle near Doneraile, during his service as secretary to the Lord Deputy of Ireland. The Irish nationalist leader Michael ⇨Collins (1890–1922) was born at Woodfield, 6 km/3.5 mi west of Clonakilty.

The ill-fated *Titanic* made its last port of call at Cobh in 1912, and the *Lusitania* was sunk off the coast of Kinsale in 1915.

CORK

Third-largest city in Ireland; port and county town of County ⇨Cork, important industrial and trading centre on the River Lee, at the head of the long inlet of Cork harbour, 21 km/13 mi from the sea; population (1996) 180,000. The lower harbour, at ⇨Cobh, can berth liners. The city has breweries, distilleries, container ports, and iron foundries. Other industries include cars, chemicals, food processing, oil refining, pharmaceuticals, pottery, steel, and tanning; manufacturing includes rubber and metal products, and computer hardware and software. St Fin Barre founded a school and an abbey here in the 7th century. The area was subsequently settled by Danes, who were in turn dispossessed by the Normans in 1172.

Cork has retained a tradition of learning; University College, founded in 1845 as the Queen's University Cork, became the University of Cork, part of the national University of Ireland in 1909. There is a Protestant cathedral dedicated to St Fin Barre, the city's patron saint, and a Roman Catholic pro-cathedral of St Mary and St Fin Barre (built in 1808). There is also an art gallery, an art school with an international

reputation, a museum, and an airport 6 km/4 mi from the city centre. The city hall opened in 1937.

location and economy

The nucleus of Cork is built on an island formed by two arms of the River Lee, known as the North and South channels; the rest of the city spreads in all directions. Large suburbs have developed, particularly since 1946. Many of the chemical and pharmaceutical industries are sited at the Little Island industrial estate between Cobh and Cork (Ringaskiddy).

Cork's principal imports are animal feed, coal, fertilizers, fruit, maize, machinery and spare parts, oil, rock containing phosphate (used to make fertilizer), iron pyrites (used to manufacture sulphuric acid), rubber, salt, steel, timber, and wheat. The principal exports are bacon, butter, clay, confectionery, eggs, malt, meat, livestock, oil products, poultry, and computer hardware and software. A natural gas field off Kinsale serves Cork City; the gas is also piped north to Dublin.

Cork harbour

The harbour at Cork is the most important on the south coast of Ireland; it is studded with islands, and

COUNTY CORK *For hundreds of years the pony and trap, seen here at Shanagarry, east of Cork, was the usual method of transport in rural Ireland. Until as late as the 1960s most farmsteads used the trap in preference to the car.*

its shores are wooded. The lower harbour is at Cobh; the upper harbour at Cork can provide berthage for certain vessels at all tides. Cork harbour is administered by a harbour board, comprised of members of the local authorities and commercial, employers', and labour organizations. Crane facilities are provided, and most quays have rail connections.

architectural features

The only monument of the Middle Ages still standing in Cork is the tower of the Red Abbey, an Augustinian foundation. The Cork skyline is dominated by the steeple of Shandon Church (built 1772). Most of the interesting buildings date from within the last 200 years. The customs house (1818), occupying a commanding position overlooking the river; the Courthouse (1835); the Cork Savings Bank (1842); the former Mansion House (now the Mercy Hospital), erected in 1767; and the County Hall (1965) are the most notable. Many of Cork's buildings are constructed in a local limestone, which is unusually pale in colour, and was also used for the stone quays.

churches

Cork has several interesting churches, many in the 19th-century Gothic style. The Church of Ireland St Fin Barre's Cathedral, a magnificent Neo-Gothic cruciform structure built between 1863 and 1878, is said to occupy the site of an ancient 6th-century church of St Fin Barre. The original buildings were demolished after the siege of 1690 and another church was erected which in turn was replaced by the existing cathedral, an imposing building in French Gothic style designed by William Burges. Its three high spires are a familiar Cork landmark and it contains some fine stone carvings. The peal of eight bells were cast by Rudhalls of Gloucester, England. The pro-cathedral of St Mary and St Fin Barre (1808) was built in a pointed Gothic style, also on the site of an older church. The 18th-century church of St Ann's, Shandon, has a remarkable tower with two sides finished in white limestone, and two in red sandstone; it is famous for its bells, which are immortalized in the song 'The Bells of Shandon'. The church of St Peter and St Paul (1866) is regarded as one of A W N Pugin's best works.

Of the many other churches in Cork, the most notable include Holy Trinity, run by the Capuchin Fathers, and erected in 1832 to commemorate Fr Matthew, the Apostle of Temperance; St Finnbarr's

South (1766), which contains the *Dead Christ* by Hogan, an eminent Cork sculptor; St Patrick's (1836); St Vincent's at Sunday's Well; Christ the King (1931) at Turner's Cross, a good example of functional architecture; the Augustinian church in Washington Street; the Franciscan church (1953) in Liberty Street, an outstanding 20th-century interpretation of the Byzantine style; and the Honan Chapel (1916) in the university grounds, which is modelled on Cormac's Chapel at Cashel, a 12th-century masterpiece in an Irish version of the Romanesque style.

history

In the 9th century the Danes devastated the settlement that had grown up around St Fin Barre's foundation. After their arrival in 1172, the Normans built walls around the city. William III took the city after a siege in 1690. During the Anglo–Irish War (1919–21) the ⇨Black and Tans caused considerable damage to the city centre. Cork was also an important strategic centre during the Irish Civil War (1922–23).

CORKERY, DANIEL (1878–1964)

Writer, born and educated in Cork, who later became professor of English literature at University College, Cork, 1931–47. His short stories accurately depict provincial life and speech and at their best have a brooding power. *The Hidden Ireland* (1925), a lyrical study of Gaelic Munster in the 18th century, had an enormous influence on contemporary Irish views of the past.

Among his collections of stories are *A Munster Twilight* (1916) and *The Stormy Hills* (1929). His criticism, as in *Synge and Anglo-Irish Literature* (1931), is often nationalistic, but he did see Ireland's history in a European context.

CORK FILM FESTIVAL

Established in 1956, Cork Film Festival was the first film festival in Ireland and its traditional strength has been its eclectic selection of short films. After a period of indecisiveness in the 1970s, it began to engage more fully with the changing Irish film cultural environment of the 1980s. While during its first 30 years it was the only Irish film festival, now there are several others: Dublin Film Festival, established in 1986, Galway Film Fleadh, established 1988, Derry Film Festival, and three children's film festivals, in Dublin, Belfast, and Galway.

CORK JAZZ FESTIVAL

One of Europe's largest jazz festivals, held annually in Cork City, over four days on the last weekend of October. Founded in 1977 by a local hotel as a means to attract custom out of season, it has grown to attract over 40,000 visitors and is spread over a number of venues in the city. It has featured leading artists including Ella Fitzgerald, Dizzy Gillespie, Art Blakey, Wynton Marsalis, Sonny Rollins, Oscar Peterson, Gerry Mulligan, Chick Corea, Dave Brubeck, George Shearing, Joe Lovano, Johnny Griffin, and Elvin Jones. It presents many styles of jazz, from Dixieland to acid jazz, and free performances in pubs and hotels are an important aspect of the festival.

CORMAC MACART (or MAC AIRT, also CORMAC UA CUINN MAC AIRT)

Pseudo-historical king of Ireland in the first half of the 3rd century, alledgedly reigning, according to various sources, for around 40 years. Grandson of Conn Cétchathach (Conn of the Hundred Battles), he established the Connachta dynasty of kings at Tara (modern County Meath). According to tradition he was proclaimed king after delivering a judgement wiser than the reigning king of Ireland, Mac Con. The *Tecosca Cormaic/Teachings of Cormac*, a legal text describing the proper behaviour for kings and warriors, is attributed to him.

Celebrated as a patron of arts and learning, Cormac MacArt was said to have founded schools of military science, law, and literature at Tara.

CORNWALLIS, CHARLES (1st Marquis and 2nd Earl) (1738–1805)

English general who served in the American Revolution, where he was forced to surrender at Yorktown in 1781. He was governor general of India 1786–92.

LIAM COSGRAVE *Leader of Fine Gael 1965–77 and Taoiseach 1973–77, Liam Cosgrave followed in the family footsteps, being the son of William Cosgrave, himself a leader of Fine Gael and prime minister of the Irish Free State.*

This combination of military and administrative experience prepared him for Ireland where, in June 1798 he was given the unique position of joint viceroy and commander-in-chief.

Cornwallis's first task was to complete the suppression of the ⇨Rebellion of 1798. His main object as viceroy was to secure legislative union between Ireland and Britain. Cornwallis wanted Catholic emancipation to accompany union. This, allied with his leniency with the defeated United Irishmen, earned him the contempt of Irish loyalists and yeomen, who dubbed him 'Croppywallis' (Croppy being a derogatory term for a United Irishman). Cornwallis resigned in 1801 when George III refused to allow emancipation to accompany union.

CORRIB, LOUGH

Lake in counties Galway and Mayo. It is the second-largest lake in Ireland, 43 km/27 mi long and 11 km/7 mi wide at its broadest point; area 176 sq km/68 sq mi. Lough Corrib is quite shallow, and contains about 300 islands; its outline is very irregular, and it flows via the River Corrib into Galway Bay. It is connected on its north side with Lough Mask, partly by means of an underground channel.

CORRS, THE

See ⇨pop and rock music.

COSGRAVE, LIAM (1920–)

Irish politician, Taoiseach (prime minister) 1973–77, leader of Fine Gael 1965–77. Cosgrave signed the ill-fated Sunningdale agreement of December 1973 with the British government and representatives of the moderate unionist and nationalist parties in Northern Ireland. The agreement, which proposed a power-sharing executive in Northern Ireland, coupled with cross-border institutions to deal with security and common socioeconomic matters, collapsed under extremist unionist pressure in 1974. At home, Cosgrave was prepared to make few concessions to reformist opinion on the Republic's social legislation, and even fewer towards traditional republicanism. He presided over severely repressive legislation to curb the Irish Republican Army (IRA) in the Republic, including the declaration of a state of emergency in September 1976.

The son of the first prime minister of the Republic of Ireland, William ⇨Cosgrave, Liam Cosgrave was born in Dublin and educated at St Vincent's College, Castleknock, and trained in law at the King's Inns, Dublin. A member of the Dáil from 1943–81, he was minister for external affairs 1954–57. In 1965 he succeeded James Dillon as leader of Fine Gael, and from 1973 headed a Fine Gael–Labour coalition government, the first non-Fianna Fáil government in 16 years. He resigned as leader when his party was heavily defeated in the general election of 1977.

COSGRAVE, WILLIAM THOMAS

(1880–1965)

Revolutionary and politician; president of the executive council (prime minister) of the Irish Free State 1922–32, leader of Cumann na nGaedheal 1923–33, and leader of Fine Gael 1935–44. He was born in Dublin and educated by the Christian Brothers. A founding member of ⇨Sinn Féin, he fought in the ⇨Easter Rising of 1916 but his death sentence was commuted. He supported the Anglo-Irish Treaty (1921) and oversaw the ruthless crushing of Irregular IRA forces during the Irish Civil War (1922–23), executing far more IRA than his British predecessors.

Cosgrave was elected to Westminster as a Sinn Féin MP in 1917, and was appointed minister for local government in the first Dáil (then the illegal republican parliament) in 1919. Following the deaths of Collins and Griffith in 1922, he succeeded them as chair of the provisional government and president of the Dáil government respectively, and became prime minister of the Irish Free State. After the civil war the Free State settled down under his leadership to a period of dull and conservative stability. Nevertheless this stability was crucial to the new state's democracy, illustrated by the peaceful transference of power to Cosgrave's old enemies in Fianna Fáil in 1932.

COSTELLO, JOHN ALOYSIUS (1891–1976)

Fine Gael politician; Taoiseach (prime minister)

1948–51 and 1954–57. Costello was born in Dublin and educated at University College, Dublin. As attorney general to the Irish Free State 1926–32, he assisted in the drafting of the 1931 Statute of Westminster, which regularized relations between the British government and the dominions. In 1949 he oversaw the withdrawal of Eire from the Commonwealth and the formal declaration of the Republic of Ireland.

Costello was elected to the Dáil (parliament) in 1933 and, untainted by a civil war background, he was the compromise candidate for Taoiseach (prime minister) in the formation of the first interparty government in 1948. He caused surprise by declaring Ireland a republic and leaving the Commonwealth in 1949. His handling of the 'Mother and Child' health care controversy of 1950–51 seemed to demonstrate the continuing domination of Irish life by the Roman Catholic church; spiritual leaders expressed concern that the planned care might offer instruction on moral issues, and argued that the right to provide for the health of children belonged to the parents and not the state. Costello's second term of office was ended by the IRA's 'border campaign', which caused the breakup of his coalition. He retired to the backbenches and resumed his legal practice.

COSTUME

Celts wore the first recorded fashions in Ireland, with their arrival around 300 BC; their brightly coloured cloaks, over tunics, or long, wide breeches were rapidly adopted. With Christianity came the next wave of costume, around the fifth century, consisting of a full-length léine, or tunic, with a brat, a large, rectangular, weatherproof woollen mantle, usually brightly coloured and embellished with a fringe, embroidery, or braid. Men sometimes wore a jacket with trews (trousers) for work during this period. These outfits were worn by both sexes for hundreds of years, the léine gradually becoming semi-fitted. The brat was worn for almost a millennium, in various forms.

With the arrival of the Anglo-Normans in 1169 came a new division in fashion, which was to last almost 500 years. This was the racial division of fashion between the urban dwellers, whose loyalties and fashion allegiance lay with London, and the native Irish, whose traditional dress styles evolved differently. The hooded mantle, brat and léine or trews continued to be worn by the native Irish at this time. In the 16th century, the léine was replaced by long-sleeved loose jackets, pleated at the waist, reaching down to mid-thigh, with tight trews. For women, the léine was now worn under a heavier woollen gown. Both sexes kept the brat. The bright colours of Irish garments continued to distinguish them from English fashions. In the 1660s the brat was finally replaced by the hooded cloak.

By the 1660s English-style clothes had become widespread among the wealthy, regardless of their racial origins, and subsequent fashion divisions related to wealth rather than race. From this date until the mid-20th century, distinctively Irish clothing tended to be the preserve of rural communities, mainly along the western seaboard. Red flannel petticoats were worn by women with bodices, shawls across the shoulders, and hooded cloaks, although by the 1840s the shawl had become larger and replaced the cloak, a separate headscarf being used to cover the head. Aran men wore wide trousers, a colourful crios (woven belt), two waistcoats, the inner one sleeved, and a báinín – a white jacket with no collar, named after the wool used in its manufacture. Elsewhere in Ireland, men wore linen shirts, wool waistcoats, knee breeches or trousers, and a heavy overcoat, or 'trusty'. These distinctive fashions gradually faded during the 20th century.

In the first half of the 20th century, the knitted Aran sweater was the main Irish fashion to be exported abroad. In the 1950s designers such as Sybil ⇨Connolly started to put Ireland on the world fashion map for their non-traditional, but distinctively Irish clothes. Since then successive waves of designers have followed, such as Paul Costelloe (1945–   ); John Rocha (1953–   ), who combines Irish textiles with Far-Eastern style; Mary Gregory (1962–   ), known for her fluid fabrics; knitwear designer Lainey Keogh (1957–   ); and milliner Philip ⇨Treacy.

COUGHLAN, ÉAMON (1952–   )

Athlete, born in Dublin. Ireland's leading athlete in the 1970s and 80s, he represented his country in three Olympic Games, narrowly missing out on the medals when finishing fourth to John Walker in the 1,500-metres final in 1976 and to Miruts Yifter in the 5,000-metres final in 1980. In 1983 he cruised past the Russian Dmitri Dmitriev to take gold in the World Championship 5,000-metres final.

His other greatest successes were for the most part restricted to the indoor athletic circuits. His record-breaking feats at middle distance earned him fame in the USA. He became known as 'the Chairman of the Boards' and in 1981 he broke world records for both 1,500 metres and the mile.

COULTER, PHIL (1942–   )

Arranger and composer of popular music. Working with Phil Martin, his hits included Sandy Shaw's Eurovision success 'Puppet on a String' (1967) and Cliff Richard's 'Congratulations' (1968). In the 1970s he managed the boy band the Bay City Rollers. Coulter has also had an impact on traditional Irish music, producing ⇨Planxty's first album and working with musicians such as the Furey Brothers and the Dubliners. More recently he has concentrated on performing and is perhaps best known for his easy-listening arrangements of traditional, popular, and his own original material. Important recordings include *Classic Tranquility* (1983) and his collaborations with the flautist James Galway, *Celtic Legends* (1997), and *Winter's Crossing* (1998).

Coulter was born in Londonderry, and studied music at Queen's University, Belfast. After emigrating to London he very quickly gained a reputation as a pianist and arranger, followed soon afterwards by a growing reputation as a composer.

COUNTER-REFORMATION

The survival and revival of Irish Catholicism in the face of official attempts to enforce the ⇨Reformation in Ireland, following the Act of Supremacy (1537) and establishment of the Church of Ireland. Though it has been argued that the Counter-Reformation movement began with the opposition to non-doctrinal reforms of the 1530s, modern research dates its origins from the reign of Queen Mary I (1553–58) and, in particular, to the energetic clerical reforms of George Dowdall (*c.* 1490–1558), archbishop of Armagh.

Dowdall's work consolidated resistance in the English Pale and the port towns, but in Munster and Ulster the Counter-Reformation took militant form, first with James Fitzmaurice Fitzgerald's declaration of war against the heretic English in 1579, and later with the Ulster lords' appeal for aid to Philip II and the Papacy in the 1590s. Though the movements occasionally overlapped, it was the institutionalized resistance of the clergy rather than the holy war of the military that characterized Counter-Reformation attitudes in the first decades of the 17th century.

COUNTRY AND IRISH (sometimes called Country and Western)

One of the most popular forms of music in modern Ireland, despite often being parodied. After the decline of the ⇨showbands in the late 1960s, 'Country and Irish' bands filled the vacuum they left, playing in smaller venues all over the country. Some artists crossed between the two genres, most notably Big Tom and the Mainliners. The material performed by these bands consists mainly of cover versions of old sentimental Irish songs in a country style as well as some showband standards. Leading performers record some original material but most perform a repertoire of standards.

Country and Irish performers such as Daniel ⇨O'Donnell, Philomena Begley, Margo, Louise Morrissey, Declan Nerney, and Dominic Kirwin have a huge following in Ireland and amongst the Irish community abroad, but are not generally known outside these communities.

COURCY, JOHN DE (died *c.* 1219)

A prince of Ulster, which he conquered in 1177. He was a member, possibly illegitimate, of a family with connections in Somerset, but established a number of monasteries in Ulster with links to northwest England, and most of those who settled with him in Ulster came from that area. De Courcy held the post of chief governor of Ireland intermittently between 1185 and 1195, but lost the favour of John (I) Lackland (acting king of England from 1189, king 1199–1216) and was ousted by the de Lacys of Meath in 1204 and never recovered his estate. He married Affreca, daughter of the king of Man and the Isles, but left no legitimate heirs.

COYNE AND LIVERY

A general term employed by English commentators to cover the various feudal and arbitrary exactions imposed by Gaelic Irish and Anglo-Irish lords in late-medieval and 16th-century Ireland, particularly in respect of the billeting of military forces. Attempts to abolish coyne and livery became a central concern of Tudor government in Ireland, but the failure of the strategies adopted towards that end, notably ⇨composition (commutation of feudal military dues), became a principal cause of the rebellions of the late Elizabethan era.

A fusion of the Irish *coinmheadh*, 'to keep; give hospitality', with the English 'livery', the obligation to care for the lords' horses, the term symbolized the degree to which both ethnic groups in Ireland had become united in their common exploitation of arbitrary taxes.

CRAFTS, TRADITIONAL

Wood, leather, iron, stone, straw, clay, and ⇨textiles are the materials of Ireland's traditional crafts.

woodwork

Apart from its use in ⇨furniture making, wood is also the foundation of many other crafts. Wooden spinning wheels and looms, both required for the manufacture of textiles, have traditionally been made in Ireland. Boat building relies heavily on woodworking skills. Boats made in Ireland range from large fishing boats, produced in coastal yards, to curraghs, small light fishing boats still in use along the west coast of Ireland, whose form remains largely unchanged since the Iron Age. The ribs and laths of these boats are wooden, and skins are stitched to this frame and then tarred.

Coopers continue to make barrels for whiskey, therefore production is based close to the main distilleries, in Cork, Dublin, and Antrim. In sport, hurling sticks are made of ash, sometimes by hurlers themselves. Wooden musical instruments have been produced for hundreds of years in Ireland, notably the harp, the earliest preserved example dating to the

CRAFTS *The methods of making baskets by hand have changed little since antiquity. Willow shoots, cane, or reeds are first softened then interwoven before the basketwork is bent into shape.*

14th century. Fiddles are also made by hand, as are uilleann pipes, bagpipes, and bodhráns (small drums).

leatherwork

Leather working focuses on four areas: bookbinding, saddlery, footwear, and sports accessories. Bookbinding is thought to have originated in the early Christian period (8th century), when many illustrated manuscripts had rich bindings, although none has survived. Remaining material indicates a growing bookbinding industry from the middle of the 17th century, particularly associated with the binding of the journals of the Irish houses of parliament. In the mid-18th century Irish bookbinding reached its peak, and became known the world over. The Act of Union in 1800, however, meant that parliament and many of the aristocracy relocated to England, so the market declined rapidly, although it was revived in a small way in the 20th century. Other leather goods include harnesses, saddles, and collars for horses; shoes, still made and repaired by a small number of craftspeople; and sliotars (hurling balls) and footballs.

working other materials

Blacksmithing as a craft has a long history, centred on the manufacture of tools, farm implements, and horseshoes. The latter is the main surviving area of production, but recent growth in demand for garden furniture, and for hand-wrought gates and railings, has led to the establishment of new ironwork craft studios.

Stone is quarried and cut in several locations around Ireland, such as Liscannor stone in County Clare, and Connemara marble in County Galway. Dry stone walling is found mainly in the West of Ireland, where stones cleared from the fields can be used to form walls. Often built without gates, stones from these unmortared walls must be removed and re-erected to move animals from field to field.

Straw, willow, reeds and rushes have a long history in Ireland's crafts, and are still used in thatching, in furniture, and in making basketwork items for homes and gardens.

See also ⇨metalwork, ⇨furniture, ⇨ceramics, ⇨glass, and ⇨textiles.

CRAIG, JAMES (1st Viscount Craigavon) (1871–1940)

Ulster Unionist politician; first prime minister of Northern Ireland 1921–40. Elected to Westminster as MP for East Down 1906–18 (Mid-Down 1918–21), he was a highly effective organizer of the Ulster Volunteers and unionist resistance to home rule before World War I. In 1921 he succeeded Edward ⇨Carson as leader of the Ulster Unionist Party, and was appointed prime minister later that year. As leader of the Northern Ireland government he carried out systematic discrimination against the Catholic minority, abolishing proportional representation in 1929 and redrawing constituency boundaries to ensure Protestant majorities.

Although a stockbroker by trade, Craig took part in the Boer War as captain of the Royal Irish Rifles in South Africa 1900–01. He saw active service in World War I, before serving for a period as a parliamentary secretary 1917–21 in Lloyd George's coalition government. He was knighted in 1918 and made Viscount Craigavon in 1927.

CRAIG, MAURICE (1919–)

Poet and architectural historian, a pioneering figure in the movement to preserve Ireland's architectural heritage, especially of the Georgian period. His book *Dublin 1660–1860* (1952) remains highly influential.

CRAIGAVON

City in County Armagh; population (1990 est) 62,000. It was created by integrating ⇨Lurgan, ⇨Portadown, and various villages and providing a new town centre and new residential and industrial areas. Craigavon was designated a 'new town' in 1965. It was named after ⇨James Craig (Viscount Craigavon), the first prime minister of Northern Ireland (1921–40).

CRANBERRIES, THE

See ⇨pop and rock music.

CROAGH PATRICK

Holy mountain rising to 765 m/2,510 ft in County Mayo, a national place of pilgrimage. An annual pilgrimage on the last Sunday of July commemorates St Patrick, who fasted there for the 40 days of Lent in 441 AD.

Crowds of people, some barefooted, climb the mountain to attend the series of masses celebrated in the oratory at the summit.

CROFTS, FREEMAN WILLS (1879–1957)

Writer of detective fiction. Crofts was born in Dublin,

CROAGH PATRICK *It was here, near Clew Bay in County Mayo, that Saint Patrick, commemorated by this statue, reputedly destroyed all the snakes and toads in Ireland by ringing his bell and then hurling it into the abyss. On a clear day there are superb views across to the strings of tiny islands lining the coast.*

and worked on the railways before taking up writing. Among his 35 novels, most of which feature the character Inspector (later Superintendent) French of Scotland Yard, are *Inspector French's Greatest Case* (1925), *The Starvel Tragedy* (1927), and *The Hog's Back Mystery* (1933).

Crofts gave up his career as chief assistant engineer on the Belfast and Northern Counties Railway in 1929 in order to concentrate on his writing and later moved to England. His novels enjoyed widespread popularity, and were noted for their meticulous plotting and attention to detail.

CROKE, THOMAS WILLIAM (1823–1902)

Catholic archbishop and prominent nationalist, born in Dromin, County Cork. Educated at the Irish College, Paris, Croke was ordained a priest in 1847. As professor of rhetoric in Carlow he became disillusioned with parliamentary politics and decided to support the Young Ireland movement, even visiting the Irish nationalist Charles Gavan Duffy in prison in 1848. Consecrated a bishop in 1870, he moved to New Zealand, but returned to Ireland in 1874,

becoming archbishop of Cashel the following year.

Croke defended the ⇨Fenians, despite much criticism, and was the most politically active cleric in the period. A public supporter of Charles Stewart Parnell's home rule movement, he only changed allegiance after the Kitty O'Shea scandal broke.

Croke was the first patron of the Gaelic Athletic Association, and its leading stadium in County Dublin, Croke Park, was named after him.

CROKE PARK

Ireland's premier sports stadium, in Dublin; it is named after the Gaelic Athletic Association's chief patron, Archbishop Thomas ⇨Croke. It was purchased in 1913, and has staged many important and memorable contests. Croke Park was also the scene of one of Ireland's greatest atrocities during the Anglo–Irish War (1919–21) when British troops fired at spectators and players during a game of Gaelic football as an act of reprisal for the murder of several of its officers. Hill 16, the main terrace of the stadium, was named after the 16 people who died on ⇨Bloody Sunday, 21 November 1920.

In recent times, with government funding, the stadium has undergone major redevelopment and it is now one of the most impressive all-seated stadiums in Europe, holding up to 80,000 people.

CROKER, JOHN WILSON (1780–1857)

Politician and journalist, born in County Galway. Educated at Trinity College, Dublin, Croker trained as a barrister but was more interested in political satire. In 1803 he wrote a defence of the Dublin Castle administration and the following year two satires on Dublin theatre and society, *On the Present State of the Irish Stage* and *An Intercepted Letter from Canton*. Croker was Tory member of parliament for Downpatrick 1807–12, Athlone 1812–18, and four other constituencies in a parliamentary career that lasted until 1832. He was acting Irish chief secretary in 1808 and was an efficient secretary to the Admiralty 1809–30. He retired from politics in 1832 after the passing of the Reform Act, which he opposed.

A talented debater and critic, Croker came up with the name 'the Conservatives' for the Tory Party. Amongst those wounded by his sharp tongue and pen were the writers and politicians Thomas Macaulay, Benjamin Disraeli, and William Makepeace Thackeray. He was a founder of the *Quarterly Review* (1809) and the Athenaeum Club in London.

CROKER, RICHARD ('BOSS CROKER', or 'KING OF THE CITY') (1841–1922)

Irish-born US Democratic politician; political 'boss' (manager) of Tammany Hall, the Democratic Party political machine in New York, 1886–1902. Born in Clonakilty, County Cork, he emigrated to New York in 1846. He became 'boss' of Tammany Hall on the death of his predecessor and patron 'Honest' John Kelly (1822–1886). An immensely talented political strategist, Croker established a virtual monopoly over New York's public affairs behind the scenes in the 1890s. He became the centre of several enquiries into municipal corruption and eventually lost control of the city in 1901 in a wave of progressive reform.

Croker was actively involved in Democratic machine politics from an early age, achieving election as alderman in 1868 and coroner in 1873. In 1870 he fought to oust 'Boss' Tweed, John Kelly's predecessor. Following his retirement from public life, Croker returned to Ireland and purchased a substantial estate in County Dublin, where he enjoyed great success as a horse-breeder. His later years were clouded by bitter family litigation.

CROKER, THOMAS CROFTON (1798–1854)

Writer and collector of Irish legends. Born in Cork, his works include *Researches in the South of Ireland* (1824), *Fairy Legends and Traditions of the South of Ireland* (1825–28), and *Legends of the Lakes* (1829).

The Grimm brothers translated Croker's *Fairy Legends* into German, and his work had considerable influence on 19th-century collectors of Irish folklore.

CROLY, GEORGE (1780–1860)

Writer, biographer, and Anglican preacher. Croly was born in Dublin and educated there at Trinity College. His literary output was based mainly on poetry and romances, including the novels *Salathiel* (1829), based on the legend of the 'Wandering Jew', and *Marston* (1846), set during the French Revolution.

Croly took holy orders in 1804 and went to London in 1810, becoming rector of St Stephen's, Walbrook, in 1835. From 1817 he published some 40 works; other titles include the tragedy *Cataline* (1822), and the satire *May Fair* (1827).

CROMMELIN, SAMUEL LOUIS (1652–1727)

French craftsman. A Huguenot, Crommelin emigrated to Ireland in 1699 after the revocation of the Edict of Nantes in 1685, invited by King William III. He arrived in Lisburn, County Antrim, with 25 families, and began importing looms from Flanders and Holland. Under his supervision the linen industry developed and thrived in Ireland, and he raised the standard to a new level. As a result of his work exports in linen increased from 0.3 to 2.4 million yards between 1690 and 1720.

CROMWELL, OLIVER (1599–1658)

Although he spent less than 10 months in Ireland (August 1649–May 1650), Cromwell's impact was profound and long lasting. A whirlwind military campaign punctuated by merciless treatment of military opponents and civilians in Drogheda (September 1649) and Wexford (October 1649) effectively ended opposition of the Irish confederates to English parliamentary rule, which he had initiated earlier in 1649.

As lord protector of England (from 1653) Cromwell was not directly involved in Irish affairs, though he both encouraged and defended the radical programme of dispossession and repression instituted and sustained by his sons-in-law Henry Ireton (lord deputy of Ireland 1650–1651) and Charles Fleatwood (lord deputy 1654–1657), and his son Henry Cromwell (between 1655 and 1659 president of the council, lord deputy, and lord lieutenant) against Ireland's Catholics. Despite the fact that the actual results of Cromwellian policy in Ireland fell far below its radical expectations in political, religious, and economic terms, the ruthlessness of the attempt was symbolized in the maleficent phrase 'the curse of Cromwell be on you' which later became a byword for hatred of English rule in Ireland.

CROSS, DOROTHY (1956–   )

Post-modernist artist who uses found objects to create assemblages and installations that explore issues relating to gender and authority. Cross emerged as a significant force in Irish art with her exhibition *Ebb* held at the Douglas Hyde Gallery, Trinity College, Dublin, in 1988. She has established an international reputation and represented Ireland at the Venice Biennale, Italy, in 1993.

Born in Cork, Cross studied art there and in England, the Netherlands, and the USA. Works such as *Shark Lady in a Balldress* (1988; Hugh Lane Municipal Gallery of Modern Art, Dublin) employ a Surrealist approach to create a complex web of references and symbolism through which she aims to deconstruct myths surrounding male and female identity. The waning power of the Catholic church in modern Ireland has also featured as a theme in her art.

CROSSES, HIGH

Intricately carved tall stone crosses, typically having a circle around the centre. Irish high crosses were the main Irish sculptural form from the 8th to 12th centuries and are widely considered to be among the most significant pieces of monumental art produced in medieval Europe. Although found in other parts of the British Isles where Celtic languages were spoken, this Christian art form was most developed in Ireland. Several hundred examples survive, some 34 largely intact.

beginnings

From remaining evidence it is likely that the Irish high cross evolved from the carving of cross shapes on to stone slabs, probably grave markers. It is believed that the next imaginative step took place in the 8th century, with the carving of the slab into a three-dimensional free-standing shape of a cross. The tall shaft fits into a large stone base, and a stone wheel or ring joins the four arms of the cross. High crosses were elaborately decorated, and probably painted in bright colours. Unlike the stone slabs from which they developed, they are not thought to have marked graves, but were probably associated with nearby monasteries, either for protection, for ritual purposes, as a boundary marker, or, in the case of the figurative crosses, to teach the largely illiterate public.

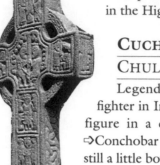

HIGH CROSSES *The origin of the circle around the cross is unproven, but it may have been a solar symbol. The segments of the cross-pieces that lie within the circle are indented, as can be seen on this example in County Meath.*

decoration

The earliest crosses were covered in abstract decoration. The Ahenny Crosses in County Tipperary epitomize this style. Sculptors began to introduce biblical scenes from both testaments in the late 8th and early 9th centuries. The crucifixion, Christ in majesty, or the Last Judgement appear in the centre of the ring of many high crosses. Te cross at Moone, County Kildare (late 8th century), and Muireadach's Cross in County Louth (early 10th century) show how the modelling and three-dimensionality of figure carving gradually increased. In the Romanesque period (late 11th and

early 12th centuries) high crosses underwent their final development. Large high-relief figures, usually Christ and an ecclesiastical figure, dominate these crosses, smaller scenes being banished to the bases, as on the cross of Dysert O'Dea, County Clare. The Norman period saw the decline and extinction in the High Cross tradition.

CUCHULAIN (or CÚ CHULAINN) (lived 1st century AD)

Legendary Celtic hero. A stupendous fighter in Irish ⇨hero-tales, he was the chief figure in a cycle associated with his uncle ⇨Conchobar mac Nessa, King of Ulster. While still a little boy, he performed his first great feat by slaying a ferocious hound. As a young man, he single-handedly kept a whole army at bay, and won battles in both the real world and the otherworld, but was slain through a combination of magic and treachery. His most famous exploits were recorded in *Taín Bó Cuailnge/The Cattle Raid of Cooley*. Cuchulain became a symbolic figure for the Irish cultural revival in the late 19th century, and a bronze statue of him stands in Dublin General Post Office, commemorating the Easter Rising.

early life

As a child Cuchlain was known as Setanta, son of the Ulster warrior Sualtam and the princess Dechtire, but his true father was the warrior god, Lugh, ruler of light, sorcery, and the crafts. He was brought up at Dun Imbrith (Louth) and, at the age of six, went to the court of King Conchobar. After killing the watchdog of Culann the smith, he guarded in its stead and acquired the name 'Culann's hound'. Later, he killed the three sons of Nechta, hereditary foes of the Ulster people.

Cattle Raid of Cooley

At the age of 17, when Medhbh of Connaught and her army attempted to capture a great bull, the Donn of Cuailnge, Cuchulain defended the frontier single-handed during the magic debility of the men of Ulster. This weakness, inflicted when Ulster was in danger, was the curse of the goddess Macha; Cuchulain was protected because he was from Leinster.

ad says, Cuchulain fought to the end like the men of Easter week. His enemies were afraid to go near him till they were sure he was dead and when the bird landed on him and drank his blood they knew. Well, says the driver, 'tis a sad day for the men of Ireland when they need a bird to tell them a man is dead.

FRANK MCCOURT Irish-American writer *Angela's Ashes: A Memoir of Childhood* (1997).

~

death

Cuchulain was slain about ten years after the cattle raid, by Lugaid and the children of Calatin Dana.

CULLEN, PAUL (1803–1878)

Roman Catholic archbishop of Armagh (1849) and archbishop of Dublin (1852), created the first post-Reformation Irish cardinal in 1866. Cullen aided Daniel ⇨O'Connell, but supported the suppression of the Fenian movement.

Born in Prospect, County Kildare, most of his early career (1832–49) was spent in Rome. In Ireland, he led the ⇨Devotional Revolution that transformed Irish Catholicism into an ultramontane church (advocating supreme papal authority in all aspects of discipline and faith). At the First Vatican Council in 1870 he supported the declaration of papal infallibility. He established schools, convents, hospitals, and churches in Ireland, as well as a Catholic university in Dublin (no longer existing) under the leadership of John Henry Newman (1801–1890).

CUMANN NA MBAN ('the league of women')

Radical women's organization. It was founded in 1913, at the same time as the ⇨Irish Volunteers, and became the women's auxiliary division of that organization in 1914. It supported the ⇨Easter Rising of 1916 and was led by Countess ⇨Markievicz and Kathleen Clarke. The group worked closely with militant republicanism and opposed the ⇨Anglo-Irish Treaty (1921) which set up the Irish Free State within the British Commonwealth. It later played a significant role in support and active service with the ⇨Irish Republican Army. Cumann na mBan was declared an illegal organization in Northern Ireland in 1922 and in the Irish Free State in 1931.

CUMANN NA NGAEDHEAL ('party of the Gael')

Political party founded in 1923 following the establishment of the ⇨Irish Free State; the principal party supporting the Anglo-Irish Treaty (1921) until it merged with the Centre Party and the semi-fascist ⇨Blueshirts to form ⇨Fine Gael in 1933. Led by William T ⇨Cosgrave, it was the party of government from its foundation until Éamon de Valera's Fianna Fáil election victory in 1932.

Claiming to be the direct successor to Sinn Féin, which split following the signing of the Anglo-Irish Treaty, Cumann na nGaedheal's support for the treaty and its conservative economic policies ensured it the support of business interests, large-scale farmers, and the Catholic hierarchy. The party's leadership comprised an uneasy combination of republican-minded figures like Richard Mulcahy (1886–1971) and more enthusiastic supporters of the Irish Free State's ties with Britain such as Kevin ⇨O'Higgins. A mutiny in the National Army in 1924 and the quashing of the Boundary Commission, which had been expected to cede territory from Northern Ireland, resulted in its increasing conservatism on national issues. Cumann na nGaedheal failed to develop a wide electoral base and struggled to remain in power following Fianna Fáil's entry to the Dáil (parliament) in 1927. After two election defeats within twelve months, it merged with other opposition parties to form Fine Gael in 1933.

CURRAGH, THE

Horse-racing course on the Curragh Plain in County Kildare, where all five Irish Classic races are run. It is primarily used for flat racing although it also stages races under National Hunt rules. The Curragh Plain is the national focus for horse breeding and training: the National Stud is on the edge of Kildare town, and overall some 1,300 horses are kept in the vicinity.

Racing has been held at the Curragh since the mid-1880s. The course is right-handed and in the shape of a horseshoe.

The Curragh was the site of the ⇨Curragh 'Mutiny' in March 1914. The Curragh Plain is also the site of the principal training camp of the Irish army. The military camp was handed over by the

British to the Irish Army in 1922, and was used as an internment camp for republicans in World War II.

CURRAGH 'MUTINY'

Outbreak of dissent on 20 March 1914 when 60 British officers of the 3rd Cavalry Brigade based at the Curragh camp, County Kildare, declared they would resign rather than enforce ⇨home rule in Protestant Ulster.

In March 1914, the British Liberal government had belatedly begun to consider measures to enforce home rule in Ireland against Ulster unionist opposition. Gen Sir Arthur Paget, commander-in-chief in Ireland, mishandled the affair by allowing his officers the option of refusing to coerce Ulster. The British secretary for war compounded this blunder by assuring the officers that the British army would not be used to force Ulster into home rule, though this was not given with cabinet authority. After a public outcry, the cabinet repudiated these assurances and secured the resignations of the secretary for war and several high-ranking army officers.

The 'mutiny' (though no orders were disobeyed) demonstrated the weakness of the Liberal government in the face of determined opposition from Ulster unionism. The suggestion that the British government would not attempt to use force to uphold British law in Ireland critically discredited public confidence in its Irish policy.

CUSACK, CYRIL JAMES (1910–1993)

Actor who joined the ⇨Abbey Theatre, Dublin, in 1932 and appeared in many of its productions, including J M Synge's *The Playboy of the Western World*. In Paris he won an award for his solo performance in Samuel Beckett's *Krapp's Last Tape*. In the UK his long career included playing many roles as a member of the Royal Shakespeare Company and the National Theatre Company.

Cusack also had a long, but secondary career in film, first appearing as an evicted child in the Film Company of Ireland's *Knocknagow* (1918). He came to prominence as a film actor when he played a member of an IRA gang in *Odd Man Out* (1947), and went on to play a number of small parts in films, including *Shake Hands with the Devil* (1959), *A Terrible Beauty* (1960), *The Spy Who Came in from the Cold* (1965), *Fahrenheit 451* (1966), Franco Zeffirelli's *The Taming of the Shrew* (1968), *The Day of the Jackal* (1973), *Poitín* (1978), and *My Left Foot* (1989).

Cusack was born in South Africa, where his father was an officer in the Natal Mounted Police, but left with his mother for Ireland when he was six. There they formed a touring company with the actor Brefni O'Rourke, and thus Cusack had a thorough theatrical training, appearing in numerous theatre productions in Dublin and London. In 1942 he was playing opposite Vivien Leigh in George Bernard Shaw's *The Doctor's Dilemma* at the Haymarket Theatre when disaster struck – he became ill and forgot his lines. He returned to Dublin and set up his own company, Cyril Cusack Productions, directing and acting in innumerable plays at the Gaiety Theatre for some 20 years. In 1963 he acted for the Royal Shakespeare Company in Peter Brook's production of Friedrich Dürrenmatt's *The Physicists* (as Möbius) and in the Stratford *Julius Caesar* (as Cassius). In 1968 he played Conn in the Abbey Theatre's production of Dion Boucicault's *The Shaughraun* at the World Theatre Season at the Aldwych Theatre, London. His Chebutykin, the drunken army doctor, in Anton Chekhov's *The Three Sisters* at the Royal Court Theatre in 1990, stole the show. It was a rare family occasion – his daughters played the sisters.

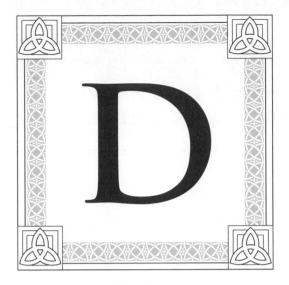

D

DAGDA (OR DAGHDHA) ('the good god')

In mythology, the father-deity in the lore of the ⇨hero-tales. He is presented as being of huge stature and strength, and his attributes were a club, magic harp, and the Undry, a wonderful cauldron in which food is cooked for all. He was the magician leader of the ⇨Tuatha Dé Danann. Originally known as the Celtic Dago-Devos, he is akin to Dyaus, Deus, Zeus, and other Indo-European sky-gods.

DÁIL ÉIREANN

Lower house of the legislature of the Republic of Ireland (Oireachtas). It consists of 166 members elected by adult suffrage through the single transferable vote system of proportional representation from 41 constituencies for a five-year term.

Legislation dealing with finance may be initiated in the Dáil only and, on being passed by the Dáil, is sent to Seanad Éireann for its recommendations, which may be accepted or rejected by the Dáil.

The government is customarily chosen from the majority party (or parties) in the Dáil and is responsible to that house. The Taoiseach (prime minister), the Tánaiste (deputy prime minister), and the minister for finance must be members of the Dáil; other government members must be members of the Dáil or Seanad Éireann, not more than two being members of Seanad Éireann. The president of Ireland summons and dissolves the Dáil on the advice of the Taoiseach, who is appointed by the president on the nomination of the Dáil. See also ⇨electoral system.

DÁL CAIS

A powerful Munster kingdom which rose to power in the second half of the 10th century. It peaked and fell within the reign of ⇨Brian Bóruma, who at the start of the 11th century became in effect Ireland's first high king from a dynasty other than the Uí Néill.

Originally part of the Déisi kingdom which settled in what is now eastern County Clare, the Dál Cais began its rise to power in the 9th century, largely

DÁIL *Members of the first Dáil, formed in January 1919. It consisted of 73 Sinn Féin candidates who, having been elected in 1918, abstained from Westminster and created their own assembly in Dublin.*

FROM KITCHEN HEARTH AND CEILIDH TO THE RENOWN OF RIVERDANCE

by Catherine E Foley

In 1994 *Riverdance*, a spectacular performance of hard-shoe step dancing at the Eurovision Song Contest in Dublin, placed traditional Irish dancing on the global stage and generated enormous popular interest in the genre. Two other forms of dance regarded as traditionally Irish are set dancing and céili dancing.

step dance

Irish step dance is predominantly a solo performance dance genre with emphasis on stepping and gestural movements with the feet, hence the name; in general, the torso and arms are not used in solo performances. Step dance may be performed by male and female, within formal and informal contexts, and with either hard shoes or light shoes depending on the dance type. Light-shoe dances emphasize a graceful and airborne aesthetic, while hard-shoe dances place emphasis on the percussive and rhythmic nature of these dances. Timing, rhythm, grace, posture, feet positions, and the actual step dance composition and its execution are considered to be important.

The three primary Irish step dances are the reel, the jig, and the hornpipe. The reel is in 4/4 time and is predominantly performed with light shoes. When performed with hard shoes, it is called the treble reel. The jig is in 6/8 time and can be sub-divided into other dance categories: the slip, double, single, and light jigs. The slip jig is in 9/8 time. The double jig is a hard-shoe dance while the other categories are light-shoe dances. The hornpipe is generally regarded to be in 4/4 time and is performed with hard shoes.

Historically, Irish step dance dates back to the 18th century when it was taught by travelling dancing masters to a predominantly rural, agricultural community, and also in the bigger Anglo-Irish houses. Together with Irish step dance and etiquette of the ballroom, they taught fashionable contemporary group dances, such as minuets, jigs, cotillons, country dances, and later Irish set dances based on the French quadrilles.

modern developments in step dance

The Gaelic League, a cultural nationalist organization whose primary objective was the de-anglicization of Ireland, emerged at the end of the 19th century. Branches of the league were established in urban areas within and outside Ireland, and although the Irish language was central to the league's programme, Irish step dance was later appropriated as a representation of cultural nationalism.

From the 1920s schools of Irish step dance emerged in the bigger towns and cities of Ireland, and subsequently in the diasporic locations of the USA, Canada, Australia, New Zealand, England, Scotland, and Africa. The urbanization of Irish step dance influenced its performance and development. In the cities children attended traditional Irish dancing classes held by a permanent teacher at a fixed venue. Aged between four and eighteen, both boys and girls (girls were the majority) were taught to embody the Irish step dance aesthetic at a dance class which they might attend two or three times a week for some 10 to 15

A team of Irish step dancers take part in a street carnival in 1991, as part of Dublin's celebrations as European City of Culture. This type of precise and ordered dancing was widely practised from the 18th century, when peripatetic teachers made their living taking classes in far-flung villages.

CULTURE   ÁTH CLIATH 1991   EUROPE

years. Competitions in Irish step dance took place more regularly and became a primary motivation factor for Irish step dancers. Over the following decades dancing costumes became very elaborate.

Another factor influencing the development of Irish step dance was the urban context of its performance. Irish step dance competitions took place on large stages in town halls and other venues, which allowed and demanded a greater use of space by the dancer. This was a marked difference to Irish step dance in 19th-century rural Ireland, where performance usually took place in more confined areas – on half doors unhinged for the purpose, the top of a barrel, or the flag stone in front of the hearth. It was said that the good step dancer could dance within six square inches (roughly 15 sq cm).

step dance competition and hierarchy

The primary context for the performance of Irish step dance is competition, commonly referred to as the *feis*, 'festival'. Feiseanna take place throughout the year at different venues and are controlled by one of the two primary organizations of Irish step dance: An Coimisiun le Rinci Gaelacha (established 1929) controls the world championships and An Comhghail (established 1969) the annual All Ireland. Dancers in one organization do not usually compete with dancers in the other.

Dancers progress through different hierarchical stages within these competitions, from beginner to championship level, and also through different age groups up to senior level. Until the 1990s champion senior step dancers who wished to continue with Irish step dance either took their teacher's examination (TCRG) with one of the organizations or performed at concerts.

However, following the performance of *Riverdance* and its translation to a full-length stage show in 1995, professionalism in Irish step dance became a reality. Other Irish step dance stage shows followed, such as *Lord of the Dance*, *Feet of Flames*, and *Dancing on Dangerous Ground*. These shows employ professional step dancers.

step dance variations

Outside the formal organizations are other regional styles of Irish step dance. The first intensive study of these traditions took place in North Kerry, where the traditional step dances of Jeremiah Molyneaux, last of the rural travelling dancing masters in Kerry and Ireland, were recorded and documented. The sean nos, 'old style', dance tradition of Connemara is another regional variation. Danced percussively to predominantly reel time music, it is performed in a more relaxed manner, differ-

ently structured to the North Kerry and 'competition' step dances. In addition to the 'national' and 'regional' styles exists the individual's style of Irish step dance, whereby the dancer internalizes the music and interprets it kinaesthetically.

set dancing

Set dances are group dances with four couples, each couple generally placed on the four cardinal points: north, south, east, and west, with the man placed to the left of the woman. A set dance comprises five or six fixed figures, with a rest in between each completed figure.

Throughout the 19th century and the early decades of the 20th century, different localities danced particular set dances based on the music types found in those areas. These could include a selection of polkas, slides, jigs, hornpipes, or reels. Examples of sets included the Caledonian Set, the Plain Set, the Jenny Lind Set, and the Baile Mhúirne Reel Set.

In the 20th century set dancing was not allowed at the informal Irish social dances known as céilithe (singular céili or céilidh); step dancing was also excluded as it was a solo genre and regarded as too complicated for a social evening. The Republic of Ireland's Public Dance Halls Act (1935), which prohibited dances held without a licence, heralded the decline of rural house dances and a consequent decline in rural set dancing practice.

However, set dancing underwent a revival in Ireland and other diasporic locations from the late 1970s, and today there are set céilithe where sets are danced all night. At present set dancing is a way of life for many set dancers, both rural and urban.

Weekend workshops, set céilithe, and weekly classes take place throughout Ireland under the direction of leading set dance teachers in the field. There is no official qualification for the teaching of set dancing.

céili dancing

The céili dance form is a group dance performed in competitions set up by the Irish dance organizations. Teachers may qualify solely as céili dance teachers. The more popular céili dances include *Ballai Luimni/The Walls of Limerick*, *Ionsai na hInse/The Siege of Ennis*, and *Baint on Fheir/The Haymaker's Jig*. The word céili is also applied to informal Irish dancing events, the first such social céili being held in 1897 by the Gaelic League in London. Its success as a social event representing Irish ethnicity and solidarity caused it to spread to Ireland and throughout the Irish diaspora.

through the strategic position it held at the lower reaches of the Shannon River. It seized the kingship of Munster in 963 by defeating the reigning Munster power the Eóganachta, and furthered its dominance in Ireland, mainly through several victories over the Vikings of Limerick.

After Brian Bóruma's death the Dál Cais lost much of the authority it had gained, and reclaimed only a short time of power in the reigns of Brian's grandson, Tairdelbach Ua Briain, who died in 1086 and great-grandson, Muirchertach Ua Briain, who died in 1119.

DALRIADA

Powerful kingdom of northeastern Ireland from the 5th to 7th centuries. Based in the north of what is now County Antrim, the Dalriada had colonized a large area of the western coast of Scotland and its islands by the end of the 5th century. For almost two centuries the kingdom was able to control its possessions both in Ireland and Scotland.

Closely associated with St ⇨Columba, the colony of the Dalriada in Scotland was instrumental in spreading Christianity to the local inhabitants. By traditional accounts, the Dalriada people were descendants of Riada of the Long Wrist, leader of the Gaelic Scots.

DAMER HOUSE

Elegant three-storey Georgian house with nine bays built by Joseph Damer in the early 18th century in the courtyard of ⇨Roscrea Castle, County Tipperary. The superbly carved staircase is of particular interest. The house was used as a barracks in the 19th century and fell into poor condition, but it has been undergoing gradual restoration by the Irish Georgian Society.

DANCE, TRADITIONAL

See feature essay on traditional Irish dance, page 94.

DANU (or DANAAN)

In Celtic mythology, the mother-goddess and land-goddess. Her name parallels those of goddesses in other Indo-European languages as well as the names of various European rivers, such as the Danube. She was also known as the war-goddess Morrigan or Mor-Ríoghain ('phantom-queen'), under which name she appears as the consort of the ⇨Dagda, leader of the mythological ⇨Tuatha Dé Danaan in Ireland's medieval ⇨hero-tales.

DARCY, PATRICK (1598–1668)

Lawyer and politician. An expert in constitutional matters, Darcy argued strongly for the legislative independence of the Irish parliament. As a Catholic, he was debarred from practising and from owning land during Oliver Cromwell's colonization of Ireland.

Born in Galway, the seventh son of a Roman Catholic baronet of English descent, Darcy sat for Navan, County Meath, in the Irish parliament of 1634. He rose to prominence by 1640, and following the uprising of 1641 supported his fellow Irish Catholics in the ⇨Confederation of Kilkenny. He was negotiator for the Catholic Confederates with Charles I's deputy Ormond in 1649, and was then made a commissioner of the peace throughout Ireland, an appointment that lasted until the arrival of Cromwell. Following the Cromwellian victories, Darcy left politics but continued to pursue his legal career until his death.

DARGAN, WILLIAM (1799–1867)

Engineering contractor and railway entrepreneur. Dargan acquired seminal experience as an engineer in England in the hey-day of railway construction. Returning to Ireland in 1831, he undertook the financing and construction of the first Irish railroads and by the early 1850s had constructed over 600 miles of track. He also played a major role in the development of Bray, at the end of his lucrative eastern coastal line, as Ireland's first commercial seaside resort. Unsuccessful investments coupled with disablement following a riding accident rendered him close to ruin by the time of his death.

DARLEY, GEORGE (1795–1846)

Poet, critic, and mathematician. Born in Dublin and educated at Trinity College, Darley later moved to London. His first volume of poetry, *The Errors of Ecstasie*, appeared in 1822. He wrote for the *London Magazine*, was a critic for the *Athenaeum*, and wrote plays and studied English dramatists. He was also an accomplished mathematician and published textbooks on geometry, algebra, and trigonometry.

DARRAGH, LYDIA (born Barrington) (1729–1789)

Quaker nurse, who put aside her pacifist views to help

the American states in their war of independence against Britain 1775–83.

Born in Ireland, she met and married William Darragh in 1753 and the couple emigrated to Philadelphia. Darragh became known as a skilful nurse and midwife but her rejection of the Quaker's extreme pacifism led to her suspension from the church. She was later readmitted.

During the American Revolution she became a Fighting Quaker, and in 1777 she left Philadelphia in order to warn the American army leaders of a coming surprise attack by the British.

DAVIES, CHRISTIAN ('MOTHER ROSS') (1667–1739)

Woman who won fame by spending some years in military service, masquerading as a man. Born in Dublin, Davies went to Flanders in search of her husband, Richard Welsh, who had been conscripted into the Duke of Marlborough's army during the War of the Spanish Succession. There she enlisted under the name of Christopher Welsh, fought in the Battle of Blenheim (1704), and was eventually reunited with her husband in 1706.

When Davies's first husband Richard was killed at the Battle of Malplaquet (1709) she married a grenadier, Hugh Jones, who was killed the following year. In England she was presented to Queen Anne, and then returned to Dublin, where she married another soldier. She died in a Chelsea Pensioners' Hospital for retired soldiers.

DAVIES, JOHN (1569–1626)

English lawyer, administrator, political writer, and poet. As solicitor general of Ireland 1603–06 and attorney general 1606–16, Davies energetically sought to increase crown revenues through the recovery of concealed lands and rents. An advocate of extensive plantation in Ulster, Davies himself received a seignory of 31,600 ha/7,800 acres in County Fermanagh. He was the author of the influential tract *A discovery of the true causes why Ireland was never entirely subdued* (1612), and has been credited by some historians as the principal author of a new legal absolutism in Ireland. However, others have contested this view, stressing the essential conservatism of his legal outlook.

Having served as speaker of the Commons in the turbulent Irish parliament of 1613–15, Davies left Ireland in 1619. He died within a month of being made lord chief justice of England.

DAVIS, JOHN T (1947–)

Film-maker, born in Belfast. After studying at Belfast Art College in the late 1960s, Davis went on to become one of Ireland's most innovative documentarists. Since his first major film, *Shell Shock Rock* (1978), which looked at the Northern Ireland punk music scene, he has made a wide range of films. Something of a hobo himself, he made a film of this title in 1991, following his earlier *Route 66* (1985) which observed disparate characters during a trans-USA trip. Echoing the themes explored as he travelled through the Bible Belt, Davis focused on fundamentalist religion in his native Northern Ireland in *Dust on the Bible* (1989) and *Power in the Blood* (1989). With his feature-length film *The Uncle Jack* which is about his uncle, cinema architect John McBride Neil, who designed many of the province's most beautiful cinemas, Davis explored the nature of memory, family, and his own art form.

DAVIS, THOMAS OSBORNE (1814–1845)

Poet and journalist. Brought up in Mallow, Cork, Davis was educated at Trinity College, Dublin, and called to the bar in 1838. Regarded as the national poet in the 19th century, Davis was a driving force behind the ⇨Young Ireland movement and highly critical of Daniel ⇨O'Connell's cautious political methods. His best work appeared in the weekly paper *The Nation*, which he helped found with Charles Gavan⇨Duffy and John Blake Dillon (1814–1866). It included such political ballads as the 'Lament for Owen Roe O'Neill' and 'The Battle of Fontenoy', and some historical sketches.

DAVITT, MICHAEL (1846–1906)

Nationalist, agrarian leader, and journalist, born in Straid, County Mayo. The son of a Mayo farmer evicted in 1850, he worked in a Lancashire cotton mill, and lost his right arm in an accident. He joined the ⇨Fenians (forerunners of the Irish Republican Army) in 1865, and was imprisoned for treason 1870–77. After his release, he and the politician Charles Stewart Parnell founded the ⇨Land League in 1879 to secure the 'three f's' (fair rents, fixity of tenure, and freedom of sale) for tenants. Davitt was jailed several times for land-reform agitation. He was elected member of parliament for North Meath in

1892 and was MP for South Mayo 1895–99, advocating the reconciliation of extreme and constitutional nationalism. Davitt earned his living from journalism and public speaking from 1879. He published six books, including *Leaves from a Prison Diary* (1885) and *The Fall of Feudalism in Ireland* (1904), numerous pamphlets, and founded a weekly newspaper, *Labour World*.

> **I** have been some five years in this House and the conclusion with which I leave it, is that no cause, however just, will find support; no wrong, however pressing or apparent, will find redress here unless backed up by force. This is the message I shall take back from this assembly to my sons.
>
> MICHAEL DAVITT resigning from the House of Commons, October 1899.

DAY-LEWIS, C(ECIL) (1904–1972)

Poet and British poet laureate 1968–72. Born in Ballintubbert, County Laois, Day-Lewis was brought up in England and educated at Oxford University. Originally one of the influential left-wing 'MacSpaunday' poets of the 1930s, alongside W H Auden, Stephen Spender, and Louis ⇨MacNeice, his poetry moved from political concerns to a more traditional personal lyricicsm. His work, which includes *From Feathers to Iron* (1931) and *Overtures to Death* (1938), is marked by accomplished lyrics and sustained narrative power. *The Complete Poems* was published in 1992.

Day-Lewis also wrote detective novels under the pseudonym Nicholas Blake, such as the popular *A Question of Proof* (1935).

DEANE, RAYMOND (1953–)

Composer, arranger, and pianist. His orchestral works include *Enchaînement* (1981–82), first performed by the RTÉ Symphony Orchestra, and *Dekatriad* (1995), first performed by the Irish Chamber Orchestra.

Deane was born on Achill Island, Mayo, off the west coast of the Republic of Ireland. He graduated from University College, Dublin, in 1974 and has since studied composition with Karlheinz Stockhausen, Gerald Bennett, and Isang Yun. His music has featured in many international festivals and has been recorded by the Black Box and Marco Polo Labels. He is now professor of Irish studies at Notre Dame University, Indiana, USA.

DEANE, SEAMUS (1940–)

Poet, novelist, and academic. Born in Londonderry, Deane was educated in Belfast and Cambridge, and settled in Dublin in 1968. His work includes *Gradual Wars* (1972), one of the first poetry collections to take 'the Troubles' as its subject; the novel *Reading in the Dark* (1998), nominated for the Booker Prize and winner of *The Guardian* Fiction Prize and the *Irish Times* Fiction Award; and *Wizard* (1999).

Deane became a Fulbright lecturer at the University of California at Berkeley 1966–68, before returning to Ireland to take up the post of professor of Modern English and American literature at University College, Dublin. In 1971 he became co-director of the ⇨Field Day Theatre Company, an appointment he held until 1993. His three-volume *Field Day Anthology of Irish Writing* was published in 1991. He has also written a book of essays, *Heroic Styles: The Tradition of an Idea* (1985).

DECLARATION OF 1460

The earliest known claim of an Irish parliament to legislative sovereignty independent of English rule. The assertion that 'the lord of Ireland is and at all times has been corporate of itself (and) free of the burden of any law of the realm of England' was made in a preamble to a statute denying the authority of the English government to summon anyone out of Ireland to answer charges of treason.

This statute was part of a programme of legislation devised by Richard, Duke of York (1411–1460), then governing Ireland, as part of his defence against the Lancastrian claim to the English throne, during the English Wars of the Roses. The gap between the declaration's constitutional implications and its immediate practical intentions has been a source of continuing controversy among Irish historians, with some arguing that it signalled the origins of an Irish home rule movement and others insisting that such inferences were never intended by its originators, whose political and material interests continued to rest upon loyalty to England.

DE DANAAN

Traditional Irish music group led by the fiddler/flute player Frankie Gavin and bouzouki player Alec Finn. Their bright, lively sound has become very distinctive. Formed in Spiddal, County Galway, in 1974, the band has been heavily influenced by recordings made in the early 1920s by Irish-American traditional musicians such as the fiddler James Morrison and the Flanagan Brothers. It has also been influenced by US and popular music, recording notable cover versions of Queen's 'Bohemian Rhapsody' and the Beatles' 'Hey Jude'. Albums include *The Star Spangled Molly* (1981), *Mist Covered Mountain* (1978), and *Half Set in Harlem* (1991).

The personnel of the band has varied over the years to include musicians and singers such as Jackie Daly, Máirtín O'Connor, Mary Black, and Delores Keane, many of whom have gone on to forge successful solo careers.

DEEVY, THERESA (1894–1963)

Playwright whose works were staged at the ⇨Abbey Theatre, Dublin, in the 1930s. Despite original rejections, the Abbey successfully produced her first full-length drama, *Reapers*, in 1930. This was followed by other plays such as *A Disciple* (1931), *The King of Spain's Daughter* (1935), and *Katie Roche* (1936). Known for her vivid characterizations and excellent dialogue, she enriched the Abbey Theatre at a time when inventive plays were lacking.

Deevy was born in Waterford. She suffered from Ménière's disease, which left her totally deaf by the time she reached adulthood. Nevertheless, she developed a passion for the theatre. A member of Cumann na mBan (the Women's League), she also fought against censorship and for the establishment of an Irish republic. In 1942 she started writing for the BBC and Radió Éireann. In 1954 she was elected to the Irish Academy of Letters.

DEFENDERS

Catholic secret society that emerged in County Armagh in the mid-1780s in opposition to the Protestant Peep o'Day Boys. In 1795 a large Defender force drawn from several counties was defeated by Protestants at the Battle of the Diamond, County Armagh, after which the Protestants formed the ⇨Orange Order. In the same year the ⇨United Irishmen allied themselves with the Defenders as part of their plan for armed rebellion. The Defender movement survived the ⇨Rebellion of 1798 and re-emerged in the 19th century as the Ribbonmen.

More than a grass-roots protest group, the Defenders soon developed a sense of political awareness as well as organizational structures copied from ⇨freemasonry. Defenderism spread from Armagh into adjacent counties in 1789, and reached Dublin and Connaught in the early 1790s.

DELANY, RONNIE (RONALD MICHAEL) (1935–)

Athlete born in Arlow, County Wicklow, who was 1,500 metres champion at the 1956 Olympic Games in Melbourne. He won the race with a trademark sprint finish, covering the final 300 metres in a remarkable 38.8 seconds to set a new Olympic record of 3:41.2. Earlier in 1956 he had become the first Irishman to run under 4 minutes for the mile. He excelled at indoor meetings, winning 40 consecutive races in the USA between 1956 and 1959, and on three occasions breaking the world indoor mile record.

DERG, LOUGH

The largest and most southerly of the lakes on the River Shannon, in County Clare; length 40 km/25 mi. Lough Derg is surrounded by hills and has many islets. It reaches north from Portumna (in County Galway) to Killaloe in the south, and is a centre for fishing and sailing. The hydroelectric power station at Ardnacrusha makes use of the 33 m/108 ft fall from the lough to sea level.

DERG, LOUGH

Lake some 6 km/4 mi northwest of Pettigo, County Donegal. It is 10 km/6 mi long by 6 km/4 mi wide, area 62 sq km/24 sq mi. Lough Derg is surrounded by a rugged landscape and contains many small islands. Station Island, the reputed scene of St Patrick's purgatory, is an important site of pilgrimage between 1 June and 15 August.

DERRY (LONDONDERRY)

County of Northern Ireland; population (1998, est) 213,000; area 2,070 sq km/799 sq mi. Its principal towns and cities are Derry (county town, also known

LOUGH DERG, COUNTY DONEGAL *Devotees of Saint Patrick prepare to cross to Station Island. It was here that the saint is said to have evicted demons from a cave, during a vision of purgatory.*

as Londonderry), Coleraine, Portstewart, and Limavady.

physical

Derry is bounded on the north by the Atlantic, and is dominated by the Sperrin Mountains which run in an arc from southwest to northeast, dividing the lowlands fringing the River Bann in the east from those of the River Foyle in the west. Mount Sawell (670 m/2,198 ft) in the Sperrin Mountains is the county's highest peak. The Roe and the Faughan are the main westward flowing streams, while the Bann forms the eastern border for most of its length.

features

The county has Ireland's longest beach, Magilligan Strand. The ruined Downhill Castle estate contains the clifftop Mussenden Temple built in classical style to accommodate a bishop's library.

economy

Farming is hindered by the very heavy rainfall; flax is cultivated and there is moorland grazing and salmon and eel fisheries on the Bann. Industries include textiles, light engineering, and stone and lime quarrying.

DERRY (LONDONDERRY) (until the 10th

century known as Derry-Calgaich)

Historic city and port on the River Foyle, 35 km/22 mi from Lough Foyle, county town of County ⇨ Derry; population (1991) 95,400. Industries include textiles, chemicals, food processing, shirt manufacturing, and acetylene from naphtha.

features

The Protestant Cathedral of St Columba dating from 1633; the Gothic revival Roman Catholic Cathedral of St Eugene (completed in 1833); the Guildhall (rebuilt in 1912), containing stained glass windows presented by livery companies of the City of London; the city walls, on which are modern iron statues by Anthony Gormley; four gates into the city still survive. The old city walls that still surround Derry/Londonderry extend for over 1 km/0.5 mi and include seven gates and several bastions. The waterside, the part of the city on the right bank of the Foyle, is connected to the old city by the Craigavon Bridge (opened in 1933), which carries a roadway 360 m/1,180 ft long.

history

Derry/Londonderry dates from the foundation of a monastery there by St Columba (Colum Cille) in AD 546. The city was subject to a number of sieges by the Danes between the 9th and 11th centuries. In 1164 Abbot O'Brolchain, the first bishop of Derry, built the Teampall Mor or 'great church', and in 1311 the town was granted to Richard de Burgo, Earl of Ulster. An uneventful period of several centuries followed until the rebellion in 1566 of Shane ⇨ O'Neill, Earl of Tyrone. O'Neill suffered a crushing defeat at the hands of Edward Randolph, commander of the English forces, and was killed. However, Randolph's successor, Edward St Low, abandoned Derry in 1568, after an accidental explosion in which the town and fort, including the Teampall Mor, were blown up.

In 1608 James I of England captured the city and in 1609, during the ⇨ Plantation of Ireland, he granted Derry, Coleraine, and a large tract of land between to the City of London. The land was distributed among the London livery companies, but in order to avoid jealousy among the companies, the City of London Corporation retained the boroughs of Derry and Coleraine. The Irish Society was formed in 1613 to administer the boroughs; its members were appointed from within the City of London Corporation. The Society was incorporated by royal charter in 1613 and was trustee for the Corporation, when the city's name was changed to Londonderry, still its official name.

The city was unsuccessfully besieged in 1689 by the armies of James II, who had fled England when William of Orange was declared joint sovereign with James' daughter Mary. James' Jacobite army was led

ÉAMON DE VALERA *Seen speaking at an election meeting at Ennis on the day of his arrest in August 1923, which led to a year in jail, de Valera stayed active in politics until two years before his death, aged 93.*

by Richard Talbot, Earl of ⇨Tyrconnell, in a conflict known as the Siege of Derry, when 13 Derry apprentices and citizens loyal to William of Orange locked the city gates against the Jacobites. The siege lasted 15 weeks, during which many of the inhabitants died of starvation and disease because of the blockade.

DESMOND

See ⇨Fitzgerald family.

DESMOND, DERMOT (1950–)

Financier and investor, a key figure in the Republic of Ireland's finance and business. Born in Dublin, Desmond worked in banking both in Dublin and for a time at the World Bank in Afghanistan. He promoted the International Financial Services Centre in Dublin, established in a derelict city area in 1979, which is now a significant international venue employing 10,000 people in banking, insurance, and associated

businesses. He also set up NCB Stockbrokers, a firm which shook up the stockbroking sector in the mid to late 1980s and grew to be one of the Republic's biggest broking firms.

DESMOND, ELEANOR

Countess of the 16th century, see Eleanor ⇨Butler.

DE VALERA, ÉAMON (1882–1975)

Nationalist politician, president/Taoiseach (prime minister) of the Irish Free State/Eire/Republic of Ireland 1932–48, 1951–54, and 1957–59, and president 1959–73. Repeatedly imprisoned, de Valera participated in the ⇨Easter Rising of 1916 and was leader of the nationalist ⇨Sinn Féin party 1917–26, when he formed the republican ⇨Fianna Fáil party. He opposed the Anglo-Irish Treaty (1921) but formulated a constitutional relationship with Britain in the 1930s that achieved greater Irish sovereignty.

No longer shall our children, like our cattle, be brought up for export.

ÉAMON DE VALERA
Speech in the Dáil, 19 December 1934.

~

De Valera was born in New York, the son of a Spanish father and an Irish mother, and sent to Ireland as a child. After studying at Blackrock College and the Royal University at Dublin, he became a teacher of mathematics, French, and Latin in various colleges. He was sentenced to death for his part in the Easter Rising, but the sentence was commuted to penal servitude for life, and he was released under an amnesty in 1917 because he was born in New York. In the same year he was elected to Westminster as MP for East Clare, and president of Sinn Féin. He was rearrested in May 1918, but escaped to the USA in 1919. He returned to Dublin in 1920 from where he directed the struggle against the British government. He authorized the negotiations of 1921, but refused to accept the ensuing treaty arguing that external association with Britain rather than the lesser status of dominion status was attainable.

His opposition to the Anglo-Irish Treaty contributed to the civil war that followed. De Valera was arrested by the Free State government in 1923, and spent a year in prison. In 1926 he formed a new party,

*W*henever I wanted to know what the Irish people wanted I had only to examine my own heart.

ÉAMON DE VALERA Speech in the Dáil, 6 January 1922.

~

Fianna Fáil, which secured a majority in 1932. De Valera became Taoiseach and foreign minister of the Free State, and at once instituted a programme of social and economic protectionism. He played the leading role in framing the 1937 constitution by which southern Ireland became a republic in all but name. In relations with Britain, his government immediately abolished the oath of allegiance and suspended payment of the annuities due under the Land Purchase Acts. Under an agreement concluded in 1938 between the two countries, Britain accepted £10 million in final settlement, and surrendered the right to enter or fortify southern Irish ports. Throughout World War II de Valera maintained a strict neutrality, rejecting an offer by Winston Churchill in 1940 to recognize the principle of a united Ireland in return for Eire's entry into the war. He lost power at the 1948 elections but was again prime minister 1951–54 and 1957–59, and thereafter president of the Republic 1959–66 and 1966–73.

DE VALOIS, NINETTE (stage name of EDRIS STANNUS) (1898–1999)

Ballet dancer and choreographer. She was principal dancer with the Diagilev Ballet Company and founder of the Royal Ballet Company. In the 1920s she sought to encourage the development of dance in Ireland through the foundation of the Abbey School of Ballet (1928); she returned to pursue her career in England in the 1930s but remained a patron of individual Irish dancers.

DEVENISH ISLAND

Small island with a group of ecclesiastical remains, in Lower Lough Erne, County Fermanagh. St Molaise founded a monastery here in the 6th century, and the ruins of an ancient small Romanesque church are named St Molaise's House. The island also has one of the most perfect round towers in Ireland, noted for its fine stonework and decorated frieze. It is thought the tower was built in the 12th century to replace an ear-

lier one that had fallen. St Mary's priory is also on the island, and dates from the 12th century.

DE VERE, AUBREY (2nd Baronet De Vere) (1788–1846)

Poet, born at the family estate of Curragh Chase, County Limerick, and educated at Harrow, England. De Vere was later noted as a reforming landlord. The patriotic *The Lamentations of Ireland* (1823) and his sonnets in *Songs of Faith* (1842) were praised by William Wordsworth as 'the most perfect of our age'. His son Aubrey ⇨De Vere appended a memoir to the verse drama *Mary Tudor* (1884).

DE VERE, AUBREY THOMAS (1814–1902)

Poet who was born at Curragh Chase, County Limerick, and educated at Trinity College, Dublin. His later verse was inspired by Irish themes; his *Innisfail* (1863) was a catalogue of the woes of Ireland and *The Foray of Queen Maeve* (1882) retold legends of Ireland's heroic age. Besides poems, he also wrote prose concerning Ireland's wrongs. He was the son of the poet Aubrey ⇨De Vere.

De Vere published *The Waldenses, or the Fall of Rora* (1842) and in the following year issued a companion volume, *The Search after Proserpine, Recollections of Greece and other Poems. English Misrule and Irish Misdeeds* (1848) was his chief prose work; *Ireland and Proportional Representation* (1885) the last. He published his *Recollections* (1897).

DEVLIN, ANNE (*c.* 1778–1851)

Patriot, born in County Dublin. A niece of the revolutionary leader Michael Dwyer, she was the servant of the revolutionary leader Robert ⇨Emmet. When his rebellion failed in 1803, Devlin carried messages between him and his friends in Dublin. She was arrested by the government, imprisoned, and brutally tortured, but refused to give any information on Emmet. Released in 1805, she spent the remainder of her life in poverty.

A monument to Devlin's life was erected over her grave in Glasnevin Cemetery by the historian R R Madden.

DEVLIN, BERNADETTE

Birth name of Bernadette ⇨McAliskey, Northern Irish political activist.

DEVLIN, DENIS (1908–1959)

Writer and diplomat, born in Greenock, Scotland, of Irish parents, and educated at University College, Dublin, in Munich, Germany, and at the Sorbonne, Paris. Devlin's verse combines a delicate interweaving of vocalic and consonantal echoes, partly derived from Gaelic poetry, and an awareness of the varieties of European poetic tradition. His *Collected Poems* (1964) significantly extended the limits of modern Irish poetry. Earlier works include *First Poems* (1930), *Intercessions* (1937), and *Lough Derg and Other Poems* (1946).

In 1935 Devlin joined the department of external affairs of the Irish civil service. He went as first secretary to Washington, DC, in 1940, and in 1958 was made ambassador to Italy.

DEVLIN, JOSEPH (1871–1934)

Nationalist leader, born in Belfast. A journalist with the *Irish News*, Devlin acquired a reputation as a fiery orator. He was elected unopposed as member of parliament for North Kilkenny in 1902, and was returned for North Belfast in 1906. He reformed the ⇨Ancient Order of Hibernians, of which he was president from 1905 until his death. A founder of the ⇨Irish Volunteers, he declined the position of leader of the Irish Parliamentary Party in 1918. Devlin defeated Éamon de Valera in the 1918 election, and was known affectionately in Belfast as 'Wee Joe'. He helped found a holiday home for working women in Belfast.

DEVOTIONAL REVOLUTION

Movement 1850–75 inspired by the Irish Catholic archbishop Paul ⇨Cullen that transformed contemporary lay-centred Irish Catholic spirituality, leading it to embrace the sacramentally centred spirituality of continental Europe, and especially Rome. This brought Irish Catholics closer to their European co-religionists, and probably increased the desire for independence from their Protestant English rulers. The term itself was coined in the 1970s by a US historian, Emmet Larkin.

The new approach was advocated by Cullen and was initially best received in the more English-speaking south and east. The main result was a more sacramentally and clerically centred Catholicism, in opposition to the lay-centred and home-based spirituality that had resulted from penal restrictions on priests and public acts of Catholic worship. In that sense, it could

be depicted as the normalizing of Catholic spirituality in the period after Catholic Emancipation. A connected development was the 1879 Marian apparition at Knock, County Mayo, one of a European-wide series of apparitions during this period.

DEVOY, JOHN (1842–1928)

Republican activist, born in Kill, County Kildare. In 1861 Devoy joined the secret society of the ⇨Fenians to struggle for an independent Ireland. In 1865 he helped rescue the Fenian leader James ⇨Stephens from prison. After serving five years in prison himself 1866–71, he was forcibly exiled to the USA, where he took US citizenship and campaigned vigorously among his fellow Irish-Americans for the nationalist cause. He was a leading figure in the formation of both 'Clan-Na-Gael', an expatriate revolutionary organization, in 1867 and the ⇨Land League in 1879.

In the USA, Devoy joined the New York *Herald* before founding his own newspaper, the *Gaelic American*. Through this journal, he adopted an increasingly anti-British position, opposing constitutional settlements and advocating armed rebellion. He helped raise funds to buy German arms for the Irish Volunteers in 1914, and strongly backed the ⇨Easter Rising of 1916. A powerful figure amongst Irish nationalist exiles, Devoy supported Éamon de Valera during his time in the USA but took the pro-Treaty side in the Civil War and became a firm supporter of the Free State.

DILLON, GERARD (1916–1971)

Painter who made a significant contribution to the development of modernism in Ireland. His work, often strongly autobiographical in content, is surreal and even naive in style. On occasion his work may be compared with that of the Russian-born French painter Marc Chagall. The vivid colour and high viewpoint of *The Yellow Bungalow* (1954; Ulster Museum, Belfast, Northern Ireland) is a case in point. In his later work Dillon used the image of the pierrot, a character from the *commedia dell'arte*, as a symbol akin to a self-portrait. A similar use of this imagery is found in the work of Picasso.

Born in the Falls Road area of Belfast, a background he drew on in his painting, Dillon was largely self-taught as an artist. This is perhaps significant for the ease with which he experimented with different media throughout his career. He also produced designs for theatre sets and costumes for the Abbey Theatre, Dublin, in the late 1960s. His work is included in the collections of the National Gallery of Ireland and the Hugh Lane Municipal Gallery of Modern Art, both in Dublin, and the Crawford Municipal Gallery of Art, Cork.

DILLON, JAMES (1902–1986)

Politician, born in Dublin, the son of John ⇨Dillon. Dillon studied business management in London and Chicago. He cofounded the National Centre Party in 1932, and was vice president of ⇨Fine Gael in 1933. He was the only member of the Dáil who was openly hostile to Irish neutrality in World War II. He served in the interparty governments of 1948–51 and 1954–57, and was a modernizing leader of Fine Gael 1959–65.

DILLON, JOHN (1851–1927)

Nationalist politician, born in Dublin. A leader of the ⇨Land League, Dillon was a vigorous supporter of Charles Stewart ⇨Parnell until the O'Shea divorce affair, when he became the leader of the anti-Parnellite Irish National Federation. He supported John ⇨Redmond as leader of the Irish Parliamentary Party and succeeded him in 1918, but was overwhelmingly defeated by Sinn Féin in the elections that year.

The son of John Blake Dillon, he qualified as a surgeon before entering parliament in 1880. Dillon was a militant agrarian in the 1880s, and served a number of periods of imprisonment. In 1916 he bitterly denounced the government's policies towards the rebels in Ireland and accurately predicted the shift in Irish national sentiment towards outright separatism. In 1918 he was defeated by Éamon ⇨de Valera at East Mayo – the seat he had held since 1885 – and retired from public life.

DINEEN, PATRICK (1860–1934)

Gaelic lexicographer. An early member of the Gaelic League, he produced the most extensive Irish-to-English dictionary to date, *Foclóir Gaedhilge agus Béarla* (1904 revised and expanded 1927). His dictionary has been superseded for contemporary uses, but not for scholarly purposes, by Tomas de Bhaldraithe's (1916–1996) *English-Irish Dictionary* (1959) which has established official modern standards of spelling and usage.

DINGLE PENINSULA *Beehive huts, known as clocháin, are round dry-stone buildings which may originally have served as monks' cells and in more recent years have provided shelter for shepherds. Similar structures have been found in the Vaucluse and Rhône Valley in France.*

DINGLE

Seaport and tourist centre in County Kerry, Republic of Ireland; population (1996) 1,400. It is situated on the north side of Dingle Bay, 48 km/30 mi southwest of Tralee, on the Dingle Peninsula. Dingle harbour allows for safe anchorage, and is a centre for flatfish and lobster fishing. The town is the most westerly town in Europe, and grew up round a medieval fortress.

The Mount Brandon (923 m/2,954 ft) area of Dingle Peninsula is rich in monuments of great antiquity, including beehive-shaped stone huts, pillar stones, stones inscribed with ogham characters, chamber tombs, earthworks, and ring forts.

Dingle had political and trade connections with Spain during the Elizabethan period. The town received a charter in 1685.

DISESTABLISHMENT

The legal separation of the (Anglican) Church of Ireland from the state. The Church of Ireland was established as the Anglican state church by Henry VIII in 1537 as a result of the Irish Reformation, but it failed to win over the Irish-speaking Catholic majority. This made Ireland the only European country in which the majority of citizens rejected the monarch's religion. The established church's link to England was strengthened when the Act of Union (1801) created the United Church of England and Ireland.

There were some attempts at reform, as in the suppression of several Church of Ireland bishoprics in 1832. Pressure for disestablishment grew after the 1860 census revealed how low a percentage of Irish people claimed allegiance to the Church of Ireland. The British prime minister William Gladstone fought an election over Irish disestablishment and, after his victory, disestablished the Church of Ireland in 1869. The church's endowments were converted to charitable ends, including a one-off grant to the Roman Catholic St Patrick's College, Maynooth.

DISSENT

Generally refers to religious movements that dissent from the state religion, but in the Irish context used to refer to non-Anglican Protestants, as exemplified in the Irish nationalist Wolfe ⇨Tone's appeal to Protestant (meaning Church of Ireland), Catholic, and dissenter to unite on common political interests in the 1790s.

The position of Irish dissenters was often better than their English counterparts as some laws did not apply, for example the Test Act (1673) which required holders of public office in England to take the sacrament in an Anglican Church. The main reasons for this difference were that the largest dissenting group, the Presbyterians, had argued since the 1640s that their church should be established in Ulster as it was in Scotland; that freedoms were granted to foreign dissenters in 1662, principally to French Huguenots; and that dissenters counteracted the overwhelming Catholic majority.

Nonetheless, restrictions applied on dissenting church activities, such as the ability to establish congregations in new areas or the conducting of marriages. The notion of dissent disappeared with the disestablishment of the Church of Ireland in 1870.

DIXON, HENRY HORATIO (1869–1953)

Botanist, born in Dublin, whose research focused on cytology (the study of cells). Dixon developed the cohesion theory with the Irish geologist and physicist John ⇨Joly, which explained why sap and water can rise great heights to the tops of trees. He also observed that cosmic rays could have a mutagenic effect.

Dixon entered Trinity College, Dublin, in 1887, winning a scholarship to study classics. He later switched to natural science in which he graduated in 1891, the move largely due to the influence and encouragement of Joly.

Dixon was intrigued by experiments that showed that sap could rise even if cells in the stem were dead. He built various pieces of apparatus to demonstrate the great cohesive force that could be established in a bubble-free column of water locked in tree cells and drawn forward by evaporation at the leaves.

DOBBS, ARTHUR (1689–1765)

Landowner and public figure, later governor of North Carolina, America, born in County Antrim. Dobbs was high sheriff of Antrim in 1720 and member of parliament for Carrickfergus 1727–30. Appointed engineer-in-chief, and surveyor general of Ireland, he became a leading advocate of land reform. He was intrigued by America, and was responsible for the commissioning of various projects to chart territory. In 1754 he was appointed governor of North Carolina, where he had acquired land. His treatment of the American Indians was benign, and he was praised for his fairness and improvements. Political disputes, however, marred his final years. He died at Town Creek, North Carolina, in 1765. Cape Dobbs in Hudson's Bay was named after him.

DOHERTY, KEN (1969–)

Snooker player, born in Ranelagh, County Dublin. Twice national champion, Doherty won both the World Under 21 and World Amateur championships in 1989. He struggled to make it as a professional before winning his first ranking tournament in 1993, when he defeated Alan McManus in the final of the Welsh Open. He finally made his big breakthrough in 1997, defeating the seemingly unbeatable Stephen Hendry in the World Championship in Sheffield, England, to become the first player to win all three world titles. In 1998 he again qualified for the World Championship final but was denied success, this time by the Scot John Higgins.

Í think my mother must have set five or six churches ablaze, she was lighting so many candles!

KEN DOHERTY Suggesting that divine help may have been a factor in his winning the 1997 snooker world championship, quoted in *The Observer*, 28 December 1997.

DONAGHADEE (Irish *Domhnach Daoi*)

Port and resort in County Down, on the North Channel and eastern gateway to the Ards Peninsula, 22 km/14 mi east of Belfast. Summer ferry services operate to the nearby Copeland Islands. The harbour was constructed to support a mail service to Portpatrick, Scotland, 13 km/21 miles to the northeast, which ended in 1849. Its massive walls and lighthouse, designed in 1819, were completed by John Rennie, creator of several of London's bridges. Other features include an 1821 castellated powder house, and Grace Neill's (established 1611), which claims to be Ireland's oldest inn; Peter the Great was a visitor in 1697. Dulse, an edible seaweed, is collected in the harbour at low tide.

DONEGAL

Mountainous county in the northwest of the Republic of Ireland, surrounded on three sides by the Atlantic Ocean, and bordering the counties of Derry, Tyrone, and Fermanagh (Northern Ireland), and Leitrim (Republic of Ireland); area 4,830 sq km/1,864 sq mi; county town Lifford; population (1996) 130,000. Ballyshannon is the largest town, and the market town and port of Donegal is at the head of Donegal Bay in the southwest. The severe climate renders much of the county barren, although the soil is suitable for potatoes, oats, and barley in places. Commercial activities include sheep and cattle raising, tweed, linen, and carpet manufacture, and some salmon and deep-sea fishing. Tourism is also very important; the county is noted for dramatic scenery and geology as well as archaeological and historic remains, and the castles of Donegal and Glenveagh as well as Glenveagh National Park are among the top visitor attractions in the county. The River Erne hydroelectric project (1952) involved the building of a large artificial lake (405 ha/1,000 acres) and a power station at Ballyshannon.

physical

Donegal is mainly mountainous with dramatic cliff scenery, being geologically a continuation of the Highlands of Scotland. The coastline is very irregular, being broken by Lough Swilly, Sheep Haven, Boylagh Bay, Gweebarra Bay, and Donegal Bay; there are high-cliffed peninsulas to the north. There are many islands off the coast, the main ones being Inistrahul, Tory Island, and Aran Island. The chief rivers are the Foyle, the Finn, the Swilly, the Erne, the Gweebarra, the Gweedore, and the Owenea, and the chief lakes Loughs Derg, Deele, Gartan, Eask, and Glen. The highest mountain is Mount Errigal (752 m/2,467 ft), and the glaciated Derryveagh Mountains have a series of peaks over 610 m/2,000 ft. At Malin Head in the west of Donegal Bay there is a sea cliff 600 m/1,969 ft in height. Malin Head is the most northerly point of Ireland.

history

The county is rich in early remains from the Bronze Age and the early Christian period, as well as early fortifications. The most interesting historical remains are perhaps those of the Grianan of Aileach, a large circular stone fort, built about 1700 BC as the stronghold of the kings of Ulster, the O'Neills. The famous St Patrick's Purgatory pilgrimage takes place on Station Island in the middle of Lough Derg. At Donegal Abbey (founded 1474) an important early literary work, *The Annals of the Four Masters*, was written between 1632 and 1636, and is an important source for early Irish history and mythology.

Donegal is strong meat: strong scenery, strong weather, strong bodies, strong spirits.

STEPHEN RYNNE Writer *All Ireland* (1956).

~

Colum Cille (St Columba) was born at Garton, where there is a heritage centre depicting his life; a flagstone on a hill near Lough Gartan is reputed to mark his birthplace. He founded an abbey at Kilmacrenan (of which nothing remains, although there are ruins of a 15th-century Franciscan friary on the site).

DONLEAVY, J(AMES) P(ATRICK) (1926–)

US-born Irish writer. His novels, which are about eccentrics, have a fierce comic energy. His picaresque masterpiece *The Ginger Man* (published in France in 1955) was banned in Ireland, Britain, and the USA until the 1960s. Later novels include *A Singular Man* (1963), *The Destinies of Darcy Dancer, Gentleman* (1977), *Leila: Further in the Life and Destinies of Darcy Dancer, Gentleman* (1983), and *Are You Listening Rabbi Löw* (1987).

*W*hen I die I want to decompose in a barrel of porter and have it served in all the pubs in Dublin.

J P DONLEAVY *The Ginger Man* (1955).

~

Donleavy was born in New York, the son of Irish immigrants. He studied at Trinity College, Dublin, and became an Irish citizen in 1967. The controversial *The Ginger Man*, set in Dublin in the 1940s, is the story of Sebastian Dangerfield, a US expatriate; his later work *The History of the Ginger Man* (1994) is part autobiography, part literary history.

DONNYBROOK

Former village, now part of Dublin, notorious until 1855 for riotous fairs.

DOWN

County of southeastern Northern Ireland; population (1981) 339,200; area 2,470 sq km/953 sq mi. The chief towns and cities are ⇨Downpatrick (county town), Bangor (seaside resort), Newtownards, Newry, and Banbridge. The northern part of the county lies within the commuter belt for Belfast, and includes part of the city of Belfast, east of the River Lagan.

physical

Down is a largely lowland county, although the south is dominated by the Mourne Mountains, the highest point of which is Slieve Donard (852 m/2,796 ft), the highest point in Northern Ireland. The coast at Dundrum Bay, where the mountains rise abruptly, is sandy, but elsewhere the coastline is mainly low and rocky. In the east it is penetrated by the long sea inlet Strangford Lough, a noted habitat for birds and grey seals.

features

There are a number of fortifications and early ecclesiastical remains in the county, including the prehistoric Giant's Ring earthwork; Legananny Dolmen, a Stone Age monument; the well-preserved tower house Audley's Castle; the 5th-century Nendrum Monastery on Mahee Island in Strangford Lough; Grey Abbey, a Cistercian foundation dating from 1193; Mount Stewart House and Gardens, the 18th-century former home of the Marquess of Londonderry, noted for its statues and carvings dating from the early 20th century; Castle Ward, an 18th-century house; and the Strangford Stone, 10 m/33 ft high, erected on the shores of Strangford Lough on Midsummer's Day, June 1999, to mark the millennium. The Ulster Folk and Transport Museum is at Holywood.

economy

County Down has very fertile land. The principal crops are barley, potatoes, and oats; there is also livestock rearing and dairying. Light manufacturing and technology businesses are also important.

DOWNEY, ANGELA (1957–)

Camogie player, born in Ballyraggert, County Kilkenny. A full forward from the club St Pauls, Downey made her debut at the age of 15, with her twin sister Anne. She captured her first senior All-Ireland Championship medal in 1974 and three years later captained the county to success over Wexford. It was her third success, and she added nine more to her tally. In all, she figured in 15 finals, coming out of retirement to play in last final of the 20th century, when Cork defeated Kilkenny.

DOWNING STREET DECLARATION

See ⇨Northern Ireland peace process.

DOWNPATRICK

County town of County ⇨Down, 45 km/28 mi southeast of Belfast; population (1991) 8,300. Local employment is mainly in service industries, but residents also commute to Belfast. Downpatrick has been an important settlement since prehistoric times, and its first church may have been founded by St Patrick in the 5th century.

Downpatrick has been the cathedral town of the (now Protestant) diocese of Down since the Middle Ages. A major borough in Anglo-Norman times, it became the market centre for the rich farming area of Lecale, but declined in importance during the 19th century. The Ulster Harp National horserace is held annually at the racecourse.

A granite stone, commissioned in 1900, with the name PATRIC engraved, stands outside the cathedral to mark the legend that St Patrick may be buried nearby. There is no historical evidence for this, although it is known that he died at Saul, 3 km/2 mi northeast of Downpatrick. A number of modern shrines in the area have become sites of pilgrimage.

DOYLE, JAMES WARREN (pseudonym JKL) (1786–1834)

Catholic bishop of Kildare and Leighlin. Having experienced as a youth the horrors of the 1798 rebellion and the Peninsular War, he became an avid promoter of social and political reform by peaceful agitation. A strong supporter of Daniel ⇨O'Connell, he used his considerable skills as a propagandist and polemicist (writing under the pseudonym JKL) to advance the interests of Irish Catholics in general and of the poor tenantry in particular. Influential in the 1830s, he gave important evidence to several parliamentary committees on Ireland, established the Catholic Book Society, and invested much of his time and resources in building schools.

DOYLE, RODDY (1958–)

Novelist, born in Dublin and educated by the Christian Brothers and at University College, Dublin. His *Paddy Clarke Ha Ha Ha*, a novel about growing up in Ireland, written from the point of view of a ten-year-old boy, won the 1997 Booker Prize. Other works include *The Commitments* (1987), *The Snapper* (1990), *The Van* (1991), and *The Woman Who Walked into Doors* (1997), all of which chronicle life in contemporary, working-class Dublin. Doyle moved into historical fiction with *A Star Called Henry* (1999), about one man's role in the 1916 ⇨Easter Rising.

DRENNAN, WILLIAM

Poet, see ⇨United Irishmen.

DROGHEDA (Irish *Droichead Átha*, 'the bridge of the ford')

Seaport, industrial town, and borough 50 km/31 mi from Dublin, and 6 km/4 mi from the estuary of the River Boyne, in County Louth; population (1996) 25,000. The port trades in cattle and textiles; industries include chemicals, foodstuffs, brewing, linen, cotton, and engineering. The salmon fishery in the Boyne has its centre here. In 1649 the town was stormed by Oliver Cromwell, who massacred most of the garrison, and in 1690 it surrendered to William III after the Battle of the ⇨Boyne.

The whole of the Boyne Valley is an area of historical and archaeological interest. In Drogheda itself, the St Lawrence gateway still remains of the ancient walls, and there are relics of the Augustinian abbey (1206), built on the site of an earlier monastery founded by St Patrick, and the Dominican friary (1224). Richard III held court here in 1394. On occasion, Irish parliamentary sessions were held at Drogheda. Poyning's Law was passed here in 1494; this law stipulated that all future laws made in the Irish parliament had to be ratified by the Privy Council in England.

The well-preserved and extensive ruins of ⇨Mellifont Abbey (1142), Ireland's first Cistercian monastery, are situated 10 km/6 mi west of Drogheda.

RODDY DOYLE *Doyle's brand of unsentimental realism, and the earthy humour with which he leavens topics such as poverty and domestic violence, have gained him a place as one of Ireland's foremost contemporary novelists.*

Jimmy said that real music was sex...
They were starting to agree with him.
And there wasn't much sex in 'Morning has Broken' or 'The Lord is my Shepherd'.

RODDY DOYLE *The Commitments* (1987).

❧

DROMOLAND CASTLE

Large 19th-century castle-house in County Clare. It was built about 1826 on the site of an earlier 18th-century house for Sir Edward O'Brien, a descendant of Brian Bóruma, High King of Ireland. The designers were James and George Richard Pain, both pupils of the English architect John Nash. The main external features of this impressive composition are three large towers, one round, one square, and one octagonal. The castle was sold in 1962 and is now a hotel.

DROMORE

Town in northwest County Down; population (1991) 3,100. It is situated on the River Lagan, 27 km/17 mi from Belfast. The present Protestant cathedral was erected after the destruction of the town during the insurrection of 1641. Nearby is the well-preserved Norman motte and bailey, Dromore Mound.

The cathedral contains the tombs of two important bishops, Jeremy Taylor (1613–1667) and Thomas Percy.

DRUID THEATRE

Theatre company in Galway, founded in 1975 by Garry Hynes, Mick Lally, and Marie Mullen, members of the Irish-language theatre company, An ⇨Taibhdhearc, and University College, Galway's student drama society. The theatre developed a reputation for fresh and original productions of Irish and continental classics, notably the 1982 staging of J M Synge's *The Playboy of the Western World*, taken on tour to New York, USA, in 1986.

Originally the company performed at the Coachman Hotel, but in 1978 an old warehouse was converted into the Druid Lane Theatre. More recently the company has promoted the work of upcoming playwrights. *At the Black Pig's Dyke* (1992) by Vincent Woods (1960–   ), inspired by the mumming tradition and by Northern Irish politics, and *The Beauty Queen of Leenane* (1996), a tragi-comedy of rural Ireland by Martin McDonagh (1971–   ), became landmarks in Irish drama. McDonagh's play won the company four Tony Awards after its successful run on Broadway in 1998.

DRURY, SUSANNAH (active from 1733, died 1770)

One of the earliest and best-known Irish women artists. With a celebrated pair of paintings of the Giant's Causeway, County Antrim (1739; Ulster Museum, Belfast, Northern Ireland) Drury made a significant contribution to the tradition of topographical landscape painting in Ireland. These paintings are also of interest as the earliest to accurately depict the Causeway, then becoming a popular attraction for tourists.

Drury came from an Anglo-Irish family which had been established in Dublin since the 16th century. Although nothing is known of her artistic training, her highly detailed technique and her accomplished use of the medium of gouache suggest she may have trained as a miniature painter. In 1740 she was awarded a premium of £25 by the Dublin Society. She was the first woman to receive such official recognition, and this was the first time such an award was made for landscape painting in Ireland.

DUBLIN

County in the Republic of Ireland, in Leinster province, facing the Irish Sea and bounded by the counties of Meath, Kildare, and Wicklow; county town ⇨Dublin; area 920 sq km/355 sq mi; population (1996) 1,058,300. The county is mostly level and low-lying, but rises in the south to 753 m/2,471 ft in Kippure, part of the Wicklow Mountains. The River Liffey enters Dublin Bay. The county is dominated by Ireland's capital city of Dublin and its suburbs, but also contains pastoral and agricultural land. Dún Laoghaire is the other major town and large port.

The coastline, stretching from 5 km/3 mi north of Balbriggan nearly as far as Bray, has many sandy beaches. The Liffey plain has the lowest rainfall in Ireland.

DUBLIN (offical Irish name *Baile Átha Cliath*, 'the town of the ford of the hurdles'; Gaelic *dubh linn*, 'dark pool')

City and port on the east coast of Ireland, at the mouth of the River Liffey, facing the Irish Sea; capital of the Republic of Ireland, and county town of County ⇨Dublin; population (1996) 481,600; Greater Dublin, including Dún Laoghaire (1996) 953,000. Around a quarter of the Republic's population lives in the Dublin conurbation, with a high density of young, professional workers. In the 1990s the city underwent a renaissance, with the restoration of many old city-centre buildings, notably in the Temple Bar area. Dublin is the site of one of the world's largest breweries (Guinness); other industries include textiles, pharmaceuticals, electrical goods, whiskey distilling, glass, food processing, and machine tools.

Dublin is a significant centre for culture and tourism, known particularly for its Georgian architecture and plethora of bars.

brief history

The earliest records of a settlement at Dublin date from AD 140. The city was captured in 840 by Viking invaders; the ruler of Dublin and his Norse and Leinster allies were defeated by Brian Bóruma in 1014 at Clontarf, now a northern suburb of the city. Dublin was the centre of English rule from 1171 (exercised from Dublin Castle; 1220) until 1922. Dublin was the scene of the 1916 ⇨Easter Rising against British rule in Ireland.

main features

In the Georgian period many fine squares and wide streets were laid out. Important buildings from this period are the City Hall (1769–79; formerly the Royal Exchange); the Bank of Ireland (1729–85; the former parliament building); the Custom House (1791; burned during 1921 but later restored); Leinster House (where the Dáil Éireann (House of Representatives) and the Seanad Éireann (the Senate) sit) with the National Library and the National Museum nearby; the Four Courts (designed in 1786 as the seat of the high court of justice); and the National Gallery.

Other notable buildings are Dublin Castle (the tower of which dates to the early 13th century); the Hugh Lane Municipal Gallery of Modern Art; Collins Barracks (now part of the National Museum of Ireland); and the Abbey and Gate theatres. There is a Roman Catholic pro-cathedral, St Mary's (1816); two Protestant cathedrals, St Patrick's and Christchurch; and three universities – Trinity College, University College (part of the National University of Ireland), and Dublin City University (formerly a technical college). Trinity College library contains the Book of Kells, a splendidly illuminated 8th-century gospel book associated with the monastery of Kells founded by St Columba in County Meath. Kilmainham Jail, where nationalists such as Charles Stewart ⇨Parnell were imprisoned, is now a museum.

city tour

The centre of the city is simple in plan. O'Connell Street (formerly Sackville Street), is the widest and most imposing thoroughfare; it runs from north to south, crossing the Liffey (which flows due east at this point) at O'Connell Bridge, and then joining Westmorland Street, which leads to College Green, the hub of the road system. College Green is dominated on one side by Trinity College and on the other by the Bank of Ireland, formerly the old Parliament House. To the west, Dame Street leads to Dublin Castle, the City Hall, and Christchurch. Between Dame Street and the Liffey is the newly restored area of Temple Bar, now a highly popular social venue. Due south is Grafton Street, leading to St Stephen's Green, whilst a turn east from the entrance to Grafton Street leads eventually to Merrion Square and the government buildings. Between Grafton Street and Merrion Square East, and parallel to both, are Dawson Street, in which is the Mansion House, the official residence of the Lord Mayor, and Kildare Street, in which are Leinster House, the National Library, and the National Museum. The Nelson Pillar, formerly Dublin's principal landmark, which stood in O'Connell Street, was damaged by a gelignite explosion in March 1966, and was subsequently demolished.

The centre for civic administration is the City Hall (1779), which is situated facing Parliament Street, on the short hill leading from Dublin Castle to St Patrick's Cathedral. There are also modern corporation offices on the south bank of the Liffey. Phoenix Park, formerly west of the city, and now enclosed by it, has an area of 713 ha/1,761 acres and a circumference of 11 km/7 mi. In it are the official residence of the president (⇨Áras an Uachtaráin), the Papal Nunciature,

DUBLIN *The city's architectural 'golden age' was the Georgian period. The Custom House, shown here, was designed by James Gandon and Thomas Cooley and was constructed over 10 years, from 1781.*

and the American Legation. The northern suburb of Glasnevin is known for the ⇨National Botanic Gardens, and its cemetery, in which many famous Irish nationalists are buried (Charles Stewart ⇨Parnell, Daniel ⇨O'Connell, Arthur ⇨Griffith, Michael Collins, and many others).

new developments in the city

Economic growth in the 1960s brought new building in the city and with it the demolition of numerous old buildings, including some of Dublin's Georgian architecture. However, by the 1990s, with an improvement in architectural standards and more wealth in the city, attractive new precincts emerged. City shopping centres, such as the Powerscourt centre, the Stephen's Green centre, and the Jervis Centre were established. The main shopping street, Grafton Street, was pedestrianized, and there are plans to pedestrianize O'Connell Street. However, in cultural terms the most interesting development is the Temple Bar area, running between Dame Street and the Liffey. It includes the Irish Film Centre, a photography gallery, a print gallery, a photography archive, an innovative children's theatre and cultural centre called The Ark, the Temple Bar Music Centre, a multimedia centre, the Project Arts Centre, and a great variety of shops, restaurants, and pubs. At weekends an open-air wholefood market and occasional concerts are held in Temple Bar's Meeting House Square.

On the north quays of the Liffey a concert centre, the Point Depot, provides a venue for large concerts and has hosted the Eurovision Song Contest, while classical music is performed in the National Concert Hall, and elsewhere. With ever-increasing levels of traffic congestion in the city – it is estimated that around 1,000 new cars come onto the streets of Dublin every week – many people have chosen to live in the city, often in new custom-built apartment blocks, rather than commute to the suburbs. This means that the city centre is now far livelier in the evenings.

architecture

The Bank of Ireland, built between 1729 and 1739, is one of Dublin's most famous buildings, and the first great Palladian building in the city. The original architect was Edward Lovat Pearce, surveyor-general of Ireland, who died before the work was completed; the remaining work was supervised by Arthur Dobbs. A Corinthian portico on Westmoreland Street was added in 1785 by James ⇨Gandon. It was used as the Irish parliament building during the period of independence from 1782 until the Act of Union in 1800, and was subsequently acquired by the Bank of Ireland in 1803 for £40,000. Although structural alterations have been made since then, many of the old features and chambers have been retained.

City Hall, formerly the Royal Exchange, was built in 1769 by the London architect Thomas Cooley, who submitted the winning design for the building in an open competition. It is square in plan with the interior designed as a circle within the square. Twelve fluted columns support the finely lit dome, and the Adam-style plasterwork is by Charles Thorp, later lord mayor of Dublin. It houses sculpture by the Irish sculptor John ⇨Foley, and others, and a fine collection of civic regalia, including a sword belonging to King Henry IV.

DUBLIN *Leinster House, now the seat of the Dáil and the Seanad Éireann, was the largest private home in Dublin when it was built (1744–48). Originally the house lay on the very outskirts of the city, but Dublin has grown so much that it is now part of the city centre.*

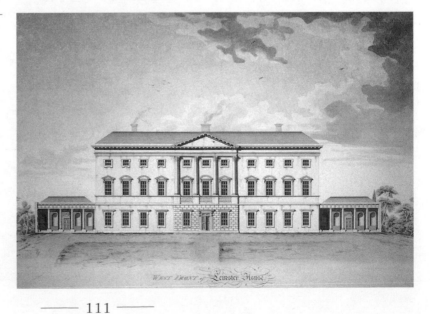

The Custom House, probably Dublin's noblest large building, was built on the north quay between 1781 and 1789, and is the creation of James ⇨Gandon, considered by many as his masterpiece. It suffered badly during the lead-up to the Irish Civil War (1922–23) when it burned for five days in 1921, following an IRA attack, and the only original interior surviving is in the North Hall. The building has been carefully restored and still retains much of the glory of the original conception. It now houses government offices.

Dublin Castle dates from 1204, when King John of England ordered that a castle should be built on the site; the original construction was completed about 1220. The largest surviving portion of the Norman building is the Record Tower, where 'Red Hugh' O'Donnell, a member of the influential ⇨O'Donnell family, was probably imprisoned in 1591. The castle was rebuilt in 1688 after a fire in 1684, and King James II spent one night in it after retreating from the Battle of the Boyne in 1690. St Patrick's Hall has an impressive ceiling of scenes from Irish history painted by Vincent Waldre in about 1790. The Chester Beatty Library in the Clock Tower, contains an excellent collection of medieval manuscripts, Babylonian clay tablets, and Egyptian and Greek papyri.

The Four Courts, a fine Neo-Classical building, once housed the courts of the Exchequer, Common Pleas, King's Bench, and Chancery; today it accommodates Ireland's High Court and Supreme Court.

Construction began in 1786 using the designs of Thomas Cooley, who died before completion; the work was finished by James Gandon in 1802. In 1922, during the Irish Civil War, the interiors were badly damaged by fire and Gandon's work was lost, but the building has since been restored. Of a much greater loss was the destruction of many important historical documents in the Public Records Office, which occupied a nearby building.

Leinster House, a magnificent Georgian mansion built between 1744 and 1748 for the 20th Earl of Kildare, has been the meeting place of the Irish parliament since 1924. Designed by Richard Castle, it is said to have influenced the Irish architect James Hoban, who created the White House (1792–99), the official residence of the president of the USA in Washington DC. The house was rented by the ⇨Royal Dublin Society in 1815; they moved to Ballsbridge, just south of the city centre in 1924. The picture gallery, redesigned by James Wyatt in 1780, is now used as the Senate chamber, while the lecture theatre of 1897 houses the Dáil. With the National Museum and National Library the house forms three sides of an open square fronting on Kildare Street.

The Royal Hospital, built in the 1680s as a hospital for veteran soldiers, is a graceful Neo-Classical building designed by William Robinson for the Duke of Ormond. Its spacious Great Hall contains excellent carved oak panelling and plasterwork, and is considered by many to be the finest interior in Dublin. The

DUBLIN *Buskers in Grafton Street, the city's smart, pedestrianized shopping area, where you can stop by at Bewley's Coffee House, once frequented by writers such as Shaw, Yeats, and Wilde.*

chapel has a magnificent ceiling and more superb woodwork. It was restored from 1980 by the Office of Public Works.

The General Post Office, designed by Francis Johnstone (1760–1829), is a granite building with an Ionic portico of Portland stone. It was the headquarters of the Irish Volunteers during the ⇨Easter Rising of 1916, when it was shelled by a gunboat on the River Liffey and destroyed by fire. It has since been rebuilt, and its impressive main hall contains a memorial to the rebels of 1916 in the shape of a statue of Cuchulain (one of Ireland's legendary heroes), on the base of which is inscribed an excerpt from the Declaration of the Republic that was read by Patrick ⇨Pearse from the steps of the Post Office at the start of the Easter Rising.

The Roman Catholic pro-cathedral in Marlborough Street, adjacent to O'Connell Street, is in Graeco-Roman style, and has a portico of Doric columns. It was completed in 1825, some years before the granting of Catholic Emancipation, the chief protagonist of which, Daniel O'Connell, became Dublin's first Roman Catholic mayor in 1841.

St Patrick's Cathedral, the principal church of the Church of Ireland, is founded on the site of a wooden church built by Sitric, the first Christian king of the Norsemen in Dublin. Construction dates from about 1220 when the existing church was elevated to the status of a cathedral by Archbishop Henri de Londres. Building continued until 1254 in the Early English Gothic style, with the Lady Chapel being added about 1270. It is the largest of Ireland's medieval cathedrals and has had many renovations, the most extensive being in 1865 by Benjamin Lee Guinness. Jonathan ⇨Swift was dean of St Patrick's from 1713 to 1745 and is buried here. In 1901 a well was discovered which legend states is the holy well where St Patrick baptized converts in the 5th century.

St Audoen's Church, the only surviving medieval church in Dublin, dates back to the late 12th century and was probably built by settlers from Bristol who had been granted Dublin by King Henry II. The tower dates from the 17th century with some restoration in the 19th century; it contains the oldest bells in Ireland, cast in 1423. There is a fine Norman font dated 1192 and in the porch is the ancient Lucky Stone, probably an early Christian gravestone, which is supposed to bring good luck when touched. St Audoen's is Dublin's oldest church in continuous use.

St Michan's Church, in Church Street, is a 17th-century building near the Four Courts. It is noted for its vaults, in whose dry atmosphere certain bodies have been preserved for centuries. One of the bodies is said to be that of a crusader.

Amongst notable 20th-century Dublin buildings are the Department of Industry and Commerce building in Kildare Street (built in 1942), and, almost in the shadow of the Custom House, the 'Busarus' or Central Bus Station (1953), and Liberty Hall (1962), headquarters of the Irish trade union movement. During the 1960s and the early 1970s, many office blocks were built, particularly in the southeast of the city. Most noteworthy of these are the Bank of Ireland in Baggot Street, the Central Bank in Dame Street, and the Department of Agriculture, in Kildare Street. In the 1990s Dublin became an important financial services centre and many new buildings were erected for this purpose on former dockland.

cultural life
Literature and the arts have flourished in Dublin: David Garrick and Sarah Siddons played at the Crow Street and Smock Alley theatres; the first performance of George Frederick Handel's oratorio *Messiah* was conducted by the composer in Fishamble Street in 1742; and the playwrights Oliver Goldsmith, George Farquhar, and William Congreve were students at Trinity College. Dublin is the birthplace of several notable writers: Richard Brinsley Sheridan was born in Dorset Street, Oscar Wilde in Merrion Square, Thomas Moore in Aungier Street, and George Bernard Shaw in Synge Street. Other famous literary Dubliners include William Butler Yeats, Charles Lever, Joseph Sheridan Le Fanu, Seán O'Casey, and James ⇨Joyce; the latter's modernist masterpiece *Ulysses* famously records the events of a single Dublin day. The satirist Jonathan Swift was also born in Dublin.

The Abbey Theatre, opened in 1904, has an international reputation; Lady Gregory and Yeats were the first directors, and the Fay brothers, T C Murray, Seán O'Casey, Barry Fitzgerald, and F J McCormick have all been associated with the theatre. The Gate Theatre opened in 1928; Mícheál Mac Liammóir and Hilton Edwards have been associated with it, and Orson Welles made his acting debut here at the age of 16. The Feis Ceoil, an annual music festival in Dublin, has a high reputation, and amongst those who won their earliest laurels at its competitions were John McCormack, a tenor popular at the turn of the 20th century, and Margaret Burke-Sheridan (1889–1958), an internationally famous soprano. The Royal Irish Academy of Music was founded in 1856.

> *g*eorgian architects, ironic / Deists, crossed over from the mainland / To build a culture brick by brick, / And graft their reason to a state / The rain is washing out of shape.

TOM PAULIN English-born poet, dramatist, and critic *The Strange Museum* (1980).

Dublin's art treasures

The National Gallery in Merrion Square, adjacent to Leinster House, has pictures by Fra Angelico, Michelangelo, Titian, El Greco, Rubens, Corregio, Tintoretto, Vermeer, Poussin, Van Dyck, Murillo, Gainsborough, and Goya, as well as works by modern Irish painters such as John Lavery, William Orpen, and Jack Butler Yeats. The Hugh Lane Municipal Gallery of Modern Art (formerly the Dublin Municipal Gallery), which occupies what was once the town house of Lord Charlemont in Parnell Square, was opened in 1907 and reconstructed in 1933. It owes much to the generosity of Sir Hugh Lane, who was lost on the *Lusitania* in 1915, and who, in an unwitnessed addition to his will, left to the Dublin Municipal Gallery his collection of 39 continental paintings then on loan to London's National Gallery. Much controversy has raged over these pictures. A compromise was reached in 1959 when a selection of them was returned to Dublin, which now hangs in a special room in the Hugh Lane Gallery. The gallery has a notable Corot collection and works by Rodin. In 1991 the Irish Museum of Modern Art (IMMA) was established in the buildings of the Royal Hospital, Kilmainham. Comprised of several galleries, it has its own collection and hosts visiting exhibitions of modern art every three to four months.

The National Library, in Kildare Street, was founded in 1877 with a collection donated by the Royal Dublin Society. It has over half a million books, important manuscripts, and map collections. Facing it is the National Museum, which has a splendid collection of antiquities, including the 8th-century Tara Brooch and Ardagh Chalice, found in Limerick in 1868, and the Cross of Cong, a beautiful crucifix in wood, bronze and silver. A new addition to the National Museum of Ireland, the museum of decorative arts and its economic, social, political, and military history, opened in 1997 at Collins Barracks. The Natural History Museum on Merrion Street, which first opened in 1857, is described as one of the world's finest and fullest collections in the old cabinet style. Trinity College Library is a copyright library. Amongst its ancient manuscripts is the incomparable Book of Kells, a superb example of the beautifully ornamented script of the early Irish monks. It also houses 'Brian Boru's Harp', a musical instrument named after the Irish high king Brian Bóruma, although the harp actually dates from about 500 years after his death in 1014; the harp appears on the presidential ⇨flag of the Republic of Ireland. The ⇨Royal Irish Academy, founded in 1785 and sited in Dawson Street since 1851, has the best collection of old Irish manuscripts in the country, while Marsh's Library, founded in 1707 by Archbishop Marsh near St Patrick's Cathedral, is the oldest public library in Ireland.

education

There are three universities in Dublin. ⇨Trinity College was founded in 1592 by Queen Elizabeth I on the site of the confiscated monastery of All Hallows. The earliest of its surviving buildings dates from 1722. For a long time it was strongly Protestant in bias. University College evolved from the Catholic University of Ireland, whose first rector was Cardinal Henry Newman. At first denied recognition in Britain, it was granted university status in 1853. It is now part of the National University of Ireland, established in 1909. Its arts and science faculties are now situated on a suburban campus (of 121 ha/300 acres) at Belfield, 5 km/3 mi southeast of the city centre, and 4 km/2.5 mi from the original site of the Catholic University in Earlsfort Terrace, part of which now houses the National Concert Hall. Dublin City University is in the suburb of Glasnevin.

sport

Three shows are held annually in the grounds of the Royal Dublin Society at Ballsbridge, the best known being the horse show, held in August, which features horse sales and international jumping competitions. There are race meetings at Leopardstown and the Phoenix Park. International rugby matches are played at Lansdowne Road, and football matches at Dalymount. The Gaelic Athletic Association has its headquarters at Croke Park (the scene of a notoriously brutal act of reprisal by the ⇨Black and Tans during the Anglo–Irish War (1919–21), and at the suburb of Portmarnock there is a championship golf course. At Tymon Park, on the outskirts of Dublin, there is a national basketball arena.

city environs

The built-up area of Dublin extends along Dublin Bay from above Howth in the north to below Dun Laoghaire in the south, a distance of about 23 km/ 14 mi. The city has a backdrop of hills (the Dublin Mountains), and many suburbs, including Sutton, Howth, Portmarnock, and Malahide to the north, and Blackrock, Dun Laoghaire, Dalkey, and Killiney to the south.

Over the years, Dublin has spread and incorporated some of its smaller neighbours. The townships of Glasnevin, Clontarf, and Drumcondra became part of the city in 1900, the urban districts of Rathmines and Pembroke in 1930, and the township of Howth in 1942. The city has grown as far north as the airport, and as far south as the foothills of the mountains. The population expansion has been accommodated mainly to the west of the present city, at Blanchardstown (north of the Liffey), and Clondalkin and Tallaght (south of the Liffey).

transport

Dublin is linked by rail to the major centres in the Republic of Ireland and Northern Ireland. Dublin is a terminus for ferries to Liverpool and the Isle of Man, Dun Laoghaire the terminus for ferries to Holyhead. The international airport is at Collinstown, 8 km/ 5 mi from the city centre. The Royal Canal originates in Dublin and joins the River Shannon, but is now disused. The Grand Canal also originates in Dublin; one branch joins the Shannon, and a second the River Barrow. It is now only used for leisure purposes. The port has over 7 km/4 mi of quays and is controlled by the Port and Docks Board, set up in 1868. A suburban rail system, the DART, runs from Bray in the south to Howth in the north, with a western spur to Maynooth; trains run every five minutes at peak time and every fifteen minutes at other times. There are plans to set up a light rail network, LUAS, and further projects for the underground are being considered in order to address a serious problem of traffic congestion in the city.

from foundation to the Act of Union

Dublin is an ancient city, and has been identified by some with the city of Eblana mentioned by the Graeco-Egyptian geographer and astronomer Ptolemy (AD 140). St Patrick is said to have visited Dublin in 448 and to have converted many of its pagan inhabitants, but the Norsemen are regarded as its real founders. The Norsemen began marauding raids towards the end of the 8th century, and Dublin was one of their first permanent settlements in Ireland. Olaf the White captured Dublin in 852. The Norse influence rose and fell for 150 years, but was finally broken in 1014 at the battle of Clontarf, when King ⇨Brian Bóruma defeated the Norsemen, who had gathered from the Orkneys and elsewhere for a trial of strength. However, Dublin remained very largely a Norse city, and in 1170 it had an Irish archbishop, St Laurence O'Toole, but a Norse governor, Asculf.

The city was captured in 1169 by the Normans, who had come to Ireland as the allies of Dermot McMurrough, a king of Leinster who had been banished. The infant city was then on the south side of the River Liffey, and some of the dispossessed Norsemen founded a small settlement called Oxmanstown on the north bank of the river. Dublin began to grow. King Henry II of England came to Dublin in 1171 to curb his own barons and receive the homage of some of the Irish chiefs. He wintered in a temporary palace built, the old chronicles say, 'of peeled osiers', entertained lavishly, gave Dublin the first of its 102 royal charters (the last was given in 1727), granted the city as a colony to the people of Bristol, and appointed Hugh de Lacy to govern it in his name.

The Normans built Christchurch Cathedral, and in 1190 John Comyn, the first Norman archbishop, began a second cathedral, St Patrick's, just outside the city walls. The population of Dublin was then less than 10,000 (it was 64,000 in 1688, 168,000 in 1798, and reached half a million early in the 20th century). Dublin Castle was completed in 1220. At this time, and for centuries after, Dublin was the chief fortress of 'the Pale', a narrow coastal strip stretching along the coast roughly from Dundalk to the Wicklow Mountains, and inland for 32 km/51 mi, over which the English had control. Neighbouring chiefs carried off its cattle at intervals, or exacted 'Black Rent' for leaving them in peace. Richard II landed at Waterford with an army of 34,000 men to punish one of these chiefs, but the Irish guerrillas harried the English all

A CHRONOLOGY OF DUBLIN

AD 140 Settlement on present site of Dublin, called Eblana, is recorded by ancient Greek geographer Ptolemy in his *Guide to Geography*.

291 The inhabitants of the village of Dubh-linn ('dark pool'), south of the Liffey, defeat an army from the surrounding province of Leinster.

841 Viking invaders from Norway and Iceland conquer Dubh-linn and establish a permanent *longphort* (fortified harbour encampment), west of the site of Dublin Castle, as a base for raiding. This soon amalgamates with Baile Átha Cliath ('the town of the ford of the hurdle'), north of the Liffey, which becomes the official Irish Gaelic name of the city.

1014 At the Battle of Clontarf (now a northeastern suburb of Dublin, on the northern shore of Dublin Bay), the high king of Munster, Brian Bóruma, triumphs over the Dublin Norse (Ostmen) and their Leinster and Norse allies. Clontarf is, henceforth, celebrated as a symbolic victory in the 250-year-long struggle between the Irish and Vikings (902–1170).

1169–71 Dermot MacMurrough, dispossessed king of Leinster, enlists the help of Anglo-Norman knights to regain his throne; in doing so, the Normans seize control of Dublin. Henry II of England, fearing a separate Norman power, invades and makes all parties swear allegiance. Dublin becomes the centre of English influence in Ireland, and is made a dependency of the English port of Bristol.

1204 King John founds Dublin Castle on a site between the River Liffey and its tributary, the Poddle, as a stronghold and centre of jurisdiction over Ireland.

1317 The townspeople put up barricades to resist Edward the Bruce, brother of Robert and self-appointed king of Ireland.

1348 Over 10,000 people perish as the Black Death sweeps Dublin between August and the New Year.

1487 The pretender to the English throne, Lambert Simnel is crowned Edward VI in Christchurch Cathedral.

1534 Following an attempted seizure of Dublin Castle in the Kildare revolt led by Thomas FitzGerald, the crown's vice deputy in Ireland, Henry VIII and later Tudor monarchs consolidate their hold over the Pale – the region around Dublin under English control.

1591–92 Trinity College is founded by Queen Elizabeth of England and Ireland. Entry is restricted to Anglicans until the 18th century, and many of the Protestant Anglo-Irish elite are educated here. Notable alumni include Jonathan Swift, Edmund Burke, Oliver Goldsmith, Wolfe Tone, and Samuel Beckett.

1649 Staunchly royalist during the English Civil War (1642–49), Dublin surrenders to Oliver Cromwell, who uses it as a bridgehead for his parliamentary army's bloody suppression of Catholic resistance in Ireland in preparation for Protestant colonization.

1662 John Ogilby opens the Royal Theatre at Smock Alley, giving Dublin its first theatre.

1667 Jonathan Swift, author of the satire *Gulliver's Travels* is born at Hoey's Court, near St Werburgh's Church. One of Dublin's most famous writers, Swift is dean of St Patrick's Anglican cathedral from 1713 until his death in 1745. Culturally, Swift's age is one of the richest in the city's history.

1685 Huguenot (French Calvinist Protestant) refugees from religious persecution, who have been arriving in Dublin since the 1650s, reach a peak after Louis XIV, King of France, revokes the Edict of Nantes that granted religious freedom. Many Huguenots settle in the Liberties area, southwest of the city centre. Their weaving skills help to establish the Irish linen industry.

1687 Richard Talbot, Earl of Tyrconnell, is viceroy in Dublin until the arrival of James II in the city in 1689; his wife rebuts James's complaint that Irish soldiers fled from the Battle of the Boyne in 1690, with the words, 'you have outstripped the fleetest of them'.

1742 George Frideric Handel's oratorio *Messiah* is first performed at the New Musick Hall on Fishamble Street, on 13 April.

1759 The Guinness family establish a brewery at St James's Gate in Dublin.

1782 The Anglo-Irish elite, or 'Protestant Ascendancy', gains an independent Irish parliament following a campaign by the patriot Henry Grattan. Grattan issues the Declaration of Rights ('Ireland is now a nation') in Dublin's parliament building (now the Bank of Ireland) on College Green. The Irish parliament is suppressed by the Act of Union in 1801.

1786 Construction begins on the Four Courts to a design by Thomas Cooley, and is completed by James Gandon after Cooley's death.

1798 Lord Edward Fitzgerald, Leinster leader of the United Irishmen, is arrested by Maj Sirr in Thomas Street on 19 May; he dies in Newgate Gaol on 4 June from a wound received during his arrest.

1803 An abortive uprising takes place in late July by 300 followers of the radical Robert Emmet. After failing to secure Dublin Castle, Emmet is captured, tried, and executed at St Catherine's Church, Thomas Street.

1841 Political leader Daniel O'Connell, 'the Liberator', who won Catholic Emancipation from the British government in 1829, elected the city's first Catholic mayor.

1849 The poet James Clarence Mangan dies in Meath Hospital during the cholera epidemic in the wake of the Great Famine.

1853 The Catholic University of Ireland is founded on St Stephen's Green, with John Henry Newman as its first rector. Its famous graduates include the nationalist politician and Taoiseach Éamon de Valera and the writer James Joyce.

1865 The poet W B Yeats is born in Sandymount Avenue on 13 June.

1872 The first tramline opens in Dublin, linking the city centre to Rathmines.

1882 Lord Frederick Cavendish, chief secretary for Ireland, and his undersecretary Henry Burke are murdered in Phoenix Park, west Dublin, by members of the Invincibles, an extremist nationalist organization. This hardens British public opinion against Irish home rule. The writer James Joyce is born in Rathgar on 2 February.

1904 The Abbey Theatre is established in Dublin by W B Yeats, Arthur Sinclair, and others; its stage is pledged to works by new Irish writers. Its founding is a major event in the Irish literary revival of the late 19th and early 20th centuries.

1905 The republican political movement Sinn Féin ('Ourselves Alone') is founded in Dublin by the journalist Arthur Griffith to campaign for independence from Britain. By the end of World War I it is the main nationalist party.

1913 In a violent industrial confrontation known as the 'Dublin lock-out', 20,000 labourers seeking trade union rights are excluded from work by their employers. As the dispute drags on, many families suffer from cold and malnutrition, and the strikers are forced to abandon their protest.

1916 In the Easter Rising, 1,200 armed nationalists seize the General Post Office and other buildings. Pitched battles and artillery fire devastate the city centre. Led by the Irish Republican Brotherhood, the revolt is put down after five days. Reprisals and executions by the British authorities consolidate support for the nationalist cause.

1919–20 An unofficial national assembly (the first Dáil Éireann) is convened at Mansion House by 73 elected Sinn Féin members who have left the Westminster parliament. Suppression of nationalism by British forces in the Anglo-Irish War (1919–21) brings violent confrontation; on 'Bloody Sunday' in November 1920, 12 spectators at a Gaelic football match at the Croke Park stadium are killed by British government troops.

1921 After the partition of Ireland under the Government of Ireland Act (1920) and Anglo-Irish Treaty (1921), Dublin becomes the capital of the new Irish Free State.

1932 Over a million people attend an open-air mass held in Phoenix Park at the 31st Eucharistic Congress, a key Catholic meeting.

1941 Parts of Dublin are bombed by German planes in World War II, leaving 34 dead, 90 injured, and 300 houses destroyed or damaged.

1961 RTÉ television station begins broadcasting.

1965 Taoiseach Seán Lemass and Northern Ireland prime minister Terence O'Neill meet in Dublin.

1966 The Nelson Pillar on O'Connell Street, long a prominent landmark north of the Liffey, is blown up by the Irish Republican Army (IRA). The Easter Rising is commemorated and a garden of remembrance opened.

1972 The British embassy is burned following the 'Bloody Sunday' shootings in Derry.

1974 22 people are killed by car bombs in Dublin.

1980 The first Anglo-Irish summit meeting takes place in the city.

1981 Over 100 Gardaí are injured during a demonstration by the H-Blocks committee, over the treatment of political prisoners in Northern Ireland.

1984 The DART, a suburban rail system, opens between Bray and Howth, with a spur to Maynooth.

1991 Dublin city centre rejuvenation takes place after it is named European City of Culture. In Temple Bar many traditional shops and pubs are preserved or renovated, making the area into a major tourist attraction.

1999 In the Liffey of Lights ceremony on 31 December, the river is permanently floodlit from Sean Heuston bridge to Memorial Bridge to mark the year 2000.

through Wicklow, and after a breathing space in Dublin, Richard sailed home again in 1394.

The Reformation reached Ireland in 1535, when a Protestant, Dr Brown, became archbishop of Dublin, and the Dublin parliament passed the Act of Supremacy in 1536. The new doctrines made little headway in the rest of the country, but were enforced with some rigour in the city. James II was welcomed in Dublin in 1689 by Irish Catholics, who felt their time had come, but he left the country hurriedly after his defeat at the Battle of the Boyne (1690), leaving the Irish and the French to fight his battles. Soon afterwards the victorious William of Orange visited Dublin, and presented a chain of office to the lord mayor.

Dublin grew considerably during the Restoration, but the 18th century was the time of its greatest development and elegance. The Georgian part of the city was laid out, and the aristocracy became patrons of art and literature. The Royal Dublin Society was founded by 1731 to encourage trade and culture, and its achievements justified in time the verdict of Lord Chesterfield: 'It did more good to Ireland with regard to Art and Industry than all the laws that could have been framed.' The Irish parliament, which had been subservient to the British parliament, became fully independent in 1782, mainly because of pressure by the Volunteers, an armed force raised originally to protect Ireland from possible French invasion during the American Revolution. The Chamber of Commerce was established in 1782, and trade flourished. Dublin prospered and grew until the passing of the Act of Union (1801) and the end of the Irish parliament.

See chronology of Dublin on page 116 for significant events in the 19th and 20th centuries.

DUBLINERS, THE

Ballad band formed in O'Donoghues Pub on Baggot Street, Dublin, in 1962. The original and most recognizable line-up consisted of Barney McKenna (banjo), Luke Kelly (vocals, banjo), John Sheahan (fiddle), Ciarán Burke (guitar), and Ronny Drew (vocals, guitar). Originally known as the Ronnie Drew Band, they became very popular throughout Ireland and Europe, even more so when their 1967 single 'Seven Drunken Nights' was banned in Ireland. Their material consisted of Drew's gravelly Dublin street ballads, Kelly's powerfully delivered socially and politically relevant contemporary folk songs, and McKenna's excellent dance music.

The Dubliners did much to popularize the tenor banjo in Ireland and laid down the song repertoire and a style of performance for many ballad bands that followed. The death of Luke Kelly in 1984 and the departure of Ronnie Drew have meant that the band has lost much of its distinctive character. Important albums include *Finnegan Wakes* (1966) and *Recorded Live at the Albert Hall* (1969).

DUBLIN INSTITUTE FOR ADVANCED STUDIES (DIAS)

Leading research institute for studies in the sciences and humanities in Dublin, Ireland. It was conceived in the late 1930s by Taoiseach (prime minister) Éamon de Valera, and established as a statutory corporation by an act of the Dáil (parliament) in June 1940. It carries out fundamental research, trains advanced students, and publishes books and research findings.

The DIAS has three constituent schools: the school of Celtic studies, the school of Theoretical physics, and the school of cosmic physics. Cosmic physics in turn has three sections: astronomy, astrophysics, and geophysics. All three carry out extensive research in their respective fields. Celtic studies publishes extensively on Irish or Gaelic, other Celtic languages, and Hiberno-Latin. Theoretical physics was headed 1939–56 by the Austrian physicist and Nobel prize winner Erwin Schrödinger, who characterized fundamental aspects of quantum mechanics, and who delivered his celebrated lecture 'What Is Life?' during his time in Dublin.

DUFFY, CHARLES GAVAN (1816–1903)

Journalist, writer, and politician. Born in County Monaghan, and educated in both Catholic and Presbyterian schools, Duffy became active in 19th-century Irish nationalist movements, and co-founded the weekly political journal *The Nation* in 1842 with the poet Thomas ⇨Davis and John Blake Dillon. He was arrested in 1848 for his involvement in the ⇨Young Ireland rising, and in 1850 founded the ⇨Tenant League for land reform. In 1852 he was elected to Westminster as MP for New Ross, supporting the Independent Irish Party until its split in 1853. He subsequently emigrated to Australia in 1855, and became prime minister of Victoria in 1871, and later speaker of the House of Assembly.

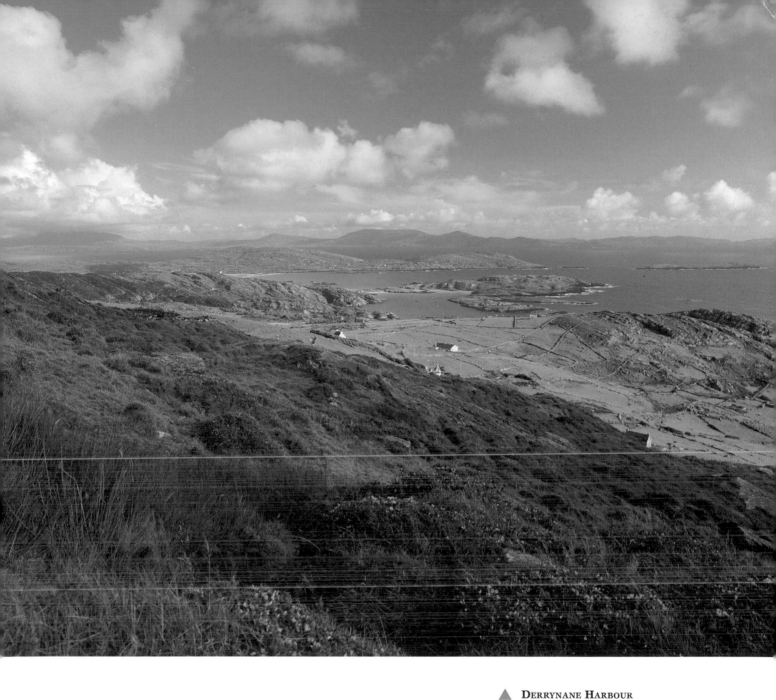

*t*here is one thing that gives a unity – a
personality, as it were – to Ireland. It is
the glory of light, which comes towards
evening and rests on every field and on every
hill and in the street of every town like a
strange tide.

ROBERT WILSON LYND (1879–1949),
Northern Irish essayist.

▲ **MACGILLYCUDDY'S REEKS**

High in the spectacular mountain range of Macgillycuddy's Reeks, above the Ring of Kerry. Ireland's highest peak, Carantuohill (1,041 m/3,415 ft), is here. The dramatic glacial scenery and peppering of lakes make it a favourite tourist destination.

▶ **CLIFFS OF MOHER**

Further north, near Galway Bay, are the dramatic Cliffs of Moher, County Clare. Among the most imposing cliffs in Ireland, they tower 200 m /700 ft above the sea, and are home to large numbers of sea birds, including fulmars, kittiwakes, and guillemots, who squeeze their nests into crevices in the deeply eroded rock face.

GLENS OF ANTRIM, TREVEBULLIAGH

Green and well-watered, the Glens of Antrim snake down to the sea from the Antrim Hills. Each valley has a name recalling its past, this being Glenballyemon, the valley of Eamon. The glens were isolated from each other until linked by a coast road in the mid-19th century.

GIANT'S CAUSEWAY

The intriguing basalt columns of the Giant's Causeway, County Antrim, have been attracting visitors since the 17th century, and since 1986 this has been a World Heritage site. Formed some sixty million years ago by molten lava, the estimated 37,000 columns range up to 12 m/40 ft high. Most are hexagonal, with some pentagons, and other polygonal shapes.

▲ **BRIAN BÓRUMA'S FORT**
This wooded spot near Killaloe, County Clare must have once rung to the shouts of Brian Bóruma's men. The high king, an ancestor of the powerful O'Brien family, who were influential in Clare's political history for many centuries, had a fort here in the 10th century.

▲ **POTATO HARVEST**
Potatoes, harvested here in Slemish, County Antrim, have played a tragic part in Irish history. In the early 19th century they were the staple food of tenant farmers and their families, many of whom would each eat 4.5 kg/10 lb or more of potatoes each day. Devastating failures of the potato crop from 1845 caused the Great Famine, which led to the deaths of around a million people.

▶ **YOUGHAL**
In a country where nowhere is further than 90 km/60 miles from the sea, fishing has always been an important source of both nourishment and livelihood. Boats like these in the harbour at Youghal, County Cork, have braved the Atlantic waters for centuries.

◀ **PEAT**
Peat was traditionally the main form of fuel in Ireland, and the right to dig 'turf' was a vital element in agreements between landlord and tenant. Although cheaper than coal, it is far bulkier to transport and can be dug only in dry weather.

▼ **FARMING**
Working the land has historically been the way of life for the majority of the population. Even in the early 1900s, half of Ireland's male workers were employed in agriculture, though by the end of the 20th century this had declined to less than 15 per cent.

▶ **THE PUB**

The Irish pub had its heyday in the mid-19th century and is still a focus for community life in most towns and villages. Thousands of bars like these in Ballydonegan (top), and Youghal (right), both in County Cork, are simple watering-holes where locals enjoy 'craic', the essentially Irish conviviality that readily involves strangers.

▲ **MUSIC FESTIVALS**
▶ *Fleadh Cheoil na hÉireann, the country's leading folk festival, is held in a different location each year – here in Listowel, County Kerry. Atmosphere is all, and the festival goes on in a succession of smoke-filled bars, where the audience rubs shoulders with players.*

◀ **HARP**

The Celtic harp, Ireland's national instrument, originated in the 12th century. It gradually fell from favour for political and social reasons, but interest revived in the 19th century.

▲ **STEP DANCING**

Traditional step dancing began in the confines of rural kitchens. Now it is the subject of fierce competition, performed in colourful and flamboyant costume.

◀ **BODHRÁN-MAKING**

The bodhrán, which is beaten with a drumstick or the hand, has roots in pre-Christian rituals, and was not brought into mainstream music until the 1960s. Here, a bodhrán-maker in Roundstone, County Galway, stretches goatskin tightly over a round frame made of beechwood.

WEAVING TWEED

Woollen fabrics have been produced in Ireland for some 600 years. The term 'tweed' was coined in the 19th century, and in the mid-20th century, designer Sybil Connolly introduced pastel tones that were a far cry from the traditional greens and browns.

BOOKBINDING

From the mid-17th century, the journals of the Irish parliament were sumptuously bound in leather embossed with gold leaf, helping Irish bookbinding to establish a worldwide reputation. The industry fell into decline after the Act of Union (1801), when many of the aristocracy left Ireland for England, taking their libraries with them.

POTTERY

A potter at work in County Wexford, carrying on a tradition that has existed since the potter's wheel was introduced to Ireland in the 12th century.

◀ **WATERFORD GLASS**
Not just the largest employer in the city, the Waterford glassworks is the biggest crystal factory in the world. No two pieces are exactly identical, and the crystal, which has a particularly high lead content, feels warm to the touch and gives out a ringing note when tapped.

▼ **STAINED GLASS**
Irish stained glass underwent a brilliant revival in the early 20th century, and Evie Hone was one of the greatest exponents. This detail from The Last Supper *shows her typical use of strong colour and powerful composition, combined with the simple figurative tradition of medieval design.*

▼ **KNITTING: ARAN**
The complex cable stitches used on fishermen's sweaters from Aran traditionally varied from area to area. The oiled, undyed wool comes from Connemara sheep, and repels moisture as well as being extremely warm. Hand-knitting is now primarily done for tourists.

▲ **BLOOMSDAY**
◄ *The action of James Joyce's novel* Ulysses
*– an account of a day in the life of Leopold
Bloom – takes place in Dublin on 16 June
1904, and on that date in 1954 a group of
Irish writers set out to mark the occasion.
Bloomsday is now a regular event in
Dublin, and players in Edwardian dress
make a pilgrimage around the city,
reciting passages from the book that
revolutionized the form of the novel in
English.*

▲ **RELIGION**

◄ *Above, a Corpus Christi procession in Clifden, County Galway. Instituted in the 13th century to celebrate the real presence of Christ in the Eucharist, the feast of Corpus Christi is still marked every year in June, throughout the Roman Catholic world. Left, a white marble crucifix at a remote viewpoint over the Caha Mountains on the Healy Pass, a spot where travellers stop to gaze at scenery that can have changed little since the arrival of the first Christians.*

▲ **DUBLIN HORSE SHOW**
◀ *Held annually in August, the Dublin Horse Show attracts entrants from all over the world, as well as the finest Irish horses and riders. A large audience attends the event, which lasts for five days and includes both national and international showjumping contests. Irish hunters, produced by crossing the Irish draught working horse with the thoroughbred, are among the best showjumpers, although they were originally intended for use in the chase.*

▲ **THE STUD FARM**
Irish thoroughbreds have a worldwide reputation, and stud farms such as this at Templemore, County Tipperary, form an important part of an industry that employs 25,000 people breeding, training, or racing. True aficionados can inspect the skeleton of Arkle, all-time great racehorse, at the museum of the Irish National Stud, Tully, in County Kildare.

▶ **THE AGRICULTURAL SHOW**
Watching horses is a favourite national pastime. Regional fairs and agricultural shows, like this one in County Clare, always pull a good crowd.

HURLING

A player chooses his hurling stick to suit his height. Most hurleys are around 1 m/3 ft long, made of ash wood and similar in shape to a hockey stick, but with a wide, flat base. The leather-covered ball, or sliotar, flies down the field at speeds of up to 110 km/68 miles per hour.

HURLING MATCH

A medieval decree attempted to ban hurling, from which, 'great evils and maims' had arisen. Here, Tipperary (in blue) play Clare in a typical match, where 15 men a side, equipped with their sticks, use a combination of strength and skill to get the ball into the goal without damaging each other too much.

Duffy published throughout his life, including the poetry collections *The Spirit of the Nation* (1843) and *The Ballad Poetry of Ireland* (1845), historical analyses such as *A Bird's Eye View of Irish History* (1882), and his memoirs. He was knighted in 1873 and served as the first president of the Irish Literary Society in London in 1892.

DÚN AENGUS

Ancient stone fort on a cliff edge on Inishmore, one of the Aran Islands in Galway Bay. It is semicircular in plan but is thought to have been circular before part of it fell into the sea from its clifftop position. There are four concentric walls. The inner wall, the largest, is 6 m/20 ft high and 5.5 m/18 ft thick. An outer bank encloses an area of 4.5 ha/11 acres. Recent excavations indicate a possible Bronze Age date for the site.

Dún Aengus was described as 'the most magnificent barbaric monument extant in Europe' by the 19th-century archaeologist George Petrie. It has undergone considerable restoration.

DUNDALK

County town of County ⇨Louth; population (1996) 25,800. It is situated on the River Castletown, near the entrance of Dundalk Bay, 19 km/12 mi southwest of Newry. Dundalk is the marketing and distribution centre of north Leinster. Its main industries are engineering, electrical goods, computer hardware, distillers, shoes, clothing, pharmaceuticals, and food processing. The Anglo-Normans built a castle at Dundalk around 1200.

King John (ruled 1199–1216) made Dundalk a royal borough; the associated settlement became a walled town, of which little remains. From the 14th to the 16th century Dundalk was subject to frequent battles as a frontier town of the English Pale, and was burnt on numerous occasions.

Seatown Castle in the town is the 15th-century tower of a Franciscan friary founded in 1244.

DUNGANNON

Market town in County Tyrone, 64 km/40 mi southwest of Belfast; population (1991) 8,300. It was the main seat of the ⇨O'Neill family, former kings of Ulster. Dungannon is now a retail centre with some fine Georgian terraces. Its industries include Tyrone crystal, mechanical engineering, meat processing, and food packaging.

Dungannon was a significant scene of conflict with the English crown during the 16th and 17th centuries.

After the formation of the kingdom of Ireland by Henry VIII in 1541, Con O'Neill, in a tactical manoeuvre, declared loyalty to the English crown and was granted the title of Earl of Tyrone in 1542. During the Nine Years' War, Hugh O'Neill (*c.* 1550–1616) engaged in open conflict with the English crown and in 1598 defeated English forces at the Battle of Yellow Ford to the south of Dungannon. After the Irish defeat at Kinsale in 1602, Dungannon was destroyed to prevent conquest by the English. Subsequently Tyrone was forfeited to the English crown and Dungannon was granted to Arthur Chichester, who replanned the town; and in 1692 it was sold to Thomas Knox. It expanded considerably as a market town under his descendants.

DUNGARVAN

Seaport town in County Waterford; population (1996) 7,200. It is situated on the bay of Dungarron and has fisheries, as well as trade in dairy and agricultural produce; the main industries are food products, engineering, tanning, and dental health-care products. The ruins of King John's Castle (built 1185) and a 13th-century Augustinian priory can be seen here.

The town is named after St Garvan, who founded a monastery here in the 7th century. It was an important military centre during the Anglo-Norman period and was attacked several times, finally surrendering to Cromwell in 1649. Dungarvan Castle has a large circular keep and the remains of a British barracks within its walls.

Local legend has it that the town was spared by Oliver Cromwell because a woman drank his health at the gateway.

DÚN LAOGHAIRE (formerly Kingstown)

Major port, residential town, and borough in County Dublin, 10 km/6 mi south of the centre of Dublin; population (1996) 190,000 (Dún Laoghaire-Rathdown). It is a terminal for ferries to Britain, and there are fishing industries. The National Maritime Museum is located here, and it is an important yachting centre and popular tourist resort. The James Joyce museum is located in a Martello tower at Sandycove, 3 km/2 mi south of the town, where the author once stayed.

Dún Laoghaire is named after Laoghaire, a king of Ireland during the 5th century, who built a fortress here of which nothing now remains. The harbour was begun in 1817 and completed in 1859; the town grew rapidly as a result of trade with Britain. The port was renamed Kingstown in 1821 to commemorate the visit of George IV, but reverted to its original name in 1920.

DUNSANY, EDWARD JOHN MORETON DRAX PLUNKETT (18th Baron of Dunsany) (1878–1957)

Writer, born in London and educated at Sandhurst military college, who succeeded to the family title and estate in County Meath in 1899. Dunsany served in the Boer War and in World War I. He wrote a series of stories, beginning with *The Travel Tales of Mr Joseph Jorkens* (1931), which employed the convention of a narrator (Jorkens) sitting in a club or bar. He also wrote short ironic heroic fantasies, collected in *The Gods of Pegana* (1905) and other books. His first play, *The Glittering Gate* (1909) was performed at the Abbey Theatre, Dublin. This and other plays, such as *The Golden Doom* (1912) and *The Laughter of the Gods* (1919), are intellectual dream-visions written from a very personal mythology.

DUNWOODY, (THOMAS) RICHARD (1964–)

National Hunt jockey, born in Comber, County Down. Dunwoody went to England in 1972, and became very successful in the 1980s. A prolific rider matched only by Tony ⇨McCoy, he has ridden well over a thousand winners in Ireland and England and at the start of the year 2000 was on a retainer with the trainers David Nicholson and Martin Pipe. A winner of the Aintree Grand National in 1986 on West Tip and in 1994 on Minnehoma, he also achieved notable success with the popular Desert Orchid on whom he won two King George VI cups. He has been champion jockey three times, 1992–93, 1993–94, and 1994–95.

DURCAN, PAUL (1944–)

Poet, winner of the Patrick Kavanagh award in 1974 and the Whitbread Poetry prize in 1990. Durcan was born in Dublin and studied archaeology and medieval history at University College, Cork. His poetry, such as *O Westport in the Light of Asia Minor* (1975), expresses a consistently humane standpoint, opposed especially against violence, and is characterized by its loose, long-line structure, and by a tone which is by turns colloquial and incantatory. His early reputation for iconoclastic satire has given way to the more meditative and reflective note evident in his autobiographical *Daddy, Daddy* (1990), and the politically charged *A Snail in my Prime* (1993). The collections *Crazy about Women* (1991) and *Give Me Your Hand* (1994) were inspired by paintings. Recent works include *Christmas Day* (1996) and *Greetings to Our Friends in Brazil* (1999). He is well known for performing his poetry around the world.

Other published works include *Teresa's Bar* (1976) and *Jesus and Angela* (1988). The formal aspects of Durcan's work are thought to have been influenced by the US 'Beat Poets' and the Russian modernists.

DURROW, BOOK OF

Late 7th- or early 8th-century illuminated gospel book, associated with the church at Durrow, County Offaly, Ireland. An early example of the illuminated insular (this refers to the script style) gospel books, the Book of Durrow contains a copy of Jerome's Vulgate text of the four Gospels. Symbols and techniques found in the artistry of the illuminated pages suggest a Northumbrian origin, and indicate that the book may have had some influence on Ireland's more famous insular Gospel, the Book of ⇨Kells.

The Book of Durrow is closely associated with St ⇨Columba and after its compilation it may have been held on Scotland's island of Iona, St Columba's most famous monastic foundation. The book was in the possession of the church at Durrow by the early 12th century, when information about the church and monastery was added to its preface. Since its donation in the late 17th century by the bishop of Meath, the Book of Durrow has been kept in Trinity College library, Dublin.

DWYER, MICHAEL

Activist, see ⇨Rebellion of 1798.

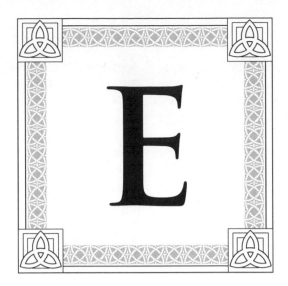

EASON, JOHN CHARLES MALCOLM

(1880–1965)

Bookseller who revolutionized the family newsagents business in Dublin, by emulating the retailing and wholesaling practices of the British bookseller WHSmith and established a nationwide business in wholesale book selling. A powerful figure in the Dublin Chamber of Commerce, he was highly influential in supporting the establishment of a national electrification scheme and in several municipal reform projects. In addition to its wholesale business, the firm has established many retail outlets in major towns and cities across the country.

EASTER RISING (or EASTER REBELLION)

Republican insurrection that began on Easter Monday, April 1916, in Dublin. The rising was organized by the Irish Republican Brotherhood (IRB), led by Patrick ⇨Pearse, along with sections of the ⇨Irish Volunteers and James ⇨Connolly's socialist Irish Citizen Army. Although a military failure, it played a central role in shifting nationalist opinion from allegiance to the constitutional Irish Parliamentary Party (IPP) to separatist republicanism.

leaders and ideology

Traditionally depicted by nationalist historiography as the inevitable culmination of centuries of separatist struggle against Britain, the Easter Rising was organized by a radical minority of advanced nationalists with little support from the general public who seemed prepared to await for the enactment of home rule secured by John Redmond, leader of the IPP, in 1914. It was organized by a number of conspirators within the military council of the IRB, including Pearse and Seán MacDiarmada (1884–1916), with poets such as Thomas ⇨MacDonagh and Joseph ⇨Plunkett also playing a prominent role. The socialist leader of the Irish Citizen Army, James Connolly, was co-opted to the military council shortly before the rising.

The 1916 myth, like malaria, is in my bloodstream.

DERVLA MURPHY Travel writer *A Place Apart* (1978).

The ideology of the rebels remains contested but was closely associated with the ideas of Patrick Pearse, who idealized the concepts of blood sacrifice and spiritual resurrection shared by many European romantic nationalists during World War I. However, Connolly was a Marxist who hoped that revolution in Ireland might spread throughout Europe and one of the rising's most influential legacies, the 1916 Proclamation of the Republic (read from the steps of the Post Office at the start of the action), combined physical force nationalism with socially progressive ideology.

series of misfortunes

The military plans for the rising remain vague but it was beset by misfortune from the start. A gunboat carrying the German-supplied weapons necessary for success was scuttled after its interception by the

British navy. John (Eoin) ⇨MacNeill, the leader of the Irish Volunteers, which the military council relied on to provide the soldiers for the rising, countermanded Pearse's orders for mobilization on Easter Sunday, 23 April. The military council pressed ahead, nonetheless, and around 1,600 rebels turned out to fight for the 'provisional government' of the 'Irish Republic' on Easter Monday. The rebels occupied a number of prominent buildings forming a ring around central Dublin and awaited the British army's assault. Little attempt had been made to mobilize separatists outside Dublin or take the offensive, suggesting that the rebellion was a bloody protest aimed at reviving sympathy for separatist objectives rather than a genuine attempt to overthrow British rule.

losses and casualties

The British forces, under Gen Sir John Maxwell, shelled the rebel positions, destroying much of central Dublin and killing numerous civilians in the process. Both sides suffered major losses: 250 civilians, 64 rebels, and 132 members of the crown forces were killed, and around 2,600 were injured. Pearse and Connolly were among the 15 rebel leaders subsequently executed in Kilmainham Jail. Others, including the future Taoiseach (prime minister) Éamon de Valera, were spared and given amnesty in June 1917: de Valera because he was born in the US, MacNeill because he countermanded the mobilization order.

the legacy

The real importance of the Easter Rising lay in its legacy. The British authorities' draconian response, including widespread arrests, deportations, and the execution of 15 republican leaders created widespread sympathy for the rebels, radicalized many young nationalists, and proved a pivotal point in the subsequent eclipse of constitutional nationalists by Irish separatists.

ECONOMIC WAR

The economic dispute between the ⇨Irish Free State and the UK which began in 1932 following prime minister Éamon ⇨de Valera's retention of the annuities owed by tenant farmers who had received British loans in order to buy their land, in the late 19th century. The British government responded by imposing tariffs on Free State exports to the UK. The dispute was not fully resolved until 1938.

The retention of the £3 million per annum annuities, coupled with the abolition of the oath of fidelity to the British crown imposed on members of the Irish Free State Parliament, marked the beginning of de Valera's campaign to remould the ⇨Anglo-Irish Treaty (1921) in order to achieve greater sovereignty.

The economic war impoverished the most prosperous farming classes, many of whom responded by joining the semi-fascist ⇨Blueshirts in their violent campaign against the payment of rates to the Irish government. However, de Valera also derived political benefits from the dispute which emphasized Fianna Fáil's willingness to adopt à confrontational yet constitutional stance against Britain. The erection of mutual trade restrictions also complemented Fianna Fáil's policy of economic protectionism, while those worst hit by the collapse of the cattle export trade were predominantly Fine Gael supporters. Britain dropped its claim for annuities in return for a final settlement of £10 million in the Anglo-Irish Agreement of 1938.

ECUMENICAL MOVEMENT

Movement for reunification of the various branches of the Christian church in Ireland; it includes any group attempting to foster greater cooperation among Irish Christians.

The Presbyterian and Methodist churches formed a joint committee in 1906 and were joined by the Church of Ireland and the Quakers in 1911. In 1923 the United Council of Churches and Religious Communions in Ireland was formed, which became the Irish Council of Churches in 1966. The Irish Inter-Church Meeting, established in 1973, is headed by the leaders of the Roman Catholic, Church of Ireland, Methodist, and Presbyterian churches. Plans are being made for the gradual amalgamation of these two organizations into a Conference of Churches in Ireland.

Ecumenical work also takes place in many organizations that bring together Christians from different denominations. Among the main examples are the Corrymeela Community (founded in 1964), the Irish School of Ecumenics (1970), the Rostrevor Renewal Centre (1974), and the Peace People (1976).

EDENDERRY

Market town in County Offaly, on the Grand Canal near the border of counties Offaly and Kildare; population (1996) 3,600. It has a vehicle-repair factory and is the centre of a large peat production area.

The ruins of Blundell's Castle are nearby and 2 km/1.2 mi to the west are the remains of Monasteroris Franciscan friary, founded in the 14th century by Johude Bermingham. There is a Norman motte 6 km/4 mi east of Edenderry and the remains of a 14th-century castle occupied by the Berminghams and later in the 16th century by the Cowleys, ancestors of the Duke of Wellington.

EDGEWORTH, HENRY ESSEX (ABBÉ EDGEWORTH) (1745–1807)

Priest who became confessor and chaplain to the French Bourbon dynasty during the French Revolution. He was present at the execution of Louis XVI in 1793.

Born in Edgeworthstown (now Mostrim), County Longford, where his father was rector, Edgeworth converted to Catholicism in 1748. He went to Toulouse in France, was ordained a priest, and took the surname De Firmont. He was appointed confessor to the princess Elizabeth in 1791, and in 1793 to her brother, Louis XVI. In 1796 he went to England, and was made chaplain to the exiled Louis XVIII.

EDGEWORTH, MARIA (1767–1849)

Novelist, born in Black Bourton, near Oxford, England, daughter of the author Richard Lovell ⇨Edgeworth. Much of Edgeworth's life was spent on her father's Irish estate at Edgeworthstown (now Mostrim), County Longford. Her first novel, *Castle Rackrent* (1800), dealt with Anglo-Irish country society as seen through the eyes of Thady Quirk, a faithful retainer, and was the first regional novel in English. Other novels about Ireland include *The Absentee* (1812) and *Ormond* (1817), both inculcating responsible attitudes in Anglo-Irish landlords. She also wrote four novels about contemporary English society, including *Belinda* (1801) and *Leonora* (1806).

Her work was marked by ingenuity, inventiveness, humour, and acute description of character. As a writer of socially concerned and historical novels, Edgeworth inspired the Scottish novelist Walter Scott, and they exchanged visits in Ireland and Scotland.

Edgeworth shared her father's progressive educational ideas and was a fervent proponent of women's education. She collaborated with a number of his literary projects, including *Practical Education* (1798) and 'Essay on Irish Bulls' (1802), a work repudiating the stereotypical view of Irishmen as foolish speakers. She went on to write two series of *Tales of Fashionable Life* (1809 and 1812), and completed her father's

Our Irish blunders are never blunders of the heart.

MARIA EDGEWORTH *Essay on Irish Bulls* (1802).

❧

Memoirs in 1829. Other works include several books for or about children, including *Moral Tales* (1801), *Popular Tales* (1804), *Frank* (1822), and *Harry and Lucy* (1825).

EDGEWORTH, RICHARD LOVELL (1744–1817)

Anglo-Irish writer, educationalist, and inventor. Edgeworth was born in Bath and studied at Trinity College, Dublin, and Corpus Christi College, Oxford. He educated his 22 children in the spirit of the philosopher Jean-Jacques Rousseau's teaching, and wrote on *Practical Education* (1798) in collaboration with his daughter Maria ⇨Edgeworth, the novelist. In Ireland he was centrally concerned with improvements to his estate at Edgeworthstown (now Mostrim), County Longford, as a model to other Anglo-Irish landlords.

Remarkable for his abilities in mechanical invention, he produced an early form of visual telegraphy, the velocipede, the perambulator land-measuring wheel, and various forms of carriage, including a phaeton and a wind-propelled version. He returned to Edgeworthston from England in 1782, following Ireland's legislative independence, and was a member of the last Irish parliament before the Union. He served as aide de camp to the Lord Charlemont, commander-in-chief of the Irish Volunteers in 1783. As member of parliament for Johnston he voted against the Act of Union on account of the corrupt means used to secure its passage, although he accepted it in principle.

Edgeworth became friendly with progressive thinkers such as the physican and naturalist Erasmus Darwin and the writer Thomas Day while studying at university. With Day he embarked on an eccentric and futile educational experiment involving the tuition of two orphan girls, one of whom Day intended to make his wife. His influence on his daughter Maria was profound and he often wrote or altered passages of her novels, adding a pro-Union epilogue to *Castle Rackrent* (1800), which was otherwise composed in his absence. His *Memoirs* (1829) were completed by her.

EDUCATION

Ireland has a long tradition of placing a high value on liberal schooling; this has contributed, in part, to Ireland's wealth of language and literature. Historically the education system has developed as a partnership between church and state, but parental responsibility is enshrined in the 1937 Constitution.

early schools

In Gaelic Ireland there were two groups of learned scholars: the fili or filidh (poets), and the guardians of brehon law, who were lawyers and judges. They were educated in the bardic schools that were an important feature of Gaelic culture. The coming of Christianity in the 5th century brought about the establishment of monastic schools, and these were strengthened following the invasion of the Anglo-Normans in the 12th century, many of whom supported foundations made by the new religious orders from Europe.

post-Reformation provision

The closure of the monastic schools during the Tudor ⇨Reformation, and the religious struggles between Catholic and Protestant forces in the 16th and 17th centuries, greatly reduced access to education for the Catholic majority. Educational initiative now passed to the newly established Anglican Church of Ireland (see ⇨Protestantism), and in 1592 the Protestant university of ⇨Trinity College, Dublin (TCD), was founded to propagate the reformed faith and English culture. During the plantation of Ulster in the early 17th century, royal schools were established by James I for the sons of Protestant settlers.

Under the penal laws of the 18th century the Catholic church was a proscribed agency of education. A clandestine system of popular schooling, known as 'hedge schools', developed whereby masters travelled around teaching in the open fields for safety. Young Catholic men were despatched to the Irish colleges and other Catholic institutions in Europe for tuition. Meanwhile, the Church of Ireland made a major effort to convert the Catholic population and Protestant charity schools and evangelical education societies were established.

nondenominational and interdenominational elementary education

By 1800 the penal laws had been repealed and there was a determined effort to provide a system of popular schooling without fear of proselytism. One of the pioneers of nondenominational education was the Kildare Place Society, founded in 1811 to support elementary schooling for the poor. The society received a government grant but its religious instruction rule of reading the Bible 'without note or comment' proved unacceptable to the Catholic church. In 1831 the state-aided elementary national schools system was established on the principle of 'combined secular and separate religious education', whereby Catholic and Protestant pupils would be educated together for 'literary' education. However, concessions won by the churches remoulded the schools, and by 1870 it was recognized that most national schools had become denominational in practice. Nondenominational model schools for teacher training, established by the Board of Commissioners for National Education from 1834, were also condemned by the Catholic church, and in 1866 Catholics were forbidden to attend.

secondary and further education

Secondary education was advanced by the Intermediate Education Act (1878), which introduced state grants for secondary schools through a system of payments by results, based on the performance of pupils in public school examinations. In 1845 Queen's Colleges were established in Belfast, Cork, and Galway, but were condemned as 'godless' by the Catholic church. The Catholic University was founded in 1854 but failed to gain a charter. Under the Irish Universities' Act (1908), the ⇨National University of Ireland (NUI), a federation of Catholic colleges, and Queen's University, Belfast were founded; Trinity College, Dublin was left unchanged.

education post-partition

In 1924 the government of the newly formed Irish Free State set up a Department of Education, and introduced a policy of compulsory Irish to the school curriculum; in Northern Ireland a Ministry of Education was established with local education authorities. Free secondary education was introduced in 1947 in Northern Ireland and in 1967 in the Republic of Ireland. National Institutes of Higher Education, established by the Republic in Limerick (1970) and Dublin (1978), became universities in 1989, while the colleges of the NUI received university status in 1997. In Northern Ireland, the University of Ulster (1968), Ulster Polytechnic (1971), and Ulster College of Art merged to form the multi-campus University of Ulster in 1984.

EIRE

Name of southern Ireland as prescribed in the 1937 Constitution.

ELECTORAL SYSTEM: REPUBLIC OF IRELAND

Method by which members of the Oireachtas (Irish legislature), comprising the ⇨Seanad Éireann (senate) and ⇨Dáil Éireann (lower house), are elected. The system is one of proportional representation (PR) through the single transferable vote (STV) or PR–STV.

Candidates for the Dáil are listed on the ballot paper alphabetically by surname with the name of their party, if any. Voters mark their ballot '1' to their first choice, '2' to their second, and so on. In this way, voters inform the returning officer where to 'transfer' their vote along if a higher preference candidate has reached the quota or been eliminated. The quota is calculated by counting the number of valid papers in a constituency, dividing this by the number of seats available in the constituency plus 1, and then adding 1 to the result. In a 4-seat constituency with 40,000 voters that is:

40,000 divided by 5 (4 seats plus 1) equals 8,000, add 1 giving a quota of 8,001.

On reaching a quota, a candidate's surplus votes are transferred to the second placed candidate on the ballot. If no candidate has reached a quota the least placed candidate is eliminated and his or her votes are distributed to the other candidates according to the next stated preference. This continues until the designated number of seats are filled or, if two candidates remain and only one seat is to be filled, the candidate with the higher number of votes is elected. Although this system allows a tendency towards the over-representation of larger parties, it enables small parties and independents to win seats. 166 TDs (Teachta Dala; member of parliament) are elected to the Dáil from 41 constituencies, each with three to five seats. 43 senators are elected to the Seanad from five vocational panels: agriculture, labour, language and culture, industry and commerce, and public administration; see ⇨Seanad Éireann.

EMAIN MACHA (or EAMHAIN MACHA)

('Macha's twins')

Gaelic name for the prehistoric earthwork of ⇨Navan Fort in County Armagh, 4 km/2.5 mi west of Armagh.

EMIGRATION

The large-scale departure of native Irish to settle in another country, particularly during the 19th and early 20th centuries.

They say there's bread and work for all, / And the sun shines always there: / But I'll not forget old Ireland, / were it fifty times as fair.

HELEN SELINA BLACKWOOD, LADY DUFFERIN Poet 'Lament of the Irish Emigrant' quoted in *The Oxford Book of English Verse 1250–1900*, edited by Arthur Quiller-Couch.

The Irish have been emigrating since the pre-Christian era. Although significant numbers left from Ulster and Munster to British colonies in North America during the 17th and 18th centuries, and others throughout the island left and settled on the European continent, mass emigration only developed after the Irish risings of the late 18th century and the Napoleonic Wars. By 1815, with a fall in agricultural prices and a rapidly rising ⇨population, many families were unable to obtain possession of a farm or gain a living from the land, and sought new prospects elsewhere. The Great Famine (historically dated 1845–49, but now believed to have lasted until 1852) accelerated the movement, with estimates of 1 million people emigrating 1845–51.

I brought up my children to read and write, and there never were children with cleverer heads for their books; but there was no place for them in Ireland, and they have all gone to America but one, and soon he too will be gone.

PEIG SAYERS Author *The Western Island* (1944).

The most common destination of emigrants has varied from Canada before the Great Famine; North America, Australia, and South Africa after the famine until World War I; and Great Britain thereafter. Unusually, an equal proportion of men and women

THE IRISH DIASPORA AND ITS FAR-REACHING CULTURAL IMPACT

by Janet Nolan

In the past two centuries, well over eight million Irish left their homeland to settle throughout the English-speaking world and beyond. Large-scale emigration from Ireland began in the second half of the 18th century when economic competition from industrializing Britain drove northern farmer and weaver families from their native Ulster. Beginning in the 1820s, and intensifying during the Great Famine (historically dated 1845–49, though recently considered as lasting until 1852), agricultural labourer families from Leinster in the east and Munster in the south joined the emigrant stream, pushed off the land by the end of potato subsistence. By 1880 economic restructuring reached isolated Connaught in the west, and the typical emigrant was now an unemployed and unmarried young person, often female, from the south or the west, seeking paid work and a mate.

destinations

Most of those leaving Ireland went to Great Britain or North America, although significant numbers journeyed elsewhere, even to the most remote corners of the globe. At all times, however, the USA was the most popular destination of all. Even before the potato famine, when passage was cheaper to Canada than to the USA, thrifty emigrants who sailed to those northern shores walked south across the border before settling down. The most destitute, however, remained in England, either too sick or too poor to buy a ticket for the voyage west. Transat-lantic crossings became safer and cheaper after the middle of the century, and more and more Irish headed directly for US ports. This pattern changed only after 1920 when US immigration restriction ended open access.

Henceforward, Irish emigrants once again chose Great Britain and the Commonwealth, especially Canada, Australia, and New Zealand, as destinations. Significant numbers also reached South Africa and many travelled even further afield as soldiers or missionaries.

Irish America

The Irish in the USA settled in northeastern cities like Boston, New York, Philadelphia, and Chicago. Irish communities also flourished in Charleston and New Orleans, while uncounted numbers of Ulster Irish settled in the Appalachian hinterlands of these southern cities. Eventually, the Irish fanned out across the entire USA, digging the canals and laying the railroad tracks that allowed Americans to extend their sway across the continent. They joined the cavalry, protecting the expanding nation's frontier as it marched west. They helped build San Francisco, Butte, San Antonio, and other cities.

Almost from the beginning of their history in the newly independent USA, the Irish were prominent in national affairs. In 1828 Andrew Jackson (1767–1845), the son of Ulster immigrants, was the first Irish American to win election to the presidency. New Yorker Al (Alfred) Smith (1873–1944) was the first Irish Catholic elected to that

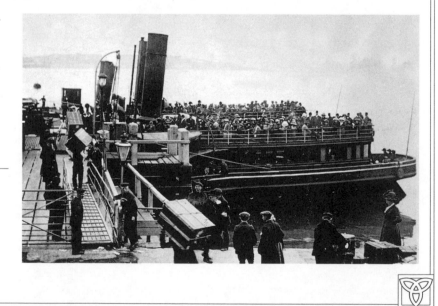

A packed tender prepares to take passengers out to a steam ship, to carry them far away from Ireland. Steam crossings regularly left Cobh, County Cork, shown here (formerly Queenstown), between 1845 and 1945. After this, air transport became cheaper and sailings dwindled.

state's governorship and in 1928, a hundred years after Jackson's election, Smith was the first Irish Catholic to run for president. The first Irish Catholic to actually win a presidential election, however, was John F Kennedy (1917–1963), who won the office only in 1960. Irish Americans, both Catholic and Protestant, were even more successful in local politics, especially in big cities. Mayor and governor James Michael Curley of Boston (1874–1958) and Mayor Richard J Daly of Chicago (1902–1976), for example, were beneficiaries of the urban political machines run by the Irish throughout the country. The Irish in America also achieved distinction in fields outside politics.

Automobile manufacturer Henry Ford (1863–1947), the son of immigrants from Cork, revolutionized how the world travelled. Prelates such as the Ulster-born archbishop of New York John Hughes (1797–1864) shaped the American Catholic church and oversaw the construction of New York's landmark St Patrick's Cathedral on Fifth Avenue.

women making their mark

Women were as important as men in fostering Irish-American mobility. Although many Irish women in America took entry level jobs in domestic service and factory work, others opened shops and became successful entrepreneurs in their adopted neighbourhoods. Irish nuns like Kilkenny-native Mother Theresa Comerford (1821–1881) founded schools, hospitals, and other pioneering social welfare institutions long before the government provided such services to its citizens. By the mid-1850s lay women like County Meath's Kate Kennedy (1827–1890) were teaching in San Francisco's public schools, setting a precedent for the thousands of other daughters of Irish America. By the end of the century, Irish-American women formed the single largest ethnic group teaching in the public schools of Boston, New York, Chicago, San Francisco, and Providence. Irish-American women were also pioneers in the American labour union movement. Margaret Haley of Chicago (1861–1939) helped found the Chicago Teachers' Federation, the nation's first teachers' union. Cork-native Mary Harris (Mother) Jones (1830–1930) led labour strikes throughout the country and fought for child labour laws.

cultural and sporting celebrity

The Irish also shaped American entertainment, and early in the 19th century minstrel shows introduced US audiences to Irish dancing, music, and drama. In the early 20th century, Irish-American song and dance men such as George M Cohan (1878–1942) produced widely popular musicals with strong Irish themes on the Vaudeville and Broadway stages. Irish America also influenced Hollywood. John Ford (1894–1973), the son of immigrants from Galway, directed some of his era's most memorable films, many with Irish subjects, and Irish-Americans such as animator Walt Disney (1901–66) and the singer Bing Crosby (1903–73) left indelible green imprints on popular entertainment throughout the world. Boxer John L Sullivan (1858–1918), baseball owner and manager Connie Mack of the Philadelphia Phillies (1862–1956), and the Fighting Irish of Notre Dame provided an equally distinctive Irish presence in American sports. Immigrant son Finley Peter Dunne's (1867–1936) 'Mr Dooley' newspaper columns recorded the voices of the working-class Irish in late-19th century Chicago. The careers of Nobel prize-winning playwright Eugene O'Neill (1888–1953), novelists F Scott Fitzgerald (1896–1940) and John O'Hara (1905–1970), artist Georgia O'Keeffe (1888–1986), and Supreme Court judge Sandra Day O'Connor (1930–   ) further attest to the importance of the diaspora to US arts and law.

exile and liberation

Irish elsewhere in the world also demonstrated the talents of the diaspora. Among the first Irish to reach Australia, for example, was political prisoner and Fenian, Thomas Francis Meagher (1823–1867), transported to Tasmania following the failed uprising of 1848. Meagher subsequently escaped his captors and fled to the USA where he rose to the rank of general during the American Civil War. In 1865 Meagher was appointed governor of the Montana Territory, becoming one of the many Irish leaders along the American frontier. Monaghan-native Charles Gavan Duffy (1816–1903) is another example of Australian Irish success. Expelled from Ireland after the failure of the Young Ireland rebellion in 1848, Duffy arrived in Australia in 1852. Less than twenty years later, in 1871, he was the colony's prime minister.

around the globe

Today, the small island of Ireland has a population of about 4 million, yet over 40 million Americans claim Irish descent and the Irish are the second largest ethnic group in Australia and Great Britain. Emigration remains a rite of passage for large numbers of Irish youth, and reliable estimates set the number of Irish around the world at 70 million.

The way with Ireland is that no sooner do you get away from her than the golden mists begin to close about her, and she lies, an Island of the Blest, something enchanted in our dreams.

KATHARINE TYNAN Writer *The Middle Years* (1917).

∽

left during this period, making it possible for the Irish-born to marry within their own ethnic group throughout the world. Although it has been estimated that between 1801 and 1921 at least 8 million people left Ireland, the tide of emigration has slowed in recent times, with many emigrés returning in light of better economic prosperity in Ireland. See feature essay on the Irish diaspora, page 126.

EMMET, ROBERT (1778–1803)

Nationalist leader, born in Dublin city and educated at Trinity College, Dublin, where he gained reknown as a brilliant speaker. Active in the radical ⇨United Irishmen organization, Emmet came to prominence in the revolutionary movement after the Irish Rebellion of 1798 and appealed for French aid. In 1803 he led an unsuccessful revolt in Dublin against British rule and was captured, tried, and hanged. His youth and courage made him an Irish hero.

Let my character and motives rest in obscurity and peace, till other times and other men can do them justice.

ROBERT EMMET Speech on his conviction for treason, September 1803.

∽

Emmet was expelled from Trinity College for his United Irish activities in 1798. He went to Paris in 1800 to seek French support for another rising, interviewing both Napoleon and his foreign minister Talleyrand, but returned to Dublin empty-handed in 1802. The following year Emmet began to organize a new rebellion. He planned to capture Dublin Castle with a surprise attack, but discovery, through an accidental explosion in his powder store, thwarted his plans and led to a premature rising on 23 July 1803.

Several people, including the lord chief justice Lord Kilwarden, were killed when Emmet's men took over Thomas Street. Although initially surprised, the authorities soon quashed the rising and Emmet, like Thomas ⇨Russell who had tried to raise the north, was executed. His speech from the dock, in which he said his epitaph would never be written till Ireland was free, led to his portrayal as a martyr by romantic nationalists of the later 19th century.

EMO COURT

Country house at Emo, County Laois, with a dome and portico designed by James ⇨Gandon for the 1st Earl of Portarlington about 1790. The house was not finished when the Earl was killed in the ⇨Rebellion of 1798. Work continued in the 1830s, when the architect was Lewis Vulliamy. The house is known for its Coade-stone capitals and the great rotunda with its copper dome, which was finished about 1860. It was sympathetically restored in the late 20th century and is lavishly furnished.

EMIGRATION *For millions of Irish emigrants, recalled in this monument at Cobh, the port was their last point of contact with Ireland, before they set sail. North America, Australia, and South Africa were popular destinations, though more Irish went to Great Britain after World War I.*

ENNIS

County town of County ⇨Clare, on the River Fergus, 32 km/20 mi northwest of Limerick; population (1996) 15,300. There are distilleries, flour mills, and furniture manufacturing. In the town are a Roman Catholic cathedral and college, and a Franciscan friary, ⇨Ennis Friary, founded about 1241. Shannon international airport is 24 km/15 mi to the south of Ennis.

Éamon ⇨de Valera, former Taoiseach (prime minister) and president of the Republic of Ireland, represented County Clare 1917–59; there is a statue of him outside Ennis Courthouse. About 2 km/1 mi south of Ennis are the ruins of the Augustinian Clare Abbey (founded in 1195), and 5 km/3 mi south are the remains of Killone Abbey (founded in 1190); both ecclesiastical sites were founded by Donal O'Brien, King of Munster.

ENNISCORTHY

Market town in County Wexford; population (1996) 3,900. It is situated on the River Slaney, 23 km/14 mi northwest of Wexford town, and across the river from Vinegar Hill, the site of the main rebel camp during the Rebellion of 1798 against the British. Below Enniscorthy the river is navigable for barges. Enniscorthy Castle dates from 1586; it is a square keep erected on the site of a 13th-century castle. It was used as a prison after the Rebellion of 1798, and is now a museum.

ENNIS FRIARY

Franciscan friary at Ennis, County Clare. Traditionally founded about 1241 by Donough Cairbreach O'Brien, the earliest of the surviving buildings probably date from the end of the 13th century and were built by Torlough O'Brien. The abbey underwent rebuilding several times and additions were made as late as the 15th century, notably the tower, to which pinnacles were added in the 19th century. It is an excellent example of early Irish Franciscan architecture and is especially noted for its many sculptured tombs and wall carvings.

ENNISKILLEN

County town of ⇨Fermanagh, between Upper and Lower Lough Erne, 184 km/114 mi from Dublin and 141 km/88 mi from Belfast; population (1991) 11,400. It is a market town and shopping centre with some light industry (engineering, food processing); it

has been designated for further industrial growth. An IRA bomb exploded here at a Remembrance Day service in November 1987, causing many casualties.

The lands of Enniskillen were held by the Maguires; under James I the lands were granted to William Cole and settled by the English. It was one of the principal strongholds of the plantation during the late 17th century. Enniskillen was granted its first charter in the 17th century, and was an important strategic centre in the time of William III. It gave its name to two regiments of the British Army: the 27th Foot (known as the Royal Inniskilling Fusiliers), and the Royal Inniskilling Dragoons. Captain Oates, a member of Scott's expedition to the South Pole in 1912, served with the 6th Inniskilling Dragoons; a commemorative plaque is located in the town hall here.

Portora Royal School (1618) is by the shore of Lough Erne; among its pupils were Reverend H F Lyte, Oscar ⇨Wilde, and Samuel ⇨Beckett. ⇨Enniskillen Castle houses both the county museum and a military museum.

ENNISKILLEN CASTLE

Castle on the River Erne at Enniskillen, County Fermanagh. Until the 18th century it stood on a small island separated from the town by a drawbridge. Little now remains of the 15th century castle of the Maguires except the lower portion of the keep. The

ENNISKILLEN CASTLE *The town of Enniskillen, which stands on an island in a narrow meander of the River Erne, was given to Sir William Cole, builder of the present-day castle, after the Tyrone rebellion. The castle keep houses the museum of the Royal Inniskilling Fusiliers.*

present castle dates from the early 17th century when it was probably built by William Cole who was fortifying the town. It is best known for its Water Gate which is thought to date from this period. The castle now houses the Fermanagh County Museum.

ENNIS, SEAMUS (1919–1982)

Traditional musician and musicologist, born in Jamestown, Finglas, County Dublin. A virtuoso uileann piper, Ennis collected and recorded a large body of Irish traditional music, songs, and stories at a time when interest in the art was fading away. Along with the broadcaster Ciaran Mac Mathuna (1925–) he was responsible for the preservation of a large archive of material which, along with his own embodiment of traditional styles of playing and singing exercised an immense influence over the revival of Irish traditional music from the late 1960s.

ENYA (EITHNE NÍ BHRAONÁIN) (1961–)

Singer, musician, and composer, born in Gweedore, County Donegal. With other members of her family she performed in the internationally known Irish band Clannad 1980–82, recording the albums *Crann Ull* (1980) and *Fuaim* (1982). As a solo artist her popularity stems from the music she composed for the BBC television series *The Celts* (1987) and her CD *Watermark* (1988). Her style of performance is influenced by that of Clannad who, out of a traditional/folk music background developed 'Celtic' or 'New Age' music. Other recordings include *LA Story* (1991), *Shepherd Moons* (1991), and *Memory of Trees* (1995).

ENYA *Since first performing with her family in the folk group, Clannad, Enya has built a highly successful solo career as a singer and composer, writing for film and TV as well as producing her own albums.*

*F*lying back home from Dublin, over the mountains before the plane comes down, I realise that the landscape is always with me, in my head, in my music.

ENYA Describing her home in Donegal in *The Times*, 6 November 1997.

ERIN

Poetic name for Ireland, derived from the dative case Érinn of the Gaelic name Ériu, possibly derived from Sanskrit 'western'.

*D*ear Erin, how sweetly thy green bosom rises!/ An emerald set in the ring of the sea, / Each blade of thy meadows my faithful heart prizes, / thou queen of the West! the world's cushla ma chree.

JOHN PHILPOT CURRAN Orator 'Cushla ma Chree'.

ERIUGENA, JOHN SCOTTUS or JOHANNES SCOTUS ERIGENA (*c.* 810–*c.* 877)

Theologian, philosopher, translator, and poet, whose views were condemned as heretical by the Catholic church. From about 845 he was employed at the court of the French king Charles (II) the Bald (823–827) near Laon, as head of the palace school. His mystical theology was based on that of Dionysius the Areopagite (living around AD 500), whose works he translated from Greek into Latin. His attacks on the Eucharist, and his treatise *De Predestinatione/On Predestination* (851), which defended the existence of free will and denied the reality of evil, were condemned at church councils in 849 and 857, as was the pantheism (a view that God is in everything) of his *De Divisione Naturae/On the Division of Nature*; the latter was placed on the Vatican's index of prohibited books in 1685.

The surname Eriugena, meaning 'born in Ireland', first appears in the 10th century, but most scholars agree that he was Irish.

ERNE, LOUGH

Lake in County Fermanagh, scattered with numerous wooded islets, comprising Upper Lough Erne to the south and Lower Lough Erne to the north. Extending for 80 km/50 mi, the two sections are linked by the River Erne as it flows towards Donegal Bay. Tourism is a major industry. The historic town of ⇨Enniskillen lies between the upper and lower loughs, and Belleek, on the western tip of Lower Lough Erne, specializes in delicate woven lustreware. The lough formed part of an ancient river highway from the coast to Leitrim, and was on a pilgrims' trail to Station Island, Lough Derg, reputed scene of St Patrick's vision of purgatory. Many of its islands contain Celtic and early Christian archaeological sites, and relics such as the intriguing 6th-century figures of ⇨White Island. Other attractions include nature reserves, boating, birdwatching, and abundant coarse and game fishing.

The main historic sites are located in and around Lower Lough Erne, including Devenish Island, site of a ruined 6th-century monastery and perfectly preserved 12th-century round tower; Boa Island, with two pagan Janus figures; and White Island. Other features include ⇨Enniskillen Castle; the 17th-century Plantation castles of Tully, Monea, and Caldwell; and the Drumskinny Bronze Age stone circle and alignment.

ERVINE, ST JOHN (GREER) (1883–1971)

Playwright, novelist, and theatre critic. Ervine was born in Belfast, but in 1900 moved to London, where he embarked on his writing career. From 1915 to 1916 he was manager of the Abbey Theatre, Dublin, where his first plays, *Mixed Marriage* (1911) and *Jane Clegg* (1914) were produced. Ervine's dramas were realistic in their setting, with pronounced local colour. His later plays include *Anthony and Anna* (1926), *The First Mrs Fraser* (1929), and *Robert's Wife* (1937).

Ervine fell out with the Abbey Theatre company over his lack of sympathy with the republican ideals of the Easter Rising in 1916, and joined the Dublin Fusiliers to serve in World War I. Pensioned off after losing a leg in battle, he settled in Devon and went on to gain a high reputation as a drama critic. He worked for the British newspapers *The Observer* and *The Morning Post*, and, from 1932 onwards, for the BBC. Aside from his dramas, his writings include seven novels and a number of biographies, among the subjects of which were George Bernard Shaw and Oscar Wilde.

ESSEX, ROBERT DEVEREUX (2nd Earl of Essex) (1567–1601)

English nobleman and soldier. Having risen to prominence in the war against Spain, Essex became a favourite of Elizabeth I in the early 1590s. He was appointed lord lieutenant of Ireland in 1599, and despatched with a massive army to crush the spreading Irish rebellion that had been launched by the Ulster chiefs Hugh ⇨O'Neill, 2nd Earl of Tyrone, and 'Red Hugh' ⇨O'Donnell, Lord of Tirconnell, in 1593.

However, Essex's failure to engage with the enemy, along with his secret negotiations and unauthorized truce with Hugh O'Neill, aroused suspicion at court and the explicit displeasure of the queen. His departure without permission from his post completed his disgrace, and he was forbidden to return to court. When he marched into the City of London at the head of a body of supporters, he was arrested and subsequently beheaded for treason in 1601.

ESSEX, WALTER DEVEREUX (1st Earl of Essex) (c. 1541–1576)

English nobleman and soldier. He was created Earl of Essex in 1572 after helping to suppress a rebellion against the crown in the north of England. A highly successful sheep breeder, he sought to develop his fortune by investment in his 'enterprise of Ulster' 1572–75, a poorly planned plantation scheme which aimed to recapture a portion of the Anglo-Norman earldom of Ulster, east of the River Bann.

Essex's attempts to subdue and colonize the region, founded on profound misconceptions of the state of affairs there, failed totally and alienated all parties in the province with its violence. Bankrupt, he withdrew from the scheme. After being recalled by Elizabeth I in 1575, he was appointed president of Ulster in 1576, but died in Dublin (by poisoning) before he took office.

EUCHARISTIC CONGRESS

Large-scale public celebration of Irish Catholicism held triennially in different cities in the early years of the Irish Free State. The first one in Ireland (and 31st of a series of international Catholic congresses) took

TRANSFORMED INTO A MODEL ECONOMY – THE EMERGENCE OF IRELAND AS THE CELTIC TIGER

by Brigid Laffan

The Republic of Ireland joined the European Union (EU) in 1973, the culmination of a process begun in the late 1950s that was designed to transform the Irish economy into an open and competitive one. Membership of the EU (originally established as the European Economic Community under the Treaty of Rome in 1957) and the embracing of Europe was part of a national project of modernization, not only of the economy but also of Irish society – the accompanying urbanization, industrialization, and secularization fostering deep social change.

Terry Eagleton, in his sardonic account of contemporary Ireland, *Eagleton* (1999), suggested that Ireland was 'a nation caught on the hop between the traditional and the modern, between the Bishop of Rome and the Treaty of Rome.' Since 1973 Ireland has moved decisively towards the Treaty of Rome.

stagnation and instability

The process of socio-economic adjustment to EU membership was long and tortuous. When Ireland joined it was the poorest member state, with average per capita incomes about 62% of the EU average. Once in the EU, Irish agriculture benefited from the price support system of the Common Agricultural Policy (CAP), which guaranteed a minimum price for part of a farmer's production, imposed levies on cheaper imports, and intervened to buy produce at a predetermined level. However, many jobs were lost in traditional industry, and the oil crises of the mid and late 1970s undermined the search for prosperity. In the 1980s the performance of the Irish economy was the worst of the EU member states on all standard indicators, in particular inflation and unemployment.

Between 1980 and 1985 annual Irish growth rates failed to reach 1%. Economic turbulence was accompanied by political instability with three elections 1981–82. Emigration, which had stalled in the 1970s, reappeared and there was a widespread perception of failure in Irish society, a sense that the promise of independence was not fulfilled.

growth and transformation

The impact of the failure of the 1980s on the Irish elite was profound, and led to a gradual consensus of opinion as to what was needed to boost the Irish economy.

The key to success was the adoption of domestic economic policies that encouraged Ireland's integration into a highly competitive single European market. In the last decade of the 20th century Ireland began to boom, experiencing unprecedented levels of growth, surplus budgets, and high consumption. Average annual growth rates between 1995 and 2000 were over 6%, with sizeable budget surpluses in 1998 and 1999. Average per capita incomes began to converge with those of the richer EU states. In stark contrast to the 1980s, Ireland became one

Computer manufacture and assembly are an area of business that has sprung up in Ireland, partly as a result of EU membership.

of the best performing EU economies in the 1990s. This growth was the outcome of a combination of strategic policies dating from the 1950s and 1960s, notably economic liberation, investment in education (the O'Malley reforms abolished fees for secondary education), and the strategic plans of the Industrial Development Authority to attract mobile foreign investment.

Transformed from the 'sick economy' of Western Europe into a 'model economy', Ireland emerged as the Celtic Tiger.

single European market

The role of the European Union was central to the transformation of Ireland. The launch of the single market for member countries of the EU on 1 January 1993, established under the Single European Act of 1987, was viewed with deep anxiety in governmental and business circles in Ireland. There were doubts that Ireland would be able to compete in a progressively harsher economic climate, but this pessimism proved unfounded.

The single European market, which created an area without internal frontiers for the free movement of goods, persons, services, and capital, benefited Ireland for a number of different reasons. Ireland became a more attractive location for US investment; in 1994 7.4% of all US investment in the EU was destined for Ireland. Generous fiscal and financial incentives, combined with access to the large EU market, gave Ireland considerable advantages in attracting US capital. US investment, particularly in the electronic and pharmaceuticals sectors, generated significant new high-skilled jobs. Moreover, it enhanced managerial capacity by giving Irish management experience of a dynamic corporate culture. The increased integration of the EU market benefited a growing number of Irish multinationals.

Furthermore, the deregulatory element of the single market put pressure on state-owned monopolies in air transport and telecommunications. Cheaper airfares in and out of Ireland reduced costs to business and led to a boom in Irish tourism. Electricity and postal utilities were also targeted for future liberalization.

Non-state-owned services such as banking and insurance have also felt the winds of competition. Both the market access and the regulatory elements of the single European market programme proved beneficial.

EU funding

Ireland also benefited from very significant financial transfers from the EU budget in the form of CAP support and the 'structural funds' assigned to Europe's poorer regions and states. As part of the internal market process, these areas extracted a sidepayment from richer European members for economic development. Big increases in structural fund monies began in 1988 when Ireland was designated as an objective one region (having a per capita income at 75% or below, of the EU average). Ireland prepared two development programmes for EU funding, 1988–93 and 1994–99. The last development programme was a remarkable success story, the EU pledging IR£ 4.35 billion to Ireland for this period. In addition to transfers to agriculture, Ireland was a net beneficiary of the EU budget to the tune of 4.1% of its gross domestic product (GDP) in 1997.

Structural funds helped to improve Ireland's infrastructure and greatly improved the manner in which public sector investment was planned and executed. Roads, water treatment plants, employment measures, rural development, environmental improvements, and the restoration of heritage sites, all benefited from EU funding.

social partnership

Ireland's economic revival in the 1990s also owed much to the manner in which the Irish elite responded to the cultural and institutional failures of the 1980s. In 1986 the government, employers, farmers, and trade unions began to hammer out a shared strategy for development. This was translated into the Programme for National Recovery (PNR) 1987–90, and followed by three subsequent agreements: the Programme for Economic and Social Progress (PESP) 1990–93, the Programme for Competitiveness and Work (PCW), and Partnership 2000, 1997–2000. In essence, during the 1990s Ireland's economic development was underpinned by a shared agreement of how the economy should be run and how public goods should be distributed among different social groups. Agreement on wage levels in the public and private sectors was paramount. Moderate wage growth was the key to competitiveness and to bringing the budget deficits back under control. Although wage bargaining was a core feature of the programmes, they also embraced agreement on a wide range of social and economic policies. Social partnership was not a direct result of EU membership, but it emerged as the best approach for Ireland in a highly competitive market.

place in 1932, when Dublin was chosen as the host city to mark the 1,500th anniversary of St Patrick's mission to Ireland. In many ways this was a follow-up to the 1929 Emancipation Centenary Festival. Some 14,000 people attended a Blackrock College garden party, one million attended an open-air mass in Phoenix Park, and 500,000 attended benediction at O'Connell Bridge.

EUROPEAN UNION (EU)

Organization of 15 European countries to which both the Republic of Ireland and Northern Ireland (through the UK) acceded in 1973, and which is an increasingly important source of social and economic decision-making. EU law, through its treaties, supersedes the national law of member countries. The union has a number of institutions including a parliament, commission, council of ministers, and court. The Republic of Ireland elects 15 members to the European Parliament from four constituencies by the single transferable vote (STV; see ⇨electoral system: Republic of Ireland). Northern Ireland elects three members from one constituency also by STV. The European Commission initiates EU legislation and has one Irish member, currently David Byrne. The UK has two members, none of whom since 1973 has come from Northern Ireland.

The Council of Ministers of the European Union is the primary decision-making forum of the EU and comprises a representative from each government. Northern Ireland is represented through UK government ministers. Both jurisdictions are net beneficiaries of the EU, mainly through its regional, structural, and common agricultural policy funds. See the feature essay on the Celtic Tiger, page 132.

EUROVISION SONG CONTEST

European song contest, which also includes some Middle Eastern neighbours. The Irish have been very successful in the competition and especially in hosting it. Since the competition's inception in Switzerland in 1956, Ireland has claimed first prize in 1970, with Dana and 'All Kinds of Everything'; 1980, with Johnny Logan and 'What's Another Year?'; 1987, with Johnny Logan again and 'Hold Me Now'; 1992, with Linda Martin and 'Why Me?'; 1993, with Niamh Kavanagh and 'In Your Eyes'; 1994, with Paul Harrington and Carlie McGettigan and 'Rock and Roll Kids'; and 1996, with Eimear Quinn and 'The Voice' (written by Brendan Graham). Perhaps the most notable Eurovision hosted in Ireland was that of 1994 which saw the first appearance of the now internationally famous dance show, ⇨*Riverdance*, as the interval act.

Í am the voice in the wind and the pouring rain / I am the voice of your hunger and pain / I am the voice that always is calling you / I am the voice, I will remain.

BRENDAN GRAHAM Songwriter 'The Voice', the Irish entry and Eurovision Song Contest winner in 1996.

∼

FACTION FIGHTING

Term used to describe the organized skirmishes between rival groups in Ireland in the early part of the 19th century. The meetings usually took place in public areas such as fairgrounds, and firearms were rarely used. This sudden rash of public fighting has been attributed to the breakdown of law and order in the countryside, or increasing social tensions, but the real cause seems to have been the relaxation of previous forms of social control.

Many of the fights appear to have originated in local feuds and jealousies, with groups of people meeting to fight over real or imagined grievances. In many ways the conflicts were tribal rather than political or social, although one skirmish between rival groups the Caravats and Shanavests was attributed to class differences. Similarly, disputes in the city often had their roots in religious or, more often, geographical rivalries. The problem gradually disappeared after the creation of the Royal Irish Constabulary in the 1830s and the Great Famine.

FAGAN, JAMES BERNARD (1873–1933)

Dramatist, producer, and actor, born in Belfast. Fagan's most successful plays were *And So to Bed* (1926) with Samuel Pepys, the diarist, as the chief character, and *The Improper Duchess* (1931).

As an actor, Fagan joined the companies of Frank Benson and Herbert Beerbohm Tree in London, and founded the Oxford Playhouse with Tyrone Guthrie in 1923. He was the producer of the British premiere of Seán O'Casey's *Juno and the Paycock* in 1924.

Some early plays by Fagan include *The Rebels* (1899), *The Prayer of the Sword* (1904), *Under Which King* (1905), and *The Earth* (1909).

FAI

Abbreviation for ⇨Football Association of Ireland.

FAIRY (or Irish *aos sí*, 'fairy folk'; *daoine maithe*, 'good people'; *bunadh na gcnoc*, 'hill people')

In Celtic mythology, immortal and ever-youthful otherworld beings who once ruled Ireland as the ⇨Tuatha Dé Danann (people of the goddess ⇨Danu). In genuine Irish literature they mostly appear in full-size human shape, and live beneath old tumuli (burial mounds). Fairies often intermix with mortals, engaging warriors to fight in their battles, carrying off children and replacing them with a *siofra* (changeling), or affecting an impassioned mortal with the fairy 'touch'; they also have a benign aspect, granting health and the gift of music. Well-known individuals include the ⇨leprechaun with his secret store of gold, and the ⇨banshee, whose cries foretell a death in the family.

Fairy Tales and Traditions of the South of Ireland (1825) by Thomas Crofton ⇨Croker (1798–1857) is regarded as the first significant collection of Irish fairy folklore, and the poet W B ⇨Yeats made extensive studies of fairy myth.

FAMINE, THE GREAT

Disastrous famine (historically dated 1845–49, but now believed to have lasted until 1852) caused by the repeated failure of the potato crop. See feature essay on the famine, page 136 and also ⇨potato blight.

THE GREAT FAMINE AND ITS LEGACY OF POVERTY, EMIGRATION, AND DEATH

by Tom Kelley

Ireland's Great Famine, also known as the Great Hunger, is historically dated 1845–1851, although its effects lingered until 1852. A parasitic fungus, Phytophthora infestans, transmitted to Ireland from North America and continental Europe by diseased potatoes and through bird droppings imported as fertilizer, first infected the Irish potato crop in September 1845. The disease, also known as blight, caused the potato to rot in the ground, making it inedible. Recurrent infestations of the blight, which led to the failure of the potato crop in three seasons out of four, had a catastrophic effect upon the Irish peasantry who were largely dependent on potatoes for subsistence. They had little opportunity to diversify because of restricted rental holdings, large families with consequent hereditary subdivision of land, and conditions of tenure that included the extortions of land agents, rack rents (excessive and frequently increased rents), and an absence of compensation for improvements. Potato consumption in Ireland just prior to 1845 was enormous, with the average male consuming 6.5 kg/14 lbs daily. Pigs, an important source of cheap meat and income for Irish farmers, ate potatoes as a basic fodder and their number dramatically fell from 1,412,813 in 1841 to 565,629 in 1848.

treated as a temporary crisis

In November 1845, Robert Peel's Tory government reacted with a grant of £100,000 to purchase Indian corn (maize) from the United States. Peel, who served as a government official in Ireland during a previous famine, 1817–1819, resolved to treat the 1845 calamity as a temporary crisis. For the most part his measures were successful in preventing many deaths. However, the ensuing Liberal administration of John Russell in 1846 espoused laissez-faire policies, motivated by beliefs in free market forces, and placed responsibility for dealing with the disaster at the door of the Irish landlords through the 1838 Poor Law. Efforts to cope collapsed as the starving flocked to the local boards and as workhouses became overcrowded and rampant with disease.

A contemporary image of the Famine's impact: an Irish tenant family prepare to leave their home, in an engraving of 1853.

In coping with such a massive loss of the potato crop, much of the burden of relief was carried out by private philanthropic organizations along with government contributions. In particular, the Society of Friends (Quakers) was at the forefront, providing food, clothing, cooking equipment, and money which was distributed by Catholic priests and Protestant ministers. For the most part all denominations worked together in distributing relief, often succumbing to famine-related sicknesses. However both fundamentalist proselytizers and the evangelical premise that the Great Famine was sent by God to punish the Irish for their sins, were looked upon with disdain by the Christian churches. Contrary to popular belief, Queen Victoria contributed generously from her own purse and sympathetic resident landlords often provided relief at their own expense. Suffering was especially acute in Connaught and Munster with the worst scenes witnessed in County Cork, particularly at Skibbereen.

horrific scenes and widespread illness

Deaths began to mount in late 1846 and tragic and horrific scenes ensued all over Ireland: mass graves, corpses gnawed by rats, hunger marches, roadside deaths, and the dying left unassisted for fear of contracting disease. Typhus and relapsing fever were the most common diseases afflicting the starved population. Famine conditions, such as the overcrowding of workhouses, provided an ideal environment for the spread of infection. Popular names for famine-related illnesses included 'gastric fever' and 'yellow fever', as many became jaundiced.

Although the blight lifted in 1847, not enough seed potatoes had been planted to supply the next season's requirements, and when the disease returned in full force in 1848, destroying two-thirds of the crop, and again in 1849, the famine reached its peak.

Russell and the Whig government began to realise that outdoor relief efforts alone were not sufficient in dealing with the famine. In the late spring of 1847 these considerations dictated a switch to direct food aid and the Destitute Poor (Ireland) Act opened up soup kitchens that fed three million daily at its height. Shortly afterwards, Russell suspended the soup kitchens and endorsed legislation to treat famine in Ireland as a long-term problem. The Poor Law was amended with the 'quarter-acre clause', proposed by William Gregory, which prohibited the relief from poor rates anyone occupying more than a quarter-acre of land. While this ensured that 'Irish property pay for Irish poverty', it also allowed large-scale evictions and the clearance of profitless land. Massive emigration ensued with many landlords organizing passage to the United States and Great Britain for tenants.

Violence and outrages were inevitable and the murder of Major Mahon, a landowner from Strokestown, County Roscommon along with the failed Young Ireland rebellion in Tipperary, led to the suspension of Habeas Corpus in 1848.

an intractable resentment of Britain

The social, economic and political consequences of the famine are greatly disputed. While living standards rose after the 1850s and average real wages increased, emigration drained Ireland of over four million people between the early 1850s and World War I. The famine left an intractable resentment of the Union with Great Britain, which even liberal Irish protestants like Isaac Butt, founder of the Home Government Association in 1870, recognized as a misnomer in view of the effectual abandonment of Ireland to her own resources by the world's richest nation during the famine crisis. It is probable that no event of Irish history was more influential in setting Irish opinion against any form of British government and its failure to stem the disaster or alleviate the misery of the people. Its immediate legacy was to radicalize Irish nationalism, which resulted in the opinion of John Mitchel (1815–1845) that, 'The Almighty sent the potato blight, but the English created the famine.' Such sentiment was shared by underground secret revolutionary societies like the Fenians in Ireland and within Irish communities established in places of emigration. Irish men and women driven overseas inculcated in their children a hatred of the British government and the pretensions of the English to just rule for Ireland.

All of these developments followed the famine's wake. Would they have occurred anyway? Several historians have answered this question affirmatively and believe that the disasters of 1845–1851 merely represented the culmination of a long-term crisis resulting from rapid population growth and gradual economic stagnation. Others are more critical of British governance in agreeing that the immediate cause of the Great Famine was blight, but there were underlying factors that had resulted in such a large percentage of the population depending on the potato for survival. Commemoration of the Great Famine in 1995 was marked by an apology from the British prime minister to the Irish people, and included widespread exhibitions, the unveiling of memorials, and the opening of Strokestown Park House, near Roscommon town, as a Famine Museum.

amilies, when all was eaten and no hope left, took their last look at the sun, built up their cottage doors, that none might see them die nor hear their groans, and were found weeks afterwards, skeletons on their own hearth.

JOHN MITCHEL Writer, revolutionary, and historian
On the Great Famine, in *Jail Journal* (1854).

∾

FARQUHAR, GEORGE (*c.* 1677–1707)

Dramatist whose most notable plays are *The Recruiting Officer* (1706) and *The Beaux Stratagem* (1707). Although typical of the Restoration tradition of comedy of manners, the good-humoured realism of his drama transcends the artificiality and cynicism of the genre.

*m*oney is the sinews of love, as of war.

GEORGE FARQUHAR *Love and a Bottle* II.
i.

∾

Farquhar was born in Londonderry, and studied at Trinity College, Dublin. He made his debut on the stage as Othello around 1695. After accidentally stabbing a fellow-actor, he retired from the stage, moved to London, and turned to playwriting. His first drama, *Love and a Bottle* (1699), was well received at Drury Lane in London. The following year *The Constant Couple* was produced, and proved an even greater success. He wrote many other dramas, of which *The Beaux' Strategem* is generally considered the finest.

FARRINGTON, ANTHONY

(1893–1973)

Born in Cork into a distinguished professional family, Farrington trained as an engineer, but discovered his true metier on his appointment to the Irish Geological Survey in 1921. Together with Robert Lloyd ⇨ Prager he established the Irish Quaternary Research Committee, and by a steady stream of original research papers dating from the late 1920s to the 1960s was responsible for major advances of knowledge in Irish glacial and vegetation history. Regarded by colleagues as the father of Irish glacial geology, Farrington was also active in broader fields. He was a member of the council of the Royal Irish Academy, editor of the Academy's proceedings, and a founder member of the Irish national heritage trust, *An Taisce*.

FASTNET ROCK

Rock situated off County Cork, 6 km/4 mi southwest of Cape Clear. It is the most southerly point of Ireland (latitude 51°23' N; longitude 9°36' W). A lighthouse erected in 1854 stands on the rock.

The light, which revolves 49 m/160 ft above the high-water mark, is visible for 29 km/18 mi. Fastnet Rock is a focal point in the Round Ireland yacht race.

FAULKNER, (ARTHUR) BRIAN (DEANE)

(Baron Faulkner of Downpatrick) (1921–1977)

Unionist politician and the last prime minister of Northern Ireland 1971–72 before the Stormont parliament was suspended. Elected to the Northern Ireland House of Commons in 1949, he held various ministerial posts 1959–71, and became leader of the Unionist Party in 1971. As prime minister he adopted a tough stance against republicans, reintroducing internment in 1971, but also tried to win middle-class Catholic support by offering nationalists a role in the parliamentary committee system. In 1973 he committed his party to the ill-fated Sunningdale power-sharing agreement.

Born in Helen's Bay, County Down and educated at St Columba's College, Dublin, Faulkner joined the family shirtmaking business before securing election to Stormont. Considered a hard–liner, Faulkner opposed prime minister Terence O'Neill's liberal policies and his resignation from the cabinet helped bring O'Neill down in 1969. He resigned from politics in 1976 and was made Baron in 1977.

FAY, WILLIAM GEORGE (1872–1947)

Actor born in Dublin. With his brother Frank Fay (1870–1931), he founded the company that in 1904 took up residence in the ⇨Abbey Theatre, Dublin. He was largely responsible for the subtlety and poetic style of its acting, producing many of its early plays himself.

Both actors were extremely versatile in their work, William concentrating more on comedy, Frank on verse speaking. They left the company in 1908, after a disagreement with the directors.

Frank later settled in Dublin as a teacher of elocution, but William continued as an actor and producer in London, the English provinces, and the USA. He also had a successful career in films. His memoirs appeared in *The Fays of the Abbey Theatre* in 1935.

FENIAN MOVEMENT

Republican secret society, founded in the USA in 1858 to campaign for Irish-American support for armed rebellion following the death of the Irish nationalist leader Daniel O'Connell and the breakup of ⇨Young Ireland. Its name, a reference to the ancient Irish legendary warrior band of the Fianna, became synonymous with underground Irish republicanism in the 19th century. The collapse of the movement began when an attempt to establish an independent Irish republic by an uprising in Ireland in 1867 failed, as did raids into Canada in 1866 and 1870, and England in 1867. In the 1880s the US-based Fenian society ⇨Clan-Na-Gael conducted assassinations and bombings through its agents in England and Ireland in an attempt to force Irish home rule.

*W*e are the Fenian Brotherhood, skilled in the arts of war, And we're going to fight for Ireland, the land that we adore.

ANONYMOUS 'Song of the Fenian Brotherhood'.

~

The Fenian movement was initiated by James ⇨O'Mahony, Michael Doheny (1805–1863), and James ⇨Stephens. O'Mahony ran operations in the USA and Stephens was in charge of Ireland, where the movement emerged as the Irish Republican Brotherhood after 1867. Fenian ideology revolved around the notion of England as an evil power, a mystic commitment to Ireland, and a belief that an independent Irish republic was morally superior to Britain. A Fenian was more likely to be an artisan than a farmer, and the movement found its greatest support in towns. Although a secret organization, James Stephens published a newspaper, *Irish People* (1863), which compromised Fenian secrecy. Charles ⇨Kick-

*S*ee who comes over the red-blossomed heather, / Their green banners kissing the pure mountain air... / ...From mountain and valley, / 'Tis Liberty's rally – / Out and make way for the bold Fenian Men!

MICHAEL SCANLAN Poet 'The Bold Fenian Men'

~

ham, its leader writer from 1863, was chairman of the Supreme Council of the Irish Republican Brotherhood 1873–82.

Fenianism was opposed by the Catholic church, but in 1867 the deaths of the ⇨Manchester martyrs, which aroused great popular sympathy, resulted in partial reconciliation as the Catholic church began to graft to the nationalist movement. The three martyrs, hanged for the murder of a police sergeant during the escape of two Fenian prisoners, were believed to be innocent victims of reprisal.

FENIANS

Another name for the ⇨Fianna, legendary Irish warriors.

FERGUSON, HARRY GEORGE (1884–1960)

Engineer who pioneered the development of the low cost tractor. He also perfected a system that linked the tractor and the implement being pulled, allowing both to be controlled from the driver's seat.

Ferguson was born in Dromore, County Down, near Belfast. He opened a car and motorcycle repair shop with his brother in 1902, but his engineering interests extended much further. He designed and built his own aeroplane and in 1909 accomplished the first recorded flight over Ireland.

Ferguson designed and manufactured a range of agricultural machinery and by the 1930s decided to develop a low cost but dependable tractor to which he added his integrated linkages and controls, which greatly improved safety for the operator. The Henry Ford company manufactured the Ferguson tractor in the US from 1938 until Ferguson set up his own US plant in 1948. This was later sold to Massey-Harris in 1953. He also manufactured his tractors at the Standard Motor Company in Coventry, England, from 1946.

FERGUSON, HOWARD (1908–)

Composer and pianist. Ferguson was a professor at the Royal Academy of Music, London, 1948–63. He made many editions of early keyboard works, and was active as an accompanist. Ferguson was educated at Westminster School and the Royal College of Music in London as a pupil of Reginald Morris.

His works include: *Chaunteclear* (1948); partita and four *Diversions on Ulster Airs* for orchestra; concerto for piano and strings (1951); Octet (1933); two violin and piano sonatas, four pieces for clarinet and piano; sonata and five bagatelles for piano; two ballads for baritone and orchestra; three *Medieval Carols* for voice and piano (1932–33); and *The Dream of the Rood* for soprano or tenor, chorus, and orchestra (1958–59).

FERGUSON, SAMUEL (1810–1886)

Antiquary and poet, and a leading figure in Protestant cultural nationalism. Ferguson was born in Belfast and educated at Trinity College, Dublin. He was appointed deputy keeper of the Irish Records in 1867 and his antiquarian works include the *Ogham Inscriptions* (1887). He was a notable president of the ⇨Royal Irish Academy. Ferguson also wrote poetry, his lyrics and ballads anticipating the Irish revival. *The Forging of the Anchor* (1883) is generally regarded as his masterpiece. His other verse includes *Lays of the Western Gael* (1865) and the epic *Congal* (1872).

Ferguson was called to the bar in 1838, became Queen's Counsel (QC) in 1859, and was knighted in 1878.

*t*here is honey in the trees where her
misty vales expand, / And her forest
paths in summer are by falling waters
fann'd, / There is dew at high noontide
there, and springs in the yellow sand, /
On the fair hills of holy Ireland.

SAMUEL FERGUSON 'The Fair Hills of Ireland'.

FERMANAGH

County of Northern Ireland; population (1991) 50,000; area 1,680 sq km/648 sq mi. It occupies the southwestern corner of Northern Ireland and is characterized by hills in the west and Lough Erne, which has many wooded islands and is used for fishing and sailing. The main towns are ⇨Enniskillen (county town), Lisnaskea, and Irvinestown.

physical
Upper and Lower Lough Erne bisect the county, the southwest portion of which consists of a series of scenic hills that rise to 663 m/2,175 ft in Mount Cuilcagh, and contain several remarkable cave systems, notably at Marble Arch. In the centre is a broad trough of low-lying land, and in the east there are low hills.

features
Fermanagh has a number of fine castles and tower houses dating from the plantation period, most notably the well-preserved remains of Monea Castle. On Devenish Island, Lower Lough Erne, are the extensive ruins of a monastery, originally founded in the 6th century by St Molaise. Florence Court, a Georgian mansion and forest park, was the home of the Earl of Enniskillen. Castle Coole is a neoclassical, late 18th-century house, and was the home of the Earls of Belmore. Tully Castle is a 17th-century fortified house, and White Island is the site of a 10th-century monastery and 12th-century church. Crom Castle Estate, on the shores of Upper Lough Erne, is an important wetland conservation area and has 770 ha/1,903 acres of woodland and parkland, and the ruins of a castle built in 1611 stand in the grounds.

economy
Agriculture and tourism provide the main occupations in the county, with clothing and tweeds being produced alongside some light engineering.

FIANNA (OR FENIANS)

Legendary band of Irish warriors, led by ⇨Finn Mac Cumhaill. His headquarters were at Almu (Allen) in County Kildare. The adventures of the Fianna are the subject of many stories, legends, and ballads.

The ballads are often attributed to Oisin, Finn's son, and are the source of James Macpherson's 18th-century epics, which he attributed to an ancient Scottish poet, ⇨Ossian.

FIANNA FÁIL ('Soldiers of Destiny')

Republic of Ireland political party, founded by the

Irish nationalist Éamon ⇨de Valera in 1926, and led since 1994 by Bertie ⇨Ahern. A broad-based party, it is conservative socially and economically, and generally right of centre. It was the governing party in the Republic of Ireland 1932–48, 1951–54, 1957–73, 1977–81, 1982, 1987–94 (from 1993 in coalition with Labour), and from 1997. Its official aims include the establishment of a united and completely independent all-Ireland republic.

Fianna Fáil was founded as a result of a split within Sinn Féin, which refused to enter the Dáil (parliament) following the establishment of the Irish Free State under the 1921 ⇨Anglo-Irish Treaty. It attracted the majority of Sinn Féin's support and became the main opposition party. In part due to skilful organization, it soon became the largest political party in the Republic, never yielding that position. In the early years of government it was associated with protectionist policies and small farmers, although it always drew support from all sections of Irish society. Although descended from the ⇨Irish Republican Army (IRA), the party was especially tough on IRA members in the early years of the Irish Free State.

De Valera, a conservative Catholic, remained leader and dominated the party until his retirement in 1959. His successor, Seán ⇨Lemass, a co-founder of the party, moved to modernize the party and the country. Fianna Fáil began to be associated with more closely with business interests, although it still retained its appeal amongst the working class. The ⇨arms crisis split the party between traditional republicans and moderates, and this division continued under the leadership of Charles ⇨Haughey, and led eventually to the establishment of a breakaway party, the ⇨Progressive Democrats. Albert ⇨Reynolds gained the leadership of the party in 1992, and he developed closer relations with the British government, a policy continued under Bertie Ahern, Taoiseach since 1997.

While remaining the most popular party in the country, it has been hit by financial scandals relating to former leaders and senior members. In 1989 Fianna Fáil abandoned its traditional refusal to enter a coalition government and it has not governed alone since that time.

FIELD, JOHN (1782–1837)

Irish-born composer and pianist. He is often regarded as one of a group of composers known as the London Pianoforte School, and all of his works include the piano, reaching their peak artistically with his noc-

turnes, a genre he named and devised. These anticipate Chopin's nocturnes by 20 years, especially regarding their forward-looking textures and passage work.

As an apprentice to Muzio Clementi, Field travelled throughout Europe demonstrating instruments for the firm of piano makers established by his master. In 1803 he settled in St Petersburg, Russia, where he composed most of his mature music.

FIELD DAY THEATRE COMPANY

Informal coalition of Irish artists created in 1980 who addressed the political situation in Ireland using artistic works, without being propagandist. The original members were playwright Brian ⇨Friel, actor Stephen Rea, poets and academics Seamus Deane, Seamus ⇨Heaney, and Tom Paulin, and singer and film-maker David Hammond. The group produced some of the finest English-language theatrical works of the 1980s, many of them studies of traditional pre-1960 Ireland.

Notable works produced by the group include Friel's *Translations* (1981) and Thomas Kilroy's *Double Cross* (1986). In 1983 Field Day began to issue pamphlets on cultural nationalism, and in 1991 the group produced the three-volume *The Field Day Anthology of Irish Writing*. Despite attacks from revisionists (for being too nationalist) and feminists (because of its underrepresentation of women), this anthology proves to be an ambitious and remarkable achievement.

FILM COMPANY OF IRELAND

The most important Irish film production company of the silent period. From 1916 to 1920 it made more than 20 fiction films, including three features. The most interesting films were the adaptations of Charles ⇨Kickham's *Knocknagow* (1918), which is a landlord/tenant drama set in 1848 during the Great Famine, and William ⇨Carleton's *Willy Reilly and his Colleen Bawn* (1920), which is set in the 1740s and 1750s and centres on the relationship between a Catholic man and a Protestant woman. Personnel associated with the company include *Willy Reilly's* director, John MacDonagh, who had been sentenced to death for his role in the 1916 Easter Rising.

FILM INSTITUTE OF IRELAND

Organization, originally established in 1945 as the National Film Institute of Ireland, a Catholic propagandist organization. It was taken over and secularized in the 1980s under the name Irish Film Institute. Following the establishment of the Irish Film Centre, a project initiated by the Irish Film Institute (IFI), it was renamed the Film Institute of Ireland, although its policies remain those of IFI. These include the development of the Irish Film Archive, which houses the largest collection of Irish film material held anywhere, two successful art cinemas, the promotion of media education, and occasional publications.

FINE GAEL ('family of the gael')

Republic of Ireland political party founded in 1933 by William ⇨Cosgrave and led by John ⇨Bruton from 1990. It has been socially liberal in recent years but fiscally conservative. Though it formed a coalition government with the Labour and Democratic Left parties 1994–97, it has typically been the main opposition party.

Fine Gael formed in 1933 as a merger of political party ⇨Cumann na nGaedheal, which governed the Irish Free State 1923–32, and two minor parties. Cumann na nGaedheal, which supported the 1921 Anglo-Irish Treaty that established the Irish Free State, was founded as the pro-Treaty side of Sinn Féin. It was traditionally associated with larger farmers and the middle class, but tended to draw support from anyone traditionally on the pro-Treaty side. Fine Gael first gained power in that guise as the main party in the coalition governments of 1948–51 and 1954–57. These coalitions also contained small leftist parties. It regained power with the Labour Party 1973–77. In 1977 Fine Gael's new leader Garret ⇨FitzGerald moved the party towards social democracy making the 1981–82 and 1982–87 coalitions with Labour more natural, yet these still ended in rancour. The party seemed to flounder after FitzGerald's departure, but regained power in 1994 as part of a rainbow coalition which included Labour and Democratic Left elements.

FINN MAC CUMHAILL (also FIONN or FINN MCCOOL) ('the fair-haired son of Cumhall')

Legendary Irish hero, the best-known character in the ⇨hero-tales of Ireland, identified with a general who organized an Irish regular army in the 3rd century. The word 'Fionn' (from Celtic *Vindos*) also has connotations of illumination and wisdom, and his most typical act was the gaining of knowledge through chewing his thumb. The Scottish writer James Macpherson featured him (as Fingal) and his followers in the verse of his popular epics 1762–63, which were supposedly written by a 3rd-century bard called ⇨Ossian.

FITT, GERRY (GERARD) (Baron Fitt) (1926–)

Northern Irish politician. Born in Belfast, Fitt was a merchant seaman 1941–53 before he entered local politics in 1955. From 1962 to 1972 he represented the Dock Division of Belfast as a Republican Labour member of the Northern Ireland parliament; he then founded and led the Social Democratic Labour Party (SDLP). He was an SDLP MP for nine years, resigning the leadership in 1979 to sit as an Independent socialist. He lost his Belfast seat in the 1983 general election.

Fitt had earlier been a member of the Northern Ireland executive 1973–75, and was its deputy chief executive in 1974. In the course of his career, Fitt, an opponent of violence, had to endure the animosity of both republican and loyalist extremists. He became Lord Fitt in 1983.

FITZGERALD (also known as the Geraldines)

One of the great Anglo-Irish houses. The dynasty was founded by the Anglo-Norman baron Maurice Fitzgerald, 'the Invader' (died 1176), who came to Ireland with Richard de ⇨Clare (Strongbow) in 1170, and was granted the manor of Maynooth, Kildare, by him in 1176. Though the Kildare branch was the first founded, it was the Fitzgerald house of Desmond, established by the direct descendants of Maurice 'the Invader', that first achieved national prominence in Ireland during the 14th century.

Maurice fitzThomas Fitzgerald, 1st Earl of Desmond (earl 1329–56) and Gerald fitzMaurice Fitzgerald, 3rd Earl (born *c.* 1338, earl 1363–98), established their authority over the Gaelic Irish lordships of Munster and occupied some of the richest lands in the province. The Desmond earls regularly served as chief governors for the crown, but the sudden dismissal and execution for treason of the 8th Earl of Desmond, Thomas fitzJames Fitzgerald (b. *c.*1426, earl 1462–68), by the English chief governor John Tiptoft, Earl of Worcester (1427–1470), put an end to their national influence.

The eclipse of the Desmond Geraldines, however, was followed by the rapid rise of their cousins in Kildare. Though the earldom of Kildare was first established in 1316, Kildare ambitions were thwarted by rivalries with the de Burgh family and the ⇨Butlers of Ormond, and by a severe succession crisis following the death of the 5th Earl of Kildare, Gerald fitzMaurice Fitzgerald (1390–1432). The Kildare ascent began with the appointment of the 7th Earl, Thomas fitzMaurice Fitzgerald (earl 1456–78), as governor of Ireland by Edward IV in 1471. There followed over 50 years of Geraldine dominance in Ireland, during which Gerald Mór Fitzgerald, 8th Earl (1456–1513), and Gerald Óg Fitzgerald ('the Young'), 9th Earl (1487–1534), enjoyed an unprecedented degree of influence over the whole of the island. Tudor attempts to reduce Kildare power provoked the rebellion of 1534–36 led by 'Silken Thomas' Fitzgerald, 10th Earl (1513–1537), and the attainder of the house in 1537. The family was restored under Gerald, 11th Earl of Kildare (b. 1525, earl 1554–85) but his own over-ambitious schemes as well as the early deaths of the 12th, 13th, and 14th Earls and consequent disputes, severely damaged the family, whose leaders remained largely absent from Irish public life during the 17th century.

The family resumed a prominent position in Irish politics under James, 20th Earl of Kildare (b. 1722, earl 1744–73), whose service to the crown was rewarded with the hereditary dukedom of Leinster in 1766. William, 3rd Duke of Leinster (1773–1804), played a central role in 18th-century Irish political life together with his wife Emily (died 1798), whose personal correspondence provides a remarkable record of the affairs of their time. After the Act of Union (1801) the family retired from national public life. The line continues in Maurice Fitzgerald, 9th Duke of Leinster (1976–   ).

FITZGERALD, BARRY (stage name of WILLIAM JOSEPH SHIELDS) (1888–1961)

Stage and film actor, born in Dublin. His first film role was in the Irish-produced *Land of her Fathers* (1925) and he later appeared as the orator in Alfred Hitchcock's 1930 film version of Seán O'Casey's play *Juno and the Paycock* (1924). Contracted by the US company RKO to play one of his most famous roles, that of Fluther Good in the 1936 film version of O'Casey's *The Plough and the Stars* (1926), directed by John Ford (1895–1973), he thereafter worked mainly in Hollywood, where he won an Academy Award for his role as a priest in *Going My Way* (1944). He returned to Ireland frequently and played his most memorable role as the impish match-maker in John Ford's *The Quiet Man* (1952).

FITZGERALD, GARRET MICHAEL

(1926–   )

Irish politician, leader of the Fine Gael party 1977–87. As Taoiseach (prime minister) 1981–82 and 1982–87, his efforts to resolve the Northern Ireland dispute led to the signing of the ⇨Anglo-Irish Agreement in 1985. He also tried to remove some of the overtly Catholic and nationalist features of the 1937 constitution.

FitzGerald was born in Dublin, the son of Desmond FitzGerald, a cabinet minister in the Irish Free State. Having entered the Seanad Éireann (Irish senate) in 1965, FitzGerald was minister for foreign affairs 1973–77 under Liam Cosgrave, and then became Taoiseach himself, leading a Fine Gael–Labour Party coalition. Always an internationalist in outlook, he recognized at an early stage the significance to Ireland of its membership of the European Community (EC; now the European Union) and, as part of that membership, the need to find a peaceful, lasting accommodation with its nearest neighbour, the UK. In 1985 he signed the Anglo-Irish Agreement with the UK prime minister Margaret Thatcher. The agreement provided for regular consultation between the two governments and the exchange of information on political, legal, security, and cross-border matters, and contained the provision that no change in the status of Northern Ireland would be made without the consent of the majority of its people.

FitzGerald studied law at University College and King's Inns, Dublin, and became a barrister in 1947. Initially he worked for the Irish airline, Aer Lingus, but then decided to pursue an academic career. After a period as a Rockefeller research assistant at Trinity College, he lectured in politcs at University College in Dublin 1959–87. He also worked as a journalist – as Irish correspondent for the BBC, the *London Financial Times*, and *The Economist*, and economics correspondent for the *Irish Times*. His books include *Planning in Ireland* (1968), *Towards a New Ireland* (1972), and an autobiography *All in a Life* (1991).

FITZGERALD, GEORGE FRANCIS

(1851–1901)

Physicist known for his work on electromagnetics. Fitzgerald was the first to suggest a method of propagating radio waves, which helped towards the development of wireless telegraphy. He also developed a theory of how bodies contract as their velocity increased, known as the Fitzgerald–Lorentz contraction, a concept reinterpreted by Albert Einstein in his special theory of relativity.

Born in Dublin, Fitzgerald studied at Trinity College, Dublin. He became a tutor there in 1877 and professor of experimental philosophy in 1881. He studied radiation and predicted that a rapidly alternating electric current would produce radiation as electromagnetic waves, a prediction proved correct in the late 1880s by the German physicist Heinrich Hertz. This early work formed the foundations of radio.

In 1892 he explained the unusual results of the Michelson–Morley experiment to detect the motion of the Earth, by suggesting that rapidly moving bodies contracted as their velocity increased. The theory was jointly named the Fitzgerald–Lorentz contraction because the idea was independently developed by Dutch physicist Hendrik Lorentz in 1895.

FITZGIBBON, JOHN (1st Earl of Clare)

Attorney-general and lord chancellor of Ireland; see ⇨United Irishmen.

FITZMAURICE, GEORGE (1877–1963)

Playwright for the ⇨Abbey Theatre, Dublin, whose peasant and folk plays often blend the realistic and the fantastical. The naturalistic play *The Country Dressmaker* (1907) was his first and most famous drama. This was followed by *The Pie-Dish* (1908), a Faustian tale in which an old man sells his soul to the devil to be able to complete an ornamental dish he is making. Later plays include *The Magic Glasses* (1913) and *'Twixt the Giltinans and the Carmodys* (1923).

A lot of his plays were ahead of their time, and the audiences often did not quite know how to react to them. Very sensitive to criticism, Fitzmaurice withdrew his plays from the Abbey after 1923, but he continued to publish material in *The Dublin Magazine*.

Fitzmaurice was born near Listowel, County Kerry, and was a clerk in the civil service for most of his life, working for the Irish Land Commission, and served in the British army during World War I.

FITZMAURICE, JAMES (1898–1965)

Aviator who, with two German companions, made the first successful east to west flight across the Atlantic in April 1928.

FITZRALPH, RICHARD (c. 1295–1360)

Scholarly archbishop of Armagh, born in Dundalk, County Louth. Educated at Oxford, Fitzralph was successively chancellor of Oxford University (1333), archdeacon of Chester (c. 1335), dean of Lichfield (1337), and archbishop of Armagh (1346), from which position he asserted his oversight over the archbishop of Dublin. In 1357 he was summoned to the papal court in Avignon, France, over his views that mendicant vows of poverty were probably unscriptural; although he was not condemned, he was never allowed to return to Armagh. His remains were transferred to St Nicholas, Dundalk, in 1370.

FITZWILLIAM EPISODE

Crisis in 1795 provoked by the appointment and prompt dismissal of William Wentworth, 2nd earl of Fitzwilliam (1748–1843) as Irish viceroy. His early plans to complete the full political emancipation of Ireland's Catholics coupled with his brusque treatment of several senior and influential office-holders led to his removal by Prime Minister Pitt, the suspension of his reform proposals and his replacement by a hard line administration under the earl of Camden. The affair greatly contributed to the bitterness and hostility between Catholics and Protestants in Ireland which preceded the 1798 rebellion.

FLAG

A tricolour of green, white, and orange, is used in Ireland as the civil and state national flag and the civil and naval ensign. It was first presented by Thomas Francis Meagher, the leader of the ⇨Young Ireland nationalist movement in Waterford in 1848. A symbol for the union of all Irish interests, the green stripe represents people of native Irish origin (Catholics), the orange represents the descendants of 17th-century British colonists (Protestants), and the white signifies hope for a truce between the two. Originally with the orange next to the staff, it was forgotten after the 1848 rebellion but revived with the green stripe next to the staff in 1916 after the Easter Rising.

The Presidential Standard is a gold harp on a blue ground, adopted as the official emblem of the Irish

Free State in 1922. The design is based on the so-called 'Brian Boru harp', a harp (which post-dates the early Irish king Brian Bóruma) kept at Trinity College, Dublin. It was the banner of the arms of Ireland from the reign of Henry VIII, although the United Irishmen changed the colour of the field to green as a symbol of revolution against the English government in the Rebellion of 1798, when it became known as the 'Green Flag'.

FLANAGAN, EDWARD JOSEPH (1886–1948)

Irish-born US Catholic priest, born in Ballaghaderreen, County Roscommon. Flanagan moved to the USA in 1904 and was ordained to the archdiocese of Omaha, Nebraska, in 1912. He opened a homeless shelter there in 1914, before establishing Father Flanagan's Boys' Home to house and reform troubled boys in 1917. The home was moved out of Omaha and became Boys' Town in 1922. Flanagan proclaimed that 'There is no such thing as a bad boy'. He travelled to Japan as a youth work consultant in 1947 and died while undertaking similar work in Germany.

FLATLEY, MICHAEL (1958–)

Irish-American dancer who transformed the choreography of traditional Irish step dancing, introducing flamboyancy, sensuality, and touches of flamenco. Flatley was born in Chicago to Irish parents, and took up step dancing at the age of 11, becoming a world champion in 1975. He first shot to fame as the principal dancer alongside Jean Butler in ⇨*Riverdance*, a stunning performance of hard-shoe step dancing at the 1994 Eurovision Song Contest that brought international acclaim to traditional Irish dancing and led to the creation of a full-length stage show in Dublin in 1995. After leaving *Riverdance* in 1995, Flatley produced and choreographed his own high-production spectaculars *Lord of the Dance* (1996–98) and *Feet of Flames* (created 1998), which incorporated dancing

MICHAEL FLATLEY *Flatley, seen here fronting his own dance company, learned step dancing as a boy, and shot to fame in the stage show* Riverdance. *He has subsequently developed and embellished traditional steps even further in* Lord of the Dance *and* Feet of Flames.

styles that were looser and more contemporary.

Flatley was educated by the Christian Brothers at the Brother Rice High School, and spent time in Ireland as a boy, where he was introduced to the art of step dancing; his grandmother had been a Leinster champion. Alongside his dancing prowess, he was also a prize-winning flautist and a champion boxer, winning the Golden Gloves championship in Chicago in 1975.

FLEISCHMANN, ALOYS (1910–1992)

German-born Irish composer, academic, researcher, and conductor. Born in Munich, Fleischmann was brought up by his parents in Cork. He was professor of music at University College, Cork, from 1934 to 1980. He established the Cork Symphony Orchestra in 1939 and was its conductor for a record 56 years. He was also a founder of the Cork Choral and Folk Dance Festival in 1954. is posthumously published *Sources of Traditional Irish Music, c. 1600–1855* (1998) contains 6,841 cross-referenced melodies and is the largest collection of Irish music ever published. His own compositions include the Piano Quintet (1938), the choral work *Clare's Dragoons* (1944), and the ballet score *The Táin* (1981).

FLIGHT OF THE EARLS

Conventional historical term for the decision, on 4 September 1607, of Hugh O'Neill, Earl of Tyrone (*c.* 1550–1616), Rory O'Donnell, Earl of Tyrconnell (1575–1608), and other leaders of the Ulster rebellion against incoming English forces (1594–1603), to abandon Ulster and go into exile. Treated ungenerously in Paris and Brussels, the earls and their party eventually found asylum in Rome, where they ended their days. Their departure provided an excuse for the English crown to confiscate their properties on the grounds that they had planned further rebellion, and so to commence the plantation of Ulster (see ⇨Ulster plantation).

An event of profound significance in Irish folk memory, where it is seen as an emblem of the demise of the Gaelic world, the 'flight' has also been a source of historical controversy. Some historians argue that indebtedness, the cost of large households, and fear of further government encroachments were the real cause of the earls' departure. Others maintain that the British government's claims – that the exposure of their plot to secure renewed Spanish intervention in Ireland caused their flight – had some foundation in fact.

FLOOD, HENRY (1732–1791)

Statesman, born in Dublin. One of Ireland's great orators, Flood entered the Irish parliament in 1759 as member for Kilkenny. He allied with Henry ⇨Grattan in the hope of establishing an independent Irish parliament, and held office as vice treasurer of Ireland 1778–81. One of the patriot leaders, he campaigned tirelessly for legislative independence and free trade, but opposed Catholic emancipation. Disputes with Grattan, however, saw him become disillusioned with Irish politics. In 1783 he was returned to the British House of Commons. He lost his seats in both parliaments in 1790 and retired from public life.

FLORENCE COURT

Mid-18th-century three-storey Baroque house in County Fermanagh, 11 km/7 m south of Enniskillen. It was probably built in 1751 for John Cole, later 1st Lord Mountflorence, but may date from as early as 1730. Arcaded wings were added about 1768 by William Cole, thought to be designed by Davis Duckart. The interior contains rococo plasterwork in the manner of Robert West, from about 1755. The main staircase is a fine example of high quality joinery. The property was given to the National Trust in 1954. It was damaged by a serious fire in 1955 but has been restored.

FOLEY, JOHN HENRY (1818–1874)

Sculptor of the 19th century. Although he spent the greater part of his career in London, Foley produced many of the monuments that are now familiar landmarks in Dublin. Most notable of these is the O'Connell Monument (1866–83; O'Connell Street, Dublin), the most important sculptural commission of its period in Ireland. The commission aroused considerable debate as it was felt that the work should be carried out by a resident Irish sculptor. Foley's statues of Oliver Goldsmith and Edmund Burke, with the combination of realism and classicism typical of his style, stand at the entrance to Trinity College, Dublin. His best-known work in London is the statue of Prince Albert for the Albert Memorial, Kensington Gardens.

Foley's equestrian monuments, such as his memorial to Field Marshall, Viscount Gough, were among his greatest achievements. This work was originally intended to stand not far from the O'Connell Monument. The proximity to the nationalist monument was, however, deemed inappropriate. It was subsequently erected opposite the entrance to the Viceregal Lodge (now Áras an Uachtaráin) in Phoenix Park. In the 1950s, having become a focus for nationalist protest, it was severely damaged and the remains were removed to the Royal Hospital, Kilmainham, Dublin.

FOLKLORE

See feature on folklore, page 148, also ⇨hero-tales.

FOMORIANS (or FOMHOIRE) ('underworld spirits')

In legend, a race of demonic beings who lived in Ireland and fought off successive waves of settlers. They were finally expelled by the ⇨Tuatha Dé Danann (people of the goddess ⇨Danu) in the second Battle of Muighe Tuireadh (Moytirra). Their most prominent leader was Balar of the Evil Eye, killed by ⇨Lugh.

FOOTBALL ASSOCIATION OF IRELAND (FAI)

Association set up in 1890, originally as the Irish Football Association (IFA), renamed in 1921 the Football Association of Ireland. The national soccer team, playing under the name of the Irish Free State, played its first senior international at the Paris Olympics in 1924, beating Belgium 1–0. With Jack ⇨Charlton as team manager, Ireland won an historic victory over England in its opening game of the European tournament Euro 88, and went on to qualify for the 1994 World Cup finals in the USA. In 1999 the FAI unveiled plans for The Arena, a new home for Irish soccer at Citywest, west Dublin.

Soccer in Ireland dates back to 1878 when an exhibition game arranged by the businessman John McAleryly was played at a cricket ground in the province of Ulster. As a result of its success,

Cliftonville, from Belfast in County Antrim, became the first official football club on the island, and the IFA was subsequently established. The game was slow to spread in the south of the country, but the Dublin Association Football Club was established in 1893. A decision by the IFA not to allow the Irish Cup Final to be played in Dublin due to civil unrest inevitably led to several Dublin clubs leaving the Irish league to form a new southern league, and in 1917 the Football Association of the Irish Free State was formed.

Though the IFA immediately blacklisted the newly formed body, the world governing body FIFA (Fédération Internationale de Football Associations) in time gave the organization its full backing, and in 1953 FIFA formally decreed that the FAI should be known as the Republic of Ireland in international competition and the IFA as Northern Ireland. The two teams met for the first time at senior international level on 20 September 1978, drawing 0–0.

FOOTBALL, GAELIC

Kicking and catching game played mainly in Ireland. The two teams have 15 players each. The game is played on a field with an inflated spherical ball. The goalposts have a crossbar and a net across the lower half. Goals are scored by kicking the ball into the net (three points) or over the crossbar (one point).

First played in 1712, it is now one of the sports under the auspices of the Gaelic Athletic Association. The leading tournament is the All-Ireland Championship (first held in 1887); its final is played in Dublin on the third Sunday in September each year, the winners receiving the Sam Maguire Trophy.

Although seen as the poor relation to hurling, the sport has nonetheless thrown up many memorable contests and produced many stars since the game was established in 1884. One team that dominated almost from the start was the Kerry side who, until the mid-1980s, proved almost invincible. They managed to win All-Ireland titles in each decade, starting with their first in 1903. During the 1950s a threat to their dominance emerged when a young full forward by the name of Kevin Heffernan came to prominence. Heffernan was part of the Dublin team beaten by Kerry in 1955. Three years later he captained them to victory over Derry before retiring in 1962. He was not seen again until the 1970s when he took up the reins as county manager. It was here that the great Dublin–Kerry rivalry took off. Their All-Ireland semi-final clash in 1977 is generally regarded as among the

GAELIC FOOTBALL *A breathtaking moment during the Laois versus Tyrone final, 1997, played at Croke Park, Dublin. Despite sporadic attempts to take the game to Irish communities in other countries, Gaelic football is rarely played outside Ireland.*

greatest games ever seen at Croke Park.

Another team to emerge in the 1980s was Meath. Trained by Sean Boylan, they elevated the game to new levels, while Ulster also managed to break the Munster–Leinster hold on football in the mid-1990s with Down, Derry, and Donegal winning four titles in a row for the province.

The following players were named as a team of the 20th century, maked by the issue of commemorative stamps: Enda Colleran (Galway), Sean Flanagan (Mayo), Kevin Heffernan (Dublin), Danno Keefe (Kerry), Joe Keohane (Kerry), Tom Langan (Mayo), Sean Murphy (Kerry), Tommy Murphy (Laois), Martin O'Connell (Meath), Mick O'Connell (Kerry), Sean O'Neill (Down), Sean Purcell (Galway), John Joe Reilly (Cavan), Mike Sheehy (Kerry), and Pat Spillane (Kerry).

FORD, PATRICK (1837 - 1913)

Journalist and Irish-American nationalist. Having emigrated to Boston from Galway at age seven, Ford retained few memories of his native country but professed to have been propelled into Irish-Nationalism by the anti-Irish nativists of Boston. After several years in journalism, Ford founded *The Irish World* in 1870 as an organ of Irish-American propaganda and defence. His radicalism and inability to compromise led him into conflict with several leading Irish nationalists including Michael Davitt and John Devoy. Yet he remained a formidable defender of Irish America

FOLKLORE – A VAST HERITAGE KEPT ALIVE BY THE LOVE OF STORIES

by Dáithí Ó hÓgáin

Folklore has survived with unusual vigour in Ireland. This is partly because centralization is a recent phenomenon in Irish social life, and so traditional custom and practice have continued to flourish. It is also due in part to the great love for conversation, conviviality, and storytelling among the people of Ireland.

written origins

Literature in Irish began in the 6th century AD and continued to flourish down through the ages, preserved in manuscript form. The literary people responsible for this tradition specialized in history, genealogy, and onamastics (the study of proper names), and couched their data in

An imagined banshee drawn by Florence Harrison and published in 1912.

the form of story. In this way, a vast heritage of mythical and historical lore was spread and reinforced among ordinary people. Most valued by the storytellers and their audiences were the hero-tales that told of ancient gods and warriors and their adventures. The origins of most of these heroes were lost in the prehistoric Celtic world, but a complex lore evolved around them with the addition of themes and imagery from other sources through the centuries.

wonder-tales

Modern scholars use the term 'international folktales' for the type of narrative-plots that circulated orally around Europe from the Roman era and through the Middle Ages to recent times. Such tales had entertainment rather than education as their main function. Most popular were the wonder-tales, which were full of imaginative themes, set in a never-never land 'long ago'. There are many Irish versions of these – such as the adventures of a widow's son who slays giants and monsters in order to save a threatened princess, or the young lover who must perform magical tasks to gain a beautiful girl, or the hero who is assisted by marvellous helpers to rescue stolen children. These wonder-tales were long and lent themselves to elaborate descriptions; they were therefore very suitable to the highly developed narrative style that was in great demand among speakers of Irish. It is notable that wonder-tales are very common in the Irish language, but are seldom found in Hiberno-English.

wit and wisdom

Other international genres are found equally in Irish and English – for instance, the novella-type tales, moral or satirical narratives, which are set against a more true-to-life background. These focus on the game of courtship and on the relations between the sexes, and variously portray men and women gaining partners through solving riddles, through quick wit, or through sincerity and perseverance.

Other stories deal with a variety of humorous situations, describing unbelievably foolish acts and clever escapades such as those of the master builder Gobán Saor. Religious tales, the product of medieval preachers, are elaborated into accounts of how humans work out their moral dilemma in a typicalized world, gaining forgiveness of sins through extraordinary penances and learning something of the mystery of God's designs. The simplest of the international-type tales concern animals, birds, and fish, and were also frequently told in Ireland. These are fanciful little adventures, telling for example of the fox and wolf, or the eagle and wren, pitting their wits against each other.

haunting memories

Popular imagination has not confined itself to such fanciful stories, but has also worked upon the living environment of the people. The range and variety of Irish folk-beliefs show how realistic knowledge, derived from observation and experience, combines with fanciful ideas that are born of curiosity and uncertainty. The life experience, the passing of time, the home and community, the different trades and skills, the physical surroundings, all have their own special lore attaching to them. Like all other peoples, the Irish are partial to stories of ghosts and spirits. These may either be of the malevolent kind who terrify or even injure benighted travellers, or the benevolent kind such as souls in distress, who return seeking prayers on their behalf or proffering assistance to the living. Respect for the dead has always been a prominent feature of Irish culture. There were various premonitions of death – such as a bird landing on the windowsill, a picture falling from the wall, or the cry of the banshee.

fairy-lore

Folk-belief and the narrative impulse come together in fairy lore. The otherworld community is known in Irish as the people of the *sí*, a word that originally designated a tumulus or burial mound. The dead were anciently believed to live on as a dazzling community in these burial chambers, and such old earthenwork structures are still claimed to be inhabited by these *sí*-people. Stories concerning elves, goblins, and the fairy realm enjoyed great popularity in medieval Europe and many such narrative plots were adopted into Ireland and merged with traditions of the *sí*. The result is that Irish folklore has preserved fairy legends in clearer and more vibrant form than other European areas. Stories tell of humans being abducted into the fairy world and changelings left in their place, of midwives being taken away to officiate at fairy births, of fairy horses and cattle appearing among a farmer's stock, of men who married beautiful women from the sea, of leprechauns and pots of gold, and other such interfaces between the realms of reality and fancy.

saints, soldiers, and sinners

Irish folklore is also rich in legends concerning historical characters. The saints, especially Patrick, Bridget, and Columba (Colum Cille) had many religious and some humourous tales attached to them, as did many more localized saints. Leaders of long ago also figure prominently – examples are the battles fought by the medieval king Brian Bóruma; the magical feats of the Gaelic-Norman Gerald Fitzgerald, 3rd Earl of Desmond; and the careers of celebrated soldiers such as Dónall Ó Súilleabháin Béarra and Owen Roe O'Neill (Eoghan Rua Ó Néill). Worthies of more recent centuries, such as Daniel O'Connell and Jonathan Swift, have attracted many anecdotes that underline their learning, quick wit, and humour. The outlaw is a very popular figure in Irish folklore, which celebrates the daring deeds of high-minded bandits and of resistance fighters. A special genre of folk legends celebrates the spontaneous compositional skill of Gaelic poets, to whose verses magical effects are often attributed.

custom and conservation

Local and indigenous customs survive with less vigour now than formerly, except where – as in the case of field-sports and music sessions – these are organized officially. Among the principal forms of traditional entertainment can be numbered dancing, hurling, Gaelic football, handball, running, weight-throwing, hunting, horse-racing, and cardplaying.

In former generations, the indigenous festivals of the Irish calendar – such as the beginning of spring (Christianized as St Bridget's Day), May Eve, the harvest-festival, the patterns (observances) of local saints, and Hallowe'en, all had their own selections of amusement and preserved vestiges of earlier rituals. Of the Christian festivals, most custom has centred on Christmas, Easter, St John's Night, and the feast of St Martin.

The Folklore of Ireland Society, founded in 1926, has a large membership. The Irish Folklore Commission was set up by the government in 1935, and down through the years has collected a vast amount of lore and ethnological data. It now functions as the department of Irish folklore at University College, Dublin.

until resigning from the editorship of the '*World*' in 1911.

FOSTER, JOHN

Politician, see Act of ⇨Union.

FOSTER, VERE HENRY LEWIS

(1819–1900)

British diplomat and philanthropist. Having first visited Ireland during 'black '47', the worst year of the famine, his subsequent reports to parliamentary commissions were instrumental in increasing poor relief and improving conditions on emigrant ships. In post-famine Ireland he funded the establishment of several hundred parish schools and devised several pedagogical innovations including a famous 'copy-book' designed to improve spelling, penmanship, and drawing. Later, while concentrating his charity work in Ulster, he continued to work to facilitate the emigration of families to North America.

FOX-HUNTING

The sport of fox-hunting in Ireland dates back to the beginning of the 19th century when there were several private hunting packs based in Galway. Among the best known was the Castle Boy Club, which took its name from the place where Robert Parsons Persse kept his hounds. Each year he went on an expedition to Birr, County Offaly, and following his death in 1829 the hunt was continued on a regular basis. The members were nicknamed 'the Blazers', reportedly after burning down a hotel after a reunion dinner. The sport's popularity spread to such places as Tipperary, Meath, and Limerick, and was particularly popular with the farming classes.

Another famous hunting club is the Ormond, which boasted such names as the jockey Walter Swinburn and the Irish showjumpers Eddie Macken, Paul Darragh, and Con Power. Today there are over 40 recognized foxhound packs, 33 harrier packs, and two staghound packs in Ireland. The formal season starts in October and ends in March. Cub hunting takes place from September to November.

FOYLE, LOUGH

Sea lough on the north coast of Ireland, traversed by the frontier of Northern Ireland and the Republic of Ireland. It is noted amongst ornithologists as a site for migratory seabirds.

FREEMASONRY

Beliefs and practices of a group of linked national organizations open to men over the age of 21, united by a common code of morals and certain traditional 'secrets'. Descended from medieval crafts guilds, modern freemasonry began in 17th-century Scotland.

The first Irish lodge was begun in the 1720s, modelled on the English grand lodge of 1717. During the 18th century freemasonry assimilated many of the progressive ideas of the European Enlightenment. Its Irish membership included aristocrats and artisans, Protestants and Catholics. Most of this membership was Catholic, despite papal hostility towards its secrecy and rituals. Freemasonry became associated with the radical politics of the 1790s, particularly in Ulster, though its political complexion varied according to locality. Masonic rituals influenced the Belfast physician and poet William Drennan (1754–1820) in his original concept for the ⇨United Irishmen, while its lodge structure was copied by both the Catholic ⇨Defenders and the ⇨Orange Order. During the 19th century it became a largely Protestant organization, attracting renewed Catholic criticism in the process. Modern Irish freemasons, of whom there are about 60,000, engage in charitable work.

FRENCH, (WILLIAM) PERCY (1854–1920)

Songwriter and painter. A civil engineer by training, French worked for a while as surveyor of drains in County Cavan, where stories of his adventures still circulate. From his student days he showed a talent and a passion for writing comic and sentimental songs. From the mid-1880s he travelled extensively in England, Europe, and the USA. With easy-to-remember words and music, his songs remained popular long after his death, and are regularly performed and recorded, among the best known being 'The Mountains of Mourne', 'Come back Paddy Reilly' and 'Gortnamona'. His reputation as a watercolourist has grown in recent years.

FRICKER, BRENDA (1944–   )

Actor, born in Dublin. Fricker came to international prominence through her Academy Award-winning performance as Christy Brown's mother in *My Left Foot* (1989), directed by Jim ⇨Sheridan. She has also worked on stage and in television, including in the first urban Irish television soap in the 1960s, *Tolka Row*, in the British television hospital series, *Casualty* from 1986 to 1990, and in the Australian television series, *Brides of Christ*.

Fricker continued to work with Jim Sheridan in *The Field* (1990), in which she played a long-suffering woman, a characterization which has become something of a trademark for her. She has also appeared in *Home Alone 2 (1991), Lost in New York* (1992), *So I Married an Axe Murderer* (1992), *A Man of No Importance* (1994), *Swann* (1996), and *Resurrection Man* (1997).

FRIEL, BRIAN (1929–)

Dramatist and short-story writer. Friel's work often addresses social and historical pressures that contribute to the Irish political situation. Born in Omagh, County Tyrone, and educated in Northern Ireland, Friel has lived in the Republic since 1967. His first success was with *Philadelphia, Here I Come!* (1964), which examines the issue of emigration in the 1960s. Later plays include the acclaimed *Dancing at Lughnasa* (1990).

In 1980 Friel co-founded the ⇨Field Day Theatre Company, which produced the groundbreaking *Translations* (1981), a study of British linguistic and cultural colonialism in 19th-century Ireland. Other plays include *The Freedom of the City* (1973), about victims of the Ulster conflict; *Faith Healer* (1980); *Making History* (1988), a treatment of the life of Hugh ⇨O'Neill, Earl of Tyrone; and *Molly Sweeney* (1994). Friel distinguishes himself as a playwright by his experiments with dramatic forms and his precise, often poetically charged language. His work dramatizes the interactions and tensions between history and myth, and change and tradition, and explores the effects of these processes on individuals, the family, and on the wider, especially rural, community.

FURNITURE

Furniture can be broadly divided into two types:

period furniture
Little furniture survives from before the 18th century.

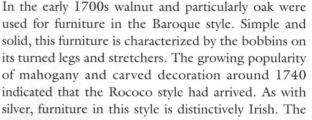

BRENDA FRICKER *The actress had a long career in theatre and television before winning an Academy Award for her portrayal of Christy Brown's mother in Jim Sheridan's 1989 film adaptation of Brown's autobiographical* My Left Foot. *She subsequently moved to America.*

In the early 1700s walnut and particularly oak were used for furniture in the Baroque style. Simple and solid, this furniture is characterized by the bobbins on its turned legs and stretchers. The growing popularity of mahogany and carved decoration around 1740 indicated that the Rococo style had arrived. As with silver, furniture in this style is distinctively Irish. The curved cabriole leg, and ball and claw or paw foot originated elsewhere, but just above the foot a small protuberance often appears, carved with stylized foliage or hair, which is uniquely Irish. Shells, leaves, masks, and flowers ornament this furniture, on aprons, arms, and legs.

Neoclassicism spread throughout Europe towards the end of the 18th century, but, unlike the Rococo, the style had no particularly Irish version. Furniture became lighter, more linear and delicate. The Irish ⇨Arts and Crafts movement helped to spread the next Irish style, Irish revival, which consisted of the use of bogwood and native woods, and the decorative use of Irish symbols (harps, shamrocks, round towers, and wolfhounds), along with early Christian designs, particularly interlace and animal patterns. In the 20th century Irish designers such as Eileen Gray were involved with international modernism, and later initiatives like the Kilkenny Design Workshop, and the establishment of the Furniture College in Letterfrack, County Galway in 1987, have ensured that Irish furniture continues to thrive.

country furniture
Styles in country furniture rarely changed, the same types of objects being made and used for hundreds of years, making country furniture difficult to date. Distinctively Irish designs are rare, but one good example is the settle-bed. Settles – high-backed wooden seats for two or more people – existed in many countries, but the Irish settle-bed has a wooden seat section that is hinged at the bottom, which swings out and downward to form a box-shaped bed.

GAA

Abbreviation for ⇨Gaelic Athletic Association.

GAELIC ATHLETIC ASSOCIATION

(GAA) (Irish *Cumann Lúthchleas Gael*)

Association founded in November 1884 in Tipperary by the Irish sportsmen Micheal Cusack and Maurice Davin. Its aims were to promote and develop traditional Irish pastimes, namely hurling and Gaelic football. After rules were drawn up for the games, the first All-Ireland finals were held three years later.

The association came to have profound political significance, often serving as a springboard for nationalist politicians and activists. It was extremely wary of outside influences, and introduced a controversial 'ban' which threatened expulsion to any member involved in foreign sports such as soccer and rugby. Although the ban was not universally approved of, it remained in place for almost a hundred years. The games themselves thrived, and hurling and Gaelic football are Ireland's two most popular sports today.

The GAA remains a significant focus for community life, with over 2,500 clubs in Ireland, and each of the 32 counties in Ireland having its own club competitions.

GAELIC FOOTBALL

See ⇨football, Gaelic.

GAELIC LEAGUE

Organization founded in 1893 to promote the use of the Irish language. Established by a Protestant academic, Douglas ⇨Hyde, a Catholic intellectual, Eoin MacNeill, and a Catholic priest, Fr Eugene O'Growney of Maynooth, the Gaelic League successfully halted the decline in the use of Irish by organizing language classes and social events, and establishing the language as a subject taught widely in national schools.

The movement was initially confined to an urban-based bourgeois intellectual elite but grew in popularity in the early 20th century to form part of what became known as the cultural nationalist movement. Although ostensibly non-political, the Gaelic League sought to promote a distinctive Irish national identity based on the revival of Gaelic culture. In both practical and ideological respects, it provided important support to the militant nationalists who would later organize the Easter Rising in 1916 and the Irish Civil War (1922–23).

GAELTACHT

Area where Irish is spoken, largely in the south and west of the Republic of Ireland, and especially in the counties Kerry, Galway, Waterford, Cork, Mayo, and Donegal. Historically the area was seen as the heart of the Irish 'soul' by generations of Irish nationalists, and it has received special help to maintain the Irish language. Amid concerns that the area of the Gaeltacht was dwindling, a radio service for the area was established in 1970, called Radió na Gaeltachta, and a television station, Telefis na Gaeltachta, opened in 1997.

The Gaeltacht enjoyed a revival at the end of the 20th century, chiefly in connection with the Irish-language poets Cathal O Searcaigh and Nuala ⇨Ní Dhomhnaill, who reflect such themes as feminism and gay liberation, as well as more traditional folkloric subjects.

GALLAGHER, RORY (1948–1995)

Blues and rock guitarist, singer and songwriter, born in Ballyshannon, County Donegal. Gallagher is credited with being 'the first Irish rock'n'roller'. By 1965 he had outgrown the showbands he had played in since his early teens and, following a brief period in Hamburg, he formed Taste, a three-piece band that was to catapult him into the 'rock' limelight. Throughout the 1970s Gallagher toured extensively in the USA, Europe, and Japan, selling over 30 million records, and recording with major figures such as Muddy Waters. Always a hard-working performer, he was known for his trademark jeans and workshirt and battered Fender Stratocaster guitar. His health declined in the 1980s and he died of complications following a liver transplant. His albums include: *Taste* (1966), *On the Boards* (1970), and *Live! In Europe* (1972).

GALLARUS ORATORY

The best preserved of all early Christian boat-shaped oratories, a small drystone church on the Dingle peninsula, County Kerry. It could date from as early as the 7th century. It resembles an upturned boat and, although rectangular in plan, it successfully employed the corbel technique used in building circular huts such as the beehive huts on Skellig Michael. This would indicate that the building work had been carried out by one or more very skilled stone masons.

GALTEE MOUNTAINS

Inland mountain range in the Republic of Ireland, stretching from southwest County Tipperary into County Limerick. The highest summit is Galtymore (920 m/3,018 ft), to the south of which are the huge Mitchelstown caves. The mountains are composed of old red sandstone and quartzite.

North of the mountains is the fertile and wooded Glen of Aherlow. Once an important pass between counties Limerick and Tipperary, the glen was the scene of a number of battles.

GALWAY

County on the west coast of the Republic of Ireland, in the province of Connacht; county town ⇨Galway; area 5,940 sq km/2,293 sq mi; population (1996) 188,900. Lead is found at Tynagh, and copper, lead, and zinc near Loughrea; marble is quarried and processed at Recess and Inverin. The main farming activity is cattle and sheep grazing. The Connemara National Park is in Galway. Towns include Salthill, a suburb of Galway city and seaside resort, Ballinasloe, Clifden, and Tuam.

The east is low-lying, fertile, limestone plain, but in the west the surface is mountainous, with the Twelve Bens group, the highest of which is Benbaun (730 m/2,395 ft), and the Maamturk Mountains, which rise to over 701 m/2,300 ft; in the south are the Slieve Aughty Mountains, which include Mweelrea Mountain (819 m/2,688 ft). Also in the south is Galway Bay, with the ⇨Aran Islands. To the west of Lough Corrib is ⇨Connemara. The Shannon is the principal river.

It is next to impossible... to toss a brick in the air anywhere in County Galway without it landing on the head of some musician.

JAMES GALWAY Flautist *An Autobiography* (1978).

Galway is rich in early archaeological remains, including ring forts, tumuli, stone circles, and *crannógs* (artificial islands); the Turoe Stone with its La Tène carvings dates from the 1st century BC. There are also a significant number of monastic remains in the county. Much of west Galway, including parts of Connemara, is a Gaeltacht (Irish-speaking area).

coast and waterways

The county is bounded to the west by the Atlantic (where the coast is much indented); to the south by County Clare; to the southeast by County Tipperary, Lough Derg, and the River Shannon; to the east by counties Offaly and Roscommon; and to the north by Roscommon and Mayo. Among the islands off the coast are Inishbofin, Inishark, and Gorumna in the northwest, and the Aran Islands in the southwest. The chief rivers, other than the Shannon, are the Shannon's tributaries the Corrib, the Suck, and the Clare. A branch of the Grand Canal connects the harbour at Shannon with Ballinasloe, but is closed to navigation.

GALWAY

Fishing port and county town of County ⇨Galway; 200 km/124 mi west of Dublin; principal city of ⇨Connacht province; population (1996) 57,200. It produces textiles and chemicals, and there is salmon and eel fishing; Galway has recently become important for its computer industry. Queen's College (founded in about 1845) was renamed University College in 1908, and is part of the National University of Ireland; teaching has been bilingual, conducted in both English and Irish, since 1929. Galway is an important centre of the Irish language; Galway Theatre, ⇨An Taibhdhearc, only stages plays in Irish.

features
Galway lies at the mouth of the short River Corrib which connects Lough Corrib with Galway Bay. It has a Roman Catholic cathedral, begun in 1957, and is home to the popular Galway Races, a three-day horse-racing fixture which takes place at the end of July. There is an important annual arts festival held in July, and an oyster festival in mid-September. The suburb of Salthill is a leading tourist resort.

history
Galway was founded in the 12th century by the de Burgo family. It was an important Anglo-Norman settlement and stronghold. Its first charter was granted in 1484 by Richard II. Until the Reformation, Galway was an important port and mercantile centre with significant trading links with Spain, France, and the West Indies. The Spanish Arch (believed to have formed part of an Anglo-Norman bastion) and Spanish Parade are named after the importance of Spanish mercantile activity during this period. Part of the medieval town walls can be seen to the south of the Spanish Arch.

I know a town tormented by the sea, /
And there time goes slow, / that the
people see it flow, / and watch it
drowsily.

MARY DAVENPORT O'NEILL Poet 'Galway'.

❧

During the Anglo-Norman period the Irish population was segregated from the city's inhabitants, being confined to Claddagh, a former fishing village demolished in the 1930s, and now a residential area in the west of the city. The Claddagh Ring (two hands holding a heart) is named after this district.

In 1651 the city was subject to lengthy conflict and surrendered to Cromwellian forces; in 1691 it fell to the troops of William III. By the early 18th century Galway's importance as a port and mercantile centre had begun to decline.

features
The Church of St Nicholas is a Norman construction of 1320; expanded in the 15th and 16th centuries, it is noted for its triple nave. Lynch's Castle, a 16th-century mansion house, has some fine carvings on its exterior, and was built by the Lynch family, who were important Anglo-Norman merchants; it is now a bank. Eyre Square in the city centre is a memorial garden to J F Kennedy, former president of the USA, who visited the city in 1963. In the centre of the square is a statue by Albert Power of Patrick O'Connor (1882–1928), a writer in the Irish language; there is also a statue of Liam Mellows, an activist in the 1916 Easter Rising who was executed during the Irish Civil War (1922–23). On Bowling Green is the former home of Nora Barnacle (1884–1951), novelist and wife of James Joyce; the house is now a museum.

GALWAY, JAMES (1939–)
Flautist, born in Belfast. He played with the London Symphony Orchestra in 1966, the Royal Philharmonic Orchestra 1967–69, and was principal flautist with the Berlin Philharmonic Orchestra 1969–75 before taking up a solo career. He also has a profile outside of classical music because of his popular recordings, particularly the cover of John Denver's 'Annie's Song' in 1978. Recent popular recordings are *Celtic Legends* (1997) and *Winter's Crossing* (1998) with Phil ⇨Coulter. Galway has done more to popularize the flute than any other instrumentalist of the 20th century.

GANDON, JAMES (1743–1823)
English-born Classical architect; one of the most important Georgian architects working in Ireland. Gandon moved from London to Dublin in 1781 to supervise the building of the new Custom House (1781–89), which is widely regarded as his masterpiece. He remained in Ireland for the rest of his life and designed some of Dublin's most significant buildings, including the Four Courts (from 1786); part of the old Irish parliament house, now the Bank of Ireland (1784–89); and the King's Inns (from 1800). He was one of the original members of the ⇨Royal Irish Academy, founded in 1785.

JAMES GANDON *The Four Courts, one of Gandon's greatest designs, are seen to best advantage from the south bank of Dublin's Liffey. Once the seat of four different courts, the building now houses only two: the High and Supreme Courts of Ireland.*

Gandon was born in New Bond Street, London, and began his career with an apprenticeship at Shipley's Drawing Academy in St Martin's Lane. He became general assistant to William Chambers, who worked in the neo-Palladian style, and started his own practice in 1765. His association with Ireland began in 1769, when he won second place in an open competition to design the Royal Exchange in Dublin (now the City Hall).

GARDA SÍOCHÁNA

Police force of the Irish Free State and later the Republic of Ireland, established in 1922. Despite its foundation in the troubled years of the Irish Civil War (1922–23), the Garda was from the beginning and remains a largely unarmed force. Expanding from an initial 2,000 officers, the force stood at over 11,000 (men and women) in 1999. Though generally perceived to be independent of serious political influence, some of its commissioners, notably Eoin ⇨O'Duffy in 1933 and Edmund Garvey in 1977, were forced to resign as a result of open conflict with the government of the day.

Since 1970 the Garda's tasks have been greatly expanded as a result of the Northern Ireland 'Troubles' and increased illegal activities on the border; 14 officers have been killed in the line of duty since 1969. However, the civil character of the force has been left largely unchanged by the Ulster crisis; political, anti-terrorist, and intelligence activities have been allocated to the Special Branch, a detective unit established for purposes of internal security in 1925.

Though the Garda continues to enjoy the respect and support of the public, increased industrial action, such as the 'Blue Flu' (a one day stoppage claiming sick-leave) in 1999, has given rise to some criticism.

GATE THEATRE

Theatre in Dublin, founded in 1928 by Mícheál ⇨Mac Liammóir and his partner Hilton Edwards (1903–1982) as a complement to the ⇨Abbey Theatre's Irish literary revival repertoire. The Earl of Longford (1902–1961) became co-director in 1931. A direct outcome of Edward Martyn's Hardwicke Street Theatre (1914–20) and the Dublin Drama League (1918–28), the Gate continued to present international drama and experimental theatre.

Originally the Gate company performed in the new Peacock Theatre, but in 1930 it inaugurated its own hall in the old Rotunda hospital on Parnell Square with a production of *Faust*. In the early years of the theatre, Mac Liammóir and Edwards looked after most of the lighting, design, acting, and production of shows. The company finally received a government subsidy in 1970, after 40 years of financial difficulties. Since 1983 its director, Michael Colgan, has continued the theatre's successful mix of modern, classical, and new Irish drama.

GELDOF, BOB (ROBERT FREDERICK XENON) (1954–)

Rock singer, born in Dun Laoghaire. He was the leader of the group the Boomtown Rats 1975–86. In the mid-1980s he instigated the charity Band Aid, which raised some £60 million for famine relief, primarily for Ethiopia.

Í don't think that the possible death of 120 million people is a matter for charity. It is a matter of moral imperative.

BOB GELDOF To UK Prime Minister Thatcher on the threatened famine in Africa (1985).

∼

In partnership with musician Midge Ure (1953–), Geldof gathered together many pop celebrities of the day to record Geldof's song 'Do They Know It's Christmas?' (1984), donating all proceeds to charity (it sold 7 million copies). The following year he organized two simultaneous celebrity concerts under the name Live Aid, one in London and one in Philadelphia, which were broadcast live worldwide. He was knighted in 1986, and in the same year nominated for the Nobel Peace Prize for his relief work.

GERALDINE

Term applied to the Anglo-Irish ⇨Fitzgerald dynasty in the medieval and early modern eras.

GIANT'S CAUSEWAY

Stretch of basalt columns forming a headland on the north coast of Antrim. It was formed by an outflow of lava in Tertiary times which has solidified in polygonal columns. The Giant's Causeway and Causeway Coast became a World Heritage Site in 1986.

According to legend, the causeway was built by the folk hero Finn Mac Cumhaill to enable the giants to cross between Ireland and Scotland.

GIBSON, MIKE (1942–)

Rugby Union player, born in Belfast. One of the game's most gifted players, Gibson won a record 69 caps for Ireland between 1964 and 1979. He won 25 caps at outside-half, four on the wing, and the other 40 in his favoured position of centre. Gibson also won 12 British Lions caps, and between 1966 and 1977 went on five Lions tours, an achievement only equalled by his fellow Irish player Willie John ⇨McBride. At club level he played for Campbell College, Trinity College, Dublin, and North of Ireland Football Club.

GILES, JOHNNY (MICHAEL JOHN)

(1940–)

Irish footballer, born in Cabra, Dublin. Giles scored five goals in 59 appearances for the Republic of Ireland between 1959 and 1979 and managed the Republic of Ireland team from 1973–1980. He joined Manchester United from Home Farm schoolboys in Dublin at the age of 15. A gifted player, he made his senior debut for Manchester United in 1959, making 98 league appearances before being sold to Leeds United in 1964. Partnering Billy Bremner in midfield under manager Don Revie, he helped Leeds win the second division championship in his first season. This marked the beginning of a successful career for Giles, who went on to win two Division 1 championships

GIANT'S CAUSEWAY *The strikingly unusual, hexagonal rock formations to be seen at the promontory of the Giant's Causeway, in County Antrim – since 1986 a World Heritage site – are the result of molten basalt cooling rapidly some 60 million years ago. The name derives from the legend that they are stepping stones used by giants.*

medals, in 1969 and 1971, and two Fairs Cups (since renamed the Union of European Football Associations (UEFA) Cup), in 1968 and 1971. His last game for Leeds was in 1975 in the European Cup final, when they lost to Bayern Munich.

Giles spent his final two seasons in England with West Bromwich Albion. In all, he scored 99 league goals for the three clubs.

Í sat under my umbrella in my
Aquascutum, like a putrid mushroom,
while a drenched mariner rowed me round
the cliffs and told me lies about them.

GEORGE BERNARD SHAW Writer Describing a visit to the Giant's Causeway on his 54th birthday, quoted in *Bernard Shaw* by Michael Holroyd (1998).

~

GILSENAN, ALAN (1964–)

Film-maker, Ireland's foremost documentarist to emerge in the 1980s. Gilsenan first came to prominence with his film version of Samuel Beckett's play *Eh Joe!* (1986) and made an impact with his influential documentary, *The Road to God Knows Where* (1988), which satirized the state's response to the social and economic crises of the decade.

In 1990, he made *Stories from the Silence*, about AIDS, which he followed with *Prophet Songs* about laicized Catholic priests. In 1996 he made *Home Movie Nights* in which he drew on amateur film footage often made by well-known Irish families. After the experimental and poorly received fiction film, *All Soul's Day* (1997), Gilsenan returned to documentary when in 1999 he made an impact with two very different films: *The Green Fields of France*, about Irish soldiers fighting in World War I, and two episodes of the history of the Irish diaspora, *The Irish Empire*.

GIRALDUS CAMBRENSIS (GERALD OF WALES) (1146–1223)

Welsh chronicler and ecclesiastic, author of the celebrated *Topographia Hiberniae/The Topography of Ireland*, a penetrating yet heavily biased description of Ireland in the 12th century. His broad yet subjective account of Ireland and its inhabitants was based on two visits, in 1183 and 1185. His other work concerning Ireland, *Expugnatio Hibernica/The Conquest of Ireland*, describes the history of Henry II's campaigns and victory in Ireland.

If an Irishman be a good man, there is no better; if he be a bad man, there is no worse.

GIRALDUS CAMBRENSIS *Topography of Ireland/Topographia Hibernica* (1186).

～

Born in Pembrokeshire of Welsh and Anglo-Norman descent, Giraldus Cambrensis studied in Paris, France, took holy orders, and became archdeacon of Brecknock, Wales. A strong promoter of church reform he was elected bishop of St David's, Wales, in 1198, but did not gain the possession of his see.

GLADSTONE, WILLIAM EWART (1809–1898)

British Liberal politician, prime minister 1868–74, 1880–85, 1886, and 1892–94. He secured several reforms for Ireland in areas of land tenure and education but two successive efforts to gain ⇨home rule for Ireland (in 1886 and 1893) failed.

Though his 'mission to pacify Ireland' was sometimes sceptically received by politicians and later historians as a ploy to manipulate and control opposing forces in his Liberal party, the sincerity of his concern for social and tenurial reform is undoubted. But his caution and failure to appreciate the depth of nationalist feelings in Ireland severely weakened his ability to manage political change.

GLASS

Flint glass production in the late 18th and early 19th centuries, and stained-glass production in the early 20th century, were the peaks of Irish achievement in the medium.

growth of the craft

Glassmaking has been practised in Ireland since the Iron Age (*c.* 300 BC–300 AD), and glass and enamel details appear on early Christian metalwork. The manufacture of glass objects, such as tableware, however, only began in the 16th century. Flint or lead glass was first made in Dublin in 1690, and as the 18th century progressed, ornaments, tableware, and apothecaries' bottles were made in this new material. A 1746 law banned the export of glass from Ireland, but in 1780 Irish glassmakers won the right to free trade, unlike those on the British mainland, and the industry suddenly bloomed. Blowers and cutters migrated from Britain, and soon Irish glass developed a distinctive style.

19th and 20th centuries

New designs for cutting, particularly deep fields of intricate diamond cutting, were developed in the early 19th century, and Irish glassworkers also began to use moulds, bearing patterns and the company name, to shape the bases of blown vessels. New forms were also introduced by Irish blowers, such as turn-over rims on large bowls, which often had square cast feet and stems. Other tableware forms came from native wooden utensils, such as the three-legged pot, and the piggin, a long-handled mug. Another innovation was the use of rows of coloured cut-glass studs to frame large wall-mirrors.

Tax on flint glass was re-introduced in 1825, and all of the major glass-producing centres – Dublin, Cork, Waterford, and Belfast – had closed by the end of the 19th century. In 1853 the Pugh glasshouse attempted to halt this decline with the production of Irish revival and other domestic wares, but it too eventually closed in 1899. Waterford glass re-opened in the mid-20th century, and a number of other glasshouses have followed suit. An interesting new approach can be seen in the recent collaboration between some of these companies and well-known designers from other fields, such as fashion design. Studio glass by self-employed craftspeople is also beginning to make inroads into the international scene at the beginning of the 21st century.

stained glass

Stained glass was popular in the 19th century in Ireland, but tended to be unoriginal in style, as Irish studios competed with larger English manufacturers. The Irish revival injected some new designs in the late 19th century, but quality of design only became a feature of Irish stained glass with the establishment of a glass department in the Dublin Metropolitan School of Art, and the simultaneous founding of ⇨An Túr Gloine (The Tower of Glass), in 1903. Rivalry between An Túr Gloine and Harry Clarke's studio early in the century spurred both on to greater heights, and by the 1930s Irish stained glass was enjoying worldwide renown. Evie ⇨Hone was still active in stained-glass production after World War II, but by this time much of the energy seemed to have left the Irish movement.

GLEESON, BRENDAN (1955–   )

Actor. More than any other film actor who came to prominence in the 1990s, Gleeson's 'honest', bumbling, and, ironically, given that he was an English and Irish teacher, inarticulate characterizations have marked him out as a unique talent. He played the lead role as real-life Dublin arch criminal Martin Cahill *The General* (1998), directed by John Boorman, as well as the small-time crook and low-lifer in the popular *I Went Down* (1997). Although he played Michael Collins in the televison series *The Treaty* (1992), he had the more minor role of Tobin in Neil ⇨Jordan's *Michael Collins* (1996).

Other films include *The Field* (1990), *Far and Away* (1992), *Into the West* (1992), *The Snapper* (1993), *Braveheart* (1995), *Trojan Eddie* (1996), *Spaghetti Slow* (1996), *Angela Mooney Dies Again* (1997), *The Butcher Boy* (1998), and *This is My Father* (1998).

GLENDALOUGH

Mountain glen in County Wicklow, situated 16 km/10 mi northwest of the town of Wicklow. Gle-

GLENDALOUGH *This monastic site takes its name from the Irish, Gleann da Loch, 'Valley of the Two Lakes'. St Kevin's Church, seen here, is also known as St Kevin's Kitchen, because the tower was once mistaken for a chimney.*

nealo Stream, a tributary of the Avonmore, runs through Glendalough, and the area is a popular beauty spot, a centre for rock climbing and hill walking. The remains of an early Christian and medieval monastic settlement attract pilgrims.

St Kevin is said to have established a hermitage here in the 6th century, but the surviving monastic ruins are later and date from the 10th century. The earliest remains are Teampall na Skellig (Church of the Rock) on the southern shore of the Upper Lough and the ruins of Reefert Church and St Kevin's cell, also on the Upper Lough. The main site, containing a large group of mainly 12th-century ruins, is situated near the Lower Lough. This takes the form of a monastic 'city', an important seat of early learning. The ruins include the gatehouse to the 'city', a round tower (31 m/103 ft high), the Romanesque church of Our Lady (the burial site of St Kevin), St Kevin's Church with its round tower and stone roof, and a mortuary chapel known as the Priest's House. The 11th-century cathedral ruins are extensive and there are remains of four other churches on the site, including St Saviour's Priory, which was reconstructed in 1875. There is also an interpretive centre and an extensive graveyard. On the eastern shore of the Upper Lough is a Bronze Age fort.

GLENVEAGH CASTLE

Victorian Scottish-style baronial castle at Church Hill, Country Donegal. It was built in 1870 by the

American J G Adair to designs by J T Trench. One of the few major country seats in Donegal, the main features of the property include Irish battlements and a round tower. Well laid-out gardens surround the castle, and it is now in the ownership of the state and open to the public.

GOBÁN SAOR (or GOIBHNIU) ('little

Goibhniu the wright')

In folklore, the ancient smith-god. A master craftsman, in folk legends he travels the countryside constructing castles, monasteries, and round-towers. Many of these legends are of a humorous variety, portraying him as outwitting his stingy and pompous employers.

GOGARTY, OLIVER ST JOHN

(1878–1957)

Writer who was born in Dublin and educated at the Royal University, and Trinity College, Dublin, later becoming a successful Dublin surgeon. A wit and a poet, Gogarty wrote several books, including the autobiographical *As I was Going Down Sackville Street* (1937). He is best known for his racy books of reminiscences, including *Tumbling in the Hay* (1939) and *It Isn't This Time of Year at All!* (1954). He took an active interest in Irish politics, being a senator of the Irish Free State 1922–36.

Virgins have done a deal of harm in this island. And marriage does nothing to soften their dissatisfaction with life. It cannot be all the fault of the men. It must be the hardness of our women that is driving men to politics.

OLIVER ST JOHN GOGARTY On Ireland, in *As I was Going Down Sackville Street* (1937).

∼

Gogarty was a member of the literary circle which included W B Yeats, George Moore, and James Joyce, and he figures in *Ulysses* as Buck Mulligan. Among his volumes of verse are *Poems and Plays* (1920), *An Offering of Swans* (1923), *Others to Adorn* (1938), and *Elbow Room* (1939). *As I was Going Down Sackville Street* was the cause of a successful libel action against him. In 1939 Gogarty moved permanently to the USA, where he wrote and lectured. He died in New York.

GOLDSMITH, OLIVER (1728–1774)

Playwright, novelist, poet, and essayist. Born in Pallas, County Longford, Goldsmith spent his early years in Lissoy, County Westmeath, and studied at Trinity College, Dublin, and Edinburgh University. Although he later travelled extensively through the British Isles and continental Europe, and settled in England for most of his life, he always retained fond memories of his Irish childhood and schooling. As a dramatist, Goldsmith is most widely celebrated for his comedy *She Stoops to Conquer* (1773). He also wrote the popular novel *The Vicar of Wakefield* (1766), and such works as the poem 'The Deserted Village' (1770) and the stage-play *The Good Natur'd Man* (1767), as well as histories and biographies.

Goldsmith's writing embodies the Enlightenment

Ill fares the land, to hast'ning ills a prey, / Where wealth accumulates, and men decay.

OLIVER GOLDSMITH *The Deserted Village* (1770).

∼

ideal of universal citizenship, but also contains a mixture of sentimentality, social satire, and displays a wondrous sense of humour. Politically conservative, he was often critical of urban society in contrast to a continued nostalgia for the rural landscape and people. *The Vicar of Wakefield*, an outwardly artless and gentle story is also social and political satire in

To begin with Ireland, the most western part of the continent, the natives are peculiarly remarkable for the gaiety and levity of their dispositions; the English, transplanted there, in time lose their serious melancholy air, and become gay and thoughtless, more fond of pleasure and less addicted to reasoning.

OLIVER GOLDSMITH *A Comparative View of Races and Nations.*

∼

which rural honesty, kindness, and patience triumph over urban values.

GOLF

Golf in Ireland dates back to the 19th century. The Golfing Union of Ireland, established in 1891, is the oldest golfing union in the world (the English and Scottish unions were not established until after World War I). The sport started out with 28 courses, by the year 2000 there were 386 clubs affiliated to the Golfing Union with 200,000 members. The popularity of the sport and ability of players increased significantly after Ireland staged the World Cup at the Portmarnock Golf Club, County Dublin, in 1960. Since then Irish golfers including Christy ⇨O'Connor, Eamon Darcy, Philip Walton, Padraig Harrington, Darren Clarke, and Paul McGinley have gone on to play top-level golf. The Ryder Cup tournament is to be played in Ireland in 2002.

GONNE, MAUD (married name MacBride)

(1865–1953)

Nationalist and political activist, founder of Inghinidhe na héireann ('daughters of Ireland') in 1900 and a founder-member of ⇨Sinn Féin in 1905. Gonne campaigned in Ireland, France, and the USA for the nationalist cause. Born in Surrey to an Irish colonel and his English wife, she moved to Ireland in 1882. A celebrated social beauty, she became one of Ireland's most colourful nationalists of the period, speaking for the rights of tenants and editing the nationalist newspaper *L'Irlande libre* in Paris.

In 1887 Gonne went to France to be with her lover Lucien Millevoye, with whom she had two children, George (1890–1891) and Iseult (1894–1954); the relationship lasted until 1899. Throughout the 1890s she took part in Irish nationalist meetings and fundraising drives in France, Ireland, and the USA.

Gonne became a lifelong friend and muse to the writer W B ⇨Yeats following their introduction in 1889. He composed his most nationalist play *Cathleen ni Houlihan* (1902) for her to act in at the new ⇨Abbey Theatre (1904). However, she refused Yeats's repeated offers of marriage and in 1903 married Maj John MacBride, whom she divorced after the birth of their son, the future revolutionary and peace campaigner Seán ⇨MacBride.

At the outbreak of World War I Gonne served in France with an ambulance corps and later returned to

*m*ore and more I realised that Ireland could rely only on force, in some form or another, to free herself.

MAUD GONNE *A Servant of the Queen* (1938), her autobiography up to 1903.

~

Ireland after John MacBride's execution for his part in the Easter Rising of 1916; she adopted her ex-husband's name for the first time after his death. She was imprisoned in 1918 but continued in nationalist politics and opposed the Anglo-Irish Treaty (1921), which established the Irish Free State within the British Commonwealth. In the 1920s and 1930s she was active in the Women's Prisoners Defence League.

GOOD FRIDAY AGREEMENT

See ⇨Northern Ireland peace process.

MAUD GONNE *A passionate devotee of the Republican cause, Gonne first organized protests in support of political prisoners during the 1890s. She spent six months in Holloway Prison in 1918, and organized the Republican Women's Prisoners' Defence League in 1922.*

GRATTAN, HENRY (1746–1820)

Patriot politician, born in Dublin. Grattan studied at Trinity College, Dublin, and trained as a barrister before entering the Irish parliament in 1775. He led the patriot opposition, and obtained free trade and legislative independence for Ireland in 1782. Disillusioned with the Protestant Ascendancy Parliament (which ironically is now known by the misnomer of 'Grattan's Parliament'), he retired from politics in 1797. Nevertheless he returned to take his seat for Wicklow in the final session of the Irish parliament, when he unsuccessfully opposed the Union Bill. He was returned as member for Malton, Yorkshire, in 1805 and for Dublin in 1806 and championed the cause of Catholic emancipation in the British parliament. He was buried in Westminster Abbey, London.

GRAVES, ALFRED PERCEVAL (1846–1931)

Poet, born in Dublin and educated there at Trinity College. His verse includes *Songs of Killarney* (1872), *Irish Songs and Ballads* (1879), and *Father O'Flynn and Other Lyrics* (1889). One of the participants in the Irish literary revival, he edited many poetry anthologies. His autobiography *To Return to All That* (1930) was a reply to *Goodbye to All That* by his son, the poet Robert Graves.

In his early career, he was a clerk and private secretary in the Home Office, and later became an inspector of schools.

GRAVES, ROBERT JAMES (1796–1853)

Physician and a leader of the Irish School of Diagnosis, which argued that clinical examination was central to the development of a diagnosis. His name is remembered in the term Graves' Disease, a condition caused by an enlarged and overactive thyroid gland which he first described in 1835.

Graves was born in Dublin. He graduated from Dublin University in 1818 and went on to study in Edinburgh, London, Göttingen, and Berlin. He returned to Dublin in 1821 to become a physician at the Meath Hospital, where he introduced radical reforms, not just in diagnosis. He gave lectures in English instead of Latin and argued that fever patients should continue to receive food and liquids, both counter to common practice. He also initiated the practice of using a watch to time the pulse.

He wrote an influential textbook, *Clinical Lectures on the Practice of Medicine* (1843), and founded the Park Street School of Medicine.

GREGORY, AUGUSTA (born Isabella Augusta Persse; Lady Gregory) (1852–1932)

Dramatist and cultural activist. Born in Roxborough, County Galway, she married Sir William Gregory of Coole Park in 1881. Her meeting with the playwright W B ⇨Yeats in the 1890s launched a life-long friendship based on a mutual love of Irish culture, that was creatively beneficial for both writers. An instrumental figure in the Irish literary revival, Gregory helped create the ⇨Abbey Theatre, Dublin, in 1897 with Yeats and other enthusiasts. Her own plays include the comedy *Spreading the News* (1904), the tragedy *Gaol Gate* (1906), *Rising of the Moon* (1907), and *Grania* (1912).

Gregory worked as an editor and theatre administrator as well as a collector and compiler of Irish folklore and music. The *Collected Works* (1970) includes her autobiography along with editions of her plays. Her journals, written 1916–30, were published in 1946.

GREYSTONES

Seaside resort in County Wicklow, 8 km/5 mi from Bray at the foot of Bray Head; population (1996) 10,000. There is a long sand and shingle beach and a golf course here, and Greystones is popular for shore angling.

Approximately 2 km/1 mi to the southwest, in the Glen of the Downs, is a nature trail through the state-owned forest.

GRIANÁN OF AILEACH ('stone palace of the sun')

Prehistoric cashel or ringfort at the entrance to the Inishowen Peninsula, County Donegal, 10 km/6 mi northwest of Derry. Situated on a 240 m-/800 ft-high mound above Loughs Swilly and Foyle, the massive circular structure, 23 m/77 ft in diameter, is further protected by three earth ramparts. Dry-stone walls, 5m/17ft high and 4 m/13 ft wide at the base, incorporate four tiers of inner terraces and two passages. Built on a site of early pagan worship, its original purpose is unknown, and construction dates differ between 1700 BC and 5 BC. From the 5th century it became the seat of the O'Neill dynasty, kings of Ulster, until sacked by Murtogh O'Brien, King of

Munster, in 1101. Reconstruction took place in the 1870s.

Grianán of Aileach appears on a 2nd-century map of Ireland by the Alexandrian geographer Ptolemy. In AD 450 Eoghán (Owen), founder of the O'Neill dynasty, was reputedly baptized here by St Patrick.

GRIFFIN, GERALD (1803–1840)

Novelist and dramatist. Griffin was born and educated in Limerick. His novels and stories capture a teeming Irish life, turbulent and sentimental by turns, in prose which is often vivid, and sometimes florid. They include *Tales of the Munster Festivals* (1827), *The Collegians* (1829), adapted as an extremely successful play (1860) by Dion Boucicault, with the title *The Colleen Bawn*, and *The Rivals* (1830). Among his other novels are *The Invasion* (1832), *Tales of My Neighbourhood* (1835), *The Duke of Monmouth* (1836), and *Talis Qualis, or Tales of the Jury Room* (1842).

*M*en thought it a region of sunshine and rest, / And they called it Hy-Brasail, the isle of the blest.

GERALD GRIFFIN 'Hy-Brasail'.

In 1823 Griffin went to London to pursue his writing career, where he was helped by John ⇨Banim. He returned to Ireland in 1827. In 1838 he joined the Society of the Christian Brothers in Dublin, and later moved to their monastery at Cork, where he died of typhus.

GRIFFITH, ARTHUR (1872–1922)

Printer, journalist, and politician; founder of Sinn Féin in 1905 and first president of the Irish Free State in 1922. Born in Dublin, Griffith was educated by the Christian Brothers and in 1893 was a founder member of the Celtic Literary Society. He became involved with the Gaelic League and the Irish Republican Brotherhood, which he left in 1910. Although a printer by trade, Griffith turned to nationalist politics after 1898 and edited several newspapers, including *The United Irishman* and *Sinn Féin*. His ideas on Irish independence found expression in his work *The Resurrection of Hungary: A Parallel for Ireland* (1904) which argued for an Irish dual monarchy. This propo-

sition, coupled with economic self-sufficiency, became the central platform for the Sinn Féin party, which he launched in 1905, uniting various nationalist parties.

Griffith joined the ⇨Irish Volunteers on its foundation and participated in its gunrunning activities through Howth. He rejected the use of force and took no part in the Easter Rising in 1916, although the government mistakenly thought Sinn Féin had led the rebellion and arrested Griffith. After his release in 1917 he was made vice-president of Sinn Féin, and was subsequently elected to Westminster as member of parliament for East Cavan in 1918. When the provisional Dáil (parliament) declared a republic in 1919, he was elected vice-president. He was imprisoned for a period during the Anglo–Irish War (1919–21), and headed the delegation assigned to negotiate the ⇨Anglo-Irish Treaty (1921), which established the Irish Free State within the British Commonwealth. He was elected the Free State's first president in January 1922 following the resignation of Éamon de Valera, but died suddenly of a cerebral haemorrhage on 12 August 1922.

GRIFFITH, RICHARD JOHN ('the Father of Irish geology') (1784–1878)

Geologist and civil engineer who produced the first complete geological map of Ireland in 1838. Griffith also carried out extensive studies of carboniferous limestone fossils, identifying many new species.

Griffith was born in Dublin and joined the Royal Irish Regiment when he was 16, resigning soon afterwards to study civil engineering in London. He went to Cornwall to gain mining experience before studying chemistry and natural history in Edinburgh for two years.

He was elected to the Royal Society of Edinburgh in 1807 and returned to Ireland where he became mining engineer to the Royal Dublin Society, and government inspector of mines in Ireland. As commissioner of valuations after the Irish Valuation Act of 1827, he created Griffith's Valuations for country rate assessments. He published the first complete geological map of Ireland in 1835, followed by large scale maps in 1838 and 1839, and an extensive revision in 1855.

He studied the carboniferous limestones of Ireland and their fossils, and also carried out elaborate surveys of the coalfields and bogs of Ireland. He was made a baronet in 1858.

GRUBB, HOWARD (1844–1931)

Engineer, who produced precision optical and astronomical instruments, some the largest of their kind at the time of manufacture. Grubb also developed a revolutionary type of optical gun sight and the first practical submarine periscope.

Born in Dublin, he was the son of the noted optical engineer, Thomas Grubb (FRS), who in the 1830s founded the telescope manufacturing business which Howard would later develop. Grubb studied civil engineering at Trinity College, Dublin, and then went to work for his father.

In 1865 he was put in charge of a major project to build a 122-cm/48-in reflecting telescope for the observatory in Melbourne, Australia, one of the largest in the world at the time. On his father's retirement in 1868, Howard assumed control of the company and moved to larger premises in Dublin. He oversaw the building of a 69-cm/27-in refracting telescope for the Vienna observatory around 1880, and also designed and built four of the rotating domes used at the observatory.

In 1925, at the age of 81, Grubb gave up active participation in the family business, which was acquired by the English engineer Charles Algernon Parsons and moved to Newcastle upon Tyne as the Sir Howard Grubb Parsons Company. Grubb was knighted in 1887.

GUERIN, VERONICA (1959–1996)

Investigative journalist, born in Dublin. Having begun her career as an accountant with close links to the Fianna Fáil party, Guerin came late to journalism, beginning to write for major Irish Sunday newspapers from 1990 onwards. Several journalistic scoops preceded her decision to become Ireland's most probing investigative journalist specializing in the exposure of

GUINNESS *One of a series of hugely successful adverts that helped make Guinness synonymous with Ireland the world over. At the Dublin brewery, 4,000 people work to produce an astonishing daily output of four million pints of the smooth, dark beer.*

the Irish drugs underworld. Her remarkable reports for the Sunday Independent from 1994 on, led to threats, at least one murder attempt and eventually to her assassination on 26 June 1996.

Guerin's murder prompted a massive reaction from the state and the public at large, which has led since her death to the vigorous suppression of the trade in drugs and the arrest and conviction of several leading criminals.

GUILDFORD FOUR

Four Irish victims of miscarriage of justice who spent 14 years in prison convicted of terrorist bombings of pubs in Guildford and Woolwich in 1974. They were released in 1989 when an investigation concluded that the arresting Surrey police had given misleading evidence and, in consequence, their convictions were subsequently quashed.

Three former Surrey police officers were subsequently accused of conspiring to pervert the course of justice.

GUINNESS

Strong dark beer with a white froth on top, generally considered to be the national drink of Ireland. Guinness has been brewed in Ireland since 1756 by one of the most successful commercial families in Irish history.

Arthur Guinness was the first to open a brewery in Leixlip in 1756, moving to Dublin in 1759 where there were around 60 other breweries. Competition was keen and the quality of the beer produced there improved rapidly. Best quality Irish barley, improved malting techniques, and the abolition of the excise tax on beer, meant that brewers in Dublin and Cork were able to virtually eliminate British imports by the end of the century.

The Guinness brewery in Dublin had started by producing ale and beer and began brewing the darker drink, porter, in the 1790s. By the 1820s Guinness's better porters were known as stouts and from then on they began to break into the British market, which by 1840 accounted for over half their sales. In 1886 Guinness became a public company with share applications of over £100 million. In the 1930s it had become one of the seven largest companies in the world.

The advertising slogan 'Guinness is good for you' first appeared in 1929 and was widely thought (or hoped) to be true.

Guinness family

Arthur Guinness (1725–1803), the son of a County Kildare land agent, set up the Leixlip brewery in 1756 with a bequest of £100. His son, Arthur (II) Guinness (1758–1858), inherited the brewery, now relocated to Dublin, along with his father's flourmilling interests. Like his father, he was an active member of the Church of Ireland, and he started many of the family's philanthropic activities; over the years they would support Catholic emancipation, restore hospitals, build almshouses, contribute to slum clearance and housing projects, and support medical research.

Benjamin Lee Guinness (1798–1868), the son of Arthur II, assumed control of the brewery in 1855 and made it the largest business of its kind in the world, exporting beer to Britain, Europe, and the USA. He was elected the first lord mayor of Dublin in 1851, and represented Dublin as a member of the Westminster parliament 1865–68. He funded the restoration of St Patrick's Cathedral 1860–65 and was made 1st Baronet in 1867.

Benjamin Lee's third son, Edward Cecil Guinness, (1847–1927) continued a devotion to public causes, including the restoration of public libraries and the construction of housing for Dublin and London artisans. He was created 1st Earl of Iveagh in 1891.

In the 1980s the family interest in the business declined to no more than 5% as the company expanded by taking over large and established firms, including Bells in 1985 and Distillers in 1986.

GUR, LOUGH

Crescent-shaped lake central to an extensive prehistoric settlement in County Limerick; one of the most complete Neolithic and Bronze Age habitation sites in Europe. Neolithic huts with stone foundations and enclosures, dating from 3500 to 100 BC, dot the marshy shore lines and the slopes of Knockadoon Hill. The lake contains a number of crannogs (dwellings on artificial islands). Wedge tombs, gallery-graves, and more than 20 stone circles have been identified. Grange Stone Circle, 4,000 years old, is the largest in Ireland, with 113 stones and a diameter of 45 m/150 ft. Artefacts recovered include the Loch Gur shield, a piece of heavily bossed armour from 600 BC. Later features include two Viking stone forts and an Early Christian earthen ring-fort. The bones of reindeer, bear, and giant Irish deer, species now extinct in Ireland, have been found in caves above the lake.

GWYNN, STEPHEN LUCIUS (1864–1950)

Poet and critic. Gwynn was born in Dublin and educated at St Columba's College, Rathfarnham, and Brasenose College, Oxford. Among his critical works are *The Masters of English Literature* (1904) and lives or studies of Alfred Tennyson (published 1899), Thomas Moore (1905), Walter Scott (1930), Horace Walpole (1932), Jonathan Swift (1933), and Oliver Goldsmith (1935). His *Collected Poems* appeared in 1923.

After graduating from Oxford, Gwynn taught classics for ten years and then became a freelance writer in London. He sat in Westminster as MP for Galway City 1906–18 and during World War I he received the Légion d'honneur.

HALL, ANNA MARIA (born Fielding)

(1800–1881)

Novelist, born in Dublin. Hall spent her childhood in County Wexford, before moving to London in 1815. Her works include *Sketches of Irish Character* (1829), *The Buccaneer* (1832), and *The White Boy* (1845). She also contributed many sketches to the *Art Journal*, edited by her husband, Samuel Carter Hall (1800–1889). Together they collaborated to produce *Ireland, its Scenery and Character* (1841).

Although Hall left Ireland at an early age, it provided the background for several of her successful books.

HAMILTON, WILLIAM ROWAN

(1805–1865)

Mathematician and astronomer. Hamilton developed quaternions, a landmark in the development of algebra. He defined the phenomenon of critical refraction and his advanced mathematics had a lasting influence on mathematical physics through its importance to quantum mechanics.

Hamilton was born in Dublin. Exceptionally bright and precocious, he was reading and could do mathematics at the age of three, was studying Greek, Latin, and Hebrew at five, and by the age of 13 had a good knowledge of 13 languages; as a 14-year-old he wrote a welcome in Persian for the visit of the Persian ambassador to Dublin.

He turned to mathematics in a more intensive way in 1820, and in 1823 went to Trinity College, Dublin. In 1827, while still an undergraduate and just 22, he was appointed professor of astronomy and Astronomer

WILLIAM ROWAN HAMILTON *Honoured by scientific societies worldwide, Hamilton named the German philosopher Kant and British poet and philosopher Coleridge among his influences. He worked in optics and dynamics, as well as making important contributions to the study of algebra.*

Royal of Ireland. This enabled him to move to Dunsink Observatory, just outside Dublin, where he lived until his death. He was knighted in 1835.

HANNAY, JAMES OWEN (pseudonym GEORGE A BIRMINGHAM) (1865–1950)

Novelist, born in Belfast, the son of a clergyman, and educated at Haileybury and Trinity College, Dublin.

Spanish Gold (1908) established him as a novelist of Irish life with a racy humour all his own. Among his other novels are *The Major's Niece* (1911), *Good Conduct* (1920), *Goodly Pearls* (1926), *Fed Up* (1931), and *Good Intentions* (1945).

Hannay was ordained in 1889, and spent many years teaching and as a curate in Ireland. He served as chaplain with the British army, and obtained a living in Somerset in 1924 before moving to a London parish in 1934.

HARDIMAN, JAMES (1782–1855)

Scholar, born in Westport, County Mayo. Hardiman grew up in Galway and temporarily studied for the priesthood. He was appointed librarian at Queen's College, Galway, in 1848. His most significant work is *Irish Minstrelsy, or Bardic Remains of Ireland* (2 volumes, 1831), an anthology of Irish poetry which uses source material from both Irish manuscript and oral traditions. The anthology, due to its size and scope, is testament to the long and distinguished history of Irish poetry, and disputes the labels of inferiority affixed by Anglo-Irish writers and chroniclers.

HARP

National instrument of Ireland. The old Irish harping tradition was a highly skilled aristocratic art. Because of a series of social, political, and economic changes, it began to decline from the 16th century onwards and as the status of the harpist diminished so the performers became increasingly poor and itinerant, and, in some cases, even blind. Despite valiant attempts to revive the harping tradition, the most notable being the Belfast Harp Festival of 1792 when Edward Bunting was employed to write down the music, the tradition was extinct by the early 19th century.

Some of the features of the older instrument and style were metal strings plucked by the fingernails, with the left hand playing the upper register. The older instrument was also nonchromatic. What is sometimes referred to as the 'neo-Irish' harp was invented in Dublin in the early 19th century by John Egan, modelled on the concert harp. This has semi-tone levers and is played with the fleshy parts of the fingertips on gut strings, creating a very different sound. The neo-Irish harp is the instrument generally known as the Irish harp today. It has been, and to a certain extent continues to be, associated with female, middle-class amateur performers, frequently as a vocal accompaniment.

HARP *Turlough Carolan's harp and manuscripts are seen here at Clonalis House, Castlerea, County Roscommon. Blinded by smallpox, Carolan travelled throughout Ireland for 45 years composing for patrons. His final piece was dedicated to the butler who brought him his last drink.*

The most famous harp composer was Turlough ⇨Carolan – almost 200 compositions attributed to him survive. In recent years the harp has become more a part of the mainstream tradition, with many prominent younger players such as Máire Ní Chathasaigh, Janet Harbison, Laoise Kelly, and Michael Rooney.

HARRIS, RICHARD (ST JOHNS) (1933–)

Actor, born in Limerick, whose international breakthrough came with his role as a North of England Rugby League player in *This Sporting Life* (1963), for which he received an Academy Award nomination and the Best Actor Award at the Cannes Film Festival. More recently he received an Academy Award nomination for Best Actor for his performance as Bull McCabe in Jim ⇨Sheridan's *The Field* (1990).

After studying at the London Academy of Music and Dramatic Art and at Joan Littlewood's Theatre Workshop, Harris appeared in minor roles in a number of films made in Ireland, including *Alive and Kicking* (1958), *Shake Hands With the Devil* (1959), and *A Terrible Beauty* (1960). His towering physical presence, often tinged with vulnerability, or even a masochistic streak, became a hallmark, as was the case in his most commercially successful role in the US film, *A Man Called Horse* (1970) (he starred in the sequels in 1976 and 1983).

After a less successful period in the 1970s and 1980s, he rediscovered religion, took up writing and in 1982 his thriller novel, *Honor Bound*, was published. Late in the 1980s he made a comeback to the screen and, following his success in *The Field*, his role in Clint Eastwood's *Unforgiven* (1992) was widely praised. Returning to Ireland, he gave a memorable performance as a traveller in *Trojan Eddie* (1996).

Other films include *The Guns of Navarone* (1962), *Mutiny on the Bounty* (1962), *Patriot Games* (1992), *Cry, The Beloved Country* (1995), and *Smilla's Sense of Snow* (1997).

HARTY, (HERBERT) HAMILTON

(1879–1941)

Conductor and composer. After much conducting experience in London he was appointed conductor to the Hallé Orchestra, Manchester, in 1920. He gave the first British performance of Mahler's ninth symphony in 1930.

He studied piano, viola, and composition under his father and became an organist at the age of 12. He later became organist in Belfast and Dublin, where he studied further under Michele Esposito. In 1900 he settled in London as an accompanist and composer and married the soprano Agnes Nicholls. He retired from the Hallé in 1933.

His works include: ORCHESTRAL arrangement of Handel's *Water Music* and *Fireworks Music*, Irish Symphony (1924), *Comedy Overture* (1907), symphonic poem *With the Wild Geese* for orchestra (1910); violin concerto. VOCAL *Ode to a Nightingale* (Keats) for soprano and orchestra (1907); cantata *The Mystic Trumpeter* (Whitman; 1913); many songs.

HARVEY, WILLIAM HENRY (1811–1866)

Botanist, a leading authority on algae who classified and named hundreds of new species of flowering and non-flowering plants, including several new forms of Irish flora, particularly mosses.

Born in Limerick, Harvey often spent summer hol-

idays at the County Clare seaside town of Milltown Malbay, where he became fascinated with seaweed. He attended a number of Quaker schools before travelling to Cape Town, South Africa, where he became colonial treasurer 1836–42. He collected many botanical specimens and wrote *The Genera of South African Plants* (1838). His abilities were remarkable, considering that he had not been educated in botany at university.

Harvey was forced to retire in 1842 due to ill health, but was able to pursue his interest in plants of all kinds. In 1844 he became keeper of the herbarium at Trinity College, Dublin, and in 1846 published *Phycologia Britannica*, a work entirely illustrated by Harvey himself. In 1849 he went on tour in the USA, where he lectured to large and enthusiastic audiences in Boston and Washington and identified and named new species in Florida. He also travelled to the southern hemisphere, writing *Phycologia Australica* in 1858. He was made chair of botany at Trinity College, Dublin, in 1856, where he died of tuberculosis.

HASLAM, THOMAS (1825–1917) AND ANNA (1829–1922)

Quaker feminist activists, from Laois and Cork respectively. They married in 1854 and settled in Dublin. In 1876 they organized the Dublin Women's Suffrage Association, which began to gain momentum at the turn of the 20th century. After cooperation with the labour movement, the group was renamed the Irish Women's Suffrage and Local Government Association (IWSLGA), which continued in various forms until 1947. Although non-militant, the IWSLGA maintained close links with more aggressive suffragist groups.

HAUGHEY, CHARLES JAMES (1925–   )

Irish politician; Taoiseach (prime minister) 1979–81, 1982, and 1987–92; leader of Fianna Fáil 1979–92. He succeeded Jack Lynch as Fianna Fáil leader and Taoiseach in 1979, to be faced with serious economic problems and an intensely difficult period in Anglo-Irish relations, as the UK's Thatcher government attempted to face down the IRA hunger strikes of 1980 and 1981. He lost office in 1981 after an early general election and regained it for a short period in 1982. His final period of office, beginning in 1987, was mired in difficulty, and saw Haughey forced to accept coalition with the ⇨Progressive Democrats. In

1998 the Irish director of public prosecutions elected to prosecute Haughey for his alleged attempts to obstruct an earlier hearing into payments made to politicians in the 1980s. His trial was set for summer 2000.

Ít seems that the historic inability in Britain to comprehend Irish feelings and sensitivities still remains.

CHARLES HAUGHEY Speech, February 1988.

❧

Haughey was born in Dublin, and studied law at King's Inns and University College, Dublin. He entered the Dáil (parliament) in 1957, becoming minister for justice in the cabinet of his father-in-law Seán Lemass in 1961. In 1970, along with Neil Blaney, he was dismissed from the government by Taoiseach Jack Lynch for alleged involvement in importing arms into the country, for use by nationalists in Northern Ireland, an incident known as the arms crisis. He was subsequently acquitted of all charges.

As Taoiseach, Haughey was rhetorically more republican than his predecessors, making relations with the UK more difficult. His early governments did nothing to remove the controversy that surrounded him as allegations were made of phone tapping and improper dealings with the Garda. He was responsible for the initiation and development of partnership agreements between unions, industry, and the state which laid the foundation for Ireland's economic development in the 1990s. However, the highly disturbing revelations of his financial and private life in the tribunal of inquiry set up to investigate his financial affairs in 1998, diminished his standing with the public at large.

HEALY, TIMOTHY MICHAEL (1855–1931)

Lawyer, politician, and first governor-general of the Irish Free State. Healy supported Irish nationalist Charles Stewart Parnell until the split in the Irish Nationalist Party occasioned by the O'Shea divorce case in 1890. Later he was in favour of reunion under the leadership of John Redmond, but in 1900 he was expelled from the party for his opposition to the United Irish League. He was readmitted in 1908, but was again expelled in 1910, in which year he formed,

with William O'Brien, the Independent Nationalist Party. Healy retired from politics in 1918. In 1922 he became the first governor-general of the Irish Free State, a post he held for five years.

Healy was born in Bantry, County Cork. He was called to the Irish Bar in 1884, and became a queen's counsel in 1899. In 1903 he was called to the English bar, and he was a bencher of Gray's Inn and of King's Inn, Dublin. He was elected to Westminster as member of parliament for Wexford in 1880, for Monaghan in 1833, for South Londonderry in 1885, for North Longford in 1887, for North Louth in 1892, and North East Cork in 1910, a seat he retained until 1918.

HEANEY, SEAMUS (JUSTIN) (1939–)

Poet and critic. Born near Castledawsen, County Derry, he has written powerful verse about the political situation in Northern Ireland and reflections on Ireland's cultural heritage. Collections include *Death of a Naturalist* (1966), *Field Work* (1979), *The Haw Lantern* (1987), *The Spirit Level* (1996; Whitbread Book of the Year), and *Opened Ground: Poems 1966–1996* (1998). Critical works include *The Redress of Poetry* (1995). His *Beowulf: A New Translation* (1999), a modern version of the Anglo-Saxon epic, won the Whitbread Book of the Year award. He was professor of poetry at Oxford 1989–94 and was awarded the Nobel Prize for Literature in 1995.

'Bogland' is an attempt to make the preserving, shifting marshes of Ireland a mythical landscape, a symbol of the preserving, shifting consciousness of the Irish people. History is the soft ground that holds and invites us into itself, century after century.

SEAMUS HEANEY Speaking about his poem 'Bogland' in *Let the Poet Choose* (1975), edited by James Gibson.

❧

Heaney was educated at Queen's University, Belfast. His *Death of a Naturalist* was the first collection from a group of Ulster poets, including James Simmons, Derek Mahon, and Michael Longley, with whom he was associated. Heaney's early work, in this

SEAMUS HEANEY *In his youth, Heaney and other Belfast poets, 'used to talk poetry day after day with an intensity and prejudice that cannot but have left a mark'. His* Beowulf: A New Translation *won the Whitbread Book of the Year award in 1999.*

collection and in *Door into the Dark* (1969), was marked by a densely descriptive evocation of rural life. The poems of *Wintering Out* (1972) and *North* (1975) explore history and prehistory as a vehicle for oblique comment on the contemporary 'Troubles' of Northern Ireland. Later collections, including *Field Work* (1979), *Station Island* (1984), *The Haw Lantern* (1987), and *The Spirit Level* (1996), mix increasingly self-conscious political language with more private love-poetry and elegy, and display a continuing concern with the natural world, and with the wider responsibilities of poetry.

The technical mastery and linguistic and thematic richness of Heaney's work have gained an international audience, and exercised a powerful influence on contemporary poetry.

HECK, BARBARA (1734–1804)

Methodist who organized the first Methodist churches in pre-revolutionary America and Canada. Born Barbara von Ruckle in County Limerick's German-speaking colony, she embraced Methodism in 1752 before marrying Paul Hescht (or Heck) and moving to New York City in 1760. She convinced her cousin Philip Embury (1728–1773) to establish a church in his home. Later, she designed North America's first Methodist church building, although it was soon replaced by a larger building (1768).

Heck left New York due to independence agitation, but her farm was burnt down by neighbours. She then fled to Montréal, where she established Canada's first Methodist class meeting.

HERBERT, VICTOR (1859–1924)

Irish-born US conductor and composer. In 1893 he became conductor of the 22nd Regiment Band, also composing light operettas for the New York stage. He was conductor of the Pittsburgh Philharmonic 1898–1904, returning to New York to help found the American Society of Composers, Authors, and Publishers (ASCAP) in 1914.

The second of his two cello concertos, written in 1894, inspired Dvořák to write his own cello concerto.

Born in Dublin, Herbert trained as a cellist at the Stuttgart Conservatory, and began his professional musical career in Vienna, Austria. He emigrated to the USA in 1886 and played with the New York Metropolitan Opera and Philharmonic Orchestra.

His works include: opera: *Natoma* (1911), *Madeleine* (1914); operettas *The Wizard of the Nile* (1895), *Babes in Toyland* (1903), and over 30 others; the orchestral symphonic poem *Hero and Leander* (1901) and three suites for orchestra; the chamber work Serenade for strings; and the vocal dramatic cantata *The Captive* (1891), as well as a range of songs.

HERO-TALES

In medieval Irish literature, stories of mythical and pseudo-historical heroes, told in prose with some interspersed verse. They include tales of Celtic deities and the ⇨mythological origins of Ireland, the Fianna and Ulster warrior cycles, and the legends surrounding supposed ancient kings. The sources were traditions which survived from ancient Celtic culture, floating folklore of medieval times, and to a lesser extent adaptations of borrowings from Latin literature and fiction. Several of these stories survived in folklore, either through continuous narrative usage or springing in recent centuries from manuscript compilations.

Mythological stories feature a range of characters called ⇨Tuatha Dé Danann ('people of the goddess ⇨Danu'), who were originally a pantheon of Celtic deities ruled by the ⇨Dagda ('the good god'). The most elaborate and influential tale is *Cath Muighe Tuireadh/The Battle of Moytirra* and describes how the Tuatha Dé Danann struggled against their oppressors, the ⇨Fomorians ('underworld spirits'), and gained their freedom. The story culminates in the victory of the hero ⇨Lugh in single combat against his adversary Balar. Other Celtic deities include Brigit ('the exalted one'), daughter of the Dagda and goddess of crafts, poetry, and healing.

The Fianna Cycle

This cycle of stories combined ancient druidic lore of the seer ⇨Finn Mac Cumhaill with the cult of young trainee warriors called ⇨Fianna. This combination seems to have occurred in prehistoric Leinster, but through the Middle Ages it attracted a myriad of narrative plots and spread throughout the whole Gaelic world. The legendary hero and bard ⇨Ossian, reputedly the son of Finn, is said to have related his father's deeds to St Patrick in the 5th century. Stories of the seer-warrior Finn and his companions were immensely popular in the literary and oral streams down to recent times.

> *y*ou hear of the Limerick fairies, and the Donegal fairies, and the Tipperary fairies, and the fairies of two adjoining counties have their faction fights, just like the inhabitants themselves.
>
> J G KOHL Writer *Ireland, Dublin, the Shannon, Limerick, Cork and Kilkenny Races…* (1843).

~

The Ulster Cycle

This was based on wars in the 5th century AD between the people of Ulster and an expansionist clan of Connacht. The cycle was developed by professional storytellers in the Middle Ages for rulers of various parts of Ireland who had a taste for warlike lore. The central story is *Taín Bó Cuailnge/The Cattle Raid of Cooley*, in which the super-hero ⇨Cuchulain (Cú Chulainn) thwarts the efforts of Queen ⇨Medhbh of Connacht to gain possession of the great brown bull of Cooley.

stories of ancient kings

Several stories dramatized the lives of supposed ancient kings, such as ⇨Conchobar, King of Ulster, and the tragic Deirdre, his betrothed. The most influential of these, in literature and folklore, concerned ⇨Cormac MacArt, a worthy king who was said to have ruled at ⇨Tara Hill. After a threatened youth, Cormac acceded to the kingship from which his father had been removed, and his reign was marked by great prosperity, wisdom, and peace.

later developments

In post-medieval times, writers continued to compose hero-tales, though the style became more picaresque (a florid episodic genre). This type of fiction combined references to ancient characters with influences from romance literature in other languages, and had a taste for burlesque and extravagance.

HICKEY, KIERAN (1936–1993)

Director and writer, born in Dublin. In the 1970s Hickey was one of the first film-makers, along with Bob ⇨Quinn, to help carve out an indigenous Irish cinema. Having studied film formally, he began his career directing sponsored documentaries for state agencies, while also producing films on writers Jonathan Swift and James Joyce. His film *Exposure* (1978), about the suppressed sexuality of three male surveyors who come into contact with a foreign woman, identified an interest with the middle class. This concern was pursued in *Criminal Conversation* (1981) in which the world of Dublin's 'nouveau riche' was explored.

Hickey's other films include *A Child's Voice* (1978), *Attracta* (1983), *Short Story: Irish Cinema 1945–59* (1986), and *The Rockingham Shoot* (1987).

HIGGINS, ALEX (GORDON) (1949–)

Snooker player, born in Belfast, County Antrim. At the age of 23, Higgins became the then youngest player to take the Embassy World Snooker Championship when he defeated John Spencer in 1972. Volatile at times, Higgins was nonetheless a hugely popular figure in the game; his 16–15 victory over Jimmy White in the 1982 World Championship ranks as a classic, and he went on to take the final, beating the Welsh player Ray Reardon. Higgins was also part of the successful Irish team that won three world titles during the 1980s.

HIGGINS, WILLIAM (1763–1825)

Chemist who wrote about the existence of atoms and the attractions between them. His theories were published almost twenty years before John Dalton's ground-breaking work on atomic weights. Higgins helped to bring down the erroneous theory of phlogiston, a substance thought to be released when material burns.

Higgins was born in Colloney, County Sligo, and was apprenticed to his wealthy uncle, a London doctor, before going to Oxford in 1786. In 1789, at the age of 26, he published the book which would establish his name, *The Comparative View of the Phlogistic and Antiphlogistic Theories*. In it Higgins was dismissive of the idea of phlogiston, instead suggesting the existence of atoms.

However, he did little more with his ideas until Dalton set out his atomic theory in *A New System of Chemical Philosophy* (1808), after which Higgins fought an unsuccessful battle claiming that he had been first with the proposition.

HILLERY, PATRICK (JOHN) (1923–)

Irish politician, president 1976–90. As minister of foreign affairs, he successfully negotiated Ireland's entry into the European Economic Community (EEC, now the European Union) in 1973. Thereupon he became Ireland's first EEC Commissioner. Hillery served as president for two terms until 1990.

Born in Miltown Malbay, County Clare, Hillery studied chemistry and medicine at University College Dublin. He entered the Dáil (lower house of the Irish parliament) for Fianna Fáil in 1951 and served various governments as minister for education, industry and commerce, labour, and foreign affairs.

HILLSBOROUGH

Market town in County Down, 20 km/12 mi southwest of Belfast; population (1991) 1,200. It mainly functions as a commuter settlement for Belfast. Hillsborough was developed by a family named Hill in the 17th century, and still retains much of its original character, with a number of fine Georgian buildings. The mansion, built in 1760 for the Hills, became the official residence of the governors of Northern Ireland, and is now the local base for the UK secretary of state for Northern Ireland. Near Hillsborough is a 17th-century star-shaped fort built for Col Arthur Hill.

Kilwalin Moravian church near Hillsborough has a model of the ancient Greek battlefield of Thermopylae in its grounds. At Moira village, 11 km/7 mi to the west of Hillsborough, a conflict took place in 637 between the high king of Ireland and the king of Ulster, as recounted in a poem by Samuel Ferguson.

HISTORIOGRAPHY

Modern Irish historiography is rooted in the books and tracts generated from the 16th century on, to justify or denounce English conquest and colonization. English propaganda and justification for the conquest, which included *View of the Present State of Ireland* (1596) by Edmund Spenser; *Discovery of the True Causes why Ireland Was Never Entirely Subdued* (1612) by John ⇨Davies; and *Hibernia Anglicana* (1690) by Richard Cox, vied with Irish works that asserted the primacy of Gaelic rights to Ireland, such as Geoffrey ⇨Keating's *Foras Feasa ar Éirinn/Groundwork of Knowledge of Ireland* (1633); the *Annals of the Four Masters* (1632–36) compiled by Mícheál Ó Cléirigh (c. 1590–1643); and John Lynch's *Cambrensis Eversus* (1662).

While English assessments quoted legal and political documents and Irish accounts were often dependent on chronicles, myth, and pseudo-history, the arguments of both schools were fundamentally prejudiced by unquestioned theoretical assumptions: the Irish asserting that a commitment to Roman Catholicism would forever separate Ireland from Protestant England, and the English assuming the absolute superiority of English laws and customs over native culture. This bitter debate, with its opposing stances, retarded historical research for over a century, although the philological (study of language) and antiquarian work of Eugene O'Curry (1796–1862) and John O'Donovan (1809–1861) laid the foundations of a scholarly approach to the study of Gaelic Ireland.

Further stimulus to historiography was added in the mid-19th century by the Irish writings of the English historian J A Froude (1818–1894) whose sharply critical views of the Anglo-Irish provoked spirited and seemingly objective defences based on solid scholarship from W E H Lecky (1838–1903) on the 18th century, and Richard Bagwell (1840–1918) on the 16th and 17th centuries. At the same time a number of Catholic scholars trained on the continent and independent antiquarians produced a body of diocesan and local studies, which immensely expanded Ireland's historical database, paving the way for a substantial increase in high quality academic publication in the early 20th century.

We Irish are always being accused of looking backwards too much. Sometimes, however, we don't look back far enough – or carefully enough, or honestly enough.

DERVLA MURPHY Travel writer *A Place Apart* (1978).

In the 1930s two academic historians, T W Moody (1907–1984) and R D Edwards (1909–1988), sought to direct and develop the energy of this movement by a variety of initiatives, most notably the founding of the peer-review journal *Irish Historical Studies* in 1938. Although their work has been highly successful, their critique of traditional nationalist views of Irish history attracted charges of ideological conservatism, evasion of fundamental issues, and the production of a bland, self-censored interpretation of history, derogatorily labelled as 'revisionism'. The revisionist controversy, sparked by Brendan Bradshaw in *Irish Historical Studies* in 1989, has since given rise to new research and has advanced several academic reputations, but it is likely that its most lasting achievement will be to encourage historians to be more critical of the assumptions underlying their research, and more conscious of the idiom and style of their writings.

HOCKEY

Hockey in Ireland dates back to the 19th century, with the men's association being founded in 1893 and the ladies' association in 1894. The greatest achievement for Irish hockey was at the 1908 London Olympic Games when the Irish team took the silver medal. The international status of the Irish team has waned since then and the Republic of Ireland has not been represented at the Olympics since the foundation of the state in 1922. Although medals were won by Ulster-born players at the 1984, 1988, and 1992 Olympics, they were won under the British team flag.

In recent years hockey has established itself as a prominent team sport throughout the island. Leagues are played on a provincial basis with a national cup competition played for annually. Ladies' hockey is currently more widespread, with 126 clubs on the island compared to 96 men's clubs.

HOLLAND, JOHN PHILIP (1840–1914)

Engineer who developed some of the first military submarines used by the US navy. He began work in Ireland in the late 1860s and emigrated to the USA in 1873. Holland's first successful submarine was launched in 1881 and, after several failures, he built the *Holland* in 1893, which was bought by the US navy in 1895. He introduced many of the innovations that would be incorporated in later attack submarines.

Holland studied engineering and then began working in the late 1860s on the design of a powered marine vessel that could travel underwater. The first submarine, the *Fenian Ram*, was built in 1881 with financial support from the Irish-American republican ⇨Fenian movement, who hoped to use it against England. The 74-tonne *Holland* had a 16 m/56 ft-long, cigar-shaped hull and was submerged by flooding internal tanks. It could travel at 7 knots while on the surface and had devices to keep the vessel level. It also carried a single, heavy gun which could fire a 45 kg/20 lb projectile over a distance of 800 m/2,800 ft. He continued to build submarines for various navies after 1895, but he died in poverty after his company became embroiled in litigation with backers.

HOLYCROSS

Village in County Tipperary, 32 km/20 mi northeast of Tipperary town; population (1996) 447. The parish church is the restored ⇨Holycross Abbey. The district is very fertile, with good pasture land.

Some 10 km/6 mi east of Holycross are the ruins of two churches on the site of the monastery of Liathmore, founded by St Mochoeniog in the 6th century.

HOLYCROSS ABBEY

Cistercian abbey at Holycross, County Tipperary. It dates from the late 12th century but was almost entirely rebuilt in the 15th century; only the west wall and some smaller portions of the original church survive. It is particularly noted for its fine stone carving and a rare example of a late medieval fresco. At the dissolution of the monasteries in 1540, Holycross was made into a secular college. It was granted to Thomas Butler, Earl of Ormond, in 1563, and remained an abbey until the 17th century. The church was reconsecrated in 1975, after being restored for the archbishop of Cashel and Emly by local craftsmen with the assistance of Percy Le Clerc.

HOLYWOOD

Town in County Down, 10 km/6 mi northeast of Belfast; population (1991) 9,500. Its priory church dates from the 12th century, but the town grew mainly in the late 19th century when it was linked by rail with Belfast.

The priory church stands on the site of a 7th-century church (founded by St Laserian) and a Franciscan monastery.

Near Holywood in the village of Cultra is the Ulster Folk and Transport Museum. Holywood has the only maypole in Ireland.

HOME RULE

Movement to repeal the Act of ⇨Union of 1801 that joined Ireland to Britain, and to establish an Irish parliament responsible for internal affairs. In 1870 Isaac Butt formed the Home Rule Association and the movement was led in parliament from 1880 by Charles Stewart ⇨Parnell. After 1918 the demand for an independent Irish republic replaced that for home rule.

a healthy nation is as unconscious of its nationality as a healthy man of his bones. But if you break a nation's nationality it will think of nothing else but getting it set again. It will listen to no reformer, to no philosopher, to no preacher, until the demand of the nationalist is granted.

GEORGE BERNARD SHAW Dramatist 'Preface for Politicians' in *Prefaces* (1934, revised 1938).

~

The British prime minister William Gladstone's home rule bills of 1886 and 1893 were both defeated. A third bill was introduced by the Liberals in 1912, which aroused opposition in Ireland where the Protestant minority in Ulster feared domination by the Catholic majority. Ireland appeared on the brink of civil war but the outbreak of World War I rendered further consideration of home rule inopportune.

In 1920 the Government of Ireland Act introduced separate parliaments in the North and South and led to the treaty of 1921 that established the Irish Free State.

HONE, EVIE (1894–1955)

Modernist painter who turned to stained-glass midway through her career, with great success. Hone was born in Dublin and, despite being severely disabled as a result of polio, studied art at Westminster, England. She went to Paris with Mainie ⇨Jellett, and studied with the Cubist painter Albert Gleizes (1881–1953). She developed a methodology for the production of abstract art and exhibited in Ireland in the early 1920s to an outraged public. Finding abstraction unrewarding, she briefly entered a convent in 1925, but returned to Ireland in 1927.

Hone decided to try working in glass, and in 1935 joined the Irish stained-glass studio An ⇨Túr Gloine (The Tower of Glass). Her glass designs combined the rhythm, shape, and colour of her abstract painting with the strength and simplicity of figurative medieval stained glass. Her biggest commission was for Eton Chapel, England, in 1947, for which she executed a massive 18-light window. Her favourite window, however, was the more intimate *Ascension* (1947–48) in Kingscourt Church in County Cavan.

HONE, NATHANIEL (1718–1784)

Portrait painter and printmaker. Hone was a founder member of the Royal Academy in London in 1768 and an outspoken critic of its president, Joshua Reynolds. His best-known work is *The Pictorial Conjuror Displaying the Whole Art of Optical Deception* (1775; National Gallery of Ireland, Dublin). This is an attack on Reynolds and the dominance of Classical taste in opposition to which Hone promoted the naturalism of 17th-century Dutch art. He was one of the most gifted painters of children of the period; a fine example is the portrait of his son John Camillus known as *The Piping Boy* (1769; National Gallery of Ireland).

Hone, born in Dublin, was the first in a dynasty of Irish artists. His sons Horace (1754/6–1825) and John Camillus (1759–1836) were painters, his grand-nephew Nathaniel Hone (1831–1917) was a leading Irish Impressionist, and Evie ⇨Hone a contemporary of Mainie ⇨Jellett, was an important modernist painter and stained-glass artist.

HORSE RACING

Horse racing in Ireland is more than just a sport, it is a national passion, some would say a national obsession. Certainly no other country has as many horses in its pantheon of national sporting heroes – from Irish Lass (the famous 'Paidrin mare') in the 18th century to Arkle, widely regarded as the world's greatest ever steeplechaser. And if the Irish reserve most of their adulation for their champion horses, they also take pride in the superlative achievements of their trainers such as Vincent O'Brien, or their jockeys such as Aubrey Brabazon and Richard ⇨Dunwoody.

HORSE RACING *Although suppressed during the 18th century as encouraging idleness and disorder, racing, seen here at Galway, has remained hugely popular. The racing industry is not only a major home employer, but also earns considerable sums of foreign income through exporting stock.*

history

The roots of racing in Ireland can be traced to the contests held at the Aenach (or Oenach) country fairs held widely in Ireland from around the 3rd century. However, what may be called organized flat racing began in Ireland in the first half of the 17th century. It took on a more regulated form in the second half of the 18th century when many races were run under English Jockey Club rules. The Turf Club, the main governing body for racing in Ireland until the establishment of the Irish Horseracing Authority in 1994, was founded in 1790. If the growth of flat racing in Ireland owed much to English precedent, the other main type of racing, steeplechasing (and the other main forms under the National Hunt umbrella, point-to-point and hurdling), has its roots in the contests for wagers between huntsmen over open country towards a visible goal such as a church steeple, which were popular in Ireland from the middle of the 18th century. The first recorded race of this kind took place in County Cork in 1752. The evolution of these contests into the modern form of steeplechasing was a joint effort with the British, though until as recently as the 1960s the Irish preference was for jumping natural obstacles such as banks or stone walls as opposed to the artificial ones of British steeplechasing. This meant that Irish steeplechasing for a long time stayed closer to its 18th-century origins.

Both flat racing and steeplechasing grew greatly in popularity in the 19th century. Irish successes in British racing, which increased significantly from the 1880s, reflected improvements in the breeding and training of Irish horses, and provided a further spur to popular interest. But if the Irish continued to enjoy success abroad, in the 20th century racing at Irish courses, particularly flat racing, suffered decades of decline and resulted in the closure of ten race tracks, including Dublin's Phoenix Park. However, in the 1990s, increased investment in Irish racing, and a major administrative reorganization, succeeded in reversing the slump.

racing in Ireland today

The breeding, training, and racing of horses has long been one of Ireland's most important industries and today employs 25,000 people in full or part-time work. Of the 27 remaining Irish racecourses, all but two of them hold meetings under both flat racing and National Hunt rules. The exceptions are Kilbeggan in Westmeath, which is exclusively a National Hunt venue, and Laytown in County Meath, where each summer a flat race fixture is held on the beach. Among the highlights of the 250 or so meetings which form the Irish racing year are the Irish Derby Sweepstakes at the ⇨Curragh in June, the Irish Grand National at Fairyhouse, in early April, the three-day ⇨Punchestown National Hunt festival in late April, and the Galway Races in late July. The flat season runs from mid-March to early November, however National Hunt racing in Ireland has no close season, and many racecourses put on mixed racing with jumping and flat races on the same card.

HORSLIPS, THE

'Celtic Rock' band of the 1970s. They were the first band ever to combine traditional music and instruments with rock music. They formed in 1970 and used aspects of Irish mythology as themes for their songs. They were very much part of the rock culture current in the Western world at the time, releasing 'concept' albums, but they did expose a young urban generation of Irish youth to traditional Irish music. By the end of their career in 1979 they had moved away from much of their traditional material but will perhaps always be remembered for it. Important recordings are *Happy to Meet Sorry to Part* (1973) and *The Book of Invasions – a Celtic Symphony* (1977).

HUGUENOTS

French Protestants, mainly Calvinists, who had been granted religious toleration under the Edict of Nantes (1598), but whose loyalty to the Catholic monarchy was always questioned. They were persecuted in the 17th century, and with the revocation of the Edict in 1685 they were expelled from France. About 10,000 emigrated to Ireland in the 1690s.

A small community had existed in Ireland since the 1660s, and by the end of the 17th century there were 21 groups in the country. One of the most prominent refugees was Samuel Louis ⇨Crommelin, who was involved in the development of the linen industry. In Dublin, the Digues La Touche family became prominent in banking, and later politics. A number of communities maintained their own liturgy, despite some official opposition, but others adopted the Church of Ireland form, thus securing financial assistance.

HUME, JOHN (1937–)

Northern Irish politician, leader of the Social Democratic and Labour Party (SDLP) from 1979. Hume was a founder member of the Credit Union Party, which later became the SDLP. A member of parliament since 1969 and a member of the European parliament, he has been one of the chief architects of the peace process in Northern Ireland. In 1998 he shared the Nobel Peace Prize with David ⇨Trimble in recognition of their efforts to further the peace process.

In 1993 Hume held talks with Sinn Féin leader, Gerry Adams, on the possibility of securing peace in Northern Ireland. This prompted a joint Anglo-Irish peace initiative, which in turn led to a general ceasefire 1994–96. Despite the collapse of the ceasefire, Hume continued in his efforts to broker a settlement. This was achieved in the 1998 Good Friday Agreement, and the subsequent devolution of ministerial powers to Northern Ireland on 2 December 1999.

HUMEWOOD CASTLE

Large, imposing Victorian house in the style of a castle, in County Wicklow. It was built in 1867 for the member of parliament W W F Hume Dick, and designed by William White. The interior contains a large stone staircase lit by one of the finest stained-glass windows in Ireland, and there are many examples of the original woodwork by White. The house remains in the ownership of the Hume family.

HUNGER STRIKE

Tactic adopted by imprisoned Irish republicans in order to secure better conditions or release. Hunger strikes frequently met with success and often proved capable of mobilizing support for republicanism from a previously unsympathetic public. The death of Irish Republican Brotherhood president Thomas Ashe in 1917, after forced feeding, led to increased support for Sinn Féin's campaign against British rule, and in 1920 the death of Cork's lord mayor, Terence ⇨MacSwiney, after 73 days on hunger strike aroused national and international sympathy.

However, the hunger strike was a less effective tactic against Irish governments, which showed a greater ruthlessness than their British predecessors. The collapse of a mass hunger strike following the Irish Civil War in the autumn of 1923 greatly damaged republican morale. Éamon de Valera's government allowed two hunger-strikers to die in 1940 and a third in 1946.

In 1981 the republican hunger strike in Long Kesh, Lisburn, County Antrim, resulted in the death of ten republicans and failed to achieve its aim of continued 'special category' status for political prisoners. The election as a Westminster MP of Bobby ⇨Sands, the best-known casualty of the ten, shortly before he died, was a pivotal point in the emergence of ⇨Sinn Féin as an electoral force in Northern Ireland.

HURLING

National game and the fastest field sport in the world, played by teams of 15 men a side with a ball and sticks. Hurling can be dated back over 2,000 years in the annals of the Celts. Irish folklore is rich with references to the game, with the Irish superhero Cuchulain being its most famous competitor. By the 16th century a law was passed that forbade the tumultuous 'hurling of the little ball with hooked sticks or staves'. This, however, did not banish the game in Ireland and since the founding of Cumann Lúthchleas Gael (the Gaelic Athletic Association) in 1884 the sport has continued to gain in popularity, both nationally and internationally.

𝓽he national sport of hurling... the blood-and-bandages game you called it.

CRÍOSTÓIR Ó FLOINN Writer *Sanctuary Island* (1971).

∼

Hurling is played on a pitch usually 137 m/150 yd long and 82 m/90 yd wide. The object is to drive the 'sliotar' (ball), 25 cm/10 in in circumference, through erect posts at opposite ends of the pitch. Each player uses a wooden hurley or 'caman', usually 1.07 m/3.5 ft long, to propel the sliotar around the playing area. The erect goalposts stand 6.4 m/21 ft apart and are usually about 6.4 m/21 ft high. There is a crossbar 2.4 m/8 ft from the ground. Hitting the ball over the crossbar scores a point and a shot under scores a goal.

The All-Ireland Hurling Championships are played annually between teams representing the Irish counties; the final is played at Croke Park, Dublin, in front of crowds of over 60,000.

HUTCHESON, FRANCIS (1694–1746)

Philosopher and religious thinker, born in Drumalig, County Down. Educated at Glasgow University, Scotland, Hutcheson studied to become a Presbyterian minister and received his preaching licence in 1719. Returning to Ireland, he established an academy in Dublin where he prepared students for university. He published two books during this period, *Inquiry Concerning the Original of Our Ideas of Beauty and Virtue* (1725) and *Essay on the Nature and Conduct of the*

Passions and Illustrations of the Moral Sense (1728). In 1730 Hutcheson became professor of moral philosophy at Glasgow University, where he continued to make important contributions to religious debate. He died on a visit to Dublin in 1746.

Hutcheson is credited with influencing the US president Thomas Jefferson and the United Irishman William Drennan. His arguments against slavery helped influence the debate in the following decades.

HYDE, DOUGLAS (pseudonym AN CRAOIBHÍN AOIBHINN) ('the pleasant little branch') (1860–1949)

Academic and cultural activist; first president of the ⇨Gaelic League 1893–1915 and first president of the Republic of Ireland 1938–45. Hyde was born in County Sligo, the son of a Church of Ireland clergyman. He led the movement to revive the Irish language and literature, and his inaugural address as president of the National Literary Society, 'The Necessity for De-Anglicising the Irish People' (1892), became an anthem for Gaelic revivalists. His writings include the first play performed in the Irish language, *Casadh an tSúgáin/The Twisting of the Rope* (1901).

Hyde moved to Frenchpark, County Roscommon, in 1867, where he acquired a passion for Irish antiquities and culture. The imitation of English manners and literature enraged him and, in works such as *Love Songs of Connacht* (1893) and *A Literary History of Ireland* (1899), he sought to create a distinct Irish literature. He was professor of Irish at the National University of Ireland 1909–32, and resigned from the Gaelic League in 1915 due to its politicization. He served in the Irish Free State senate 1925–26 and was elected president of the Republic of Ireland after the declaration of the new constitution in 1937. *Mise agus a Connradh*, an account of his work in the Gaelic League, was published in 1937.

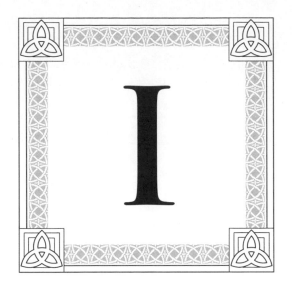

IMPRESSIONISTS

Group of Irish artists who studied and painted in France and Belgium between about 1850 and 1914. Prior to the mid-19th century, artists aiming to study or work abroad looked to London or Rome. This shift of location may be accounted for by the rise of Paris as an artistic centre with a greater diversity available in art training, and also by the fact that these artists, largely from middle-class backgrounds, were no longer catering for aristocratic patrons. In contrast to the previous concentration of Irish emigrées in France, the exiles from the Rebellion of 1798, the Irish Impressionists did not have a political agenda.

One of the first artists to go to Paris was Nathaniel ⇨Hone. Working in Paris and Barbizon between 1853 and 1870, painting out of doors allowed him to capture with immediacy the light and tone of a scene. Settling in Malahide, County Dublin, on his return to Ireland, he was an important channel for foreign artistic influences on younger artists. Frank O'Meara (1853–1888), from County Carlow, also worked at Barbizon and at the nearby village of Grèz-sur-Loing. There he painted his best-known works, such as *Towards Night and Winter* (1885, Hugh Lane Municipal Gallery of Modern Art, Dublin), one of a series of images of solitary women in wintry landscapes. These are in contrast to the sunny, untroubled images also painted at Grèz, by his friend John ⇨Lavery, in which he attempted to capture his immediate impressions of a scene. Lavery acknowledged the enduring importance of this experience for his later success as a portrait painter. The portraits of Sarah Purser (1848–1943) also show the impact of these ideas. The number of women, such as Edith ⇨Somerville and Helen Mabel Trevor (1831–1900), who feature among the Irish Impressionists reflects how Irish women were increasingly becoming part of the professional art world at this time.

A number of artists, including Walter ⇨Osborne, chose to study in Antwerp. He went there in 1881 in the company of fellow students J M Kavanagh (1856–1918) and Nathaniel Hill (1860–1930). For these artists the picturesque interiors and rural scenes of the Hague School were an important influence. In the 1890s Osborne became more directly influenced by Impressionism as the heightened colour and broken brushwork of *The Lustre Jug* (National Gallery of Ireland, Dublin) shows. William Leech (1881–1968) was strongly influenced by Osborne, who taught him in Dublin. His most ambitious work, *The Convent Garden* (National Gallery of Ireland), dates from his period in Brittany, from 1903 to 1908.

Ultimately, the impact of the Irish Impressionists on Irish art was not the adoption of radical French styles but a greater concern with naturalism, which became an important part of the nostalgic, nationalistic imagery of Paul Henry (1876–1958) and Sean Keating (1889–1978) among others in the early years of the Irish Free State.

INLA

Abbreviation for ⇨Irish National Liberation Army.

INNISFREE

Islet near the southeast shore of Lough Gill, County Sligo. It was the inspiration for W B Yeats's poem 'The Lake Isle of Innisfree' (1893).

INTERNMENT

Detention of suspected criminals without trial. Internment had been practised since the 18th century in times of crisis under the suspension of the writ of habeus corpus. In the 20th century a number of public order and security acts were passed by the UK or Irish governments, making provision for internment after the ⇨Easter Rising in 1916, and during the ⇨Anglo–Irish War, the ⇨Irish Civil War, and the ⇨Irish Republican Army (IRA) bombing campaigns of World War II and 1957–62. In 1971 internment was reintroduced by the UK government for the detention of people suspected of terrorist acts in Northern Ireland. The practice was suspended in December 1978, and the legislation for internment lapsed in 1980.

INVINCIBLES, THE

Group of Irish terrorist revolutionaries formed in 1881 to carry out political assassinations. Established in Dublin as the Irish National Invincibles, an offshoot of the Irish Republican Brotherhood, their leaders included James Carey, John McCafferty, and P J Tynan. Notoriety soon followed their first, and only real attack, the ⇨Phoenix Park Murders in 1882, when they assassinated the chief secretary for Ireland, Lord Frederick Cavendish, and his undersecretary, Thomas Burke.

*t*wenty years a child; twenty years running wild; twenty years a mature man – and after that, praying.

ANONYMOUS Irish proverb.

In a massive investigation, Carey was soon identified as a suspect and he turned Queen's evidence (gaining immunity by naming others involved), which led to the arrest of 20 main conspirators. Attempting to flee to Cape Town, South Africa, Carey was shot dead by Patrick Donnell, a bricklayer and former Invincible. Five of the Invincible leaders were hanged, and the remainder were given lengthy prison sentences. It was revealed that Edmund Burke had been their intended target, and they had been unaware of the importance of Cavendish.

IRA

Abbreviation for ⇨Irish Republican Army.

*t*he geography and history of Ireland hold my imagination in a melancholy magic spell. Dublin and Limerick are cities beautiful to me not only with some of the most superb and most neglected architecture in Europe but with a compelling litany, a whole folklore, of tragic and heroic associations.

BRIGID BROPHY English writer 'Am I an Irishwoman?' in *Don't Never Forget* (1966).

IRELAND

An island lying to the west of Great Britain, between the Atlantic Ocean and the Irish Sea. It comprises the provinces of Ulster, Leinster, Munster, and Connacht, and is divided into the Republic of ⇨Ireland (which occupies the south, centre, and northwest of the island) and ⇨Northern Ireland (which occupies the northeastern corner and forms part of the United Kingdom).

The centre of Ireland is a lowland, about 60–120 m/200–400 ft above sea level; hills are mainly around the coasts, although there are a few peaks over 1,000 m/3,000 ft high, the highest being Carrantuohill ('the inverted reaping hook'), 1,041 m/3,415 ft, in Macgillycuddy's Reeks, County Kerry. The entire western coastline is an intricate alternation of bays and estuaries. Several of the rivers flow in sluggish courses through the central lowland and then cut through valleys to the sea. The ⇨Shannon in particular falls 30 m/100 ft in its last

*F*or the great Gaels of Ireland / Are the men that God made mad, / For all their wars are merry, / And all their songs are sad.

G K CHESTERTON English novelist, essayist, and poet 'The Ballad of the White Horse' (1911).

The Irish, with their glowing hearts and reverent credulity, are needed in this cold age of intellect and scepticism.

LYDIA MARIA CHILD US writer and editor Letter dated 8 December 1842 in *Letters from New York* (1843).

~

26 km/16 mi above Limerick, and is used to produce hydroelectric power.

The lowland bogs that cover parts of central Ireland are intermingled with fertile limestone country where dairy farming is the chief occupation. The bogs are an important source of fuel in the form of peat (see ⇨peat bog), Ireland being poorly supplied with coal.

Politics is the chloroform of the Irish people.

OLIVER ST JOHN GOGARTY Writer *As I was Going Down Sackville Street* (1937).

~

The climate is mild, moist, and changeable. The annual rainfall on the lowlands varies from 76 cm/30 in in the east to 203 cm/80 in in some western districts, but much higher falls are recorded in the hills.

The people are thus inclined: religious, frank, amorous, sufferable of infinite paines, verie glorious, manie sorcerers, excellent horsemen, delighted with wars, great alms-givers, passing in hospitality.

RALPH HOLINSHED English historian On the Irish, in *Chronicles* (1577).

IRELAND, JOHN (1838–1919)

Irish-born US prelate. Born in County Kilkenny, Ireland emigrated to the USA with his parents in 1849, settling in St Paul, Minnesota. He later studied in France and was ordained priest in 1861. He served as a US Civil War chaplain and cathedral rector before becoming successively coadjutor bishop (1875), bishop (1884), and first archbishop (1888) of St Paul, Minnesota.

A founder of the Catholic University of America, Ireland was regarded as a liberal and the probable target of an 1899 papal encyclical condemning 'Americanism'. He took stands on many controversial issues, including the ordination of black Americans.

The luck of the Irish is a wish more than a characteristic.

JAN MORRIS English travel writer and journalist 'Do You Think He Should Have Gone Over' in *Travels* (1976).

It is impossible to eat or drink out in Ireland without getting into conversation with at least two people you have never met before.

LISA O'KELLY Journalist *The Observer*, 7 December 1997

~

IRELAND, REPUBLIC OF

Country occupying the main part of the island of Ireland, bounded to the east by the Irish Sea, south and west by the Atlantic Ocean, and northeast by ⇨Northern Ireland; area 70,282 sq km/27,135 sq mi; population 3,705,000 (1999 est). There are 26 counties. The capital is ⇨Dublin, and major towns

There is perpetual kindness in the Irish cabin – butter-milk, potatoes – a stool is offered or a stone rolled that your honour may sit down and be out of the smoke, and those who beg everywhere else seem desirous to exercise free hospitality in their own houses.

WALTER SCOTT Scottish novelist and poet Diary entry of 21 November 1825 in *Memoirs of the Life of Scott* (1838), John Lockhart.

~

and ports include Cork, Limerick, Galway, Waterford, Wexford, and Dun Laoghaire.

Essentially a central plateau surrounded by hills, such as Macgillycuddy's Reeks and the Wicklow Mountains, the Republic of Ireland has three main rivers, the Shannon, Liffey, and Boyne. The Bog of Allen is source of domestic and national power.

It was not until I went back to Ireland as a tourist, that I perceived that the charm of my country was quite independent of the accident of my having been born in it.

GEORGE BERNARD SHAW Preface to *Immaturity* (1930).

≈

Economically, the country benefits from tourism but also manufactures textiles, machinery, chemicals, electronics, motor vehicles, with some food processing and brewing. Agriculture is important and exports include beef and dairy products and live animals, as well as machinery and transport equipment, electronic goods, including computer software, and chemicals. Since joining the ⇨European Union the Republic has received regional development funding.

Ireland still remains the Holy Isle, whose aspirations must on no account be mixed with the profane class-struggles of the rest of the sinful world.

FRIEDRICH ENGELS German philosopher Letter to Karl Marx, 9 December 1869.

history
The Irish Free State, the precursor to the Republic of Ireland, came into being under the terms of the Anglo-Irish Treaty of December 1921, which gave southern Ireland dominion status within the British Commonwealth. Six out of the nine counties of Ulster remained part of the UK, with limited self-government, as Northern Ireland. For events leading up to partition, and what has happened since, see the chronology at the end of the book.

See also the feature essays on post-independence Ireland, page 182, on ⇨social change, page 324, also ⇨population, and ⇨emigration.

The roof has always had an almost mystical importance in Ireland because of the incessant rain. Throughout the ages a quite inordinate amount of unsuccessful Irish time and energy has been spent trying to do something about the roof.

CAROLINE BLACKWOOD Novelist *Great Granny Webster* (1977).

≈

IRISH-AMERICAN NATIONALISM

Form of nationalism largely resulting from the mass emigrations in the 1840s, which created a distinct, anti-English group of people who shared a national identity. By 1900 over 3 million Irish people had emigrated to the USA since the Great Famine, and their sense of alienation in their new country helped foster deep feelings of resentment and bitterness towards the British. This was exploited by nationalist groups, such as the Fenians, and later Sinn Féin, and their hostility was channelled into various attempts to win Irish independence. One prominent movement was Clan-Na-Gael, a secret society formed by the Fenians in the USA around 1883, aimed at winning home rule for Ireland. Its headquarters were in Chicago, but it had agents in England and Ireland who were responsible for assassinations and bombings in the 1880s.

A major feature of Irish-American nationalism was the extent to which the emigrants' descendants, often

With the exception it may be of Malta and Iceland, no European island lies in so lamentable and hostile a solitude as Ireland, who has no neighbour on her right hand but her conqueror, and nothing at all on her left hand but the desolate ocean, not one dry step until you get to America.

MICHEÁL MAC LIAMMÓIR Actor and director

≈

with little real knowledge or awareness of Ireland, inherited their beliefs and asserted their own Irish-American identity. The treatment of the emigrants upon arriving in the USA influenced their views significantly. The 1840s and 1850s witnessed a major surge in nativist groups in the USA, and deep-seated anti-Irish prejudices were a major factor in encouraging the emigrants to think of themselves as a distinct and separate group. The Irish-Americans developed their own social, cultural, and religious life, and slowly became involved in politics. Anti-Catholicism, which was rife, was another major influence in preventing the assimilation of many emigrants into American society, and reinforced the idea of national difference.

By the 20th century the Irish-Americans had become a significant lobby, and played an important role in US political life. Their support was courted by the main political parties, most notably the Democratic Party, and their Anglophobia helped dictate the national reaction to international events. American unwillingness to enter World War 1 was partly attributed to the large Irish immigrant community. Irish affairs remained important, even after independence, and the problem of Northern Ireland's 'Troubles' after 1969 became a major factor for US politicians concerned with the 20 million citizens who claimed some form of Irish descent.

IRISH COLLEGES

Network of seminaries set up throughout Europe from the end of the 16th century, at a time when Catholic education in Ireland was severely restricted by the Protestant Dublin government. Established primarily for the education of priests, they also provided shelter for students of other professions. As financial, social, and political centres for Irish communities in Europe, the colleges played an important role in maintaining Ireland's European links in the 17th and 18th centuries.

The first officially established college was in Salamanca, Spain, in 1592. Others were established in the main university cities of Catholic Europe. By 1670 there were over 30 of them, the largest in Paris, France. By the time of the French Revolution there were about 400 seminary places available to Irish students. Many colleges were closed during the French Revolution, but those that reopened maintained an important link between Ireland and Europe until after World War II. Today only the Irish College in Rome survives as a seminary.

IRISH FILM BOARD (BORD SCANNÁN NA HÉIREANN)

Statutory body, established in 1981, which is charged with aiding Irish film production. With the exception of sums from the Arts Council, it was the first state body to invest directly in indigenous productions. Although loans (rather than grants) of only about IR£500,000 were made by the board until 1987, when it was wound down as part of Government cutbacks, it took minority stakes in films and made culturally significant investments in pre-production. It was re-activated in 1993 under Chairperson Lelia Doolan, with an initial budget of IR£1.1 million, an amount which was to rise to IR£4 million by the late 1990s.

The board membership has included film director Neil ⇨Jordan and actor Gabriel ⇨Byrne. Films supported by the Board include Jordan's first feature *Angel* (1982), Pat Murphy's *Anne Devlin* (1984), Pat O'Connor's *Circle of Friends* (1995), and Paddy Breathnach's *I Went Down* (1997).

IRISH FREE STATE

Name of the former state of southern Ireland 1922–37, established as a result of the Anglo-Irish Treaty (1921). It was replaced by Eire in 1937 and the Republic of ⇨Ireland in 1949. The treaty established a 26 county dominion, which exercised a significant degree of autonomy but was formally subordinated to the British crown through the appointment of a governor-general and an oath of fidelity to be taken by its representatives.

The Irish Free State Constitution, a liberal democratic document with safeguards for the Protestant minority, was approved by the Dáil (parliament) on 25 October 1922 and ratified by Britain on 5 December. The Free State was formally inaugurated the following day, in the midst of the Irish Civil War (1922–23), with William ⇨Cosgrave as first president of the executive council

The Free State was not recognized by republicans, who set up a rival government under Éamon ⇨de Valera, leader of Sinn Féin, in 1922. It was not until Fianna Fáil entered the Dáil in 1927 that the Free State's legitimacy was fully established. After leading Fianna Fáil to power in 1932 de Valera instigated a series of reforms including the abolition of the governor-general and substitution of the 1922 constitution with his own, which effectively dismantled the Irish Free State by 1937.

IRELAND AFTER INDEPENDENCE – FROM ISOLATION TO MODERNIZATION

by Ciaran Brady

The Anglo-Irish Treaty (December 1921), which established the Irish Free State within the British Commonwealth, also confirmed the partition of the island and precipitated civil war. For some nationalists the clauses requiring an oath of fidelity to the crown, confirming the state's indebtedness to British landowners, and recognizing the state of Northern Ireland, were unacceptable.

Attempts to find a compromise failed, and war began in June 1922 when pro-Treaty forces fired upon anti-Treaty forces occupying the Four Courts, seat of the Supreme and High courts in Dublin. Lasting for 11 months and costing at least 927 lives, the Irish Civil War was still a mild affair compared to the Anglo–Irish War of 1919–21, yet it shaped the character of Irish politics for over 40 years, subordinating matters of economic and ideological dispute to questions of sides taken in 1922.

early years

The victorious pro-Treaty side consolidated its gains politically in August 1923 when William Cosgrave's Cumann na nGaedheal party took office and initiated a series of reforms in local government and education. Its most lasting achievement was in foreign affairs where it successfully asserted the right of Commonwealth nations to pursue policies independent of Britain. However, economically and socially it was highly conservative, accepting Ireland's dependent trading status with Britain, and abjuring any interventionist role in the domestic economy. The government's economic and social conservatism was crucial to the rise of Fianna Fáil, the political party formed by a group of anti-Treatyites under Éamon de Valera in 1926 that took power in 1932.

economic war and neutrality

Committed to the ending of payments to British landlords (land annuities) and the development of economic self-sufficiency, the policies pursued by Fianna Fáil in the depression-ridden 1930s produced mixed results. The suspension of the land annuities in 1932 provoked the Economic War with Britain, a tariff dispute during which Irish exports (largely cattle) fell from £35.8 million in 1929 to £13.5 million in 1935, and standards of living fell sharply. However, cuts in imports greatly aided Ireland's nascent industrial sector while the drive for self-sufficiency produced significant development in Irish arable farming.

Moreover, the 1938 Anglo-Irish Agreement ending the war gave rise to unforeseen benefits, as Britain surrendered several naval installations in Ireland. This rendered feasible de Valera's delicate (though quietly pro-Allied) neutrality in World War II, while the war further justified Fianna Fáil's commitment to self-sufficiency. Ireland's isolation also consolidated important changes enframed in the constitution drafted by de Valera in 1937. The constitution, which nominated Eire as the country's official name, further distanced Ireland from the Commonwealth, creating an elected Irish president and strengthening the powers of the Taoiseach (prime minister). However, several articles affirmed conservative positions on education, the family, the role of women, and the special position of the Catholic church.

post-war conservatism and economic decline

Ireland thus emerged into the post-war world as a deeply inward-looking country. Its conservatism, highlighted by narrow-minded censorship and by the display of church power in quashing a modest state scheme for the support of mothers and children, functioned more systemically in the refusal of successive governments (both Fianna Fáil and coalitions of their opponents) to undertake any sustained economic planning. Domestic industries failed, exports stagnated, and emigration rose to an unprecedented 40,000 per annum.

free trade and expansion

Rapid recovery began with the election of Seán Lemass as Fianna Fáil Taoiseach in 1959 and his endorsement of a key programmatic document drafted by the secretary of the Department of Finance, Thomas Whitaker. Under the 'Programme for Economic Expansion' 1959–63, protectionism was abandoned and new initiatives in industrial development, capital financing, and employment effected a striking recovery in the 1960s, as industrial output doubled, agricultural output increased by 50%, emigration fell to 25% of 1950s levels, and a hoped for annual growth rate of 2% was doubled within five years.

By 1969 Ireland's economic progress had encouraged new demands for a more liberal and tolerant society. Commentators looked confidently toward Ireland's admission into the European Economic Community (EEC); few anticipated the challenges that were ahead.

IRISH INDEPENDENT

Newspaper founded by businessman William Martin ⇨Murphy in 1905. It was established on the back of a less successful newspaper, the *Irish Daily Independent*, which had unsuccessfully challenged the *Freeman's Journal*, then the paper of the emerging Catholic middle classes. Founded with the help, encouragement, and technical advice from Dublin-born Alfred Harmsworth (later Lord Northcliffe), it pioneered modern journalism in Ireland and did so on the basis of an editorial policy which specifically appealed to the middle ground in Irish politics.

In the quarter of a century after the paper's foundation, and especially after the demise of the *Freeman's Journal* (whose title it acquired) in 1924, it had the Irish newspaper market virtually to itself; it extended its hegemony through acquisition of the *Evening Herald* (1891; 1999 circulation 110,510), and the establishment of the *Sunday Independent* (1905; 1999 circulation 315,600). The 1999 circulation of the flagship *Irish Independent* was 165,660.

The establishment of the *Irish Press* (1931), and the more expansionary approach of the *Irish Times* in the 1960s, began to challenge the *Irish Independent*'s dominance of the indigenous newspaper market, but it was not until 1973, when the ownership interests of the Murphy and Chance families were bought out by the young entrepreneur A J F O'Reilly, that it began seriously to expand. Its 1978 purchase of the newly-established *Sunday World* (1973; 1999 circulation 308,040) gave it a foothold in the tabloid Sunday market; and its joint venture the *Star* (1999 circulation 89,300), an operation carried out in partnership with the UK-based *Express Newspapers*, achieved the same result in the daily tabloid market. Within Ireland, it acquired an important stake in the *Sunday Tribune* (1999 circulation 84,570) in 1990, and a similar holding in the *Irish Press* group in 1994.

The newspaper has been active internationally, acquiring a range of print media and radio interests abroad, including the *Independent* (UK), as well as publications and radio stations in Australia, New Zealand, and South Africa. By 1999 it was effectively an Irish-based multinational with revenues in excess of £1 billion annually, and with major interests in other media-related enterprises such as MMDS (the micromedia distribution system established across Ireland on a franchise basis), and Newspread, one of the country's two print media distribution companies.

IRISH LAND ACTS

Series of 19th-century laws designed to improve the lot of the Irish peasantry. The first act in 1870 awarded tenants compensation for improvements they had made to land, but offered no protection against increased rents or eviction. The second act in 1881 introduced the 'three 'f's' – fair rents, fixity of tenure, and freedom of sale. The third act in 1885, part of the British prime minister William Gladstone's abortive plans for home rule, provided £5 million for tenants to buy out their landlords. This scheme was further strengthened by the Wyndham Act of 1903, which offered inducements to landlords to sell. Before the end of the Union with Britain, some 11 million acres were purchased with government assistance.

IRISH LANGUAGE (GAELGE)

First official language of the Irish Republic, known simply as 'Irish', but much less widely used than the second official language, English. More than half a million citizens today claim to speak Irish though there are fewer than 20,000 native speakers, mostly situated in the ⇨Gaeltacht. In addition to enhanced cultural and educational standards and a generally more relaxed and more imaginative sense of national identity in the Republic, cultural and political nationalism associated with the 'Troubles' in Northern Ireland has given a considerable impetus to language-learning, especially in west Belfast, during recent decades.

Irish is a branch of the Indo-European family of languages, which is divided into two groups: the Goidelic or Q-Celtic (Irish, Scottish, and Manx Gaelic languages) and the Brythonic or P-Celtic (Welsh language, Cornish, Breton, and Gaulish). Of these, Irish, Welsh, Scottish, and Breton are the sole surviving branches, while Scottish is actually a dialect variation of Irish, having been carried into north Britain by an 11th-century Gaelic hegemony emanating from Ulster. Most people in Ireland spoke Irish until the middle of the 18th century, but English gradually came to dominate thereafter, driven by social and economic changes.

In the mid-19th-century the so-called language-shift was powerfully accelerated by the demoralising effects of the Famine on the native Irish population, especially in areas where emigration became a natural resort for younger generations. The Irish cultural renaissance of the 20th-century was significantly fuelled by the desire to revive the native language, chiefly under the stimulus of the ⇨Gaelic League (Connradh na Gaeilge) founded by Douglas Hyde and others, while Irish scholars today are still concerned to estimate the degree of trauma occasioned by the 'loss' of Irish as the vernacular in the colonial period.

The extent and population of the traditional Irish-speaking areas, collectively known as the Gaeltacht, continues to decline in spite of incentives provided by the modern Irish state on a per capita basis. A radio station opened in 1970 in County Galway greatly added to the vitality of Irish-language culture and also accelerated the development of a up-to-date vocabulary, alert to the inflections of popular culture as well as technological changes in the modern world. A television station added in the 1990s enjoys something of a cult following outside the Gaeltacht, while the policy of 'parity of esteem' associated with the Belfast Agreement in Northern Ireland has resulted in Irish-language broadcasting within the state-sponsored media.

The Irish language is far from dying today, though it increasingly enjoys the role of a special-interest group rather than a minority language in the older demographic sense. Paradoxically, a turning-point was reached in the early 1970s when the Irish State rescinded laws that had made Irish compulsory in schools, necessary for entrance to the National University of Ireland, and as a qualification for a range of professional courses as well as government employment.

IRISH LITERARY THEATRE

Three-year theatre project of the contemporary Irish literary revival set up in Dublin, in 1899 by W B Yeats, Lady Gregory, and Edward Martyn (1859–1923) to produce new drama by Irish authors and on Irish subjects. In 1901, the final year of the experiment, the performances were held in the Gaiety Theatre instead of the Ancient Concert Rooms. This brought the theatre out of its elitist position, inspired a wave of dramatic activity in the capital, and eventually prepared the ground for the ⇨Abbey Theatre.

The first play produced by the Irish Literary Theatre, Yeats' *The Countess Cathleen*, in which a landlady sells her soul to the devil to save the lives of the famine-stricken peasants, caused a controversy because of its alleged blasphemy. Most of the other plays, such as Martyn's *The Heather Field*, *The Bend-*

If we turn to early Irish literature, we find ourselves wandering in delighted bewilderment through a darkness shot with lightning and purple flame.

SEÁN Ó FAOLÁIN Writer and critic *The Irish* (1948).

❧

ing of the Bough by George Moore (1852–1933), and *The Twisting of the Rope* (*Casadh an tSugáin*) by Douglas Hyde (1860–1949), were extremely well received.

IRISH LITERATURE

Writing by Irish authors, generally on Irish subjects, in the English language or in modern Irish. See feature essay on Irish literature, page 185.

IRISH NATIONALISM

Political and cultural expression of the concept of an Irish nation. Although a sense of Irishness probably existed in the Gaelic period before the 12th-century Norman invasion, the exact origins of an imagined Irish nation is debatable. Political Irish nationalism developed from the early 16th century following the reaction of Protestant reformers to Counter-Reformation Catholicism, which included measures such as the ⇨plantation of Ireland by Protestant settlers. Irish nationalism was given further cohesion during the 17th century, as various Catholic cliques were welded together in opposition to their exclusion from the Protestant state establishment.

Radical nationalism received inspiration from the American and French revolutions in the 18th century, leading to the United Irishmen's unsuccessful ⇨Rebellion of 1798. After this, Irish political nationalism adopted a constitutional approach under the leadership of 19th-century reformist politicians such as Daniel ⇨O'Connell and Charles Stewart ⇨Parnell. However, while constitutionalism dominated Irish politics, more radical groups such as ⇨Young Ireland and the ⇨Fenian movement continued the militant trend in Irish nationalism.

Nationalism in Ireland lacked a basis in language or culture until a literary revival at the turn of the 20th century promoted Irish cultural ideology in opposition to anglicization. The 20th century saw militant nationalism expand after the ⇨Easter Rising in 1916,

IRISH LITERATURE – A UNIQUE VOICE

by Bruce Stewart

The near-eradication of Gaelic culture and vernacular Irish literature during the colonial period in the centuries following the Norman invasion resulted in a vacuum that was only slowly filled by a new form of recognizably Irish literature, though written in the English language. This was for a long time known as Anglo-Irish literature, the term 'Irish literature' being reserved for the new literature written in Irish that emerged in the early 20th century.

Anglo-Irish beginnings

Whilst earlier centuries threw up such figures as James Ussher and George Farquhar, the Anglo-Irish literary tradition begins in the age of George Berkeley and Jonathan Swift. In the ensuing decades, Trinity College, Dublin, produced such writers as Oliver Goldsmith, Edmund Burke, and R B Sheridan, all of whom made their livelihoods and reputations in England. Maria Edgeworth, the daughter of an 'improving' landlord in County Longford, wrote the first distinctly Irish novel (*Castle Rackrent*) in 1800. Throughout the 19th century such Protestant Irishmen as Charles Lever, Joseph Sheridan Le Fanu, and Bram Stoker wrote to serve the English taste for romantic or else supernatural tales from Ireland. At the same time others such as Lady Morgan, Sir Samuel Ferguson, and Lady Wilde – the mother of Oscar – reflected a fascination with the remnants of Gaelic culture that served to lay foundations for the literary revival of the 1890s, out of which modern Irish literature was born.

a convergence of traditions

No modern literature could exist in Ireland without a convergence of Protestant (colonist) and Catholic (native) traditions. In the early 19th century, native Irish writers such as John and Michael Banim, Gerald Griffin, and William Carleton established a line of native Irish fiction writing which was later to flourish as the modern Irish short story and novel. In the Romantic period, J J Callanan and James Clarence Mangan adapted Irish matter to the modes of English poetry, often translating earlier Irish poems and songs preserved by oral tradition. A lively ballad literature centrally concerned with the political woes of Ireland emanated from *The Nation*, a journal founded in 1842 by Thomas Davis, while John O'Donovan and others carried on the translation of ancient Irish manuscripts. It was with the return of W B Yeats to Dublin and the foundation of a National Literary Society in 1892 that the claims of a separate tradition of Irish literature in English began to take definite shape.

The literary revival that he fostered with Lady Gregory and others produced a succession of writers who achieved international reputations, among them chiefly John Millington Synge and Seán O'Casey, who bestowed their fame on the Abbey Theatre. A somewhat younger writer, James Joyce, came to dominate literary modernism in continental exile during the 1920s, while Catholic Ireland retired into social and religious conservatism.

the weight of censorship

Seán Ó Faoláin, Frank O'Connor, and Liam O'Flaherty were among those whose work was banned in Ireland under the 1929 Censorship Act, which inaugurated a period when it was said that no Irish writer worth their salt wrote books that could be bought in Ireland. Among those whose writing represented a complex and often brilliant reaction to the prevalent clerical and petty bourgeois ethos were the poet Patrick Kavanagh, the playwright Brendan Behan, and the novelist Flann O'Brien.

In the second half of the 20th century, writers such as Thomas Kinsella and John McGahern exposed the cracks in the official culture and produced writing of the first order, while John Montague and Brian Friel generated a postcolonial literature based on an amalgam of modern and particularly US models and Irish subject-matter. Irish writing in the 1970s was dominated by an upsurge of poetic talent in Northern Ireland led by Seamus Heaney, Michael Longley, and Derek Mahon, while the poets Brendan Kennelly, Richard Murphy, and Eavan Boland added lustre to the southern tradition. In the Republic, the official era of PQ ('Peasant Quality') in Irish drama eventually gave way to a turbulent new realism spearheaded by Thomas Kilroy and Tom Murphy, as well as a more sophisticated conception of literary fiction developed by John Banville. The 1980s brought a flood of new talent exemplified in all genres and styles by Frank McGuinness, Roddy Doyle, Dermot Bolger, Jennifer Johnston, and others. A second generation of Ulster poets, including Paul Muldoon and Mebdh McGuckian, produced a poetry remarkable for its wit.

Novels and stories by writers such as Michael Collins and Colm McCann have been alert to the plight of young Irish people in an age of renewed emigration, while Patrick McCabe and Eoin MacNamee have portrayed the dysfunctional aspects of modern Irish life in various comical and tragic lights.

and remain active throughout the ⇨Anglo–Irish War (1919–21) and the Irish Civil War (1922–23).

While a vocal minority tradition of Protestant nationalism survived in Ireland after the declaration of the Irish Free State in 1922, political groups enjoyed a close relationship with the Roman Catholic church and Catholicism emerged as a perennial element to Irish identity.

IRISH NATIONAL LIBERATION ARMY (INLA)

Guerrilla organization committed to the end of British rule in Northern Ireland and Irish reunification. The INLA, founded in 1974, is a left-wing off-shoot of the ⇨Irish Republican Army (IRA). The INLA initially rejected the IRA's call for a ceasefire in 1994; its assassination in 1997 of loyalist leader Billy Wright threatened to destabilize the peace process and bomb attacks occurred in London in 1998. However, after the Omagh bomb atrocity in 1998 the INLA became the first republican subversive group to explicitly state that the war was over and voice strong support for the peace process.

The INLA has repeatedly been devastated by internecine feuds. In 1987 alone, 13 members were killed in a vendetta between rival factions. Its leader, Gino Gallagher, was shot and killed in Belfast in January 1996, by feuding INLA members.

IRISH PRESS

Newspaper established in 1931 by Éamon ⇨de Valera, to counter the anti-Fianna Fáil ethos of Ireland's national daily press. While not owned by the Fianna Fáil party, which de Valera led from 1927 to 1959, the paper played a major part in de Valera's general election victory in 1932. The paper's links with Fianna Fáil did not hamper its growth as a vibrant expression of nationalist Irish journalism, and its overall penetration of the market was assisted by the establishment of the highly successful *Sunday Press* (1949) and *Evening Press* (1954).

The press's financing was a matter of controversy: part of the capital was drawn from funds originally contributed to the Irish nationalist cause in the USA in the early 1920s, and subsequently allocated to the *Irish Press* enterprise after enabling legislation had been passed in the Dáil while de Valera was head of government.

The Press group of newspapers reached a high point during the 1950s. When Fianna Fáil was out of power 1948–51 and 1954–57, it provided a rallying point for the party's electoral base and, in addition, openly supported modernizing tendencies within the organization. Its circulation base, however, was by then vulnerable, consisting as it did largely of older readers with relatively limited purchasing power. As Fianna Fáil became increasingly prone to leadership struggles in the 1970s, the Press newspapers' circulation first grew, then declined rapidly. Despite attempts to move the papers away from the party into a position of greater independence to attract more readers, the group was plagued by industrial unrest and lost even more readers. A 1987 re-launch of the daily *Irish Press* as a tabloid failed to turn the tide, and the group folded in 1995.

IRISH REPUBLICAN ARMY (IRA)

Militant Irish nationalist organization formed in 1919, the paramilitary wing of ⇨Sinn Féin. Its aim is to create a united Irish socialist republic including Ulster. To this end, the IRA has frequently carried out bombings and shootings. Despite its close association with Sinn Féin, it is not certain that the politicians have direct control of the military; the IRA usually speaks as a separate, independent organization and has, until recently, been the dominant half of the partnership. The chief common factor shared by Sinn Féin and the IRA is the aim of a united Ireland.

The IRA was founded in 1919 by Michael ⇨Collins as the successor to the Irish Volunteers, a militant nationalist body dating from 1913. The IRA strategy was to make British rule ineffective by the use of armed force, the belief being that political activity alone would not achieve this end. Although the IRA and Sinn Féin share a common goal, and there is overlapping membership, the IRA has always operated independently and in times of crisis has appeared to be free from political control. During the War of Irish Independence 1919–21, employing guerrilla tactics, it forced the British government to negotiate a political settlement which involved the creation of the Irish Free State in the south, with dominion status within the British Commonwealth. This settlement proved unacceptable to some IRA members and the organization split into two groups. The larger, which supported the settlement, became the nucleus of the Irish Free State army, and the rest, styled 'the Irregulars', began a campaign of violence against the new independent government in the south. A civil war ensued

1922–23 which, after heavy fighting, ended with the defeat of the Irregulars. The IRA did not disband or surrender its arms but remained a clandestine organization, turning its efforts towards achieving the unification of Ireland. It was declared illegal in 1936, but came to the fore again in 1939 with a bombing campaign in Britain. Its activities intensified from 1968 onwards, as the civil-rights disorders ('the Troubles') in Northern Ireland increased.

In 1969 the IRA split into two wings, one 'official' and the other 'provisional'. The official wing sought reunification by political means, while the Provisional IRA, or Provos as they became known, carried on with terrorist activities, their objective being the expulsion of the British from Northern Ireland. It is this wing, of younger, strongly sectarian Ulster Catholics, who are now generally regarded and spoken of as the IRA.

*t*his is not just another glorious phase in Irish history. We must win. We can't afford to lose. We will keep the campaign going regardless of the cost to ourselves, regardless of the cost to anyone else.

SEÁN MACSTÍOFÁIN Activist, Chief of Staff of the Irish Republican Army's militant Provisional wing, quoted in *Time*, 10 January 1972.

∾

The IRA announced a cessation of its military activities in August 1994, in response to a UK–Irish peace initiative. However, the insistence by the government in London that Sinn Féin could enter into all-party negotiations about the future of Ireland only after the IRA had decommissioned its weaponry was seen as unacceptable by the more militant members of the organization, who broke the ceasefire in February 1996. Subsequent bombing cast doubt over the whole peace process and raised the question of how much influence Sinn Féin has over its military allies, and how much control the leadership of the IRA has over its active members. UK–Unionist plans for elections to select representatives to the talks also met with opposition from Sinn Féin.

In October 1996, two IRA car bombs exploded at the British army's headquarters in Lisburn, County Antrim, killing a British soldier (the first to die since the August 1994 ceasefire was announced) and injur-ing 30 people. In July 1997 the IRA announced another ceasefire but doubts about its validity were expressed by Unionist politicians. 'Continuity IRA', a republican splinter group opposed to the ceasefire, carried out a number of bomb attacks during 1997–98. An extremist splinter group, 'Real IRA', was believed to have been behind a brutal car bombing attack in Omagh, County Tyrone, in August 1998, which claimed more than 26 lives. The IRA's political wing, Sinn Féin, unreservedly condemned the atrocity.

The left-wing Irish Republican Socialist Party, with its paramilitary wing, the ⇨Irish National Liberation Army, split from the IRA in 1974.

The IRA has carried out bombings and shootings in Northern Ireland as well as bombings in mainland Britain and in British military bases in continental Europe. In 1979 it murdered Louis Mountbatten, and its bomb attacks in Britain included an attempt to kill members of the UK cabinet during the 1984 Conservative Party conference in Brighton, Sussex.

IRISH REPUBLICAN BROTHERHOOD

Secret revolutionary society which grew out of ⇨Fenianism, in the wake of the failed insurrection of 1867, in an effort to reform its organization and improve its security precautions. Though very successful in the 1870s and 1880s in attracting membership and in encouraging secret agrarian agitation, internal frictions over the question of support for Home Rule hampered the movement thereafter. By the early 1910s, thanks to increasing frustration with constitutional politicians and the organizational skills of Tom Clarke (1857–1916) and Sean MacDermott the movement had revived and was a considerable force behind both the 1916 ⇨Easter Rising and the ⇨Anglo-Irish War. Damaged by splits among it leaders over the ⇨Anglo-Irish Treaty, the brotherhood was said to have been dissolved in 1924, but rumours that it has survived in the USA, until the time of the Northern Ireland peace process, have persisted.

IRISH REVIVAL (also known as the literary revival, or Celtic revival)

Movement that sought to create, promote, and sustain Irish art, starting in the late 19th century. An extraordinary period of artistic and cultural activity, it had its roots in the earlier Celtic revival of the late 18th century, which developed a keen interest in Irish history, antiquities, music, and poetry of 'ancient Ireland'. The later revival, by contrast, aimed to restore Irish culture forms in literature and music, though naturally the literature produced was distinctly modern in theme and treatment. In this way, the ideals and practices of the Irish revival continues to influence contemporary artists. Although the term is most often used to refer to the literary movement, the exploration and affirmation of Irish identity was evident in other areas, such as architecture, the visual arts, and sports; the movement also paralleled a growth in nationalist politics.

Aspects of the Irish revival were wide and varied. Key elements included the publication of W B ⇨Yeats's *Fairy and Folk Tales of the Irish Peasantry* (1888); the foundation of the ⇨Gaelic League (1893) with the express purpose of maintaining Irish as a living, spoken language; the development of the ⇨Gaelic Athletic Association, established in 1884 to promote national sports; and the establishment of the ⇨Abbey Theatre (1897) by W B Yeats, Edward Martyn, George Moore, and Lady Gregory. The ethos of the revival, in the creation of an idea and an image of Ireland that was idealistically rural, mythically powerful, and decidedly not British, was in turn criticized and even mocked by writers such as James ⇨Joyce and Samuel Beckett. Nevertheless the movement influenced even its critics.

IRISH SEA

Arm of the North Atlantic Ocean separating England and Wales from Ireland; area 103,600 sq km/ 39,990 sq mi. Its greatest width, between Morecambe Bay, Lancashire, and Dundalk Bay, Louth, is 240 km/150 mi. It joins the Atlantic to the south by St George's Channel and to the north by the North Channel.

IRISH STEW

Traditional Irish dish of lamb or mutton, potatoes, and onions, flavoured with herbs. Layered in a deep pot, the stew is cooked slowly over a long period to enrich its cooking liquids. The dish was originally made with young kid.

IRISH SWEEPSTAKE

Lottery run by the Irish government, on three horse races each year, with proceeds going to the nursing services. The best known race is the Irish Derby.

IRISH TIMES

Newspaper established in 1859 to reflect primarily the interests of the Protestant and Unionist middle class. It evolved to become a central force in the Irish print media, especially from the 1960s.

Initially the paper functioned largely as a bulletin board for Irish Protestants. It adapted, chameleon-like, to the establishment of the Irish Free State in 1922, and to the even greater challenge posed by Fianna Fáil's election victory in 1932. Throughout the 1930s and 1940s it supported artists and writers, more especially those who experienced criticism or even ostracism at the hands of the Catholic church. Its editor from 1934 to 1954, Robert Maire ⇨Smyllie, despite his personal hostility to Germany, helped it to accept the declaration of Irish neutrality in 1939. A later editor, Douglas Gageby, successfully adapted its somewhat old-fashioned mien to the emergence of new social and cultural trends after 1963.

In 1999 it had the second largest circulation of any morning newspaper in the Republic (112,620), and the highest proportion of readers in the upper socio-economic groups. It is owned by a trust, and publishes one subsidary paper, a weekly devoted to the horse industry.

IRISH VOLUNTEERS

National defence force formed at the Rotunda, County Dublin, on 25 November 1913 to defend the principle of home rule. It took its name from the Volunteers, a part-time militia which had been formed 1778–79 to protect the country from invasion. The Volunteers had played an important role in securing legislative independence in 1782, and their name still evoked strong memories in the 1910s. Inspired by an article by Eoin MacNeill in *An Claideamh Soluis*, the newspaper of the Gaelic League, the formation of the Irish Volunteers was also a response to the Ulster Volunteer Force (UVF), which had been formed the previous year. Among the organizers was the Irish revolutionary and socialist Liam ⇨Mellows.

Recruitment took place throughout the country. By March 1914 membership stood at 8,000, and guns and ammunition were smuggled into Ireland that year in the Howth gunrunning incident, led by (Robert) Erskine Childers (1870–1922). An Englishman by birth, Childers gradually became a committed republican, and was involved in the negotiations for the Anglo-Irish Treaty, which he later opposed; he was executed during the Irish Civil War (1922–23). His son, Erskine H Childers (1905–1974), was later president of Ireland, 1973–74.

Come closer, boys, it will be easier for you.

(ROBERT) ERSKINE CHILDERS Sinn Féin politician
Words to the firing squad taking up position across
the prison yard, quoted in Burke Wilkinson *The Zeal of the Convert* 1976 ch. 26.

~

With the outbreak of World War I, the Irish Volunteers split. The bulk of the then 160,000-strong movement followed the Irish Parliamentary Party leader John Redmond's plea and enlisted to join the British army, as the National Volunteers. Unlike the UVF, however, they were not given distinct regiments and were deliberately separated. Only a small number remained in Ireland, rising to 11,000 in 1915. Infiltrated by the nationalist Irish Republican Brotherhood, the Irish Volunteers became embroiled in the plans for the 1916 Easter Rising to overthrow British rule.

IRISH WOMEN WORKERS' UNION (IWWU)

Women's labour association, founded in 1911 to act as the sister organization to the Irish Transport and General Workers' Union (ITGWU) and led by Delia Larkin. Under the lengthy tenure of Louie Bennett (1870–1956) from 1917 to 1955, the women-only union sought to improve worker–employer relations and expanded its membership, although controversy arose within the IWWU in 1932 over the admittance of married women with employed husbands. The union vigilantly policed the application of the Conditions of Employment Act (1935) and opposed the 1937 constitution, which made Ireland a republic, as an obstacle to women's working opportunities. The 1950s saw changing economic conditions and new leadership, and in 1984 the IWWU merged with the Federated Workers' Union of Ireland.

IRISH YEOMANRY

Military force active from 1796 until 1834. Yeomen were civilians who volunteered for part-time service to help magistrates cope with the threat of the ⇨United Irishmen, a radical reformist secret society, and to assist the regular army if Ireland was invaded by France. There were 20,000 men enlisted throughout Ireland by late 1796. The force played a major role in the defeat of the United Irishmen's ⇨Rebellion of 1798.

The Irish Yeomanry was organized in small companies or corps of between 50 and 100 men. Yeomen normally only served in their home district. Each corps had a captain, often the men's landlord. Ultimate control of the entire force rested with the Irish government, which issued officers' commissions, pay, arms, and uniforms. Most yeomen were Protestants, though there were some Catholic yeomen, particularly in Leinster and Connaught.

Contemporary critics accused the force of brutality during the Rebellion of 1798, while supporters believed it had saved the country. Its most important role after 1798 was as an anti-invasion reserve. Numbers peaked in 1810 at 85,000 but declined after 1815, with only Ulster retaining substantial concentrations. The yeomanry was largely inactive during the 1820s and was disbanded completely in 1834.

IRVINE, EDDIE (1965–)

Formula 1 motor-racing driver, born in Newtownards, County Down. Irvine began his career in the Formula Ford category, winning two championships between 1983 and 1987. He then moved to Japan where he raced in the Formula 3,000 series, before signing for Eddie ⇨Jordan's Formula 1 team in 1993.

I'm doing all I can to encourage people to believe I'm ruthless, but at the same time trying to steer clear of trouble.

EDDIE IRVINE *The Mirror*, 3 May 1998.

~

His first race at Suzuka saw him finish sixth and he raced for three seasons in the Jordan car before moving to Ferrari where he partnered Michael Schumacher. He won his first Formula 1 race at the Australian Grand Prix in 1999, but subsequent victories in Germany, Hungary, and Malaysia were not enough to take the drivers' championship; Mika Hakkinen won the final race in Japan to take his second successive title.

JACOBITE

A supporter of the royal Stuart dynasty following the overthrow of James II in 1688. Although fears of Jacobite conspiracies were pervasive in Protestant Ireland in the early 18th century and resulted in the enforcement of repressive anti-Catholic legislation, Ireland featured little in the actual strategies of the exiled Jacobite court in France. However, it provided a steady stream of recruits, known as 'wild geese', for Jacobite brigades in the French army, which were intended to play a central role in projected invasions of Scotland and England.

Following the defeat of the 1745–46 Jacobite rising in Scotland, both the perceived threat and the actual appeal of Jacobitism declined sharply in Ireland, though the dream of the triumphal restoration of the house of Stuart remained a powerful theme in the literary and oral culture of Ireland's dispossessed Catholics.

JELLETT, MAINIE (MARY HARRIET) (1879–1944)

Painter, a pioneer and key figure in the promotion of modern art in Ireland. In an international context she is remarkable for being a woman in this role.

Born in Dublin, Jellett developed her own highly analytical interpretation of cubism while studying in Paris. She combined this with the academic rigour of her early training and increasingly her own deeply spiritual outlook, as can be seen in works such as *The Ninth Hour* (1941; Hugh Lane Municipal Gallery of Modern Art, Dublin). Her meticulous geometric abstract compositions were savagely attacked when first exhibited in Dublin in 1923. The cultural imperative in Ireland at this period was the assertion of a national identity rather than embracing such international developments. Nevertheless she was unflagging in her efforts during the next decades as an educator and administrator. In 1943 she chaired the founding committee of the Irish Exhibition of Living Art, a vital forum for Irish modern artists until the 1970s.

JENNINGS, PAT(RICK) (1945–)

Footballer, born in Newry Town, County Down. One of the world's greatest goalkeepers, he won 119 international caps for Northern Ireland between 1964 and 1986, and appeared in both the 1982 and 1986 World Cup finals.

Jennings began his club career for Newry Town before moving to Watford in 1963. He was transferred to Tottenham Hotspur in 1964 and spent 13 seasons there before joining Arsenal in 1977. By the time he retired he had played in over 1,000 senior matches at club or international level.

JERPOINT ABBEY

One of the best-preserved abbey ruins in Ireland and the most interesting of the early Cistercian houses, near Thomastown, County Kilkenny. It has the tallest tower of any Cistercian church in Ireland. It is believed to have been founded in 1180, although it could have been founded by the king of Ossory about 20 years earlier. The finely decorated cloister arcade is of particular interest, although of a later date than the church.

JERPOINT ABBEY *The 15th-century decorated cloister is unique among Irish Cistercian abbeys. Among the carved figures that border the cloister walls are those of St Margaret standing on a dragon, St Christopher, a creature – possibly a monkey – and a knight.*

JOHN F KENNEDY ARBORETUM

Arboretum at New Ross, County Wexford, dedicated to the memory of the former US president and opened in 1968. It comprises 252 ha/623 acres and overlooks the Kennedy ancestral homestead at Dunganstown. The property has a collection of over 4,500 plant varieties arranged in botanical circuits, and there is a Visitor Centre that includes an audiovisual display and a Kennedy memorial fountain.

JOHNSTON, (WILLIAM) DENIS

(1901–1984)

Dramatist and writer, born in Dublin. His works include the highly successful *The Old Lady Says 'No'* (1929), and *The Moon on the Yellow River* (1931).

Johnston trained in law at Cambridge, England and Harvard, USA, and in 1925 joined both the English and Irish Bars. His first play, the impressionist piece *Shadowdance*, was rejected by Lady Gregory, director of the Abbey Theatre, Dublin. However, retitled *The Old Lady Says 'No'*, it was a major hit at the city's Gate Theatre in 1929. During World War II he worked as a reporter and producer for the British Broadcasting Corporation (BBC). Over the next three decades, Johnston wrote several other dramas.

He was also the author of two autobiographical works, *Nine Rivers from Jordan* (1953), which recounts his experiences as a war correspondent, and *The Brazen Head* (1977), and a book about Jonathan Swift, *In Search of Swift* (1959). His daughter is the novelist Jennifer ⇨Johnston (1930–   ).

JOHNSTON, JENNIFER (PRUDENCE)

(1930–   )

Writer, notable for her intimate portraits of struggling relationships between families, friends, lovers, and communities. Born in Dublin and educated at Trinity College, Dublin, Johnston settled near Londonderry, in the 1970s. Some of her best-known works are *The Captains and the Kings* (1972); *Shadows on Our Skin* (1977), shortlisted for the Booker Prize; *The Old Jest* (1979), winner of the Whitbread Award for fiction; and *Fool's Sanctuary* (1987). Her style is lucid but always attuned to subtleties of human emotion and political reality; one of the strengths of her fiction is her ability to create sympathetic but complex characters.

JOHNSTOWN CASTLE

Multi-towered Victorian castle at Murrinstown, County Wexford. The present castle, dating from about 1840, was built around an older property that formerly belonged to the Esmonde family. It was designed in the Gothic and Norman styles by Daniel Robertson of Kilkenny for the member of parliament H K Grogan-Morgan. The original medieval tower house at the heart of the structure was owned by Cornelius Grogan, who was executed after the Rebellion of 1798. The castle is now an agricultural institute.

JOLY, JOHN (1857–1933)

Geologist and physicist. Joly demonstrated that radioactive elements in the Earth could account for much of the heat produced by the planet, and developed the idea of using radioactivity as a way to calculate the age of rocks. He also pioneered the use of radioactivity in the treatment of cancers.

Born in Clonbulloge, County Offaly, he was the son of a Church of Ireland rector. He entered Trinity College, Dublin, in 1876 and was appointed assistant to the professor after graduating in engineering in 1882. He became professor of geology in 1897, a post he held until his death.

In the 1890s he estimated the age of the Earth at 80–90 million years by measuring the salt content of the seas, but after the discovery of radioactivity he realized that much better estimates might be obtained by studying the radioactivity contained in rocks. In 1903 he was the first geologist to recognize the significance of radioactivity in maintaining heat inside the Earth.

Joly, with Walter Stevenson of Dr Steevens' Hospital, Dublin, introduced the use of radiation in cancer therapy. In 1914 he persuaded the Royal Dublin Society to purchase a supply of radium and set up the Radium Institute which provided radioactive materials for medical treatments until the 1940s. Other achievements included the invention of a system of colour photography.

JONES, 'MOTHER' (MARY) (born Harris) (1830–1930)

Irish-born US labour leader who, beginning in the 1890s, organized coal miners and strikes for the United Mine Workers in Virginia, West Virginia, and Colorado. Known for her bold tactics, Jones fought on for decades; at the age of 89 she joined in a major steel walkout, earning a prison term.

Jones was born near Cork city, and emigrated to Canada and then the USA as a child. She was widowed in 1867 when her husband, and four children, died of yellow fever. She lost her home in the Chicago fire of 1871. She resumed earlier work as a dressmaker, and worked with the Knights of Labor as an organizer. In the 1960s a socially conscious periodical, *Mother Jones Magazine*, was named after her.

JORDAN, EDDIE (1948–)

Motor-racing team owner, born in Dublin. A winner of 11 races as a driver, his success was restricted mainly to the Formula Three circuit. He retired in 1980 to set up Eddie Jordan Racing but it was not until 1987 that he had his first taste of success, winning the Formula Three title with the British driver Johnny Herbert. Jordan then entered a team into Formula One in 1991 but had to wait another seven years before winning his first Grand Prix in Belgium with the former world champion Damon Hill. The 1998–99 season proved his most successful when the Jordan car powered by the Mugen Honda engine finished third in the constructors' championship behind Ferrari and McClaren.

EDDIE JORDAN *Heinz-Harald Frentzen races a Jordan car in the 1999 British Grand Prix. The team's greatest success was the 1998 Belgian Grand Prix, when Jordan netted both first and second place, despite terrible weather causing one of the biggest pile-ups in Formula 1 history.*

JORDAN, NEIL (1950–)

Film director and writer, born in Sligo. Despite its non-conventional material, *The Crying Game* (1992) established Jordan as a commercial director and won him an Academy Award for best original screenplay. It was one of the most successful non-US films ever released in the USA, with cinema box office takings alone in excess of $60 million. Jordan returned to the USA to make the big-budget *Interview With a Vampire: The Vampire Chronicles* (1994), and with his two further Irish films, the epic *Michael Collins* (1996) and the adaptation of Pat McCabe's novel *The Butcher Boy* (1998), he secured his position as the foremost commercial Irish film-maker of his generation.

> **I**f I make a good movie they say I'm a British director and if I make what they think is a bad one, they say I'm Irish!
>
> NEIL JORDAN Quoted in *The Independent*, 3 February 1993.

∼

The Irish themes in Jordan's work include a concern with the effect of political violence on individuals involved with Northern Ireland's paramilitary organizations and their attempts to start a new life, and the psychic link made between acts of terrorism and sexuality (*Angel*; *The Crying Game*). This aspect of his work also informs *Michael Collins*, which became an Irish national event both at production and exhibition stages. The earlier, and more modest scale of *The Miracle* (1990), was an effective exploration of an American woman's re-discovery of her Irish son after a long absence. *The Butcher Boy* put a coach-and-horses through the spate of 1950s nostalgia which was overwhelming Irish cinema in the 1990s. The film brought to the fore a version of small-town and rural Ireland which ensured that the rose-tinted spectacles of many other film-makers would be permanently darkened.

JOURNALISM

Journalism in Ireland was closely associated initially with printing and then with politics. In the 17th and 18th centuries it was exclusively the preserve of Protestants, not least because the majority of the population was impoverished, spoke only Irish, or both.

The end of the 18th century and the Rebellion of 1798 saw the emergence of new publications and forms of journalism which, though still Protestant, argued for more self-government for Ireland and, in some cases, for separatism. As party lines hardened, official bribery, corruption, and intimidation influenced the conduct of many early newspapers.

the grip of party journalism

The 18th century saw the arrival of an increasing number of Catholics in the profession, especially in the O'Connellite era, and the acquisition by the emerging Catholic middle class of its first influential daily paper, the *Freeman's Journal*, in 1853. Party journalism was still the norm, however, and it was not until the establishment of the ⇨*Irish Independent* in 1905 that concepts of journalistic independence – at least from party interests, if not from business interests – began to take root. The final flowering of the older tradition can be seen in the proliferation of newspapers and party papers published by various elements within emerging Irish nationalism between 1897 and 1922, which helped to underpin and consolidate the rise of Sinn Féin after 1905, despite the watchfulness of the British authorities. That tradition found its ultimate expression in the ⇨*Irish Press*.

pressure from the UK

The mainstream broadsheet press was, especially in the last quarter of the 20th century, supplemented by indigenous tabloid papers, as Irish journalism defended itself against the commercial pressure from UK-edited papers, which at the turn of the century accounted for almost one in four daily newspapers and one in three Sunday newspapers sold in the Republic. See also ⇨*Irish Times*.

journalism in Northern Ireland

In Northern Ireland journalism began in its modern sense with the publication of the *Belfast Newsletter* (1737), which was famously the first newspaper in the British Isles to publish the news of the American Declaration of Independence; it is now the oldest daily newspaper published on the island. Unionist in political leaning, it became *The Newsletter* in 1962, and also published a Sunday newspaper, the *Sunday News*, from 1965 to 1993. The publication of the nationalist *Morning News* (1855) marked the start of the bi-polar tradition in Irish journalism which has continued until the present, with the nationalist and unionist communities catered for almost exclusively by newspapers reflecting their own political views.

The only paper to bridge the divide was the *Belfast Evening Telegraph* (1870). Particularly after its name change to the *Belfast Telegraph* (1918), and its emergence as the only evening newspaper in Northern Ireland, it achieved a notable cross-community readership and considerable profitability. Originally the property of a Belfast family, it was bought in 1966 by Roy Thompson, the Canadian media magnate, and subsequently re-sold to the UK Trinity/Mirror Group in 1996. Its circulation in 1999 was 124,530. It also owns a profitable Sunday newspaper (*Sunday Life*, founded in 1992; 1999 circulation 98,200).

The role of the *Morning News* as the house journal of Northern nationalism was sharply challenged by the foundation of the *Irish News* (1891), founded with the support of the Catholic hierarchy, which was angry at the pro-Charles Stewart ⇨Parnell line taken by the editor of the *Morning News*. The dismissal of that editor by the proprietor did not satisfy the paper's critics, and the *Morning News* was overtaken (and eventually bought out) by its younger rival. Although both the *Irish News* (1999 circulation 50,300) and the *Newsletter* (1999 circulation 33,958) still reflect their predominantly nationalist and unionist readerships, each employs journalists from both sides of the religious divide, and attracts a small readership from the opposite community.

See also ⇨periodicals.

JOURNALISM, RELIGIOUS

Religious journalism in the 18th and 19th centuries mirrored communal divisions, often sharply. The *Christian Examiner* (1828) was founded to undermine Catholicism; the *Irish Catholic Magazine* (1829) to defend it. A more intellectual tradition found its expression in the *Catholic University Gazette*, founded by John Henry Newman in 1854; in *Studies*, edited by the Jesuits since 1912; and in *The Furrow*, edited from Maynooth since 1950. The *Church of Ireland Gazette* (1856; 1999 circulation 6,000) is one of a number of house journals for other denominations which continue in existence, as does the weekly *Irish Catholic* (1888; 1999 circulation 30,000), which, despite its name, is owned by a private company rather than by a specifically religious group.

JOYCE, JAMES (AUGUSTINE ALOYSIUS)

(1882–1941)

Foremost Irish novelist, and poet. Joyce was born in Rathgar, Dublin, one of a large and poor family, and educated at University College, Dublin. His originality lay in evolving a literary form to express the complexity of the human mind; he revolutionized the form of the novel in English with his 'stream of consciousness' technique. His key works are the short story collection *Dubliners* (1914); *A Portrait of the Artist as a Young Man* (1916); *Ulysses* (1922), which is regarded as a masterpiece; and *Finnegans Wake* (1939).

Ulysses, which records the events of a single Dublin day, experiments with language and combines direct narrative with the unspoken and unconscious reactions of the characters. Banned at first for obscenity in the USA and the UK, it made a huge impact. *Finnegans Wake*, a story about a Dublin publican and his family, continued Joyce's experiments with language. In this work the word-coining which is a feature of *Ulysses* is pushed to its limits, and punning language and allegory are used to explore various levels of meaning while attempting a synthesis of all existence.

early years

Joyce's father, John Stanislaus, who appears in his son's books as Simon Dedalus, was a middle-class Catholic with a great love of music, but his drinking habits led to the loss of inherited income and property and the constant moving of his family from one rented home to the next. Joyce's mother, May, was a devout Catholic who died of cancer in 1903.

Educated at University College, Dublin, where he studied languages as well as mathematics and philosophy, Joyce showed strong literary tendencies very early in life. However, on completion of his degree he was rebuffed by the leaders of the Irish literary revival: he was anti-clerical, comparing the Catholic clergy to 'tyrannous lice'; he attacked W B ⇨Yeats for surrendering to a nationalistic Ireland; and he demonstrated his antipathy to Patrick ⇨Pearse in a satirical sketch. In June 1904 Joyce met and fell in love with Nora Barnacle (1883–1951), who was working as a chambermaid in Dublin; they married in 1932. He drew upon his love for Nora for descriptions of several female characters in his books.

Riverun, past Eve and Adam's, from swerve of shore to bend of bay, brings us by a commodius vicus of recirculation back to Howth Castle and Environs.

JAMES JOYCE The opening sentence of *Finnegans Wake* (1939).

the start of an exile

At this time Joyce had published a few sketches and reviews but was unable to make a living, and on 8 October 1904 he and Nora travelled to Trieste, Italy, where he taught English; Joyce's two children Giorgio and Lucia were both born here, in 1905 and 1907 respectively. This was a more fruitful writing phase, but Joyce's work was plagued by delays in publication. A book of lyrics called *Chamber Music*, which Joyce had completed some years earlier, was published in 1907, while a volume of short stories, called *Dubliners*, was completed in 1906 but remained unpublished for nine years, because of wrangling with publishers over their demands for excisions. Meanwhile the partly autobiographical *A Portrait of the Artist as a Young Man* was serialized by Ezra Pound in *The Egoist* (1914–15).

As World War I gained momentum, Joyce left Trieste for Zürich, Switzerland, where he lived until 1919. There he formed a company of Irish players who performed his drama *Exiles* (1918), modelled on the work of Ibsen, with whom he had corresponded.

Ulysses

Joyce, with the financial support secured by W B Yeats and critical support of Ezra Pound, had begun writing his major work, *Ulysses*, in 1914. It appeared serially in the New York magazine *Little Review* (1918–20), until publication was halted in early 1921 because of a prosecution for obscenity. Meanwhile, in Zürich, Joyce's eyesight began to fail, and he moved to Paris, where *Ulysses* was published as a book in 1922, in time for Joyce's 40th birthday in February. It was, however, banned in both the USA and the UK, being finally published there in 1932 and 1936 respectively.

The novel relates the mental and physical history of Leopold Bloom, a Jewish advertisement canvasser, and Stephen Dedalus, scholar-philosopher, during a single day in Dublin, Bloom's day being paralleled to the wanderings of Odysseus in the Homeric epic. Joyce claimed to have discovered the literary device of the interior monologue, used in *Ulysses*, in Edouard Dujardin's forgotten work *Les lauriers sont coupes* (1888). The device was used by Marcel Proust and Dorothy Richardson, among other writers, and the development of the 'stream of consciousness' technique had a far-reaching influence on many modern authors.

> **S**tephen Dedalus watched through the webbed window the lapidary's fingers prove a timedulled chain. Dust webbed the window and the showtrays. Dust darkened the toiling fingers with their vulture nails. Dust slept on the dull coils of bronze and silver, lozenges of cinnbar, on rubies, leprous and winedark stones.
>
> JAMES JOYCE 'The Wandering Rocks', *Ulysses*.

breaking with literary conventions

In 1922 Joyce began his next novel, known as *Work in Progress*, which began to appear in parts under various titles in 1927. During this time Joyce was under great emotional, physical, and mental strain resulting from numerous eye operations, worries concerning his son Giorgio, and his daughter Lucia's schizophrenia. The book was published in full in 1939 as *Finnegans Wake*. This difficult but engrossing work breaks with many literary conventions, creating a continuous entity (the opening words run on from the last words of the book) which can be entered at any point. It also sidesteps the basic convention of using a single language throughout – in its merging of different languages it has been hailed as ultra-modernistic. Its evasion of conventional form and its linguistic obscurities make the work so complex that few readers can follow the meaning without the assistance of a commentary.

the final years

The Joyces moved to Gerand-le-Puy, near Vichy, France, at the outbreak of World War II but then on 14 December 1940 the family, except Lucia who was in a sanatorium, entered Switzerland. On 10 January 1941 Joyce was taken to hospital suffering severe stomach pains, where he died three days later after an operation for an ulcerated duodenum.

JAMES JOYCE *His novel* Ulysses, *published in 1922, is seen as a masterpiece that revolutionized the form of the novel. This classic photo was taken shortly before Joyce's death.*

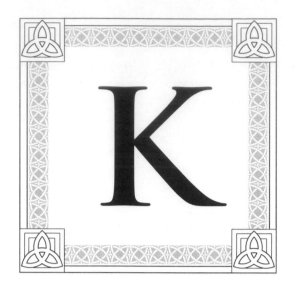

KANE, ROBERT (1809–1890)

Chemist and educationalist. Kane conducted extensive chemical experimentation, isolating acetone from wood spirit in 1836, and producing the first cyclic hydrocarbon from a straight-chain hydrocarbon. He analyzed the mineral kaneite, which was later named after him.

Kane was born in Dublin, and was a slow starter, taking seven years to complete his primary degree at Trinity College, Dublin. He went on to publish numerous papers in chemistry, eventually becoming a professor and qualifying as a doctor. He also published a textbook on pharmacy, and carried out work on the chemistry of the natural dyestuffs, achil and litmus.

He advised the government on education and wrote a three volume textbook on chemistry in 1841. Other works include *The Industrial Resources of Ireland* (1844). He was knighted in 1846.

KAVANAGH, PATRICK (JOSEPH) (1905–1967)

Poet, born in Inniskeen, County Monaghan, who moved to Dublin in 1939. Kavanagh's poetry creates a sense of small-scale, parochial Ireland, and expresses a variety of moods, from the gentle and elegiac to the satiric and savage. The collections include *Ploughman and Other Poems* (1936); *The Great Hunger* (1942), a long, energetic poem about life in rural Ireland; *Come Dance with Kitty Stobling* (1960); and *Collected Poems* (1964).

Until 1939 Kavanagh farmed on a small scale in County Monaghan. In Dublin he worked for various

Í returned to Ireland. Ireland green and chaste and foolish. And when I wandered over my own hills and talked again to my own people I looked into the heart of this life and saw that it was good.

PATRICK KAVANAGH *The Green Fool* (1938), his autobiography.

∼

newspapers and as a broadcaster, as well as briefly editing a review, *Kavanagh's Weekly*, in 1952.

KEANE, JOHN B(RENDAN) (1928–)

Writer, born in Listowel, County Kerry, and educated at a Christian Brothers school. Keane's most important work, *The Field* (1965), set in County Kerry, chronicles how one man's obsession with the land leads to tragic, deadly consequences. Staged across the world, *The Field* was made into a film in 1990. Although best known as a playwright, Keane has also published collections of poetry, essays, and a best-selling novel, *Durango* (1992).

Before turning to writing, Keane worked as a chemist's apprentice and as a manager of a public house. His first play *Sive* (1959) won the All-Ireland drama festival in Athlone.

KEANE, MOLLY (MARY NESTA) (born Skrine) (1905–1996)

Novelist, born into an Anglo-Irish family in County

MOLLY KEANE *Keane gave up a successful writing career for 20 years following her husband's sudden death. She made a sensational comeback at the age of 77, with* Good Behaviour, *a highly praised black comedy.*

Kildare, and raised in County Wexford. Keane's comic novels chronicling the loves, lives, and pursuits of the Anglo-Irish gentry include *Good Behaviour* (1981), *Time After Time* (1983), and *Loving and Giving* (1988). While her fiction often takes place in a big-house setting, she writes with a keen sense of class tensions and the difficult question of Irish nationalism. She has also published under the name M J Farrell.

KEANE, ROBBIE (1980–)

Footballer, born in Tallaght, County Dublin. The most gifted striker to come out of Ireland since the 1970s, he spent two seasons with Wolverhampton Wanderers scoring 24 goals in 79 appearances before signing for Coventry City in September 1999, for a fee of £6 million. He played a pivotal role up front for the Republic of Ireland in the qualifiers for the European 2000 campaign.

KEANE, ROY MAURICE (1971–)

Footballer, born in Cork. A dynamic and combative midfield player, he made his full international debut for the Republic of Ireland in 1991, and by 2 September 1999 had won a total of 43 caps. Keane was signed by Nottingham Forest from Cobh Ramblers in 1990. He moved to Manchester United for the 1993–94 season for £3.75 million, and as captain has helped the club to win a succession of honours including the European Cup, and three league and cup doubles. He was voted the Republic of Ireland Player of the Year in 1997.

In November 1999 Keane signed a £50,000 a week contract to stay with Manchester United until 2003. This deal made him the highest-paid player in the Premiership.

KEATING, GEOFFREY (SEATHRÚN CÉITINN) (*c.* 1580–*c.* 1645)

Gaelic poet and historian, and Roman Catholic priest. Born in Burges, County Tipperary, he was educated on the Continent at Bordeaux and Salamanca. His *Forás Feasa ar Éirinn/Groundwork of Knowledge about Ireland* (about 1630) refutes other commentators on Ireland, particularly the Elizabethan chroniclers of the preceding generation, and produces the first attempt at a complete compendium of history and legendary material. He also wrote poetry, in densely wrought assonantal metres.

KEATING, RONAN (1977–)

Pop singer, band manager, and TV presenter, born in Dublin. Keating was the unofficial front man of the boy band Boyzone. Following a string of successful songs with Boyzone, Keating has since gone on to record his own solo album and is joint manager of Westlife, a new boy band that has already proved immensely popular.

KEATING, SÉAN (1889–1977)

Painter, mainly of figure subjects and landscapes, His work is traditional in style and presents a romantic, picturesque, and sometimes heroic image of his country. In particular, his most famous picture, *Men of the West* (*c.* 1915), now in the Hugh Lane Municipal Gallery of Modern Art, Dublin, became something of a patriotic icon. Keating also painted various other types of work, including murals, religious pictures, and portraits. Throughout most of his career he was regarded as one of Ireland's leading artists.

Born in Limerick, Keating studied at the Technical College there and at the Metropolitan School of Art in Dublin, where he was taught by Sir William Orpen (1878–1931). He worked in London as Orpen's assistant 1951–16, then returned to Dublin, where he taught at the Metropolitan School from 1919. He was professor of painting there from 1936 until his retirement in 1954, and he was also President of the Royal Hibernian Academy from 1948 to 1962.

KELLS

Market town in County Meath, 60 km/37 mi northwest of Dublin; population (1996) 2,200. Kells Monastery was founded here by ⇨Colum Cille (St Columba) in the 6th century. The surviving buildings were constructed on the same site by monks from the monastery of St Columba on Iona in the early 9th century, to house the relics of the saint safely. The monks of this order are best known for their association with the Book of ⇨Kells. A facsimile of the book is displayed in the church.

The town has an ancient round tower (30 m/99 ft high), and there are carved stone crosses in the marketplace. Colum Cille's House is a 9th-century, stone-roofed, two-storey building. On the summit of the Hill of Lloyd (130 m/428 ft) is a folly resembling a lighthouse, erected in memory of the Earl of Bective.

KELLS, BOOK OF

Eighth- or ninth-century illuminated gospel book, associated with the church at Kells, County Meath. Once described as the 'chief relic of the western world', the Book of Kells represents the crowning achievement in insular illuminated gospel books. Spanning 340 folios, it contains a Latin copy of the four Gospels as well as numerous richly decorated canon tables.

Its association with ⇨Colum Cille (St Columba) and his church at Kells dates back at least as far as the early 11th century when the *Annals of Ulster* record its theft and later its return to the great stone church there. Once thought to be written in Columba's own hand, the book was most likely started at the island monastery of Iona, off the western coast of Scotland, and completed at Kells. Its size and splendour suggest that it was probably intended as an altar book. Since its donation in the late 17th century by the bishop of Meath, the Book of Kells has been kept in Trinity College library, Dublin.

KELLY, HUGH (1739–1777)

Playwright, born in Killarney, County Kerry, and apprenticed in Dublin before moving to London in 1760. His poem *Thespis, or a Critical Examination into the Merits of all the Principal Performers* *belonging to Drury Lane Theatre* (1767) attracted David Garrick's attention, and his comedy *False Delicacy* (1768) was produced under Garrick's direction.

Kelly also wrote the plays *A Word to the Wise* (1770), *Clementina* (1771), *The School for Wives* (1773), *The Romance of an Hour* (1774), and *The Man of Reason* (1776).

When he first moved to London, Kelly took a succession of jobs before before finding a good post in an attorney's office. From about 1762 he wrote essays, poetry, criticism, and comments on politics for various newspapers and magazines.

KELLY, MICHAEL (1762–1826)

Tenor, actor, and composer. Kelly made his operatic debut in Naples, Italy, in 1781. He began composing dramatic works in 1789, and produced over 60. His entertaining *Reminiscences* (1826), though not fully reliable, contain valuable information on his contemporaries, especially Mozart.

Kelly studied with Michael Arne and others, and went to Naples in 1779 to study with Fedele Fenaroli (1730–1818) and Giuseppe Aprile (1732–1813). At the Court Opera in Vienna, Austria, 1784–87, he was the first Basilio and Curzio in Mozart's *The Marriage of Figaro* (1786). He returned to London in 1787. His works include: *A Friend in Need* (1797), *The Castle Spectre* (1797), *Blue Beard* (1798), *Pizarro* (Sheridan; 1799), *The Gipsy Prince* (1801), *Love Laughs at Locksmiths* (1803), *Cinderella* (1804), *Polly* (1813).

KELLY, SEAN (JOHN JAMES) (1956–)

Cyclist, born in Carrick-on-Suir, Tipperary. One of the top riders of the modern era, he won a total of 193 races in a professional career spanning 17 years from 1977 to 1994. Kelly achieved 12 victories in the one-day Classics, and won the Paris–Nice stage race a remarkable seven years in a row, 1982–88. He won the Tour of Spain in 1988, and the Tour of Lombardy in 1983, 1985, and 1991. In 1989 he won the inaugural World Cup series, and also became the first cyclist to win the green points jersey in the Tour de France four times, having previously won it in 1982, 1983, and 1985.

KELVIN, WILLIAM THOMSON (1st Baron Kelvin) (1824–1907)

Scientist who helped to lay the foundations of modern

WILLIAM THOMPSON KELVIN *A prodigious inventor, Kelvin developed the Kelvin scale of thermodynamic temperature, still used today, which includes the concept of absolute zero. He was president of the Royal Society for five years in the late 19th century.*

physics. He developed the kelvin temperature scale, and his work on a theory of heat transfer helped lead to the second law of thermodynamics.

Born in Belfast, Kelvin was taught mathematics by his father from a young age and went to Glasgow University at the age of ten; his first published scientific article appeared when he was 16 years old. He worked in Paris for a time before taking the chair of natural philosophy, and later physics, at Glasgow University 1846–99. He had a very productive scientific career, penning 600 scientific papers and holding dozens of patents.

Kelvin's achievements ranged right across physics. He pursued the goal of a unified theory given his experimental results, which linked light, energy, and electromagnetism. In 1848 he proposed his absolute zero temperature scale, a system of measurement

which is used today. He developed the work of English scientist Michael Faraday into a full theory of magnetism, and expanded ideas derived from the work of the English physicist James Joule on the determination of the mechanical equivalent of heat. He also crystallized theoretical and experimental findings on the movement of heat from a hotter to a cooler body into a theory now known as the second law of thermodynamics.

An inventor and a consultant, Kelvin participated in the laying of some of the early submarine telegraph cables. In 1858 he patented a telegraph receiver called the mirror galvanometer. He was concerned with the accurate measurement of electricity, and developed an absolute electrometer in 1870. He was instrumental in achieving the international adoption in 1881 of many of today's electrical units. His inventions included a tide gauge and predictor, an improved compass, and simpler methods for fixing a ship's position at sea.

Kelvin was knighted for his work in 1866 and was made Baron in 1892. He was president of the Royal Society 1890–95. He died in December 1907 and was buried in Westminster Abbey, London.

KENMARE

Market town in County Kerry, at the head of a sea inlet known as Kenmare River; population (1996) 1,400. Situated at the southern end of the Ring of Kerry, Kenmare is a popular tourist centre. It produces handmade lace.

Kenmare was founded in 1670 by William Petty (1623–1687), Oliver Cromwell's surveyor general in Ireland, to support his mining developments nearby. The town's two main streets, which intersect each other in a distinctive X-shape, were laid out by the 1st Marquess of Landsdowne in 1775. Cromwell's Fort, a 17th-century castle, is situated close to the centre of the town. Nearby are the ruins of Dunkerron Castle (2 km/1 mi west), Cappanacushy Castle (8 km/5 mi west-southwest), and Dromore Castle (10km/7 mi west-southwest).

KENNELLY, BRENDAN (1936–)

Writer, best known for his poetry. Kennelly was born in Ballylongford, County Kerry, and educated at Trinity College, Dublin, and the University of Leeds. His verse extols the infinite complexity and variety of the human condition: its loves, its hatreds, its history of violence, and its desire for understanding and compassion. He has published several poetry collections, as well as long poem sequences, such as *Cromwell* (1983) and *The Book of Judas* (1991), and novels and plays. In 1973 he became professor of Modern English at Trinity College, Dublin.

KERRY

County of the Republic of Ireland, west of Cork, in the province of Munster; county town ⇨Tralee; area 4,700 sq km/1,814 sq mi; population (1996) 126,100. Industries include engineering, woollens, shoes, cutlery, fishing, and farming (dairy farming in the north, cattle grazing in the south). Tourism is important; Muckross House and Abbey are among the top visitor attractions. Other towns include Caherciveen, Castleisland, Dingle, Killarney, and Listowel. Kerry is low-lying in the north and mountainous in the south, with the Slieve Mish and Caha Mountains, and ⇨Macgillycuddy's Reeks, where Carrauntoohill (Ireland's highest peak at 1,041 m/3,415 ft) is situated; other peaks include Brandon (953 m/3,127 ft) and Mangerton (840 m/2,756 ft).

Kerry's western coastline is deeply indented, with three large peninsulas (Beara, Iveragh, and Dingle), and large bays at Tralee and Dingle. Islands off the west coast include the Skelligs, the Blaskets, and Valentia Island. There are many rivers and lakes, notably the Lakes of ⇨Killarney.

> Íreland! Ireland! Ireland! the word falls on the ear with the gentle persistence of rain on the shores of Kerry.
>
> HONOR LILBUSH WINGFIELD TRACY Anglo-Irish writer 'Mind You, I've Said Nothing' (1953) quoted in *The Oxford Book of Ireland*, edited by Patricia Craig.

~

The area is rich in archaeological remains, most notably Staigue near Sneem, Leacanabuaile Fort near Caherciveen, and the large site of Fahan on the Dingle Peninsula. There are also significant early ecclesiastical ruins, including the monastic site on Skellig Michael, which is a place of pilgrimage. The western half of the Dingle Peninsula is a Gaeltacht (Irish-speaking area).

KERRY, RING OF

Coastal strip around the broad Iveragh Peninsula in

RING OF KERRY *Although this stretch of shoreline, between Caherciveen and Glenbeigh, is serenely beautiful, in other parts of Kerry the scenery is far more wild and rugged. This variety, plus the mild climate, make the circular route known as the Ring of Kerry one of the most popular tourist itineraries.*

County Kerry; length 176 km/109 mi. It contains some of the most popular tourist scenery in Ireland, encompassing ⇨Killarney, Parknasilla, Sneem, Derrynane, Waterville, Caherciveen, Glenbeigh, and Killorglin. The Iveragh Peninsula is 64 km/40 mi by 24 km/15 mi.

KICKHAM, CHARLES JOSEPH (1828–1882)

Writer and political activist, born in Cnoceenagaw, County Tipperary. A member of the republican ⇨Fenian movement, Kickham contributed to nationalist newspapers, such as *The Celt* and *The Nation*, and advocated armed rebellion. He was arrested in 1865 and sentenced to 14 years' imprisonment for treason, but was released in the 1869 amnesty. From the mid-1870s until his death, Kickham was chairman of the Supreme Council of the Irish Republican Brotherhood.

Kickham's republican activities and support of land reform through the ⇨Tenant League, in addition to his novel *Knocknagow; or, the Homes of Tipperary* (1873), significantly influenced the Irish nationalist movement in the 19th century. His popularity and renown extends to the large Irish emigrant communities in North America and Britain.

KIELY, BENEDICT (1919–   )

Journalist, and novelist who has successfully married modern fiction methods with a content and technique based on the oral conversational methods of the traditional folk-story. Born and educated in County Tyrone, Kiely entered the Jesuit novitiate but soon left with spinal tuberculosis. While working for a succession of Irish newspapers as a journalist and literary editor, Kiely wrote *Land Without Stars* (1946), concerning the fate of two brothers living on the border, and *In a Harbour Green* (1949), dealing with the seduction of a woman by one man and the loyalty of another. He also wrote *Modern Irish Fiction: A Critique* (1950), the first study of its kind.

Later novels deal with more political issues: *Proxopera* (1977), based on the notorious kidnapping of a Dutch industrialist in Ireland, registered his disgust at the violent methods of the modern IRA, while *Nothing Happens in Carmincross* (1985) deals with sectarianism and extremism in Ulster. Kiely has worked in America as writer-in-residence and lecturer since the early 1960s. He is much loved as a radio-broadcaster of long-standing whose cultivated and amusing intelligence finds natural expression in local stories and reminiscences.

KILDARE

See ⇨Fitzgerald family.

KILDARE

County of the Republic of Ireland, in the province of Leinster; county town ⇨Naas; area 1,690 sq km/652 sq mi; population (1996) 135,000. The principal rivers are the Barrow, the Boyne, the Lesser Barrow, and the Liffey. Kildare is wet and boggy in the north with extensive grassy plains and rolling hills, and includes part of the Bog of Allen. The town of Maynooth houses a constituent part of the National University of Ireland; originally the college was a seminary for Roman Catholic priests. The Curragh, at Tully, is a plain that is the site of the national stud and headquarters of Irish horse racing; steeplechase racing also takes place at Punchestown. Cattle are grazed in the north, and in the south products include oats, barley, potatoes, and cattle. Other main towns include Athy, Droichead Nua, and Kildare.

KILDARE

Market town in County ⇨Kildare, 48 km/30 mi southwest of Dublin; population (1996) 4,300. Kildare is the centre of the Irish horse-breeding and training industry, and the national stud is located at nearby Tully; the town also has meat-processing industries. An ecclesiastic settlement was founded at Kildare by St Brigid in AD 470. The Protestant St Brigid's Cathedral incorporates a 10th-century round tower and the ruins of a 13th-century church.

Tully, 1 km/0.6 mi away, also has the remains of a community of Knights Hospitallers (the Order of St John); Japanese gardens laid out in 1906; and a horse museum at the Irish National Stud.

KILKEEL

Fishing port and resort in County Down. Situated at the foot of the Mourne Mountains, Kilkeel is the chief market town for the Mourne region and a centre for quarrying and dressing Mourne granite. There is a large dolmen stone 2 km/1 mi northeast of Kilkeel, and to the southwest a large ring fort and a chambered Mesolithic tomb.

KILKENNY

County of the Republic of Ireland, in the province of Leinster; county town ⇨Kilkenny; area 2,060 sq km/795 sq mi; population (1996) 75,300. It has the rivers Nore, Suir, and Barrow. Industries include coalmining, clothing, footwear, brewing, and agricultural activities include cattle rearing and dairy farming. Principal towns include Castlecomer, Callan, Graiguenamanagh, and Thomastown.

There are several medieval ruins in the county, including Kells Monastery and Jerpoint Abbey, founded in 1158 by Donagh MacGillapatrick, King of Ossory.

KILKENNY

County town of County ⇨Kilkenny; population (1996) 8,500. Kilkenny lies on the River Nore. Local industries include food processing and textile and shoe manufacture. The town's medieval buildings are better preserved than in any other centre in Ireland. The cathedral of St Canice dates from 1255. Kilkenny Castle was the former residence of the Earls of Ormond.

A number of parliaments were held in Kilkenny during the 14th century. The Statute of Kilkenny (1366) forbade Anglo-Norman men to marry Irish women and prevented Irishmen from living within the town walls.

Dunmore Caves, 11 km/7 mi north of Kilkenny, are a national monument. These limestone caves are extensive and have large stalagmites and stalactites.

architecture

Kilkenny Castle was built in the 13th century to replace an earlier motte; it is now open to the public. St Canice's Cathedral is built partly in Early English Gothic style with an older round tower (30 m/100 ft high). Near the cathedral is St Canice's Library, which contains important 16th- and 17th-century texts. The town also contains ruins of a Dominican and a Franciscan monastery.

Between 1642 and 1648 there was an independent Irish parliament here, the ⇨Confederation of Kilkenny. A tablet in Parliament Street marks the site of the Confederation Parliament House, demolished in the mid-19th century. The Tholsel in the High Street, now the town hall, was built in 1761 as a toll house and exchange. It has an unusual clock tower.

Kilkenny College is the former Protestant College of St John (1666), where the writer Jonathan Swift and the philosopher George Berkeley received part of their education.

KILKENNY DESIGN WORKSHOP (KDW)

Design workshop, established in 1963, that immeasurably raised design awareness in industry and among consumers in Ireland.

The workshop was set up by by An Córas Tráchtála (Irish Export Board) to assist Irish industrial designers and craftspeople in developing the potential of craft-based industries, and to raise public consciousness of design. The main areas of training and production were woven and printed textiles, woodwork, silversmithing, and ceramics, and later graphic design, furniture, and candlemaking.

Two Kilkenny Design shops, in Kilkenny and in Dublin, raised the public profile of the Workshop and of Irish design generally. However, following the financial failure of a London shop, KDW was wound up, with the sale of the Irish shops, and the Crafts Council of Ireland's adoption of the workshop's responsibility for Irish design.

KILLALOE

Town in County Clare, on the River Shannon at the edge of Lough Derg, 27 km/17 mi from Limerick; population (1996) 1,400. Killaloe was the former seat of Brian Bóruma, High King of Ireland, and is now the cathedral town of a Protestant diocese.

A ring fort dating from the 11th century, 2 km/1 mi to the west, was reputedly a stronghold of the O'Brien family, the descendants of Brian Bóruma.

KILLANIN, MICHAEL MORRIS (3rd Baron Killanin) (1915–1999)

English sports administrator, born in London. Killanin began his career in 1952 with the Irish Olympic Council, later renamed the Olympic Council of Ireland. His appointment came after internal bickering had seen two separate Irish teams entered for the London Games in 1948. By the mid-1960s Killanin's profile was such that he was elevated to vice-president of the International Olympic Council before eventually succeeding Avery Brundage as president in 1972. He spent eight years in office and resisted international pressure to cancel the 1980 games in Moscow after the withdrawal of the US team. Killanin also pushed for the return of China into the Olympic movement, which he lived to see.

KILLARNEY

Market town and tourist centre in County ⇨Kerry; population (1996) 8,800. It is a famous beauty spot in Ireland; the mountain range ⇨Macgillycuddy's Reeks and the Lakes of Killarney lie to the southwest. Industries include hosiery and container cranes. The Catholic Cathedral of St Mary was designed by Pugin in 1855. The 19th-century Church of Ireland St Mary's Church is noted for its rich internal decoration. The National Museum of Irish Transport is located at Killarney.

the Lakes of Killarney

The Lakes of Killarney are 2 km/1.3 miles from the town, and are enclosed by wood-crowned mountains. The lower lake, called Lough Leane, is dotted with 30 wooded islands, the most important being Inisfallen Island, with the beautiful ruins of the abbey, founded about AD 600. Between 950 and 1320 the *Annals of Inisfallen* were written here; the manuscript is now held at the Bodleian Library in Oxford. ⇨Muckross Abbey, which was built by the Franciscans about 1440, is on a peninsula which divides the lower lake from the middle lake or Lough Torc (also known as Lough Muckross). The upper lake connects with the middle and lower lakes by means of the Long Range, a channel 4 km/2.5 mi long.

Other places of great beauty in the area are Mount Torc (537 m/1,762 ft) and Mount Purple (835 m/2,740 ft, so called because it is covered in heather in summer); the gardens at Muckross; and the famous gap of Dunloe, a narrow mountain gorge. Of historic interest are the church at Aghado, and the ruins of Ross Castle, a large, heavily fortified, 14th-century construction on the shore of Lough Leane. The 19th-century Muckross House in Killarney National Park houses a folk museum.

KILLORGLIN

Town in County Kerry, 26 km/16 mi south of Tralee; population (1996) 1,300. There is an annual cattle, sheep, and horse fair. The surrounding glacial scenery has many small lakes within it.

Killorglin is the scene of the Puck Fair and Pattern, where a goat is enthroned for three days each August. Although the fair has pagan origins, this particular ritual is also reputed to commemorate the wild goats whose stampede through the village warned the inhabitants of the approaching Cromwellian army in the 17th century.

KILMAINHAM TREATY

Informal secret treaty reached in 1882 between the British prime minister William Gladstone and the Irish nationalist Charles Stewart ⇨Parnell, securing his release from Kilmainham jail, Dublin.

KILRUDDERY HOUSE

Country house at Bray, County Wicklow. It is one of the earliest Tudor revival mansions in Ireland, designed by Sir Richard ⇨Morrison for the 10th Earl of Meath about 1820. It has three fronts, pointed gables, and a domed conservatory, which was designed by William Burn and added in 1852. The house was altered in the 1950s and reduced in size. The original entrance hall, great hall, and dining room were some of the rooms lost in this reconstruction, which was to the design of Claud Phillimore.

KINANE, MICK (MICHAEL JOSEPH) (1959–)

Flat racing jockey, born in County Tipperary, who was flat racing champion a record ten times between 1983 and 1994. He has ridden winners in many of the world's top races, including the Prix de l'Arc de Triomphe on Carroll House in 1989, the Belmont Stakes on Go and Go in 1990, the Epsom Derby on Commander-in-Chief in 1993, the Melbourne Cup on Vintage Crop in 1993, and the Japan Cup on Pilsudski in 1997. With victories in the 2,000 Guineas in 1982 and 1986, the 1,000 Guineas in 1988, the Oaks

in 1989 and 1996, and the St Leger in 1993 and 1994, he has won a total of seven Irish Classics. Additionally, he rode the winner of the Irish Champion Stakes in 1989, 1994, and 1997.

Kinane rode his first winner in 1975. Son of the jump jockey Tommy Kinane, and originally apprenticed to Liam Browne, he began a highly successful 15-year partnership with the Irish trainer Dermot Weld in 1983. In 1999 he teamed up with Aidan O'Brien.

KING, CECIL (1921–1986)

Painter, printmaker, designer, and art collector. Although he was a late starter in art, King became recognized as one of Ireland's leading abstract painters.

Born in Rathdrum, County Wicklow, King initially pursued a career as a businessman, and his success enable him to build an impressive collection of paintings, including many Irish works. In the early 1950s, he turned his own hand to painting, in which he was mainly self-taught. He had his first one-man exhibition in Dublin in 1959 and he became a full-time artist in 1964, at the age of 43. By this time he had moved from representational works to abstracts. Initially, his abstracts were exuberant, with suggestions of natural forms, but by the late 1960s he had developed a cool, hard edged style.

KING JOHN'S CASTLE

See ⇨Limerick Castle; name also used for ⇨Trim Castle.

KINSELLA, THOMAS (1928–)

Poet and translator, born in inner-city Dublin, and educated at the Model School, Inchicore, and University College, Dublin. Kinsella is a prolific and highly regarded poet, whose publications range from *Poems* (1956) to *From Centre City* (1994). His early work tended to be personal and lyrical, dealing with the difficulties of love, family illness, and the almost ghostly calm of an unpopulated countryside. Collections such as *Fifteen Dead* (1979) and *Butcher's Dozen* (1972) confront violence and what Kinsella perceived as a moral vacuum in contemporary Ireland.

Kinsella was very active in the Irish publishing industry, serving as a director of Dolmen Press and starting his own, called Peppercanister. His translations from Irish Gaelic into English show a keen awareness of Gaelic tradition; *The Táin* (1969), a translation of *Táin Bó Cuailnge/The Cattle Raid of*

Cooley and the central saga of the ancient Ulster cycle, is his most celebrated.

KIRWAN, RICHARD (1733–1812)

Chemist and mineralogist. He helped advance methods of analytical chemistry through his work on the relevant densities of saline substances, and was an authority on chemical affinity.

Kirwan was born in Cloughballymore, County Galway, and studied at the University of Poitiers, France 1750–54. He entered the Jesuit seminary at Saint Omer, France, hoping to become a priest, but the death of his elder brother in a duel in 1755 brought him back to Ireland.

Kirwan practised law but gave this up to pursue scientific studies. He lived in London 1777–87 and was elected to the Royal Society in 1780. He wrote papers on chemical reactions and a book *Essay on Phlogiston*. An early supporter of the theory of phlogiston, a substance thought to be released during combustion, Kirwan later accepted the views held by opponents of the theory, led by the French chemist Antoine Lavoisier.

He helped found the Royal Irish Society in 1779 and became its president for a time. His writings covered a wide range of subjects, most notably mineralogy but also climatology, logic, and metaphysics.

KITCHENER, HORATIO (HERBERT) (1st Earl Kitchener of Khartoum) (1850–1916)

General and politician, born near Ballylongford, County Kerry. He established his reputation as a leading British military figure with the Egyptian army, winning notable victories against the Sudanese at Atbara and Omdurman in 1898, when he recaptured Khartoum for Egypt. Commander-in-chief of British forces during the second Boer War (1900–02), his revolutionary tactics helped defeat the Boers although he was criticized for introducing concentration camps for prisoners and civilians. Later commander-in-chief in India (1902–09), he was made secretary of state for war upon the outbreak of World War I. He oversaw a radical reorganization of the army, and led a successful campaign for voluntary recruitment.

Raised to an earldom in 1914, Kitchener was criticized for the failure of the Gallipoli campaign the following year, in which Allied forces attempted to gain control of the Dardanelles strait. An opponent of home rule for Ireland, in politics he was a conserva-

tive. He died at sea, when his ship struck a mine. He was made KCMG in 1894, Baron in 1898, Viscount in 1902, and Earl in 1914.

KNOCK

Village and parish in County Mayo, 11 km/7 mi northeast of Claremorris. A national place of pilgrimage, Knock is known as the site of alleged apparitions of the Virgin Mary (the first on 21 August 1879), and for its church shrine, the Basilica of Our Lady, 'Queen of Ireland', which seats 12,000 and was opened in 1976. Horan International Airport, opened in 1986, receives transatlantic flights; it was named after Monsignor James Horan, a parish priest who launched the project to attract pilgrims.

In the first alleged apparition the Virgin Mary, St Joseph, and St John initially appeared to two women in 1879. A church commission investigated the witnesses and accepted their account; a second commission ratified this in 1936. Although the Catholic Church has made no official statement, interest in the shrine has been great, and large numbers of pilgrims arrive each year from Ireland and around the world. In 1979 Pope John Paul II, the first pope to set foot on Irish soil, celebrated mass here for the sick on the centenary of the first apparition. There is a folk museum on the site.

KNOCKMEALDOWN MOUNTAINS

Mountain range in south County Tipperary and the northwest of County Waterford; 20 km/12 mi by 7 km/4 mi. Knockmealdown, the highest summit, is 795 m/2,608 ft. The mountains are composed of old red sandstone and quartzite.

KNOCKNAREA ('hill of executions')

Massive prehistoric cairn perched on the summit of Knocknarea Mountain, County Sligo. Unexcavated, its 40,000 tonnes of stone are believed to cover a passage-grave, reputedly the tomb of ⇨Medhba, the legendary queen of Connacht. Other sources place her burial place at Rathcroghan. The cairn, 10 m/33 ft high and 57 m/197 ft wide, is believed to be about 5,000 years old.

KNOWLES, JAMES SHERIDAN (1784–1862)

Dramatist, born in Cork, and second cousin of the dramatist Richard Brinsley Sheridan. His only Irish play was *Brian Boroimhe* (1811), produced by the company of Andrew Cherry (1762–1812). In

London Knowles became part of the literary circle of Charles Dickens, Charles Lamb, and William Hazlitt. His tragedy *Caius Gracchus* (1815) won much praise. Five years later his *Virginius*, suggested by his friend the actor Edmund Kean, was performed at Drury Lane. *William Tell* (1825) was produced by William Macready at Covent Garden, and *The Beggar's Daughter of Bethnal Green* was produced in 1828.

Among his other plays were *Alfred the Great* (1831), *The Hunchback* (1832), and *The Love Chase* (1837). Knowles later became a Baptist preacher.

KNOX, ALEXANDER (1757–1831)

Lay Anglican (Church of Ireland) theologian and letter writer, a prominent figure in the Irish High Church revival. Knox published *The Doctrine Respecting Baptism Held by the Church of England* and *Treatise on the Use and Import of the Eucharistic Symbols* (1824). His main influence was through his published letters, both his 30-year correspondence with his co-revivalist Bishop Jebb of Limerick and his posthumously published *Remains* (1834–37). He prefigured (and influenced) the English Tractarians in combining Catholic sentiments with an opposition to Roman Catholicism.

Knox was born in Dublin. His first career was in politics, which he abandoned due to illness, turning instead to writing sacramental theology.

KYLEMORE ABBEY

19th-century castle between Letterfrack and Leenane in the Pass of Kylemore, County Galway. It was designed about 1860 by James Franklin Fuller and Ussher Roberts for Michael Henry, a wealthy Liverpool merchant and member of parliament, and was afterwards the seat of the 9th Duke of Manchester. In 1920 the abbey was bought by the Irish Dames of Ypres, an order of Benedictine nuns, and is now a convent and school. The castle is undergoing restoration and is one of the most photographed buildings in the west of Ireland.

KYTELER, ALICE (DAME ALICE)

A Kilkenny woman accused of heresy and witchcraft in 1324. Dame Alice, having married and outlived four husbands, was charged by the bishop of Ossory, Richard Ledred, with forming and leading a band of witches and sorcerers in the town and environs of Kilkenny. A wealthy woman, through birth as well as through her first marriage, she twice escaped the charges, the second time fleeing to England where she was not heard from again.

The accused who remained in Kilkenny, including her son and heir William Outlaw, were prosecuted and, after full admissions of guilt, jailed. In lieu of Dame Alice's arrest, Petronilla of Meath, clearly the situation's scapegoat, was burned alive in the marketplace, the first such execution reported in Ireland.

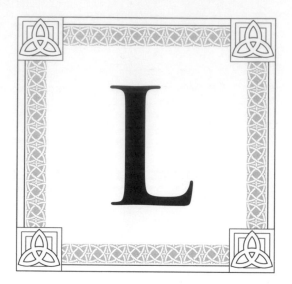

LABOUR PARTY

Oldest surviving political party in the Republic of Ireland, established in 1914 by the Irish Trade Union Congress (ITUC), at the instigation of radical republican James ⇨Connolly and the labour leader James ⇨Larkin. Moderately left-of-centre, it supports the privatization of some state industry and is relatively liberal on social issues, although it still has a significant number of socially conservative TDs (members of the Irish parliament). Ruarí Quinn, appointed party leader in 1997, continued the Labour Party's rightward shift economically but oversaw the merger with the more left wing Democratic Left party in 1999. Since its foundation, the party has not widened its electoral base beyond the status of the minor third party of Irish politics.

Various factors account for Labour's weakness. Partition left a small urban working-class base in the south while high levels of land ownership limited the potential for agrarian radicalism. The anti-communism of the predominantly Catholic state limited the appeal of socialism. Labour's image as the political wing of trade unionism, despite separating from the ITUC in 1930, restricted its appeal although the party's later leaders, including Dick Spring (1982–1997), extended this beyond its traditional base. Labour's greatest problem has been the dominance of the national question, which has led to the party's marginalization as long as divisions stemming from the ⇨Irish Civil War (1922–23) dominated Irish politics.

The ITUC voted to form a Labour Party in 1912 in response to the urging of Connolly. Congress adopted a new constitution and changed its name to the Irish Trade Union Congress and Labour Party in 1914 but no real party organization was established until the following decade. Pre-war Irish Labour leaders thought syndicalism (industrial agitation) of more importance than electoral politics. World War I had a radicalizing effect and the 1918 Congress praised both Connolly, executed as a leader of the Easter Rising in 1916, and the success of the Bolsheviks in Russia.

Despite the expansion of Irish trade unionism in the post-war period, Labour, under the conservative leadership of Thomas Johnson (1872–1963) from 1918 to 1927, chose not to contest the general elections of 1918 and 1921 that set the pattern for the party system. Labour's first general election performance in 1922, winning over 21% of the vote, was a success. On that occasion the party had benefited from popular disillusionment with the divided Sinn Féin's electoral pact and its performance was never repeated. Its vote slumped to 11% the following year, reaching a low of 6% in 1933, and achieving a high of 19% in 1992, when it took 33 seats under the leadership of Dick Spring.

LADIES' LAND LEAGUE

Peasant-rights organization set up by Anna and Fanny ⇨Parnell in 1881; its supporters and activists were women.

LALOR, JAMES FINTAN (1807–1849)

Nationalist politician and journalist, born in County Laois. The son of a gentleman farmer and member of parliament, Lalor was educated at Carlow College but was forced to retire from all activity for a number of years because of poor health. After a partial recovery, he became interested in agrarian reform and began work in 1847 as a journalist for *The Nation*. Working to repeal the Act of ⇨Union (1801), he assumed control of the *Irish Felon* in 1848, after the suppression of the *United Irishman*. Arrested in July 1848 after attempting to organize a rising, he was soon released because of his declining health.

LAND LEAGUE

Peasant-rights organization, formed in 1879 by Michael ⇨Davitt and Charles Stewart ⇨Parnell to fight against tenant evictions. Through its skilful use of the boycott against anyone who took a farm from which another had been evicted, it forced British prime minister William Gladstone's government to introduce a law in 1881 restricting rents and granting tenants security of tenure.

Charles Boycott (1832–1897) was an English land agent in County Mayo who strongly opposed the demands for agrarian reform by the Irish Land League, with the result that the peasants refused to work for him; hence the word 'boycott', meaning to isolate an individual, organization, or country, socially or commercially.

LANDSCAPE PAINTING

Landscape painting developed in Irish art from the later 17th century. The early landscapes were mostly topographical, but by the mid-18th century the Italianate Classical landscape style was being imitated by Irish painters. Romanticism emerged in the later 18th century. In the 19th century historical interests and French influences (Impressionism) were incorporated into Irish landscape painting, and the 20th century saw a variety of uses for the landscape subject in modernist works.

topographical and ideal landscapes
Early interest in landscapes in art coincided with the military requirement to map Ireland in detail. Works by artists such as William van der Hagen (died 1745) and Joseph Tudor (died 1759) tended to be topographical in approach. By the mid-18th century the taste for Italianate Classical landscapes fostered a similar style among Irish painters. One of the most talented exponents of the genre was Thomas Roberts (1748–1778) who achieved a synthesis between

Italian and Dutch influences and combined this with his own observation of the Irish landscape. The English artist William Ashford (1746–1824) went to Ireland at the age of 18 and established himself there as the leading landscapist with paintings that bring together the topographical and ideal traditions.

Romantic landscapes and views of Ireland
It is in landscape painting of the later 18th century that Romanticism first appears in Irish art. The writings of the philosopher Edmund Burke inspired George Barrett (1728/32–1784) in paintings such as *A View of Powerscourt Waterfall* (c. 1764; National Gallery of Ireland, Dublin). This imaginative response to the rugged, picturesque terrain of areas such as Kerry and Wicklow is also to be seen in the work of James Arthur ⇨O'Connor. The work of the Cork artist Nathaniel Grogan (c.1740–1807), derived from 17th-century Dutch art, is an early example of an Irish landscapist dealing with the subject of peasant life. The period also saw the development of the taste for volumes of prints depicting views of Ireland. The *Views of Killarney* and *Malton's Views of Dublin* (1790s) of Jonathan Fisher (1763–1809) may be seen as the culmination of the topographical landscape tradition.

historical and French influences
In the 19th century the growing interest in Ireland's early Christian and medieval past is reflected in landscape painting where it led to a widening of subject matter. A leading figure in promoting this was the artist and antiquarian George Petrie (1790–1866). His romantic imagery occupies an important place in the history of the ⇨Irish revival. From the middle of the 19th century many landscape painters were influenced by developments in French art. This group of artists, known as the Irish ⇨Impressionists, brought a new naturalism to Irish landscape painting. Paul Henry (1876–1958) was influenced by post-Impressionism while studying in Paris and brought his concerns with colour and form to bear in his archetypal images of the west of Ireland. This preoccupation with rural, native, often nostalgic subject matter was shared by many artists in the years after independence as a new cultural identity was being forged in Ireland.

the modernist period
Landscape has continued to be of enduring importance to Irish artists in the modernist period. The almost abstract images of Patrick Collins

(1911–1996) evoke a sense of place and deal with ideas surrounding land ownership, historically an important issue in Ireland. Poetic responses to the Irish landscape recur in the work of Jack Butler ⇨Yeats, Camille Souter (1929–), and Gwen O'Dowd. In contrast, Martin Gale (1949–) and Trevor Geoghan (1946–) work in a detailed realist style. The surreal imagery of Dermot Seymour (1956–) often uses the landscape to deal with political issues.

LANE, HUGH PERCY (1875–1915)

Art dealer and collector. In 1908 Lane founded the Municipal Gallery of Modern Art in Dublin, now named after him and situated on Parnell Square. He was knighted in 1909 and became director of the National Gallery of Ireland, Dublin, in 1914.

Born in Ballybrack, County Cork, Lane was the nephew of the Irish dramatist and cultural activist Lady Augusta Gregory. He made his name as a connoisseur of Old Masters and Impressionism. Now famous works by Manet and Renoir were among the collection of paintings he offered to donate to the Municipal Gallery of Modern Art. However, as a result of the reluctance of the civic authorities to finance the project, Lane removed 39 of the works to London in 1913. The unwitnessed codicil to his will found after his death (on the *Lusitania*, torpedoed at the start of World War I) in which he bequeathed these paintings to Dublin was deemed invalid. After much legal wrangling, in 1959 it was finally agreed to periodically rotate the paintings between Dublin and London.

LANYON, CHARLES (1813–1889)

English-born civil engineer and architect, who created some of the most important Victorian buildings in Ireland, chiefly in the industrial city of Belfast. As county surveyor for Antrim, Lanyon's engineering projects included the Antrim coast road, numerous railways, and the Queen's (1843) and Ormeau bridges over the River Lagan, Belfast. His architectural designs include Belfast's Queen's College (1845–49), now Queen's University; the Institute for the Deaf, Dumb and Blind; the Custom House (1857); and the County Gaol and Courthouse. He was elected president of the Royal Institute of Architects in Ireland in 1862.

Lanyon was born in Eastbourne, Sussex. Initially appointed county surveyor for Kildare, he requested transfer to Antrim but resigned the county surveyorship in 1860 to concentrate on his architectural work.

LAOIS (or LAOIGHIS) (previously spelt Leix; also formerly known as Queen's County)

County of the Republic of Ireland, in the province of Leinster; county town ⇨Portlaoise; area 1,720 sq km/664 sq mi; population (1996) 52,900. Other towns are Abbeyleix, Mountmellick, Mountrath, and Portarlington. Laois is flat, except for the Slieve Bloom Mountains in the northwest, the highest point of which is Mount Arderin (529 m/1,734 ft), and there are many bogs. The Barrow and the Nore are the chief rivers. Agriculture includes dairying, and mixed cattle and arable farming (sugar beet), and industries include peat, woollens, and agricultural machinery. Part of the Leinster coalfield lies within the county. There is a large peat-fired power station near Portarlington, and at the Clonsast Bog (1,619 ha/4,000 acres) is an important peat industry.

LARKIN, JAMES (1876–1947)

Labour leader and Labour politician; founder of the Irish Transport and General Workers' Union (ITGWU) in 1908, the Irish Workers' League in 1923, and the Workers' Union of Ireland in 1924.

Larkin was born in Liverpool, England, to working-class Irish parents, and became a committed trade unionist and socialist. In 1907 he was sent to Belfast by the British-based National Union of Dock Workers in an unsuccessful attempt to unionize the Belfast docks, where he encountered disparity and sectarianism. He founded the ITGWU in 1908, and was imprisoned for organizing the bitter 1913 lockout in Dublin. Following his release in 1914 Larkin went to the USA where, as a delegate to the founding convention of the American Communist Party, he was imprisoned for three years for 'criminal anarchy'. Deported from the USA in 1923, Larkin returned to Ireland and feuded with the new ITGWU leader William O'Brien (1852–1928). On being expelled from the ITGWU in 1923, he founded the Irish Workers' League and became a founder member of the Workers' Union of Ireland in 1924. He later joined the Labour Party and served in Dáil Éireann (Irish parliament) 1943–44.

Although he clashed with many of his peers, Larkin's dynamic personality and organizational abilities helped to establish trade unionism in Ireland.

His wife, Delia Larkin, was the first general secretary of the ⇨Irish Women Workers' Union (IWWU).

LARMOR, JOSEPH (1857–1942)

Physicist and mathematician. Larmor was the first to calculate the rate at which energy is radiated by an accelerated electron, and he explained the splitting of spectrum lines by a magnetic field. He also wrote extensively on hydrodynamics.

Born in Magheraghall, County Antrim, Larmor studied at Queen's College, Belfast, and later St John's College, Cambridge. He was professor of natural philosophy at Queen's College, Galway 1880–85 before returning to Cambridge, where he was Lucasian professor of mathematics 1903–32.

His main work, *Aether and Matter* (1900), discussed the prevailing theory that matter moved through a wave-bearing medium present in all space known as ether. The work also gave the complete formulae for the Fitzgerald–Lorentz contraction, which described the contraction of bodies moving at high speed and played a key part in the development of Albert Einstein's theory of relativity.

Larmor's most important work involved experiments on the interaction of charged matter and electromagnetic fields, but he also made important contributions in the radiation of energy by accelerated electrons, and in the development of a theory on how magnetic fields affected electron orbits. He was knighted in 1909 and represented Cambridge in parliament at Westminster 1911–22.

LARNE

Seaport and industrial town of County Antrim, on Lough Larne, 30 km/19 mi north of Belfast; population (1991) 17,500. It is the terminus of sea routes principally to Cairnryan near Stanraer in Scotland, and has a turbine generator works and an electronics industry.

The Curran is a raised gravel beach running south from Larne, on which many Neolithic flint implements have been found. The Norse used Lough Larne in the 10th and 11th centuries as a port. Edward Bruce (brother of Robert) landed at Larne with his army in 1315; his campaign was supported by the Bissett family whose castle (Olderfleet, dating from the 13th century) and lands were confiscated by the British crown as a result. The ruins of Olderfleet Castle can still be seen on the Curran.

LAVELLE, PATRICK (1858–1886)

Catholic priest, who was closely associated with the National Brotherhood of St Patrick, a front organization for the Fenians. Following papal censure Lavelle became parish priest of Cong, County Mayo, and although for the most part contented himself with pastoral work from then on, he was involved with the Land League before his death.

Lavelle was born in Mullagh, County Mayo. He entered St Patrick's College, Maynooth, in 1844 and was ordained in 1854. An intelligent, but by no means brilliant student, he was appointed to teach theology at the Irish College in Paris, France. He was as turbulent in Paris as he had been at Maynooth and returned to his diocese, Tuam, in 1858 when the Parisian college was given over to the administration of the Vincentian Order. Back in Ireland he immersed himself in social and political agitation.

LAVERY, JOHN (1856–1941)

Portrait painter of Edwardian society, born in Belfast. Lavery worked in Glasgow and France before settling in London and establishing a successful portrait practice. Though influenced by Impressionism, James Whistler and Velázquez made a greater impact on his work. He was knighted in 1918.

Lavery emerged as an important figure during the negotiation of the Anglo-Irish Treaty in 1921, acting as an envoy for Winston Churchill and becoming a close friend of Michael Collins. His portrait of Collins lying in state entitled *Love of Ireland* (Hugh Lane Municipal Gallery of Modern Art, Dublin) is a highly emotive political image. He continued to take an interest in artistic affairs north and south of the border. In 1927 his wife, Hazel, was proposed as the model for the figure of Eire on the new Irish pound note. Though his academic style was ultimately eclipsed by modernism, since the mid-1980s reappraisals of his work have resulted in a new appreciation of his artistic achievement.

LAVIN, MARY (1912–1996)

US-born Irish short-story writer and novelist. Her many collections, which focus on the complexities beneath the surface of small-town life in Ireland, include *A Memory and Other Stories* (1972), *The Shrine and Other Stories* (1977), *A Family Likeness* (1985), and *The House in Clewe Street* (1987). Her first collection *Tales from Bective Bridge* (1942) received the James Tait Black Memorial Prize. Other awards include the 1961 Katherine Mansfield prize, two Guggenheim awards, and the Gregory Medal, founded by W B Yeats as 'the supreme award of the Irish nation'.

Lavin was born in East Walpole, Massachusetts, into an Irish immigrant family, who returned to Ireland when she was 14. After studying English at University College, Dublin, she went to live in County Meath. Her first short story, 'Miss Holland', was published in the *Dublin Magazine*, where it was admired by the writer Lord ⇨Dunsany, who encouraged her and later wrote an introduction to *Tales from Bective Bridge*. Apart from two early novels – *The House in Clewe Street* (1945) and *Mary O'Grady* (1950) – she concentrated on the short story.

LE BROCQUY, LOUIS (1916–)

Painter, resident in the south of France. Le Brocquy is best known for his paintings of the faces of writers such as W B Yeats, Samuel Beckett, and James Joyce, evoking the presence rather than the physical likeness of the subject.

Born in Dublin, Le Brocquy travelled in Europe between 1938 and 1940. Formative influences included Rembrandt, Velázquez, Goya, and Manet, while the influence of Picasso is evident in his angular approach to form. He settled in London in 1946 where his circle included Francis Bacon and William Scott. There he emerged as a designer of tapestries and as a graphic artist, later illustrating Thomas Kinsella's translation of the *Táin-Bo-Cuailgne* (1969). In the mid-1960s Le Brocquy began to produce ethereal images of the human face inspired by Irish Celtic and early Christian art. His ongoing concern with the isolation of the individual lies behind his series of paintings made in the early 1970s in response to violence in Northern Ireland.

LEE

River in County Cork; length 80 km/50 mi. It rises on the border of counties Kerry and Cork, forming Lough Gougane Barra and Lough Allua, and divides into two main channels through the city of Cork before flowing into Cork harbour. With its tributaries it is an important centre of salmon and trout fishing. It has been developed for electrical power on a large scale between Macroom and Inniscarra.

LE FANU, (JOSEPH) SHERIDAN
(1814–1873)

Writer, journalist, and newspaper proprietor, born in Dublin and educated at Trinity College, Dublin. Le Fanu amalgamated the *Warden*, the *Evening Post*, and the *Dublin Evening Mail* as the *Evening Mail*. He wrote tales of mystery and suspense, included in *Ghost Stories and Tales of Mystery* (1851) and *In a Glass Darkly* (1872), and the dark, psychological novel *Uncle Silas* (1864).

Le Fanu excelled in writing about the uncanny and the supernatural, and with his work the tradition of the Gothic novel took on a new psychological and literary power. Other publications include *Wylder's Hand* (1864), *The Tenants of Malory* (1867), and *Willing to Die* (1873). He was a grand-nephew of the playwright Richard Brinsley Sheridan.

LEGAL SYSTEM

In the Republic of Ireland the legal system is based on common law. Initially ruled by the custom-based ancient Gaelic 'Brehon Laws', Ireland saw the introduction of common law with the Anglo-Norman invasion in 1169. Common law is a body of law based on judicial decisions rather than written legislation. Through the practice of precedent, decisions gain binding effect as law. The common law itself shapes the law, and this can only be overridden by legislation. In this way it is distinguished from continental civil law systems based on written civil codes of law, which give less weight to precedent. As the British Empire expanded, so too did the common law, developing into a central body of law. On gaining independence in 1921, the Irish Free State maintained its common law system.

Irish law, however, has a number of varied sources. The primary source is its common law basis. Legislation, law enacted by the Oireachtas (legislature), enjoys supremacy over common law under the 1937 Irish constitution. The constitution is itself a vital source of law, governing the authority of state institutions and protecting human rights. It is a touchstone for all law, as any common law or legislation which is inconsistent with the constitution is unlawful. Finally, as a European Union member state, the Republic of Ireland must honour its obligations under the Treaty of Rome (1957) and subsequent treaties. The Irish constitution thus recognizes the applicability of European law over national legislation and its constitution.

solicitors and barristers

The legal profession is split into two distinct branches: solicitors and barristers. Solicitors are general legal advisers in a wide range of areas, typically property, probate, company law, and litigation. In court work solicitors usually instruct specialist advocates or barristers. A barrister's work is traditionally the drafting of court pleadings, presenting cases in court, and advising on more complex legal issues. This division may be distinguished from the US 'attorney' who occupies both roles, but loosely likened to the continental 'notaire' and 'avocat'. Other legal offices include the attorney general, who is the government's chief legal adviser, and the director of public prosecutions, who brings criminal proceedings on the state's behalf.

hierarchy of courts

Irish law operates within a court hierarchy. The local district courts handle minor criminal and civil matters. There are eight circuit court areas of higher jurisdiction. Civil matters of up to a monetary value of £30,000 are dealt with at this level. The Circuit Criminal Court enjoys authority in all matters, except treason, murder, and rape. The High Court has full original jurisdiction in all civil and criminal cases. It may also consider the constitutionality of legislation. In criminal matters it sits as the central criminal court in jury trials and the Special Criminal Court for more serious non-jury trials. The High Court has appellate jurisdiction from the circuit in civil law only.

The Court of Criminal Appeal hears appeals from the circuit, central criminal, and special criminal courts. Its decisions can be challenged to the Supreme Court on point of law only. The Supreme Court, headed by the Republic of Ireland's chief justice, is an appeal court only and represents the final court of appeal. It may consider referrals from the Irish president on the constitutionality of legislation. In limited circumstances, appeal may lie to the European Court of Human Rights or the European Court of Justice.

independence from government

The Irish legal system is strictly independent from its government. By the separation of powers, the judiciary has the power to regulate the authority of the legislature and executive. Both superior courts may declare legislation unconstitutional or award damages where individuals' rights have been breached by the state. While judicial appointments are political, the constitution protects the judiciary's independence. No legislation may fetter the jurisdiction of the superior courts. Similarly, superior court judges can only be removed by full resolution of the Oireachtas for 'stated misbehaviour' or 'incapacity'. Judges may not be legislature members and traditionally avoid political comment.

model of common law system

Distinguished by origin from its continental civil law neighbours, and in modern practice from the USA, the Irish system is a uniquely classical model of a common law system.

LEGENDS

See feature essay on ⇨folklore, page 148, for a discussion of the survival of legends.

LEINSTER

Southeastern historic province of the Republic of Ireland, comprising the counties of Carlow, Dublin, Kildare, Kilkenny, Laois, Longford, Louth, Meath, Offaly, Westmeath, Wexford, and Wicklow; area 19,630 sq km/7,577 sq mi; population (1996) 1,924,700.

The MacMurroughs were kings of Leinster until the mid-12th century. Their descendants ruled independently in Wexford and Carlow until the 16th century. Richard ⇨Strongbow accepted Leinster from Henry II, although it was still under the control of the crown.

LEITRIM

County of the Republic of Ireland, in the province of Connacht, bounded on the northwest by Donegal Bay; county town Carrick-on-Shannon; area 1,530 sq km/591 sq mi; population (1996) 25,100. Carrick-on-Shannon, Mohill, and Manorhamilton are the only important towns. The rivers Shannon, Bonet, Drowes, and Duff run through Leitrim. There is some coal, and iron and lead in the mountainous areas, but the county is generally not very productive – even the soil is heavy – and is the poorest county in the Republic of Ireland. Potatoes and oats are grown, and some cattle and sheep are reared. Industries include linen, woollens, and potteries. Parke's Castle is one of the most popular tourist attractions in the county.

physical

The surface of the county varies: the north and east is mountainous, with the Truskmore Mountains and Slieve Anierin range, and the south has low hills.

There are numerous loughs, of which Lough Allen (3,604 ha/1,459 acres) is the largest; east of Lough Allen, in the Iron Mountains, is Slieve Anierin (586 m/1,923 ft), the highest point of the county, noted for rocks containing important marine fossil evidence.

LEIX

Former spelling, used 1922–35, of County ⇨Laois.

LEIXLIP (Danish

Lax-Hlaup, 'salmon leap')

Town in County Kildare, at the confluence of the River Liffey and Rye Water, 18 km/ 11 mi west of Dublin; population (1996) 13,500. Situated on a turbulent stretch of the Liffey, its former waterfall and salmon leap have been replaced by a hydroelectric dam. Industries include packaging, electronic publishing and communication, and the production of computer components (Intel, Hewlett Packard). Leixlip was founded by the Danes in 915 AD, and its rivers once marked the historic boundary between the kingdoms of Leinster and Brega. Leixlip Castle, erected soon after 1172, is now owned by the Guinness family; the first pint of ⇨Guinness was brewed here by Arthur Guinness.

LEMASS, SEÁN FRANCIS (1899–1971)

Nationalist politician and Taoiseach (prime minister) 1959–66. Born in Ballybrack, County Dublin, Lemass joined the nationalist Irish Volunteers at the age of 15 and became a loyal follower of Éamon ⇨de Valera, who was the captain of his company. He was a founder member of the ⇨Fianna Fáil party in 1926, and minister for industry and commerce from 1932.

SEÁN LEMASS *Committed to goals of economic and industrial development throughout his long political life, Lemass believed that partition could eventually be ended peacefully through promoting and maintaining economic progress.*

During World War II he was minister of supplies. His greatest achievements were the modernization of the Republic's economy (through industrialization and free trade with Britain) and the improvement of relations with Northern Ireland. In 1965 he made a historic visit to Belfast to meet Northern Ireland's prime minister Terence ⇨O'Neill.

Lemass fought at the General Post Office in the ⇨Easter Rising of 1916 but escaped deportation. He joined the ⇨Irish Republican Army (IRA) as an officer and was interned 1920–21. Like de Valera, Lemass rejected the Anglo-Irish Treaty (1921) which established the Irish Free State within the British Empire, and he became a republican leader in the Irish Civil War (1922–23) until his capture and imprisonment.

Elected to the Dáil (parliament) in 1924 Lemass, like other republicans, refused to take his seat until 1927. As the chief architect of the Republic's economic expansion from 1932, he built up Irish industry behind a wall of high tariffs before adopting free-trade practices, promoted the foundation of a national shipping company and airline, and made Ireland's first attempt to join the European Economic Community (EEC) in 1961. He became de Valera's deputy in 1945, and succeeded him as prime minister and head of Fianna Fáil in 1959. Ill health prompted his resignation in 1966.

LEONARD, HUGH (pseudonym of JOHN KEYES BYRNE) (1926–)

Playwright, born in Dublin, and raised in Dalkey, County Dublin. He took the name of his protagonist in *The Italian Road* (1954), a play rejected by the Abbey Theatre, Dublin. Although Leonard later staged several works with the Abbey, he is chiefly associated with the Dublin Theatre Festival. While his dramatic style ranges from the satiric to the bittersweet, Leonard's best-known and most successful play was the autobiographical *Da* (1973). He has also written for television, including *Parnell and the English-woman* (1990) and the eight-part *Insurrection* (1966), commemorating the ⇨Easter Rising of 1916.

Before joining the theatre, Leonard worked in the civil service.

LEPRECHAUN (Irish *leipreachán*, 'small body')

In folklore, a ⇨fairy shoemaker with a hidden treasure or 'crock' of gold. If caught, the leprechaun must tell the location of the treasure, but he always tricks the captor into looking away for an instant, after which he has disappeared. The leprechaun's part in genuine Irish folkore is a minor one, but his importance has been greatly exaggerated in the literature of recent generations, and he has been promoted as a genial otherworld character in the tourist trade.

> Do you not catch the tiny clamour, /
> Busy click of an elfin hammer, / Voice of
> the Lepracaun singing shrill, / As he mer-
> rily plies his trade?
>
> W B YEATS *Irish Fairy and Folk Tales* (1893).

LETTERKENNY

County town of County ⇨Donegal, 24 km/15 mi northwest of Lifford; population (1996) 7,600. Its industries include clothing, health-care products, confectionery, telecommunications equipment, and a large synthetic-fibre plant. The Donegal Motor Rally takes place here each June and the Letterkenny International Folk Festival in August.

Letterkenny is joint county town with Lifford. It has a large 19th-century Gothic revival cathedral, St Eunan's. Conwal, 3 km/2 mi west of Letterkenny, is the site of an ancient monastery and the burial place of the O'Donnells. Conwal Dun stone fort is said to have been the stronghold of the O'Cannons, and there is a large standing stone.

LEVER, CHARLES JAMES (1806–1872)

Writer, born in Dublin and educated in medicine at Trinity College. Lever wrote novels of Irish social, political, and army life, such as *The Confessions of Harry Lorrequer* (1839), *Charles O'Malley: The Irish Dragoon* (1841), and *Tom Burke of Ours* (1844). His later novels, such as *Lord Kilgobbin* (1872), often have a gravity and seriousness of theme, an aspect of Lever's work that has tended to be neglected.

At the beginning of the 20th century Lever was regarded as a literary exploiter of Ireland, who poked fun at the Irish character to provoke comfortable English laughter, but in latter years his esteem has risen. In 1842 he gave up medicine to become editor of the *Dublin University Magazine*, gathering round him the Irish writers and wits of the time. He later moved to Europe, was appointed British consul in Spezia, and died in Trieste.

LEVIATHAN TELESCOPE

See William ⇨Parsons, 3rd Earl of Rosse, and Robert ⇨Ball.

LEWIS, C DAY

Poet; see Cecil ⇨Day-Lewis.

LIBERATOR, THE

Title given to the Irish politician Daniel ⇨O'Connell.

LIFFEY

River in the east of the Republic of Ireland; length 129 km/80 mi. The Liffey is formed by two streams that rise in the Wicklow Mountains near Enniskerry. It flows through County Kildare, past Kilcullen and Newbridge, and into Dublin Bay. The Liffey Plain is excellent land for pasture, and has the lowest rainfall in the Republic of Ireland.

The city of Dublin is divided into two by the Liffey, and here there are 14 bridges over the river, including a railway bridge and Ha'penny Bridge, a footbridge erected in 1816 for which tolls were levied until 1919. There is a hydro-electric power station at Golden Falls.

LIFFORD

County town of County ⇨Donegal; population (1996) 1,300. It is situated on the River Foyle, opposite Strabane in County Tyrone. There is salmon fishing in the Foyle, and greyhound racing in Lifford.

Lifford is joint county town with Letterkenny.

LIMAVADY

Town in County Derry, 26 km/16 mi east of the city of Londonderry; population (1991) 8,000. There is a large clothing manufacturer, and smaller light industries. The town was founded in the 17th century by Thomas Phillips during the plantation of Ulster by English settlers.

St Canice was born near Limavady at Drumramer in 526. Limavady was also the birthplace in 1856 of William Massey, prime minister of New Zealand 1912–25.

Roe Valley country park nearby includes an exhibition centre; in the park is the Mullagh, a small hill reputed to be the site of the Convention of Druim Ceatt in 575, attended by St Columba (St Colum Cille), at which various political matters were discussed, including the future of the kingdom of Scotland.

The Irish melody known as the *Londonderry Air*, better known as 'Danny Boy', was first written down in Limavady by Jane Ross in 1851 (although it originally derived from an itinerant fiddler called Mac-Cormick).

LIMERICK

County of the Republic of Ireland, in the province of Munster; county town ⇨Limerick; area 2,690 sq km/ 1,038 sq mi; population (1996) 165,000. The principal river is the ⇨Shannon, and towns include Abbeyfeale, Kilmallock, Newcastle West, and Rathkeale. Limerick is hilly in the southwest (Mullaghreirk Mountains) and in the northeast (Galtee Mountains). The low-lying region in the west is very fertile, and is known as the 'Golden Vale'. Dairy cattle, sheep, pigs, and poultry are reared extensively, and corn, sugar-beet, and potatoes are grown. Lace is also produced.

County Limerick is rich in archaeological remains, with evidence of human habitation dating back to Neolithic times; the most significant sites are on the shores of Lough ⇨Gur (Cush and Reevassta ringfort). There are also remains of a large number of strongholds and castles of the kings of Munster, and several significant 12th-century monastic ruins in the county.

LIMERICK

County town of County ⇨Limerick and fourth-largest city in the Republic of Ireland, on the Shannon estuary; population (1996) 52,000. The city is divided into three parts: English Town, which is the old city on King's Island (an island in the Shannon estuary); Irish Town; and Newtown Pery, which now forms the centre of the modern city. Industries include flour milling, tanning, meat products, and

brewing. The University of Limerick, 5 km/3 mi north of the city, is a modern campus.

The origins of settlement at Limerick have been traced back to a Danish stronghold in the 9th century. It was retaken by the Irish under Brian Bóruma and later, at the end of the 12th century, occupied by the Anglo-Normans. The city was subject to a number of sieges until the end of the 17th century and changed hands several times. Until the late 17th century Limerick was an important port with trading links with France and Spain.

features

⇨Limerick Castle, or King John's Castle, a fine Norman building, was constructed on King's Island and inaugurated by King John himself in 1210. The Church of Ireland Cathedral of St Mary on King's Island, dating from 1168, was founded by Donal Mór O'Brien, a member of the successful Gaelic ⇨O'Brien dynasty. One of the most interesting of Ireland's medieval cathedrals, its 15th-century choir stalls with grotesque carvings on the black oak misericords are unique in Ireland, and it also has a fine 12th-century Romanesque doorway. The cathedral has been much restored and remodelled, particularly by William Slater and others in the mid-19th century. The Catholic Cathedral of St John is in the Gothic revival style, and has a marble Madonna by the sculptor Benzoni. The Dominican, Redemptorist, Jesuit, Augus-

COUNTY LIMERICK *This circle of 13 standing stones, dating back to 4000 BC, can be found between Lough Gur and the road to Limerick. The discovery of vessels and axe heads suggest that a thriving Neolithic community must have once inhabited the site.*

tinian, and Franciscan churches are among many examples of contemporary church architecture. There are fine Georgian houses in John's Square.

history

Originally a Viking settlement, Limerick has had a stormy history. The Irish struggled to take it from the Vikings, eventually gaining control under the leadership of Brian Bóruma, King of Ireland at the end of the 11th century. Walls were built to secure the city, and under Henry II North Munster was split between the Normans and the Irish. Parliamentary legislation also resulted in the division of Limerick into English Town and Irish Town during the 13th and 14th centuries.

After the Battle of the ⇨Boyne, those Jacobite supporters who had not surrendered rallied in Limerick under Patrick Sarsfield, a Jacobean army commander, who defended the city against William III and Gen Ginkel for more than a year. Eventually the Jacobites agreed to the terms of the Treaty of ⇨Limerick (3 October 1691), although these were not subsequently ratified by the English parliament. On the Thormond Bridge is a large limestone slab, known as the Treaty Stone, on which the 1691 treaty was reputedly signed.

LIMERICK CASTLE (commonly called King John's Castle)

Late 12th-century castle forming part of the city walls of Limerick, County Limerick. Only the north and south walls, and three of the four very large corner drum towers survive. The gateway is in the north wall, flanked by two rounded gate turrets. A new tower was added about 1608 in the southeast corner by Josias Bodley. Barracks were built inside the castle in the 18th century. It was restored in 1990 and now houses a museum.

LIMERICK, TREATY OF

Treaty signed on 3 October 1691 in Limerick, dictating the terms of surrender of the Jacobite forces of James II who had resisted the invading armies of William (III) of Orange. The Jacobites were promised retention of their property, limited freedom of religious practice, freedom from suit for damage caused in the war, and the right to carry arms, while those who wished were given safe passage to France.

These concessions infuriated Irish Protestants who worked to undermine the terms of the treaty in prac-

tice. In 1697 the act ratifying the treaty deliberately excluded the greatest concessions, such as the guarantee of religious freedom, while drafting errors in the treaty itself allowed for the evasions of concessions protecting pro-Jacobite civilians. Successive enactments of legislation in the Protestant Irish parliament gradually repealed the remaining concessions.

LISBURN

Town in County Antrim, on the River Lagan, 14 km/ 9 mi from Belfast; population (1991) 27,400. The main industries are engineering and the production of soft drinks, yarn and thread, and packaging; it is a busy shopping centre. Many inhabitants commute to Belfast. Lisburn was founded in the 17th century and planted with English settlers and French Huguenot refugees.

The development of the linen industry, which came to be important in the town, owed much to the Huguenot settlers. The Church of Ireland cathedral was built in 1623.

There is a monument to Bishop Jeremy Taylor (died 1667) in the cathedral; Lisburn is the seat of the bishop of Connor. Lisburn Museum, in the Assembly Rooms, has exhibitions on the linen industry; and 2 km/1 mi from Lisburn, in Lambeg village, is a linen research institute.

LISMORE CASTLE

Castle at Lismore, County Waterford. On the site of a medieval monastery and a former castle built by King John, the present building is mostly of early 17th- and 19th-century construction. It was granted in 1589 to the adventurer Walter Raleigh, and in 1602 passed to the Boyle family. In ruins by that time, it was rebuilt by Richard Boyle, 1st Earl of Cork. It fell into disrepair again and was rebuilt between 1812 and 1858 by the 6th Duke of Devonshire, having passed to the Devonshires in 1753; several architects were employed, including William Atkinson from 1812 to 1822. The Banqueting Hall was designed by Crace and A W N Pugin (1812–1852) from 1850. The English architect Joseph Paxton made further alterations and additions between 1853 and 1858.

LISTOWEL

Town in County Kerry, on the River Feale, 26 km/ 16 mi northeast of Tralee; population (1996) 3,400. There is a ruined castle built here by the Fitzmaurices, lords of Kerry.

A week-long writers' festival is held here each June. The Listowel Races are held in the third week of September. The town has a heritage centre with a theatre for traditional Irish music.

LLOYD GEORGE, DAVID (1st Earl Lloyd-George of Dwyfor)

British prime minister; see ⇨Anglo-Irish Treaty.

LOFTUS, ADAM (c.1533–1606)

English-born Protestant archbishop of Dublin 1567–1606 and founder of Ireland's first university, ⇨Trinity College, Dublin, in 1592. Though often portrayed as an insensitive enforcer of the Elizabethan Reformation and as a devious self-promoter and nepotist, Loftus is now regarded as a shrewd and able administrator whose attempts to persuade his clergy to accept doctrinal change were hampered both by the entrenched conservative resistance and by the indifference and occasional opposition of several secular governors.

Loftus came to acknowledge the defeat of his efforts among the Dublin clergy and laity in the 1580s, but his greatest achievement came with the establishment of Trinity College, which was intended to serve as a seminary for an indigenous Protestant clergy. By the time of his death, however, the college had abandoned its missionary ambitions and had become a centre of Puritan exclusiveness.

LOMBARD, PETER (1554–1625)

Archbishop of Armagh and active promoter of the Irish ⇨Counter-Reformation. Lombard was born into an Old English family in Waterford, and studied at Louvain in 1575, later becoming professor of philosophy and theology there. While in Rome in 1598, he wrote *De regno Hiberniae sanctorum insula commentarius* to secure papal support for the rebellion of Hugh ⇨O'Neill, 2nd Earl of Tyrone, against English government forces which had begun in 1593. In the aftermath of O'Neill's defeat in 1603 and the subsequent ⇨Flight of the Earls from Ireland in 1607, Lombard advocated a conciliatory policy toward James I to reduce anti-Catholic feeling, arguing for his recognition as king by the Irish, criticizing confrontation with the English government in Ireland, and discouraging plans for renewed rebellion.

Estranged from the exiled O'Neill, Lombard pursued a successful career in the Vatican and was actively involved in several doctrinal decisions, including the condemnation of Copernicus in 1616, who had defied church doctrine with his hypothesis that the Sun was the centre of the Solar System. Despite plans to assume an Irish see, he never returned to Ireland.

LONDONDERRY

See ⇨Derry.

LONDONDERRY, MARQUESS OF

Title of an influential political family from County Down. In the 18th century the family came to prominence when Robert Stewart (1739–1821) purchased an estate at Newtownards, County Derry, later renamed Mount Stewart. He was member of parliament for County Down 1771–83 and encouraged his son, Robert Stewart (1769–1822), to follow him into politics; the latter was MP for the constituency 1790–1801. Best remembered for his title of Viscount Castlereagh, the younger Stewart built a formidable political career and was Irish chief secretary during the ⇨Rebellion of 1798 and the passage of the Act of ⇨Union through the Irish and British parliaments in 1800, enacted 1801. He was later British foreign secretary in the 1810s. His father benefitted from these successes, becoming Marquess of Londonderry in 1816.

Continuing the dynasty, the 6th Marquess of Londonderry, Charles Vane-Tempest-Stewart (1852–1915), was Irish lord lieutenant 1886–89. The 7th Marquess, Charles Stewart (1878–1949), was minister for education in the first Northern Ireland government, and was British secretary of state for air in the 1930s.

LONGFORD, EDWARD ARTHUR HENRY PAKENHAM (6th Earl Longford) (1902–1961)

Playwright and theatre director, affectionately known as 'the Lord'. Longford inherited the family seat of Pakenham Hall (now called Tullynally) at Castlepollard, County Longford. He was director of the ⇨Gate Theatre, Dublin, from 1931, and founded Longford Productions with his wife, Christine Longford, in 1936. His first play *The Melians* (1931) exhibited his interest in Greek history and culture, and his later productions included translations and adaptations of Aeschylus and Moliére. Together, the Longfords were a major force in bringing world literature to the Irish stage.

LONGFORD

County of the Republic of Ireland, in the province of Leinster; county town ⇨Longford; area 1,040 sq km/ 401 sq mi; population (1996) 30,200. The county is low-lying (the highest point is Carn Clonhugh 279 m/916 ft), and the western border is formed of the River Shannon and part of Lough Ree, one of several lakes. Other rivers are the Camlin, a tributary of the Shannon, and the Inny, which flows into Lough Ree. Agricultural activities include cattle and sheep rearing, and the production of oats and potatoes.

In the ⇨Rebellion of 1798, one of the decisive battles to crush the rising took place at Ballinamuck, County Longford. The novelist Maria ⇨Edgeworth spent most of her life in Edgeworthstown in the county.

LONGFORD

County town of County ⇨Longford, on the River Camlin; population (1996) 6,400. The principal industries are textiles, component manufacture, pet-food production, engineering, and timber processing.

Longford was the seat of the O'Farrells, who had a fort here and founded a Dominican friary in 1400. Nothing remains of these structures but there are some remains of a castle erected by the Earl of Longford in 1627. St Mel's Cathedral, built in 1840 in the Italian Renaissance style, is regarded as one of the finest of its kind in Ireland. The crosier is held in the county museum.

LONSDALE, KATHLEEN (born Yardley)
(1903–1971)

X-ray crystallographer who developed several technologies for the study of crystal structures. She was among the earliest to determine the structures of organic molecules and was the first to confirm the hexagonal arrangement of carbon in benzene compounds.

Born in Newbridge, County Kildare, Lonsdale moved with her family to England at the age of five. After graduating from Bedford College for Women in London, she joined the research team of the physicist William Bragg at University College, London, and later the Royal Institution. Her collaboration with Bragg extended over the periods 1922–27 and 1937–42. She was interested in X-ray work at various temperatures and in thermal motion in crystals. She used beam X-ray photography to investigate the textures of crystals, the pharmacological properties of crystal structures, and the composition of bladder and kidney stones. In 1968 Lonsdale became the first woman president of the British Association for the Advancement of Science.

LOUGHREA

Market town in County Galway, on Lough Rea, 30 km/19 mi southwest of Ballinasloe; population (1996) 3,400. Loughrea was a Norman stronghold built in the 14th century by Richard de Burgo, and the ruins of a Carmelite priory he founded can be seen in the town centre.

Loughrea is the seat of the Roman Catholic bishop of Clonfert, and has a cathedral, St Brendan's, built in 1897, with stained-glass windows by Irish artists.

The area round Loughrea has a number of prehistoric crannogs (Celtic lake dwellings) and souterrains (underground dwellings). On Monument Hill is a stone circle, and 6 km/3.5 mi from Loughrea at Bullaun is the Turoe Stone, dating from the 1st century, with abstract designs, a fine example of La Tène art (see ⇨Celt. Nearby is the ring fort of Feerwone.

LOUTH

Smallest county of the Republic of Ireland, in the province of Leinster; county town ⇨Dundalk; area 820 sq km/317 sq mi; population (1996) 92,200. It is mainly fertile and low-lying. The chief towns are

COUNTY LOUTH *King John's Castle, on the south side of Carlingford Lough, was built on the king's orders to defend the town against invaders from the other side of the water. The boundary between the Republic and Northern Ireland still runs down the middle of the Lough.*

Dundalk at the north end of Dundalk bay, Drogheda, and Ardee, and the chief rivers are the Fane, Lagan, Glyde, and Dee. There is cattle rearing and fishing; oats and potatoes are grown. Greenore on Carlingford Lough is a container shipping port. Louth is rich in ancient buildings and remains, and was of strategic importance during the 12th–18th centuries. Important monastic sites with extensive remains include Monasterboice (founded in the 5th century), and Mellifont Abbey (founded in the 12th century).

topography

Louth is bounded on the east by the Irish Sea, and the River Boyne constitutes part of the southern border. The Cooley Mountains are in the northeast (highest point Slieve Foye, 590 m/1,935 ft), bordering Carlingford Lough, on the coast of which are the resorts of Carlingford and Greenore.

LOVER, SAMUEL (1797–1868)

Novelist and songwriter, born in Dublin. Lover wrote a number of songs, 'Molly Bawn' and 'The Low-Backed Car' being particularly popular. One of the founders of the *Dublin University Magazine* in 1833, he also wrote several novels, the best known of which are *Rory O'More* (1837), originally a ballad, and *Handy Andy* (1842). His short Irish sketches were combined with his songs into one-man shows called 'Irish Evenings' and 'Paddy's Portfolio'.

LUGH (or LUG) ('the shining one')

In mythology, god of light, sorcery, and the crafts, and a leading champion in ⇨hero-tales, described as possessor of all arts and skills. A prophesied child, Lugh succeeded Nuadha of the Silver Hand as king of the ⇨Tuatha Dé Danann, and led them at the second second Battle of Muighe Tuireadh (Moytirra) against the ⇨Fomorians, killing the tyrant Balar, whose blazing eye destroyed all on which it looked. He is the divine father of the hero ⇨Cuchulain. His feast, Lughnasadh, a harvest festival, was celebrated on 1 August.

Lugh is the Irish version of the Celtic deity Lugus, worshipped widely across the Celtic world from Ireland to central Europe, who left his name on several places anciently called Lugudunum, such as modern Lyon, Leiden, and Laon.

Brian Friel's play *Dancing at Lughnasa*, later filmed (1998), was based on a 1930's celebration of Lugh's festival in a small Irish village.

LUNNY, DONAL (1945–)

Folk musician, composer, and record producer. He first began playing folk music with the 1960s ballad band Emmett Spiceland. Lunny was a founder member of Planxty and helped create the Bothy Band in 1975 and Moving Hearts in 1981, three of the most influential groups in modern Irish folk music. Since being involved in Moving Hearts, he has devoted more of his time to production, and has been a leading figure in the successful blending of Irish traditional music with rock.

Lunny was born in Newbridge, County Kildare. He first learned to play the drums, but later switched to the guitar and then to the bouzouki, as well as playing keyboards. While pursuing his performing career, he also ran a record company, Mulligan, in Dublin. He was involved in the eclectic 'Common Ground' project in 1996, fusing folk and rock. From this he developed his present band, Coolfin (1998).

His brother, Manus Lunny, is a member of the Scottish folk-rock group Capercaillie.

LURGAN

Town in County Armagh; population (1991) 21,000; in 1965 it was joined with Portadown to form ⇨Craigavon, though the two towns still retain a measure of individual identity. Lurgan was a major centre for the linen industry and textile production is still important.

In the early 17th century the lands around Lurgan were planted with English settlers. The settlement was destroyed by Irish forces under the leadership of Phelum O'Neill in 1641, and again in the mid-17th century by troops of James II. The linen industry was established at the end of the 17th century, and during the 18th century the area was colonized by Huguenot and Flemish weavers.

LYNCH, JACK (JOHN MARY) (1917–1999)

Politician, leader of ⇨Fianna Fáil 1966–79, and Taoiseach (prime minister) 1966–73 and 1977–79. Born in Cork city, he trained as a barrister in Dublin, and entered the Dáil (parliament) in 1948. He was Ireland's most successful Taoiseach electorally, achieving a 20-seat majority in the Dáil in 1977, and has been described as its most popular politician since the 19th-century reformist Daniel ⇨O'Connell. Lynch steered the country through a turbulent time at the beginning of 'the Troubles' in Northern Ireland and

Í have never and never will accept the right of a minority who happen to be a majority in a small part of the country to opt out of a nation.

JACK LYNCH *The Irish Times*, 14 November 1970.

~

through the ⇨arms crisis (see Charles ⇨Haughey).

Lynch was appointed minister for education in 1957, succeeded Seán ⇨Lemass in industry and commerce when Lemass became Taoiseach in 1959, and then became minister for finance. He was a compromise candidate for leader in 1966 when Lemass retired, at the time being widely regarded as weak, but Lynch showed determination when allegations of ministerial involvement in arms imports surfaced 1969–70, and he fired a number of his cabinet colleagues, including Charles Haughey. Fianna Fáil lost power in 1973 but regained it in 1977 with a large majority, assisted by Lynch's personal popularity and some generous campaign promises such as the abolition of domestic rates. However, some by-election defeats and calls for his removal by rivals prompted his retirement in 1979.

Lynch was educated at North Monastery, Cork, and worked as a civil servant in Dublin while studying to be a barrister, being called to the Bar in 1945. Before his election to the Dáil in 1948, he was already well known as a hurler and footballer from Cork, having obtained a record six All-Irelands in a row.

LYNCH, LIAM
Activist, see ⇨Anglo-Irish Treaty.

MCALEESE, MARY PATRICIA (1951–)

Irish lawyer and academic, president of the Republic of Ireland from 1997. When President Mary Robinson announced her resignation, McAleese was nominated by the ruling Fianna Fáil and Progressive Democrats as their candidate in preference to former prime minister Albert Reynolds. She went on to secure a clear victory over all other candidates.

After completing her legal studies at Queen's University, Belfast, and the Inn of Court of Northern Ireland, McAleese held academic posts at Trinity College, Dublin 1975–87 and was pro-vice-chancellor 1994–97 at Queen's University, Belfast.

MCALISKEY, BERNADETTE JOSEPHINE

(born Devlin) (1947–)

Northern Irish political activist, prominent in the civil rights movement in Northern Ireland in the late 1960s. In 1969, at the age of 21, she was elected a member of the Westminster parliament. In the same year she was arrested while leading Catholic rioters in the Bogside, Londonderry, and was sentenced to six months' imprisonment. She stood down as an MP at the 1974 general election. In 1981, along with her husband, Michael McAliskey, whom she married in 1973, she survived an assassination attempt after actively supporting IRA hunger strikers. She is chair of the Independent Socialist Party of Ireland.

McAliskey was born into a poor Catholic family in County Tyrone. While studying at Queen's University, Belfast, she won the Mid-Ulster by-election as an Independent Unity candidate, becoming the youngest MP at Westminster since William Pitt.

BERNADETTE MCALISKEY *Once an extremely familiar figure, and known in the 1970s as the 'five-foot firebrand', during her involvement in the Battle of the Bogside, civil rights activist McAliskey has now largely disappeared from the public eye.*

MCANALLY, RAY(MOND) (1926–1989)

Stage and screen actor. McAnally first appeared on stage aged 16, and joined the company at Dublin's prestigious ⇨Abbey Theatre in 1947, where he often returned to direct and teach later in his career. From the late 1950s, he was active in cinema and television. His numerous screen credits included the films *Cal* (1984), *The Mission* (1986), and *My Left Foot* (1989), and the television dramas *A Perfect Spy* (1988), and *A Very British Coup* (1989).

McAnally, who was born in Buncrana, Donegal,

made his professional debut in *A Strange House* in 1942. Among his many celebrated performances at the Abbey Theatre were *The Shadow of a Gunman* (1951), and *The Country Boy* (1959), while London appearances included *A Cheap Bunch of Nice Flowers* (1962), *Who's Afraid of Virginia Woolf?* (1964), and *The Best of Friends* (1988).

His long film career included roles in *Shake Hands With the Devil* (1959), *Billy Budd* (1962), *The Looking Glass War* (1970), *Fear is the Key* (1972), *Angel* (1982), *Empire State* (1987), *The Fourth Protocol* (1987), *The Sicilian* (1987), *White Mischief* (1987), *High Spirits* (1988), *Taffin* (1988), *Jack the Ripper* (1988), and *We're No Angels* (1989), his last film. He won a number of British Academy of Film and Television (BAFTA) awards for his later TV and film work.

At the Abbey Theatre, between 1947 and 1963, McAnally appeared in some 150 productions, attributing his phenomenal versatility to the experience of delivering 'five lines one week, King Lear the next'.

McAuley, Catherine Elizabeth
(1787–1841)

Religious founder, educator, and social reformer, depicted on the Irish five punt note. In 1831 she founded the Sisters of Mercy, which grew into one of the largest Irish religious orders for women, dedicated to educating orphans and the poor with convents and orphanages throughout the USA, Canada, Australia, and the UK.

McAuley was born in Dublin and brought up by Protestant foster parents. With their legacy, she bought a site for a school for poor children and a residence for working women, which was named the House of Our Blessed Lady of Mercy.

MacBride, Seán (1904–1988)

Revolutionary, politician, lawyer, and peace campaigner. He became chief of staff of the IRA in 1936 but left the movement after the 1937 constitution, and broke with it completely over its 1939 bombing campaign. He won a reputation as a great barrister for his defence of IRA suspects during the war years and founded ⇨Clann na Poblachta (Children of the Republic) in 1946. He took his party into coalition as part of the interparty government, 1948–51, in which he was minister for external affairs, and split the second interparty government in 1957 over its handling of the IRA's border campaign.

After leaving politics in 1961 MacBride began a new career in human rights. He was secretary general of the International Commission of Jurists 1963–70, and chair of Amnesty International 1961–74. He was co-author of the United Nations Declaration of Human Rights, and was awarded the Nobel Peace Prize in 1974 (jointly with the Japanese politician Eisaku Satō) and the Lenin peace prize in 1977.

MacBride was the son of Maj John MacBride, who was executed as a rebel in the Easter Rising of 1916, and Maud ⇨Gonne, the radical nationalist and muse of W B Yeats. Born in Paris, he was educated there and at University College, Dublin. He joined the IRA during the Anglo–Irish War (1919–21) and supported the republicans who opposed the Anglo-Irish Treaty (1921).

In 1937 he was called to the Irish Bar, and he was admitted to the Inner Bar in 1943. He was vice-president of the Organization for European Economic Cooperation 1948–51, and was delegate for Ireland to the Council of Europe in 1954. He was also chairman of the Irish Association of Jurists, and of the International Peace Bureau.

His publications include *Civil Liberty* (1948) and *Our People Our Money* (1951).

McBride, Willie John (William James) (1940–)

Rugby Union player, born in Toomebridge, County Antrim. A formidable second-row forward and inspirational leader, McBride won 63 caps for Ireland between 1962 and 1975, including 12 as captain. He played on five Lions tours, in 1962, 1966, 1968, 1971, and 1974, winning a record 17 caps. As captain in 1974, he famously led the Lions to a 3–0 Test series victory over South Africa. In retirement he coached Ireland and was the manager of the 1983 British Lions tour of New Zealand.

McCabe, Patrick (1955–)

Novelist, born in Clones, County Monaghan. His best-selling *Butcher Boy* (1992) was shortlisted for the Booker Prize, won the *Irish Times*/Aer Lingus Award for Literature (Fiction), and was made into a successful film by Neil Jordan. McCabe has an arresting style that offers vivid characters. When he writes using first-person narration, as in *Butcher Boy*, his uncanny ability to create unique voices is startlingly original. Other works include *Carn* (1989) and *The Dead School* (1995).

McCANN, DONAL (1943–1999)

Actor, born in Dublin. Noticed early for the rich quality of his voice and deft mimicking skills, his ability to capture a character made him an exceptional actor. He joined the ⇨Abbey Theatre Company at the Queen's Theatre in 1962. Major credits include *On Baile's Strand*, *Tarry Flynn*, *Waiting for Godot*, *The Shadow of a Gunman*, and *Faith Healer*, for which he was awarded the Harvard Award for Best Actor in 1980. He won the Critic's Circle Award for Best Actor in 1995 with his performance in *The Steward of Christendom*.

McCann also played numerous roles in television drama and appeared in films such as *Cal* (1984), *Out of Africa* (1985), John Huston's *The Dead* (1986), and *Stealing Beauty* (1995).

MacCARTHY, DENIS FLORENCE
(1817–1882)

Poet and academic, born in Dublin and educated at Maynooth and King's Inns. MacCarthy was the first professor of English at the Catholic University, Dublin. Among his works were *Ballads, Poems and Lyrics* (1850), *The Bellfounder* (1857), *Under-Glimpses* (1857), and *Poems* (1882). His *Shelley's Early Life* (1872) chronicled an Irish visit in 1812. He also translated the plays of the Spanish dramatist Calderón de la Barca, for which he received a medal from the Royal Spanish Academy.

MacCarthy's early verse appeared in the *Dublin Satirist*, and by 1843 he was a regular contributor to the cultural and political journal *The Nation*.

McCORMACK, JOHN (1884–1945)

Irish-born US tenor. With no formal training, he won a gold medal at the 1902 National Irish Festival. Following studies and recitals, he made his operatic debut in London, England, in 1907, with instant success. His US debut followed two years later in New York City. He became a favourite throughout the USA, primarily, after 1914, as a concert singer specializing in sentimental Irish songs. He initiated a tradition of Irish tenors that is still popular in Ireland and abroad, with artists such as Wright and the recordings and performances of the Three Irish Tenors.

McCormack was born in Athlone, County West-

meath. He became a US citizen in 1919 and a papal count in 1928 as a reward for his charitable work; by this time he had returned to live in Ireland. He is regarded as an iconic figure to whom all Irish tenors will be compared.

McCOURT, FRANK (FRANCIS) (1933–)

Irish-American writer, born in Brooklyn, New York, and raised in Limerick. McCourt's memoir *Angela's Ashes* (1996) became the literary sensation of the 1990s, winning the National Book Critics Circle Award (US), the *Los Angeles Times* Book Award, and the 1997 Pulitzer Prize for autobiography. The poignancy, humour, and honesty with which he wrote of his impoverished youth in Ireland before emigrating to the USA captivated readers around the world. British director Alan Parker made a film of *Angela's Ashes* in 1999. McCourt has also published a second memoir, *'Tis* (1999), chronicling his life in the USA.

McCOY, TONY (1975–)

National Hunt jockey, born in Toombridge, County Antrim. He joined Jim Bolger's flat yard at the age of 14, but after an accident turned his attention to the National Hunt discipline. He made his debut at Leopardstown. After moving to Britain in 1994, he made an almost immediate impact on the sport and by the end of the century he had won the Jockey's championship four times. A year later he became only the fourth rider to win both the Champion Hurdle, on Make A Stand, and the Gold Cup, on Mr Mulligan, at the same Cheltenham Festival. On 12 November 1999, he became the fifth jump jockey in history to ride 1,000 winners, when he steered Majadou to victory at Cheltenham.

McCRACKEN, HENRY JOY

Radical, see ⇨Rebellion of 1798.

McCRACKEN, MARY ANN (1770–1866)

Radical and philanthropist. She was born into a prominent Belfast Presbyterian business family, and ran her own textile firm for many years. Outward looking and progressive, she supported the revolutionary politics of her brother Henry Joy McCracken (1767–1798) and his friend Thomas ⇨Russell, both founder members of the Belfast Society of ⇨United Irishmen in 1795. After the failure of the United Irish cause in the Rebellion of 1798, she channelled her formidable energies into charitable and educational work with the poor of the rapidly industrializing town of Belfast.

McCracken's brother was hanged in 1798 for leading the United Irishmen at the Battle of Antrim; Russell, whom she secretly adored, was executed in 1803 for trying to organize another rebellion.

MacCurtain, Thomas (1884–1920)

Republican and revolutionary, born in Ballyknockane, County Cork. MacCurtain was commander of the ⇨Irish Volunteers in Cork city during the ⇨Easter Rising of 1916. Although he obeyed the last-minute order of John (Eoin) MacNeill, leader of the Volunteers, not to fight, his refusal to disarm held British government forces at bay for a week and he was imprisoned. While commandant of the Cork No 1 Brigade of the ⇨Irish Republican Army (IRA), MacCurtain was elected ⇨Sinn Féin's lord mayor of Cork in January 1920 and was murdered by the Royal Irish Constabulary (RIC) in March 1920.

MacCurtain joined the Gaelic League in 1901 and Sinn Féin in 1907. He became a member of the secret revolutionary organization the Irish Republican Brotherhood, and joined the Volunteers in 1914. After his death a coroner's jury found the RIC guilty of his murder.

MacDiarmada, Seán (or John MacDermott)

Republican; see ⇨Easter Rising.

MacDonagh, Donagh (1912–1968)

Dramatist, lawyer, and broadcaster, born in Dublin. After studying and practising law, MacDonagh became known as a playwright for his exuberant *Happy as Larry* (1946). His other dramas include *God's Gentry* (1951, a study of tinker life) and *Step-in-the-Hollow* (1957).

MacDonagh's father, Thomas, was executed for his part in the 1916 Easter Rising, and the following year, his mother drowned while swimming. After being educated at Belvedere College and University College, Dublin, he became a barrister in 1935 and was made a district justice in 1941. He co-edited *The Oxford Book of Irish Verse* (1958), which was criticized for its loose interpretation of Irishness. He also published a number of poetry collections, including *The Hungry Grass* (1947) and *A Warning to Conquerors* (1968), as well as a perceptive essay on his father.

McDonagh, Martin (1971–)

English-born writer and playwright, raised in London of Irish parentage. McDonagh's treatment of Irish life in the rural west has brought him critical acclaim. His trilogies *The Leenane Trilogy* (1995–97) and *The Aran Trilogy* (1997–98) revise stereotypes of rural Ireland. Often characterized as dramatic fairy tales, McDonagh's portrayals of Irish life are at once familiar and coyly ironic. *The Beauty Queen of Leenane* (1995), for example, begins with an entirely recognizable Irish kitchen with turf fire and rocking chair, but also presents contemporary criticisms of religion and generational conflict.

He has also written a history of Irish theatre, based on the works of Seán O'Casey and J M Synge.

MacDonagh, Thomas (1878–1916)

Writer, teacher, and republican revolutionary, born in Cloughjordan, County Tipperary. A founder member of the ⇨Irish Volunteers in 1913, he was one of the signatories of the Proclamation of the Irish Republic in the ⇨Easter Rising of 1916, and was executed by firing squad for his part in the rebellion.

MacDonagh was assistant professor of English at the National University, Dublin, but had a passion for the Irish language. He joined the ⇨Gaelic League in 1901 and assisted Patrick ⇨Pearse at his bilingual secondary school, St Enda's, from 1908.

Volumes of MacDonagh's verse, which has been compared to that of English religious poet Richard Crashaw, are *Through the Ivory Gate* (1902), *Songs of Myself* (1910), *Lyrical Poems* (1913), and *Poetical Works* (1916). He also wrote a book on English poet and musician Thomas Campion as a stylist of verse. His most significant literary contribution, *Literature in Ireland*, published posthumously in 1916, attempted to define an 'Irish mode', a distinctively Irish note, in English.

McEntee, Seán (1889–1984)

Nationalist politician, born in Belfast. McEntee moved to Dublin and took part in the ⇨Easter Rising of 1916, for which he was sentenced to death but reprieved. Opposed to the Anglo-Irish Treaty (1921) which endorsed the partition of Ireland, he became a firm supporter and close ally of Éamon ⇨de Valera, and was a founder member of ⇨Fianna Fáil in 1926. As a minister in de Valera's government after 1932, he proved one of the more socially conservative figures in the Fianna Fáil cabinet and clashed with his more progressive cabinet rival, Seán ⇨Lemass, throughout their careers.

His ministerial posts included finance 1932–39 and 1951–54, industry and commerce 1939–47, and health and social welfare 1957–65.

MacEOIN, SEÁN (known as the 'Blacksmith of Ballinalee') (1893–1973)

Soldier and nationalist politician. Born in Bunlahy, Granard, County Longford, MacEoin was leader of the North Longford flying column (mobile guerilla unit of the ⇨Irish Republican Army) in the ⇨Anglo–Irish War (1919–21). Celebrated for his defence of Ballinalee against British forces in 1921, he was captured, sentenced to death, but reprieved. Elected to the Dáil (parliament) in 1921, he became a strong supporter of the 1921 Anglo-Irish Treaty, which established the Irish Free State, and served in the National Army during the Irish Civil War (1922–23). He resigned as chief of staff in 1929 to reenter the Dáil where he served until 1965, being Fine Gael's minister for justice 1948–51 and defence 1954–57.

McGAHERN, JOHN (1934–   )

Novelist, born in Dublin. McGahern grew up in Cootehill, County Cavan, and later returned to Dublin to attend University College. He won early acclaim for *The Barracks* (1963), a study of the mind of a dying woman. His books explore Irish settings and issues as in *Amongst Women* (1991), about an ageing member of the IRA. His other works include *The Dark* (1965), *Nightlines* (1970), *The Leavetaking*, and *The High Ground* (1985).

Originally a primary school teacher, McGahern travelled widely to London, Spain, and the USA, eventually settling in County Leitrim. He lectured frequently in the USA, becoming professor of literature at Colegate University, New York, where he taught in 1969, 1972, 1978, and 1980.

MacGILL, PATRICK (1890–1963)

Writer, born into a poor farming family in the Glenties, County Donegal. MacGill was hired out to an employer by his parents, but escaped to Scotland, where he found work as a farm labourer. His first novels were uncompromising depictions of the brutal existence of Irish migrant workers. He served in

World War I, and wrote powerful accounts of trench warfare such as *The Amateur Army* (1915) and *The Red Horizon* (1916).

MacGill's brilliantly naturalistic novel of migrant worker life, *Children of the Dead End*, was published in 1914; it was followed a year later by *The Rat-Pit*, which showed how Irish labouring women were driven to prostitution by poverty. He emigrated to the USA in 1930, but his later years were blighted by poverty and the onset of multiple sclerosis.

MACGILLYCUDDY'S REEKS

Range of mountains in southwestern Ireland, west of Killarney, in County Kerry. It has several high peaks, including Carantuohill, the highest mountain in Ireland (1,041 m/3,415 ft). The Gap of Dunloe is a narrow rocky gorge 457 m/1,500 ft deep, running for 6 km/4 mi between Magillycuddy's Reeks and the Purple Mountains. The area is a centre for tourism because of its dramatic glacial scenery.

McGRATH, PAUL (1953–   )

Footballer, born in London and raised in Dublin. McGrath signed for Manchester United from the League of Ireland side St Patrick's Athletic in 1985. He went on to win over 200 appearances for the club before being released by Alex Ferguson to Aston Villa. Generally acknowledged as a world-class player, he received the highest accolade in 1993 when collecting the Players' Player of the Year award.

McGrath is the second most capped Irish player of all time behind Tony Cascarino.

MacGREEVY, THOMAS (1893–1967)

Poet and art critic. His works include *Poems* (1934) and numerous articles and studies of influential writers and artists such as T S Eliot and Jack Butler Yeats. Born in Tarbert, County Kerry, MacGreevy studied at Trinity College, Dublin, following service in World War I. He was a friend of the writers James Joyce and Samuel Beckett, whom he met while lecturing at the École Normale in Paris 1927–29. After working as a critic in London, he returned to Dublin in 1941, and was appointed director of the National Gallery in 1950.

McGUIGAN, BARRY (FINBAR PATRICK) (1961–   )

Boxer who was World Boxing Association (WBA)

world featherweight champion between 1985 and 1986. Born in Clones, County Monaghan, McGuigan first came to the fore in 1978 when he won the Irish and Commonwealth bantamweight titles. He turned professional in 1980 after competing at the Moscow Olympic Games, and steadily established himself as one of Irish boxing's brightest ever talents. He won the British featherweight title in 1983 and two years later, after a string of victories over world-class opponents, he unanimously outpointed Eusebio Pedroza of Panama for the WBA crown. He lost the title in 1986 and retired briefly. When he finally bowed out of the ring he had a career record of 30 victories from 32 fights.

McGUINNESS, FRANK

(1953–)

Dramatist, born in Buncrana, County Donegal, and educated at Carndonagh College and University College, Dublin. A versatile and sometimes controversial artist, he does not hesitate to engage difficult political questions in his theatre. He addressed Londonderry's ⇨Bloody Sunday (1972) in *Carthaginians* (1988), which includes a moving litany of victims' names, while his play *Observe the Sons of Ulster Marching Toward the Somme* (1985) was a powerful portrait of the bravery and vulnerability of young Ulster Volunteers during World War I.

McGuinness's original drama has also tackled issues such as Alzheimer's disease and hostage-taking in the Middle East. Other works include translations of Henrik Ibsen's *Peer Gynt* (1988), Bertolt Brecht's *The Threepenny Opera* (1991), and Anton Chekhov's *Three Sisters* (1990).

McGuinness began his career teaching drama, linguistics, and Old and Middle English at University College, Dublin, and the National University of Ireland; he has also directed plays.

BARRY MCGUIGAN *In 1986, after a gruelling bout in the extreme heat of Las Vegas, McGuigan lost his World Boxing Association Featherweight Champion title to Steve Cruz, after which he retired. He returned to the ring in April 1988 for four last fights.*

MACHALE, JOHN (1791–1881)

Roman Catholic archbishop of Tuam, County Galway (1834), who supported non-separatist Irish nationalism and opposed coeducation of Catholics and Protestants. MacHale also translated religious works into Connaught Irish. He was the first Irish Catholic bishop since the 16th century to be educated entirely in Ireland.

MacHale was born in Tobbernavine, County Mayo, and studied at St Patrick's College, Maynooth. At a meeting led by Daniel O'Connell in 1845 he supported Irish legislative independence. Later, he enlisted O'Connell's support in successfully opposing non-denominational Queen's Colleges (1849), which strengthened the link between nationalism and Catholicism. He spoke against papal infallibility at the First Vatican Council in 1870.

MACINTYRE, TOM

(1931–)

Playwright whose drama is best known for its experimentation with dance, mime, and surrealistic imagery. Born in County Cavan, MacIntyre was educated at University College, Dublin, and first published short stories before turning to the theatre with *Eye-Winker, Tom Tinker* (1972). Several of his plays are very short, the most intriguing of which is *The Great Hunger* (1983), an adaptation of a poem by Patrick Kavanagh. Other works include *The Bearded Lady* (1984), *Fleurs-du-Lit* (1991), a volume of poetry, and short stories such as 'The Harper's Turn' (1982).

After leaving college, MacIntyre began his career teaching English in Ireland and at Ann Arbor, Michigan, and other centres in the USA.

McKENNA, SIOBHÁN (1922–1986)

Actor who made her reputation on the stage of the ⇨Abbey Theatre, Dublin. McKenna gave memorable performances in such works as George Bernard Shaw's *St Joan* and J M Synge's *The Playboy of the Western World. Bailegangaire*, a play written especially for her by Tom Murphy (1935–   ), was her last stage production, at the Druid Theatre, Galway, in 1986.

McKenna was born in Belfast. Reared in an Irish-speaking family in Galway, she made her acting debut in the Irish language, in ⇨An Taibhdhearc. In 1944 she joined the Abbey company and in 1946 she married a fellow actor, Denis O'Dea. She received several honorary degrees at Irish and US universities, was granted life membership of the Royal Dublin Society, and in 1975 was appointed president of the Council of State of Ireland.

MacKenna, Stephen (1872–1934)

English-born translator and journalist, celebrated in the world of classical studies for his unparalleled translation of Plotinus' *Enneads* (1917–1930). MacKenna was born in Liverpool of Irish parents, and first moved to Dublin after failing an entrance exam to London University. He served as a European news correspondent during the Russo-Japanese War (1904–05), and interviewed the Russian novelist Leo Tolstoy before returning to Ireland in 1907. He was a close friend of the dramatist J M Synge as well as the poets George Russell and James Stephens, and other leading figures of the Gaelic revival. After the Irish Civil War (1922–23), he moved to London where he worked continually on the Plotinus project.

Macken, Walter (1915–1967)

Actor, director, playwright, and historical novelist. Macken was born in Galway and at 17 joined An Taibhdhearc, the Gaelic League Theatre, which he continued to support as an actor, director, and playwright long after he moved on to the Abbey Theatre, where his own play *Mungo's Mansion* had a long run in 1946. *I Am Alone* (1949), a novel about an Irishman's experiences in London, was banned in Ireland but a series of historical novels were long-standing successes with the Irish public. These include *Seek the Fair Land* (1959), on the Cromwellian War in Ireland, *The Silent People* (1962) on the Irish Famine, and *The Scorching Wind* (1964), on the Irish Troubles 1916–1922.

Mackey, Mick (1912–1982)

Hurler, born in Castleconnel, County Limerick. Mackey was rated alongside Christy ⇨Ring as one of the game's greatest exponents. He made his debut for Limerick at the age of 18 in a national league game against Kilkenny in 1930, but was reduced to playing club football with the local side Ahane for another two years before regaining his place. Alongside his brother, John, he was on the losing side to Kilkenny in 1932, but in 1934 he collected his first senior All-Ireland Championship medal when Limerick beat Dublin in the replay. There were further successes in 1936 and 1940 when he captained the side.

Macklin, Charles (or M'Laughlin) (c. 1700–1797)

Actor and dramatist. His portrayal of Shylock in Shakespeare's *The Merchant of Venice* at Drury Lane, London, in 1741 was significant. The part had long been played by a comedian, and Macklin raised it again to a dignified and tragic status.

Macklin joined a company of strolling players in 1716, and in about 1730 began playing minor parts in London. He was a fine actor but a quarrelsome person, and moved constantly from one company to another. He was at his best in such parts as Scrub (a servant in *The Beaux' Stratagem* by George Farquhar) and Peachum (a criminal in *The Beggar's Opera* by John Gay), and as Sir Pertinax MacSycophant in his own play *The Man of the World* (1781).

MacLaverty, Bernard (1942–   )

Writer. Born in Belfast, McLaverty worked there as a medical technician before studying English and eventually settling in Glasgow. His prose is often dedicated to vexed relationships between lovers, families, and communities. Starting his career with short stories, he is best known for his novel of tragic love *Cal* (1983) and his masterful portrait of a female composer in *Grace Notes* (1997). His style is marked by a delicacy that bespeaks an intense respect for human emotions and frailties. Other works include *Lamb* (1980) and the short story collection *Walking the Dog, and Other Stories* (1994).

McLaverty, Michael (1904–1992)

Writer who was born in Carrickmacross, County Monaghan, and lived for a short time on Rathlin Island, County Antrim, before moving to Belfast. His fiction, both short stories and novels, is directly related to his experiences as a headmaster of a Belfast Catholic boys' school. Beginning with stories that concentrate on young and marginalized characters, then moving into autobiographical fiction, and finally writing Catholic novels dealing with morality, McLaverty is known for caring but unnostalgic prose that is often praised for its straightforward style. His best-known works are the short story 'Pigeons' and the collection *The Road to the Shore* (1976).

MAC LIAMMÓIR, MÍCHEÁL (ALFRED LEE WILMORE) (1899–1978)

Actor, artist, and writer. After establishing a reputation as a painter and designer, Mac Liammóir founded the ⇨Gate Theatre Company in Dublin in 1928 with his partner Hilton Edwards (1903–1982). He is perhaps best known for his internationally acclaimed one-man shows *The Importance of Being Oscar* (1960), about the life of Oscar Wilde; *I Must Be Talking to My Friends* (1963), on Irish history and literature; and *Mostly About Yeats* (1970).

Mac Liammóir was born into an Irish family in London and became a child actor, playing alongside Noel Coward in Herbert Beerbohm Tree's production of *Peter Pan*. He studied art at the Slade School and toured Ireland with the Shakespearean company of Anew McMaster (1894–1962). With the Gate Theatre, as well as promoting contemporary Irish writing and presenting innovative productions of classical works, he introduced Dublin audiences to new European drama. His written works includes fiction, plays, and memoirs, both in Irish and in English. His film roles include Iago in Orson Welles's *Othello* (1949) and the narrator in *Tom Jones* (1963).

MACLISE, DANIEL (1806–1870)

Painter of historical subjects. Maclise is remembered mainly for his series of portrait drawings of eminent literary men and women (1830–38) and for his frescoes *The Meeting of Wellington and Blucher at Waterloo* (1861) and *The Death of Nelson at Trafalgar* (1865) in the UK parliament's House of Lords, London.

Born into a Presbyterian family in Cork, Maclise trained as an artist there before moving to London in 1827 where he soon established himself as a history and portrait painter. His circle included many of the leading literary and theatrical figures of the day, among them Charles Dickens whose book *The Chimes* (1844) he illustrated. Maclise's large narrative paintings depicting the literary and historical themes so popular with his Victorian audience were painted in a meticulously detailed style, influenced by the German Nazarene movement. An example is *The Marriage of Strongbow and Aoife* (1854; National Gallery of Ireland, Dublin); this work also reveals the artist's enduring interest in Irish subjects which he treated in a nostalgic, Romantic manner. In this sense Maclise may be seen as a central figure in the early stages of the ⇨Irish revival.

MACMURROUGH, DERMOT (DIARMAIT MAC MURCHADA UÍ, or DERMOT MURPHY) (1110–1171)

King of Leinster from around 1132. Following the death in 1166 of his powerful ally Muirchertach Mac Lochlainn, King of Tír Eógain (modern counties Tyrone and Derry), MacMurrough was deposed by Rory O'Connor, High King of Ireland, and sailed with his wife and daughter to Bristol, England. After winning the support of Henry II, King of England, MacMurrough returned to Ireland in 1167 with a small Anglo-Norman force recruited from southern Wales. He was able to win back much of his kingdom, and in 1169 captured Wexford. In 1170, with the aid of the Anglo-Norman earl Richard de ⇨Clare (Strongbow), he defeated Rory O'Connor but was allowed to keep his Leinster kingship. Later in the same year he took Dublin, prevailing after a concerted effort upon the city walls by an English detachment. He died at Ferns, County Wexford, in 1171, passing the kingship of Leinster to Strongbow, who had married his daughter Aoife, the first such bequest to a non-Irish heir.

MacMurrough has traditionally been regarded in Ireland as the archetypal traitor who helped to instigate English rule, as for example in W B Yeats's play *The Dreaming of the Bones* (1921).

MACNAMARA, BRINSLEY (pseudonym of JOHN WELDON) (1890–1963)

Writer and dramatist. Born in Devlin, County Westmeath, MacNamara lived most of his life in Dublin and was long associated with the ⇨Abbey Theatre as an actor and director. His first novel *The Valley of the Squinting Windows* (1918), which is representative of his critical portrayal of romantic notions of Irish rural life, caused such negative reactions that boycotts and litigation resulted. Disillusionment remained a key tone to his plays and novels, such as *The Clanking of*

Chains (1920) and *Mirror in the Dusk* (1921). His later novels, such as *The Various Lives of Marcus Igoe* (1929), show an experimentation with fantasy and dream states unexpressed in his earlier work.

MacNamara began his career acting with the Abbey Theatre and toured with them to the USA in 1911, remaining as a freelance actor until 1913. His first play *The Rebellion in Ballycullion* was produced by the Abbey, and he continued to work for them throughout his life, although a brief period as director ended with his resignation over the theatre's rejection of Seán ⇨O'Casey's *The Silver Tassie* (1928).

MacNeice, (Frederick) Louis

(1907–1963)

Poet and dramatist, born in Belfast and educated at Merton College, Oxford. MacNeice developed a polished ease of expression, reflecting his classical training, as in the autobiographical and topical *Autumn Journal* (1939). His debut as a poet was made with *Blind Fireworks* (1929). MacNeice is noted for his low-key, socially committed but politically uncommitted verse; and his ability to reflect the spirit of his times in his own emotional experience earned him an appreciative public. Although his parents had ties to the west of Ireland, MacNeice did not really concentrate on Irish culture or topics; rather, his Irish background encouraged a general mistrust of religious and secular rigidity.

MacNeice lectured at British and US universities, served during World War II, and worked with the BBC as a writer and producer. Other works include the play *The Dark Tower* (1947); a verse translation of Goethe's *Faust* in 1949; a study of the poetry of ⇨Yeats (1941); and the poetry collections *The Last Ditch* (1940), *Springboard* (1944), *Ten Burnt Offerings* (1952), *Autumn Sequel* (1954), *Visitations* (1957), and *Solstices* (1961). He was made a CBE in 1958.

Í come from an island, Ireland, a nation / Built upon violence and morose vendettas. / My diehard countrymen like dray-horses / Drag their ruin behind them.

Louis MacNeice *Eclogue from Ireland* (1936).

~

MacNeill, Eoin (John) (1867–1945)

Historian, Gaelic scholar, and politician, born in Glenarm, County Antrim. MacNeill was educated at St Malachy's College and Royal University, Belfast, and was professor of early and medieval Irish history at University College, Dublin 1908–45. Co-founder of the Gaelic League with Douglas ⇨Hyde, he was also a founder member and commander-in-chief of the ⇨Irish Volunteers. He reluctantly supported the plans for the 1916 ⇨Easter Rising, and his last-minute countermand of the rebellion, after it became evident that German aid would fail, prevented national insurrection, the action being confined to Dublin. Arrested but released in 1917, he became minister of finance in the first Dáil (parliament) in 1919 and minister for industries 1919–21.

MacNeill supported the Anglo-Irish Treaty (1921), which separated the six counties of Northern Ireland from the Irish Free State, and was minister of education 1922–25 in Cumann na nGael's government. After representing the 1926 Boundary Commission, which confirmed partition and shattered nationalist hopes of a revision of the border with Northern Ireland, MacNeill resigned from politics.

MacPherson, Conor (1971–)

Playwright and co-founder of the Fly By Night Theatre Company. Born in Dublin, he studied philosophy at University College, Dublin, and went on to hold a term as writer-in-residence with the Bush Theatre, London. His first major London success was *This Lime Tree Bower* (1995), but *The Weir* (1997), staged at the Royal Court Theatre, received even greater acclaim. Seemingly straightforward, his drama is punctuated with moments of intense moral questioning that put the characters' lives in relief against a contemporary Irish society which is quickly changing. A master of the dramatic monologue, MacPherson's work constantly questions the nature of identity, criminality, and morality.

McQuaid, John Charles (1895–1973)

Roman Catholic archbishop of Dublin 1940–72. An influential figure in the religious formation of the Republic of Ireland, he opposed mixed religious education and in 1944 banned Catholics from attending Trinity College, Dublin.

McQuaid was born in Cootehill, County Cavan, and was educated there and in Dublin and Rome. He was ordained priest in the Holy Ghost Fathers in 1924. He fell out with his one-time acquaintance Éamon ⇨de Valera when he supported striking schoolteachers in 1947, and thereafter became a vehement opponent of state policy. He played a leading part in the Irish bishops' successful objection to the 'Mother and Child Scheme', a national health proposal, in 1951.

MacRORY, JOSEPH (1861–1945)

Catholic archbishop of Armagh from 1928 and cardinal from 1931. He supported the creation of a Catholic Irish state and officially opposed the Irish Republican Army.

Although based in Northern Ireland, his primary influence was on the Irish Free State. At William Thomas Cosgrave's instigation, he issued a pastoral letter in 1931 condemning republicanism, especially the 'communist' Saor éire party. He never forgave Éamon de Valera for politicizing the ⇨Eucharistic Congress of 1932 and opposed his mention of the Church of Ireland in the constitution of 1937.

MacSWINEY, TERENCE (1879–1920)

Republican politician. In March 1920 Terence MacSwiney, a writer and revolutionary, was elected lord mayor of Cork, following the murder of his predecessor by police. In August he was arrested and sentenced to two years' imprisonment. He went on hunger strike and died in Brixton Prison after a fast of 74 days which attracted worldwide attention.

Terence MacSwiney was born in Cork where he trained as an accountant. As a nationalist playwright, he co-founded the Cork Dramatic Society in 1908. He was instrumental in the creation of the Cork Volunteers in 1913, but obeyed John (Eoin) MacNeill, the leader of the Volunteers, in his countermand of the order for rebellion during the Easter Rising of 1916. In 1918 he was elected to Westminster as Sinn Féin member of parliament for West Cork, but abstained to the first Dáil and helped to establish its arbitration courts while continuing his efforts as an Irish Republican Army (IRA) organizer.

MacSWINEY, MARY (1872–1942)

Republican politician. Born in England, MacSwiney spent most of her life in Ireland. Following the death of her brother, Terence, Mary became a prominent republican leader and was elected to the Dáil (parliament) in 1920 where she opposed the Anglo-Irish Treaty (1921), which established the Irish Free State within the British Commonwealth. She broke with Éamon de Valera in 1926 when he founded Fianna Fáil. In 1933 she set up Mná na Poblachta (Women of the Republic), a breakaway from ⇨Cumann na mBan.

MAGHERAFELT

Market town in County Derry, on Lough Neagh, 13 km/8 mi southeast of Maghera; population (1991) 5,100. There are building contractors, brick and concrete manufacture, and peat processing; it is also a centre for angling. The town was laid out during the 17th century by the Salters' Company of London after they were granted the lands during the plantation.

MAGRATH, MEILER (c. 1523–1622)

Ecclesiastic, notorious for the flexibility of his attitudes towards the ⇨Reformation in Ireland, which his critics claimed were unprincipled. A Franciscan friar, he was appointed papal bishop of Down and Connor in 1565 but, with his acceptance of the royal supremacy in 1570, was made Church of Ireland archbishop of Cashel in 1571, a position he held with an accumulation of lesser sees until his death. Though regarded with suspicion by Protestants and contempt by Catholics, Magrath was, in fact, a shrewd observer of men and affairs. His memoranda on the politics of Ulster and the Munster plantation in the 1580s and 1590s remain invaluable to historians, and deserved to have exerted more influence over English administrators than they did.

MAHON, DEREK (1941–)

Poet, born in Belfast and educated at Belfast Institute and Trinity College, Dublin. Together with Seamus ⇨Heaney and Michael Longley (1939–), he was associated with the Northern Poets in Belfast in the 1960s. His poetry, such as *Night-Crossing* (1968) and

M aguire, I believe, suggested a blackbird / And over your grave a phrase from Euripides / Which suits you down to the ground, like this churchyard / With its play of shadows, its humane perspective.

DEREK MAHON An elegy, at his graveside, to Louis MacNeice, 'In Carrowdore Churchyard'.

The Snow Party (1975), is characterized by squalid landscapes and desperate situations.

After a brief teaching career, Mahon turned to journalism and creative writing. His early works, such as *Twelve Poems* (1965), show the influence of Louis MacNeice and W H Auden. Later publications include *The Hunt by Night* (1982), *A Kensington Notebook* (1984), and *Antarctica* (1985). The anthology *Poems 1962–1978* (1979) contained some revised versions of earlier works, and a new collection *Selected Poems* appeared in 1991.

MAHONY, FRANCIS SYLVESTER
('FATHER PROUT') (1804–1866)

Humorous writer and poet. Born in Cork, he was educated at Clongowes Wood, where he later taught while training as a Jesuit priest. Expelled for taking the boys on a drunken outing, he was ordained as a secular priest in Italy in 1832, but left the church and took up writing on his return to Ireland. His contributions to *Fraser's Magazine* were collected in *Reliques of Father Prout* (1836), and he is remembered for his poems 'The Bells of Shandon' and 'The Lady of Lee'.

MALACHY, ST (MALACHY O'MORGAIR)
(1094–1148)

Church reformer, the first Irishman to be canonized (1190). Born in Armagh, he was successively abbot of Bangor (1121), bishop of Connor (1125), and archbishop of Armagh (1134). His reforms brought the Celtic era to an end by giving the Irish Church a closer relationship with Rome. He replaced Celtic with Roman liturgy, renewed sacramental practice, and established a regular hierarchy. He introduced the Cistercians into Ireland in 1142, after meeting St Bernard of Clairvaux in 1139. On the way to Rome in 1148 he died at Clairvaux, and St Bernard subsequently wrote his biography. Malachy's feast day is 3 November.

MALAHIDE CASTLE

Twelfth-century castle at Malahide, County Dublin, held by the Talbot family from 1174 until 1976. Many of the internal features survive due to this long and continual ownership. These include the old family chapel (the Oak Room) with elaborate wooden carvings, the Great Hall, built with a minstrel's gallery in the reign of Edward IV, and two Georgian drawing rooms, each with a corner turret and plasterwork attributed to Robert West. The castle is now owned by Dublin City Council.

MALLON, SEAMUS (1936–)

Northern Ireland Social and Democratic Labour Party (SDLP) politician: deputy leader of the SDLP (since 1979) and deputy first minister (December 1999 to February 2000) in the Northern Ireland power-sharing executive.

Born in Markethill, County Armagh, Mallon first became involved in politics during the campaign for civil rights in Northern Ireland in the 1960s. In 1973 he was elected a member, for the Catholic community-oriented SDLP, of Armagh district council and the Northern Ireland Assembly. In 1982 he was appointed to the Irish Senate, which led to his expulsion from the Northern Ireland Assembly. A blunt-speaking spokesman for the nationalist cause, he gained respect through also being ready to denounce IRA atrocities.

Mallon was elected to Westminster, as MP for Newry and Armagh, in 1986. A firm supporter of the peace process, he became a member of the Forum for Peace and Reconciliation, established in 1994 by the Irish government, and a member of the new Northern Ireland Assembly from June 1998.

MANCHESTER MARTYRS

Three Irish activists hanged by the British in 1867, for the murder of a police officer during the escape of two Fenian prisoners on their way to court in Manchester; see ⇨Fenian movement.

MANGAN, JAMES CLARENCE (1803–1849)

Poet and translator. Mangan was born in Dublin, and worked as a clerk until 1828 while establishing his career as a writer. Much of his writing is concerned with Irish history and legend, and among his chief works are *Anthologia Germanica* (1845) and *Romances and Ballads of Ireland* (1850). He published English versions of Irish poems in *The Poets and Poetry of Munster* (1849), notably 'Dark Rosaleen' and 'The Nameless One'. He is one of the few Anglo-Irish poets before W B Yeats.

Mangan wrote for the *Dublin Satirist*, the *Comet*, and *The Nation* (founded 1842), and contributed to many Irish newspapers under various pseudonyms. The account of his life given in his *Autobiography* is filled with images of fearful misery, deprivation, and persecution. His poetry is fitful and neurotic; at times he reached a masterly eloquence (often in his very free 'translations' of Irish or even Arabic, two languages of which he had no knowledge). An opium addict and an alcoholic, he died from cholera.

MANNIX, DANIEL (1864–1963)

Irish-born Catholic archbishop of Melbourne 1917–63, who became a spiritual director to leading republican figures during the Anglo–Irish War (1919–21) and Irish Civil War (1922–23).

Born in County Cork, Mannix trained for the priesthood at St Patrick's College, Maynooth, and became its president in 1909. He left Ireland to become coadjutor archbishop of Melbourne in 1913 and was appointed archbishop four years later. He opposed conscription and was generally outspoken, leading the Australian government to complain to Rome. In 1920 he was arrested onboard a liner off the coast of County Cork, near Cobh, taken to England, and detained there until 1921, despite protests from Irish bishops. He led the funeral cortège of Terence MacSwiney, mayor of Cork, who died in Brixton Jail, London. In 1921 he was permitted to go to Rome, where he drafted a papal encyclical that opposed Irish violence without condemning nationalists. He corresponded with anti-Anglo-Irish Treaty leaders and may have influenced Éamon de Valera's decision to renounce abstentionism.

MANT, RICHARD (1776–1848)

English-born Church of Ireland bishop and leader of the High Church revival in Ireland. Mant was successively bishop of Killaloe (1820–32) and bishop of Down, Connor, and Dromore (1823–48). He banned the (Evangelical) Established Church Home Mission from his diocese in 1828 and published *Episcopal Jurisdiction Asserted as the Law of the Church and the Rule of the Clergy's Ministrations* against clergy who operated in his diocese without consent. He set up the Church Architecture Society which was responsible for building 22 Belfast churches during his episcopacy.

MANUSCRIPTS, ILLUMINATED

Decorated religious manuscripts associated with Irish Christianity appeared in the 6th and 7th centuries, and Irish illuminators quickly developed a distinctive, imaginative, and sophisticated style.

earliest example

The earliest Irish manuscript in existence is the 6th-century 'Cathach' (battler) of St Columba, with decoration confined to simple enlarged initials at the beginning of every paragraph. Its half-uncial (rounded cursive) script is distinctively Irish. Manuscripts were made of vellum, or calf-skin, and up to 150 skins were used for the ⇨Book of Kells, along with expensive materials and extensive labour, to glorify God through the pages. It is difficult to say whether many 'Irish' manuscripts were illustrated in Ireland, or in various monastic centres established by Irish monks in Britain, such as Iona and Lindisfarne. For this reason, the term 'insular' is used, rather than 'Irish', to describe the common style which emerged in these locations and on the Irish mainland.

the insular style

The ⇨*Book of Durrow* (*c.* 675) is the earliest fully illustrated manuscript known in the insular style, but it is likely that others preceded it, as it demonstrates dramatic advances on the illumination of the Cathach. Its decorative plates include 'carpet' pages of pure ornament, and pages with stylized symbols of the evangelists (man, lion, ox, and eagle). Pages of text are enlivened with elaborately designed and enlarged initial letters. Only four colours were used – red, yellow, green, and black – and the decoration is also restrained, with a controlled use of empty space. As with ⇨metalwork and high ⇨crosses in this Early Christian period, ornament combined the flowing curves of the Celtic La Tène style with newer ribbon and animal interlace patterns.

Book of Kells

The Book of Kells (*c.* 800) was the highest achievement of insular manuscript illumination, believed to have been begun in Iona, Scotland, and finished when the monks fled from the Vikings to Kells, County Meath, in 806. In addition to portraits of the evangelists, carpet pages of decoration, and canon tables, like the *Book of Durrow*, the Kells manuscript illuminators depicted a small number of scenes from the Gospels, and dedicated an entire page to illustrating the first word of each Gospel, beginning with each enormous first letter. The Chi Rho page, with the letters XPI (Christ), is one such, and is often considered the highlight of the book. Motifs reappear on different scales, little animals enliven the page, and the most awkward spaces between letters are filled with intricate designs. This manuscript contains none of the austerity of the *Book of Durrow* – in its exuberance, lively variety of colours, and inventive design, it displays the inspiration and skill of several illustrators.

variety of style

The *Book of Armagh*, completed only a few years after the Book of Kells, demonstrates the variety of the insular style, in its simple, bold, black and white line drawings of the Evangelists' symbols. Other insular manuscripts of note from the early Christian period are those of *Dimma*, *Mulling*, the *Lindisfarne Gospels*, the *Stowe Missal*, and the *Southampton Psalter*.

MARIA DUCE (Latin

'under the leadership of Mary')
Conservative Catholic movement founded in 1942 by Father Denis Fahey (1883–1954) to popularize Catholic social teaching. In practice, it tended towards fundamentalism, which caused it to lose popular support even though its anticommunist stance was shared by many in both the church and state. In its most high-profile public campaign, it lobbied unsuccessfully to enshrine the Catholic church's teaching in the Irish state constitution.

Some bishops were initially sympathetic to the organization but grew increasingly embarrassed by its extremism. The founder's death gave them the excuse they needed to distance themselves from the organization, which survived until the 1960s.

ℳhen she died in a pauper bed, in love / All the poor of Dublin rose to lament her.

CECIL DAY-LEWIS Poet About Constance Markievicz, in *'Remembering Con Markievicz'* (1970).

MARKIEVICZ, CONSTANCE GEORGINA

(born Gore Booth; Countess Markievicz)
(1868–1927)

CONSTANCE MARKIEVICZ *A hugely popular figure, known as the Red Countess, Markievicz garrisoned 120 Republican soldiers in the Royal College of Surgeons during the Easter Rising. Upon surrender, she kissed her revolver before giving it up to the British.*

Socialist, revolutionary, and politician. Born in London to a family from Sligo, she was educated at Slade School and Paris, where she met and married the Polish Count Casimir Markievicz. She was prominent in the Gaelic revival before becoming involved in nationalist politics. She joined Sinn Féin in 1908 and founded Na Fianna, the republican youth organization, in 1909. Active with Maud ⇨Gonne in the women's movement Inghinidhe na héireann, she later became honorary president of the ⇨Irish Women Workers' Union. In the strike known as the 'Dublin lock-out', she ran a soup kitchen. She joined James ⇨Connolly's socialist Irish Citizen Army and fought in the ⇨Easter Rising of 1916, but her resulting death sentence was commuted.

In 1918 Markievicz was elected to Westminster for Sinn Féin (technically becoming the first British woman MP), but did not take her seat, instead serving as minister for labour in the first Dáil (then the illegal republican parliament). Markievicz opposed the Anglo-Irish Treaty (1921), which established the Irish Free State within the British Empire, and was elected for Fianna Fáil shortly before her death in 1927.

MARTIN, JAMES (1893–1981)

Aeronautical engineer, born in Crossgar, County Down. Martin designed World War II fighter aircraft, and designed and manufactured ejection seats to improve pilot safety.

Before World War I Martin designed a three-wheeled car and set up a business for its manufacture in London. By the 1930s he was designing aircraft, the first being a two-seater monoplane made of thin-gauge steel tubing. It was called the Martin-Baker

MB-1, named for Martin and his chief test pilot and partner, Capt Valentine Henry Baker.

For the next 10 years to 1944 Martin designed three fighter aircraft. Although they performed well and could be produced cheaply, he received no government orders. Before World War II, however, Martin had designed a barrage-balloon cable cutter, which was brought into widespread use by aircraft under RAF Bomber Command.

The ejection seat was invented during World War II to improve a Spitfire pilot's chances of escape by parachute. The Martin–Baker design was fitted in new British military jet aircraft from 1947 and Martin continued to modify his designs to accommodate higher speeds, greater altitudes, vertical takeoff, multiple crew escape, and underwater ejection. By the early 1980s about 35,000 Martin–Baker ejection seats were in service with air forces and navies in 50 countries.

MARTIN, VIOLET FLORENCE (pen name MARTIN ROSS) (1862–1915)

Novelist, born in County Galway. Martin collaborated with her cousin Edith ⇨Somerville in the writing partnership ⇨Somerville and Ross, on tales of Anglo-Irish provincial life, such as *The Real Charlotte* (1894) and *Some Experiences of an Irish RM* (1899).

MATTHEW, THEOBALD (1790–1856)

Roman Catholic priest, founder of the Irish Total Abstinence Society in 1838. By 1844 some 5,500,000 people were registered with the Society and a further 1,500,000 had taken the abstinence pledge without registering, although many later renounced their pledge. He was ecumenical and nonpolitical, and fell out with Daniel O'Connell over an attempt to politicize the Society.

Matthew was born in Thomastown, near Cashel, County Tipperary. He entered the Capuchin Franciscans in 1812 and was ordained priest in 1814. He was encouraged to form the Society by Quakers while working among the poor in Cork.

MATURIN, CHARLES ROBERT (1782–1824)

Novelist and dramatist. Born into a Huguenot family in Dublin, Maturin was educated at Trinity College, Dublin, and ordained in 1803. He is best remembered for his 'horror' novels *Montario* (1807), *The Milesian Chief* (1812), and *Melmoth the Wanderer*

(1820), which the French writer Honoré de Balzac considered one of the greatest novels in the English language. He also wrote several plays, including the tragedy *Bertram* (1816), which was successfully produced by Edmund Kean at Drury Lane, Londonderry, in 1816.

MAYNOOTH

Town and commuter settlement in County Kildare, 24 km/15 mi west of Dublin; population (1996) 8,500. It accommodates part of the National University of Ireland, originally established in 1795 with government funding as ⇨St Patrick's College, a training college for Roman Catholic priests, also known as Maynooth College. Lay students have been admitted since 1966.

The ruins of Maynooth Castle, built by the Fitzgeralds and dating for the most part from the 13th century, lie by the college gates. There is also an ecclesiastical museum and ⇨Carton House, the former residence of the Dukes of Leinster, in Maynooth.

The university is dominated architecturally by Pugin's mid-19th-century Gothic revival St Mary's Square complex, including St Patrick's House and St Mary's Chapel. In 1846 Sir Robert Peel carried a parliamentary bill for an increased and permanent endowment for the college; a further endowment of £369,000 from public funds was granted in 1871. It was accorded the status of a pontifical university in 1896 and in 1908 became part of the National University of Ireland, which awards degrees to lay students at St Patrick's.

MAYNOOTH COLLEGE

See ⇨St Patrick's College, Maynooth.

MAYO

County of the Republic of Ireland, in the province of Connacht; county town ⇨Castlebar; area 5,400 sq km/2,084 sq mi; population (1996) 111,500. Its wild Atlantic coastline is about 400 km/249 mi long. The principal towns are Ballina, Ballinrobe, and Westport, and the principal rivers are the Moy, the Robe, and the Owenmore. Loughs Conn and Mask lie within the county. Agriculture includes pig, sheep, and cattle farming, and salmon fishing (particularly in the River Moy). The soil of the central plain is fertile, and crops include potatoes and oats. An excellent marble is found in the northwest district.

Two of Ireland's national places of pilgrimage are situated in County Mayo: ⇨Croagh Patrick (765 m/2,510 ft), where St Patrick spent the 40 days of Lent in AD 441; and ⇨Knock, the site of alleged apparitions of the Virgin Mary. There are several ecclesiastical remains and early fortifications. The county has a number of important archaeological sites, the most significant of which is Céide Fields, an extensive Neolithic site with evidence of field systems and dwellings, 10 sq km/4 sq mi in extent.

topography

The coastline of Mayo is much indented with bays, the chief of which are Killala Bay, Clew Bay, Westport Bay, Newport Bay, Achill Sound, and Blacksod Bay. Achill Island lies just off the coast. The interior is very flat, forming the western part of the large plain that runs across central Ireland. In the west of the county are two ranges of mountains, separated from each other at the coast by Clew Bay. The highest point in the two southern ranges (the Partry Mountains and the Mweelrea Mountains) is Mount Mweelrea (817 m/2,680 ft), and in the northern range, the Nephin Beg Mountains, Mount Nephin (807 m/2,648 ft).

antiquities

Four round towers survive. At Cong there are also remains of a splendid 12th-century abbey, founded in 1128 for the Augustinians by Turlough O'Connor, King of Ireland. The 'Cross of Cong', a beautifully decorated Celtic crucifix, is now in the National Museum of Ireland, Dublin.

MEAGHER, THOMAS FRANCIS

(1823–1867)

Nationalist, born in County Waterford, the son of a Waterford merchant. Meagher became a founder member of the Irish Confederation and served as a member of its war council; he is said to have proposed the tricolour as the Irish national flag. Meagher was condemned to death for his revolutionary propaganda during the 1848 ⇨Young Ireland rebellion, but the sentence was commuted to transportation to Van Diemen's Land (Tasmania). In 1852 he escaped to the USA where, on the outbreak of the American Civil War in 1861, he commanded the pro-Union Irish brigade for the Federals.

Meagher was educated at Clongowes and Stoneyhurst College. He joined the Repeal Association but left in 1846 after attacking Daniel ⇨O'Connell's constitutional approach to nationalism, for which he was named 'Meagher of the Sword'. In 1848 he unsuccessfully contested the Waterford by-election.

On his arrival in the USA Meagher became a journalist in New York. Following the civil war, he was appointed temporary governor of Montana territory where he drowned in 1867.

COLM MEANEY *As well as spending six years as a regular on the TV series* Star Trek, *Meaney played three different roles in the film versions of Roddy Doyle's Dublin-based novels,* The Commitments, The Snapper, *and* The Van, *all made in the 1990s.*

MEANEY, COLM

(1953–   )

Stage, television, and film actor. Meaney was born in Dublin and trained at the Abbey Theatre before going to London where his first television appearance was in the series *Z Cars*. He emigrated to New York in 1982, and had roles in various television series before becoming a regular in *Star Trek* from 1987 to 1993. He has regularly played native Irish roles and his screen persona is often characterized by a devilish smile, as in the case of his hugely popular roles in the adaptations of Roddy Doyle's books: as the harassed father in *The Snapper* (1993), the Elvis-loving Mr Rabbitte in *The Commitments* (1991), and unemployed entrepreneur in *The Van* (1996).

Other films include *Far and Away* (1992), *Into the West* (1992), *War of the Buttons* (1994), *Last of the High Kings* (1996), and *This is My Father* (1998).

MEATH

County of the Republic of Ireland, in the province of Leinster; county town ⇨Navan; area 2,340 sq km/903 sq mi; population (1996) 109,700. The chief river is the Boyne, of which the Blackwater is a tributary. The principal towns are Kells, Trim, Athboy, Bettystown, and Laytown. Cattle and sheep are reared, and oats and potatoes are grown. The largest working lead mine in Europe is located near Navan. ⇨Tara Hill, 155 m/509 ft high, was the site of a palace and was the coronation place of many kings of Ireland; St Patrick also preached here. The Book of Kells (now held in the Trinity College Library) was produced at Kells in the early 9th century.

topography

Meath is bounded in the east by the Irish Sea, in the south by Kildare, in the north by Monaghan, in the southwest by Offaly, in the northwest by Cavan, and in the west by Westmeath. The coast is low and sandy, and the surface is mainly flat, limestone plain rising towards the west, the highest point being Slieve na Caillighe (276 m/906 ft).

historical remains

There are beautiful 12th century ruins at Duleek, originally a monastic settlement founded by St Patrick in the 5th century. There are also the ruins of Bective Abbey, once a powerful Cistercian abbey that owned a large part of the county of Meath; and Trim Castle, the largest Anglo-Norman castle in Ireland. Tara Hill is a very ancient site, and was probably orginally a religious rather than a residential centre. Its heyday was in the 3rd century AD, and the site was still in use in the 10th century. There are significant monastic remains at Kells, founded in the 6th century by St Columba (St Colum Cille).

MEDHBA (MEADHBH or MEDB) (Irish

Meduva, 'she who is mead')

In mythology, a warrior queen of the ⇨hero-tales. She symbolized the kingship of Tara, which was ritually portrayed as an otherworld woman serving that drink. In the Ulster cycle, she is the warrior-queen of the province of Connacht who lords it over her male admirers.

MEGALITH (Greek *megas* 'great', *lithos* 'stone')

Prehistoric stone monument of the late Neolithic or early Bronze Age (4000–2000 BC). Ireland has about 1,000 tombs and stone circles. Grave sites include portal tombs or wedge dolmens, enormous slabs supported by uprights; court cairns, compartmented chambers with ritual forecourts; and passage-graves, corridors with chambers. Tombs are sometimes grouped together in large cemeteries, as in the ⇨Boyne Valley, and at ⇨Carrowkeel and ⇨Carrowmore. The structures were buried under earthen mounds or stone cairns, but some have been laid bare by erosion, as at Poulnabrone Dolmen in the ⇨Burren. Stone circles such as those found at Lough ⇨Gur and burial sites such as Newgrange in the Boyne Valley probably performed a ritual function, possibly linked to seasonal and astronomical events.

Intricate abstract decorative carvings adorning the megalithic monuments include spirals, diamonds, suns, lozenges, and concentric circles and arcs. Similar symbols and designs are found on megaliths in Brittany, France, and on Malta.

MELLIFONT ABBEY

The earliest Cistercian abbey in Ireland, near Drogheda, County Louth. It was founded in 1142 by St Malachy, assisted by a group of French monks from Burgundy. The remains include the chapter house, the church foundations, and, most notably, the only extant example of a lavabo in Ireland (where the monks washed their hands before and after meals). After the Reformation the monastery was dissolved and the abbey was turned into a fortified house. Part of the cloister arcade was re-erected in the 1950s.

MELLIFONT, CONSPIRACY OF

The 13th-century revolt by members of the Irish Cistercian community against the mother house in Cîteaux, France, led by the abbot and community of the monastery at Mellifont, County Louth. The conspiracy, while indicative of contemporary tensions between native and Anglo-Norman Cistercian communities, was initially a reaction against disciplinary measures incurred by the absenteeism of Irish abbots from the annual Cistercian general chapter held at Cîteaux. The reaction escalated in 1217 when the abbot of Mellifont barred visiting Cistercian inspectors from entering the monastery's grounds.

By 1221 reports to the Pope from further inspectors portrayed a state of affairs lacking in discipline and religious observance throughout the many Cistercian houses in Ireland, particularly the daughter house of Mellifont. In 1228 Stephen of Lexington, an

English abbot, was sent to Mellifont to tackle the problem. After initial opposition, the situation was abated by reaffiliating the Irish daughter-houses to Cistercian monasteries outside Ireland, as well as introducing stricter requirements for new members.

MELLOWS, LIAM (1892–1922)

Revolutionary and socialist. A prominent Irish Republican Army (IRA) leader during the ⇨Anglo–Irish War (1919–21) and a leading anti-Treaty republican during the civil war following the ⇨Anglo-Irish Treaty of 1921, Mellows was executed by the Irregulars of the Provisional Government in December 1922 in reprisal for the killing of two pro-Treaty Dáil (parliament) deputies. His published *Jail Notes* greatly influenced the development of republican socialism.

The Manchester-born son of a soldier, brought up in Wexford, Mellows was sworn into the Irish Republican Brotherhood in 1912 and got involved in the organization of Fianna éireann and the Irish Volunteers. He was deported to England but returned to fight in the ⇨Easter Rising of 1916, later escaping to the USA where he acted as agent for Éamon de Valera's US tour. He returned to Ireland in 1921 to become IRA director of purchases and Sinn Féin Teachta Dála (member of the Dáil) for Galway. An opponent of the Anglo-Irish Treaty, Mellows was arrested following the fall of Dublin's Four Courts garrison and subsequently executed on 8 December 1922.

MERRIMAN, BRIAN (or BRYAN MAC GIOLLA MEIDRE) (1747–1805)

Gaelic poet, born in Ennistymon, County Clare. Merriman became a schoolmaster and small farmer in Feakle, and later settled in Limerick as a mathematics teacher. His reputation rests on a single work, the 1,000-line mock-heroic epic *Cúirt an Mheáin Oíche/The Midnight Court* which he wrote in around 1786. An attack on Irish Catholic puritanism, the poem was the subject of fierce controversy between religious traditionalists and liberal intellectuals in post-independence Ireland.

Merriman's work was banned after Irish independence, but only in English translation (the Irish language was deemed incapable of being a corrupting influence). An English translation of Merriman's work by Frank O'Connor appeared in the *Penguin Book of Irish Verse* (1970). The Merriman Summer School has been held annually in Clare in August since 1967.

METALWORK

Highpoints in Irish metalwork were the 8th, 11th–12th, and 18th centuries, and the discipline continues to thrive.

early Christian work

The arrival of Christianity in the 5th century brought new patronage for Irish metalwork. By the 8th century religious objects were as lavishly ornamented as secular ones. Both combined Irish pre-Christian designs in the curvilinear La Tène style with newer influences from the Mediterranean and Scandinavia. Irish metalsmiths distinctively combined these three decorative styles in silver objects with gilt and enamelled details. The best-known objects from this period include the Ardagh Chalice, from County Limerick, and the Tara Brooch, from County Meath. After this golden era of Irish design, Viking immigration led to a great demand for silver, often worked as bracelets or brooches, but quantity rather than quality was the focus of production.

METALWORK *A fine George II silver basket, made by John Hamilton in Dublin, 1736. Richly decorated with lions, winged cherubs, corn sheaves and garlands of fruit, the piece probably belonged to Sir Ralph Gore of Wicklow.*

Romanesque

The next high-point of metalwork occurred in the late 11th and early 12th centuries. Reliquaries or shrines, in gilt bronze or silver-gilt, were made to enclose sacred objects, often associated with saints. The curves of La Tène all but disappeared in this Romanesque style, and decoration on crosses, croziers, book-shrines, and house-shaped shrines, among other items, consisted mostly of Scandinavian Urnes-style animal interlace. The Clonmacnoise Crozier, from County Offaly, and the Cross of Cong, from County Galway, show this style at its peak. A small number of objects, such as the Breac Maedoic, a house-shaped shrine, were decorated with figures, but this new development ended abruptly at the end of the 11th century. Little of the Gothic style which followed survives, apart from the finely crafted early 15th century O'Dea mitre and crozier from Limerick.

17th century to the present

Apart from some simple chalices, little or no silver remains from between the late medieval period and the Cromwellian wars. The Company of Goldsmiths of Dublin was founded in 1637, and by the second half of the 17th century a demand for domestic silver emerged. This early tableware was decorated with leaves, flowers, animals, and Chinese-style figurative scenes. From 1700 to 1740 the Baroque style predominated, characterized by plain surfaces and geometric designs. This was followed by the lightness of French Rococo style, featuring shells, asymmetrical waves and curves, flowers, foliage, and animals. Irish silversmiths produced a particularly Irish interpretation of this style and distinctively Irish objects, such as the dish ring, thought to have supported hot dishes.

1775 saw the arrival of Italian Neo-Classicism, based on classical Greek and Roman architecture. Urns, swags, and medallions decorated the silver of this time, which was more rational in structure than in the Rococo period. The mid-19th century Irish revival led to a rediscovery of Early Christian designs in silver, which continued into the early 20th century. Silver- and goldsmithing, taught in art colleges around the country, continue to thrive, particularly with growing public awareness of, and interest in, craft design in recent times.

See also ⇨art, prehistoric and pre-Christian.

MIDDLEMEN

Term used to describe tenants who rented large properties in Ireland from landlords (who were usually absentees) and then sublet them to other tenants. The rapid rise in property value after 1750 allowed such adventurous farmers to make substantial profits by securing property on a long lease for a fixed sum, and then allowing other tenants to work the land on a much shorter lease. Some middlemen were unscrupulous and raised rents to maximize profits whenever possible (rack-renting). Their influence declined in the early 19th century, as landlords began to rent directly to the tenants and the middlemen's role was bypassed completely. The Great Famine (historically dated 1845–49, but now believed to have lasted until 1852) precipitated their demise.

MIDLETON

Market town in County Cork; population (1996) 3,300. It is a commuter settlement for the city of Cork, 21 km/13 mi to the west. Midleton is the main centre in the Republic of Ireland for whiskey distilling, producing the majority of Irish whiskey and gin; it also has pottery manufacturing and food-processing industries. At Whitegate 14 km/9 mi to the southeast is an oil refinery.

The distillery is open to the public and there is an interpretive centre at the site. Some 8 km/5 mi to the east at Castlemartyr is a Carmelite college.

MITCHEL, JOHN (1815–1875)

Journalist and political activist. Born in Dungiven, County Derry, and educated at Trinity College, Dublin, Mitchel wrote extreme nationalist articles for *The Nation* before working on the *United Irishman* with James Clarence ⇨Mangan and James Fintan ⇨Lalor. In 1848 he was convicted of treason–felony and transported, eventually reaching Van Diemen's Land (now Tasmania). His *Jail Journal, or Five Years in British Prisons* (1854) is a central 19th-century text of anti-British imperialism and Irish nationalism. He escaped in 1853 and settled in the USA, returning to Ireland in 1875, where he died at Newry just days after being elected to Westminster as member of parliament for County Tipperary.

Mitchel's published works also include *The History of Ireland From the Treaty of Limerick to the Present Time* (1868) and an 1859 edition of Mangan's poetry.

MITCHELL, GEORGE FRANCIS (FRANK)

(1912-1997)

Geologist, archaeologist, and naturalist. Though academically a slow starter, Mitchell developed rapidly as a geologist under the encouragement of Anthony ⇨Farrington and built upon the latter's seminal work in quaternary studies. Noted for his audacity in formulating original theses, all of which proved fruitful, even if some of them were disproved, Mitchell was also an energetic popularizer. The first edition of his *Shell Guide to Ireland* (1952) is a treasure trove of geographical, archaeological, and local historical knowledge, and his book *The Irish Landscape* (1976) an essential starting point for the subject. His characteristically modest memoir *The Way That I Followed* (1990) is a valuable source for the cultural history of 20th-century Ireland.

MODERNISM

In the early part of the 20th century Ireland was resistant to art forms that were anything other than realistic. The first modern, nonrealistic images and influences that were to change this came from abroad. Avant-garde art gradually gained support and interest, with exhibitions and changes in art education opening up to modernist ideas, so that by the end of the 20th century modernist art had entered the mainstream.

foreign influences

In 1912 an exhibition organized by Ellen Duncan, an associate of the collector Sir Hugh Lane, presented the work of modern artists such as Picasso and Matisse for the first time in Ireland, heralding the impact that foreign avant-garde art was to have on Irish art. In the 1920s a new wave of Irish artists went to study in Paris. Among these were Mainie ⇨Jellett and Evie ⇨Hone who, on their return, were to become key advocates of modern art in an Ireland which in the 1920s and 1930s was culturally isolated and whose artistic institutions were often unsympathetic to such influences. Official taste in the visual arts was at that time dominated by the nationalist realism of artists such as Sean Keating (1889–1978) and Maurice McGonigal (1900–1979).

modernism encouraged

The establishment of the White Stag Group in Dublin in the early 1940s was the first time a modernist cultural group had been set up in Ireland. Including English artists such as Basil Rakoczi (1908–1979), it gave an important impetus to providing a platform for artists concerned with modernism. In 1943 the Irish Exhibition of Living Art was established as an alternative to the Royal Hibernian Academy, founded in 1823. Its exhibitions continued until the late 1970s. The Arts Council of Ireland, founded in 1951, became in the ensuing decades a vital source of encouragement for avant-garde art in Ireland both through its collecting and its financial and practical support for artists. The student protest of 1969 at the National College of Art, Dublin (now the National College of Art and Design), was a watershed for the modernization of art education in Ireland.

reaching a wider audience

From the 1960s modernism began to reach a wider audience in Ireland with the establishment of private galleries such as the Dawson Gallery and the Hendriks Gallery in Dublin and the public commissioning of works such as the minimalist sculptures of John Burke (1946–   ) and Michael Bulfin (1939–   ). Cecil King (1921–1986) and Patrick Scott (1921–   ) embraced US influences with their hard-edge abstract paintings. Abstraction has remained a key concern for Irish artists, many of whom have responded to it in terms which are informed by their nationality. In 1961 the founding of the Graphic Studio in Dublin by the foremost printmaker of the period, Patrick Hickey (1927–1997), was of great significance for the development of this area. In 1967 the multimedia Project Arts Centre was established; it has recently reopened in refurbished premises in Dublin's Temple Bar. Criticism of contemporary art, so limited in the 1930s and 1940s, is now accessible in broadsheet newspapers and in specialized publications such as *Circa*. Since the 1980s conceptual art in the form of installation and performance has become an important means of expression for a new generation of Irish artists.

MOHER, CLIFFS OF

Spectacular sheer cliffs of dark sandstone topped by black shale in County Clare, on the southwest edge of the ⇨Burren, overlooking the Aran Islands. Extending for 8 km/5 mi, they rise from 115 m/400 ft, at the southern extremity of Hag's Head, to a height of 200 m/700 ft. The stratified layers of shale and sandstone lie on a bed of limestone, and contain a band of unusual fossils. Breanan Mór, a 70 m/244 ft-high sea stack, stands offshore at the northern end of the cliffs. A coastal path leads along the clifftops to O'Brien's

Tower, a circular folly built near the highest point by Cornelius O'Brien (1801–1857) in 1835. A visitors' centre lies 5 km/3m northwest of Liscannor.

The cliffs are named after the ancient fort of Mothar on Hag's Head, now the site of a signal tower built during the Napoleonic Wars.

MOLLOY, M(ICHAEL) J(OSEPH)

(1917–1994)

Folk-dramatist, born in Milltown, County Galway. Molloy was greatly influenced by the work of J M ⇨Synge, a leading figure of the early 20th-century Gaelic revival. His drama is essentially folk theatre that sympathetically portrays the poverty of rural life and the ever-threatened culture of traditional Ireland. His first play, *Old Road* (1943), was produced at the Abbey Theatre, Dublin, and his best-known work is the love story of Bartley Dowd in *The King of Friday's Men* (1948).

Molloy originally trained for the priesthood at St Columba's College, Derry, but left due to ill health.

MOLLY MAGUIRES

Irish-American secret society active in the Pennsylvania coalfields, USA, where it was responsible for the assassination of several law officers and coalmining officials in the late 1860s and 1870s. The outgrowth of an Irish agrarian secret society, the Mollys were so-named because its members used women's clothes as a disguise. The society developed under the protection of the ⇨Ancient Order of Hibernians, an Irish-American benevolent society, amidst severe industrial discontent in the Pennsylvania anthracite mines.

The success of conventional unions led to a cessation of the Molly's activities in the early 1870s, but a return of depression produced a renewed spate of strikes and violence against coal-company property and officials for which the Molly were held responsible. Intensive penetration of the society by Pinkertons (agents planted by the Pinkerton Detective Agency), and ruthless repression in 1877 led to the arrest of over 50 individuals, 20 of whom were given long prison sentences and 20 of whom were hanged.

MOLYNEUX, WILLIAM (1656–1698)

Philosopher, political writer, and scientist. Born in Dublin, Molyneux was educated at Trinity College, Dublin, and the Middle Temple. An important philosophical presence in the 17th century, he translated the French philosopher Decartes' *Meditations* in 1680 and was the author of the question: 'What knowledge of the visual world can a blind man have?' In the context of Irish history, his most influential work was a defence of Irish autonomy in *The Case of Ireland's Being Bound by Acts of Parliament in England, Stated* (1698), a treatise later adopted by nationalist and republican movements.

One of the founders in 1683 of the Dublin Philosophical Society, he also corresponded with the English philosopher John Locke on various topics, including mathematics and the science of optics. Molyneux explored these subjects in his *Sciothericum Telescopium* (1686) and *Dioptrica Nova* (1692).

MONAGHAN (Irish *Mhuineachain*)

County of the Republic of Ireland, in the province of Ulster; county town ⇨Monaghan; area 1,290 sq km/498 sq mi; population (1996) 51,300. The county is low and rolling, with hills in the northwest, the highest point being Slieve Beagh (381 m/1,217 ft). The principal towns are Clones, Carrickmacross, and Castleblayney. Rivers include the Finn and the Glyde in the south, and the Blackwater in the north. Much of the county is fertile. The main form of agriculture is dairy farming, but cattle and pigs are also raised, and cereals and potatoes grown. Industries include leather, linen, knitwear, footwear, furniture, and lace-making.

waterways

None of Monaghan's rivers is navigable. The Ulster Canal, which unites loughs Neagh and Erne (both in Northern Ireland), traverses the county near Monaghan and Clones, but is now disused.

MONAGHAN

County town of County ⇨Monaghan; population (1996) 5,600. Monaghan lies in an agricultural area and is a popular fishing centre.

The 19th-century St Macartan's cathedral in Monaghan is in Gothic revival style. Rossmore Forest Park is adjacent to the town.

Monaghan was the birthplace of the nationalist leader Charles Gavan Duffy (1816–1903), who went on to become prime minister of Victoria, Australia. St Macartan's College, the seminary of the Clogher diocese, is 2 km/1 mi to the north.

MONASTERBOICE

Ancient monastic settlement in County Louth, Republic of Ireland; 10 km/6 mi northwest of Drogheda. It is said to have been founded by St Buite in the 5th century and contains the ruins of two churches, three sculptured early Christian crosses, and the tallest round tower in Ireland (33 m/110 ft), now missing its cap.

Muireadach's Cross is over 5 m/17 ft high and highly ornamented. The West Cross is 6.5 m/21 ft high.

MONASTERIES

When the first Christian missionaries came to Ireland in the 5th century they brought with them the ideal and practice of the monastic life, whereby men and women lived lives of prayer and either did good work in the community or became hermits. The monastic life flourished in Ireland and became an important part of its domestic and missionary activity in Britain and Europe. Some, such as Clonard, County Meath, housed centres of learning that enjoyed a reputation throughout Europe, but all played important pastoral and political roles and many produced significant works of religious art. The wealth of the Irish monastic sites attracted marauding Vikings from the mid-8th century.

In the 12th century, church structures, discipline, and authority were centralized in Europe, and new monastic orders, such as the Cistercian order, were introduced to Ireland from the continent. Their influence grew after the Norman invasion and some of Ireland's most splendid church architecture dates from this period. The strict contemplative orders were joined by the more pastorally engaged groups, such as the Dominican and Franciscan friars.

All orders suffered during the 16th-century Reformation, losing their property and status. The monastic system as it existed in the Middle Ages disappeared, along with the educational, health, and social services provided by many of the houses. Some orders did survive, however, and the Franciscans in particular played a role in the internal reform of Catholicism in the 17th century. While the Franciscans, Dominicans, Augustinians, and some others maintained a presence in the 18th century, it was the following century that saw the return of the contemplative orders, male and female, to monasteries such as Mount Mellary in County Waterford and Roscrea in County Tipperary.

In the latter part of the 20th century, vocations to the monastic life declined.

MONTAGUE, JOHN (1929–   )

Poet, born in Brooklyn, New York. Montague spent his childhood on the family farm in County Tyrone, and studied in Dublin. His collections of verse include *Tides* (1970); *The Rough Field* (1972), about Northern Ireland; *A Slow Dance* (1975); *Selected Poems* (1982); and *New Selected Poems* (1990). His Catholic background, unusual for a poet of Northern Ireland, is reflected in his political verse and poems about his family. He has also edited several verse anthologies.

Montague worked in France and the USA before returning to Ireland to lecture at Cork University.

The whole landscape a manuscript / we had lost the skill to read, / A part of our past disinherited; / But fumbled, like a blind man, / Along the fingertips of instinct.

JOHN MONTAGUE 'The Rough Field' (1972).

❧

MOONEY, RIA (1903–1973)

Actor and drama teacher. She had a long association with the ⇨Abbey Theatre in Dublin, her home town, and was its first woman director (1948–63).

Mooney was on stage from the age of six. She first appeared at the Abbey in 1924, won acclaim for her performance in Seán O'Casey's *The Plough and The Stars* in 1926, and made her US acting debut in 1927. After a short spell at Dublin's Gate Theatre, she returned to the Abbey in 1935, and was put in charge of its experimental Peacock Theatre two years later.

MOORE, BRIAN (1921–1999)

Irish-born novelist, born into a Catholic family in Belfast. Moore emigrated to Canada in 1948 and then to the USA in 1959. His books include *Judith Hearne* (1955), reissued in the USA as *The Lonely Passion of Judith Hearne* in 1956; *The Temptation of Eileen Hughes* (1981); *Black Robe* (1985); and *The Colour of Blood* (1987), shortlisted for the Booker Prize. After 1987 his style became far more economical and accessible; novels from that period include the Booker-shortlisted *Lies of Silence* (1990), *No Other Life*

(1993), *The Statement*, and *The Magician's Wife*. Catholicism, obsession, and the contrast between dreams and reality are recurrent and powerful themes, depicted with stylistic economy and realism.

Other works include *The Luck of Ginger Coffey* (1960) and *The Emperor of Ice-Cream* (1966). Moore's earliest novels were published under the pen name Michael Bryan.

MOORE, CHRISTY

(1945–)

Folk singer born in Dublin whose first solo album, *Prosperous* (1972), is regarded as ground breaking in the history of Irish song and the folk revival, departing from the performance style of previous ballad bands such as the Clancy Brothers and the Dubliners. He was a co founder of the bands Planxty (1971) and Moving Hearts (1981), two of the most influential groups in Irish contemporary music, but is best known as a solo performer. His live appearances combine folk guitar and hand-played bodhrán with powerful political and social messages contained in covers, traditional, and self-penned songs.

Moore began as a solo singer, working the folk clubs and pubs between spells of manual labouring and bank work in both the Republic of Ireland and England. His songs confront controversial issues such as nuclear power and the political situation in Northern Ireland (and elsewhere), but are also tinged with surreal humour. His last recording, *Traveller*, was released in 1999 but ill health forced him to retire from performance soon afterwards. Other important recordings include *Ride On* (1984).

MOORE, GEORGE (AUGUSTUS)

(1852–1933)

Writer, born at Moore Hall, Ballyglass, County Mayo, the son of a Catholic landowner and nationalist MP.

CHRISTY MOORE *Moore has acknowledged how the support of his fans helped him come to terms with having to retire from live performance because of ill health, in 1999. Since then he has concentrated on songwriting and recording.*

Moore was educated in England at Oscott College, Birmingham. Moore's early fiction did much to revitalize the Victorian novel. His debut *A Modern Lover* (1883) was sexually frank for its time and was banned in some quarters. His *Esther Waters* (1894) is a masterpiece of realism, recounting the life of a domestic servant.

As a young man Moore studied painting in Paris but quickly decided he was not a painter; as a writer, his realistic presentations of both his own experiences and historical moments prove his talent as a storyteller. His many works, some of which are highly acclaimed plays, include the drama *The Bending of the Bough* (1900), and the novels *The Untilled Field* (1903), *In Single Strictness* (1922), and *Heloïse and Abelard* (1921).

MOORE, THOMAS

(1779–1852)

Poet, born in Dublin. Moore studied law and was appointed registrar to the Admiralty Prize Court in Bermuda. In 1801 his collection of amorous poetry, *The Poetical Works of the Late Thomas Little, Esq.*, appeared. His most lasting achievement were the *Irish Melodies* (1807–34), for which the music was arranged by John Stevenson (1761–1833). *Lalla Rookh* (1817), with its Eastern setting, was one of the most popular verse romances of the day.

*e*rin, thy silent tear shall never cease, / Erin, thy languid smile ne'er shall increase, / Till, like the rainbow's light / Thy various tints unite / And form in heaven's sight / One arch of peace!

THOMAS MOORE 'Erin! The Tear and the Smile in thine Eyes' in *Irish Melodies* (1807–35).

Silent, oh Moyle, be the roar of thy waters, / Break not ye breezes your chain of repose, / While mournfully weeping Lir's lonely daughter / Tells the nightstar her sad tale of woes!

THOMAS MOORE 'Song of Fionnula'.

~

The amusing *Fudge Family in Paris* (1818) was written in the manner of his *Intercepted Letters; or Twopenny Post-bag* (1813), in which he lampooned the Prince Regent and his associates. Other works include *The Memoirs of Captain Rock* (1824), an ironic and effective indictment of English policy in Ireland. Moore was a close friend of the English poet Byron.

MORAN, DAVID PATRICK (1869–1936)

Author and journalist, born in County Waterford. Moran was founder and editor of the *Leader* (1900–40), a weekly journal which combined classic Irish nationalism with a rejection of some Sinn Féin policies, notably trade protectionism. He was also critical of W B Yeats and of aspects of the Irish literary movement which he considered ersatz. His book *The Philosophy of Irish Ireland* (1905) won him a wide following, but his journal did not long survive his death.

MORGAN, SYDNEY (LADY MORGAN)

(born Owenson) (*c.* 1783–1859)

Writer, born at sea. Morgan was educated at the Huguenot school in Clontarf, County Dublin, and accompanied her actor–manager father Robert Owenson on his tours through Ireland. Her volume of poems set to Irish tunes, *Twelve Original Hibernian Melodies* (1805), were a forerunner of Thomas ⇨Moore's *Irish Melodies*. She then wrote the novels *St Clair* (1804), *The Novice of St Dominick* (1805), and *The Wild Irish Girl* (1806), the book which established her reputation. Mature works include *O'Donnell* (1814) and *The O'Briens and the O'Flaherties* (1827), which strongly supported Catholic emancipation, and describes the variety of life in Connacht, which she knew well, having spent time there as a young girl. *Passages from my Autobiography* appeared in 1859.

MORRISON

Dynasty of Irish architects, spanning four generations in the 18th and 19th centuries. Its most eminent members were the Neo-Gothic architect Richard Morrison (1767–1849), author of the influential *Useful and Ornamental Designs in Architecture* (1793), and his son, William Vitruvius Morrison (1794–1838). Designers of numerous country houses, together they created one of the most significant architectural alliances in Ireland during the early 19th century.

Richard Morrison was a student at Dublin Society's School of Architectural Drawing, where he reputedly studied under the Classical architect James ⇨Gandon, before starting a practice in Clonmel. His career was launched with *Useful and Ornamental Designs in Architecture*, copies of which penetrated as far as Philadelphia, USA, by the end of the 18th century. In the early 1800s Morrison introduced the Neo-Gothic style of English architect James Wyatt to Irish architecture, which was still being built in the Classical Gandonian manner, and built his reputation redesigning country houses outside Dublin. These included the houses of Carton and Lyons in County Kildare, and Pakenham Hall, County Westmeath.

Richard's son, William Morrison, trained as an architect and spent time in Europe. After entering partnership with his father, their joint projects included Ballyfin, County Leix; Fota House, County Cork; Borris House, County Carlow; and Templemore Priory, County Tipperary.

MORRISON, GEORGE (1922–   )

Director and archivist. Morrison's film-making career is forever linked to two major actuality films, *Mise Eire/I Am Ireland* (1959) and *Saoirse?/Freedom?* (1961). These, as well as tracing the struggle for Irish independence up to the outbreak of the Irish Civil War in 1922, helped save a large portion of contemporary Irish newsreel film from being lost or destroyed. In the process, national awareness was raised about this period of Irish history and the valuable use that could be made of archival material.

Morrison went on to make other documentaries, but none of them matched the impact of his first two films.

MORRISON, VAN

Singer, songwriter, and saxophonist; see ⇨Van Morrison

MORTIMER

Family from the Welsh Marches, who acquired Dunamase in Leinster, Ireland, in 1247 and the lordship of Trim in 1308. Roger Mortimer, 1st Earl of March (died 1330), served as lieutenant to the English crown in Ireland, as did several of his heirs. In 1368 the 3rd Earl, Edmund Mortimer (died 1381), inherited the de Burgh claim to Connacht and Ulster through marriage to King Edward III's granddaughter Philippa, heiress to the territories. Though frequently absent from Ireland because of their prominent role in English affairs, they sought hard to exploit their Irish lands, but the line came to an end with the death of Edmund Mortimer, 5th Earl of March and 8th Earl of Ulster (1391–1425), and their vast Irish estate eventually became vested in the crown in 1461.

MORYSON, FYNES (1566–1630)

English adventurer and writer. Moryson travelled extensively in Europe and the Middle East before visiting Ireland in 1600 as secretary to Lord ⇨Mountjoy, lord deputy of Ireland. His observations and experiences of wartime Ireland during the rebellion of 1593–1603, led by Hugh ⇨O'Neill, 2nd Earl of Tyrone, form part of his massive work *An Itinerary*, published in 1617. Although colourful and informative, and a much-mined source by historians and other commentators, his account is deeply biased, not only by Moryson's own unquestioned sense of cultural superiority, but also by his implicit attack on those who still regarded the native Irish as being capable of peaceful assimilation into English culture.

MOUNT IEVERS COURT

Country house at Sixmilebridge, Country Clare, built on the site of an earlier castle by Henry Ievers to designs by the architect John Rothery. Famously resembling a doll's house with its elegant four-storey, seven-bay proportions in pink brick, this property is widely considered one of the finest early country houses in Ireland and may have been based upon Inigo Jones's Chevening House in Kent, England.

MOUNTJOY, CHARLES BLOUNT (1st Earl of Devonshire, 8th Baron Mountjoy)

See Charles ⇨Blount.

MOUNTJOY CASTLE

Square castle on the shores of Lough Neagh, County Tyrone. It was built in the early 1600s for Charles Blount, 8th Baron Mountjoy. A central keep and two corner towers survive. The castle was used during the campaign against Hugh O'Neill, Earl of Tyrone, and ownership changed between English and Irish forces several times in the 1640s. It was also used by the armies of William III and James II in the late 17th century.

MOUNT STEWART HOUSE

Country house near Greyabbey, County Down. The oldest part of this Classical 1820s house dates from the early 1800s, or possibly as early as the 1780s, when the 1st Marquess of Londonderry built a modest house designed by the English architect George Dance the Younger. Three rooms and a staircase and balustrade of the original house still survive. It was enlarged in the 1820s to its present size, the architect being William Vitruvius ⇨Morrison. In the grounds is one of the finest 18th-century garden buildings in Ireland, the octagonal banqueting house known as the Temple of the Winds.

The house was the childhood home of Lord Castlereagh (1769–1822), member of parliament for County Down, who helped steer through the Irish parliament the 1801 Act of Union, that created the United Kingdom of Great Britain and Ireland.

MOUNT USHER GARDENS

Gardens created by the Walpole family near Ashford, County Wicklow. They date from 1868, cover about 8 ha/20 acres, and contain many exotic tender plant species as well as native flora. The River Varity winds through the gardens and is flanked by plants from all parts of the world.

MOURNE MOUNTAINS (or MOUNTAINS OF MOURNE)

Mountain range in the south of County Down, extending from above Newcastle to Carlingford Lough. The highest summit is Slieve Donard; height 852 m/2,795 ft. The mountains are of granite.

MUCKROSS ABBEY

Franciscan abbey situated on a peninsula separating the upper and lower Lakes of Killarney, County Kerry. It was founded about 1440 by Donal MacCarthy, the chieftain of Desmond. Despite the abbey being formally repressed in 1542, the friars remained until about 1589. They regained possession later and restored the abbey in 1626, but the Cromwellian forces burned it in 1652, after which time the site was abandoned. The most attractive features include the east window and the cloisters that surround a gigantic and ancient yew tree.

MULLEN, KARL (1926–)

Rugby player, born in Wexford. Ireland's most successful captain ever, he led his team to three Five Nations titles in four years, between 1948 and 1951. Making his debut in 1947, his leadership saw Ireland take the Grand Slam a year later, a feat that no other Irish team has since managed to do. Playing as a hooker, he was capped 25 times for his country and also captained the British Lions for their tour to Australia and New Zealand in 1950.

MULLINGAR

County town of County ⇨Westmeath, on the River Brosna; population (1996) 8,000. It is an important road and rail junction and was a harbour on the (now disused) Royal Canal that links Dublin and the River Shannon. It is a cattle market and trout-fishing centre. Industries include tobacco, vinyl, furniture, and pencils.

MUCKROSS ABBEY *Despite the destruction of the abbey at the hands of Cromwell's troops in 1652, burials continued here, and the remains of three Kerry poets of the 17th and 18th centuries, Geoffrey O'Donoghue, Egan O'Rahilly, and Owen Roe O'Sullivanlie, lie within the abbey grounds.*

Mullingar was the base for the troops of William III during the siege of Athlone in 1691 against the Jacobites. Nearby on Lough Ennell is the ring fort of Dun na Sciath, former seat of Malachy, High King of Ireland. The Catholic Cathedral of Christ the King was dedicated in 1939.

MULLINS, BRIAN (1954–)

Gaelic footballer, born in Dublin. A towering presence in midfield for Dublin, he won three All-Ireland medals under Kevin Heffernan in 1974, 1976, and 1977. He suffered serious injuries in a car accident in 1980 but made a miraculous recovery to win his fourth championship in 1983. One of the greatest of all Irish sportsmen, he was at the peak of his powers in the mid-1970s. His exceptional aerial skills later saw him switch to rugby, playing for the Dublin clubs Blackrock College and Clontarf.

MUNSTER

Historic southern province of the Republic of Ireland, comprising the counties of Clare, Cork, Kerry, Limerick, North and South Tipperary, and Waterford; area 24,140 sq km/9,318 sq mi; population (1996) 1,033,900.

Before Henry II's reign, Munster was divided into two kingdoms, Desmond and Thomond, whose rulers bore the title and rank of king of Munster alternately. The English conquest of Ireland began during Henry II's reign, and the province was settled by the English in plantations from 1586.

MUNSTER PLANTATION

A major confiscation of native Irish lands in counties Cork, Kerry, Limerick, and Waterford by the English crown in 1586, following the death in rebellion of Gerald Fitzgerald, 14th and last Earl of Desmond (*c.* 1533–1583). Originally estimated at some 245,000 ha/600,000 acres, the surveys and claims

*T*he Spaniard and others have reported a long time since that, if the Princes of England knew what a jewel Ireland were, they needed not to seek the discovery of foreign countries to settle in.

SIR GEORGE CAREW English governor of Munster
Plan for the Reformation of Ireland (1603).

were greatly overstated and ultimately only half that amount was actually confiscated for Protestant English colonization.

Rapid growth of the plantation in the 1580s and early 1590s was accompanied by severe disputes between both English settlers and native Irish, and among the settlers themselves. In 1598 a native Irish uprising effectively destroyed the first colonies and ruined several of the early investors, including the planter poet Edmund ⇨Spenser. Re-established following the rebels' defeat in 1601, the plantation grew steadily. The extraction of timber and iron yielded large profits but the plantation areas also rapidly developed a strong export trade in cattle and sheep. By 1641 the plantation was securely established with an expanding population that had grown from just over 3,000 in 1592 to an estimated 22,000.

MURPHY, ARTHUR (1727–1805)

Playwright, lawyer, and writer, born in Clomquin, County Roscommon. Murphy turned to the stage to pay off his debts, writing and producing his first successful farce, *The Upholsterer*, in 1758. His later writings include a translation of Tacitus (1793), and two poorly received biographical works, 'Essay on Johnson' (1792), and *Life of David Garrick* (1801).

Murphy was educated at St Omer, France, and worked as a clerk in Cork and then London 1747–51. In 1757 he entered Lincoln's Inn, and in 1762 became a barrister. Throughout his legal career he maintained his theatrical and literary interests, publishing the weekly *Gray's Inn Journal* (1752–74), through which he made the acquaintance of Samuel Johnson, and writing farces and adaptations for the stage.

MURPHY, DERVLA MARY (1931–)

Travel writer, born in Lismore, County Waterford.

*t*he bards in their beds once beat out ballads, / under leaky thatch listening to sea-birds, / But she in the long ascendancy of rain / Served biscuits on a tray with ginger wine.

RICHARD MURPHY 'The Woman of the House' in *Sailing to an Island* (1963).

Murphy's first journey was an intrepid bicycle ride through Afghanistan and India. Her books include *Full Tilt* (1965), *Tibetan Foothold* (1966), *In Ethiopia with a Mule* (1968), *Eight Feet in the Andes* (1983), *Cameroon with Egbert* (1989), *The Ukimwi Road* (1993), *South from the Limpopo* (1997), and *One Foot in Laos* (1999). Travelling with minimal resources in the UK as well as in Asia, Africa, and South America, her responses to both people and landscapes are reported with warmth and originality.

MURPHY, JIMMY (JAMES BARRY) (1954–)

Gaelic footballer and hurler, born in Cork. From the St Finbar's club, Murphy was first spotted as a minor hurler by the legendary Christy ⇨Ring. He won his first senior medal in 1973, playing Gaelic football for Cork in the All-Ireland win over Dublin. In 1976 he was part of the Cork hurlers three-in-a-row side, where he played at forward. He captained the team in back-to-back finals in 1982 and 1983, being defeated by Kilkenny on both occasions, but collected two more championships in 1984 and 1986. He retired the following year, but in 1999 he managed the Cork Senior Hurlers to victory in the All-Ireland final against Kilkenny.

MURPHY, PAT (1951–)

Director and scriptwriter, born in Dublin. Murphy has made only three feature films: *Maeve* (co-director, John Davies, 1982), *Anne Devlin* (1984), and after a gap of 15 years, *Nora* (2000) but they are amongst the most culturally critical of the new Irish cinema. *Maeve* explores the relationship between republicanism and feminism in Northern Ireland. In *Anne Devlin*, Murphy sought to uncover the 'hidden history' of this woman whose association with the 1803 rebellion against British rule in Ireland has been submerged and overshadowed by the elevation to mythic status of the rebellion's leader, Robert Emmet. *Nora* is the story of Nora Barnacle and James Joyce.

MURPHY, RICHARD (1927–)

Writer and eclectic poet, whose work reflects a life of many travels. Born at Milford House, County Mayo, he lived in Ceylon (now Sri Lanka) as a child, where his father worked in the colonial service, and was educated at Magdalen College, Oxford, and the Sorbonne, Paris. He ran a school in Crete 1953–54

TRADITIONAL IRISH MUSIC – DISTINCTIVE, VIBRANT AND PLAYED BY THOUSANDS

by Niall Keegan

Traditional Irish music was the music historically played and sung by the peasant and, to some extent, the working classes of Ireland. Although only one of the many musical traditions of Ireland, and no longer confined to these two social groups, it is considered distinctly Irish. An important part of this music genre is the instrumental tradition, although its roots are largely from outside Ireland.

instruments

The instrumentation of traditional Irish music is relatively recent and very few of the instruments used are indigenous, those most distinctively Irish being the uilleann pipes and the bodhrán. The uilleann pipes, a complex bellows-blown bagpipe, with up to seven different pipes, is probably descended from an Irish war-pipe, similar to the Scottish bagpipes, which is thought to have disappeared by the 18th century for political reasons. The bodhrán is an Irish frame drum usually struck with a stick but sometimes by the hand. It is constructed from a round wooden frame, often containing a wooden cross, and has a head normally made from goat skin. Although the origins of the bodhrán are unknown, it is associated with pre-Christian ritual, particularly the Wren Hunting Festival of St Stephen's Day (26 December) and the festival of St Bridget, a Christianized pagan goddess, on 1 February. Seán Ó Riada (1930–1971) brought the bodhrán into the mainstream tradition with his innovative ensemble performances of the 1960s.

Virtually all the other major instruments of the tradition have been imported into Ireland over the past 300 years. Perhaps the most important instrument, the fiddle, appeared in Ireland in the mid-17th century, soon after its development in Italy, although bowed instruments, also referred to as fiddles, had been played in Ireland for centuries prior to this. The flute came from England in the last half of the 19th century, the precursor to the modern classical flute. However, 19th-century English wooden flutes are preferred by traditional players to this day. The accordion and concertina, introduced around the end of the 19th century, were the first instruments to be associated with female performers. At the beginning of the 20th century the adaptation of traditional music to the new dance halls of the USA, and especially the new phenomenon of the dance band, led to the acquisition of instruments from popular jazz at the time, most notably the tenor four-string banjo and the piano. The folk revival of the 1950s and 1960s, and the development of concert bands, involved the introduction of the guitar, bouzouki (a form of mandolin from Greece), various keyboards, and much of the instrumentation used in modern popular music.

The repertoire performed by these instruments is also recent. Generally traditional dance music has a very sym-

Eugene Lambe with the uilleann pipes. Instead of being blown with the mouth, this instrument rests on the player's lap and is operated by a bellows tucked under the arm, and pumped with the elbow.

metrical structure related to the structure of the various traditional Irish dances. The most popular tune type today, the reel, is believed to have been brought to Ireland in the 17th century by the Scots-Irish ancestors of the Protestant community in Northern Ireland. The reel can most accurately be accounted for in split common time or 2/2, where each beat is divided into 4. The jig was probably introduced earlier and is believed to be of English origin. Its various forms, related to different dances, included the double jig, the single jig, the slip jig, and the slide. Most types of jig can be accurately represented in 6/8 time, where each beat is divided into 3.

The 19th century saw the creation of other dance-tune forms to match the styles of social dancing popular in Europe and North America at that time. These included the hornpipe, polka, barn dance, mazurka, scottische, and highland dancing. Many of these 19th-century tune types declined during the 20th century, but in some areas, particularly County Donegal, a number have survived. The aesthetics of dance music performance are naturally tied up in rhythm, a good performance being noted by its accentuation of rhythm using a variety of stylistic factors.

The instrumental tradition meets the song tradition in slow air playing, most often to accompany Irish language songs. Here the rhythm is free and performance more lyrical.

changes in performance practice

During the 20th century the sound of traditional music was radically altered by new performance contexts. Traditional Irish music had formerly been a rural, amateur, recreational activity for the peasant classes; its playing was mainly for dancing, and most music was to be heard at the house dance or at religious festivals, such as the patterns, or fair days. Individual local musicians developed local styles of music, some of which survive to this day, such as Sligo–Leitrim style, Ballinakill style (a parish in East Galway), South West Clare style, or Sliabh Luachra style (a culturally defined area around the border between counties Cork and Kerry). Traditonal music was non-harmonic and its performance was probably mostly solo. The only musicians that could be regarded as professional or semi-professional were the travelling musicians who would have earned part of their income from teaching music. Many of these were from the travelling community, in which the tradition of music playing would have been passed from parent to child.

The first significant changes in performance practice

came in America at the beginning of the 20th century, when traditional musicians had to provide music in an acoustic dance hall setting. This led to the formation of the first formalized ensembles. Bands such as Dan Sullivan's Shamrock Band and The Flanagan Brothers dominated the American music scene and produced loud, rhythmical music for Irish and popular American dances. The Ballinakill Ceili Band from Galway, formed in 1926, was the first traditional dance band in Ireland. More bands were formed when much of the Republic of Ireland's music and dancing was forced into halls after the 1936 Dance Hall Act. In the same period, new technological advances in the media, such as 78 rpm records, cylinder recordings, and radio, aided the dissemination of traditional Irish music. In this way, musicians such as the fiddler Michael Coleman gained rapid popularity by reaching an audience throughout Ireland. Despite these early triumphs, traditional music went into decline between the 1930s and 1950s; like much of traditional culture, its music was regarded as something backward.

revival and renewal

Since the 1960s the international folk revival has brought about a reversal in these fortunes, with bands like the Clancy Brothers, Tommy Makem, and the Dubliners performing alternative traditional music attractive to a new and younger audience. Ceoltóirí Chualainn and Seán Ó Riada placed traditional music into a formal, classical music environment, while in the 1970s bands like the Bothy Band, DeDanann, and Planxty introduced traditional music into the popular music scene. Bands such as the Horslips, Stockton's Wing, and Moving Hearts have sought to fuse traditional music and rock directly by adding electric guitars, drum kits, and other rock instruments to their traditional instrumentation. Deiseal, Sharon Shannon, and others have attempted to draw from jazz in the way they arrange traditional material. Many composers, such as Mícheál Ó Súilleabháin, Sean Davey, and Bill Whelan, have mixed classical and traditional idioms. Some have drawn from the repertoire, instrumentation, and style of other folk traditions; Bill Whelan's music for the stage-show *Riverdance* draws on Balkan rhythms, Spanish flamenco, rock instrumentation, and classical music arrangements.

However, the strength of Irish traditional music lies in the thousands of excellent amateur traditional musicians who perform regularly in informal pub sessions throughout the island.

before settling on Inishbofin Island, off Galway. Murphy often uses journeys and rites of passage as topics for his writing. His several collections of poetry include *Sailing to an Island* (1963), which concentrates on life at sea; *High Island* (1974); *The Price of Stone* (1985); and *The Mirror Wall* (1989), which incorporates Sri Lankan artistic influences. He won the Æ Memorial Award in 1951 and the Guinness Poetry Award in 1962.

MURPHY, TOM (1935–)

Dramatist, born in Tuam, County Galway. His work directly confronts human violence, exploring late 20th-century Irish life as it contradicts the ideals of the Catholic church and the Republic's founding poets and politicians.

Murphy was educated by the Christian Brothers and originally trained as a metalworker. After his early plays were rejected by the Abbey Theatre, Dublin, he moved to London where he achieved success with *A Whistle in the Dark* (1961) and *Famine* (1968). He returned to Ireland in 1970. *Morning After Optimism* (1971) is his most experimental play, while *Conversations on a Homecoming* (1985) presents sympathetic female characters who are sources of both inspirational hope and generosity of spirit.

MURPHY, WILLIAM MARTIN (1844–1919)

Business executive and newspaper proprietor, and an Irish Party member of parliament 1885–92. He developed the faltering *Irish Daily Independent* into the successful ⇨*Irish Independent* in 1905, crushing the *Freeman's Journal* with a combination of price-cutting, modern technology, and an appeal to the middle ground in Irish nationalist and Catholic sentiment. He also owned the *Irish Catholic*.

Murphy was born in County Cork, and was already a successful builder when he became a newspaper proprietor. As president of the Dublin Chamber of Commerce 1912–13, he oversaw employer resistance to the Irish Transport and General Workers' Union, which culminated in the lock-out of the James Larkin-led workers in 1913. He refused a knighthood in 1906.

MURRAY, ANN (1949–)

Soprano, born in Dublin. She has performed extensively as an operatic soloist with the English National Opera; the Royal Opera House, Covent Garden; the Metropolitan Opera, New York; La Scala, Milan; the Vienna State Opera; the Bavarian State Opera; and the Saltzburg Festival. She has also sung as a concert performer with the Orchestre de Paris under Rafael Kubelik, the Chicago Symphony Orchestra under Georg Solti, and at both first and last nights of the Proms at the Royal Albert Hall, London. She has an extensive discography and recorded as Purcell's Dido under Nikolaus Harnoncourt, Mozart's Dorabella under James Levine, and Humperdinck's Hansel under Colin Davis.

MUSIC, TRADITIONAL

See feature essay on traditional music, page 246.

It is remarkable how the Irish maintain a musical balance while moving their fingers so rapidly. They play their various instruments with consummate artistry, keeping them in close harmony. The resulting melody is complete and satisfying, played softly or at great speed, with what one can only call a smooth unevenness or a discordant concord.

GIRALDUS CAMBRENSIS Welsh chronicler and ecclesiastic *Topographia Hibernica/Topography of Ireland* (1186).

One point, for Saint Patrick's Day, about Irish music; only the Irish can bear it for long. That is, true Irish music, of course.

MARY KENNY Journalist 'The Real Sound of Ireland', in *The Guardian*, 17 March 1965.

MUSSENDEN TEMPLE

Circular, domed temple in the grounds of the ruined Downhill Castle, Castlerock, County Derry. It is surrounded by Corinthian columns and is sited on a cliff top overlooking the Atlantic. The temple was built in 1783 by Frederick Hervey, 4th Earl of Bristol and Earl Bishop of Derry, and it contained a library. The entrance gates are inspired by the Roman monument at St Rémy, France.

MYTHOLOGICAL ORIGINS OF IRELAND

In legend, an epic struggle was fought for control of the island between successive waves of supernatural and mortal settlers. These included the demonic ⇨Fomorians, the original inhabitants of Ireland, led by the giants Balar and Bres; the Fir Bolg; and the ⇨Tuatha Dé Danann ('people of the goddess ⇨Danu'), a race with magical powers.

The Tuatha Dé Danann, led by Danu's son Nuada, defeated their predecessors, the Fir Bolg, in the first battle of Moytirra. The Fir Bolg were permitted to retire to Connacht, but Nuada lost his arm in the battle and Bres of the Fomorians took control. After Bres was ousted, Nuada, fitted with a cunningly wrought silver hand by the healer Dian Cécht, retrieved his throne. The Fomorians were finally defeated at the second battle of Moytirra, which culminated in the victory of the god-hero ⇨Lugh in single combat against Balar. The Tuatha Dé Danann were eventually defeated by the Milesians (the Celts), mortal ancestors of the Gaels.

According to Gaelic tradition, many tribes of the Tuatha Dé Danaan retired to a distant country beyond the western horizon known as Tír na n'Óg ('land of eternal youth'), while the remainder withdrew to a subterranean otherworld to rule over the ⇨fairy folk, leaving Ireland to the mortals.

Stories of the legendary conquest of Ireland are recounted in the early medieval *Lebor Gabála Érenn/Book of Invasions*, which chronicles the history of Ireland from Creation to the 12th century, and in medieval ⇨hero-tales, such as the epic *Cath Muighe Tuireadh/The Battle of Moytirra*.

MYTHOLOGY

See ⇨hero-tales.

N

NAAS

County town of County ⇨Kildare, 32 km/20 mi southwest of Dublin; population (1996) 14,100. The town has agricultural vehicle manufacturers and distribution industries. Naas was the ancient seat of the kings of Leinster. The 17th-century Jigginstown House, 2 km/1 mi to the south, is one of the earliest brick buildings in Ireland.

There is a racecourse at Naas, and Punchestown racecourse, used for steeplechasing, is 5 km/3 mi to the southwest.

The North Mote in Naas is said to be the site of one of the strongholds of the kings of Leinster. Jigginstown House was built for the Earl of Strafford but was never completed.

NAGLE, NANO (1718–1784)

Catholic nun, founder of the Congregation of the Sisters of Presentation in 1775. She devoted her life to improving the status of Irish Catholics through education. She was born in Ballygriffin, County Cork, but (due to penal law restrictions) was educated in France. She entered the Ursuline Order in France to pray for Irish Catholics who were denied education. Later she returned to Cork and in 1752 established the first of 20 schools in Cork city. To continue her work she introduced the Ursuline Order in 1771, but was frustrated by their rule of enclosure and four years later founded the Sisters of Presentation.

NATIONAL BOTANIC GARDENS

Gardens covering 20 ha/49 acres in the residential Dublin suburb of Glasnevin, established in 1795 but redesigned from 1834 by Ninian Niven; the fine collections of plants include many rare and exotic varieties. The palm houses were built in phases from 1843 to 1876 by Richard Turner of Dublin, who later built the Great Palm House in Kew Gardens, London. The last wing of the palm house had to be rebuilt in 1884 after it collapsed.

The property was once owned by the English poet Thomas Tickell before being sold to the Royal Dublin Society and is famous as having been a meeting place of some of the greatest literary figures of the 18th century. These included Joseph Addison, Patrick Delany, Richard Brinsley Sheridan, Richard Steele, Jonathan Swift, and Thomas Parnell.

NATIONAL BOTANIC GARDENS *Nineteenth-century Dublin ironfounder Richard Turner, who built the greenhouses of Kew Gardens, was also responsible for the Palm House in the National Botanic Gardens in Dublin. The gardens spread over 50 acres, and were founded in 1795.*

NATIONALIST PARTY (of the Republic of Ireland)

The main parliamentary party 1882–1922. Growing out of the ⇨home rule movement, and holding home rule as its main aim, the party was led initially by Charles Stewart ⇨Parnell and latterly by John Redmond (1856–1918). From the mid 1880s, the party held over 80% of the 103 Irish seats in the UK parliament, but this did not prevent three home rule bills being defeated, in 1886, 1893, and 1912. In 1918 the Nationalist party gained only six parliamentary seats.

NATIONALIST PARTY (of Northern Ireland)

Political party which succeeded the all-Ireland Nationalist Party (1882–1922) and became active in the politics of the Northern Ireland parliament after partition in 1921. The party, initially led by Joseph ⇨Devlin, chiefly represented northern Catholics but struggled to gain any political influence through its failure to establish a concrete programme or party discipline. By adopting a non-violent platform and supported by the Catholic church, it mainly appealed to the rural population. Under the leadership of Eddie McAteer (1914–   ), the party acquired new energy and it became the official opposition at the Stormont parliament in 1965. However, in ignoring the civil rights movement of the 1960s, the Nationalist Party was largely supplanted by the ⇨Social Democratic and Labour Party after 1970.

NATIONAL UNIVERSITY OF IRELAND (NUI)

Federal university of the Republic of Ireland. Founded under the Irish Universities' Act (1908) to provide acceptable higher education for Catholics, it originally consisted of three constituent colleges: University College, Dublin; University College, Cork; and University College, Galway. St ⇨Patrick's College, Maynooth, established in 1795 for the training of Catholic priests, became a 'recognized college' of the university in 1913. In 1997 the four colleges became constituent universities of the National University of Ireland.

The Irish Universities' Act was a compromise measure resulting from a protracted struggle between the Catholic church and the state. The secular Queen's Colleges, founded in 1845, were condemned by the Catholic church as 'godless colleges', but the government refused to grant a charter to the denominational Catholic University founded in 1854. The Royal University of Ireland (1879–1908), an examining university, served as a stop-gap measure while the Royal Commission on University Education (1901–03) sought an alternative solution. The subsequent Irish Universities' Act dissolved the Royal University and created the Queen's University of Belfast and the National University of Ireland, leaving ⇨Trinity College, Dublin (TCD) untouched.

NATION, THE

Newspaper, printed 1842–97, that attempted to fuse the Catholic and Protestant religious traditions in Ireland. It was the brainchild of several gifted political journalists, notably Thomas ⇨Davis. Very widely read in its early years, it advocated the repeal of the 1800 Act of Union between Britain and Ireland and the re-establishment of a native Irish parliament.

The paper popularized patriotic ballads and Irish culture, invented the tricolour (symbolizing the union between orange and green) which is now the national flag of the Republic of Ireland, and called for the development of native industry. Its readers (and many of its writers) formed the nucleus of the ⇨Young Ireland movement, which was to lead to the 1848 rebellion. In later years, however, the prosecution and exile of some of its most gifted writers led to a slow decline. The title was briefly revived by other political groups in the early 20th century.

NAVAN

County town of County ⇨Meath; population (1996) 3,400. The rivers Boyne and Blackwater converge at Navan. The chief industry is mineral exploration and mining; large lead and zinc mines are located west of the town. There are also food-processing industries, engineering, and furniture manufacturers here. In the Middle Ages Navan was a strategic outpost of the Pale (the English-held territory around Dublin).

Navan Motte was built during the Anglo-Norman period. Athlumney Castle, 2 km/1 mi to the south, is a 16th-century fortified house; there is also a large souterrain (prehistoric underground dwelling) here. The ruins of Bective Abbey, a 12th-century Cistercian foundation, are 8 km/5 mi south of Navan, and the ruins of Ardbraccan monastery, founded by St Brecan in the 7th century, are 5 km/3 mi to the west. Rathaldron Castle, 3 km/2 mi to the northwest, has a 15th-century tower incorporated into the 19th-century castle. At Donaghmore, 3 km/2 mi north of Navan, are the ruins of a 16th-century church and round tower on the site of a larger church allegedly built by St Patrick. ⇨Tara Hill lies 10 km/6 mi to the south.

NAVAN FORT (Irish *Emain Macha*)

Enormous circular earthwork or hill fort, 4 km/2.5 mi west of Armagh, Northern Ireland; capital and seat of the ancient kings of Ulster. Excavation has revealed that the large mound was constructed in the late Bronze Age, and covered five concentric circles of massive timber posts set around a central mast, possibly a temple or palace. The structure appears to have been roofed over in 100 BC, but was later filled in with stones and burned. Beneath this lies a previous series of circular houses, possibly dating back to 700 BC.

NEAGH, LOUGH

Lake in Northern Ireland, 25 km/15 mi west of Belfast; area 396 sq km/153 sq mi. It is the largest lake in the British Isles, being 27 km/17 mi long, 16 km/10 mi wide, with an average depth of 12 m/39 ft. The shores are mostly flat and marshy; there are a few islands of which Ram's Island is the largest, on which is an early round tower. The lake is famous for trout and eel fishing, and breeding waterbirds.

Lough Neagh is fed by the rivers Blackwater, Ballinderry, and Upper Bann, and is drained north to the Atlantic through the Lower Bann.

NEESON, LIAM (1953–)

Stage and film actor, born in Ballymena, who received an Academy Award nomination for Best Actor for his performance in *Schindler's List* (1993) and starred in the the title role in Neil ⇨Jordan's *Michael Collins* (1996).

Neeson's early career in Ireland included work at the Lyric Players Theatre, Belfast, and the Project and Abbey theatres, Dublin. He made his feature film debut in *Excalibur* (1981), directed by John Boorman. Tall and ruggedly handsome, Neeson has mostly worked in the British and US film industries, where he has played a variety of roles, often that of a lover: to Diane Keaton in *The Good Mother* (1988) and to Mia Farrow in *Husbands and Wives* (1992). His Irish roles have included *Lamb* (1985), in which he plays a Christian Brother who takes a boy away from a penal educational institution and goes on the run; as an IRA

hit man in *A Prayer for the Dying* (1987); and as a ghost in Neil Jordan's *High Spirits* (1988). Neeson's Broadway performance in *Anna Christie* won him a Tony Award (1993) and brought him to the attention of Stephen Spielberg who cast him in the title role in *Schindler's List*.

Other films include *The Mission* (1986), *Duet for One* (1986), *The Dead Pool* (1988), *Next of Kin* (1989), *The Big Man* (1990), *Ethan Frome* (1993), *Deception* (1993), *Nell* (1994), *Rob Roy* (1995), *Before and After* (1996), *Les Misintrables* (1998), *Star Wars: The Phantom Menace* (1999), and *The Haunting* (1999).

NENAGH

Town in northern County Tipperary; population (1996) 5,600. It is situated 18 km/11 mi northeast of Killaloe and 8 km/5 mi from Lough Derg. The principal industry is pharmaceuticals. Nenagh Castle is a Norman circular keep built around 1200 by Theobald Fitzwalter, an ancestor of the Earls of Ormond. The upper part was restored in 1860.

Nenagh has the ruins of a Franciscan friary founded in the 13th century, and there is a heritage centre in the heptagonal governors' house of the old county jail. The ruins of the Augustinian Tyone Abbey, founded in 1200, are 2 km/1 mi southeast of Nenagh, and 6 km/4 mi east, at Rathurles, is a ring fort with the ruins of an early gatepost and a 15th-century church inside.

NEUTRALITY

Cornerstone of Irish foreign policy in the Irish Free State/Eire/Republic of Ireland, adopted following the outbreak of World War II. From the 1960s Irish neutrality was usefully combined with a prominent 'nonaligned' role in Cold War diplomacy and United Nations (UN) peacekeeping operations. Moves in the 1990s towards creating a European military force, with NATO backing, saw the debate on neutrality once again become a central issue.

Neutrality became possible when control of the 'treaty ports' in southern Ireland, which Britain had retained after the Anglo-Irish Treaty (1921), was handed to Éamon de Valera's Fianna Fáil government in 1938. Following the outbreak of World War II, and despite Irish membership of the Commonwealth, de Valera declared Ireland neutral, an action that provoked much hostility from critics in Britain and the USA.

Neutrality was adopted for reasons of pragmatism rather than morality. Entry into World War II would have destabilized Ireland, and de Valera actually authorized secret cooperation with the Allies on defence issues. Despite this, and Ireland's failed attempts to join NATO in 1949, neutrality came to be seen as a moral principle.

NEWBRIDGE (Irish *Droichead Nua*)

Town in County Kildare; population (1996) 6,600. It is situated on the River Liffey, 10 km/6 mi northeast of Kildare town; the ➪Curragh racecourse is 2 km/1 mi away. The chief industry is the processing of peat from the Bog of Allen; dental health-care products, carpets, and cutlery are also manufactured. On the banks of the Liffey is a large motte 12 m/40 ft high.

Newbridge is a former garrison town. At Great Connell, 2 km/1 mi to the southeast, are the ruins of the Augustinian priory of Our Lady and St David, founded by Myler FitzHenry in 1202, which was an important monastery during the Middle Ages. The Hill of Allen, 8 km/5 mi to the northwest, was the site of a stronghold of the kings of Leinster. The large stone tower on the summit was erected in 1859

NEWCASTLE WEST

Market town in County Limerick, 40 km/25 mi southwest of the city of Limerick; population (1996) 3,300. In the centre of the town is a ruined castle that was built in 1184 for the Knights Templars (Order of St John) and later passed to the Earls of Desmond.

The castle remains include two 15th-century halls, one of which (Desmond Hall) has been restored and is used as a cultural centre.

NEWGRANGE

Outstanding Neolithic passage-grave and the world's oldest known astronomical observatory; one of four great Neolithic burial mounds in the ➪Boyne Valley necropolis, 3 km/5 mi east of Slane, County Meath.

NEW ROSS

Market town in County Wexford, on the River Barrow, 37 km/23 mi west of Wexford town; population (1996) 5,000. New Ross retains its medieval appearance but is now a thriving industrial centre. The main employers are fish exporters and haulage and shipping companies, but there are also many small manufacturers.

New Ross was founded in the 13th century by

NEWGRANGE *This richly engraved threshold stone is one of Ireland's greatest ancient remains, and partly conceals the entrance to a passage-grave dating from 2500 BC. The site was once ringed by standing stones, of which only 12 are left.*

William the Marshall, 1st Earl of Pembroke, and in the medieval period was an important seaport. It was the scene of many conflicts from the 14th to the 16th century and of rebel resistance against the British in 1798 by the United Irishmen. The Gothic ruins of St Mary's Church, founded by William the Marshall, can still be seen.

NEWRY

Town in counties Armagh and Down; population (1991) 19,400. It is situated at the head of Carlingford Lough, 53 km/33 mi southwest of Belfast. It manufactures products for veterinary care and also textiles and electrical goods, and has food and drink processing. An important seaport since medieval times, Newry was connected with Lough Neagh by canals in the 18th century; the first inland canal constructed in Ireland and the UK was at Newry. The canals are now used for angling.

Nothing remains of the Cistercian abbey founded here in 1153 by Maurice MacLoughlin, King of Ireland, and the castle built by de Courcy in 1177. In the 16th century the confiscated lands of Newry were granted to Nicholas Bagenal and the Protestant St Patrick's church includes a tower he built in 1578.

Patrick Brontë, or Prunty (1777–1861), father of the English novelists Anne, Charlotte, and Emily Brontë, was born in Ballynaskeagh, 24 km/15 mi from Newry.

NEWTOWNARDS

Town in County Down, near the head of Strangford Lough; population (1991) 21,000. Synthetic fibre, linen yarn, carpets, and jeans are manufactured here. The town is a shopping centre for a rich farming district and there is food processing. Newtownards was planned in the 17th century, centred on a large square.

The ruins of a Dominican friary founded in 1244 by Walter de Burgh can be seen here, but most of the present town originated during the plantation period.

Scrabo Hill (165 m/540 ft), 2 km/1 mi from Newtownards, is a red sandstone and basalt hill. On its summit is Scrabo Tower, erected as a memorial to the Marquis of Londonderry in 1857. Newtownards has a small airfield.

NICHOLSON, ASENATH (1792–1855)

Teacher, reformer, writer, and traveller. Born in Chelsea, western Vermont, Nicholson spent her life as a teacher advocating reform through temperance, vegetarianism, and abolitionism. She was brought up in the Congregational church, a branch of US Protestantism that emphasized the Bible and individual freedom. In 1944 she travelled to Ireland to distribute Bibles in both English and Irish. She worked in soup kitchens and handed out clothing during the famine. The Protestant colonies at Achill and Ventry attracted her interest, however the published account of her travels, *Ireland's Welcome to the Stranger*, criticized the activities of vigorous evangelicals. Nicholson left Ireland in 1848 and died in relative obscurity from typhoid fever in New Jersey in 1855. Her recently rediscovered *Annals of the Famine in Ireland* (1850–1) provides an invaluable contemporary account of the Irish subsistence crisis.

NICHOLSON, JOHN (1821–1857)

British general and colonial administrator in India, born in Ireland. During the Afghan Wars, Nicholson assisted in the defence of Ghazni in 1841, but was ultimately captured and imprisoned at Kabul. He was eventually rescued by Sir George Pollock. He was administrative officer at Bannu in the Punjab 1851–56, and was highly regarded for the justness of his rule. Promoted to brigadier general in 1857 on the outbreak of the Indian Mutiny, he defeated resistance in the Punjab, but was killed on 14 September during the storming of Delhi.

NÍ CHONAIL, EIBHLÍN (c. 1743–1800)

Poet, born into the O'Connells of Derrynane (County Kerry). Eibhlin (who was later to become an aunt of Daniel O'Connell) was married twice by arrangement of her parents. Twice widowed she then married Art Ó Laoire in 1769, against her parents' will. A fiery individual, Ó Laoire was killed by the sheriff of Cork, reportedly for refusing to sell a prize-winning racehorse for the mandatory price of £5 (the highest legal value of a horse owned by a Catholic). The brutal circumstances of his death prompted his pregnant widow to begin her long elegy 'Caoineadh Airt Uí Laoghaire' (Lament for Art Ó Laoire). Her powerful poem which embraced both bardic forms and older folk traditions, while developing a novel and individual mode of expression, enjoys a place of signal importance in the Gaelic literary tradition.

NÍ DHOMHNAILL, NUALA (1952–)

Poet and playwright, born in Lancashire, but raised in

an Irish-speaking area of County Kerry. Her writing fuses Gaelic folklore and language with a vibrant female voice that creates poetry at once timely and ancient. Ní Dhomhnaill studied both English and Irish, and lived in Holland and Turkey before settling in the Kerry Gaeltacht (Irish-speaking area). Her collections of poetry, such as *An Dealg Droighin* (1981) and *Feis* (1991), have led to English verse translations and international critical recognition. Recent works include *The Astrakhan Cloak* (1992) and *Cead Aighnis* (1997).

NIVEDITA, SISTER (born Margaret Noble)
(1867–1911)

Born into a Church of Ireland family, Noble moved to Calcutta, India, in 1897 and converted to Hinduism a year later. She was a disciple and biographer of Swami Vivekananda (1863–1902), who spread the message of Hinduism in the West. At her conversion, Vivekananda renamed her Nivedita ('Dedicated One'). After Vivekananda's death, Nivedita became actively involved in the campaign for an independent India.

Nivedita established schools in England, in 1892, and Calcutta in 1898. She assisted Calcutta plague victims, and publicly defended Hinduism in the USA in 1899. She died after ministering to Bengali flood victims. Her epitaph reads: 'Here reposes Sister Nivedita, who gave her all to India'.

NORE

River of the Republic of Ireland. Rising in the ➪Slieve Bloom Mountains in County Offlay, it flows southeast through the counties of Wexford and Kilkenny to join the River Barrow, north of ➪New Ross, before entering the estuary at Waterford Harbour. Fishing is popular on the river, which is well-stocked with trout and pike. In 1991 a breeding programme began to save the Nore freshwater pearl mussel, a species unique to Ireland and the Nore, from extinction.

NORMANS

See feature essay on the ➪Vikings and Normans, page 352.

NORTHERN IRELAND

Constituent part of the United Kingdom, in the northeast of the island of Ireland, bounded to the east by the Irish Sea, to the north by the Atlantic sea, and to the south by the Republic of ➪Ireland; area 13,460 sq km/5,196 sq mi; population (1993 est) 1,632,000. It is made up of the counties Antrim, Armagh, Down, Fermanagh, Derry, and Tyrone, which are divided into 26 regional districts for administrative purposes.

> *The eggs of danger which were always incubating got hatched out very quickly.*
>
> SEAMUS HEANEY Describing violent events in Northern Ireland between 1968 and 1974 in 'Crediting Poetry – The Nobel Lecture 1995'.

NORTHERN IRELAND *Looking down on the Bogside, from Derry Walls, County Derry. Scene of notorious riots in the summer of 1969, the Catholic Bogside stayed a barricaded no-go area until 1972.*

NORTHERN IRELAND'S COMPLEX HISTORY FROM CREATION TO DEVOLUTION

by Alan O'Day

A political entity created under the UK's Better Government of Ireland Act (1920), the six counties of Northern Ireland do not correspond to the historic nine-county province of Ulster, to natural geographical boundaries, to a pre-existing administrative unit, or to a clear religious divide. The chief factor in the separation of Northern Ireland was the existence of Protestant-majority populations in Armagh, Antrim, Down, Fermanagh, Derry, and Tyrone, who were generally opposed to inclusion in a Roman Catholic-dominated all-Ireland state. However, although leading Unionist politicians persisted in calling the province 'a Protestant state for a Protestant people', from the outset it contained a substantial one-third Catholic minority which now exceeds 40%. Protestants are a considerable majority in the northern and eastern parts of Northern Ireland; Catholic pluralities exist in the west and south. In many districts, especially in rural areas, Protestants and Catholics reside in close physical proximity. However, in cities, notably Derry and Belfast, residential segregation is the norm.

partition

The formation of Northern Ireland was controversial. In 1912 almost half a million men and women signed the Ulster covenants, pledging armed resistance to home rule. Yet, despite unionist opposition, the third home rule bill was passed (1914). Its enactment was suspended following the outbreak of World War I and superseded in the south by demands for a republic. Ulster unionists never sought a separate parliament, but the 1920 Act, passed by a Conservative-dominated coalition government, established two subsidiary jurisdictions of Northern and Southern Ireland with an overarching Council of Ireland (moribund from its inception).

In 1921 the Anglo-Irish Treaty, which set up the Irish Free State within the British Commonwealth, confirmed the separation of the six northern Protestant-majority counties. Ironically, although bitterly opposed to home rule, Northern Ireland became the only part of Ireland to be given this form of government.

Protestant unionist government

From the outset the Ulster Unionist Party, which debarred Catholics from membership, dominated the government. Although many of the charges made against the regime were exaggerated, unionists certainly used the powers of the state for the benefit of their followers, particularly in such sensitive areas as electoral arrangements, education, and, to a lesser extent, law and order.

Northern Ireland enjoyed a considerable degree of stability between the beginning of the 1920s and the late 1960s. Yet, underneath the surface, the region experienced political and economic problems. The province's nationalists never accepted partition and between the 1920s and the 1950s the militant Irish Republican Army launched a number of bombing campaigns to subvert the State. Northern Ireland's chief industries, shipbuilding, engineering, textile production, and agriculture, suffered during the inter-war years. After 1945 Northern Ireland's economy was relatively buoyant until the later 1960s and its people benefited from the UK's social welfare schemes. Fear of subversion from within and mistrust of the London government reinforced the new State's intense preoccupation with security; and, in addition to an armed policeforce, an all-protestant armed militia, the B Specials, was established to suppress republicanism.

Northern Ireland continued to enjoy higher per capita standard of living than the Republic until the 1980s, when the confluence of structural changes in the economy and 'the Troubles' led to high levels of unemployment, especially in the western, more Catholic, portion of the province. Thereafter, the relative economic positions of Northern Ireland and the Republic were reversed.

civil rights movement

Terence O'Neill, prime minister of Northern Ireland 1963–69, gave the regime a more conciliatory image through his overtures to the Republic of Ireland, and unsuccessful attempts to improve the political representation of Catholics. Although welcome in London, they met with criticism within Ulster Unionism. However, the real challenge to the Protestant regime came from the Northern Ireland Civil Rights Movement (NICRM), founded in 1967, which wanted the government's good intentions translated into positive actions for the improvement of Catholic rights. It demanded reforms such as 'one person, one vote' in local government elections, equal rights in the allocation of council housing, and an end to discrimination in the public employment sector.

'the Troubles' begin

Unionist reluctance to redress grievances prompted the NICRM to stage a series of marches 1968–69; these were disrupted by hostile Protestant mobs, sometimes abetted by the police. Destabilization followed rapidly. O'Neill resigned in April 1969 and was eventually succeeded by Brian Faulkner in March 1971. The UK government attempted to defuse the civil disorder, but the introduction of internment of republican suspects without trial alienated the Catholic community. Open warfare on the streets of Belfast followed. On 24 March 1972 the Northern Ireland parliament was suspended, and government passed directly to Westminster through the secretary of state for Northern Ireland, and the Northern Ireland Office. IRA attacks in Northern Ireland and mainland Britain expanded. The UK government attempted to conciliate Catholic opinion in 1972 by introducing 'special category' status for some prisoners, holding secret talks in London with IRA representatives, and guaranteeing the constitutional position of Northern Ireland while recognizing an 'Irish dimension'. Meanwhile opposition to the republican movement had emerged in the shape of the Protestant paramilitary Ulster Defence Association. Now both communities possessed an armed, potentially aggressive force and a wave of sectarian, reprisal killings followed.

London–Dublin initiatives

In December 1973 the Sunningdale agreement between the UK and Irish governments, and the Northern Ireland executive, provided for a devolved power-sharing executive. The executive, composed of Ulster Unionists, the Alliance Party and the mainly Catholic Social Democratic and Labour Party (SDLP), was established on 1 January 1974 and headed a new Northern Ireland assembly. However a general strike on 14 May by the Ulster Workers' Council, opposed to the Sunningdale agreement, forced the executive to resign on 28 May and control returned to Westminster.

After Margaret Thatcher became prime minister of the UK in May 1979, regular meetings began between the prime ministers of the UK and the Republic of Ireland, which formed frameworks for cooperation. However, this process received a setback in the spring and summer of 1981 when republican prisoners staged a hunger strike over the refusal to grant new prisoners 'special category' status, ending with several deaths and retaliation by republican paramilitaries on mainland Britain. In November 1985 the Anglo-Irish Agreement, which gave the Republic a consultative role in the affairs of Northern Ireland, heralded a new era of cooperation between London and Dublin, though disquieting both republicans and Ulster Unionists and causing the mass resignation of Ulster Unionist members of parliament. In the early 1990s loyalist paramilitaries became more active, killing Catholics in greater numbers than republicans did Protestants. A grim equilibrium emerged.

progress towards peace

In December 1993 the Downing Street Declaration, a joint statement of the London and Dublin governments, set out general principles for holding all-party talks on securing peace. IRA ceasefires followed in August 1994 and in May 1997. Multi party talks from February 1998 culminated in the 1998 Good Friday (Belfast) agreement. Its terms included the devolution of a wide range of executive and legislative powers to a Northern Ireland Assembly, in which executive posts would be shared on a proportional basis; the establishment of a North/South Ministerial Council, accountable to the assembly and the Dáil (Irish parliament). The agreement, which was overwhelmingly endorsed by polls in the north and south, was coupled to paramilitary decommissioning of weapon arsenals, and the relinquishing of the Republic of Ireland's territorial claims on the north. In late November 1999 an understanding was reached between the main parties, with the exception of the Democratic Ulster Unionists led by Ian Paisley, and devolution of ministerial powers from Westminster to Northern Ireland was enacted on 2 December. However, a number of problems including decommissioning, which led to a suspension of the Assembly February–May 2000, and the character of policing in the province, continue to present serious problems for the new executive.

The capital is ⇨Belfast, traditionally a town producing linen and, later, ships; see ⇨textiles and ⇨shipbuilding. Other main towns are Derry (Londonderry), Enniskillen, Omagh, Newry, Armagh, and Coleraine. Among the topographical features in Northern Ireland are Europe's largest inland stretch of water, Lough Neagh, and the Giant's Causeway, a major tourist attraction and a World Heritage site. The mountains of Mourne Mountains are also popular with visitors.

As well as having some tourism, Northern Ireland manufactures and exports engineering products, ships, textile machinery, aircraft components, linen and synthetic textiles, processed foods (especially dairy and poultry products), rubber products, and chemicals.

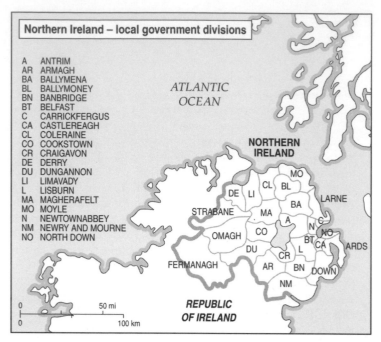

Northern Ireland – local government divisions

A	ANTRIM
AR	ARMAGH
BA	BALLYMENA
BL	BALLYMONEY
BN	BANBRIDGE
BT	BELFAST
C	CARRICKFERGUS
CA	CASTLEREAGH
CL	COLERAINE
CO	COOKSTOWN
CR	CRAIGAVON
DE	DERRY
DU	DUNGANNON
LI	LIMAVADY
L	LISBURN
MA	MAGHERAFELT
MO	MOYLE
N	NEWTOWNABBEY
NM	NEWRY AND MOURNE
NO	NORTH DOWN

history

The creation of Northern Ireland dates from 1921, when the Irish Free State (subsequently the Republic of Ireland) was established separately from the mainly Protestant counties of north and northeastern Ireland, which were given limited self-government as Northern Ireland, but continued to send members to the House of Commons in Westminster. See the feature essay on Northern Ireland, page 256, for an account of the area's history from 1921 up to the creation of the ⇨Northern Ireland Assembly. For history before 1921, see the chronology at the end of the book, page 369.

NORTHERN IRELAND ASSEMBLY

In the UK government, power-sharing assembly based in Belfast. The assembly came into being as a result of the 10 April 1998 Good Friday peace agreement between the contending unionist and Irish nationalist communities in Northern Ireland. The agreement negotiated the devolution of a range of executive and legislative powers – in areas such as agriculture, economic development, education, the environment, finance, health, and social security – from the secretary of state for Northern Ireland to an elected assembly. The assembly effectively took over much of the work of the Northern Ireland Office, although the post of secretary of state for Northern Ireland remains. Elections were first held on 25 June 1998. The assembly met for the first time on 1 July 1998, and became fully operational with the first meeting of the power-sharing executive on 2 December 1999. The Assembly was temporarily suspended on 11 February 2000 but was once again reconvened on 30 May 2000.

Based at the Castle Buildings, Stormont, the assembly comprises 108 members, 6 from each of the 18 Westminster constituencies in Northern Ireland. Its members are elected by proportional representation, using a system of single transferable votes.

The assembly has legislative powers and is specifi-

> **O**ur locations are our greatest attraction. We have countryside which has never been seen on film before, and an incredible diversity of geography. We have mountains, lakes, plains, glens, and dramatic coastlines, and you can get anywhere within two hours. There's a low density of population and the roads are empty. That means a film-maker has a better rapport with the local community.
>
> ANDREW REID Locations manager of the Northern Ireland Film Commission Quoted in 'Northern Ireland's Booming Film Business: Troubles Aside, Ulster Packs in Movie-makers' by John Mullin, *The Guardian*, 20 October 1997.

*t*he Troubles were an endless series of small military skirmishes. The objective was to go on killing the enemy wherever you could find him, and thereby wear out his will to fight on... It is the longest war the world has ever known.

KEVIN TOOLIS Writer *Rebel Hearts* (1995) quoted in *The Oxford Book of Ireland*, edited by Patricia Craig.

～

cally charged with setting up interconnecting bodies between Northern Ireland and the Republic of Ireland to cooperate and take decisions on matters of mutual interest. Important decisions of the assembly are made by a weighted majority system, which is designed to ensure that minority interests in the assembly can influence legislation.

The first minister of the assembly (from 1999) is David ⇨Trimble of the Ulster Unionist Party. On Saturday 27 May 2000 Trimble managed to secure a vote from the Ulster unionist council supporting the return of his party to government. The first minister and deputy first minister sit in an executive committee, which includes up to ten departmental ministers, with posts allocated on the basis of party support.

'Reconciliation' is the name given to Maurice Harron's pair of bronze figures with hands linked across a symbolic divide, situated at the west end of Craigavon Bridge in Derry.

NORTHERN IRELAND OFFICE (NIO)

UK government department established in 1972 to take responsibility for the direct government of Northern Ireland, including administration of security, law and order, and economic, industrial, and social policies. In 1999 Peter Mandelson was appointed its secretary of state, replacing Marjorie ('Mo') Mowlam. The terms of the 1998 Good Friday agreement established power-sharing with an executive drawn from the Northern Ireland Assembly. Fol-

lowing devolution on 2 December 1999, the department's responsibilities were reduced to matters of security, and law and order.

NORTHERN IRELAND PEACE PROCESS

Generally considered as beginning in 1993 when London and Dublin issued the Downing Street Declaration, a joint peace proposal for consideration by all parties, but probably better thought of as a continuation of efforts made between the British and Irish governments and some Northern Ireland political parties for nearly two decades. IRA ceasefires followed the British general elections in August 1994 and again in May 1997. Multiparty talks began in January 1998 culminating in the Good Friday agreement on 10 April 1998. This agreement was endorsed overwhelmingly by voters in both Northern Ireland and the Republic of Ireland in May 1998, and finally came to fruition with the devolution of ministerial powers to Northern Ireland on 2 December 1999. Unresolved issues concerning the status of the Royal Ulster Constabulary and the decomissioning of paramilitary weapons, as well as continuing tensions within the unionist parties mean that doubts continue to hang over the progress of the peace process.

Since the beginning of 'the Troubles' in 1968, there had been various attempts to reach a peaceful compromise. The 1973 Sunningdale agreement between the UK and Irish governments, together with the Northern Ireland executive, included provisions for a power-sharing executive in Northern Ireland but was brought down by a massive strike of Protestant workers. In 1985 the ⇨Anglo-Irish agreement (or Hillsborough agreement), which increased cross-border cooperation between police and security forces and gave the Republic of Ireland a greater voice in Northern Ireland's affairs, was also rejected by the Protestant unionists.

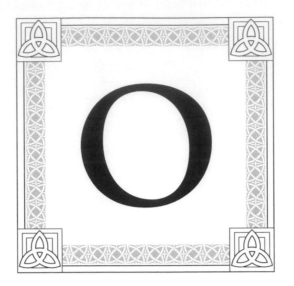

O'BRIEN

Successful Gaelic Irish dynasty claiming descent from the great chieftain ⇨Brian Bóruma, who became high king of Ireland in 999. The O'Briens established a key strategic position in Thomond, County Clare, in the 13th century through resistance to and negotiation with the Anglo-Norman invaders. Their lordship was divided into the houses of Thomond and Inchiquin in the 1570s, but these were joined after 1774 when the earldom of Thomond died out.

Having successfully repulsed several challenges from the Anglo-Normans, notably with their victory over the Anglo-Normans at the Battle of Dysert O'Dea in 1318, the O'Briens entered into a ⇨surrender and regrant treaty with the crown in 1543, under which they surrendered their lands and received them back with confirmation of their title. However, highly complicated succession disputes led to the division of their lordship into the house of Thomond and the house of Inchiquin. The division proved highly stabilizing, and the O'Briens survived the turmoils of the 17th century maintaining a largely Royalist stance throughout. Though some of the ruling family remained loyal to the Catholic ⇨Jacobite supporters of James II, the majority supported the cause of the Protestant king William (III) of Orange, and prospered in the 18th century. Although the earldom of Thomond became extinct in 1774, the Inchiquin line, amalgamated with Thomond, survives to the present.

O'BRIEN, AIDAN (1969–)

Racehorse trainer, born in County Wexford. A former champion amateur jockey, O'Brien spent three years as assistant to Jim Bolger before taking up a full licence in 1993. That season he won the Irish champion jumps training title, and again in 1997/98 and 1998/99. He has enjoyed considerable success on the flat, training three Irish classics winners in 1997 – Desert King won the Irish Derby and the Irish 2,000 Guineas while Classic Park triumphed in the 1,000 Guineas. Abroad he was equally successful, registering back-to-back wins in the 1998 and 1999 Champion Hurdle at Cheltenham with Istrabraq. Other classic wins included King of Kings in the 1998 2,000 Guineas and Shantoush in the Epsom Oaks.

O'BRIEN, CHARLOTTE GRACE

(1845–1909)

Author and social reformer, born in County Limerick. The youngest daughter of the nationalist leader William Smith ⇨O'Brien, she was educated in Brussels, Belgium, where her father lived after his release from Tasmania. She returned to Ireland in 1856, living in Dublin after her mother's death in 1861. In 1878 she published *Light and Shade*, a novel about the Fenian rising. In 1880 she moved from Dublin to Foynes, where she published *A Tale of Venice* and *Lyrics*. Soon she became involved in nationalist politics, and in 1881 founded a boarding house to protect emigrating women. She retired in 1886 and spent her final years writing.

O'BRIEN, CONOR CRUISE (DONAL CONOR DERMOD DAVID DONAT)

(1917–)

Politician, journalist, and historian. O'Brien entered

Irishness is not primarily a question of birth or blood or language; it is the condition of being involved in the Irish situation and usually of being mauled by it.

CONOR CRUISE O'BRIEN 'Irishness' in the *New Statesman*, January 1959 – reprinted in *Writers and Politics* (1965).

❧

the Department of External Affairs in 1944, and was a member of the Irish delegation to the United Nations 1956–60. He was vice-chancellor of Ghana University 1962–64 and Schweitzer professor of the humanities at New York University 1965–69. He returned to Ireland to stand for the Dáil (parliament) as a member of the Irish Labour Party in 1969, and had a controversial career as minister for posts and telegraphs (1973–77), when he introduced legislation prohibiting the appearance of representatives of Sinn Féin on Irish radio and television, and as Labour Party spokesman on Northern Ireland. In 1977 he was appointed editor of *The Observer*.

In 1961 O'Brien was the United Nations secretary general Dag Hammarskjöld's representative in Katanga, Congo; his book, *To Katanga and Back* (1962), described the crisis in Congo following that country's independence. His other publications include *Maria Cross* (1952), a study of French Catholic writers, *Parnell and His Party* (1957), *Writers and Politics* (1965), *Camus* (1969), *A Concise History of Ireland* (1972), *States of Ireland* (1972), and his study of Edmund Burke *The Great Melody* (1992).

Although O'Brien participated as a civil servant in early anti-partition campaigns, his strong political opposition to the IRA led him increasingly to criticize traditional Irish nationalism and irredentism, particularly the variety espoused by Fianna Fáil. His views always generated fierce controversy in the Republic, and eventually he left the Irish Labour Party and joined the UK Unionist Party.

O'BRIEN, FITZ-JAMES (1828–1862)

Irish-born writer, born in Cork. O'Brien emigrated to New York in 1852, seeking money and adventure. He is best known for his macabre horror stories, such as 'The Diamond Lens', first published in the *Atlantic Monthly* in 1858.

In New York O'Brien worked as a journalist and freelance writer, and wrote poetry, short stories, and plays. After volunteering for service in the Union army in the American Civil War (1851–56), he was wounded and died of tetanus.

O'BRIEN, FLANN (pen name of BRIAN O'NOLAN) (1911–1966)

Humorist, novelist, and essayist. Born in Strabane, County Tyrone, he was educated in Dublin, where he later worked as a civil servant. He wrote in Irish Gaelic and English, and his exuberant style is a blend of seriousness, surrealism, and farce. For 30 years he was a brilliant columnist on the *Irish Times* under the pen name Myles na Gopaleen. His first novel, the ambitious, exploratory *At Swim-Two-Birds* (1939), was influenced by James ⇨Joyce and is also indebted to Gaelic comic tradition. *The Third Policeman* (1967), written in 1940, is an experimental work with fantastic and satirical elements.

I fear that being a patient in any hospital in Ireland calls for two things – holy resignation and an iron constitution.

FLANN O'BRIEN *Myles Away from Dublin* (1990).

❧

An Béal Bocht/The Poor Mouth (1941) was the only novel he produced in Gaelic. Other works include *The Hard Life* (1961) and *The Dalkey Archive* (1964). A selection of his newspaper columns appeared posthumously in *The Best of Myles* (1968).

O'BRIEN, (JOSEPHINE) EDNA (1932–)

Writer, born in Tuamgraney, County Clare, and educated at various convents as well as the Pharmaceutical College of Dublin. O'Brien first gained acclaim for her trilogy, *The Country Girls* (1960); *The Lonely Girl* (1962), later renamed *The Girl With Green Eyes*; and *Girls in their Married Bliss* (1964), about two girls who flee restrictive rural Ireland for excitement in Dublin and London, but end in bleak disillusionment.

O'Brien's writing is often infused with sensuality, and female characters struggling toward self-realization. Although loneliness, guilt, and loss tend to dominate her work, her lyrical prose style is beautiful and haunting, and there are moments of joyful self-fulfilment. Much of her early work was banned by Irish

hour after hour I can think of Ireland,
I can imagine without going too far
wrong what is happening in any one of
the little towns by day or by night, so
steadfast is the rhythm of life there.

EDNA O'BRIEN *Mother Ireland* (1976).

~

censors due to sexual content, and her honesty and lack of inhibition has led to comparisons with French writer Colette. Other novels include *August is a Wicked Month* (1965), *Casualties of Peace* (1966), *A Pagan Place* (1970), *Night* (1972), *Johnny I Hardly Knew You* (1977), *Time and Tide* (1992), and *House of Splendid Isolation* (1994).

O'BRIEN, KATE (1897–1974)

Novelist and playwright. Born in Limerick, O'Brien was educated at University College, Dublin, and worked as a journalist in London. Her first novel, *Without My Cloak* (1931), won Hawthornden and Tait Black Memorial prizes. *The Ante-Room* (1934) and *The Last of Summer* (1943), set in County Clare, contain shrewd pictures of the Irish temperament. Other novels are *Mary Lavelle* (1936), *Pray for the Wanderer* (1938), and *That Lady* (1946). Among her plays are *The Bridge* (1927) and *The Schoolroom Window* (1937). *Farewell Spain* (1937) is a travel book. Her later works include *The Flower of May* (1953), *My Ireland* (1962), and *Presentation Parlour* (1963).

O'BRIEN, WILLIAM (1852–1928)

Journalist and nationalist, born in Mallow, County Cork. In 1880 O'Brien established the journal *United Ireland* to popularize the aims of Charles Stewart ⇨Parnell and the ⇨Land League. He was a leader of the Plan of Campaign (1886–91), a nationalist proposal to address tenant eviction and distress, and in 1898 he founded the United Irish League. O'Brien took the anti-Parnellite side in the split in the Irish Parliamentary Party, following Parnell's citation in the O'Shea divorce case. A leader of the tenant side in the Dunraven Land Conference (1902–03), he directed his influence towards the conciliation policy which looked for the union of Irishmen of all creeds and classes.

O'Brien was repeatedly imprisoned under the Crimes Act in connection with the National League and Tenants' Defence League 1887–91. In the Westminster parliament he represented South Tyrone 1885–86, Northeast Cork 1887–92, Cork City and Northeast Cork 1892, and Cork City 1910–18, when he and his friends stood aside in favour of ⇨Sinn Féin.

O'BRIEN, WILLIAM SMITH (1803–1864)

Nationalist, born at Dromoland, County Clare. O'Brien sat in parliament at Westminster and, although a Protestant, favoured Catholic emancipation. He joined the Repeal Association of Daniel ⇨O'Connell, but in 1846 seceded to the Young Ireland party. In 1848 he led an abortive rising in Tipperary against the British. He was captured and sentenced to death, but the sentence was commuted to transportation.

Ó BRUADAIR, DÁIBHI (or DAVID O'BRUADAIR or BRODER) (c. 1625–1698)

Gaelic poet who was born in east County Cork, and received formal training as a bard. A ⇨Jacobite (supporter of the deposed Catholic James II), he violently castigated the English and those Irish who betrayed their native traditions, and his verse records and focuses upon the turbulence of the 17th century in Ireland. Conscious both of the dignity of his calling, and of the crumbling of the ancient order he represented, his poems are in the old, strict metres (*dán díreach*) but he also makes use of the newer, looser type of metre, the *amhrán*, which was beginning to emerge with the fall of the Irish order.

O'BYRNE, FIACH MacHUGH (c. 1544–1597)

Prominent leader of Gaelic resistance to Elizabethan penetration in County Wicklow. O'Byrne rose to prominence after his celebrated defeat of a major English force under Lord Deputy Grey de Wilton (1536–1593) at Glenmalure in 1580. After successfully resisting several punitive campaigns, he became reconciled to the crown in the later 1580s but once again came under suspicion in the early 1590s. In 1594, in punishment for his suspected complicity in the murder of the sheriff of Kildare, the government launched a surprise offensive against him during which his chief house was destroyed and his wife, Rose, taken hostage. Forced again into rebellion and into alliance with Hugh ⇨O'Neill, leader of the Ulster lords in their war of 1593–1603 against the crown, O'Byrne returned to his guerrilla tactics. Half-hearted attempts at reconciliation failed, and he was finally captured and executed in May 1597.

Ó CADHAIN, MÁIRTÍN (or MARTIN KANE) (1906–1970)

Gaelic short-story writer and novelist. Ó Cadhain was born in Spiddal, Connemara, the Gaeltacht (Gaelic-speaking area) of Galway. His work reflects his staunch support of revolutionary republicanism, and is also stylistically highly inventive. His collection of short stories *An Braon Broghach/The Hare Lip* (1948) established him as a stern critic of accepted social conventions. His novel *Cré Na Cille/The Clay of the Churchyard* (1949), a bitter commentary by the dead of the Irish Civil War (1922–23) on the treachery of politicians, is now regarded as a major work of modern Irish literature. He exerted a strong influence on subsequent generations of writers

Ó Cadhain worked for a time as a schoolteacher, but was interned during World War II for his active involvement in the IRA. In 1969 he was appointed professor of Irish at Trinity College, Dublin. His collection *The Hare Lip* was reprinted in Seamus ⇨Deane's *The Field Day Anthology of Irish Writing* (1991).

O'CASEY, SEÁN (adopted name of JOHN CASEY) (1884–1964)

Dramatist, born in Dublin. His early plays are tragicomedies, blending realism with symbolism and poetic with vernacular speech: *The Shadow of a Gunman* (1923), *Juno and the Paycock* (1924), and *The Plough and the Stars* (1926). Later plays include *Red Roses for Me* (1946) and *The Drums of Father Ned* (1959).

Born into a working-class Protestant family, poverty dominated O'Casey's childhood after his father's death. Like George Bernard Shaw, he was a regular patron at the popular nationalist Queen's Theatre in Dublin. He was active in a number of nationalist and socialist organizations, but his subsequent scepticism over the politics of nationalism is prominent in the drama he wrote for the Abbey Theatre: *The Shadow of a Gunman, Juno and the Paycock,* and *The Plough and the Stars.* Later on he became increasingly experimental with plays such as *The Star*

Turns Red (1940) and *Oak Leaves and Lavender* (1947).

O'Casey moved to London in 1926, where his antiwar drama *The Silver Tassie* was produced in 1929, after a controversial rejection from the Abbey Theatre. While his plays became increasingly successful in the USA, O'Casey remained in England until his death. *The Drums of Father Ned* was submitted to the 1958 Dublin Theatre Festival, but was withdrawn because of clerical intervention; as a result, O'Casey banned all professional productions of his plays in Ireland. The ban was lifted after his death. The six-volume *Autobiographies* (1939–54), evokes his early impressions and memories of his childhood and dramatic career.

Ó CONAIRE, (SEAN-)PÁDRAIC (or PATRICK CONROY) (1882–1928)

Gaelic writer who was born in Galway and educated in Gaelic-speaking Rosmuc. He began to write stories while working as a civil servant in London, but devoted himself to writing full-time in 1913 after winning literary prizes. His work, which was part of the 'Gaelic revival' in literature, embraced novels, short stories, essays, travel accounts, and children's books. His short-story collections *Nóra Mharcuis Bhig agus Sgéalta Eile* (1909) and *An Chéad Chloch* (1914), along with a novel *Deoraíocht/Exile* (1910), are his most acclaimed works.

Ó Conaire spent some time at sea before entering the civil service, where he remained for many years. His writing was marked by its deceptive simplicity and subtle construction, and touched on themes of psychological complexity that alarmed the more puritanical exponents of the Gaelic revival. His later years were spent writing and teaching Irish, chiefly in Galway.

O'CONNELL, DANIEL (known as 'the Liberator') (1775–1847)

Lawyer and politician, born in Carhan, near Cahirciveen, County Kerry. After a successful career as a barrister, in 1823 he formed the Catholic Association, to campaign for Catholic emancipation and the repeal of the 1801 Act of Union between Britain and Ireland. As a young man O'Connell had possessed a fiery temper, on one occasion killing a man in a duel. However, he became more opposed to violence as his career went on. As a Catholic, the higher legal posts were closed to him, but he made a good living by pleading large numbers of small cases, his work taking him all over Ireland. When he was elected member of parliament for County Clare in 1828, he was debarred from taking his seat, but by his election to parliament helped secure Catholic emancipation in 1829.

In his attempt to oppose the Act of Union, he organized mass meetings all over Ireland, and formed an alliance with the Whigs in Britain, but was jailed for sedition. A few months after his release from prison, the Great Famine (historically dated 1845–49, but now believed to have lasted until 1852) had pushed repeal of the Act of Union into the background. O'Connell's influence began to wane when his reserved and vacillating leadership and conservative outlook on social questions alienated his most active supporters. They broke away to form the more radical nationalist ⇨Young Ireland movement. Broken in health, O'Connell died in Genoa while undertaking a journey to Rome.

O'CONNELL, EILÍS

(1953–)

Sculptor, born in Cork, who has established an international reputation for her abstract work. She represented Ireland at the São Paolo Biennale, Brazil, in 1985 and has been the recipient of a fellowship administered by the Arts Councils of Ireland and Northern Ireland, which allowed her to work for a time in New York, USA.

O'Connell has created a number of public sculptures in Ireland, such as *The Wind Column* (1982; Londonderry, Northern Ireland), a monument to the US aviator Amelia Earhart, and her works are also on display in other countries. A recent project is the design for a bridge in concrete and steel for the River Avon at Bristol. In her smaller-scale work she uses a huge variety of media from organic materials such as

DANIEL O'CONNELL *O'Connell was lionized by 19th-century moderate nationalists. Over half a million people are said to have attended the Dublin ceremony when the foundation stone for his statue was laid in what became O'Connell Street.*

feathers to steel, stone, and slate, as illustrated by *Skillet* (1986; Allied Irish Bank collection, Dublin).

O'CONNOR, CHRISTY (1924–)

Golfer, born in Dublin. Ireland's greatest golfer, and a leading player in European golf in the late 1950s and 1960s, O'Connor won 24 tournaments on the British PGA Tour, and twice topped the Order of Merit. He never won a major title, but between 1958 and 1969 he finished in the top five of the British Open on seven occasions, and was runner-up in 1965. He was ten times Irish Professional Champion, 1958–78, and in partnership with Harry Bradshaw (1913–1990) won the 1958 World Cup for Ireland. Between 1955 and 1973 he played in ten Ryder Cups, an all-time record until surpassed by Nick Faldo in 1997. His nephew, Christy O'Connor Jr (1948–), also became a leading player.

O'CONNOR, FEARGUS EDWARD (1794–1855)

Parliamentarian, born in Connorville, County Cork, and educated at Trinity College, Dublin. O'Connor was a repeal member of parliament for Cork 1832–35 and a follower of Daniel ⇨O'Connell, but they soon had a serious rift. An active supporter of the Reform

*t*he hospitality of an Irishman is not the running account of posted and ledgered courtesies, as in other countries; it springs like all his qualities, his faults, his virtues, directly from the heart.

DANIEL O'CONNELL Speech made against the Marquess of Headfort (July 1804).

Bill of 1832, he was unseated for failing to satisfy the required property qualifications, and he embraced radical extraparliamentary opposition. As founder and editor of the *Northern Star* (1837) he became an influential figure of the radical working-class Chartist movement. In 1840 he was imprisoned for seditious libel. From 1847 he represented Nottingham in the House of Commons, and led the great Chartist demonstration at Kennington in 1848. He was declared insane in 1852.

O'CONNOR, FRANK (pseudonym of MICHAEL O'DONOVAN) (1903–1966)

Writer, born in Cork. His short stories are rooted in the provincial life of his native county, but he brings to his work a wide human sympathy and careful elegance. Collections include *Bones of Contention* (1936), *Crab Apple Jelly* (1944), *Traveller's Samples* (1950), *Collection Two* (1964), and *Collection Three*, published posthumously in 1969. He also wrote two novels, several plays, poetry – both original and in translation – and a history of Irish literature. His study of the short story, *The Lonely Voice* (1963), is recognized as a basic work in the field.

O'Connor worked as a librarian in Cork and Dublin, where he was a director of the ⇨Abbey Theatre 1935–39.

O'CONNOR, JAMES ARTHUR (*c.* 1792–1841)

Landscape painter, born in Dublin. Despite enduring the frustration of a lack of patronage throughout his career, he produced some of the most remarkable landscapes by an Irish artist in the early 19th century. His early topographical work, such as his views of Bridge House, Ballinrobe, County Mayo (National Gallery of Ireland, Dublin) were followed by a more picturesque style in the 1820s, which coincided with his settling in London in 1822. His dark, forbidding landscapes of the 1830s are the most accomplished paintings of his career.

The dramatic power of works such as *The Frightened Wagoner* (1832; National Gallery of Ireland, Dublin), with its emphasis on the power of natural forces, is characteristic of his later work. In *The Poachers* (1835; National Gallery of Ireland) a striking sense of mood is conveyed through complex handling of light and shade. Such concerns place O'Connor's work in the context of European Romanticism.

O'CONNOR, PAT (1943–)

Film and television director, born in Ardmore, County Waterford. He first came to prominence while working at RTÉ (the national TV station) as a director, especially with his *The Ballroom of Romance* (1981), which recreated 1950s rural Ireland and explored the sexual repression of the people attending the local dancehall, and for which he won a British Academy award. His first feature film, *Cal* (1984), was set in Northern Ireland, and told of the relationship between the driver of an IRA gang and a widow whose policeman husband was killed by the unit. His adaptation of Maeve Binchy's coming-of-age novel *Circle of Friends* (1995) was a considerable commercial success.

Another of O'Connor's Irish features, *Fools of Fortune* (1990), is set amongst the Anglo-Irish in rural Ireland during the War of Independence. Their world is shattered as the events impinge on their lives, but as in *Cal*, O'Connor's concerns are less with the political and historical events, than with an exploration of a love affair and the possibilities of redemption through retribution.

O'CONNOR, RORY (or RUADRÍ UA CONCHOBAIR) (died 1198)

Last high king of Ireland, 1166–70. He succeeded his father as king of Connacht in 1156 and secured high kingship of Ireland after one of his chief rivals Diarmait Mac Murchada was temporarily exiled to England. In the same year he marched on Dublin, offering its Hiberno-Norse citizens 4,000 cows, whereupon they recognized him as high king. He lost high kingship after the English invasion of 1170, yet retained status as king of Connacht and continued to hold sway over much of the northern half of Ireland.

Attempting to recapture his lost position as well as to hold his remaining territory, O'Connor spent much of the next decade in sporadic warfare against the English invaders, as well as their settled allies in Dublin and throughout Leinster. Slowly losing the effort, in 1183 he retired to a monastery at Cong, County Mayo, leaving the kingship of Connacht to his son Conchobar.

O'CONNOR OF CONNACHT

Gaelic Irish royal dynasty of Connacht. Having established dominance over the O'Rourkes and other major dynasties of Connacht in the early 11th century, the O'Connors asserted tenuous claims to the high kingship of Ireland over the next century which were never fully accepted. In 1166 the high king Rory O'Connor (died 1198) deposed Dermot ⇨MacMurrough, King of Leinster, who retaliated by inviting a number of Anglo-Norman barons to support his reinstatement; their arrival in 1169 was followed by a full-scale Anglo-Norman invasion under Henry II in 1171. Although Rory O'Connor made peace with Henry II at Windsor in 1175, by which he retained all of Connacht, internecine disputes paved the way for Anglo-Norman penetration into Connacht led by the de Burghs. By the time of the death without heir of Áodh, the last king of Connacht, in 1274, the O'Connors had already been reduced to vassals of the de Burghs.

The O'Connors then split into two dynasties: O'Connor Roe (the red-haired) and O'Connor Don (the brown-haired). The former became vassals of the de Burghs while the latter retained a position of some independence in Connacht down to modern times.

O'Connor Faly (Offaly) was an unrelated dynasty that survived between the often hostile Anglo-Irish lords of Ormond and Kildare until 1556, when the Tudor government undertook a major plantation in their territory along with that of their neighbours, the O'Moores in County Laois.

O'CONOR, JOHN (1947–)

Concert pianist, born in Dublin. He has performed as a soloist with orchestras such as the Vienna Symphony, Orchestre National de France, Royal Philharmonic, Scottish Chamber, Dallas, Montréal, and the Republic of Ireland's National Symphony Orchestra. He is a co-founder of the Guardian Dublin International Piano Competition and director of the Royal Irish Academy of Music in Dublin. He has been influential in the proposed development of an Irish College of Performing Arts, the establishment of which was announced in 1999. His recordings include the complete Sonatas of Beethoven (1987) and John Field's Nocturnes (1990).

O'Conor studied at University College, Dublin, and later at the Hochschule für Musik in Vienna, Austria, with Dieter Weber and Willhelm Kempff. He won first prize at the international Beethoven Competition in Vienna in 1973 and the Bösendorfer Competition in 1975.

O'CONOR, RODERIC (1860–1940)

Painter whose work occupies a significant place in the history of Post-Impressionism. While he was influenced by the work of Van Gogh and Gauguin in the 1890s, he retained his own distinctive artistic personality. Gauguin, a particular admirer of his work, dedicated two prints to O'Conor and invited him to accompany him on his return to Tahiti in 1895.

O'Conor was born in County Roscommon, into a family descended from the high kings of Ireland. He was educated at Ampleforth, England, and began his artistic studies in Dublin and Antwerp before moving to Paris in 1888. There the milieu of the avant-garde seems to have sparked his individual creativity. Much of his best-known work was inspired by the coastline and rural society of Brittany in the north of France. In his most radical paintings, such as *Farm at Lezaven* (1894; National Gallery of Ireland, Dublin) and *Woman Knitting* (Hugh Lane Municipal Gallery of Modern Art, Dublin), he took a deliberately unnatural approach to colour, anticipating the experiments of the Fauves in the early 1900s. He lived in Paris, where he knew Picasso and Matisse, from 1904 until his death. Increasingly reclusive, he exhibited only once in these years, in 1933.

Ó DÁLAIGH, MUIREADHACH ALBANACH (1180–1250)

Poet, probably born in County Meath; one of the first of the learned bardic Ó Dálaigh family to rise to prominence. He was a student of bardic poetry and may have been educated in monastic schools. His intensely mournful poem on the death of his wife 'M'anam do sgar riomsa a-raoir'", which opens with the line 'I was robbed of my soul last night', is one of the most celebrated in Irish literature.

After murdering a tax collector with an axe, Ó Dálaigh abandoned his home in County Sligo and fled to Scotland.

O'DONNELL, DANIEL (1961–)

⇨Country and Irish artist who has had several successes in the UK country and pop charts. His carefully cultivated 'boy next door' image has played a large part in his success and his Christian, caring, and romantic persona is represented fully in the style and content of his songs. His career has also been marked by a large amount of charity work, notably for

Romanian orphans and following the Omagh bombing of 1998. His recordings include *Don't Forget to Remember* (1987) and *Love Songs* (1998).

O'Donnell was born in Kincasslagh, northwest Donegal. He is the brother of the country music artist Margo. His initial success was amongst the Irish communities of Britain. O'Donnell is perhaps the only Country and Irish singer to break out of the Irish markets in Ireland and elsewhere.

O'DONNELL, PEADAR (1893–1986)

Republican activist and writer, born in Meenmore, County Donegal. Ireland's most prominent socialist republican, he campaigned for numerous radical causes throughout his life. O'Donnell was the son of a small farmer. He fought in the Anglo–Irish War (1919–21) and became a leading figure in the Irish Civil War (1922–23), when he fought for the Irish Republican Army (IRA) against the Anglo-Irish Treaty (1921). He later joined the International Brigade in the Spanish Civil War (1936–39). His most celebrated works, which depict the harsh lives of the underprivileged, are *Islanders* (1927) and *The Big Windows* (1955).

O'Donnell began his working life as a teacher, then a trade union organizer, before becoming engaged in revolutionary politics. During the Irish Civil War (1922–23), he was captured by forces of the provisional government, but escaped after a 41-day hunger strike. A vigorous publicist and editor of *An Phoblacht*, the official IRA newspaper, he gave (and then withdrew) qualified support for Éamon de Valera during the election of 1932. He left the IRA in 1934 to establish Republican Congress, an unsuccessful fusion of socialism and republicanism.

O'Donnell wrote extensively on his experiences – the novel *Storm* (1925) had the Anglo–Irish War as its theme, *The Gates Flew Open* (1934) was about his imprisonment, *Salud!* (1937) concerned the Spanish Civil War (1936–39), and *There Will Be Another Day* (1963) reflected his campaign against land annuities which led to the Anglo-Irish ⇨Economic War of the 1930s. As editor of the literary monthly *The Bell* 1946–54, O'Donnell strongly promoted Irish writing.

O'DONNELL OF TIRCONNELL (or Ó DOMHNAILL OF TÍR CONAILL)

Major dynasty of Irish Gaelic chiefs in northwest Ulster (modern County Donegal); a significant power in Ireland from the mid-13th to early 17th centuries.

The O'Donnells rose to prominence through their successful resistance both to the Anglo-Norman colonists, who had penetrated deep into Ulster in the 13th century, and the O'Neills, the ascendant family in Ulster. Strong lines of succession coupled with shrewd alliances with gallowglass families such as the MacSweeneys, descendents of Scottish mercenary troops imported by the Irish chiefs in the 13th century, allowed them to exercise control over a large portion of north Connacht (now counties Sligo and Mayo) during the late 15th and early 16th centuries. The family even gained brief dominance over the O'Neills under Aodh Ruadh O'Donnell (1461–1505). The height of O'Donnell achievements was reached under Manus O'Donnell (1535–1563) who extended their claims in Connacht, supplanted the O'Neills as the ally of the Kildare ⇨Fitzgeralds, and was a generous patron of the arts.

Manus O'Donnell's deposition by his son Calvach in 1555, coupled with fierce invasions by Shane O'Neill (c. 1530–1567), severely weakened the dynasty. Calvach was granted the title Earl of Tyrconnell by the English crown, but died before receiving the royal charter. Aodh Dubh O'Donnell (chief 1566–93) attempted to shore up the O'Donnell's position by marriage alliances and careful diplomacy with the English government. However, on his death 'Red Hugh' (Aodh Ruadh) O'Donnell (chief 1593–1602), Aodh Dubh's son by his Scots wife Fionualla MacDonnell, seized power and, with Hugh ⇨O'Neill, 2nd Earl of Tyrone, led the O'Donnells into war against the crown in 1593. Following the defeat of the Ulster army at Kinsale in 1601, Hugh O'Donnell went to Spain seeking further support and died (possibly by poisoning).

After the surrender of the Ulster rebels in 1603, Hugh's brother Rory was created Earl of Tyrconnell, but he joined with Hugh O'Neill and other Ulster lords in the ⇨Flight of the Earls from Ireland in 1607. In the aftermath the family's title was suppressed and their lands confiscated, destroying their power base.

O'DONOVAN ROSSA, JEREMIAH

Fenian activist; see Patrick ⇨Pearse.

O'DUFFY, EIMAR (ULTAN) (1893–1935)

Satirical playwright and novelist. Born in Dublin, he was educated at Stonyhurst (Jesuit) College, Lancashire, and University College, Dublin. Influenced by the Irish poet Thomas ⇨MacDonagh, he embraced Irish cultural and political nationalism, joining the ⇨Irish Volunteers. However, during the 1916 ⇨Easter Rising he obeyed Volunteer leader John (Eoin) MacNeill's countermand of the insurrection. His subsequent work took a more sceptical view of revolutionary nationalism. The play *Bricriu's Feast* (1919) satirized neo-Gaelicism, and his first novel, *The Wasted Island* (1919), examined critically the origins of the rising.

O'Duffy's first play, *The Walls of Athens*, was published and produced by Edward Martyn's Irish Theatre; he also staged O'Duffy's *The Phoenix on the Roof* (1915).

A perceptive literary critic, O'Duffy was one of the first to recognize as a masterpiece James Joyce's *Ulysses* (1922). He emigrated to England in 1925, and his autobiography *Life and Money* appeared in 1932.

O'DUFFY, EOIN (1892–1944)

Politician and soldier. Born in County Monaghan, he joined the Irish Volunteers in 1917, and took a leading part in the ⇨Sinn Féin movement and the ⇨Irish Republican Army. He supported the Anglo-Irish Treaty (1921) and was appointed the first commissioner of the Garda Síochána (civic guard), established to police the Irish Free State in 1922. Following his dismissal by the president of the executive council (prime minister) Éamon de Valera in 1933, he joined the oppositon, and became director general of the semi-fascist National Guard (formerly the ⇨Blueshirts).

The Blueshirts merged with Cumann na nGaedheal and the Centre Party to form Fine Gael with O'Duffy as its first president in 1933. O'Duffy's radicalism and pro-fascist sympathies resulted in his resignation from the party the following year. His next political ven-

> **O**ur sins are tawdry, our virtues childlike, our revolts desultory and brief, our submissions formal and frequent. In Ireland a policeman's lot is a supremely happy one.
>
> SEÁN Ó FAOLÁIN 'The Dilemma of Irish Letters', in *The Mouth*, December 1949.

ture, the fascistic National Corporate Party, failed to gain popular support. In 1936 he led the Irish Brigade to Spain to fight for Gen Franco during the Spanish Civil War (1936–39), but it returned home within six months due to infighting and poor military performance.

O'Duffy was the author of *The Crusade in Spain* (1938).

Ó FAOLÁIN, SEÁN (JOHN WHELAN) (1900–1991)

Novelist, short-story writer, critic, and biographer, born in Cork. Ó Faoláin was educated at the National University of Ireland and Harvard University. His first collection was *Midsummer Night Madness and Other Stories* (1932), after which he wrote *A Nest of Simple Folk* (1933), his first novel. He also wrote biographies of Daniel ⇨O'Connell in 1938; Éamon ⇨de Valera, beside whom he had fought in the IRA, in 1939; and Cardinal Newman in 1952.

In 1940 Ó Faoláin founded the Irish literary journal *The Bell*, editing it until 1946. *The Bell* was influential not only because it published many significant writers such as Brendan Behan, Patrick Kavanagh, and Frank O'Connor, but also because the commentaries by Ó Faoláin and others challenged predominant notions of Irish identity as well as contemporary censorship policy.

Ó Faoláin's *Collected Short Stories* was published 1980–82. Previous volumes of his stories were *A Purse of Coppers* (1937), *The Stories of Seán Ó Faolain* (1958), *The Heat of the Sun* (1966), and *The Talking Trees* (1971). His novels include *Bird Alone* (1936), *Come Back to Erin* (1940), and *Teresa* (1946). He edited the works of Thomas ⇨Moore in 1929 and an autobiography of Wolfe ⇨Tone in 1937. *She Had To Do Something* (1938) is a play; *A Summer in Italy* (1950) and *South Sicily* (1953) are travel books. *Vive Moi!* (1964) is an autobiography

During the Irish Civil War (1922–23), Ó Faoláin fought on the republican side and he was also director of publicity for the IRA. He lectured at Boston College in 1929, before teaching in Middlesex, England, 1930–33. After this he returned to County Wicklow, where he devoted himself to writing. In his fiction, as in his biographical and editorial work, Ó Faoláin charted the transition from idealistic nationalism to a more critical and disillusioned engagement with cultural conditions in Ireland.

OFFALY

County of the Republic of Ireland, in the province of Leinster, between Galway and Roscommon in the west and Kildare in the east; county town ⇨Tullamore; area 2,000 sq km/772 sq mi; population (1996) 59,100. It is low-lying, with part of the Bog of Allen to the north.

Features include the rivers Shannon (along the western boundary), Brosna, Clodagh, and Broughill, and the Slieve Bloom Mountains in the southeast. The chief towns are Tullamore, Birr, Banagher, and Edenderry. Peat is used to fuel power stations. Agricultural products include oats, barley, and wheat; cattle, sheep, pigs, and poultry are bred. The area is noted for ecclesiastical remains, the most extensive and important of which is Clonmacnois, founded by St Ciarán in AD 548, and once the most significant theological centre and centre of learning in Ireland; many of the high kings of Connaught and Tara are buried here, and it is a site of pilgrimage.

The county on the whole is flat, the northern part being occupied by the Bog of Allen. There are rich pasture lands on the borders with Westmeath in the north, and Tipperary in the west, and also in the Slieve Bloom Mountains, which lie along the border with Laois.

O'FLAHERTY, LIAM (1896–1984)

Writer and radical, born on the Aran Islands, off the coast of Galway, and educated at the National University, Dublin. O'Flaherty is best known for his volumes of poetic short stories, such as *Spring Sowing* (1924), *The Tent* (1926), and *Two Lovely Beasts* (1948). He also wrote novels, including *The Informer* (1925), which won the Tait Black Memorial Prize and was translated into an award-winning Hollywood film by John Ford. His novels are often set in Dublin and chronicle a violence and despair resulting from a spiritless, urbanized world.

Other works include *The Mountain Tavern* (1929), *The Wild Swan* (1932), *The Martyr* (1933), *Land* (1946), and *Insurrection* (1950).

During World War I O'Flaherty enlisted in the Irish Guards and fought in Belgium, but was invalided out in 1917. For the next few years he roamed all over the world and wrote of his experiences in autobiographies. In the Irish Civil War (1922–23) he fought for the Irish republicans. A left-wing radical, O'Flaherty was a member of the group that founded the first Irish

I was born on a storm-swept rock and hate the soft growth of sun-baked lands where there is no frost in men's bones. Swift thought and the flight of ravenous birds, and the squeal of hunted animals are to me reality.

LIAM O'FLAHERTY On his own background, in *Joseph Conrad: an Appreciation* (1925).

❧

Communist Party in 1921. He travelled to Moscow in 1930, but was disillusioned by what he found. Many of his books were banned in Ireland.

O'GRADY, STANDISH JAMES (1846–1928)

Historian and novelist. He was born in Castletown Bere and educated at Trinity College, Dublin. O'Grady is best known for his *History of Ireland: Heroic Period* (1878), which kindled interest in the legendary material used by later writers of the Irish literary revival. Among his historical romances are *Finn and his Companions* (1892), *The Bog of Stars* (1893), *In the Wake of King James* (1896), *The Flight of the Eagle* (1897), and *In the Gates of the North* (1901).

O'Grady also edited Thomas Stafford's *Pacata Hibernia* (1896), and was owner–editor of the *Kilkenny Moderator* and the *All Ireland Review*.

O'HARA, MAUREEN (born Fitzsimmons) (1920–)

Actor, born in Dublin. Ireland's premier Hollywood actor of the 1940s and 1950s, she appeared in more than 50 films. O'Hara began performing as a child on radio and later appeared as a teenager with the Abbey Players, with whom she trained. In 1938 she made her film debut in the English film *Kicking Around the Moon* and was given a leading part the same year in the Irish-theme film *My Irish Molly*. In 1939 she went to Hollywood where her first role was as Esmerelda in Charles Laughton's *The Hunchback of Notre Dame* (1939). Her career took a major advance when she played the female lead in *How Green Was My Valley* (1941), directed by John Ford. She went on to act in many of Ford's films, perhaps the best known being *The Quiet Man* (1952). Her role in that film as Mary Kate, with flowing red hair and fiery temperament, came to characterize the quintessential assertive Irish woman. Most of her roles, however, were not as a distinctive Irish character.

The films in which O'Hara appeared include *Jamaica Inn* (1939), *The Black Swan* (1942), *Rio Grande* (1950), just one of the many films in which she plays opposite John Wayne, *The Redhead from Wyoming* (1953), and *The Parent Trap* (1961). She retired from acting in 1971, the year she starred in *Big Jake*, but made comeback appearances in *The Red Pony* (1973), *Only the Lonely* (1991) as Chicago Irishwoman Rose Muldoon, and *The Christmas Box* (1995).

O'HEHIR, MICHEAL (1920–1997)

Sports commentator, born in Dublin. He gave his first official commentary on 14 August 1938, for the All-Ireland Gaelic football semi-final in Mullingar, County Westmeath. He was only 18 years old at the time and still a student at O'Connell's secondary school in Dublin. From then on, his dramatic and infectious style made him a household name for the next 50 years. He was also well known in the UK for his commentaries on the Grand National steeplechase with Peter O' Sullevan. After retiring as head of sport for RTÉ (the national TV station) in 1972, he continued to broadcast until 1985.

O'Hehir's father had trained Clare to victory in the 1914 All-Ireland hurling final, and it was this background, together with a fascination for the radio, that introduced the young O'Hehir into sports broadcasting.

Ó hEÓDHASA, EOCHAIDH (or EOCHAIDH Ó hEÓGHUSA) (*c.* 1570–1617)

Writer, a major bardic poet in traditional Gaelic society, and head of the learned and poetic Ó hEódhasa family of Ballyhose on Castlehume Lough, Lower Lough Erne, County Fermanagh. He was *ollamh* (highest ranking poet under the *áes dána*, a Gaelic guild system) to three Maguire (Mág Uidhir) chieftains of Fermanagh. His poetry of praise, loyalty, and adoration of Hugh Maguire (died 1600) most typifies the often complex relationship between high-born patron and poet, and indicates the privileged position of the bard in Gaelic society.

O'HERLIHY, DAN (1919–)

Actor, born in Wexford. Although he trained as a set designer, he soon began acting at the Abbey Theatre and on Irish radio. He first film appearance was in the Irish historical drama *Hungry Hill* (1946), and shortly afterwards he was in the landmark film about the IRA in Northern Ireland, *Odd Man Out* (1947), which featured many Abbey players. Thereafter, he worked mainly in the USA in a wide range of films such as *Macbeth* (1948), *The Adventures of Robinson Crusoe* (1952), for which he was nominated for an Academy Award, *The Virgin Queen* (1955), *The Cabinet of Dr Caligari* (1962), *MacArthur* (1977), and *Halloween III* (1982). Amongst his last films were *The Dead* (1987) and *RoboCop 2* (1990).

O'HIGGINS, AMBROSIO (AMBROSE HIGGINS) (1726–1801)

Viceroy of Chile and Peru, born in County Meath. O'Higgins emigrated to South America as a young man and built rest places for a living. In 1770 he was appointed captain of a cavalry unit by the viceroy of Chile in a campaign against the Araucanian Indians. He won a key victory and established the fort of San Carlos. Rising in the military, he was appointed viceroy of Chile in 1789, lieutenant general in 1794, and viceroy of Peru in 1795. A highly respected and admired leader, O'Higgins helped defend the country in the Anglo-Spanish war of 1797.

O'HIGGINS, KEVIN CHRISTOPHER (1892–1927)

Revolutionary and politician. Known as the 'strong man' of the ⇨Cumann na nGaedheal government, he was vice-president of the executive council from 1922 until his assassination by republicans. O'Higgins was born in Stradbally, County Laois, and joined Sinn Féin while a student at University College, Dublin. Unsympathetic to republican aspirations, he sought a united Ireland under a dual monarchy with Britain. He was a ruthless advocate of the Anglo-Irish Treaty (1921), which set up the Irish Free State, vigorously defending the government's execution of 77 rebels during the Irish Civil War (1922–23). His establishment of an unarmed police force was a major success.

O'Higgins was elected to Westminster in 1918 as Sinn Féin member of parliament for Queen's County while under arrest in jail. He abstained and in 1919 was appointed assistant minister for local government in the first Dáil (then the illegal republican parliament). While vice-president of the Irish Free State, he also held successive ministerial posts for economic affairs, justice, and external affairs. On 10 June 1927 he was assassinated by three members of the Irish Republican Army (IRA), although without central IRA sanction, while walking to mass.

OIREACHTAS

Name of the legislature or parliament of the Republic of Ireland. It consists of the president of the Republic, a lower house called ⇨Dáil Éireann, and a senate called ⇨Seanad Éireann.

O'KEEFFE (or O'KEEFE), JOHN (1747–1833)

Dramatist and actor, born in Dublin, whose plays were popular in London. They include comedies, farces, and operas, such as *The Poor Soldier* (1783) and *Wild Oats* (1791).

O'Keeffe started acting at the Smock Alley Theatre in Dublin. After about 1770 he moved to London and turned to writing plays, generally full of Irish characters. More prolific than his contemporaries Oliver Goldsmith and Richard Brinsley Sheridan, his success was, however, less enduring. His weak eyesight made him totally blind by 1790 and ended his acting career. He wrote 68 pieces for the theatre, mostly comedies. His *Recollections* appeared in 1826. The Abbey Theatre revived *Wild Oats* in 1977.

Ó LAOGHAIRE, AN TATHAIR PEADAR (or FATHER PETER O'LEARY) (1839–1920)

Writer, born and raised on a farm in the then Irish-speaking parish of Clondrohid, County Cork. Ó Laoghaire was a prolific and bilingual writer of Irish fiction, in particular after the establishment of the ⇨Gaelic League in 1893. Besides his translations into Irish of Aesop and Lucian, among others, he also published an autobiography, *Mo Sgéal Féin*, contributed to periodicals, and wrote *Séadna* (1904), a serialized collection of folk tales intended as a reader for students of the Irish language.

O'LEARY, DAVID (1949–)

Anglo-Irish footballer, born in London. He was brought up in Dublin before returning to London in 1975 to join his compatriots Liam Brady and Frank Stapleton at Arsenal. A regular at centre-half for Arsenal, he won two FA Cup winners' medals but had to wait 14 years for his first league medal when a late Micheal Thomas goal enabled Arsenal to steal the title from Liverpool. His loyalty to the club saw him set an all-time record of 723 appearances. Capped 68 times for the Republic of Ireland, his winning penalty in the shoot-out against Romania sent his side through to meet Italy in the World Cup quarter-finals in 1990.

O'Leary succeeded George Graham as manager of Leeds United in 1998, guiding them to a place in the UEFA (Union of European Football Associations) Cup at the first attempt.

O'LEARY, LIAM (1910–1992)

Actor, director, and archivist, born in Cork. One of the founders of the Irish Film Society in 1936, O'Leary also worked as a director in both independent theatre and at the Abbey Theatre. In the 1940s he began to produce documentaries, some of which were sponsored by government departments. He also made one of Ireland's most effective political propaganda films, *Our Country* (1948), which helped defeat Fianna Fáil in the 1948 general election.

O'Leary acted in a number of films including the thriller *Stranger at My Door*/*At A Dublin Inn* (1948), and as a missionary priest in *Men Against the Sun* (1953). His publications include the first Irish book on cinema, *Invitation to the Film* (1945), *Silent Cinema* (1965), and a biography of the Irish-born Hollywood director of the 1920s and 1930s, Rex Ingram (1980).

OMAGH

County town of County ⇨Tyrone, in the foothills of the Sperrin Mountains, on the River Strule, 48 km/30 mi south of Londonderry; population (1991) 17,300. Industries include dairy produce, food processing, footwear, shirt manufacturing, and engineering. Omagh was planned in the early 17th century; its chief buildings are the Catholic church, with its irregular twin spires, the courthouse, built in Classical style, and the County Hall. It is now a tourist centre, and there is salmon fishing.

Omagh was the scene of a terrorist attack when a republican car bomb exploded on 15 August 1998 in a busy shopping area, killing 29 people and injuring scores of others. The breakaway republican group, the Real IRA, claimed responsibility for the bombing. This tragic incident appeared to have a bonding and strengthening effect which spurred the Northern Ireland peace process forward. Over 50,000 people gathered in Omagh for the remembrance ceremony, and in September 1998 the Real IRA announced a permanent ceasefire.

O'MAHONY, JOHN (1816–1877)

Political leader, born in Kilbeheny, County Limerick, and educated at Trinity College, Dublin. After taking part in the abortive rebellion of 1848 led by William Smith ⇨O'Brien, he fled to France, and from there to the USA in 1852. In New York, he became acquainted with the revolutionary publicist John Mitchel, and in 1858, with James ⇨Stephens in Dublin, he founded the Irish-American ⇨Fenian Brotherhood.

O'MALLEY, DONOGH (1921–1968)

Fianna Fáil politician. Although an engineer by trade, O'Malley made politics his career. He represented the constituency of Limerick East in the Dáil (parliament) from 1954, and served as minister for health 1965–66 and education 1966–68. As minister for education, he made post-primary education free in September 1967.

O'MALLEY, ERNEST (1898–1957)

Revolutionary and intellectual. He was born into a prosperous family in County Mayo, and was a medical student at University College, Dublin. An ⇨Irish Republican Army (IRA) organizer during the Anglo–Irish War (1919–21), he became a leading opponent of the Anglo-Irish Treaty (1921) in the Irish Civil War (1922–23). In 1936 he published *On Another Man's Wound*, one of the finest memoirs of the Irish struggle for independence.

O'Malley dropped out of medical studies in 1916. He joined the ⇨Irish Volunteers in 1917, becoming an experienced activist under Michael Collins, who became the IRA's director of organization. He was imprisoned in 1920 but escaped in February 1921 and became commander of the IRA's 2nd Southern Division.

In 1922 O'Malley was appointed to the anti-Treaty IRA Army Council as assistant Chief of Staff for the Irregulars and was seriously wounded by Free State forces in the civil war. While imprisoned, he was elected to the Dáil (parliament) for anti-Treaty Sinn Féin in 1923. Later, he drifted out of republican activism and pursued his interests in literature and art in Ireland and abroad.

O'NEILL

Major Gaelic Irish dynasty of Ulster in the later Middle Ages, descended from the Cenél nEóghain branch of the Uí Néill, an ancient family which dominated mid-Ulster in the 9th and 10th centuries.

Having suffered eclipse in the 11th century, the O'Neills recovered status through their leadership of Gaelic resistance to the Anglo-Norman invaders of Ulster, consolidating their pre-eminent position in Ulster at the Battle of Caimeirghe in 1241. However, their defeat at the Battle of Down (1260) ended O'Neill ambitions to restore the high kingship of Ireland. Thereafter, successive O'Neill chieftains sought to stabilize their position through complex armed alliances with other Ulster lords, the Scots, and the great Anglo-Norman houses. Such aspirations reached their peak in 1480 with the conclusion of a marriage alliance with the powerful ⇨Fitzgeralds of Kildare.

The fall of the Kildare Fitzgeralds in 1536 left the O'Neill's vulnerable to reprisals from factional rivals. They sought escape by means of a ⇨surrender and regrant treaty with the English crown in 1542, under which Conn Bacach O'Neill (1484–1559) surrendered his lands to Henry VIII and received them back, along with the title Earl of Tyrone.

Succession problems arising from the illegitimacy and political weakness of Conn's nominated heir, Matthew (died 1559), led to the rise of another legitimate son, Shane (1530–1567), and violent internecine war. Rejecting Shane's claims to the succession, the crown had him assassinated and restored the original succession through Matthew's younger son Hugh ⇨O'Neill, who was created 2nd Earl of Tyrone in 1585. Hugh proved to be highly independent and, after some hesitation, became leader of the Ulster rebellion against government forces in 1594. Following the surrender of the Ulster chiefs in 1603, their sudden departure from Ireland in 1607, known as the ⇨Flight of the Earls, was intended to be temporary but ended in prolonged exile in Rome. Although Hugh's nephew, Owen Roe O'Neill, returned to lead an army for the ⇨Confederation of Kilkenny in their rebellion of the 1640s, the main O'Neill line died out with Hugh in Rome.

O'NEILL, HUGH ('THE GREAT O'NEILL') (2nd Earl of Tyrone) (1550–1616)

Ulster chieftain and rebel. The younger son of Matthew, Baron of Dungannon, who was the nominated heir of Conn Bacach O'Neill, Earl of Tyrone, Hugh barely escaped death at the hands of Shane

O'Neill (1530–1567). Educated in the English ⇨Pale (the Anglo-Irish region around Dublin) and for some time in England, Hugh was restored to a small part of the O'Neill lordship in 1568.

Heavily reliant on English protection in his early years, O'Neill had begun to assert his independent influence in Ulster politics before his creation as 2nd Earl of Tyrone in 1585. Thereafter his attempts to extend his authority over the Ulster lords, while simultaneously supporting the English reform policy of ⇨composition (which imposed a tax instead of feudal military dues), imposed severe strains on him. These problems, coupled with the provocative actions of the English lord deputy, William Fitzwilliam (1526–1599), in his partitioning of Monaghan, eventually forced him to join with his son-in-law Red Hugh O'Donnell (1572–1602) and Aodh Maguire (died 1600) in rebellion against the government in 1594. Success in Armagh at the Battle of the Yellow Ford (1598) allowed O'Neill to carry the war into Ireland as a whole, but defeat of his overstretched forces in County Cork at Kinsale in 1601 spelled a virtual end to the rising.

Following their surrender in 1603, O'Neill and his allies secured remarkably generous terms, but he was unable to sustain his dual role of Gaelic chief and English peer. His participation in the ⇨Flight of the Earls from Ireland in 1607 was intended to be preparatory to a triumphal return, but plans never matured and he died in exile in Rome.

O'NEILL, SHANE (1530–1567)

Ulster dynastic lord. Displaced from possible succession to the O'Neillship and the earldom of Tyrone through his father's decision to nominate an older but illegitimate brother as his heir under the terms of surrender and regrant, Shane fought a violent campaign to overthrow the settlement. By the mid-1550s he had overpowered his father and brothers and established himself as the O'Neill. But the war had left him heavily dependent on Scottish mercenaries – most particularly the MacDonnells (MacDonalds) – whose extortions alienated his own people and aroused the hostility of the English government. After his father's death in 1559, O'Neill made several efforts to rid himself of the Scottish alliance by reaching an agreement with the English. But the government's mistrust and intrigues with other Ulster Lords forced him to even greater demonstrations of his power including a bold declaration of war of the Scots themselves. In

1567, an overconfident mission to punish the O'Donnells of Tyrconnell led to his surprise defeat at Farsetmore, and while seeking to revive the old alliance with the MacDonnells, he was assassinated in the midst of negotiation, most probably through the intrigues of the Dublin government.

O'NEILL, TERENCE (Baron O'Neill of the Maine) (1914–1990)

Unionist politician who was minister of finance 1956–63, then prime minister of Northern Ireland 1963–69. He expounded liberal policies and in 1965 exchanged visits with the Republic of Ireland's Taoiseach (prime minister) Seán ⇨Lemass to improve cross-border relations, but his government achieved little substantial reform. He resigned when opposed by his party on measures to extend rights to Roman Catholics, including a universal franchise in local elections.

O'Neill was born in London into a wealthy Anglo-Irish family. He was sent to Eton public school, then entered the Irish Guards, serving as a captain in World War II. He was a Unionist member of parliament at Stormont (the Northern Ireland parliament) from 1946–70 and was made a life peer in 1970.

O'NOLAN, BRIAN

see ⇨O'Brien, Flann.

ORANGEMAN

A member of one of the Ulster Protestant Orange Societies established within the ⇨Orange Order (founded 1795).

ORANGE MUSIC

Traditional music of the Unionist population in the north of Ireland. Orange music is often ignored in discussions of traditional Irish music, the vast majority of which is normally associated with the Catholic, nationalist communities. The ⇨Orange Order, a social and political organization within the unionist communities of Ireland, has played a role in parts of Northern Ireland in the preservation of certain country dances and song. The marching band tradition of the Orange Order, and particularly the flute bands (although brass and reed and accordion bands also exist), have maintained a repertoire of Orange marching tunes and songs with roots in British military music, traditional dance music, and church music.

The instrument most commonly associated with these bands is the Lambeg drum, originating from the military long drum of the 18th century. It is regarded very much as a symbol, both visual and audible, of Unionism, although this was not always the case.

ORANGE ORDER

Solely Protestant organization founded in County Armagh in 1795 in opposition to the ⇨Defenders, a Catholic secret society. It was a revival of the Orange Institution founded in 1688 to support William (III) of Orange, whose victory over the Catholic James II at the Battle of the Boyne in 1690 has been commemorated annually by Protestants in parades since 1796. The new order was organized into Orange Societies in a similar way to ⇨freemasonry, with a system of lodges. It has institutional ties with the ⇨Ulster Unionist Party.

The Orange Order was established following the victory of the Protestant Peep o'Day Boys over the Defenders in the sectarian Battle of the Diamond (1795) near Loughgall, County Armagh. During the late 1790s the order spread to many Irish counties and centralized its leadership in Dublin in 1798. Initially a proletarian organization, this development reflected growing support amongst the gentry officials who saw its wider military and political potential in opposing the radical reformist ⇨United Irishmen. Orangemen served as armed auxiliaries in the suppression of the ⇨Rebellion of 1798, and lodges spread into the armed forces.

Orangemen resisted Catholic emancipation in the early 19th century. This opposition was sometimes violent and the government banned the Orange Order in 1825, along with the Catholic Association. Gentry support had declined and the Grand Lodge voluntarily dissolved in 1836. Orangeism survived at a popular level and was reactivated as a political force in the 1880s by landlords opposed to ⇨home rule. This revival continued as the Orange Order became an integral part of unionist resistance to home rule. The link continued with the formation of Northern Ireland in 1921 and the Orange Order still retains institutional ties with the Ulster Unionists. Its political prominence is cyclical. In the late 1990s nationalist opposition to some of its traditional marches led to parades, like that at Drumcree in 1997 and 1998, assuming immense significance during attempts to create new political structures in Northern Ireland.

Ó RATHAILLE, AODHAGÁN (or LITTLE HUGH O'RAHILLY) (1670–c.1730)

Gaelic poet who was born in Kerry, on lands ruled in the middle ages by the MacCarthy Earls of Clancarty. He idolized the memory of the MacCarthys, and regarded himself as a descendant of their court bards. His poetry embodies the great ⇨Jacobite lament for the demise of Catholic Gaelic Ireland. A characteristic feature of his elegant, elegiac poems is the *aisling*, or patriotic dream-vision.

Although they were largely orally transmitted, his Gaelic poems survived in part and were edited bilingually for the Irish Texts Society in 1900, a revised edition being produced in 1911.

ORCHESTRAS

Ireland supports four professional orchestras: the Ulster Orchestra in Northern Ireland and the National Symphony Orchestra, Radió Telefís Éireann (RTÉ) Concert Orchestra, and Irish Chamber Orchestra in the Republic of Ireland.

Northern Ireland

The Ulster Orchestra is based in the Ulster Hall, Belfast. It was established in 1969, currently has 63 full-time players, and is conducted by Dmitry Sitkovetsky. Past principal conductors include Bryden Thomson, Vernon Handley, Yan Pascal Tortelier, and En Shao. It has made over 50 recordings and has toured extensively in Britain, Ireland, Europe, and the USA.

Republic of Ireland

The two longest established professional orchestras in the Republic are the Dublin-based National Symphony Orchestra and the RTÉ Concert Orchestra, both of which developed in association with the national broadcasting agency. The first professional ensemble out of which they emerged was 2RN's (as the national radio broadcaster was called at the time) 'station trio'. By 1946 Radio Éireann (the renamed

*t*elevision contracts the imagination and radio expands it.

TERRY WOGAN Radio and television broadcaster 'Sayings of the Year' in *The Observer*, 30 December 1984.

ORCHESTRAS *The RTÉ (Radio Telefís Éireann) Concert Orchestra prides itself on being one of Europe's most versatile ensembles, with a repertoire covering musical styles from* Messiah *to* Les Misérables. *It has visited the USA three times with its* Spirit of Ireland *programme.*

national broadcaster) supported the Radio Éireann Light Orchestra of 22 players and the Radio Éireann Symphony Orchestra of 61 players. By the early 1950s these orchestras began to tour outside Dublin. In the late 1960s the Light Orchestra developed into what is know now as the RTÉ Concert Orchestra. This is a versatile ensemble, conducted for 22 years by Proinnsías Ó Duinn, performing a variety of repertoires from opera to Eurovision. By 1989 the larger ensemble was renamed the National Symphony Orchestra and was based at the National Concert Hall, Dublin. It now has over 90 musicians and is conducted by Alexander Anissimov, with Gerhard Markson as principal guest conductor; past conductors have included Tibor Paul, Gerald Victory, and Milan Horvat. It has recorded extensively, including its series of Malcolm Arnold and Bruckner symphonies.

The most recent professional orchestra in the Republic is the Irish Chamber Orchestra. Formed in 1970, mostly from musicians in the RTÉ ensemble, it became a full-time professional orchestra in 1995 with its move from Dublin to Limerick, where it is based at the University of Limerick. This ensemble of 18 string players is led by Fionnuala Hunt and is committed to works by contemporary Irish composers. They have performed and recorded with Bruno Giuranna (principal guest conductor), Franco Gulli, Nicholas Kraemer, Jerzy Maksymiuk, John O'Conor, Günter Pichler, and Hugh Tinney. The orchestra has also established an International Chamber Music Festival in Killaloe, County Clare, which takes place annually in July.

Ó REACHTABHRA, ANTOINE

Versifier and wandering minstrel; see Antoine ⇨Raiftearaí.

O'REILLY, JOHN BOYLE (1844–1890)

Irish-born writer and republican. Born at Dowth Castle, County Louth, he was apprenticed as a journalist, and worked in Ireland and England. O'Reilly is best known for his collections of poetry, such as *Songs, Legends and Ballads* (1878). In 1866 he was arrested and tried for his ⇨Fenian activities; he was sentenced to life imprisonment and later transported to Australia in 1868. He escaped to the USA in 1869, settled in Boston, and resumed his career as a journalist. In 1876 he became co-owner and editor of the *Pilot*, an influential Irish-American newspaper. He was also a popular lecturer.

O'REILLY, TONY (ANTHONY JOHN FRANCIS) (1936–   )

Rugby Union player and business executive, born in Dublin. In 1954, aged 18, he made his debut for Ireland and the following year he was chosen to travel on the British Lions tour. He played with Old Belvedere Rugby club from 1955 to 1970 and won 29 international caps during his record-breaking 16-year career, playing at wing three-quarter. He is the most capped

Lions test winger and his tally of 38 tries for his country still stands as a record. He scored a record six tries in his ten appearances for the Lions. He is currently the worldwide president of Heinz and chairman of Independent Newspapers.

Ó RIADA, SEÁN (JOHN REIDY)

(1931–1971)

Composer, arranger, and academic. Though he was fluent in many different musical idioms, he is best remembered for the pioneering role he played in the revival of traditional Irish music, particularly with his group Ceoltóirí Cualann (from which the folk group the ⇨Chieftains evolved).

Ó Riada was born in Cork and studied at University College, Cork. He was assistant music director at Radio Éireann in Dublin 1954–55. After a short period in Paris, he returned to Dublin for perhaps the most prolific period of his life as musical director of the ⇨Abbey Theatre until 1962. He was also involved in the other major classical ensembles in Dublin of the time but most famously founded Ceoltóirí Cualann (in which he played the bodhrán and harpsichord) to perform his music to Brian MacMahon's play *The Honey Spike* in 1962. It was at this time also that he wrote the influential orchestral scores for the films *Mise Éire* and *Saoirse*. From 1963 until his death he taught in the Music Department of University College, Cork, under Aloys Fleischmann.

Other important works include his two masses *Aifreann 1* and *Aifreann 2* and his series of orchestral Nomos pieces 1–6, composed between 1957 and 1966.

Ó RIÓRDÁIN, SEÁN (1916–1977)

Poet, born in Ballvourney, in the Gaeltacht (Irish-speaking area) of west Cork. Considered one of the best modern Irish-language poets, Ó Riórdáin believed that writing is a form of prayer and a process of self-discovery. He had a strong influence on younger poets who wrote in Irish such as Nuala ⇨Ní Dhomhnaill. Collections of his poetry, which include *Eireaball Spideoige* (1952) and *Brosna* (1964), reflect a struggle with the nature of identity, language, and faith.

Diagnosed with tuberculosis in 1938, Ó Riórdáin often commented on the ironic relationship between his illness and his creative vitality.

O'RIORDAN, CONAL HOLMES O'CONNELL (pseudonym F NORREYS CONNELL) (1874–1948)

Novelist and playwright. Born in Dublin, he was educated at Clongowes Wood College, and moved to London at the age of 16 to pursue a career as an actor and dramatist. His first book was *In the Green Park* (1894); later novels include the 'Adam' trilogy, beginning with *Adam of Dublin* (1920); and the 'Soldier' series, including *Soldier Born* (1927), *Soldier of Waterloo* (1928), and *Soldier's End* (1938). O'Riordan succeeded J M Synge as director of the ⇨Abbey Theatre, Dublin 1909–15. His plays include *Rope Enough* (1913), *His Majesty's Pleasure* (1925), and *The King's Wooing* (1929).

ORMOND (or ORMONDE)

See ⇨Butlers of Ormond.

ORPEN, WILLIAM NEWENHAM MONTAGUE (1878–1931)

Portrait painter who exerted a huge influence on the succeeding generation as a teacher in Dublin 1900–14. He later achieved enormous financial success in London as a society portrait painter. His nudes are among the most significant of the period, and as an official war artist 1914–18 he produced one of the greatest bodies of war art.

Born in Dublin, Orpen enjoyed a brilliant student career in Dublin and London. He was a consummate draughtsman. The influence of James Whistler is evident in his early works, and he saw the work of Velázquez in Madrid with his close friend Hugh Lane. In London he enjoyed accentuating his Irishness to the point of caricature. Despite the demand for his services in fashionable society, he continued his personal artistic explorations. His nude portraits, characterized by a lack of idealization, emphasis on the sitter's personality, and frank positions, invite comparison with the work of the German-born British artist Lucian Freud.

OSBORNE, WALTER (1859–1903)

Painter, a leading artist of the later 19th century. Though a successful portraitist, Osborne's first love was landscape where he depicted the scenes from everyday rural and urban life for which he is best known and enduringly popular.

Born in Dublin into an artistic family, Osborne received his artistic training in Dublin. He continued his studies in Antwerp, Belgium, as a number of Irish artists did around this time. There, in common with many European artists of the day, he began to paint outdoors, hence his inclusion in the group known as the Irish ⇨Impressionists. During the 1880s he spent much of his time painting in France and England. Though impressionistic in their emphasis on the effects of light, these works demonstrate Osborne's concern with clarity of line and draughtsmanship, reflecting his sound academic training.

From 1892 Osborne lived permanently in Dublin. Some of his best-loved works, such as *Dublin Park, Light and Shade* (National Gallery of Ireland, Dublin) and *Tea in the Garden* (Hugh Lane Municipal Gallery of Modern Art, Dublin), date from this period. He was elected a member of the Royal Hibernian Academy in 1886 and through his teaching at the academy schools exerted an important influence on the next generation, most notably William Leech (1881–1968).

WALTER OSBORNE *A much-travelled artist, Osborne was influenced by the Impressionists, as seen in this portrait of J B S MacIlwaine (1892), which hangs in Dublin's National Gallery of Arts.*

O'SHEA, MILO (1925–)

Stage and film actor. Following a long stage career with the Abbey Theatre, O'Shea began playing character roles in films, with his signature as a somewhat confused and ineffective person. Although his first screen appearance was in a minor role in *Talk of a Million* (1951), it was not until the 1960s that he began to appear regularly in films. Among his more prominent roles were those in *Ulysess* (1967), *Sacco and Vanzetti* (1971), *The Verdict* (1982), *The Purple Rose of Cairo* (1985) directed by Woody Allen (1935–), *Only the Lonely* (1991), and *The Playboys* (1992).

OSSIAN (Irish *Oisín*)

Legendary Gaelic hero and bard, claimed by both Ireland and Scotland. He is sometimes represented as the son of ⇨Finn Mac Cumhaill, in about AD 250, and as having lived to tell the tales of Finn and the Ulster heroes to St Patrick, in about 400. The publication in 1760 of James Macpherson's poems, attributed to Ossian, made Ossian's name familiar throughout Europe.

Ó SÚILLEABHÁIN, EOGHAN RUADH (or RED OWEN O'SULLIVAN; also known as EOGHAN AN BHÉIL BHINN, 'EOGHAN OF THE SWEET MOUTH') (1748–1784)

Gaelic poet who was born in Meentogues, near Killarney, County Kerry. His work followed Irish patriotic poetic traditions, epitomizing the last phase of native Irish vernacular poetry, and has been compared to that of his Scottish contemporary Robert Burns. W B Yeats's character 'Red Hanrahan' is based on him, as is 'Owen MacCarthy' in Thomas Flanagan's *The Year of the French* (1979).

During his life he taught in the banned Catholic ('hedge') schools, worked as an itinerant labourer, sailed under Admiral George Rodney in the West Indies, and served in the British army.

Ó SÚILLEABHÁIN, MÍCHEÁL (1950–)

Composer, performer, and academic. He has had parallel careers in the academic and performance worlds, with a concentration on Irish traditional music. A pioneer in writing for combined ensembles of traditional and classical musicians, his work *Oileán/Island*, a 'concerto for Traditional Musician and String Orchestra', was released in 1989.

Born in Clonmel, County Tipperary, Ó Súilleabháin studied music at University College, Cork, where he became a lecturer in music in 1975. In 1994 he was appointed first professor of music at the University of Limerick where he established the Irish World Music Centre, honouring different traditions of music and dance in the same academic and performance environment. He made nine commercial recordings between 1976 and 1999.

O'SULLIVAN, MAUREEN (1911–1998)

Film and stage actor, born in Boyle, County Roscommon, who appeared in over 60 films but is best known for her role as Jane in a number of films in the *Tarzan* series. Discovered by US director Frank Borzage in Dublin in 1929 while preparing for Ireland's first sound feature, the John McCormack vehicle *Song O' My Heart*, O'Sullivan, who had no previous acting experience, went to Hollywood shortly afterwards to play Jane to Johnny Weissmuller's Tarzan. She was largely confined to secondary roles in first-line pictures or lead parts in B films.

She retired from films in 1942 to raise her seven children by director John Farrow, including future actor Mia Farrow. In the 1950s she hosted a television show, *Irish Heritage*, and in the 1960s she appeared in a number of Broadway productions, including *Never Too Late*, a role she repeated in the film version of the play in 1965.

O'SULLIVAN, SEUMAS (pseudonym of JAMES SULLIVAN STARKEY) (1879–1958)

Poet, born in Dublin, and the founder-editor of the *Dublin Magazine* 1923–58. A mystical poet, and a follower of 'AE' (George ⇨Russell), his volumes of verse include *The Twilight People* (1905), *Verses Sacred and Profane* (1908), *Collected Poems* (1912 and 1940), *Requiem* (1917), *Personal Talk* (1936), *Dublin Poems* (1946), and *Translations and Transcriptions* (1950).

Collections of O'Sullivan's essays are *Impres-*

SONIA O'SULLIVAN *Seen here in the women's 1500m heat at the World Athletics Championships, Athens, in 1997, O'Sullivan took a break from sport for the arrival of her first baby in 1999, returning to train for the Sydney Olympics in 2000.*

sions (1912), *Mud and Purple* (1917), *Common Adventures* (1926), and *The Rose and Bottle* (1946).

O'SULLIVAN, SONIA (1969–)

Athlete, born in Cobh, County Cork. A brilliant and versatile middle- and long-distance runner, equally strong on the track or in cross-country, she came to the fore in 1992 when she won the 1,500-metres world title at the World Student Games. In 1994 she won the European 3,000-metres title. Stepping up to 5,000 metres, she took the gold medal at the 1995 world championships. Affected by illness she underperformed at the 1996 Olympic Games; however, in 1998 she won both the short- and long-distance events at the World Cross-Country Championships, and then at the European Championships she won golds at 5,000 and 10,000 metres.

O'SULLIVAN, THADDEUS (1948–)

Director and cameraman, born in Dublin. O'Sullivan's most accomplished and commercially popular film, *December Bride* (1990), an adaptation of the novel by Sam Hanna ⇨Bell, is set in Northern Ireland and concerns the tensions generated in a largely Protestant community when a housekeeper has children with both brothers who employ her. His feature *Nothing Personal* (1996) focuses on the activities of loyalist and republican paramilitaries in Belfast in the 1970s. O'Sullivan has also worked in television, making *In the Border Country* (1991) about the border area between Northern Ireland and the Republic of Ireland.

O'Sullivan's debut film as director was the short *A Pint of Plain* (1975), while his feature-length *On a Paving Stone Mounted* (1978) used an experimental form to explore an Irish migrant's experience in London, and the migrant's return to Ireland. Later he abandoned this avant-garde practice as he made mainstream commercial cinema and television films.

O'TOOLE, PETER (SEAMUS) (1932–)

Actor, born in Connemara. After leaving school at a young age,

POULNABRONE

Ireland has some of Europe's best-preserved prehistoric remains. Believed to date from 3800 BC, this huge Neolithic dolmen, or portal tomb, known as Poulnabrone, is one of over a hundred megaliths in the Burren, an outstanding area of limestone pavement in County Clare. Standing beside the road from Ballyvaughan to Corrofin, the dolmen's uprights support a large capstone, and the structure would have had earth sides, forming a burial mound. Its silhouette is used as the symbol of the Burren National Park.

NEWGRANGE

The brilliant white quartzite surrounding the enormous burial mound of Newgrange, County Meath, is a modern reconstruction that has not been without its critics. This huge passage grave, dating from 3100 BC, lies within the Valley of the Boyne, which has a number of Neolithic burial sites. Newgrange is a near-circular construction, 80 m/278 ft in diameter, with a passage leading to an inner chamber.

CARROWKEEL

Standing above the still waters of Lough Arrow, County Sligo, are 14 round cairns, known collectively as Carrowkeel, grouped on a hilltop of the Bricklieve Mountains. Inside are megalithic cruciform passage graves with side recesses, dating from around 2500 BC.

DUN AENGUS

Hanging on the edge of a sheer drop of 92 m/300 ft to the sea, the stone fort of Dun Aengus on Inishmore, Aran Islands, is believed to be of Bronze Age origin, and may once have been circular, the remainder of the building having fallen into the sea as the cliffs were eroded.

▶ **ORATORY OF GALLARUS**

Such skill went into the construction of the drystone Christian Oratory of Gallarus on the Dingle Peninsula, County Kerry, that the building stands intact to this day, having been erected between the 7th and 12th centuries. A door is believed to have hung from a horizontal hinge across the entrance.

WHITE ISLAND

These eight solemn images dating from the 7th and 10th centuries stand in atmospheric splendour in a ruined Romanesque church on White Island, Lough Erne, County Fermanagh. The lough was on an ancient pilgrims' trail, which may account for why so many carved figures have been found here.

GLENDALOUGH

Once there were many monastic round towers, but now only 65 remain, some as mere stumps. Dating from the 7th century, and possibly used as observatories, storehouses, or strongholds, their slender height made them vulnerable to destruction by high winds and lightning. This one, at Glendalough, County Wicklow, is over 30 m/100 ft high.

CLONMACNOISE HIGH CROSS

Carved high crosses are a notable feature of medieval Irish religious art. This Cross of the Scriptures at Clonmacnoise monastery, County Offaly, is a replica, the original having been moved to the nearby Visitors' Centre. Various biblical carvings can be deciphered, including the crucifixion and other Passion scenes. The original cross was made in the 10th century for high king Flann Sinna.

SHRINE OF ST PATRICK'S BELL
This small shrine was made in about 1100 for the king, Domhnall Ua Lochlainn, to hold one of Ireland's most important relics, St Patrick's bell. The workmanship on the bronze casket is variable, the finest being on the gold filigree openwork panels with their patterns of large beasts interlaced with snakes.

ARDAGH CHALICE
The Ardagh Chalice shows the remarkable skills of 8th-century Celtic metalworkers. The borders and roundels on the beaten silver are decorated with the finest filigree, enamelwork, embossing, and engraving. Animals used in the decoration show the beginnings of a German influence that became more evident in later centuries.

BOOK OF KELLS

The intricacy and detail of the illuminations in the Book of Kells show the astonishing creativity of the artists who worked on it, for no design is repeated. Dating from the 8th or 9th century, the partly finished book of gospels was probably brought to Kells from Iona, the holy island off the west of Scotland, by monks escaping from a Viking raid.

TARA BROOCH

Superbly worked, the bronze and gold Tara Brooch, an early 8th-century artefact found on a beach near Bettystown, County Meath, is over 22 cm/8 in long, and was designed to be worn on the shoulder. Its owner must have been wealthy, although there is no known connection with royalty, despite its name.

CLONMACNOISE

The remains of Clonmacnoise, once a bustling monastic city founded in 548 by St Ciaran, stand by the River Shannon. The complex grew up near a key crossroads of first-millennium Ireland, where the river met the main road from east to west. This proximity, while good for trade, also made invasion a constant threat.

ARDMORE

The ruins at Ardmore, County Waterford, are probably those of a 12th-century cathedral, built on the site of an earlier monastery. The reliefs on the western façade are Romanesque, a style that originated in France and was introduced into Ireland by the English who would have seen Romanesque churches along the pilgrims' route to Compostela in Spain.

MELLIFONT

Monasteries flourished in Ireland from the 5th to the 12th centuries, and many were like small, wealthy towns. In 1142, St Mallachy, founder of Mellifont Abbey, County Louth, left, acted with others to reform the monasteries. This pattern of decline and revival continued until the 16th century, when the monasteries were dissolved by the Tudor monarchy.

◀ **ROCK OF CASHEL**
The cluster of medieval buildings that top the Rock of Cashel dominate the Tipperary skyline above the Golden Vale. Brian Bóruma was crowned here, and an earlier fortress was the seat of kings of Munster until 1101, when the Rock was given to the church. The Rock was made a protected site in 1999.

▶ **JERPOINT ABBEY**
The height of Jerpoint Abbey's tower makes it unusual, since typically a Cistercian tower would be wide but squat. Like the decorated cloister, the tower was a 16th-century addition to the 12th-century abbey, which was built on a cruciform plan, with two square chapels in each transept.

BUNRATTY CASTLE
Surrounding the 15th-century castle at Bunratty, County Clare is a reconstruction of an Irish community of the late 19th/early 20th centuries. Peasants' cottages are set up with the tools, furniture, and equipment of the time, as are various shops, a school, and a doctor's surgery.

BLARNEY CASTLE
Best-known for the famous stone set in its battlements, the 15th-century Blarney Castle, County Cork, occupies a commanding position over the River Martin, and there are magnificent views from the top of the square keep. The castle is surrounded by beautiful gardens that include several ancient standing stones.

ROSS CASTLE
The setting of the early 16th-century Ross Castle on the banks of Lough Leane, just outside Killarney, County Kerry, is particularly romantic in the early evening. Innisfallen Island, which Thomas Babington Macaulay described as 'a bit of heaven itself', can be reached by boat from the pier below the castle.

MOUNT STEWART GARDENS

On the east coast of County Down, between Strangford Lough and the Irish Sea, the 80-acre Mount Stewart estate benefits from the warmth of the Gulf Stream. Edith, Lady Londonderry, wife of the seventh Marquess of Londonderry, laid out spectacular gardens here from the 1920s, including the Shamrock Garden with its Celtic harp.

KNOCKMEALDOWN MOUNTAINS

A quintessential County Tipperary view, deep in the Knockmealdown Mountains which form the border with County Waterford. Rough moorland latticed with brooks and edged by pine forests stretches away from the border down to the valley of Clogheen with the Galtee Mountains in the distance.

MOUNT STEWART HOUSE

The original Mount Stewart House was a simple family home dating from the early 19th century. It was greatly enlarged in neoclassical style for the third Marquess of Londonderry, by William Vitruvius Morrison, one of a dynasty of Irish architects.

▲ THE FOUR COURTS

The Georgian period saw a great surge of architectural activity in Ireland. Architect James Gandon set to work on the famous Dublin landmark, the Four Courts, in 1786, designing the huge central rotunda, with its green dome, as a focus from which the four courts radiated out. The interior was replanned when the building was reconstructed following shell-damage during the Irish Civil War in 1922.

▼ CARTON HOUSE, CHINESE ROOM

Queen Victoria once slept in the Chinese bedroom of Carton House, County Kildare, which was originally decorated in 1759. The Palladian style in which the house is built originated in Italy, and the movement dominated Irish architecture from about 1715 to 1760. It is characterized by richly decorated interiors contrasted with simple exteriors.

▲ CARTON HOUSE, SALOON

The saloon at Carton House, seat of the Fitzgeralds, has a highly ornamented baroque plasterwork ceiling by the Lafranchini brothers. Elaborate stucco was characteristic of 18th-century stately houses and became increasingly ornate, until the style took a more understated turn towards the end of the century.

GALWAY

Galway was founded at the mouth of the River Corrib in the 12th century and became a major port for international trade – Christopher Columbus is believed to have called here. Today it has a thriving computer industry and is an important centre of the Irish language – a theatre company based here, An Taibhdhearc, only stages plays in Irish.

CORK

In Cork, St Fin Barre's cathedral, built between 1863 and 1878, is said to occupy the site of a church founded by St Fin Barre in the 6th century. Lying on an island between two arms of the River Lee, the city centre has a wealth of quays and bridges.

DUBLIN

Dublin's O'Connell Bridge and O'Connell Street, the city's main thoroughfare, named after one of Ireland's greatest heroes, Daniel O'Connell (1775–1847), who campaigned for the emancipation of Catholics and for an end to the Act of Union with Britain.

▼ **THE GUINNESS FACTORY**

In 1759, a young brewer called Arthur Guinness signed a 1000-year lease on the St James's Gate site that is now home to Ireland's most celebrated brewery, covering 64 acres. As well as supplying a thirsty home market, Guinness is the biggest exporter of beer in the world.

◀ **TEMPLE BAR**
Artists, cultural organizations, businesses, bars, and restaurants co-exist in Temple Bar, Dublin's cultural quarter and one of Europe's most successful urban renewal projects. Saved from demolition in the 1980s, the area was targeted for development and now attracts 50,000 pedestrians daily.

▶ **IRISH FILM CENTRE**
The Irish Film Centre, in the Temple Bar district, houses cinemas, a bar, and shop, plus an important film archive built on a collection of Irish films accumulated since 1945. This unique resource is owned and run by the Irish Film Institute.

◀ **TRINITY COLLEGE LIBRARY**
The superb Long Room of Trinity College Library, which houses the richest collection of rare books in Ireland. The Book of Kells, the extraordinarily beautiful volume of illuminated manuscript, is kept here.

▲ **BELFAST SHIPBUILDING**
The Harland and Wolff shipyard, seen here in the distance, with Cave Hill in the background, is still important to Belfast's economy, which boomed in the 18th and 19th centuries as a result of shipbuilding. The yard lies at the mouth of the River Lagan, where it opens out into Belfast Lough.

◄ **BELFAST PUB**
There is no shortage of pubs and bars, both in the city centre and in more peaceful settings, such as the riverside Cutters Wharf, left. The city's most famous pub, The Crown, is under the protection of the National Trust.

STORMONT

Completed in 1932 for the government of Northern Ireland, the white, neo-classical building of Stormont, 8 km/5 mi from the centre of Belfast, is now the seat of the Northern Ireland Assembly.

LINEN HALL STREET

The modern buildings of Belfast's Linen Hall Street lead the eye to the elegant dome of the City Hall, built in 1906. The street takes its name from the White Linen Hall, which stood here in the 18th century. Other nearby reminders of the textile industry include the former Linen Merchants' Warehouse of 1869, now a chain store, and the Linen Hall Library, built in 1781.

CITY HALL GARDENS

Looking across the City Hall gardens from the west side of Donegall Square, with a statue of Sir Daniel Dixon, three times lord mayor of Belfast, standing in the foreground.

▲ **THE BURREN**

Tourism is a key industry for modern-day Ireland, and away from the tourist honeypots, Ireland remains peaceful and underpopulated. This group of walkers is exploring the Burren, County Clare, an extensive area of weathered limestone perched high above Galway Bay.

◄ **COBH**

Visitors in need of sustenance will find hospitality in any of the thousands of bars and pubs throughout the land. These pavement tables are outside a bar in Cobh, famous as the departure point for Irish emigrants, many of whose descendants now make nostalgic trips to the land of their forebears.

O'Toole made his stage debut at Leeds Civic Theatre aged 17 and began a professional acting career with the Bristol Old Vic Theatre in 1955. He came to prominence in a production of *The Long and the Short and the Tall* in 1959. He made his film debut as Rob Roy in the Disney production *Kidnapped* (1960) and became an international star when he played the lead in *Lawrence of Arabia* (1962), for which he won a British Academy award and the first of seven Academy Award nominations.

Other films for which O'Toole received Academy Award nominations (though no wins) include the critically acclaimed *Becket* (1964), *The Lion in Winter* (1968) which was shot in Ireland, *Goodbye Mr Chips* (1969), *The Ruling Class* (1972), and *My Favourite Year* (1982).

In the 1970s O'Toole's public notoriety as a drinker began to take precedence over his acting, but

I'm not a philosopher. Guilty bystander, that's my role.

PETER O'TOOLE *Sunday Times* 20 May 1990.

~

he received the American Film Critics award in 1979 for *The Short Man* and continued to act in a wide range of films for both television and theatrical release, including *The Last Emperor* (1987) and, in his one distinctive Irish role in Neil ⇨Jordan's *High Spirits* (1988). More recent films include *King Ralph* (1991), *Gulliver's Travels* (1996), *Fairy Tale: A True Story* (1997), and *Phantoms* (1998). In 1990 he took the lead role, with great success, in *Jeffrey Bernard is Unwell* in London's West End.

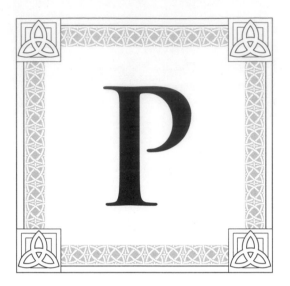

PAISLEY, IAN (RICHARD KYLE)

(1926–)

Northern Irish politician, cleric, and leader of the Democratic Unionist Party (DUP) from 1971. An imposing and deeply influential member of the Protestant community, he remains staunchly committed to the union with Britain. His political career has been one of high drama, marked by protests, resignations, fierce oratory, and a pugnacious and forthright manner.

Paisley was born in Armagh, the son of a Baptist minister. He preached his first sermon at the age of 16, and in 1951 established the Free Presbyterian Church of Ulster in Belfast. When Catholic civil-rights agitation began to flourish in the 1960s, Paisley organized numerous marches and speeches in opposition, which led to his imprisonment for six weeks in 1968 for unlawful assembly. In April 1970, one year into 'the Troubles' in Northern Ireland, Paisley won the seat for Bannside in Northern Ireland's Stormont assembly, and he went on to win the North Antrim seat two months later. The following year, he established the DUP as a more hardline rival to the ruling dominant Ulster Unionist Party.

Throughout the 1980s Paisley stuck rigidly to his 'no surrender' policies, resigning his seat in 1985 in protest at the Anglo-Irish Agreement, which set up cross-border cooperation between police and security forces and gave the Republic of Ireland a greater voice in Northern Ireland's affairs. He re-entered the UK parliament early the following year. His Presbyterian beliefs were inextricably bound up with his political aims, and in 1988 he was ejected from the European

Í would rather be British than just.

IAN PAISLEY *The Sunday Times*, 12 December 1971.

❧

Parliament for interrupting an address by Pope John Paul II.

Paisley opposed the 1998 Good Friday agreement on power-sharing in Northern Ireland and in the May 1998 referendum his North Antrim constituency was the only one of Northern Ireland's 18 seats in which there was a majority against the accord. He went on to lead the opposition to the agreement within the new Northern Ireland Assembly.

PALE, THE ENGLISH

The fortified area round Dublin, where English rule operated after the English settlement of Ireland in 1171. The term soon came to include the surrounding counties of Dublin, Meath, Kildare, and Louth, and was recognized politically until the early 17th-century, when medieval boundaries were overtaken by the ⇨plantation of Ireland 1556–1660.

PARKER, STEWART (1941–1988)

Dramatist, born in east Belfast and educated at Queen's University, Belfast. Parker achieved popularity by tackling timely issues but always with a belief that theatre should be enjoyed. Plays such as *Spokesong* (1975) and *Pentecost* (1987) are representative of his style in that they are set during 'the Troubles' but affirm the ability of language, and in particular theatricality, to affect change and illustrate individual goodness.

Parker's other works include the history plays *Northern Star* (1984) and *Heavenly Bodies* (1986), radio and television scripts, and two early pamphlets of verse.

PARKE'S CASTLE

Plantation-style castle with bawn (grass or meadow area) on the shore of Lough Gill, County Leitrim. It was built in the 1620s by Robert Parke on the site of a former tower house belonging to the O'Rourkes. The castle was captured by Irish forces and, in the mid-1600s, Cromwellians, before being returned to the Parke family in 1660. A considerable amount of restoration work has been carried out to the interior, and an original forge has been rebuilt.

PARNELL, CHARLES STEWART

(1846–1891)

Nationalist politician born in Avondale, County Wicklow. Elected member of parliament for Meath in 1875, he was a key member of the Irish Home Rule party led in the House of Commons by Isaac Butt. Parnell was instrumental in disrupting the business of the House and in securing the support of the ⇨Fenians. He became the president of the Home Rule party in 1877, and in 1879 helped form the ⇨Land League. This led to his imprisonment in 1881 in Kilmainham jail for incitement to violence, but he was released the following May, when an arrangement concerning Irish affairs, called the 'Kilmainham Treaty', was arrived at with the British prime minister William Gladstone. The treaty was an informal secret agreement, reached in April 1882 when the British government realized that Parnell could quell violence more easily out of prison than in it. In return for his release, he agreed to accept the Land Act of 1881. It marked a change in British policy in Ireland from confrontation to cooperation, with the government attempting to conciliate landowners and their tenants, who were refusing to pay rent.

Parnell welcomed Gladstone's Home Rule Bill, and continued his agitation after its defeat in 1886. In 1887 his reputation suffered from an unfounded accusation by *The Times* of complicity in the ⇨Phoenix Park Murders, though he had no connection with the crime and denounced it in the House of

*W*hy should Ireland be treated as a geographical fragment of England… Ireland is not a geographical fragment, but a nation.

CHARLES STEWART PARNELL Speech in the House of Commons, 26 April 1875.

~

Commons. His career was ruined in 1890 when he was cited as co-respondent in a divorce case, after his affair with Kitty O'Shea. He died suddenly of rheumatic fever at the age of 45. Because of his great influence over his followers, Parnell was called the 'uncrowned king of Ireland'.

CHARLES STEWART PARNELL *Seen here, in an engraving of the time, addressing supporters from the Victoria Hotel in Cork, shortly before his early death, the nationalist Parnell attracted deep loyalty and was colloquially known as 'the Chief'. As leader of the nationalist party he pressed for land reform and home rule, but his career faltered when he was cited in the O'Shea divorce case, and he died soon after.*

PARNELL, FRANCES ('FANNY') (1849–1882) AND ANNA (1852–1911)

Sisters of the Irish nationalist leader Charles Stewart Parnell. They set up the Ladies' Land League in 1881, in support of the ⇨Land League founded by their brother and Michael Davitt two years earlier. Anna was the more radical of the pair, and was a fund-raiser in the USA in the 1870s. After setting up the Ladies' Land League her extremism was denounced by the Catholic church. Considered the first modern Irish female agitator, she became estranged from her brother after he withdrew support for her movement. Fanny was a poet who gave Anna the idea for the Ladies' Land League. Her health was always poor and her poems became increasingly dark.

PARNELL, THOMAS (1679–1718)

Poet, born in Dublin, and educated there at Trinity College. Parnell wrote various isolated poems, showing a fine descriptive touch, the most important being 'The Hermit', 'The Night Piece', and 'The Hymn to Contentment'. He was a friend of Jonathan ⇨Swift, and the English poet Alexander Pope, whom he helped with his translation of the *Iliad*.

Parnell was ordained in 1700, and appointed vicar of Finglas and archdeacon of Clogher. He visited London 1712–18 where he contributed verse to the *Spectator* and *The Guardian*.

PARSONS, CHARLES (1854–1931)

Ireland's most eminent engineer, who invented the high-speed marine steam turbine and designed a much more efficient marine propeller blade which greatly increased thrust.

Parsons was born at Birr Castle, Birr, County Offaly, the youngest son of the astronomer William ⇨Parsons, 3rd Earl of Rosse. He never attended school and was tutored at home until he went to Trinity College, Dublin, and then Cambridge University in the 1880s. He left to establish Parson's Works at Newcastle upon Tyne where he built versions of his newly developed steam turbine.

His work received little attention until he launched the *SS Turbinia* in 1894, powered by his turbine and incorporating his new propeller design. With a speed of 34 knots, it was conspicuously faster than existing Royal Navy vessels and when demonstrated at a naval review for Queen Victoria's Diamond Jubilee at Spithead in 1897, Parsons' turbines were immediately bought by the Royal Navy. Within 20 years his new designs had revolutionized marine transport.

PARSONS, WILLIAM (3rd Earl of Rosse) (1800–1867)

Astronomer and engineer. He designed and built a 1.8-m/72-in reflector and telescope, which was the world's largest in the 19th century, and used it to study nebulae and photograph the moon. He found 15 spiral nebulae and named the Crab nebula.

Parsons was born in York, England, the son of a titled landowner. He studied at Trinity College, Dublin, and then Oxford, where he graduated in mathematics in 1822. While still a student in 1821 he was elected to parliament at Westminster to represent King's County (now County Offaly) as Lord Oxmantown, a seat he held for 13 years. In 1831 he became lord lieutenant of County Offaly and resigned his seat in the Commons in 1834. He entered the House of Lords as an Irish peer on the death of his father in 1841.

Parsons wanted to build a telescope larger than that used by the German-born English astronomer William Herschel, and began experiments in 1826 to find a suitable metal alloy for casting a large mirror which would not crack as it cooled. Much of the work was done by Parsons himself at the family seat at Birr Castle, Parsonstown, County Offaly, with the assistance of local workers. He developed a suitable alloy, combining four parts copper to one part tin to achieve a highly reflective surface.

In 1842 Parsons cast the Leviathan of Parsonstown, a disc 1.8 m/72 in in diameter which weighed nearly 4 tonnes and was incorporated into a telescope with a focal length of 16.2 m/54 ft. It took three years to complete its installation in the the observatory at Birr Castle, and was in operation 1845–78, mainly for the observation of nebulae and clusters. The Irish astronomer Robert ⇨Ball refined observational methods at the Birr observatory while working as a tutor at the castle. In 1999 the telescope and mirror were repaired and remounted to working order.

PARTITION

Division of Ireland into ⇨Northern Ireland and the ⇨Irish Free State (now the Republic of Ireland) under the Government of Ireland Act (1920). Partition was one factor which stopped Sinn Féin leader Éamon de

⇨Valera declaring the Irish Free State a republic, as it was felt that this would cement the separation which affected six of the nine counties of Ulster. Under the terms of the 1998 Good Friday agreement, the Republic of Ireland on 2 December 1999 recognized the partition of 1920 for the first time, rescinding articles 2 and 3 of the 1937 Irish constitution which staked a territorial claim on Northern Ireland.

PASSAGE EAST

Historic fortified settlement and fishing village in County Waterford, on the River Suir, strategically situated 10 km/7 mi below the entrance to Waterford Harbour. Founded by the Vikings in the 10th century, it is now a tourist centre noted for its charming streets and thatched cottages. A car ferry connects with Ballyhack, County Wexford, on the Hook Peninsula. Local salmon fishing is a long-established industry. To the south lie the ruins of Geneva Barracks, a British army base and notorious prison during the ⇨Rebellion of 1798; atrocities committed towards the insurgents are commemorated in the ballad 'The Croppy Boy'.

The barracks were constructed in the 18th century to house Swiss refugee gold- and silversmiths, and were originally intended to be part of a planned town following plantation of the area.

PATRICK, ST (c. 389–c. 461)

Patron saint of Ireland, whose feast day, 17 March, has become an international celebration of Irish identity. There is little definite information about him, as the traditional legends are late, untrustworthy, and often contradict his two surviving texts, *The Confession* and *Letter to Coroticus*.

Born in Britain, possibly in western Scotland (or south Wales or southwest England), he was kidnapped by pirates and during six years' slavery in

*e*go Patricius peccator rusticissimus et minimus omnium fidelium et contemptibilissimus apud plurimos.

I am Patrick, a sinner, the least learned of men, least of all the faithful, most worthless in the eyes of many.

PATRICK, ST *Confessions*.

∿

County Mayo (not County Antrim, as tradition has it), he embraced his father's Christian faith. He escaped to Britain, probably entering monastic life there. Ordained as a missionary bishop to Ireland in 432 (probably by the British church), he played a vital part in the conversion of northern and (possibly) western Ireland, but definitely not of the whole island. Patrick's traditional centre was Armagh, although some scholars argue that he never lived there.

PATTERN (Irish *pátrún*, 'patron')

The traditional celebration of the feast-day of a saint who is a local 'patron'. A pattern was usually held at a holy well dedicated to the saint, with devotees kneeling in veneration and 'making rounds' (walking sunwise around the well while praying for the relief of ailments or other favours). The patterns developed from the 17th century into important social occasions, and were often accompanied by dancing and sports. Due to the prevalence of drinking and fighting, they earned the disapproval of the clergy in the later 19th century and were largely discontinued, although there has been some revival in recent years.

PEARSE, PATRICK HENRY (1879–1916)

Writer, educationalist, and revolutionary, born in Dublin of an English father and Irish mother. Pearse was initially a cultural activist in the ⇨Gaelic League and founded the bilingual secondary school St Enda's, Dublin (1908). He later embraced radical nationalist politics, becoming a founder member of the ⇨Irish Volunteers and member of the Irish Republican Brotherhood (IRB) in 1913. As commander-in-chief of the Volunteers and president of the provisional government during the ⇨Easter Rising in 1916, he read aloud the 'Proclamation of Independence' and signed the unconditional surrender of the rebels. He was executed for his role in the rising on 3 May 1916 at Kilmainham Jail in Dublin.

Pearse was educated by the Christian Brothers and

*D*á gcaillfí an Ghaeilge chaillfí Éire.
If Irish were to be lost Ireland would perish.

PATRICK HENRY PEARSE 'An Barr Buah', 4 May 1916.

∿

at the Royal University, Dublin, where he became convinced of the necessity of encouraging Irish nationalism through native culture and language. He joined the Gaelic League in 1896, and edited their journal *An Claidheamh Soluis* 1903–09. Although he lectured in Irish at University College, Dublin, his main work in education targeted the young. He established St Enda's to foster all things Irish and instil a love of Ireland's cultural heritage.

Although Pearse initially supported some version of home rule for Ireland, he became disillusioned with the government's indecision in handling unionist opposition, and began to accept the use of force. Soon after joining the Volunteers and the IRB, he was coopted to its secret military council. In 1915 his celebrated graveside oration at the funeral of Jeremiah O'Donovan Rossa (1831–1915), director of the first nationalist bombing campaign in mainland Britain 1881–85, revealed his notions of a blood sacrifice for Irish freedom, and fuelled inspiration for the ill-fated rebellion of 1916.

Pearse wrote extensively in both Irish and English. While he did not receive international acclaim, he was well known to Irish intellectuals, and is noted for his play *The Singer* (1915), and the poems 'Renunciation' (1914) and 'The Fool' (1915).

PEAT BOG

Type of wetland where slow-growing mosses have accumulated over centuries to form thick blankets of a material called peat or turf. Peat can be dried and used for fuel, or ground and used to enrich poor soils. Peat bogs once covered 17–20% of Ireland.

Bogs are waterlogged habitats that are strongly acid with a pH of 3.2–4.2. Sphagnum mosses are the predominant plant in bogs and there are more than 30 species growing in Ireland, but peat is also built up of the roots, leaves, flowers, and seeds of heathers, grasses, and sedges. The bogs started growing at the end of the last glacia-

tion about 10,000 years ago, with living plants growing on layer upon layer of dead plant material, forming peat depths of up to 12 m/42 ft.

Generally referred to as 'turf' in Ireland, peat is brownish-black in colour and in its natural state is 90% water and only 10% solid material. When cut into slabs and dried it burns like wood with a bright flame. Harvesting of peat accelerated as Ireland's population grew, and by the 1940s large-scale mechanized peat extraction developed under the state-owned company Bord na Mona. Today, the Bog of Allen, occupying 958 sq kn/370 sq mi of the counties of Offaly, Laois, and Kildare is the country's main source of peat.

Intensification of farming has also served to deplete Ireland's bogs and today only about 20% of the peatland resource remains relatively intact. Only 8% of the original peatland area can be considered suitable for scientific study and conservation purposes.

PATRICK PEARSE

Famous both as a writer and nationalist, Pearse was executed in 1916 for his part in the Easter Uprising. A Memorial Cottage can be found in the remote seaside village of Rosmuck, Connemara, where Pearse came to find solitude and inspiration.

PENAL LAWS

Series of discriminatory laws passed in the 1690s against Roman Catholic clergy and laity. They were a direct result of the turmoil created by the Glorious Revolution of 1688 in which the Catholic James II of England was replaced by his Protestant daughter Mary and her husband William of Orange, and the subsequent attempt by James to use the Irish Catholics to regain his throne. Under the penal laws, Catholics were forbidden from bearing arms, going abroad to be educated, and, under the Bishop Banishment Act (1697), all clergy and bishops with ecclesiastical jurisdiction were ordered to leave the country. Another act in 1704 limited the number of regular clergy to one per parish. The most restrictive law was the Act to Prevent the Further Growth of Popery (1704). This banned Catholics from buying land and inheriting land from a Protestant, and declared that Catholic landowners had to divide their land equally between their male heirs.

With agitation from the ⇨Catholic Committee

PEAT *Peaty wetlands once covered one-fifth of Ireland. A Connemara turf man is seen here leaning on his stacks of peat, which is dug increasingly by machine, rather than by traditional methods.*

after 1760, and the pressures of a British empire and war, significant relief acts were passed in 1778, 1782, and 1792–93. By the end of the 18th century the most contentious of the penal laws had been removed, and the remaining restrictions ended with the passing of the Catholic Relief Act in 1829.

PERIODICALS

Publications largely devotional or confessional in character, that broadened into other fields with the cultural revival of the 1880s. The lack of a substantial public for periodical journalism, however, meant that many titles were short-lived, and very few from before 1900 survived.

The Leader (1900–40) provided an eclectic overview of Irish nationalism; *The Bell* (1940–52), particularly under the editorship of Seán Ó Faolain, originated and defended much good literary and political journalism. A more intellectual version of *The Bell, The Crane Bag* (1977–86), also combined culture, politics, and literature.

The latter part of the 20th century saw the emergence of numerous sectoral publications, such as those for popular music (*Hot Press* 1977; 1999 circulation *c.* 21,000); women (*Women's Way* 1963; 1999 circulation 65,500); agriculture (*Irish Farmers' Journal* 1958; 1999 circulation 76,100); and a plethora of current affairs journals such as *Hibernia* (1969–80), *Magill* (1977; 1999 circulation 36,000), and the satirical journal *Phoenix* (1983; 1999 circulation 21,000). *An Phoblacht/Republican News*, which is the official journal of Sinn Féin (1979; 1999 circulation

around 15,000), can trace its origin to a republican paper originally established in 1906.

periodicals in Northern Ireland

These have also been marked by confessionalism in both religion and politics, ranging from the *Protestant Telegraph* (founded in 1966; 1999 circulation 24,000), the organ of Ian Paisley's Democratic Unionist Party, to the *Andersonstown News* (founded in 1972; 1999 circulation 20,000), a weekly publication reflecting the republican aspirations of west Belfast. Notable exceptions have been *Fortnight* (founded in 1971; 1999 circulation 3,500), a monthly journal of current affairs owned and edited by a loose cooperative of Catholics and Protestants; and *Lá* (founded in 1992; 1999 circulation 3,500), a weekly Irish-language newspaper which, although taken over in 1999 by the *Andersonstown News*, has achieved a reputation for a certain independence of spirit, and is the only Irish-language newspaper to have been subsidized by the UK government.

PETERS, MARY ELIZABETH (1939–)

Athlete who won the Olympic pentathlon title at Munich in 1972. Born in Lancashire, England, but raised in Northern Ireland, she competed in her first pentathlon at Ballymena in 1955. After finishing fourth in the pentathlon at the 1964 Olympics, and ninth four years later, she won the event in 1972 with a world record score of 4,801 points. In 1970 she won the Commonwealth pentathlon and shot put gold medals. After retiring from competition she became a leading sports administrator in Northern Ireland.

PETRIE, CHARLES (1789 – 1866)

Antiquarian, painter, musicologist, and folklorist. Through his skills as an artist, Petrie was commissioned to illustrate several early Irish guidebooks with sketches of ancient Irish historic sites and ruins. He then began a more systematic collection of sketches and paintings of Irish antiquities which he undertook under the auspices of the Royal Irish Academy. Petrie supplemented his visual depictions by several essays on antiquarian, archaeological, and architectural subjects; but on his travels throughout the island he began to collect a large body of Irish airs which he published as *The Ancient Music of Ireland* (1855). Petrie's highly competent sketches provide an invaluable archive of many ancient sites and antiquities which have since deteriorated badly or disappeared entirely.

PHOENIX PARK MURDERS

The assassination on 6 May 1882 of the chief secretary for Ireland, Lord Frederick Charles ⇨Cavendish, and his undersecretary, Thomas Burke, outside the Viceregal Lodge in Phoenix Park, Dublin. Having just arrived in Ireland following his appointment by the British prime minister William Gladstone, Cavendish was attacked by the ⇨Invincibles, a splinter group of the Irish Republican Brotherhood. The murders, carried out with surgical knives, shocked public opinion in Britain and Ireland and led to a tightening of the repressive measures that had been relaxed after the Kilmainham Treaty.

Charles Stewart ⇨Parnell denounced the killings in parliament, but was later implicated in a series of letters that were soon revealed to have been forgeries. Innocent, Parnell had in fact offered his resignation to Gladstone after the killings, but it had been refused.

PHOTOGRAPHY

Several photographic studios were established in Dublin, Cork, and Belfast in the early 1840s, and the Photographic Society of Ireland was founded in 1854. Early photographers focused on the scenery and people that surrounded them, and many women, such as the Countess of Rosse (1813–1885) placed themselves behind the lens, as photography was considered an acceptable pastime for ladies.

early 20th century

In the early 20th century, 'art photography' became popular, mostly reproducing the sentimental style of late Victorian painting. At the same time documentary photographers were finding plenty of exciting material, between the slums and poverty, the Easter Rising (1916), the Anglo–Irish War (1919–21), and the Irish Civil War (1922–23). In 1921 the *Camera* magazine was launched in Dublin, and influences from across the Atlantic and from Europe started to affect Irish photography, although the emphasis on national identity and tradition in the early years of the Free State stifled Irish photographers somewhat. Father Frank Browne (1880–1960) is the best-known popular documentary photographer from the 1920s to the 1950s.

post-World War II

Following World War II Irish photography expanded greatly, with biennial Irish Photographic Society exhibitions raising awareness of the medium. In 1978 the Gallery of Photography was established in Dublin. In recent years the widespread availability of sophisticated cameras has meant that amateur photography has become enormously popular, driving many professional photographers to specialize. Photojournalism and art photography are the two main areas of professional practice. Documentary photography in Ireland tends to be polarized around two stereotypes – romantic Ireland, its landscape and inhabitants, which is primarily aimed at the tourist market and industry; and political Ireland, specifically Northern Ireland, where bleak images of 'the Troubles' are distributed through the media.

Art photographers have to some extent tried to overcome this imbalance by looking at everyday experiences from an independent point of view. Apart from this social documentary, other areas explored by contemporary photographers include portraits, still lives, and Irish history, and they approach their subjects in a variety of ways, including expressionism, irony, and a sense of personal healing. Probably the best known (although not necessarily in Ireland) contemporary photographers are Willie Doherty (1959–   ), for his northern landscapes overlaid with text, Victor Sloan (1945–   ), with his interpretation of the rituals of the Orange Order in Northern Ireland, and Karl Grimes (1955–   ), who plays with the differences between eastern and western cultures, and, more recently, with subjects inspired by science and medicine.

PIGOTT, RICHARD (1828–1889)

Journalist, born in County Meath. He supplied *The Times* with forged documents, which it used in good faith as the basis of the article series 'Parnellism and Crime' in 1887. The Parnell Committee was appointed to investigate the matter, and the forgeries were exposed; Pigott fled to Madrid, Spain, and shot himself to escape arrest. His *Personal Recollections of an Irish Journalist* was published in 1882.

PLANTATION

Colonization and conquest of Ireland by English and Scottish settlers from 1556 to 1660; see feature essay on rebellions and plantations, page 288, also ⇨Ulster plantation and ⇨Munster plantation.

PLANXTY

Band of the 1970s, notable for its innovative arrangements of traditional and contemporary folk song. Together with the ⇨Bothy Band, it is regarded as one of the most influential traditional music bands of modern times. Formed out of a group of musicians gathered to record Christy ⇨Moore's 1972 solo album *Prosperous*, the original line-up included Christy Moore (vocals, guitar, bodhrán), Donal Lunny (bouzouki, guitar), Andy Irvine (bouzouki, guitar, harmonica, vocals), and Liam O'Flynn (uileann pipes, whistles).

The band went through many changes in personnel, including the singers Delores Keane and Paul Brady and musicians Matt Molloy (flute), Bill Whelan (keyboards), and Nollaig Casey (fiddle). It split between 1975 and 1978 and finally split in 1981 when Donal Lunny and Christy Moore formed the Celtic rock band Moving Hearts.

Planxty performed excellent arrangements of dance tunes, but was best known for its arrangements characterized by complex contrapuntal multiple guitar, bouzouki, and mandolin parts. Albums include *Planxty* (1972), *After the Break* (1979), *The Woman I Loved so Well* (1980), and *Words and Music* (1983). Perhaps the band's most important performance was as the 1981 Eurovision Song Contest interval piece with Timedance, which included Bill Whelan and influenced directly his composition of the 1994 Eurovision interval piece Riverdance.

PLASTERWORK

Decorative stucco or plaster reached its peak in the 18th century with the flowering of the Rococo and Neo-Classical styles.

Immigrant stuccodores introduced the craft into Ireland during the middle ages, and a 16th-century plasterwork ceiling survives in County Tipperary. Many 17th-century ceilings were plain, but motifs such as flowers, leaves, and fruit sometimes appeared, as on the ceiling of the Royal Hospital Kilmainham, Dublin (*c.* 1680). The Italian Francini brothers, Paolo (1695–1770) and Filippo (1702–1779), did the first full-scale figurative work in Ireland in the 1730s and 1740s, in bold relief, often based on mythological themes, such as the dining room ceiling at Carton, County Kildare, in 1739. Bartholomew Cramillion (active 1755–62), also from continental Europe, executed the plasterwork of the Rotunda Hospital Chapel, Dublin, (1755–58) in a lively, vigorous Rococo style. A native stuccodore, Robert West (died 1790), active from the 1750s onwards, worked in a more delicate version of this Rococo style. His specialities were birds and musical instruments, and both feature in his house at 20 Lower Dominic Street, Dublin (1755).

In the late 18th century, inspired by the architecture of classical Greece and Rome, architects such as William Chambers (1723–1796), Robert Adam (1728–1792), and James Wyatt (1746–1813) designed ordered, restrained, low-relief plasterwork

PLASTERWORK *The superb rococo ceiling in the drawing room of Russborough House, County Wicklow, is the work of the Lafranchini brothers, Swiss experts in stuccowork, who took the form to its most ornate heights in the mid-18th century.*

REBELLIONS AND PLANTATIONS – 200 YEARS OF CONFLICT

by Ciaran Brady

In the early 16th century, having consolidated their authority in England and Wales, the Tudor kings Henry VII (reigning 1485–1509) and Henry VIII (reigning 1509–47) sought to reassert English influence in Ireland, where long years of neglect had strengthened the independence of great Gaelic and Anglo-Irish families. The characteristic Tudor policy of conciliation mixed with occasional coercion went badly wrong in 1534 when the most powerful of the families, the Fitzgeralds of Kildare, rejected reform proposals being pressed on them and rose in rebellion. The rebels were crushed, their leaders executed, and their lands confiscated.

integration of the Irish lordships

The defeat of the Kildare Fitzgeralds presented the Tudors with more problems than it solved. Despite their faults, the great dynasty had, by careful diplomacy and shrewd power-politics, established a degree of influence over all the lordships of the island which, with its inadequate administrative and financial resources, the English government could never equal. Over the next 50 years attempts to develop an alternative to Fitzgerald rule constituted the principal aim of Tudor Irish policy, as successive English lord deputies from Anthony St Leger in the 1540s to John Perrot in the 1580s, sought a means of assimilating the Irish lordships under English government. This was achieved in some measure through agreements such as the surrender and regrant programme in which the lords surrendered their Gaelic titles and assumed an English one with a royal grant confirming their lands and their local political and social standing. However, this long-term aim was occasionally overridden by more urgent security concerns arising from fears of French, Scottish, or Spanish invasion. Such fears exercised a profoundly disruptive effect on domestic Irish policy, as lord deputies associated with conciliation were forced to suspend operations or were replaced with short-term military governors.

failure of conciliation

The credibility of conciliation was severely damaged among the dynasties as severe divisions arose within the lordships between landholders who stood to benefit from anglicization and professional soldiers who stood to lose most. The great lords sought strenuously to contain such divisions, but with increasing lack of success. This combination of English security concerns and internal pressures underlay the majority of the rebellions of the Elizabethan period, most notably the Munster rebellion of 1579–83 and the massive rebellion of Hugh O'Neill and other Ulster lords 1594–1603. From the 1560s, moreover, divisions had begun to emerge among English officials in Ireland between those who continued to favour conciliation and those who favoured a more coercive approach, the latter often garrison commanders and settlers in the post-rebellion plantation in Munster.

religious dissent

Rising criticism of conciliation by interested parties on both sides was reinforced by religious division. Though the statutory changes of the Reformation had been introduced peacefully in the Irish parliaments (1536, 1560), religious dissent first became politicized in the open appeals for aid to Spain and the papacy made by the Munster and Ulster rebels in the 1570s and 1590s.

However, a more deep-seated and lasting effect of confessional division lay in the increasing refusal of the politically loyal 'Old English', as the descendants of the Norman conquest pointedly referred to themselves, to permit intermarriage with 'New English' arrivistes or to attend services of the Church of Ireland.

Catholic confederacy

In the years following the defeat of the Ulster lords and the Flight of the Earls in 1607, it was these Catholic loyalists who presented the greatest obstacle to the advance of an English planter interest that was steadily encroaching on native lands, not only in the official Ulster plantation of 1609, but in a host of private speculations in all provinces. The attempt of Thomas Wentworth, lord deputy 1633–41, to play both sides to the crown's advantage further alienated the Old English, and when the remaining native Irish of Ulster rose again in rebellion in 1641 the Old English took their side. Although achieving a stunning victory at Benburb in 1646 under the generalship of Owen Roe O'Neill, the 'confederation' of Old English and Gaelic Irish Catholics was never solid enough to enable them to form a powerful military force during the critical 1640s. When Oliver Cromwell, fresh from his triumphs in England, came to Ireland in 1649 he crushed both groups with ease, meting out exemplary punishments at Drogheda and Wexford.

consolidation of Protestant ascendancy

In 1653 the Cromwellian act of settlement aimed at the confiscation of the bulk of the lands of the Irish Catholics and its redistribution to English soldiers and adventurers. However, the practical problems involved in such a revolution proved insurmountable and at the time of the Restoration of the Stuart monarchy in 1660 dispossession had been only partial. A second act of settlement in 1662 reduced the extent of confiscation, but land held by Irish Catholics had fallen from 59% in 1641 to 22%. With the accession of the Catholic James II in 1685, Irish Catholics under Richard Talbot, Earl of Tyrconnell, looked for redress of their former status and holdings.

However, the installation of William (III) of Orange as king of England in 1688 forced James II to fight for his crown in Ireland. Two successive defeats at the Boyne and Aughrim 1690–91 ended the hopes of Irish Catholics, whose landholdings were further reduced in the ensuing confiscations to a mere 15%.

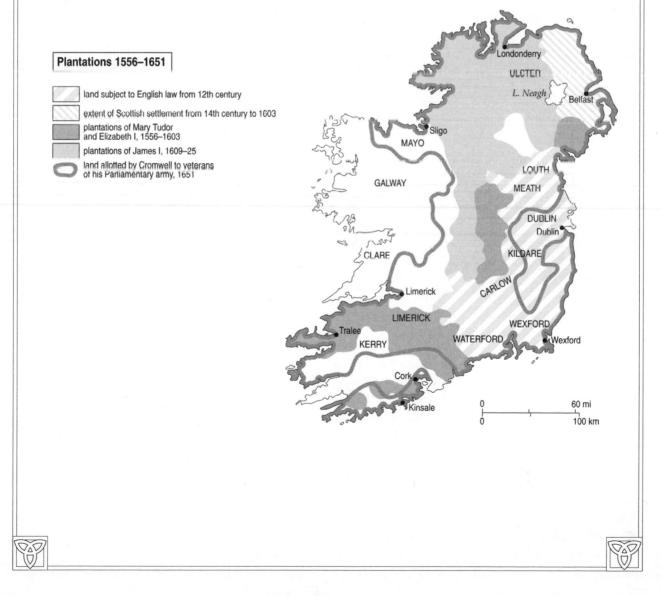

Plantations 1556–1651

land subject to English law from 12th century

extent of Scottish settlement from 14th century to 1603

plantations of Mary Tudor and Elizabeth I, 1556–1603

plantations of James I, 1609–25

land allotted by Cromwell to veterans of his Parliamentary army, 1651 ceilings, which were executed by stuccodores such as Dubliner Michael Stapleton (died 1801). Powerscourt House, Dublin, completed in 1771, shows the hallmarks of Stapleton's rich, symmetrical Neo-Classical work. The achievements of 18th-century Irish plasterwork were never equalled, as the medium gradually became less important in interior schemes.

PLUNKETT, HORACE CURZON

(1854–1932)

Agricultural reformer, founder of the Irish agricultural cooperative movement. The third son of Lord Dunsany, a County Meath landowner, Plunkett was educated at Eton and Oxford and spent time cattle-ranching in the mid-western USA. He returned to Ireland determined to transform agricultural commerce. His cooperative movement was based on a model set up by Danish farmers, who established creamery societies that used the recently invented mechanical cream separator and steam-powered churn, enabling farmers to control the processing of their milk.

Plunkett became a member of parliament at Westminster in 1892. In 1900 he persuaded the government to establish the Department of Agriculture and Technical Instruction for Ireland, the first fully-fledged Irish government department, with himself as vice-president.

In 1904 his publication *Ireland in the New Century*, a critique of Irish social and economic life, was attacked, and in 1907 he was forced to resign. In 1917 Plunkett was elected head of a government-sponsored Irish Convention, aimed at allowing nationalists and unionists to reach an accommodation. The convention failed but Plunkett was later nominated to the Free State senate.

PLUNKETT, JOSEPH MARY (1887–1916)

Poet and revolutionary. Born in Dublin, the son of a papal count, he was mainly educated by the Jesuits. He became director of operations for the ⇨Irish Volunteers at their inception in 1913, and joined the Irish Republican Brotherhood the following year. In 1915 he went to Germany with Roger ⇨Casement to seek military aid for a nationalist rebellion. Sentenced to death for his part in the 1916 ⇨Easter Rising, he married Grace Gifford in the chapel of Kilmainham Jail, Dublin, on the eve of his execution.

HORACE PLUNKETT *Plunkett pioneered the Irish agricultural co-operative movement in 1889. He learned much about farming during a 10-year spell of ranching in Wyoming and this knowledge, plus his experience of running the family estate at Dunsany, underpinned his reforming zeal.*

PLUNKETT, OLIVER (1629–1681)

Catholic archbishop and canonized saint (1975), who was executed, along with 30 or more other victims, in the panic surrounding the fictitious Popish Plot to murder Charles II, burn London, and put the Catholic James II on the throne.

A native of County Meath, Plunkett spent most of his adult life in Rome until his appointment as archbishop of Armagh in 1669. There he initiated an energetic policy which combined reconciliation with the Dublin government with the enforcement of his episcopal authority of the secular and regular clergy of his diocese. Early successes on both fronts were undermined in the anti-Catholic hysteria of the Popish Plot, which led to Plunkett's arrest on groundless charges of treason, sustained largely by the evidence of clergy whom he had antagonized. His trial in Ireland collapsed, but in a second trial a London jury convicted. Though certain of Plunkett's innocence, Charles II was afraid to intervene and Plunkett was hanged, drawn, and quartered at Tyburn on 11 July 1681.

POP AND ROCK MUSIC

The Irish popular and rock music scene filled the vacuum left by the demise at the end of the 1960s of the ⇨showbands and the dance culture that supported them. Many of the rock stars of the early 1970s had previously performed on the showband circuit. ⇨Van Morrison began his performing career with the Belfast-based showband the Monarchs, Rory ⇨Gallagher first worked with the Fontana showband, and Phil Lynott (⇨Thin Lizzy) played support to showbands. Prior to the 1970s popular music artists such as Phil ⇨Coulter, Van Morrison, and Rory Gallagher went abroad to work, but bands like Thin Lizzy and the ⇨Horslips were among the first to live and work successfully in Ireland. These bands and those that came after them, such as Mama's Boys from Londonderry, were stylistically part of the developing international 1970s rock scene in their guitar-driven sound, outrageous clothes, concept albums, and drug culture, but they did also create a distinctive Irish-rock image.

from punk to U2

Ireland produced two notable bands during the punk era, the Boomtown Rats from Dublin and the Undertones from Derry. Both these bands were British-based, but lesser known bands such as the Radiators, the Atrix, and the Virgin Prunes remained in Ireland for the most part and had some impact. The first Irish 'supergroup' and the first band to portray Ireland to the world as having a unique popular music voice, was the Dublin band ⇨U2. Despite the efforts of the record companies, Ireland has not since produced a rock band of comparable stature, although bands like Ash, A House, and Therapy have enjoyed some popularity.

1980s and 1990s

One of the most successful Irish pop artists in the 1980s was Sinéad O'Connor, who had her biggest success with the single 'Nothing Compares 2 U' (1990). Perhaps the first successful, truly indigenous

Show business is Shamanism, music is worship.

BONO Lead singer of the rock band U2
Introduction to The Book of Psalms (1999), quoted in *The Mail on Sunday*, 24 October 1999.

pop band was Bagatelle, formed in the late 1970s, whose song 'Summer in Dublin' (1981) is still very much an anthem of that city. The Pogues emerged in 1984 and survived up to the mid-1990s, when there was a veritable explosion of Irish pop music. Pre-teen bands such as Boyzone, B*witched, and Westlife of the Louis Walsh stable met with enormous overseas success in the 1990s, exploiting underdeveloped markets like the Far East. More mature pop acts, such as Divine Comedy and Brian Kennedy have gained some degree of popularity in the UK and Europe, while the Cranberries became a major international act of the 1990s. One of the other success stories of recent years is the sibling group the Corrs, from Dundalk. As is typical of successful contemporary pop artists, their combination of soft, lilting melodies and attractive appearance proves irresistible to the music-buying public.

POPULATION

The populating of Ireland began with the arrival of small groups of Mesolithic hunter-gatherers in Ulster in 8000 BC, across the landbridge from Scotland. Tentative figures set Ireland's population at the end of the Neolithic period (about 2500 BC) between 100,000 and 200,000, reaching 250,000 by the introduction of Christianity in AD 431. These numbers continued to rise in close parity with English figures up into the early modern period; by the 1750s the population had reached 2–2.3 million.

A new pattern had emerged by the end of the 17th century which saw a greater part of the population clustered into towns, and the population slope running east–west, rather than north–south. At this time people married earlier than in England, providing a longer childbearing period for women and larger families. Towards the end of the 18th century, the population began to expand rapidly with numbers rising to 4.4 million by 1791. These increases have been attributed to economic prosperity as demands for Irish agricultural products opened in overseas markets and in British industrial cities. However, from 1815 the fall in agricultural prices after the Napoleonic Wars made population growth increasingly difficult to sustain. Numbers rose rapidly from 6.8 million in 1821 to 7.8 million in 1831, but slowed towards a population peak of 8.2 million by 1841, indicating a decline in growth before the Great Famine (historically dated 1845–49, but now believed to have lasted until 1852). Death and emigration resulting from the famine saw the population plunge to 6.5 million by 1851.

The trend since the 1840s has been a period of decline followed by stagnation. By 1911 the population had fallen to 4.4 million. The Irish Free State saw figures descend even further from just below 3 million in 1926, to 2.8 million in the Republic of Ireland by 1962. In the same period Northern Ireland experienced a steady increase from 1.25 million to 1.4 million in 1956; by 1991 Northern Ireland's population had expanded to nearly 1.6 million. The Commission on Emigration and other Population Problems, which reported in 1954, reflected concern in the Republic of Ireland regarding population decline. However, since the 1960s, with emigration tailing off, the population of the Republic of Ireland has increased, reaching 3.6 million by 1996. This growth is mostly associated with new economic opportunities, and population density in the Republic of Ireland remains much below the European average.

PORTADOWN

Part of the new town of ⇨Craigavon, County Armagh; population (1991) 21,400. It is situated on the River Bann, 40 km/25 mi southwest of Belfast, and was joined with Lurgan to form Craigavon in 1965. Manufactures include domestic appliances, plastics, and clothing; and there are service industries, food processing, and newspaper printing and publishing.

Portadown developed first as a result of the construction of the Lough Neagh canal in the 1730s, and later as a result of the linen industry and as a railway junction in the 19th century.

PORTLAOISE (OR PORTLAOIGHISE)

(formerly Maryborough)

County town of County ⇨Laois, 80 km/50 mi southwest of Dublin, situated on a tributary of the River Barrow; population (1996) 3,300. It has woollen, flour-milling, and malting industries, and is the site of a top-security prison. On the Rock of Dunamase, 6 km/4 mi east of Portlaoise, are the castle ruins of the 12th-century king of Leinster, Dermot MacMurrough.

PORTRAITURE

Portraiture first emerged in Irish art in the latter part of the 17th century and flourished under the patronage of wealthy Protestant ascendancy (Anglo-Irish) landowners, politicians, and professionals in the 18th century. The Act of Union of 1801 saw the departure of many of these patrons and a subsequent decline in demand for portraits. Towards the end of the 19th century and during the 20th century the art of portraiture was revived, with foreign and modernist influences working on artists to produce a new style of work.

17th- and 18th-century portraiture

Stylistic conventions of English portraiture were introduced to Ireland by visiting artists such as Stephen Slaughter (1697–1765). Garret Morphey (active 1680–1716) was the first Irish portrait painter of note. Henrietta Dering (later Johnston; c. 1675–1729), one of the earliest known women artists in Ireland, produced pastel portraits in Dublin and later settled in Charleston, South Carolina, USA, where she continued her practice. Charles Jervas (c. 1675–1739), a friend of the satirist Jonathan Swift and principal painter to King George I, was the most successful portrait painter of the next generation, though James Latham (1696–1747) had greater talent. On his death his place as the leading portrait painter in Dublin was taken by Robert Hunter (active 1745–1803). A number of highly accomplished portraits in oils and pastels by Thomas Frye (1710–1762) are known. He also made important stylistic and technical contributions to the print process of mezzotint. Frye spent much of his career in London, as did a number of Irish portraitists at this time such as Nathaniel ⇨Hone.

The influence of contemporary French art may be seen in the pastels of Robert Healy (c. 1743–1771), who also produced a series of remarkable portraits depicting the Connolly family engaged in sporting activities (1768–69). There was also a thriving school of miniature painting in Dublin in the second half of the 18th century. Notable practitioners included Gustavus Hamilton (c. 1739–1775), Horace Hone (c. 1754–1825), and John Comerford (1770–1832). In the same period a number of foreign artists such as Francis Wheatley (1747–1801) from England and Gilbert Stuart (1755–1828) from the USA spent time in Ireland.

19th- and 20th-century portraiture

After the Act of Union, patronage for art in Ireland remained limited until the later part of the 19th century. In the 1890s Walter ⇨Osborne established himself as the leading portrait painter bringing the techniques of Impressionism to the genre as did Sarah Purser (1848–1943). John Butler Yeats (1839–1922), the father of both W B Yeats and Jack Butler Yeats, was also an outstanding exponent though he spent much of his career in London and New York. William ⇨Orpen and John ⇨Lavery achieved huge success as portrait painters in London. Orpen's pupil Leo Whelan (1892–1956) became prominent from the 1920s, painting many of the leading political figures of the day. Edward McGuire (1932–1986) features among modern artists who have made portraiture their field of interest. The stylized realism of his portrait of the poet Seamus Heaney (1974; National Gallery of Ireland, Dublin) is a good example of his work. The most comprehensive historical collection of Irish portraiture is held by the National Gallery of Ireland in Dublin. The National Self-Portrait Collection was established at the University of Limerick in 1982.

POTATO BLIGHT (also known as 'late blight')

Disease of the potato caused by the parasitic fungus *Phytophthora infestans*. It can cause massive damage to growing crops but can be controlled using fungicides. The disease wiped out the Irish potato harvest in 1845 and brought about the Great ⇨Famine (historically dated 1845–49, but now believed to have lasted until 1852).

The fungus spreads readily on the air to affect plants over distance. Spores can infect a plant within hours and new spores are released in four to six days, continuing the infectious cycle. Once infected, potatoes will rot in the ground in as little as two weeks, and the fungus survives in stored potato tubers, in fields, in piles of dumped crops, and in greenhouses.

Other fungi and bacteria can follow late blight infection causing rot during storage. The blight can strike other crops and *Phytophthora infestans* wiped out half the tomato crop in the eastern US in 1946. It must have warm, humid conditions to spread. Blight is still a major problem and new strains are evolving that are resistant to commonly used fungicides.

POTEEN (Irish *poitín*, 'small pot')

Very strong alcoholic Irish drink made in private stills from potatoes or barley and yeast. Poteen (pronounced 'potcheen') acquires regional distinction according to differences in local water. According to legend it has been distilled in Ireland since the first potato harvest (early 17th century). It was made

illegal by the English in 1661, stimulating a vigorous underground trade and turning many Irish people into criminals. Over the centuries doctors have warned of possible alcoholic poisoning and mental illness, although one doctor in 1730 claimed that it held off old age, aided digestion, and 'delighted the heart'. Commercial brands of poteen were legalized in 1997 but many people still prefer the illicit version.

POWERSCOURT

Country house at Enniskerry, County Wicklow, built in 1731 by Richard Castle for the Wingfield family, the Viscounts Powerscourt. Its gardens, among the last formal gardens to be constructed in Europe, are famous worldwide; they include a Japanese and an Italian garden. Set against the dramatic backdrop of Sugarloaf Mountain, the demesne was partially reconstructed in 1843 by Daniel Robertson based upon the design of the Villa Butera in Sicily. The house was burnt by an accidental fire in 1974 and has been restored.

POYNINGS'S LAW

Statute of 1494, introduced by Lord Deputy Edward Poynings (1459–1521), that decreed that all bills and amendments introduced in the Irish parliament must first be approved by the English Privy Council before being returned for passage in Ireland. Originally a device to curb the independence of the great feudal lords of Ireland, the act became an obstacle to effective government, and it was frequently suspended. Weakened by Yelverton's Act (1782), which asserted the power of the Irish parliament to initiate legislation, it was effectively suppressed by the Act of Union (1800).

Poynings's Law was exploited by Lord Deputy Thomas Wentworth (1593–1641) in his outright attack on the Irish parliament in the 1630s, but was rarely employed in this way thereafter.

PRAEGER, ROBERT LLOYD (1865–1953)

Natural historian who dominated the subject in Ireland during much of his lifetime. He co-founded and edited the journal *The Irish Naturalist* and completed major research in the field of botany.

Praeger was born in Holywood, County Down, and graduated from Queen's College, Belfast, in 1886 as an engineer. He began to study the fossil shells being unearthed during the construction of the Alexandra Dock in Belfast. He published papers on the post-glacial geology of northeast Ireland, and left engineering to join the National Library of Ireland, Dublin, in 1893.

His publications were extensive and included *Irish Topographical Botany* (1901), *A Tourist's Flora of the West of Ireland* (1909), and *The Botanist in Ireland* (1934). He was elected president of the Royal Irish Academy, the British Ecological Society, the Royal Zoological Society of Ireland, and the Geographical Society of Ireland. He also received honorary doctorates from Queen's University, Belfast; Trinity College, Dublin; and the National University of Ireland.

PRENDERGAST, KATHY (1958–)

Contemporary artist. Using a huge range of media, she deals mainly with issues relating to the female body. She has received a number of awards, including the Carroll's Award at the 1980 Exhibition of Living Art for *Waiting* (1980; Hugh Lane Municipal Gallery of Modern Art, Dublin), a Henry Moore Sculpture Fellowship (1986), and a prize for outstanding young artist at the Venice Biennale, Italy (1995).

Among Prendergast's best-known work is a series of drawings entitled *To Control a Landscape* (1983; Irish Museum of Modern Art, Dublin) in which she represents her own body as a map, depicting it in terms of contours and its bodily functions as a series of mechanical apparatus. More recent projects such as *The End and the Beginning* have been inspired by the birth of her daughter and show her employing a more surreal means of expression. Prendergast was born in Dublin.

PRENDERGAST, PADDY (PATRICK J) (1909–1980)

Racehorse trainer whose 21 classic wins put him second after Vincent O'Brien in the all-time list in Ireland. In 1963 he became the first Irish trainer to capture the trainers' championship in Britain, an achievement he repeated for the next two years in succession. At home, Prendergast was leading trainer seven times. In all, he won the Irish 2,000 Guineas on four occasions, first with Kynthos in 1960 and ending 20 years later with Nikoli. Other successes included eight Irish Derby winners and winners in the English 1,000 and 2,000 Guineas with Pourparler in 1964 and Martial in 1960 respectively.

PRESTON, THOMAS (1860–1900)

Physicist who established empirical rules for the analysis of spectral lines, which are still associated with his name. He discovered the Anomalous Zeeman Effect, a phenomenon noted when the spectral lines of elements were studied in the presence or absence of a magnetic field. His authoritative textbooks *The Theory of Light* (1890) and *The Theory of Heat* (1894) remained in continuous use for over 50 years.

Preston was born in Kilmore, County Armagh. He enrolled in Trinity College, Dublin, in 1881, and worked under the physicist George ⇨Fitzgerald, known for his work in electromagnetics. He later won the second Boyle Medal presented by the Royal Dublin Society, but died of a perforated ulcer just as he was reaching the height of his academic powers.

POWERSCOURT GARDENS *Backed by the wild and rugged granite heights of the Wicklow Mountains, the 18th-century gardens, designed by Richard Castle, seem all the more ordered. They were among the last formal gardens to be constructed in Europe.*

PROGRESSIVE DEMOCRATS (PD)

Political party in the Republic of Ireland, founded in 1985 by Desmond O'Malley following a power struggle with Charles ⇨Haughey in ⇨Fianna Fáil. The PDs are socially liberal but more right wing economically, and are less nationalist than the other major parties. The party won 14 seats in its first general election in 1987 but failed to maintain that strength. However, it entered coalition with Fianna Fáil 1989–92 and again with Fianna Fáil from 1997. It has been led since 1994 by Mary Harney, the first woman party leader in the Republic of Ireland.

PROTESTANTISM

Main division of Christianity that emerged from Roman Catholicism at the Reformation in the 16th century. It refers both to the Christian denominations founded at that time and also to more recent churches with a similar theological outlook. The three largest denominations in Ireland are the (Anglican) Church of Ireland, the Presbyterian Church in Ireland, and the Methodist Church in Ireland. Protestants are found predominantly in Northern Ireland, with approximate numbers being (in total/in Northern Ireland/in the Republic of Ireland): Anglican (378,000/280,000/98,000), Presbyterian (297,000/285,000/12,000), and Methodist (60,000/55,000/5,000). There are many smaller groupings, including the Free Presbyterian Church of Ulster (18,500/18,250/250), the Elim Pentecostal Church (15,500/15,250/250), the Charismatic Christian Fellowships (10,000/8,000/2,000), the Baptist Union of Ireland (8,400/7,800/600), the Christian Brethren (7,000/6,000/1,000), and the Reformed Presbyterian Church in Ireland (2,400/2,200/200).

The Church of Ireland was formed in 1537, although it traces its origins to St Patrick. It was an established church, originally separate from England, but became part of the United Church of England and Ireland in 1801 until disestablishment in 1870. Priests, with the assistance of lay select vestries, run local parishes, which are grouped into 33 dioceses, governed by ten bishops and two archbishops. Legislative power rests in the annual (lay and clerical) general synod, which is elected triennially by the annual diocesan synods. The church is led by the archbishop of Armagh.

The Presbyterian Church in Ireland was founded in 1642 among Scottish immigrants. Local congregations are run by a kirk session made up of elders (or presbyters), including the minister (or teaching elder). Local congregations elect members for both the 13 presbyteries and the annual (lay and clerical) general assembly. A moderator is elected each year as spokesperson.

The Methodist Church was formed in 1738 as a consequence of John Wesley's 22 Irish preaching tours. Local congregations are grouped into a preaching circuit, which is governed by a quarterly circuit meeting, in association with the lay leaders' meeting. It has 76 preaching circuits, grouped into eight districts. The legislative body is the annual (lay and clerical) conference, whose members are elected from district synods, after consultation with the circuits. Each year the conference elects a president of the church.

PROUT, FATHER

See Francis ⇨Mahony, Irish writer.

PROVISIONAL IRA

Radical faction of the ⇨Irish Republican Army (IRA), now the main republican terrorist faction. In 1969, against a background of mounting violence in Northern Ireland, the IRA split between its left-wing (the Official IRA) and militarists (the Provisional IRA). In the violent 1970s the latter became the dominant force within Irish republicanism. In the 1980s the Provisional IRA adopted the strategy known as 'the armalite and the ballot box', which combined militarism with political activism. Use of the term Provisonal IRA has become synonymous with the IRA.

PUNCHESTOWN

Ireland's premier National Hunt racecourse, in County Kildare, 5 km/3 mi southeast of Naas. It hosts the National Hunt Festival in April each year. The Punchestown International Horse Trials in May attract top competitors from around the world. The cross-country course is spread over 200 ha/500 acres of natural landscape with opportunities to jump fallen trees, stone walls, double banks, and so on.

Punchestown also has one of the finest schooling facilities in Ireland, catering for horses and riders of all abilities. There are over a hundred jumps available, and the Punchestown horse sales, held periodically throughout the year, cover an impressive spectrum of the equestrian arena.

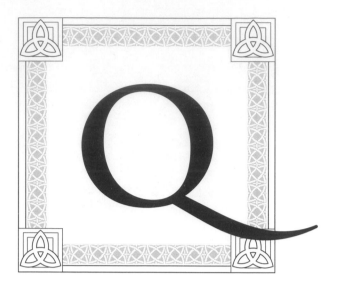

QUINN, AIDAN (1959–)

Actor. Although born in Chicago, Quinn spent much of his youth in Birr, County Offaly, and in Dublin where he started acting in plays. When he returned to Chicago he played a rebellious teenager in *Reckless* (1984) and in 1985 came to prominence through *Desperately Seeking Susan* (1985). A tall, handsome actor with piercing blue eyes he has made numerous television and screen appearances, including *The Mission* (1986), *Stakeout* (1987), *The Lemon Sisters* (1989), and *An Early Frost*, the first television drama to deal with AIDS. In the 1990s he became a regular visitor to Ireland again, appearing in *The Playboys* (1992) and in Neil ⇨Jordan's *Michael Collins* (1996). With his brothers, director Paul and cinematographer Declan, and his actor sister, Kathleen, he starred in *This is My Father* (1998), an Irish emigrant story.

QUINN, BOB (1939–)

Director and writer, born in Dublin. Quinn is the most prolific Irish film-maker, who worked in RTÉ (the national TV station) in the 1960s before establishing an independent production company, Cinegael, in an Irish-speaking area of the west of Ireland. He made the first Irish-language fiction film, *Caoineadh Airt Uí Laoire/Lament For Art O'Leary* (1975), which explored the relationship of the 18th century to the present in a formally innovative manner. His *Poitín* (1978) inserted a realist aesthetic into the depiction of rural Ireland. Continuing to work in often quirky contrast to other Irish film-makers, Quinn made a three-part television series, *Atlantean*, which sought to overturn the Celtic myth of Irish origins, and argued that the Irish came, via the Atlantic, from North Africa. Quinn's largely silent feature, *Budawanny* (1987), later developed in *The Bishop's Story* (1994), explored the relationship between a priest and his housekeeper with whom he has a child.

QUINN, EDEL (1907–1944)

Missionary, born in Cork. Intensely spiritual, Quinn had intended since early youth to join the enclosed order of the Poor Clares but was prevented by family finances and ill-health. In 1927 she joined the Legion of Mary, a Catholic lay voluntary organization, founded by Frank Duff (1884–1980) in 1921 and devoted to social care and religious prosletysm among Dublin's poor. Despite increasingly poor health, Quinn became the Legion's first missionary in Africa where in less than four years she founded missions in Kenya, Uganda, Malawi, and Mauritius. Overwork and the return of tuberculosis hastened her early death. But for more than 20 years since her death was granted informal recognition as Ireland's greatest female martyr.

RAIFTEARAÍ, ANTOINE (or Ó REACHTABHRA; also ANTHONY RAFTERY) (*c.* 1780–1835)

Versifier and wandering minstrel. Born in Killedan (Cill Liadáin), near Kiltimagh, County Mayo, he was blinded in childhood as a result of smallpox infection. A character surrounded by folkloric rumour and gossip, his songs and poetry were revitalized by Isabella Augusta ⇨Gregory and W B ⇨Yeats during the Gaelic literary revival. His best-known works are 'Mise Raiftearaí/I am Raftery', a self-lament; and 'Bua Uí Chonaill', a poem about Daniel ⇨O'Connell's 1828 election victory, which typifies Raiftearaí's strongly Catholic stance.

RALEIGH, WALTER (*c.* 1552–1618)

English-born Elizabethan courtier and soldier, and Irish planter. He first served in Ireland during the Desmond rebellion (1579–83), participating in the massacre of Irish, Spanish, and Italian troops garrisoned at Smerwick in 1580. Already a favourite of Queen Elizabeth I, Raleigh received preferential treatment in the Munster plantation, securing the largest grant with his estate of 17,000 ha/ 42,000 acres.

At first Raleigh sought to develop his Irish holdings around Youghal, County Cork, but other business interests, increasing difficulties at the English court, and recurring disputes with the Dublin government persuaded him to sell out in 1602, his lands passing to Richard Boyle (1566–1643), later 1st Earl of Cork. After this he showed no further interest in Ireland.

Claims that Raleigh was the first to introduce the potato into Ireland have not been substantiated.

RATHDRUM

Town in County Wicklow; population (1996) 1,200 It is situated high in the Avonmore Valley, 16 km/ 10 mi from Wicklow town. Nearby are Glendalough and Avondale (now a forestry school). ⇨Avondale House, to the south, was the birthplace of the nationalist politician Charles Stewart ⇨Parnell. The house and grounds are open to the public and there is a museum dedicated to Parnell.

Nearby on the summit of Cronebane Hill (249 m/816 ft) is the Moltee Stone, a large glacial granite boulder which in mythology is reputed to be the hurling stone of Finn Mac Cumhaill.

RATHLIN ISLAND

Island in Northern Ireland, 10 km/6 mi off the north coast of County Antrim, opposite Ballycastle. Its main industries are fishing and tourism; there is also some farming.

The Kebble national nature reserve is a breeding ground for such seabirds as razorbills and puffins. There is also a scuba-diving centre.

Rathlin Island has had a long history of conflict: it was raided by Vikings in 790 and later occupied by the McDonalds of Scotland; later still, English forces slaughtered the Scottish inhabitants in 1575 and 1584. In 1617 Rathlin Island was subject to a legal dispute over ownership between Scotland and Ireland which finally settled it as Irish.

The island was the refuge of Robert Bruce, King of Scotland, in 1306. Legend has it that this is where the exiled king learned his lesson in perseverance from watching a spider weave its web in a basalt cave now known as Bruce's Cave.

REA, STEPHEN (1946–)

Actor, born in Belfast. While Rea came to international prominence with his performance in Neil ⇨Jordan's *The Crying Game* (1992), for which he was nominated for an Academy Award, he was already an experienced stage, television, and film actor. He also played in other Jordan productions: *Angel* (1982), *The Company of Wolves* (1984), *Interview with a Vampire* (1994), *Michael Collins* (1996), and *The Butcher Boy* (1998). As a director of the Field Day Theatre Company, he has helped to rejuvenate Irish theatre. His television and film work also includes *The House* (1985), *Life is Sweet* (1991), *Bad Behaviour* (1993), *Pret-a-Porter* (1994), and *Trojan Eddie* (1996).

REAL IRA

An extremist Irish republican terrorist group which split away from the ⇨IRA in 1997. Based in the republican stronghold of Dundalk, County Louth, close to the border with Northern Ireland, its political mouthpiece has been the 32 County Sovereignty Committee. On 15 August 1998 it was responsible for the deadliest terrorist atrocity in Northern Ireland's history, when 28 innocent bystanders were killed by a car bomb detonated in the shopping centre of Omagh, County Tyrone. Following condemnation of the attack by ⇨Sinn Féin and revulsion within Dundalk, the Real IRA apologized for the deaths and claimed that the warnings given had not been misleading, as the media and police claimed. Soon afterwards, it announced a suspension to its military operations.

REBELLION OF 1798

Unsuccessful nationalist rising of the Society of ⇨United Irishmen against government forces May–September 1798. The society's main aims were parliamentary reform and escape from English dominance. Fired by the example of the French and American Revolutions, it planned a coordinated, national insurrection backed by French aid, which would overwhelm government forces with superior numbers. In fact the rebellion was hurried and uncoordinated, hampered by arrests of leaders, changes in French strategy, and divisions between the remaining United Irish leadership. The fighting, which occurred mainly in the counties around Dublin and those of Wexford, Antrim, and Mayo, took place in stages, depriving the rebels of their numerical superiority. Up to 30,000 died during the rising. (See map on page 299.)

The fact that elements of both the United Irishmen and government forces committed sectarian atrocities meant that Protestant and Catholic folk memories of the rebellion were very different. Historical writing on the rising reflects the fact that interpretations of the rebellion also became embroiled with nationalist politics and various separatist movements in the 19th century.

chronology of events

The first outbreaks in the counties around Dublin were intended as preparatory to the seizure of the

REBELLION OF 1798 *Armed with pikes, the rebels depicted here at the Battle of New Ross, 5 June, by the 19th-century illustrator George Cruikshank, had little chance against the rifles and cannons of the government forces. More than 30,000 people died during the five-month insurrection.*

capital itself. However, these outbreaks were partial and were easily and bloodily suppressed. The Wexford rising, which began 26–27 May, was more serious. Here the United Irishmen were better organized and were led by charismatic local priests as well as some liberal Protestant gentry. The Wexford insurgents defeated government forces at Oulart Hill and captured the towns of Enniscorthy and Wexford, where they established a rudimentary administration. They tried to spread the rebellion into other counties but were heavily defeated at the battles of New Ross (5 June) and Arklow (9 June). The tide turned completely against the rebels with their defeat at the Battle of Vinegar Hill (21 June). Some leaders like Michael Dwyer (1771–1826) retreated with remnants of the rebel army into the Wicklow mountains, maintaining a guerrilla campaign until 1803.

The Ulster rising did not begin until 6 June when the mainly Presbyterian United Irishmen of County Antrim rose under Henry Joy McCracken (1767–1798). They were defeated at the Battle of Antrim on 7 June. The County Down United Irishmen did not rise until the following week. After initial success at Saintfield, they were decisively defeated at the Battle of Ballynahinch on 13 June, after which their leader, Henry Munro, was executed.

The last campaign in 1798 came in August, when a small French force under Gen Jean Joseph Amable

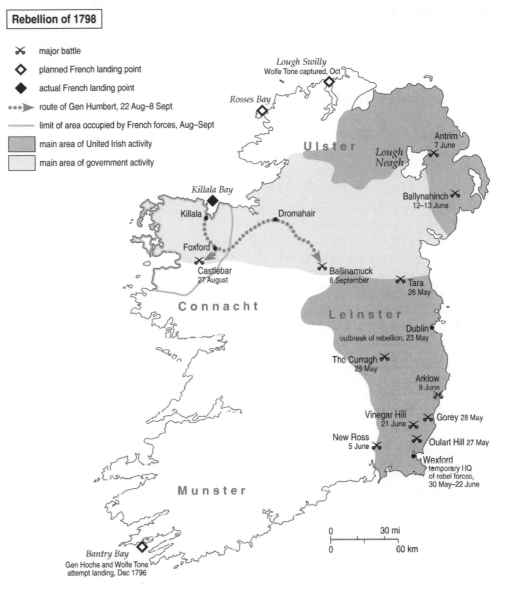

Rebellion of 1798

- ⚔ major battle
- ◇ planned French landing point
- ◆ actual French landing point
- •••▶ route of Gen Humbert, 22 Aug–8 Sept
- —— limit of area occupied by French forces, Aug–Sept
- ▨ main area of United Irish activity
- ▨ main area of government activity

Lough Swilly
Wolfe Tone captured, Oct

Rosses Bay

Ulster

Lough Neagh

Antrim 7 June

Ballynahinch 12–13 June

Killala Bay

Killala   Dromahair

Foxford

Castlebar 27 August

Ballinamuck 8 September

Tara 26 May

Connacht

Leinster

Dublin outbreak of rebellion, 23 May

Tho Curragh 29 May

Arklow 9 June

Vinegar Hill 21 June   Gorey 28 May

New Ross 5 June   Oulart Hill 27 May

Wexford temporary HQ of rebel forces, 30 May–22 June

Munster

0   30 mi
0   60 km

Bantry Bay
Gen Hoche and Wolfe Tone attempt landing, Dec 1796

Humbert (born 1767) landed in Killala Bay, County Mayo. Humbert armed local United Irishmen and inflicted a defeat on a larger government force at Castlebar, which became known as the 'Races of Castlebar' due to the rapidity of the retreat. Leaving parts of Mayo under a makeshift garrison, Humbert moved towards Dublin with a small force of the French and Irish. He was defeated by Gen Charles ⇨Cornwallis at the Battle of Ballinamuck, County Longford, on 8 September, and the 'Republic of Connaught' ended with the recapture of Killala on 23 September. These battles effectively ended the fighting in 1798.

REDMOND, JOHN EDWARD (1856–1918)

Nationalist politician and barrister; leader of the Irish Parliamentary Party (IPP) 1900–18. He rallied his party after Charles Stewart ⇨Parnell's imprisonment in 1881, and came close to achieving ⇨home rule for all Ireland in 1914. However, the pressure of World War I, unionist intransigence, and the fallout of the 1916 ⇨Easter Rising destroyed both his career and his party.

Born in Wexford and educated by the Jesuits at Clongowes Wood College and Trinity College, Dublin, Redmond was elected to Westminster as member of parliament for New Ross in 1881. A loyal supporter of Parnell, following 'the chief's' death in 1891 Redmond led the Parnellite minority which had split from the party, and rose to political prominence as leader of a reunited IPP in 1900.

In 1910, with the Conservatives and Liberals evenly split in terms of seats, Redmond's party held the balance of power. Redmond exploited this position to secure the passage of the Third Home Rule Bill in May 1914. However, opposition from the Ulster Unionists and the outbreak of World War I delayed its implementation.

*F*or us, the Act of Union has no binding moral or legal force. We regard it as our fathers regarded it before us, as a criminal act of usurpation carried by violence and fraud.

JOHN REDMOND Speaking in 1905, quoted in *The Irish Question* (third edition, 1975), by Nicholas Mansergh.

~

In September 1914 he encouraged recruiting for the British army with his Woodenbridge Speech, which angered radical nationalists in the Irish Volunteers. The Easter Rising caught Redmond completely by surprise, and his condemnation of it as a 'German intrigue' displayed the extent to which he was out of touch with a new generation of Irish nationalists. The rising marginalized Redmond's influence and by 1917 he was squeezed between a reorganized Sinn Féin and unionist demands for the partition of Ireland. He died the following year, shattered personally and politically

*W*hat you have done for Frenchmen in Quebec... for Dutchmen in the Transvaal, you should now do for Irishmen in Ireland.

JOHN REDMOND Speech in favour of Irish home rule in the House of Commons, 30 March 1908.

~

by the Easter Rising and subsequent events.

REE, LOUGH

Lake on the River ⇨Shannon in the Republic of Ireland, between counties Roscommon, Westmeath, and Longford; 24 km/15 mi long and 1 km/0.6 mi to 11 km/7 mi wide. Lough Ree contains many small islands, which have the remains of ancient churches. It is used for game fishing and sailing.

Hare Island has the ruins of a church reputedly founded by St Ciaran in the 6th century; Inchmore, Inchbofin, and Saint's islands also have early church remains, and Inchcleraun is the site of a monastery founded by St Diarmait in 540 on which are six early churches.

REFORMATION

European-wide ecclesiastical and religious revolution, which ended papal supremacy in the western church and led to the formation of the Protestant churches. In Ireland, as in England, the Reformation was instituted by the Tudor monarchy and was precipitated by dynastic concerns, namely Henry VIII's desire to divorce Catherine of Aragón in order to remarry and produce a male heir.

Following the pope's refusal to grant Henry VIII a divorce, the crown abolished papal jurisdiction in its dominions in the mid-1530s. The king himself assumed the pope's authority, adopting the title of supreme head of the English and Irish churches, sanctioned by the English and Irish parliaments under the Act of Supremacy in 1537 (the act was repealed under Queen Mary but royal supremacy was restored by a second act in 1560). Dissolution of the monasteries followed, although modern studies suggest that this had less cultural and social impact than once claimed, the function of the monasteries in Irish society already being in decline.

The new Anglican state churches acquired Protestant doctrine in the reigns of Henry's heirs, Edward VI and Elizabeth I. Apart from a brief interlude in the 1540s, when the English government successfully promoted the Reformation as part of a general programme of political reform, the Church of Ireland (see ⇨Protestantism) failed to win the support of the indigenous population in Ireland. For a variety of political and cultural reasons, the Gaelic Irish and colonial communities remained loyal to their traditional religion and attached themselves to the newly emerging ⇨Counter-Reformation Catholic church in the late 16th and early 17th centuries.

REGINALD'S TOWER

Circular tower in the county town of Waterford. Traditionally built in 1003, it is named after the Viking chief Ragnvald. It seems unlikely that the tower was constructed at such an early date, although the core of the structure may have existed before the Norman occupation of the town in 1170. Amongst its famous visitors were King Henry II and King Richard II. Reginald's Tower has been used as a mint (15th century), a munitions store, and a prison (19th century); it now accommodates the city museum.

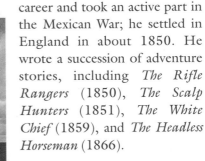

RELIGIOUS ORDERS *Far fewer people now turn to the religious life than was the case in previous centuries. This Benedictine monk belongs to Glenstal Abbey, near Limerick. The doctrine of the fifth-century Italian hermit St Benedict, formed the basis of Western monasticism.*

REID, FORREST (1875–1947)

Writer, born in Belfast. Reid is best known for his deft recreations of boyhood in the trilogy of novels about Tom Barber: *Uncle Stephen* (1931), *The Retreat* (1936), and *Young Tom* (1944), the latter winning the James Tait Black Memorial Prize. All Reid's novels focus on the coming of age of a young male protagonist and are often strongly autobiographical.

Reid studied at the Royal Belfast Academical Institute, and was encouraged to write by English novelist E M Forster. He also wrote critical analyses of the poets W B Yeats and Walter de la Mare.

REID, MAYNE (pseudonym of THOMAS MAYNE REID) (1818–1883)

Novelist, born in Ballyroney, County Down. Reid went to the USA in 1838, where he had a varied career and took an active part in the Mexican War; he settled in England in about 1850. He wrote a succession of adventure stories, including *The Rifle Rangers* (1850), *The Scalp Hunters* (1851), *The White Chief* (1859), and *The Headless Horseman* (1866).

RELIGIOUS ORDERS

The religious orders have played a dominant role in Ireland since the 6th century, although their influence lessened following the Protestant ⇨Reformation and dissolution of the monasteries in the 16th century. They have had a major influence on Roman Catholicism. A few Anglican orders exist, including the Society of St Francis.

The Celtic monasteries of early Christian Ireland, such as Clonmacnoise, County Offaly, founded in the mid-6th century by St Ciarán, were not organized into religious orders, but were self-governing. In 1142 St ⇨Malachy of Armagh introduced the Cistercians, a reformed Benedictine order founded in Cîteaux, France, in 1098, who lived mainly by agricultural labour. He also persuaded most Irish monastics to become Augustinian Canons (followers of the rule of the 5th-century St Augustine of Hippo). In this way Ireland's Celtic monasteries differed from those on the continent, which became Benedictine.

The first Cistercian foundation was ⇨Mellifont Abbey, County Louth; others included ⇨Boyle Abbey, County Roscommon; ⇨Holycross Abbey, County Tipperary; and ⇨Jerpoint Abbey, County Kilkenny. By 1228 the order had established 34 monasteries, and reached the limit of its expansion.

In the 13th century the recently-formed mendicant orders arrived and became very influential in Irish life. Dependent on alms for their living, they included the

Dominicans (from 1224), Franciscans (from around 1230), Carmelites (from around 1271), and Augustinian friars (from 1282). The Jesuits appeared in the 16th century. The largest and most influential Catholic order, founded by Ignatius Loyola in 1534, the Jesuits were instrumental in preserving Irish loyalty to Catholicism during the Protestant Reformation. The 19th century saw the arrival of missionary orders such as the French Congregation of the Holy Ghost Fathers, who established Blackrock College, Dublin, in 1860.

Irish-founded orders include the educational orders, Nano ⇨Nagle's Presentation Sisters (1775) and Ignatius ⇨Rice's Christian Brothers (1802); Catherine ⇨McAuley's welfare-centred Sisters of Mercy (1831); and the missionary Columban Fathers, founded by Edward Galvin and John Blowick in 1916.

REPUBLICANISM

See feature essay on republicanism, page 304, also ⇨United Irishmen, ⇨Young Ireland, ⇨Sinn Féin, ⇨Easter Rising, and ⇨Northern Ireland.

REYNOLDS, ALBERT (1932–)

Irish Fianna Fáil politician, Taoiseach (prime minister) 1992–94. He was born in Rooskey, County Roscommon, and established a successful business career before entering politics. He was minister for industry and commerce 1987–88 and minister of finance 1988–92. In December 1993 Reynolds and UK prime minister John Major issued a joint peace initiative for Northern Ireland, the Downing Street Declaration, which led to a ceasefire by both the Irish Republican Army (IRA) and the loyalist paramilitaries the following year.

But in 1994, after a deep disagreement with its leader Dick Spring, Reynolds lost the support of the Labour Party. His coalition collapsed and he lost a vote of confidence in the Dáil (parliament). He gave up the leadership of Fianna Fáil and left politics to pursue his international business interests.

REYNOLDS, OSBORNE (1842–1912)

Physicist and engineer, born in Belfast. He accomplished ground-breaking work in fluid mechanics and devised a mathematical model for fluid flow, known as the Reynolds number. His work also led to a radical redesign of boilers, condensers, and turbine pumps.

Reynolds studied at Cambridge University, England, and from 1868 was a professor at Owens Col-

lege (now Manchester University). His key area of study was in fluid flow and he established the standard mathematical frameworks used to model turbulent flow, wave engineering, and tidal measurement. He applied much of what he learned to the behaviour of the water in river channels and estuaries. One study involved a model of the mouth of the River Mersey, and he pioneered the use of such models in marine and civil engineering projects.

His studies of condensation and heat transfer between solids and fluids led to significant improvements in boiler design. Reynolds also worked on steam turbines and turbine pumps.

RING, CHRISTY (CHRISTOPHER NICHOLAS) (1920–1979)

Hurler, born in Cloyne, County Cork. A nimble team member who played at half forward and left full forward, Ring won eight All-Ireland titles with Cork between 1941 and 1954. Only a brilliant save from the Wexford keeper Art Foley deprived him of a record ninth. It was a measure of the esteem in which Ring was held that, after that game, he was chaired off the field on the shoulders of the victorious and very sporting Wexford side. His vast array of skills made him extremely hard to mark. He was the leading player of his generation, and arguably the greatest hurler the country has ever produced.

RIVERDANCE

Phenomenally successful 1990s Irish musical that

RIVERDANCE *The dance production started life in 1994 with just 26 performers, but now over 180 dancers are involved in Riverdance, in three different companies. The show has been performed to resounding success across America, Europe, Asia, and Australasia.*

placed Irish music and traditional Irish step dancing on the global stage, and opened real professional opportunity to dancers trained within the competitive hierarchy of the Irish step dance organizations. Originating as a spectacular seven-minute mass display of highly disciplined, drumming hard-shoe step dance on television's 1994 *Eurovision Song Contest*, with centrepieces by the Irish-American world champion step dancers Michael ⇨Flatley and Jean Butler and the choral group Anúna, its wide acclaim led to a full-length stage show, premiered in Dublin in 1995.

The success of subsequent tours in London, Europe, and the USA eventually led to the formation of three *Riverdance* companies, the Lagan, Lee, and Liffey. With original music and lyrics composed by Bill Whelan, produced by Moya Doherty, and directed by John McColgan, *Riverdance* integrates traditional and modern music with choral writing, and with sensual dynamism focuses on the evolution of Irish dance and its meeting with other cultures during the Irish diaspora of the 19th century.

ROBINSON, (ESMÉ STUART) LENNOX

(1886–1958)

Dramatist, editor, and writer. He was manager of the ⇨Abbey Theatre, Dublin 1909–14 and 1919–23, after which he also became a director of the theatre. He wrote many plays, the best of them comedies of Irish rural life. He edited Lady Gregory's *Journals* (1946), and in 1951 published *Ireland's Abbey Theatre, 1899–1950*.

Robinson also compiled *The Golden Treasury of Irish Verse* (1925) and *The Little Anthology of Irish Verse* (1929), and wrote a study of the poet W B Yeats in 1939. His major dramatic successes include *The Whiteheaded Boy* (1912), a light-hearted play about small-town life, and *The Big House* (1926), about the ascendancy class. He was born at Douglas, County Cork.

ROBINSON, MARY (1944–)

Irish Labour politician, president of the Republic of Ireland 1990–97. Born in County Mayo, Robinson was educated at Trinity College, Dublin, and Harvard University, USA, and became a professor of law at the age of 25, the youngest at Trinity College. A strong supporter of women's rights, she campaigned for the liberalization of Ireland's laws prohibiting divorce and abortion. In 1997 she became the UN high commissioner for human rights.

MARY ROBINSON *As first woman president of Ireland 1990–97, Robinson overturned a long masculine tradition. She saw her success, won after a hard campaign, as, 'a great boost for the confidence of women', and went on to press for changes to laws affecting divorce and abortion.*

Robinson won a seat in the Irish senate (Seanad Éireann) in 1969 and held it for 20 years. As a lawyer she achieved an international reputation in the field of human rights. She surprisingly won the presidency of her country after failing to win a Labour seat in the Dáil (parliament) in two earlier elections in 1990.

At the start of the presidential campaign she was the 100–1 outsider, but campaigned strongly and was well placed when the leading contestant, the Fianna Fáil candidate Brian Lenihan (1930–), was sacked as deputy prime minister by Charles Haughey, following indications he had tried improperly to influence the president's decision to dissolve the Dáil in 1982. The first woman to hold the post, Robinson raised the profile of the presidency considerably, campaigning for greater equality for women and holding an outward-looking, pro-European stance.

*t*here are 70 million people living on this globe who claim Irish descent. I will be proud to represent them.

MARY ROBINSON Speech at her inauguration as president of the Irish Republic (1990).

REPUBLICANISM – THE HISTORIC WISH FOR A WHOLE AND SEPARATE STATE

by Feargal MacGarry

From the United Irishmen of the 1790s to the Irish Republican Army (IRA) of the 20th century, Irish republicanism has generally been associated with organizations prepared to use physical force to achieve their aims. Its political ideology emphasizes the need for Ireland's complete separation from British rule and the attainment of a united 32-county republic. Although influenced by the republicanism of the American and French revolutions, characterized by egalitarianism and opposition to monarchy, Irish republican organizations place greater attention on the importance of separatist nationalism.

Wolfe Tone and the United Irishmen

The first influential republican movement in Ireland was the Society of United Irishmen founded in 1791 in Belfast and Dublin, and predominantly supported by middle-class Presbyterians and Catholics. It advocated a non-sectarian independent republic based on universal male suffrage. After its suppression by British government authorities, it became a secret society and planned for armed rebellion. Its most famous leader, Wolfe Tone, urged Irishmen of all denominations to unite against British rule, which he described as 'the never failing source of all Ireland's ills'. He accompanied an unsuccessful French military expedition to Ireland during the Rebellion of 1798 but was captured and committed suicide. His grave at Bodenstown became a focus of commemoration for Irish republican organizations.

Young Ireland

In the 1840s Young Ireland, led by Thomas Davis, stressed the importance of the spiritual rebirth of Ireland and its people's shared history of opposition to British domination. It comprised social radicals such as Fintan Lalor, who urged a peasant revolution, alongside social conservatives such as John Mitchel who was an extreme nationalist. In 1848, against the background of the Great Famine and inspired by European romantic nationalist ideas and the legacy of the Rebellion of 1798, Young Ireland organized a disastrous rebellion.

Irish Republican Brotherhood

Irish republicanism remained a conspiratorial elite throughout the 19th century. The most significant strain to emerge was the Fenian movement which originated among Irish-Americans in the USA in the 1850s, and was dedicated to insurrection. Its Irish branch, known as the Irish Republican Brotherhood (IRB), was founded by James Stephens in 1858. Following a futile rising in 1867, the IRB regrouped and began a 'New Departure', cooperating with Charles Stewart Parnell's Home Rule Party to agitate for land reform in the Land War 1879–82.

At the turn of the century, the revival of Gaelic culture and the growth of Arthur Griffith's Sinn Féin, reinvigorated republicanism. The formation of the Irish Volunteers in 1914 (its leadership infiltrated by IRB members) and the outbreak of World War I offered the potential for another strike against the British government.

Easter Rising

Irish Parliamentary Party (IPP) leader John Redmond's support for Britain in the war split the Irish Volunteers, and backing from its anti-war minority enabled the IRB military council, led by Patrick Pearse, to attempt another rising. The Irish Republic was proclaimed at Dublin's General Post Office on Easter Monday 1916. The rhetoric of the Proclamation combined the physical force nationalism of the IRB with the socialism of James Connolly, whose Irish Citizen Army also fought in the rising.

The Proclamation, with its commitment to achieving a united Irish Republic through force of arms, was the most influential document of 20th-century republicanism. Although the rising was a military failure, its aftermath of executions and reprisals increased public support for republicanism.

independence

The 1918 general election saw the republican Sinn Féin party, led by the 1916 veteran Éamon de Valera, crush Redmond's IPP, and indicated the first widespread support for republican objectives. In 1919 Sinn Féin members of parliament abstained from Westminster and established the Dáil Éireann (Irish parliament) in Dublin, declaring the Irish Republic. At the same time, the Irish Volunteers (soon known as the IRA) began the Anglo–Irish War, a campaign of guerrilla warfare against British government authorities that ended with the Anglo-Irish Treaty (1921).

The treaty, which established the Irish Free State within the British Commonwealth and endorsed partition, divided pro-Treaty republicans, willing to accept a compromise that fell short of an independent Irish republic, from anti-Treaty republicans, who wanted to continue the military struggle for full independence.

Following the defeat of the anti-Treaty faction in the Irish Civil War (1922–23), Irish republicans abstained from the Free State Dáil. The most important section of republican opposition, led by de Valera, split from Sinn Féin to form Fianna Fáil and entered the Dáil in 1927. Sinn Féin dwindled into insignificance but the IRA remained a potent force. When de Valera gained power in 1932 he succeeded in drawing most Irish republicans into the democratic process and the influence of the IRA (divided between left-wing socialists and militarists) declined. For more extreme republicans, who accused de Valera of selling out, the characteristics of true republicanism became abstention from parliament, a deep-rooted suspicion of politics, and a commitment to physical force.

'the Troubles'

The IRA's bombing campaign in England 1939–40 and border campaigns of the 1950s were failures. In 1969, against a background of mounting violence in Northern Ireland, the IRA split between its left-wing, the Official IRA, and militarists, the Provisional IRA. In the violent 1970s the latter became the dominant force within Irish republicanism.

In the 1980s the Provisional IRA adopted the strategy known as 'the armalite and the ballot box', which combined militarism with political activism. The 1990s, with two extended ceasefires and years of negotiations, saw Sinn Féin, the political wing of the republican movement become more dominant than the IRA. The republican movement also modified its demand for a complete British withdrawal from Northern Ireland to acceptance of an interim stage of power-sharing under British authority.

The General Post Office in Sackville Street, Dublin, on fire during the Easter Rising of 1916. It was here that the Irish Republic was proclaimed, before the fire drove the nationalists out of the building. Though a military failure, the Easter Rising increased Irish support for the republican cause.

ROCHE, REGINA MARIA (born Dalton) (1764–1845)

Writer, born in County Waterford where she remained throughout her life. Roche wrote romantic novels that bordered on the Gothic. Her most successful work was the four-volume *Children of the Abbey* (1796). While several of her novels are set on the Continent or in Britain, her later fiction concentrates on Irish settings and issues such as absentee landlordism and Irish nationalism. Other works include *The Munster Cottage Boy* (1820) and *The Castle Chapel* (1825).

ROCHE, STEPHEN (1959–)

Cyclist, born in Dublin. One of the outstanding riders of his generation, in 1987 he became only the second cyclist after Eddy Merckx of Belgium to win the Tour de France, the Giro d'Italia (Tour of Italy), and the world professional road-race championship in the same year. He turned professional in 1981, a year after competing at the Moscow Olympic Games, and rode until persistent injuries forced him to retire in 1993.

ROCHE, TOM (1916–1999)

Industrialist; the founding figure behind Cement Roadstone Holdings (CRH), the Republic of Ireland's largest industrial group. Born in Dublin, Roche purchased a small coal and sand business for IR£800 in the early 1940s, and in 1944 established a gravel concern, Castle Sand Company. In 1949 the company floated on the stockmarket as Roadstone. In 1970 Roadstone took over the Cement Group to form CRH, the most significant acquisition of its time in the Republic; Roche served as chairman until 1974. CRH has grown to become one of Ireland's major companies, quoted on the Dublin and London stockmarkets, and operating a building materials business in Ireland, the UK, Europe, and the USA.

Roche was also involved in establishing the Bula lead and zinc mine near Navan in County Meath. The owners later got involved in a complex legal battle with the state and with neighbouring Tara Mines. Roche also established National Toll Roads, a company which built and now operates the Republic's first two toll bridges, east and west of Dublin.

ROCK OF CASHEL

See ➪Cashel, Rock of.

RODGERS, W(ILLIAM) R(OBERT) (1909–1969)

Writer, born in Belfast and educated at Queen's University, Belfast. Rodgers was a Presbyterian minister at Loughgall, County Armagh, 1935–45. His early poetry was uneven, but his second collection, *Europa and the Bull* (1952), contained original and energetic rewritings of both Christian stories and classical mythology.

Rodgers worked for the BBC in London 1947–65, where his literary portraits of W B Yeats, J M Synge, and James Joyce, among others, were very popular and later published. In 1966 he became writer in residence at Pitzer College, California, but died soon after in Los Angeles.

ROLLESTON, THOMAS WILLIAM (1857–1920)

Writer, born in Glasshouse Shinrone, County Offaly, and educated at Trinity College, Dublin, and in Germany. He played a leading part in the Irish literary revival as joint editor, with Stopford Brooke, of *A Treasury of Irish Poetry* (1900), and published *Imagination and Art in Gaelic Literature* (1900) and *Myths and Legends of the Celtic Race* (1911).

Other works include the volume of verse *Sea Spray* (1909) and a life of the German writer Gotthold Lessing in 1889.

ROMAN CATHOLICISM

See ➪Catholicism.

ROSCOMMON (originally Ros-Comain 'wood around a monastery')

County of the Republic of Ireland, in the province of Connacht; county town Roscommon; area 2,460 sq km/950 sq mi; population (1996) 52,000. It has rich pastures and is bounded on the east by the River Shannon, with bogs and lakes, including Lough Key and Lough Gara. The three largest lakes (loughs Allen, Boderg, and Ree) lie only partly within the county. There is agriculture, especially cattle rearing. Roscommon was established as a county in about 1580. Other important towns are Castlerea, Elphin, and Boyle.

Roscommon town contains the remains of a Dominican priory founded in 1253 by Felim O'Conor, King of Connacht, and a castle dating from the 13th century, originally built by the Normans. At Castlestrange, 10 km/6 mi from Roscommon, is a sculptured standing stone of the early Iron Age. There is a large ring fort and tumuli at Rathcroghan, in pre-Christian and early Christian times the site of the palace of the kings of Connacht, and coronation site for the high kings of Ireland. A well-preserved Cistercian abbey, founded in the 12th century, can be seen at Boyle. At Frenchpark, near Castlerea, is the birthplace of Douglas ⇨Hyde (1860–1949), President of the Gaelic League and first president of the Republic of Ireland.

ROSCOMMON, WENTWORTH DILLON

(4th Earl of Roscommon) (1633–1685)

Poet and translator. He was born in Dublin, and educated in France at the University of Caen. His works include a poetical *Essay on Translated Verse* (1684), which argued the case for freeing poetry from the constraints of rhyme, and a translation of the Roman writer Horace's *Ars Poetica*.

ROSCOMMON CASTLE

Imposing castle in Roscommon town, County Roscommon. It was built in the 13th century by the justiciar of Ireland, Robert de Ufford, and was later held by the O'Conors, kings of Connacht. It is quadrangular and has a tower at each corner, with two towers on each side of the gateway. One of the towers retains its vaulted roof. Many alterations have been made, including the mullioned windows added by Sir Nicholas Malbie about 1580 which still survive. In 1652 the castle was surrendered to the Cromwellian forces who partially dismantled it.

ROSCREA

Market town in County Tipperary, 52 km/32 mi north of Cashel; population (1996) 4,200. Clothing, fabric, and pharmaceuticals are manufactured. It is a centre for climbing and walking in the Slieve Bloom Mountains. Roscrea developed around a monastery founded in the 7th century by St Cronan.

features
Within the ruins of the 13th-century ⇨Roscrea Castle is ⇨Damer House, an 18th-century Georgian mansion which houses a collection of furniture and paintings.

The 8th-century illuminated manuscript known as the Book of Dimma (Trinity College Library, Dublin)

was produced in the first monastery in Roscrea. The ruins of St Cronan's abbey, a 12th-century Augustinian priory on the site of the original monastery, include a Romanesque doorway and a round tower. Roscrea also has the ruins of a 15th-century Franciscan friary.

The 12th-century St Cronan's Cross, which has been heavily restored, stands in the grounds of the modern Protestant church. There is a large modern Trappist monastery in Roscrea, with a school and agricultural college attached.

The ruins of Mona Incha abbey, 3 km/2 mi east of Roscrea, include a 12th-century church and cross. In the Timoney Hills, 8 km/5 mi south of Roscrea, are 300 standing stones, of which eight form a stone circle.

ROSCREA CASTLE (also known as Ormond

Castle; sometimes referred to as King John's Castle)

Thirteenth-century keepless castle in Roscrea, County Tipperary. A tall rectangular gate tower and a portion of the curtain walls with two D-shaped towers survive of this well-preserved ruin. The castle was granted to the Butler family in 1315. It was captured by the forces of Oliver Cromwell in 1650 but was given back to the family after 1660. In 1722 it was purchased by the Damer family, who built ⇨Damer House inside the castle walls.

ROSS, MARTIN

Pen name of Violet Florence ⇨Martin, Irish novelist.

ROSSE, WILLIAM PARSONS (3rd Earl of

Rosse)

Astronomer, see William ⇨Parsons.

ROSSLARE HARBOUR (or BALLYGEARY)

Port in County Wexford, 15 km/9 mi southeast of Wexford; population (1996) 1,000. It has been the Irish terminus of the ferry route from Fishguard since 1906, and is the terminus for ferries from Pembroke, Le Havre, and Cherbourg. It was founded by the English in 1210. The seaside resort of Rosslare is about 8 km/5 mi north along the coast; population (1996) 900.

Lady's Island is situated in a lagoon nearby on the south coast near Carnsore Point. It is the site of an ancient monastery, and a pilgrimage is made annually on 15 August, the feast of the Assumption. On the island are the ruins of an Augustinian priory and a 12th-century Anglo-Norman castle.

ROTHE HOUSE

Country house in Kilkenny, County Kilkenny. One of the earliest surviving country houses in Ireland, it was built in 1594 in the then walled town, for John Rothe. The Tudor-style structure was enlarged in the early 17th century, restored in 1965, and is now the museum of the Kilkenny Archaeological Society where an audiovisual show gives the history of the house and those associated with it. Rothe House also holds a collection of Charles Stewart Parnell memorabilia.

ROUND TOWERS

Free-standing towers built in association with Irish monastic sites from about AD 900 until possibly 1300, representing some of the earliest stone structures to survive in Ireland. Most are gently tapering buildings, 20–30 m/66–98 ft high, topped with a conical cap. The entrances are usually some 3 m/10 ft above ground level. Internal supports suggest that some may have had as many as seven floors. The top floor had four windows – one facing in each main direction. This type of building is almost exclusive to Ireland; elsewhere only three examples are known, two in Scotland and one on the Isle of Man. Some 65 round towers survive intact or as stumps.

Although the old Irish name for a round tower was 'bell house', the use of these structures remained a mystery until 1845 when the Irish archaeologist George Petrie established that they were not only bell towers but also places of refuge and storehouses for monastic treasures such as bells, croziers, and even books.

Many round towers seem to have vanished without trace. Irish annals (chronologies prepared from the late 11th century to the 16th century) record numerous incidents of towers being blown over, struck by lightning, or burnt out with laypeople, monks, and even kings perishing inside them.

ROWALLANE HOUSE

Nineteenth-century house at Saintfield, County Down. It was built in 1861 by J R Moore and is now owned by the National Trust. The property is famous for its fine gardens, mainly created between 1903 and 1955 by H Armytage Moore, whose sister was the first wife of the songwriter and artist Percy ⇨French.

ROUND TOWERS *Standing beside the ruins of St Declan's Church, this round tower at Ardmore, County Waterford is one of the best-preserved examples. The original conical cap is still in place, and the decorative brickwork rings indicate the position of the floors within.*

ROYAL DUBLIN SOCIETY (RDS)

Association established in Dublin in 1731 to promote the sciences and to improve agricultural practices. It has had a central role in the development of Irish scientific thinking and funded many of Ireland's early scientists. The society has helped to establish many national institutions including the National Library, the National Gallery, the National Botanical Gardens, and the Veterinary College which is now part of University College, Dublin. It formerly occupied the buildings of the Dáil (parliament) 1815–1924, but is now based in Ballsbridge, just south of central Dublin.

The RDS had its first meeting on 25th June 1731, setting itself objectives which included the improvement of 'husbandry, manufactures, and other useful arts'. The words 'and sciences' were only added to its aims at its second meeting, but it is in the promotion of the sciences that the society has had its greatest impact. By the end of the 18th century the society appointed professors in the sciences who were required to carry out research and give public lectures on scientific advancements. Before a living could be made from science the RDS funded the research efforts of leading Irish scientists such as the chemists Richard ⇨Kirwan, Robert ⇨Kane, and William ⇨Higgins, and the geologist Richard ⇨Griffith. The physicist George Stoney coined the term 'electron' at an RDS lecture.

Royal Irish Academy (RIA) (or the Royal Irish Academy for Science, Polite Literature, and Antiquities)

Institution founded in Dublin in 1785 to promote academic endeavour across all fields of scholarship, including the sciences. It carries out extensive publication of academic papers and holds frequent meetings for the presentation of new research in the sciences and humanities. The *Proceedings of the Royal Irish Academy* have been published since 1787. The academy has no laboratories, but has funded scientific research in the past, and offers annual research fellowships in all disciplines. Originally housed at 115 Grafton Street, Dublin, it moved to its present location in Dawson Street in 1851.

The RIA was established at a time when similar scholarly bodies were being formed in other cities. Its founders, led by the Earl of Charlemont, believed that it was in the national interest to have an institution where all branches of learning might be pursued. Its motto is 'We will endeavour'.

The academy is divided into national committees that pursue scholarly study in areas as varied as archaeology, philosophy, biochemistry, and Irish antiquities. It organizes international meetings and negotiates for Ireland with similar institutions overseas, assisting in international exchange programmes. It also elects distinguished foreign scientists and academics to honorary membership of the academy, a list which includes the German-born US physicist Albert Einstein, and the Danish physicist Niels Bohr.

RUGBY

Rugby in Ireland can be traced back to 1854 when students at Trinity College, Dublin, set up the Dublin University Football Club, having learnt the game at English public schools. Other clubs that followed were Wanderers (1869), Lansdowne (1872), Dungannon (1873), UC Cork (1874), Ballinasloe (1875), NIFC (1868), and Queen's University, Belfast (1869). From 1874 to 1879 there were two Unions. The Irish Football Union had jurisdiction over clubs in Leinster, Munster, and parts of Ulster, while the Northern Football Union of Ireland controlled the Belfast area. When the first International was played against England in 1875, the Irish team included 12 players from Leinster and 8 from Ulster. The first 15-a-side match was in 1877, and the first Munster players were chosen in 1879. In 1879 the two Unions agreed to amalgamate. Subsequently branches of Ulster, Leinster, and Munster were formed, and the Connaught branch was formed in 1886.

By the turn of the century the game was in a healthy state, and in 1899 Ireland had won both the triple crown and the home nations championship. Yet the golden age of Irish rugby was to come nearly half a century later, when Ireland's rugby side won three International Championship (Five Nations) tournaments between 1948 and 1951. Their finest moment was in 1948 when the Irish side, which included such greats as Karl Mullen and Jack Kyle, took on Wales in Belfast before a crowd of 30,000. A win would assure them the grand slam but at half time the sides were locked at three points apiece. Finally the Welsh gave way to a try from Chris Daly, which enabled Ireland to capture their first triple crown win since 1899. They repeated the feat again in 1982 and 1985.

Since then there have been some other successes. At provincial level Ireland have defied the odds. In 1978 Munster wrote themselves into folklore when they defeated the mighty All Blacks before a packed attendance at Thomond Park. Ulster's rugby team completed the last century on a memorable note when they defeated Colomiers 21–6 to win the 1999 European Cup, before a record attendance of 49,000 at Lansdowne Road, Dublin.

RUGBY *'A crazy game, which bears a strong resemblance to the windswept, rugged wastes of Connemara,' remarked Jean Lacouture, former foreign editor of* Le Monde. *The players' expressions tell their own story, in this match between Connemara and Galwegians, played in Galway.*

RUSSBOROUGH HOUSE

Palladian house near Blessington, County Wicklow, dating from 1740. It is the longest house in Ireland, with a frontage measuring 210 m/700 ft, and is considered by some the most beautiful. Russborough was built for the 1st Earl of Milltown by Richard Castle and is regarded as his finest creation. It remains virtually unaltered since its construction and has the finest stucco decorated rooms in Ireland. The plasterwork of the staircase area is particularly ornate.

RUSSELL, GEORGE WILLIAM
(pseudonym Æ) (1867–1935)

Poet and essayist. Born at Lurgan, County Armagh, Russell was educated at Rathmines School, and trained as a painter. An ardent nationalist, he helped found the Irish national stage at the ⇨Abbey Theatre, Dublin. His poetry includes *Gods of War* (1915) and reflects his interest in mysticism and theosophy. Together with W B ⇨Yeats, Russell is regarded as a leading figure in the Irish literary revival of the late 19th and early 20th centuries.

Russell became leader of the circle that published the journal *The Irish Theosophist*, in which his first poems appeared. These were later published as *Homeward: Songs by the Way* (1894) and *The Earth Breath* (1897). These early poems were characterized by great lyrical beauty, and were heavily influenced by his study of Eastern mysticism. Other works include the essay 'Ideals of the New Rural Society' (1911); the poem 'Salutation' (1917), concerning the Easter Rising of 1916; and the poetry collection *Enchantment and Other Poems* (1930).

In 1897 Russell gave up his job as an accountant for Pim's drapery, Dublin, and embarked on a bicycle tour of Ireland, during which he interviewed country people. Thereafter, he devoted much of his life to promoting agricultural reform, becoming editor of the *Irish Homestead*, the journal of the cooperative farming movement, from 1906 until 1923. The *Irish Statesman*, his own venture, ran from 1923 until 1930.

RUSSELL, MOTHER MARY BAPTIST
(KATHERINE) (1829–1898)

Irish-born Catholic religious leader. In 1854 she travelled to the USA as head of a group of nuns aiding the sick and poor. She opened many charitable and educational institutions in California.

RUSSELL, THOMAS (1767–1803)

Radical who campaigned for parliamentary reform. Born in County Cork, he played an active role in the establishment of the Society of ⇨United Irishmen in Belfast and Dublin from 1791 until his imprisonment in 1796. He conspired with the radical nationalist Robert ⇨Emmet to raise rebellion in 1803, and made a futile attempt to raise the north, but was arrested and later hanged.

Russell joined the British army and served in India for several years before returning to Dublin in 1787. Here he established a lasting friendship with the Irish nationalist Wolfe ⇨Tone. Russell was posted to the garrison of Belfast in 1791. A dashingly handsome man with wide intellectual interests, he mixed well in Belfast society and made a lasting impression on the radical philanthropist Mary Ann ⇨McCracken. In late 1791 Russell and Tone co-founded the first Society of United Irishmen, at that stage a pressure group for radical political reform. Russell later became a travelling organizer for the United Irishmen but was jailed between 1796 and 1802. During his imprisonment he planned with Emmet to organize a new rebellion. Russell was to organize the north in 1803 but received negligible support. He was arrested and sent to Downpatrick where he was convicted and hanged. He is popularly remembered as 'the man from God knows where', but the title is not contemporary, coming from a poem of 1918.

RYAN, WILLIAM PATRICK (or LIAM P
O'RIAIN, W P O'RYAN) (1867–1942)

Journalist and historian. His journal, the *Irish Peasant*, which he owned and edited, spread socialist views with the aim of fostering a distinctive Irish culture. After it was closed down in 1911 by Church censorship, he wrote novels, anticlerical tracts, and critical studies, while serving as assistant editor of the London *Daily Herald*.

Born in Templemore, County Tipperary, Ryan went to work in London as a journalist, but returned to Ireland in 1906 to start his journal. He expressed his anger at its suppression in *The Pope's Green Island* (1912), and *The Plough and the Cross* (1918). His other works include *The Irish Literary Revival* (1894), *The Irish Labour Movement* (1919), and *Gaelachas i Gléin* (1933), a study of European contributions to Gaelic scholarship.

SABINE, EDWARD (1788–1883)

Astronomer and geophysicist. He was noted for his experiments to determine the shape of the Earth and for his intensive studies of its magnetic field. He also linked the incidence of magnetic storms with the sunspot cycle.

Sabine was born in Dublin and was educated at the Royal Military Academy, Woolwich, London. He served in the Royal Artillery, rising to the rank of major general in 1859. He was appointed astronomer to an Arctic expedition in 1818 led by the Scottish explorer John Ross in an effort to find the Northwest Passage, and on a second search with the English admiral William Parry in 1819.

In 1821 Sabine began experiments on the coasts of Africa, North America, and the Arctic to determine the shape of the Earth by observing the motion of a pendulum. He supervised the establishment of magnetic observatories all around the world and in 1851 he discovered the 10–11-year periodic fluctuation in the incidence of magnetic storms. He linked this cycle with data collected by the German astronomer Samuel Schwabe, who had observed variation in solar activity.

Sabine held the presidency of the Royal Society 1861–71 and was made a KCB in 1869.

ST PATRICK'S COLLEGE, MAYNOOTH

(also called Maynooth College)

The largest Catholic seminary in Ireland, founded by an act of the Irish parliament in 1795. Its foundation was a Protestant effort to win Catholic support in a time of increasing political and economic unrest in the country. It was also a response to the closure of many European ⇨Irish Colleges due to the French Revolution. It had a lay college until 1817, its theological schools were recognized as a pontifical university in 1896, and its arts and science schools constituted a recognized college of the National University of Ireland from 1908. In 1997 these latter schools were established as a separate civil institution, and St Patrick's continued as a seminary and pontifical university.

The college was established on the site of an earlier college which had been founded by the Earl of Kildare in the 16th century but closed about 20 years later by Henry VIII. The earliest part of the college is Stoyte House, which was extended from 1796. The library contains some rare manuscripts and books and the museum has a fine collection of antiquities.

Through the priests it educated, St Patrick's exercised a formative influence on the political, social, and religious life of Ireland in the 19th and 20th centuries and through its missionary activities it was influential all over the English-speaking world, especially in the USA. In recent years it has undergone a modernization process, part of the Catholic church's effort to redefine its role in contemporary Ireland.

ST PATRICK'S DAY

National holiday to honour ⇨St Patrick, the patron saint of Ireland, celebrated in Ireland and all over the world, especially in the USA. St Patrick's Day (March 17th) is one of America's earliest holidays, declared in 1737 by a group of Irish Protestants at a meeting in Boston, Massachusetts.

ST PATRICK'S DAY *A holiday for those at home and for Irish all over the world, March 17th is celebrated with get-togethers, street parades like this one in New York, and the wearing of shamrocks.*

In the USA it is a day of Irish bonding celebrated with riotous parades in over 100 cities, especially New York and Chicago. The day is marked by traditional Irish symbols. Cards, cakes, clothing, and other items are all decorated with shamrocks, shillelehs, leprechauns, and harps. The holiday is also associated with spring, and green is the colour of the day. Anyone caught not wearing green on the parade can be pinched. Food and drinks, including beer, are coloured green for the day; in some cities even the rivers flow temporarily green. Corned beef and cabbage (probably never eaten in Ireland) is the official dish of the day, and ⇨Irish stew, boxty (Irish potato bread), and other Irish dishes are served.

SAINTS, CELTIC

Following the introduction of Christianity to Ireland by St ⇨Patrick in the mid-5th century, and the establishment of the Celtic church, Ireland became a centre for sending out missionaries to Britain and Western Europe, many of whom were canonized. Although the saints of the Celtic church are primarily known for their exploits abroad in the 6th and 7th centuries, an exception is St Finnian whose great monastic school at Clonard, County Meath, founded in the 6th century, was responsible for training many of those who went overseas.

The first moves abroad were to Britain, where ⇨Colum Cille (St Columba) introduced Christianity to western Scotland from the abbey he founded on the Scottish island of Iona in 563. St Aidan (*c.* 600–651) founded the monastery of Lindisfarne on Holy Island, off the northeast coast of England, in 635, and began the evangelization of Northumbria. Aidan admitted Begh, an Irish princess also known as Bee or Bega (died 681), to religious orders and she established St Bees in Cumbria, northwest England. St Brendan (484–577) of Clonfert, Galway, set up monastic communities in Ireland and Scotland, before sailing to a unknown 'Land of Saints', possibly North America. The greatest Celtic missionary was St Columbanus (543–615) who travelled throughout Western Europe and established the renowned monastic centres of Luxeuil, France, and Bobbio in Italy. Columbanus's disciple, St Gall (*c.* 550–645), settled in Switzerland, where he became one of the country's apostles; the town and canton of St Gallen are named after him. Columbanus inspired an influx of Irish monks to the continent, especially to France, the most renowned of which is probably the anchorite St Fiacre (died *c.* 670), whose relics have made Meaux Cathedral a centre of pilgrimage in France.

Although St Brigid is one of Ireland's best-known Celtic saints, she probably derived from the Christianization of a pagan goddess. Her legendary exploits include the foundation of a religious settlement at Kildare in around 473.

SANDS, ROBERT (BOBBY) (1954 – 1981)

Republican. Born in Belfast, Sands came of age at the height of 'the Troubles' in the early 1970s. Intimidation by loyalists and the introduction of internment in 1971 radicalized his politics and by 1972 he was an active service member of the Provisional IRA. Imprisoned in the H Blocks of Long Kesh for arms offences in 1976, Sands became the leader of a prisoner's protest demanding the restoration of 'political status'. The failure of 'the dirty protest', which involved the prisoners remaining naked and smearing excrement on cell walls, led to the adoption in 1980 of the more extreme strategy of hunger strike. At first the principal organizer and negotiator for the prisoners, Sands joined the Hunger Strike in 1981. In April, he was elected UK member of parliament for Fermanagh. Despite the extremity of the situation and the intense mood of support among Northern Ireland's Catholics, the Thatcher government refused to restore the privileges, and Sands died after 66 days of refusing food. His death and those of nine other prisoners in the following months immeasurably deepened the crisis in Ulster in the 1980s.

SARSFIELD, PATRICK (Earl of Lucan) (c. 1655–1693)

⇨Jacobite commander and patriot. Sarsfield was born in Lucan, County Dublin, into an Old English family with lands in counties Dublin and Kildare. He joined the English Life Guards and served in France and England, returning to Ireland in 1687 to enter the administration of the Earl of ⇨Tyrconnell, James II's lord lieutenant of Ireland.

After the revolution of 1688 brought William (III) of Orange to the English throne, Sarsfield fought bravely to hold Ireland for James in the Williamite War (1689–92), notably as leader of a daring raid which destroyed a siege train at Ballyneety, County Limerick, on 11 August 1690. He was also present at the battles of the ⇨Boyne (1690) and Aughrim (1691). A principal negotiator for the Jacobites at the Treaty of Limerick (1691), he left Ireland under amnesty immediately after its conclusion. He went to France where he served in the Irish Brigade for the French army, and was killed in action at the Battle of Landen in Flanders in July 1693.

SAUL

Village in County Down, 3 km/2 mi northeast of Downpatrick. St Patrick is reputed to have landed at Saul in 432. Sliabh Padraig Hill (126 m/415 ft) west of Saul is a pilgrimage site; there is an altar and on the summit a granite statue of the saint.

Some 4 km/2 mi from Saul are the ruins of Raholp church, said to have been founded by St Tassach, and 2 km/1 mi south of Saul are the ruins of a church, well, and bathhouses, known as St Patrick's Wells, another site of pilgrimage.

Above the village of Saul is a modern Protestant church dedicated to St Patrick.

SAYERS, PEIG (1873–1958)

Storyteller and writer. She was born into a storytelling family in Dunquin, County Kerry, a Gaelic-speaking community, and spent most of her life on the Great Blasket Island. Sayers had great powers of recollection, which she used to record numerous folk tales in clear, straightforward language. The stories were collected in *Peig* (1936), her autobiography which she dictated to her son Micheál; and *Machtnamh Sean-Mná/An Old Woman's Reflections* (1939; translated 1962). Her stories draw upon a great store of folklore and have a balance of rhythm, thought, and phrasing which has inspired many writers. Around 360 of Sayers's tales were recorded for the Irish Folklore Commission. The preservation of traditional narratives in the Irish language has left an important body of work for later Gaelic scholars.

SCOTT, MICHAEL (1905–1989)

Widely regarded as one of the foremost Irish architects of the 20th century as well as a famous wit and patron of the visual arts, Scott had an immense influence on Ireland's cultural and artistic development. Born in Drogheda, County Louth, Scott began his career designing St Ultan's Children's Hospital in Dublin (1928–29) and went on to provide many notable infirmaries, cinemas, and council buildings throughout Ireland, including the celebrated Department of Social Welfare Building, Dublin (1953) which was received with acclaim as the first major post-war building in Ireland.

Scott retired from practice in 1975 after completing the New Abbey Theatre (1966), the RTÉ offices, Donnybrook (1960) and designs for University College, Galway (from 1964). In the same year he was awarded the Royal Gold Medal for Architecture by the Royal Institute of British Architects, presented for the first time by Queen Elizabeth II.

SCOTT, WILLIAM (1913–1989)

Scottish-born Irish modernist painter. He is best known for his elegant and austere abstracted images of mundane domestic objects. He stands out as one of the most fascinating still-life painters of the 20th century.

Scott was born in Scotland of an Irish father, and the family moved to Enniskillen, County Fermanagh, in 1924. There he was first introduced to the work of artists such as Cézanne and Picasso. Having studied in Belfast and London, he spent time in Italy and France 1937–39. Based in England throughout his career, he explored the formal tensions between abstraction and representation, developing a monumental sense of design in works such as his mural for Altnagelvin Hospital, Belfast (1958–61). A key characteristic of both his oils and prints is their emphasis on the flatness of the surface where the rhythms create a highly refined harmony analogous to that of music.

SCULPTURE

Early Irish sculpture is primarily religious, featuring the high ⇨crosses of the 9th to 12th centuries, church decoration, and tombs, the focus of much fine work until the 17th century. In the 17th and 18th centuries European craftsmen dominated Irish sculpture and began to train sculptors. Ornamental sculpture and portrait busts were much in demand in the 18th century. Nationalistic themes emerged in the 19th century, followed by modernism in the 20th century.

religious sculpture

The high crosses with their combination of abstract and figurative ornament were the major form of sculpture in the early Christian period. They served a didactic function as well as indicating the Christian nature of monastic sites. Highly original in the context of contemporary European developments, the Cross of Muireidach at Monasterboice, County Louth, and the Cross of the Scriptures at Clonmacnois, County Offaly, are well-known examples. In the Romanesque period sculpture features mainly as an integral part of churches. The tiers of carved heads surmounting the doorway of Clonfert Cathedral in County Galway echo the ancient Celtic concern with the same motif. In the area of Anglo-Norman control their craftsmen worked in the Early English style, as can be seen in capitals at Christchurch Cathedral, Dublin. The tomb with carved effigies of the dead became a major focus for sculptural decoration from the 13th century to the mid-17th century. A good example is that of Piers Butler, 8th Earl of Ormond, and his wife (c. 1539, St Canice's Cathedral, Kilkenny). The late 16th and early 17th centuries saw English sculptors producing tombs for settlers such as that of Robert Boyle, 1st Earl of Cork (1620, St Mary's Church, Youghal, County Cork). It is in this period that Renaissance ornament appears in Irish sculpture for the first time.

European influences

From 1660 to about 1750 sculpture in Ireland was dominated by foreign craftsmen. The elaborate Baroque ornament of the Kilmainham Royal Hospital, Dublin, was the work of the Huguenot sculptor James Tabary between 1682 and 1688. The arrival of John van Nost (died 1780) in Dublin in about 1749 saw the establishment of sculptural training in the city. His pupils included Christopher Hewetson (c. 1736–1798) who later established himself in Rome from where he sent the monument to Dr Richard Baldwin (1784; Trinity College, Dublin), the first Neo-Classical funerary monument in Ireland. The upsurge in building in the 18th century created a demand for ornamental sculpture with Simon Vierpyl (c. 1725–1810) and Edward Smyth (1749–1812) producing notable work at the Casino Marino, County Dublin, and the Customs House, Dublin, respectively. From the middle of the century portrait busts also became a common form.

*t*o build, to plant, whatever you intend, / To rear the Column, or the Arch to bend, / To swell the Terras, or to sink the Grot; / In all, let Nature never be forgot.

ALEXANDER POPE English poet and satirist Celebrating the work of Richard Boyle, 3rd Earl of Burlington, in 'An Epistle to the Right Honourable Richard, Earl of Burlington, Occasioned by his Publishing Palladio's Designs of the Baths, Arches, Theatres & c. of Ancient Rome' (1731).

~

19th- and 20th-century sculpture

In the 19th century John Henry ⇨Foley established himself as a leading sculptor in both Ireland and Britain. Cork-born John Hogan (1800–1858) spent much of his career in Rome and produced some of the most important religious sculpture of the period. The turn of the century saw the ⇨Irish revival impacting on Irish sculpture and growing concern with nationalistic themes, as in the *Cu Chulainn* (1911–12; General Post Office, Dublin) by Oliver Sheppard (1865–1941). This trend continued in the work of Albert Power (1881–1945) and Yann Renard Goulet. After 1945 the stylized naturalism of Oisin Kelly (1915–1981) exerted an important influence. The 1950s onwards saw the emergence of modernism in the work of sculptors such as Hilary Heron (1923–1977), Edward Delaney (1930–   ), and Gerda Fromel (1931–1975).

SDLP

Abbreviation for ⇨Social Democratic and Labour Party, a Northern Ireland political party.

SEANAD ÉIREANN (Irish senate)

Upper house or senate of the ⇨Oireachtas (legislature) in the Republic of Ireland. It has 60 members or senators, and its term of office is up to five years, concurrent with that of the ⇨Dáil (lower house of the

Irish legislature). The Seanad has limited powers, being able only to delay bills; in the case of money bills, it can only refer a bill back to the Dáil. Although nominally a vocational chamber it tends to mirror the Dáil's political composition, making it even less powerful.

Of its 60 members, 43 are elected by a constituency of TDs (Teachta Dála; member of the Dáil), senators, and local councillors through the single transferable vote. These are elected from five vocational panels: agriculture, labour, language and culture, industry and commerce, and public administration. Six are elected by the graduates of two of the Republic of Ireland's universities and 11 are nominated by the Taoiseach (prime minister).

SEMI-STATE COMPANY

Semi-state companies (owned by the State but managed independently of government) have been major influences on the Irish economy since the foundation of the Irish Free State. Early Irish governments pursued a policy of protectionism and used state-owned industry as a means to promote economic development. One of the first such bodies to be established was the Electricity Supply Board (ESB), set up in 1927, which undertook the country's first major power station at Ardnacrusha on the River Shannon, a major investment project of the time. The ESB was quickly followed by the Sugar Company, which produced sugar from native beet. Further semi-state companies formed in the 1930s included Bord na Mona, responsible for peat production from bogland and a major employer in the midlands; Aer Rianta, which managed the national airports; and the Industrial Credit Corporation, a state bank supporting industry.

Semi-state companies were used as instruments of economic policy by successive governments and grew to be major employers in many sectors of industry, usually operating as monopolies. Recent years have seen a change of approach as state industry has been opened to competition. This has meant companies in sectors such as aviation, telecommunications, and power supply had to compete against private companies, often because of European Union regulations. In 1999 the government completed its first major privatization, selling off the state telecommunications company Telecom Éireann, now Eircom, in a flotation in which more than 500,000 members of the public bought shares.

SHAMROCK (Irish *seamróg*, 'trefoil')

Low-growing clover-like plant, whose leaves comprise three leaflets that fold up at night; the unofficial emblem of the Irish and their descendants overseas, traditionally worn on ⇨St Patrick's Day (17 March), when many people try to gather their own wild plant. Its association with St Patrick stems from his preaching about the Holy Trinity. Unlike other plant emblems, the shamrock has been commercially adopted to promote a number of Irish products.

SHANNON

Longest river in Ireland, rising 105 m/344 ft above sea level in the Cuilcagh Mountains in County Cavan, and flowing 386 km/240 mi to the Atlantic Ocean past Athlone, and through loughs Allen, Boderg, Forbes, Ree, and Derg. The estuary, which is 110 km/68 mi long and 3–16 km/2–10 mi wide, forms the northern boundary of County Limerick. The river is navigable as far as Limerick city, above which are the rapids of Doonas and Castletroy. The river is known for its salmon farms, Castleconnell being an important centre. It also has the first and largest hydroelectric scheme in the Republic of Ireland (constructed 1925–29), with hydroelectric installations at and above Ardnacrusha, 5 km/3 mi north of Limerick.

SHAW, GEORGE BERNARD (1856–1950)

Dramatist, critic, and novelist, and an early member of the socialist Fabian Society, although he resigned in 1911. His plays combine comedy with political, philosophical, and polemic aspects, aiming to make an impact on his audience's social conscience as well as their emotions. They include *Arms and the Man* (1894), *The Devil's Disciple* (1897), *Man and Superman* (1903), *Pygmalion* (1913), and *St Joan* (1923). He was awarded the Nobel Prize for Literature in 1925.

Shaw was born in Dublin, and went to London in 1876 to work as a critic. *Our Theatre in the Nineties* (1932) contains many of his reviews published in the

he hasn't an enemy in the world, and none of his friends like him.

OSCAR WILDE Writer On George Bernard Shaw, quoted in *Bernard Shaw: 16 Self Sketches* (1949).

Saturday Review between 1895 and 1898. He became a brilliant debater and supporter of the Fabians. His first play, *Widowers' Houses*, was privately produced in 1892. Attacking slum landlords, it allied him with the realistic, political, and polemical movement in the theatre, pointing to people's responsibility to improve themselves and their social environment. His first public production was *Arms and the Man*, a cynical view of war, published as one of seven plays entitled *Plays: Pleasant and Unpleasant* (1898). Also in the volume was *Mrs Warren's Profession* (1898), dealing with prostitution, which was banned until 1902. *Man and Superman* expounds his ideas of evolution by following the character of Don Juan into hell for a debate with the devil.

The 'anti-romantic' comedy *Pygmalion*, first performed in 1913, was written for the actor Mrs Patrick Campbell (and after Shaw's death was converted to a musical as *My Fair Lady*). Shaw combined treatment of social issues with a comic technique that relied on brilliantly witty serio-comic dialogue and playfully ironic inversion of audience expectations about character and situation. As a result, he put himself in the vanguard of the intellectually serious and progressive English theatre, yet also became a successful popular playwright. Later plays included *Heartbreak House* (1920), about the decline of Edwardian England; *Back to Methuselah* (1922), an ambitious

GEORGE BERNARD SHAW *Shaw first came to public attention as an arts critic, and went on to achieve a legendary reputation as a playwright, wit, and prolific letter-writer who could tackle emotive political issues as well as poke fun at social mores. Shaw continued to write for the theatre until his death at the age of 94.*

cycle of plays offering a view of history from human beginnings to the distant future; and the historical *St Joan* (1923), which examines the nature of religious belief.

Altogether Shaw wrote more than 50 plays and became a byword for wit. His theories were further explained in the voluminous prefaces to the plays, and in books such as *The Intelligent Woman's Guide to Capitalism, Socialism and Fascism* (1928).

SHEEHAN, PATRICK AUGUSTINE (1852–1913)

Novelist, born in Mallow, County Cork, and ordained as a priest in 1875. His fiction was a personal response to the increasing modernization of Ireland, much of which he perceived as a threat to Catholic values; in many ways, his novels are sermons in print. His first book, *Geoffrey Austin* (1895), a story of student life, was followed in 1899 by its sequel, *The Triumph of Failure*. Other works include *Glenanaar* (1905), *Lisheen* (1907), *The Blindness of Dr Gray* (1909), and *The Graves at Kilmorna* (1915).

Sheehan began his pastoral work in England, but in 1877 returned to Ireland. From 1895 he was priest at Doneraile in Cork, being made a canon of Cork Cathedral in 1905. His best-known work, *My New Curate* (1900), contains sketches of the life of a typical Irish priest.

SHEEHY, NICHOLAS (*c.* 1728–1766)

Catholic priest. As parish priest of Clogheen, County Tipperary, he was hated by landlords because of his sympathies with the poor. Agrarian unrest by the Whiteboys (a secret agrarian protest society) was met by the repressive 'Whiteboy Act' of 1765, under which Father Sheehy was retired in March 1766 for involvement in the murder of a local landlord; he was hanged at Clonmel the same month. Popular tradition claims the alleged victim had survived an attempt

> **Í** don't believe in circumstances. The people who get on in this world are the people who get up and look for the circumstances they want, and, if they can't find them, make them.
>
> GEORGE BERNARD SHAW *Mrs. Warren's Profession* 2.

on his life and was later seen in Nova Scotia. Father Sheehy's case is regarded as a miscarriage of justice, and he became a martyr figure among the destitute tenants.

SHEEHY-SKEFFINGTON, FRANCIS JOSEPH CHRISTOPHER (1878–1916)

Pacifist, writer, and journalist. He was the husband and fellow campaigner of Hannah ⇨Sheehy-Skiffington.

SHEEHY-SKEFFINGTON, HANNAH (born Sheehy) (1877–1946)

Patriot and feminist, born in Kenturk, County Cork. One of the first women in Ireland to study and teach at a university (the National University of Ireland (University College, Dublin)), she was a founder member of the Irish Women Graduates' Association (1901) and campaigned ardently for votes for women. In 1908, together with fellow suffragist Margaret Cousins and her husband, the pacifist Francis Sheehy-Skeffington, she established the Irish Women's Franchise League – in her own words 'an avowedly militant association'. She was imprisoned for three months in 1912 while protesting at Dublin Castle at the exclusion of women from the Home Rule Bill.

Francis Sheehy-Skeffington was murdered by troops during the 1916 Easter Rising.

The ministering angel of the ambulance class, who provides the pyjamas and the lint, but who sinks below the human the moment she asks for the vote.

HANNAH SHEEHY-SKEFFINGTON Protesting at the treatment of women in the Irish Volunteers, quoted in *Hannah Sheehy-Skeffington: A Life* by Margaret Ward.

SHEELA-NA-GIG (Irish *Síle na gcíoch*, 'Sheila of the teats')

Primitive Irish carving of a naked female displaying exaggerated genitalia. Mainly found outside medieval churches and buildings, the figures have been variously interpreted as pagan fertility symbols, Christian morality tableaux, Celtic war goddesses, or fetishes against evil – early sagas refer to warriors, such as the hero ⇨Cuchulain, being subdued by women exposing their genitals. Examples of the effigies may be found on ⇨White Island, Lower Lough Erne, County Fermanagh and at Bunratty Castle, County Clare.

SHEILS, GEORGE (*c.* 1881–1949)

Playwright whose realistic dramas often satirize the role of greed and financial despair in political and familial decisions. Born in Ballymoney, County Antrim, Sheils emigrated to Canada but returned to Ireland after being crippled in a railway accident. Closely associated with the Abbey Theatre, Dublin, in the 1930s and 1940s, he is best known for *The Passing Day* (1936), a play which showcases his themes and sardonic wit.

SHERIDAN, JIM (1949–)

Film and theatre director and writer, born in Dublin. His first three films, *My Left Foot* (1989), *The Field* (1990), and *In the Name of the Father* (1993), received a total of 13 Academy Award nominations. Sheridan's career began in the 1970s as a theatre director and playwright. Eight of his own plays have been produced. He moved to New York where he was Artistic Director of the Irish Arts Centre and studied film at New York University. He spent many years attempting to gain backing for his adaptation of the autobiography of writer Christy Brown, who suffered from cerebral palsy, before he was able to make *My Left Foot*. It was nominated for five Academy Awards and won two: for actors Daniel Day-Lewis and Brenda ⇨Fricker. Sheridan's second film, *The Field* was also nominated for an Academy Award: for Richard Harris's performance as Bull McCabe, a farmer who is seeking to purchase a field he has long tilled. Sheridan's third feature, *In the Name of the Father*, explores the Guildford Four miscarriage of justice case when Irish people were wrongly convicted of terrorist offences and as a result spent 15 years in jail. Continuing his remarkable critical success in the USA, Sheridan's film was nominated for seven Academy Awards. Sheridan was also the script-writer for the children's film *Into the West* (1992), and, with director Terry George, of *Some Mother's Son* (1996). With George he co-wrote *The Boxer* (1997), which he also directed.

SHERIDAN, RICHARD BRINSLEY (1751–1816)

Dramatist and politician, born in Dublin. His social

comedies include *The Rivals* (1775), celebrated for the character of Mrs Malaprop, whose unintentional misuse of words gave the English language the word 'malapropism', and his best-known piece, *The School for Scandal* (1777). He also wrote a burlesque, *The Critic* (1779), on the staging of inferior dramatic work. In 1776 he became lessee of the Drury Lane Theatre, London.

Sheridan became a member of parliament in 1780 as an adherent of the English Whig politician Charles Fox. A noted orator, he directed the impeachment of the former governor general of India, Warren Hastings, and was treasurer to the Navy 1806–07. His last years were clouded by the burning down of his theatre in 1809, the loss of his parliamentary seat in 1812, and by financial ruin and mental breakdown.

SHILLELAGH

Village in County Wicklow, 26 km/16 mi southwest of Arklow; population (1996) 300. The district was once covered by the Shillelagh Wood, and the village gives its name to a rough cudgel of oak or blackthorn, now manufactured as a tourist souvenir. Oak from the wood was supplied for the roofing of St Patrick's Cathedral in Dublin, and Westminster Hall in London.

Coolattin Park lies 2 km/1 mi east of Shillelagh; once the estate of the Earls of Fitzwilliam, it is now a golf course. At Aghowle, 8 km/5 mi to the west, are

RICHARD BRINSLEY SHERIDAN *The son of an actor-manager, Sheridan always disliked the theatre despite the popularity of his plays, and once said that he never saw a play if he could help it. He much preferred parliamentary life.*

Mr Speaker, I said the honourable member was a liar it is true and I am sorry for it. The honourable member may place the punctuation where he pleases.

RICHARD BRINSLEY SHERIDAN Attributed remark, when asked to apologize for calling a fellow member of parliament a liar.

~

the remains of a 12th-century church with a Romanesque carved doorway and windows, and a cross on the site of a monastery founded by St Finian of Clonard.

SHIPBUILDING

As an island, Ireland always had shipwrights. The earliest written accounts refer to construction on the west coast in the time of St Brendan in the 6th century, his legendary voyages being described in *Navigation of St Brendan* (*c.* 1050). Later the Vikings introduced their technically advanced boats and skills; many Irish terms for parts of ships are borrowed from Old Norse, such as *ancaire* (anchor) and *stiúir* (rudder). By the early 19th century shipbuilding was well established in several centres, based on the construction of wooden sailing vessels. In the first half of the century, the leading developments were in Munster, especially in the Cork and Waterford yards – Ireland's first steamship was built in Cork in 1815. However, from the middle of the 19th century, although iron steamships were built at Waterford 1847–80, the importance of the Munster yards was eclipsed by the dynamic growth of works in Belfast.

The rise to pre-eminence of Belfast shipbuilding may be traced to several factors. With the transition to iron, and later steel, hulls and steam rather than sail power, there was an evident trend in the manufacture of ships in both Britain and Ireland to relocate nearer to sources of iron and coal in the northern districts of Britain. Belfast became part of a network based around the River Clyde and benefited from the boom in world trade in the latter part of the 19th century. Improvements in the port facilities carried out by the Belfast Harbour Commissioners made it an attractive location for the industry.

Belfast's shipbuilding was carried out by two enterprises: Harland and Wolff, originally established in 1853; and Workman, Clark and Company, founded in 1879. Harland and Wolff was by far the largest and

SHIPBUILDING *Belfast has always been the main centre for Irish shipbuilding. Major maufacturer Harland and Wolff, whose yard is seen here, has struggled to survive the worldwide decline in demand, but remains an important force in the European industry.*

owed its position as a world leader to its technical superiority and innovative designs. It specialized in the construction of liners for companies such as Bibby's and the White Star Line, whose most famous ship was the ill-destined ⇨*Titanic*, which sunk on its maiden voyage in 1912. Workman, Clark and Company built smaller vessels. By the beginning of the second decade of the 20th century the two shipyards together accounted for 8% of world output, employed over 15,000 workers and, along with infra-structure industries such as ropemaking, made an enormous impact on the economy of Belfast.

Following a boom during World War I, inter-war economic problems and over-capacity sent Belfast shipbuilding into decline. In 1935 Workman Clark ended production. A brief recovery in the shipyards during World War II was followed by an even more serious drop in demand and the industry has ceased to be the cornerstone of the region's economy. Harland and Wolff continues to operate, but on a lesser scale.

SHOWBANDS

Bands playing cover versions of mainly US popular music to large dancing audiences in the 1950s and 1960s; they ushered in the first popular music movement in Ireland. Showbands grew out of the big-band era, which was coming to an end in the early 1950s. Despite opposition from the church, ballrooms that could hold between 2,000 and 4,000 people were built all over the country, with names like the Las Vegas, the Royal, the Jetland, and the Majestic Bal-

loon. The heyday of the showband era was between 1960 and 1968; it was deeply influenced by popular US culture and bands included the Royal, Capitol, and Miami Showbands, the Dixies, and the Freshmen.

At the height of the craze 500 full-time bands were working in Ireland. The showbands' decline was probably due to the changing social habits of a new generation, when the lounge bar, club, disco, and cabaret replaced the ballroom. The younger generation looked to the new guitar-driven popular music of the early 1970s. However, some of the most popular artists of the showband era, such as Dickie Rock, Joe Dolan, and Brendan Bowyer, have survived and work abroad, mainly in the USA.

See also ⇨Country and Irish.

SHOWJUMPING

Showjumping was born at the Royal Dublin Society, Leinster Lawn, in 1868. The man behind it was Lord Howth, who conceived the idea of the first Royal Dublin Horse Show. The prize money at that time was £55 – compared to about £200,000 in the 1990s. The Dublin Horse Show moved to its current home at Ballsbridge in 1889 with the financial backing of Sir Arthur Guinness. Today the show is regarded as one of the best in the world and is attended by over 1,000 competitors annually. Millstreet in County Cork is another popular showjumping venue.

SIGERSON, DORA (1866–1918)

Poet, born in Dublin, who eventually settled in London. She is best known for her elegiac *Sixteen Dead Men and Other Ballads of Easter Week* (1919), dedicated to the men executed after the Easter Rising of 1916. Her *Collected Poems* (1907) and *New Poems* (1912) reflect her interest in the ballad form and in Celtic lore. *The Sad Years* (1918) is often understood to be the poetic expression of her own broken heart with the failure of the rising.

SINN FÉIN ('we ourselves')

All-Ireland political party founded in 1905, whose aim is the creation of a united republican Ireland. The driving political force behind Irish nationalism between 1916 and 1921, Sinn Féin returned to prominence with the outbreak of violence ('the Troubles') in ⇨Northern Ireland in the late 1960s, when it split into 'Provisional' and 'Official' wings at the same time as the ⇨Irish Republican Army (IRA), with which it is closely associated. Official Sinn Féin later became the Workers' Party, a left-wing socialist party rather than a nationalist party, but never achieved more than a handful of seats in the Dáil (parliament). Provisional Sinn Féin assumed a more active political role from the late 1960s, fielding candidates in local and national elections. It became known simply as Sinn Féin and developed as a significant electoral force in Northern Ireland. It won two seats in the 1997 UK general election and one seat in the 1997 Irish general election. Gerry ⇨Adams became party president in 1978. Sinn Féin participated in the multiparty negotiations (known as the Stormont Talks) and became a signatory of the agreement reached on Good Friday, 10 April 1998.

history
Sinn Féin was founded by Arthur ⇨Griffith, and Éamon ⇨de Valera became its president in 1917. Sinn Féin MPs won a majority of the Irish seats in the 1918 UK general election, set up a secessionist Dáil (parliament) in Dublin, and declared Irish independence in January 1919. The party split over the 1921 Anglo-Irish Treaty, which created the Irish Free State within the British Commonwealth and partitioned Ireland. The refusal of a section of Sinn Féin, led by de Valera, to accept the terms of the treaty, led to armed conflict between his followers and the forces of the new Free State. In the aftermath of the Irish Civil War (1922–23), Sinn Féin pursued a policy of abstention from the Dáil. The party rapidly declined in importance after Éamon de Valera resigned the presidency of Sinn Féin to form his new ⇨Fianna Fáil party in 1926.

Talks in 1993 between Provisional Sinn Féin and the moderate nationalist ⇨Social Democratic and Labour Party (SDLP) on achieving a non-violent political settlement in Northern Ireland were followed by the Downing Street Declaration by the British and Irish prime ministers (December 1993), and the IRA ceasefire of August 1994. In May 1995 Sinn Féin engaged in the first talks with British government officials since 1973, but the 'peace process' remained deadlocked over Sinn Féin's refusal to accept the demands of the British government and the Ulster Unionists (see ⇨Ulster Unionist Party) that all-party talks could not proceed until the IRA had begun decommissioning their arms. The IRA ceasefire was broken in February 1996 with a renewed bombing campaign in London.

all-party discussions
The British Labour government made clear its wish for Sinn Féin to participate in all-party talks on the political future of Northern Ireland, provided that the IRA declared another ceasefire. A second IRA ceasefire was duly declared in July 1997, though Unionists remained opposed to Sinn Féin participating in all-party negotiations without the IRA having first decommissioned their weapons. Although the IRA maintained that its ceasefire was intact, the killings of loyalists resulted in Sinn Féin's temporary exclusion from the all-party talks in early 1998. In February, however, the party returned to the negotiations (known as the Stormont Talks) and became a signatory of the agreement reached on Good Friday, 10 April 1998. It secured 18 of the 108 seats in the new Northern Ireland assembly, elected in June 1998.

Northern Ireland Assembly
On 10 May 1998 Sinn Féin decided to opt for involvement in a new Northern Ireland government, and an internal vote cleared the way for Sinn Féin members to take their seats in the Northern Ireland Assembly. The party also decided to call for a 'Yes' vote in referendums on the Good Friday agreement held in Northern Ireland and the Republic of Ireland; the agreement was voted in by the people of Ireland, north and south, on 22 May 1998. When devolution of ministerial powers took place on 2 December 1999, two members of Sinn Féin took seats on Northern Ireland's power-sharing executive: Martin McGuinness, ex-IRA Chief of Staff, became minister for education, and Bairbre de Brún received responsibility for health, social services, and public safety.

SIX COUNTIES
The six counties that form Northern Ireland: Antrim, Armagh, Down, Fermanagh, Derry, and Tyrone.

SKELLIGS, THE
Group of three islets off the coast of County Kerry, 15 km/9 mi southwest of Valentia Island. Great Skellig has the ruins of a monastery; its twin peaks rise to 218 m/715 ft and 198 m/649 ft above sea level. Little Skellig is the most southerly breeding place for gannets in the area.

The monastic settlement on Great Skellig is associated with St Michael. Its ruins are well preserved and are now a tourist attraction. They include two churches from before the 10th century, six beehive-shaped cells, two oratories, and many early grave-stones and crosses.

SKERRIES

Seaside resort and fishing port in County Dublin, 29 km/18 mi north of Dublin; population (1996) 7,300. Some 3 km/2 mi south of Skerries are the ruins of Baldongan Castle, and on St Patrick's Island, one of three small islands opposite Skerries, are the ruins of an early church.

SKIBBEREEN

Market town and seaport in County Cork; population (1996) 1,900. It lies on the River Ilen, 29 km/18 mi southwest of Bantry. The ruins of a Cistercian abbey can be seen here. On Lough Ine (or Hyne) 6 km/4 mi southwest of Skibbereen, are the ruins of Cloghan Castle, a former stronghold of the O'Driscolls, and a marine biological research station.

Skibbereen is the cathedral town of the Ross diocese.

SLIEVE BLOOM ('Mountains of Bladhma')

Old red sandstone and quartzite mountain range of the Republic of Ireland, extending from north County Tipperary through County Laois to south-west Offlay. Rising dramatically from low-lying boggy plains, its gently rounded slopes reach 498 m/1,734 ft at Arderin, the highest peak. The range is dotted with conifer plantations and is a centre for walking; the Slieve Bloom Way, a long-distance foot-path, circles the peaks for 50 km/31 mi. An interpre-tive centre is located at ⇨Birr in County Offlay. The mountains are reputedly named after a Celtic warrior who took refuge in their hills.

SLIGO

County of the Republic of Ireland, in the province of Connacht, situated on the Atlantic coast of northwest Ireland; county town ⇨Sligo; area 1,800 sq km/695 sq mi; population (1996) 55,800. Limestone mountains rise behind a boggy coastal plain. There is some mineral wealth, including barytes, coal, lead, and copper. Agricultural activity includes cattle farm-ing and dairy farming. The other principal town is Ballymote.

Sligo is notable for its important megalithic remains, including the cemetery site at Carrowmore

COUNTY SLIGO *The vast megalithic burial site at Carrowkeel has been widely damaged by quarrying. Around 50 sets of remains have been saved, among them graves dating back to 5000 BC. Scorched bones found nearby indicate that mass cremations probably also took place here.*

Hill. W B ⇨Yeats wrote much of his poetry about Sligo, where he lived for many years.

topography

Sligo is bounded on the north by the Atlantic, on the southwest and west by County Mayo, on the east by Leitrim, and on the southeast by Roscommon. The bays of Killala and Sligo indent the shore, and the mountains behind the coastal plain are the Slieve Gamph or Ox Mountains, the highest point of which is is Mount Knockalongy (545 m/1,788 ft), and the Dartry Mountains, the highest point of which is Mount Truskmore (641 m/2,103 ft) on the eastern border. The principal rivers are the Garavogue and the Owenmore. The lakes include loughs Arrow, Easky, Gara, Gill, Glencar, Talt, and Templehouse.

SLIGO

Seaport and county town of County ⇨Sligo; popula-tion (1996) 17,800. It is situated on the River Gar-avogue, between Lough Gill and the Atlantic. Health-care products, pharmaceuticals, animal vac-cines, rubber, and videotape are manufactured, and Sligo has engineering, food-processing, and service industries. The town contains the 15th-century ruins of a Dominican abbey founded in 1252; 5 km/3 mi away at Carrowmore is a collection of megalithic remains.

Sligo is a popular centre for tours of the 'Yeats Country'. In Lough Gill (8 km/5 mi by 2 km/1 mi)

lies the islet of Innisfree, made famous by W B Yeats's poem 'The Lake Isle of Innisfree' (1893). Drumcliff, the poet's burial place, is 8 km/5 mi to the north of Sligo. The art gallery in the Yeats Memorial Building contains a collection of drawings and paintings by Jack Yeats, J B Yeats, and other 20th-century artists.

history and archaeology

Sligo was a strategic site as a ford for the River Garavogue and was the site of conflict between English and Irish forces from the 13th century onwards.

On Cairns Hill, 4 km/2 mi south of Sligo, are the remains of two stone ring forts and a stone circle; nearby is a stone altar known as Tobernalt, which was used for Mass during the period in which Catholicism was prohibited. At Magherannish, 6 km/4 mi to the east, are the remains of a large court tomb, a ring fort, and a souterrain (underground dwelling). ⇨Carrowmore is the site of an extensive Neolithic cemetery. There is also a group of dolmens, stone circles, and ring forts. There is a visitor centre here. Nearby is a horseshoe-shaped tomb, Cloverhill, with Bronze Age carvings. On the summit of Knocknarea (330 m/ 1,083 ft), 6 km/4 mi from Sligo, is Miscaun Meadhbh, a large cairn 24 m/80 ft high, and the remains of other tombs. Also 6 km/4 mi from Sligo, near Fermoyle, is Leacht Con Mhic Ruis, a large megalithic chambered tomb.

SLOANE, HANS (1660–1753)

Physician who is credited with introducing the scientific method into medicine. His achievements earned him a baronetcy in 1716, the first medical practitioner to receive a hereditary title.

Born in Killyleagh, County Down, Sloane studied medicine in London and took his doctorate at the University of Orange, France. He returned to London and in 1721 founded the Chelsea Physic Garden. He was first physician to George II and was president of the Royal College of Physicians 1719–35. He succeeded the English physicist Isaac Newton as president of the Royal Society in 1727, a post he occupied until 1740. He was a great believer in the importance of diet and also helped to establish the practice of inoculation for smallpox.

In 1712 Sloane bought large tracts of land in the Kensington and Chelsea area, where his name lives on in Sloane Square, Sloane Street, Hans Crescent, and other roads. He also had the distinction of inventing a recipe for chocolate mixed with milk, Sir Hans Sloane's Milk Chocolate, which was used by Cadbury's until 1885.

Sloane was a distinguished collector, amassing over 58,000 manuscripts and books as well as curiosities and plants. He brought back no fewer than 800 plant specimens from a trip to Jamaica during 1687–88. His library was bequeathed to Britain and formed the nucleus of the British Museum, which opened in Bloomsbury, London, in 1759.

SMURFIT, MICHAEL (1936–)

Industrialist who built the Jefferson Smurfit Group into one of the world's biggest paper and packaging companies. Smurfit was born in England in St Helen's, Lancashire. In 1955 he joined the packaging company founded in Dublin by his father, Jefferson Smurfit, and was joint-managing director 1966–77 and appointed chairman and chief executive in 1977. Under his leadership the Smurfit Group expanded into a multinational business with substantial investments in the USA, South America, mainland Europe, the UK, and Ireland.

Four of the 15 directors of the group are members of the Smurfit family: Michael, his brothers Alan and Dermot, and Michael's son Tony.

Michael Smurfit also developed the K Club, County Kildare, the country club just west of Dublin named as the venue for the 2005 Ryder Cup golf match between the US and Europe. He is also a significant figure in the Irish horse racing and breeding industry and owned Vintage Crop, which won the 1993 Melbourne Cup in Australia.

SMYLLIE, ROBERT MAIRE (1894–1954)

Journalist and editor. He joined the ⇨Irish Times at the end of World War I, and played a critical role as its editor from 1934 until his death. He encouraged the evolution of the newspaper from an old-fashioned, Protestant and Unionist house organ into a liberal and literate daily.

Smyllie was born in Glasgow and educated at Trinity College, Dublin. A larger-than-life bohemian, he was reputed to sing parts of his leading articles in operatic recitative, and to carve the nail on his little finger into a pen nib, as did Keats. Early in his career he achieved notable success by interviewing Lloyd George at Versailles.

SOCIAL CHANGE

See feature essay on social change, page 324.

*t*he shopping mall is fast replacing the Church as a place of worship and it has to be said that Ireland is not a nicer place because of it.

ITA O'KELLY-BROWNE Writer *The Mirror*, 1 January 1998.

~

SOCIAL DEMOCRATIC AND LABOUR PARTY (SDLP)

Northern Ireland left-of-centre political party, formed in 1970. Inspired by the civil-rights movement, it was intended to be a broad cross-community labour party but soon became known as a mainly Catholic and moderately nationalist party, and has consistently been the largest representative of the Catholic population. It aims ultimately at Irish unification, but through constitutional means. Its leader, John ⇨Hume, played a key role in the negotiations which culminated in the 1998 Good Friday agreement on power-sharing. It secured 24 of the 108 seats in the new Northern Ireland Assembly, elected in June 1998; the party's deputy leader, Seamus Mallon, was voted deputy first minister (to Ulster Unionist David Trimble) by the first meeting of the assembly.

The SDLP took part in the failed 1973 Sunningdale agreement, which provided for a power-sharing executive in Northern Ireland. Led by John Hume, the SDLP was responsible for setting up the unsuccessful New Ireland Forum in 1983, and for initiating talks with the leader of Sinn Féin (the political wing of the IRA), Gerry Adams, in 1993, which prompted a joint UK–Irish peace initiative and set in motion a Northern Ireland ceasefire 1994–96. The party won three seats in the 1997 general election. The SDLP is very influential on the Republic of Ireland's government policy toward Northern Ireland.

SODA BREAD

Round loaf leavened with a mixture of sodium bicarbonate and buttermilk, traditional to Ireland. Originally baked on a hot griddle over an open fire, the bread is moist and close-textured with a hard crust.

SOLOMONS, ESTELLA (1882–1968)

Painter. Born into a distinguished Dublin Jewish family, Solomons studied under two of Ireland's lead-

ing artists, Walter Osborne and William Orpen and was an early member of the Irish impressionist school. Becoming increasingly politically active, she joined the republican feminist organization Cumman na mBan and was active in the 1916 rising. During the Anglo–Irish War her studio was used as a safe house by republican volunteers. Her politics, combined with an increasing interest in Rembrandt, may have influenced her shift from landscape and still-life studies to a greater concentration on subtle and critical portraiture.

SOMERVILLE, EDITH (ANNA OENONE) (1861–1949)

Novelist, born into a wealthy Anglo-Irish family. Somerville lived on the family estate in the village of Castletownshend, County Cork, and wrote stories of Anglo-Irish life jointly with her cousin, Violet ⇨Martin (Martin Ross). Works by ⇨Somerville and Ross include *An Irish Cousin* (1889), *The Real Charlotte* (1894), *The Silver Fox* (1897), *Some Experiences of an Irish RM* (1899), and *Further Experiences of an Irish RM* (1908). Books by Somerville alone include *Irish Memories* (1917) and *The Big House at Inver* (1925).

Somerville was born on the Greek island of Corfu, the daughter of an Irish army officer, who soon returned with his family to Ireland. She studied art in Paris, Düsseldorf, and London, and later illustrated her own books. She collaborated with her cousin from 1886 until the latter's death in 1915; they completed 14 books. Besides novels, they also wrote *Through Connemara in a Governess Cart* (1893) and *Some Irish Yesterdays* (1906).

Somerville became the first woman master of foxhounds in 1903, and edited an anthology of hunting verse, *Notes of the Horn* (1934).

SOMERVILLE AND ROSS (joint pseudonym of VIOLET MARTIN (1862–1915) and EDITH SOMERVILLE (1858–1949))

Writers. Somerville and Ross were both members of the Anglo-Irish ascendancy, Martin living at Ross House, County Galway, and Somerville in the village of Castletownshend, County Cork. Their best-loved collaboration is the 'Irish RM' trilogy: *Some Experiences of an Irish RM* (1899), *Further Experiences of an Irish RM* (1908), and *In Mr Knox's Country* (1915),

SOCIAL CHANGE AS THE REPUBLIC HAS GROWN MORE OUTWARD-LOOKING

by Carla King

In the wake of the Great Famine (historically given as 1845–49, though more recently considered as having continued until 1852), Irish society adopted a pattern that was to characterize it for over a century. The country, apart from Dublin and the northeast corner, remained very little urbanized or industrialized, high levels of emigration persisted well into the 20th century, and Ireland had the highest rate of celibacy in Europe, population levels remaining low. Recent decades have seen an end to this model, as Ireland underwent a period of rapid and radical change associated with increased industrialization and urbanization, and higher living standards. Earlier portrayals of Irish society as transitional between a developing and a modernized society gave way as it increasingly converged with Western European patterns.

As the economy grew more buoyant, society became increasingly consumer-oriented, although pockets of poverty and lack of opportunity remain. Nevertheless, as noted in the European Values Survey (1990), social values continue to display a tension between the adoption of European practices and national distinctiveness, the latter based on Ireland's history and on the influence of the social teachings of the Roman Catholic church.

population

In the 1996 census the population of the Republic of Ireland stood at 3,626,000, 58% of which lived in urban areas and 26.3% in the Greater Dublin area. More people live in the east of the country than the west.

Since the 1960s, family structure has shifted away from the post-famine pattern of very high rates of celibacy coupled with high levels of fertility within marriage, towards smaller completed family size. The average number of children per family in 1996 was 1.8, while the number of households made up of couples without children rose by 22% between 1991 and 1995. Limitation of family size has been assisted by the lifting of legal bans on the importation of contraceptives in the 1970s. Although by European standards the Irish population is relatively young, with an average age of 33.6 in 1996, the average age is rising owing to lower birth and mortality rates. Life expectancy has risen from 58 in 1926 to 78 for women and 72 for men in 1991. Infant mortality has fallen owing to improvements in nutritional and living standards.

employment

Traditional work patterns within the family have altered considerably, as the farm household has generally given way to an industrial model in which men and unmarried women engage in waged labour outside the home, and married women concentrate on looking after the home and child rearing. In 1992 unpaid work in the household was the principal occupation of over 60% of women – a higher than average proportion for western countries.

Nevertheless in recent years, with rising demands for labour in Ireland, there has been a growing number of dual-earner households.

marriage

Equality between spouses appears to have grown in recent years, indicating a move away from traditional marriage models. However, in common with other modern states, Irish society has experienced rising levels of marital break-

The Family Planning Association selling condoms over the counter. From 1935 until the 1970s, the sale of contraceptives was illegal in the Republic of Ireland.

down. The 1996 census revealed that there were more than twice as many broken marriages in that year than ten years previously.

In 1995 the country voted narrowly in a referendum to permit divorce, Ireland becoming the last country in Europe to legalize divorce, although provision for judicial separation without re-marriage was introduced in 1989. In the absence of divorce, the most typical pattern of breakdown was desertion, which showed a particularly sharp increase in the 1980s and 1990s, deserted women numbering 16,785 in 1996, compared with 6,363 deserted men.

birth

Following international trends, non-marital births have also increased. In 1991 these accounted for just under a third of all first births in Ireland. Abortion is not only illegal in Ireland but its prohibition was written into the constitution (Article 40.3.3) by a referendum in 1983. This was somewhat modified by a finding by the Supreme Court in the 'X' case in 1992, which allowed Irish women to travel legally to secure an abortion outside the state if their lives were in danger. In fact, several thousand Irish women travel abroad every year to seek abortions.

the Catholic church

In certain of its trends, particularly those family-related, Irish society may be seen to be moving away from the social teaching of the Catholic church. Indeed it appears to be following a general Western pattern in which modernization has brought a tendency towards secularization. Nevertheless, Ireland's religious profile is unusual in a number of respects. It is the only country in the English-speaking world with a Catholic majority, 92% of the population claiming membership of the Catholic church in 1991, and Irish society is characterized by very high levels of religious practice. Although on measurements such as regular confession and mass attendance, church loyalty has fallen in recent decades, it is still unusually high in European terms.

The Catholic church is also uniquely powerful, not only in terms of its influence on public opinion (particularly on social and moral issues), but also institutionally, in view of its continuing role in the provision of education, health, and social welfare. Catholic social teaching is evident in the 1937 constitution and has permeated aspects of Irish law, particularly family law and censorship issues.

In Ireland the Catholic church controls significant resources, such as hospitals, schools, refuges for single mothers, orphanages, and reformatories, that in other countries would usually be vested in the state. Catholic orders also own a large amount of land and buildings throughout the country. This situation, which arose for historical reasons, has resulted in the religious character of a great deal of social provision, even though this is now mostly state-funded. However, a decline in religious vocations is leading the orders to relinquish this role. Moreover, in the late 1990s past abuse was uncovered within these institutions, especially in the institutional care of children. State agencies may be forced to take a more interventionist approach.

government

During the 20th century Ireland matched general Western trends towards state involvement in economic and social spheres. A major provider of employment, the state also played an important part in encouraging investment and stimulating economic growth through state agencies such as the Industrial Development Agency (IDA); Foras Áiseanna Saothair (FÁS), the Training and Employment Authority; and Bord Fáilte, the Irish Tourism Board. Increasingly, the state has become a guarantor of social rights – welfare, equality, and security – to which Irish citizens are entitled by virtue of their membership of the national community. Despite a slow start to social welfare provision in Ireland, the expansion of those rights has characterized the decades since the 1960s. This has been intensified by Ireland's membership of the European Union (EU), the EU somewhat limiting the state's autonomy through its attempts to standardize social provision.

culture

In cultural terms Irish society has moved away from the extreme insularity that marked the early decades of independence. This is the result of a combination of factors, including the influence of the mass media, the effects of travel by Irish people seeking work and taking holidays abroad, increased contact with Europe through the institutions of the EU, and an expansion of tourism bringing interaction with foreign visitors. Unfortunately, this has not prevented the emergence of some hostility to refugees and asylum-seekers who have recently sought to make their homes in Ireland.

Since the provision of free secondary education in the 1960s the Irish population has become better educated. Across a range of cultural activities – sport, music, theatre, literature, and film – the Irish have achieved international success and acquired a greater degree of national self-confidence. There is also greater participation in cultural activities, not just in urban areas but throughout the country.

but their masterpiece was *The Real Charlotte* (1894). Chronicling the financial and amorous ambitions of Charlotte, the novel displays Somerville and Ross's characteristic wit and astute analysis of late 19th-century life in upper-class rural Ireland.

Their work is celebrated as some of the most subtle and entertaining of the period.

SPENSER, EDMUND (*c.* 1552–1599)

English poet, part-time administrator, and Munster planter. After serving as secretary to Lord Deputy Arthur Grey during the Munster rebellion in 1580, he became clerk to the council of the Munster plantation in 1586, acquiring Kilcolman Castle and an estate of 1,200 ha/3,000 acres in County Cork.

While living in Ireland he completed his epic poem *The Faerie Queene*, books I–III published in 1590, and IV–VI in 1596. He also composed *A View of the Present State of Ireland* (1596), a political dialogue which argued for the abandonment of conventional policies of assimilation by education and acculturation, and the adoption of total repression of the native population – this was to be enforced by dispossession, plantations, and where necessary the application of a ruthless policy of starvation.

The representative character of Spenser's ideas and their influence over Elizabethan policy-makers remains a matter of contention among historians. Having been expelled from his holdings in 1598 during Hugh ⇨O'Neill's rebellion, Spenser died in London before his *View* received widespread notice.

SPORT

See feature essay on great moments in Irish sport, page 327.

> Í miss things like the camaraderie in the gym. I don't miss being smacked in the mouth every day!
>
> BARRY MCGUIGAN Boxer On his retirement from boxing, quoted in the *Irish Times*, 18 April 1998.

❧

SPRING, DICK (RICHARD) (1950–)

Irish Labour Party leader from 1982. He entered into a coalition with Garret ⇨FitzGerald's Fine Gael in 1982 as deputy prime minister (with the posts of minister for the environment 1982–83 and minister for energy 1983–87). In 1993 he became Tánaiste (deputy prime minister) to Albert ⇨Reynolds in a Fianna Fáil–Labour Party coalition, with the post of minister for foreign affairs. He withdrew from the coalition in November 1994 in protest over a judicial appointment made by Reynolds, and the following month formed a new coalition with Fine Gael, with John Bruton as prime minister, in power until 1997. He retired from the leadership in 1997 following the poor performance of Labour's presidential candidate.

Born in Kerry in 1950, the son of a Labour TD (member of the Irish parliament), Spring was educated at Trinity College, Dublin, and trained as a barrister at King's Inns. He was elected to the Dáil (parliament) in 1981 for Labour in Kerry North.

STACK, TOMMY (1946–)

National Hunt jockey, born in Moyvane, County Kerry. Twice a champion jockey in Britain 1974–75 (82 winners) and 1976–77 (97 winners), he made history in 1977 when he rode the legendary Red Rum to a third win in the Grand National at Aintree. Prior to that he had spent three months in traction after breaking his pelvis. After retiring from the saddle he took up training in Ireland, winning the 1,000 Guineas at Newmarket with Meninas in 1994 and the Irish 1,000 Guineas with Tarascon in 1998.

STACKALLAN

Property in County Meath, built about 1716. It is a rare example of a pre-Palladian style house, being one of the few surviving grand Irish houses of its era. Formerly known as Boyne House, it was built for one of King William III's generals, Gustavus Hamilton, 1st Viscount Boyne, and considered to be designed by Thomas ⇨Burgh, the architect of Trinity College's Great Library in Dublin. It has two formal fronts and is three storeys high with wide eaves.

STACPOOLE, HENRY DE VERE (1863–1951)

Physician and writer who used his experiences as a ship's doctor and his life at sea to write more than 50 popular novels.

Stacpoole was born in Kingstown, now Dun Laoghaire, County Dublin, and was educated in England at Malvern College, Worcester, and at St George's and St Mary's hospitals, London. He then went on a series of voyages as a ship's doctor. His

GREAT MOMENTS FOR IRISH SPORT, FROM FOOTBALL TO SNOOKER

by Rory Kerr

For an island of five million people, it is remarkable that Ireland has managed to produce so many great sporting moments. From boxing to cycling, athletics to snooker, there have been many success stories.

football

In the world of soccer, June 6 1988 is ingrained on the minds of those who watched Ireland score a celebrated victory over England in the European Championships in Germany. A late goal from Scotland's Gary McKay against Bulgaria had seen Ireland qualify for their first major championship in their history. Prior to that, there had many frustrations along the way with Eoin Hand's side narrowly missing out on qualification for the 1986 World Cup finals.

Hand's successor was Jack Charlton, a player for Leeds United in the late 1960s and early 1970s. Although he had helped England to win the World Cup in 1966, his appointment was nonetheless a surprise one, given that the soccer authorities chose to go outside the country for Ireland's manager. However, successive championships saw Charlton, or 'Big Jack' as he came to be known, become one of Ireland's adopted sons.

Charlton's approach relied on keeping possession and making the opposing team as uncomfortable as possible. His first test in the World Cup championships against England was to prove a daunting one. With players like Gary Lineker and Paul Gascoigne on the English team, the odds were stacked high against Ireland, but against all expectations they achieved victory, with Ray Houghton scoring the only goal with a looping header. The match proved a magnificent start for the Irish, but they were unable to make it through to the next stage, with a freak goal from Holland denying them entry in their final group game after it seemed that they would hold on for a required draw. Ireland went on to qualify for the World Cup finals in 1990 and 1994 under Charlton, whose achievements earned him the freedom of Dublin.

cycling

On the cycling circuits, Stephen Roche's success in the Tour de France in 1987, along with the Giro d'Italia (Tour of Italy) and the world professional road-race championships that year, delighted all Ireland. In the Tour de France Roche performed heroics on the slopes of La Plagne when it seemed that Spain's Pedro Delgado had pulled away from him. However, Roche dug deep in, and by end of that crucial stage he trailed by just 39 seconds. Coming to the final trial he had knocked a further 18 seconds off his time, before gaining the coveted yellow jersey in the penultimate stage at Dijon. Having already won the Giro d'Italia, Roche completed a tremendous treble when he won the world professional road-race championships in Austria, becoming only the second rider ever to win all three titles in the same year.

boxing

In the boxing ring, one man whose sporting achievements were celebrated both north and south was featherweight boxer Barry McGuigan from Clones, County Monaghan. McGuigan took up amateur boxing in 1978 and turned professional in 1980, packing the King's Hall, Belfast, as he slowly made his way up the rankings. Finally, in 1985, the opportunity came to fight for the World Boxing Association World Championship against Panama's Eusebio Pedroza. Pedroza, champion for the previous seven years, showed his durability under intense pressure from McGuigan, who hit him with a barrage of punches over the 15 rounds. Pedroza was eventually floored in the seventh round and McGuigan went on to take the contest on a points decision.

The triumphal returns of Ireland's soccer team, Roche, and McGuigan managed to bring traffic to a standstill in Dublin, with thousands lining the streets to greet their heroes.

Olympic and other successes

There have been, of course, many other notable achievements. For Ireland the Olympic Games saw Ronnie Delaney's outstanding 1,500-metre final in 1956; a bronze medal in the marathon for John Treacy in 1984, in his third Olympics; and Micheal Carruth's gold in the 1992 welterweight boxing final. Northern Ireland's Olympic champion Mary Peters won golds representing Great Britain in the shot and pentathlon in 1970 and in the pentathlon in 1974. The World Snooker Championship was captured by Northern Ireland's Alex Higgins in 1982 and Dennis Taylor in 1985, and by Dublin's Ken Doherty in 1997, Doherty having won the world under-21 and amateur championships ten years previously.

resulting works include *The Blue Lagoon* (1909), *The Pearl Fishers* (1915), and *Green Coral* (1935). He also wrote two volumes of autobiography, *Men* (1942) and *Mice* (1945).

STAIGUE FORT

Prehistoric *cashel* or ring fort, 3 km/1 mi northeast of Castlecove, County Kerry. Dating from 1500 BC, it consists of a circular dry-stone wall, 35 m/115 ft in diameter, surrounded by a large bank and ditch. The walls, 4–1.5 m/13–5 ft thick and originally 5.5 m/ 19 ft high, contain steps leading to a platform overlooking the coast. The fort is considered to be the best-preserved *cashel* in Ireland.

STANFORD, CHARLES VILLIERS

(1852–1924)

Composer and teacher, born in Dublin. Stanford was a leading figure in the 19th-century renaissance of British music. His many works include operas such as *Shamus O'Brien* (1896), seven symphonies, chamber music, and church music. Among his pupils were Ralph Vaughan Williams, Gustav Holst, and Frank Bridge.

In 1870 Stanford became a choral scholar at Queens' College, Cambridge, England, and in 1873 organist of Trinity College, where he took classical honours the next year; he was also conductor of the Cambridge University Musical Society. He studied with Carl Reinecke at Leipzig 1874–76 and with Friedrich Kiel in Berlin, and in 1876 Alfred Tennyson suggested him as composer of incidental music for his *Queen Mary*. He received a doctorate from Oxford in 1883 and in 1888 from Cambridge, where he had succeeded George Macfarren as professor of music in 1887. He was also conductor of the Bach Choir in London and professor of composition at the Royal College of Music, where he conducted the orchestral and opera classes. He collected traditional Irish songs and edited an edition of George Petrie's *The Complete Petrie Collection of Irish Music* (1902–1905, three volumes).

His works include: OPERA *Shamus O'Brien* (after Le Fanu; 1896). ORCHESTRAL seven symphonies (1876–1911); five Irish rhapsodies (1901–14); cello concerto (1919); clarinet concerto. CHAMBER two sonatas for cello and piano, clarinet and piano sonata, some smaller instrumental pieces with piano; piano works including sonata, three *Dante Rhapsodies*

STAIGUE FORT *According to legend, it took just one day and one night to construct this massive prehistoric fortress. Flights of steps leading to the top were built on the diagonal.*

(1875); 11 organ works including five sonatas. CHORAL oratorios *The Three Holy Children* (1885), *Eden* (1891); Magnificat; *Stabat Mater*, *The Revenge* (1886), *Songs of the Sea* (1904), *Songs of the Fleet* (1910). OTHER two psalms, six services, three anthems; 20 op. nos. of songs.

STANIHURST, RICHARD (1547–1618)

Historian, classical scholar, alchemist, and Counter-Reformation activist. Born into a long-established Dublin family, he became tutor to the children of the 11th Earl of Kildare (1525–1585). Commissioned to write the early Irish section of Holinshed's *Chronicles* in 1577, his work was subjected to extensive editorial censorship for its version of the 1534–35 rebellion of Thomas ⇨Fitzgerald, 8th Earl of Kildare. In 1581 he was driven into exile in the Spanish Netherlands through suspicions of his Catholic sympathies. Celebrated there for his, possibly whiskey-based, medicinal elixirs, he was invited to El Escorial, Philip II's palace and monastery near Madrid, where he was given a laboratory and became involved in a number of intrigues concerning Ireland.

Stanihurst was the son of James Stanihurst, speaker of the Irish parliament 1569–71. He was educated at Oxford University, where he met the English Jesuit and later Catholic martyr Edmund Campion. Stanihurst's *De rebus in Hibernia gestis* (1584), a historical and topographical account from an Old-English viewpoint, was later criticised by more radical ⇨Counter-

Reformation historians for its sympathetic attitude towards the English in Ireland and reported to the Inquisition. His translation of the first four books of Virgil's *Aeneid* was derisively received by several English critics, notably Edmund ⇨Spenser. Towards the end of his life Stanihurst became a Jesuit.

STEELE, RICHARD (1672–1729)

Essayist, playwright, and politician. Born in Dublin, he entered the Life Guards, and then settled in London. He founded the journal *The Tatler* (1709–11), in which Joseph Addison collaborated. They continued their joint work in the *Spectator* (1711–12), also founded by Steele, and *The Guardian* (1713). He also wrote plays, such as *The Conscious Lovers* (1722). In 1713 Steele was elected to parliament. He was knighted in 1715.

STEPHENS, JAMES (1882–1950)

Poet and novelist. Born in Dublin, where he was sent to an orphanage as a child, he later moved to London as a full-time writer in 1924. His work first came to wide attention through the success of his prose fantasy *The Crock of Gold* (1912). His later publications include *Songs from the Clay* (1914), *The Demi-Gods* (1914), and *Reincarnations* (1917). Many of his works drew on his enormous knowledge of Irish history, myth, and legend.

Stephens's first publication was a volume of poems, *Insurrections* (1909), followed by his first novel, *The Charwoman's Daughter* (1912), which described poverty in the Dublin slums. His *Collected Poems* were first published in 1926, and revised in 1954.

STEPHENS, JAMES KENNETH (1825–1901)

Nationalist activist, born in County Kilkenny. He worked as a railway engineer before becoming involved in the ⇨Young Ireland Party. He was wounded at Ballingarry during the failed revolution of 1848, hid for three months in the mountains, and then escaped to France. In 1858, along with John ⇨O'Mahony, he founded the ⇨Fenian movement (later known as the Irish Republican Brotherhood) to campaign for Irish-American support for armed rebellion. In the USA, he undertook extensive fund-raising activities, and established the newspaper *Irish People* (1863). After abandoning a promised uprising in 1866, he was ousted from the Fenian leadership. He remained in exile until permitted to return to Ireland in 1886.

STERNE, LAURENCE (1713–1768)

Writer who was born in Clonmel, County Tipperary, and ordained in 1737. He created the comic anti-hero Tristram Shandy in *The Life and Opinions of Tristram Shandy, Gent* (1759–67). An eccentrically whimsical and bawdy novel, its associations of ideas on the philosophic principles of John Locke, and other devices, foreshadow in part some of the techniques associated with the 20th-century novel, such as stream-of-consciousness. His other works include *A Sentimental Journey through France and Italy* (1768).

*D*igressions, incontestably, are the sunshine; – they are the life, the soul of reading! – take them out of this book, for instance, – you might as well take this book along with them; – one cold eternal winter would reign in every page of it.

LAURENCE STERNE *Tristram Shandy* (1759).

❧

Sterne became vicar of Sutton-in-the-Forest, Yorkshire, in 1738, and married Elizabeth Lumley in 1741, an unhappy union largely because of his infidelity. He had a sentimental love affair with Elizabeth Draper, recorded in his *Letters of Yorick to Eliza* (1775).

STEWART

Family name of the Marquesses of ⇨Londonderry.

*I*t was like a miracle; but before our very eyes, and almost in the drawing of a breath, the whole body crumbled into dust and passed from our sight. I shall be glad as long as I live that even in that moment of final dissolution there was in the face a look of peace, such as I never could have imagined might have rested there.

BRAM STOKER The destruction of the vampire in *Dracula* (1897).

❧

STOKER, BRAM (ABRAHAM) (1847–1912)

Novelist, actor, theatre manager, and author. Born in Dublin, he was educated there at Trinity College, and followed his father into the civil service. His celebrated novel *Dracula* (1897) crystallized most aspects of the traditional vampire legend and became the source for all subsequent fiction and films on the subject.

Stoker wrote a number of other stories and novels of fantasy and horror, such as *The Lady of the Shroud* (1909). Employed as a civil servant 1866–78, he was subsequently business manager to the theatre producer Henry Irving at the Lyceum Theatre, London 1878–1905.

STOKES, GEORGE GABRIEL (1819–1903)

Physicist, born in Skreen, County Sligo, and educated in England at Bristol and Cambridge, where he was appointed Lucasian professor of mathematics in 1849. Stokes studied the viscosity of fluids in the late 1840s, and formulated Stokes' law to describe the force acting on a sphere falling through liquid. In 1852 he gave the first explanation of the phenomenon of fluorescence, a term he coined for the visible light re-emitted from a material following its absorption of ultraviolet light. Using fluorescence as a method to study ultraviolet spectra, he realized in 1854 that the Sun's spectrum is made up of the spectra of the elements it contains.

Stokes's works include *Mathematical and Physical Papers* (1880–1905), *On Light* (1884–87), and *Memoirs and Scientific Correspondence* (1907). He was made a baronet in 1889.

STOKES, WHITLEY (1830–1909)

Academic and lawyer. Born in Dublin, Stokes was an influential scholar of Celtic and Gaelic philology (the study of the historical development of languages), pursuing his interest while working in the Indian legal administration. He published several translations and commentaries explaining medieval Latin and Gaelic texts and manuscripts, before producing his major glossary, *Thesaurus Palaeohibernicus* (1901–03).

STOKES, WILLIAM (1804–1878)

Irish-born doctor who promoted the idea of clinical examination as a means towards diagnosis, and was the author of seminal works on cardiology and pulmonary disease. He was considered the leading Irish

BRAM STOKER *As creator of Dracula, who featured first in Stoker's 1897 novel of the same name, Bram Stoker sowed the seeds of horror fiction based on vampires. Stoker describes Count Dracula as tall and thin, with pointed ears, cruel features, and 'peculiarly sharp white teeth'.*

physician of his time and one of the greatest contemporary practitioners in Europe.

Born in Dublin, Stokes was the son of a regius professor of medicine at Dublin University. He studied medicine at the University of Edinburgh in 1825 before returning to Dublin to practise at the Meath Hospital. He brought about sweeping reforms in the education of medical students, encouraging them to conduct physical examinations and to do rounds on the wards in the company of senior doctors. He also pioneered new methods of clinical diagnosis.

On the death of his father in 1845 he was chosen to succeed him as regius professor. He published 100 scientific works, including one as a student on the use of the stethoscope.

Stokes became associated with Cheyne–Stokes respiration, a characteristic of advanced myocardial degeneration first defined in 1818 by Scottish physician John Cheyne, after referring to Cheyne's paper on periodic respiration in his book *The Diseases of the Heart and Aorta*. Stokes defined a second condition, Adams–Stokes syndrome, which brings about slow pulse and cerebral attacks in his paper 'Observations on Some Cases of Permanently Slow Pulse' (1846).

STONEY, GEORGE JOHNSTONE

(1826–1911)

Physicist who coined the term 'electron' and calculated an approximate value for the charge of the particle. He was also a pioneer in the field of spectroscopy and made important contributions to the theory of gases.

Born in Dun Laoghaire, a few miles south of Dublin, Stoney studied at Trinity College, Dublin, and was professor of natural philosophy at Queen's College, Galway, 1852–57. He served as an administrator at Queen's University, Belfast, 1857–82 and as superintendent of civil service examinations in Dublin 1882–93, but continued his research in physics.

In 1868 he calculated the number of molecules in a cubic millimetre of gas from data obtained from the kinetic theory of gases. He proposed that light waves were produced by periodic 'orbital motions' within atoms or molecules. As early as 1874 he had calculated the magnitude of the electron. His 1891 paper to the Royal Dublin Society proposed the 'electron', also describing it as travelling in elliptical orbits in the molecule.

Stoney became a fellow of the Royal Society in 1861 and vice-president in 1898. He received the first Boyle Medal for scientific achievement awarded by the Royal Dublin Society in 1899.

STORMONT

Suburb 8 km/5 mi east of Belfast. It is the site of the new Northern Ireland Assembly, elected as a result of the Good Friday agreement in 1998 and functioning from 1999 when some powers were transferred back to Northern Ireland from Westminster. It was previously the seat of the government of Northern Ireland 1921–72.

The official residence of the prime minister of Northern Ireland was at Stormont, and parliament met in Parliament House, a large, white Neo-Classical building, completed in 1932. Following increasing civil unrest from 1968, the UK government suspended the constitution and parliament of Northern Ireland in 1972, and imposed direct rule from London. By the Northern Ireland Act (1972) the UK parliament was to approve all legislation for Northern Ireland, and the Northern Ireland department was placed under the direction of the secretary of state for Northern Ireland, with an office at Stormont Castle.

STRABANE

Market town in County Tyrone; population (1991) 10,800. It is situated on the River Mourne, 32 km/20 mi north of Omagh. Clothing is manufactured, and there is a food-processing industry. The town was developed by the Abercorn family in the 18th century as a linen-manufacturing centre.

The novelist Flann O'Brien was born here.

Strabane was also the birthplace of John Dunlap (1747–1812), the printer who printed the American Declaration of Independence and founded one of the first daily newspapers in the USA, the *Pennsylvania Packet*. James Wilson, grandfather of the US president Woodrow Wilson, worked in the printing trade in Strabane and his home is open to the public. The hymn writer Frances Alexander, author of 'There is a Green Hill Far Away', was also born in Strabane.

Sion Mills village, 5 km/3 mi south of Strabane, is a planned settlement of half-timbered housing established in the 1840s to promote the textile industry.

STRANGFORD LOUGH

Island-dotted inlet in the east of County Down. The entrance to the lough lies between Strangford and Portaferry in the south, and it is bounded from the sea on the east by the Ards Peninsula, 32 km/20 mi long by 8 km/5 mi wide.

Violent tides enter the lough through the narrow inlet. Strangford Lough is an important habitat for wildlife, especially for overwintering Arctic birds. Queen's University, Belfast, has a marine biological research station and sea-water aquarium at Portaferry on the south of Ards Peninsula. There are many monastic and castle ruins along the shores of Strangford Lough. On Mahee Island, reached by a causeway, are the ruins of Nendrum monastery founded in the 5th century. The Nendrum Bell is now in Belfast Museum.

STRONGBOW

See Richard de ⇨Clare, Earl of Pembroke and Striguil.

Suir

River in the Republic of Ireland; length 160 km/ 99 mi. It rises in County Tipperary and flows south past Cahir and Thurles to the city of Waterford, where it joins with the River Barrow to form Waterford harbour.

Sunningdale Agreement

See ⇨Northern Ireland peace process.

SURRENDER AND REGRANT

Term used to summarize the Tudor diplomatic process whereby Gaelic lords were to be assimilated into English political and social culture without significant loss of power or status. The lords revoked their Gaelic title, assumed an English one, and gained a royal grant of their lands. Initiated under the 1541 act, which declared Ireland as a kingdom in which all subjects were equal in the eyes of the crown, the policy was developed in the 1540s by the English lord deputy Anthony St Leger. A growing awareness of the tenurial and political difficulties involved caused the policy to be displaced by the more detailed and flexible strategy of ⇨composition (commutation of feudal military dues) in the 1570s.

However, although concerns with foreign invasion and domestic conspiracy caused surrender and regrant to be periodically disrupted, the Tudor government never abandoned it entirely. Almost all the Elizabethan lord deputies made efforts to conclude surrender and regrant arrangements with several of the lesser Gaelic lords throughout Ireland, the last significant programme being in the 1580s.

SUTHERLAND, PETER (1946–)

Lawyer, representative, administrator, and international business figure. Born in Dublin, he studied law there at University College, practised as a barrister 1969–81, and was attorney general of the Republic of Ireland 1981–85. As a European Union (EU) commissioner 1985–93, he made his mark in the competition portfolio, taking an active approach to breaking down cartels in such areas as the airline sector. He was appointed director general of the General Agreement on Tariffs and Trade (GATT) organization in 1993, and its replacement body, the World Trade Association (WTO), until 1995. A passionate advocate of free trade, he played a significant role in the international agreement reducing trade barriers completed in December 1993. In 1995 he became chairman and managing director of Goldman Sachs International, the international arm of the major US investment bank.

Sutherland was non-executive chairman of Allied Irish Banks plc (AIB) 1989–93, Ireland's largest banking group, and now serves as non-executive director of BP/Amoco plc, having overseen the merger between the former British Petroleum (BP) and Amoco in 1988. He is also a board member of the multinational groups Investor, Asea Brown Boveri (ABB), and LM Ericcson.

SWAN, CHARLIE (CHARLES FRANAN THOMAS) (1959–)

Jockey, born in Tipperary, County Tipperary, who was Irish National Hunt champion jockey nine years in succession 1989–90 and 1997–98. Son of the trainer, Capt Donald Swan, Swan rode his first winner in 1983. He has also enjoyed success abroad, most notably at the Cheltenham Festival in England, finishing top jockey in both 1993 and 1994, and riding Istabraq to victory in the Champion Hurdle in 1998 and 1999. In September 1998 Swan gave up riding chasers to concentrate on training and riding over hurdles.

SWEEPSTAKE, IRISH

See ⇨Irish Sweepstake.

SWIFT, JONATHAN (1667–1745)

Satirist and Anglican cleric. Born in Dublin, he was educated there at Trinity College, and ordained in 1694. He wrote *Gulliver's Travels* (1726), an allegory describing travel to lands inhabited by giants, miniature people, and intelligent horses. His other works include *The Tale of a Tub* (1704), attacking corruption in religion and learning; and the satirical pamphlet *A Modest Proposal* (1729); written in protest of the on-going famine in Ireland, it suggested that children of the poor should be eaten. His lucid prose style is simple and controlled and he imparted his views with fierce indignation and wit.

*t*hey laughed at such an Irish blunder, / To take the noise of brass for thunder.

JONATHAN SWIFT *Wood the Ironmonger* (1725)

Swift became secretary to the diplomat William Temple (1628–1699) at Moor Park, Surrey, where his friendship with the child 'Stella' (Esther Johnson; 1681–1728) began in 1689. Returning to Ireland, he was ordained in the Church of England in 1694, and in 1699 was made a prebendary of St Patrick's, Dublin. He made contributions to the Tory paper *The Examiner*, of which he was editor 1710–11. He obtained the deanery of St Patrick in 1713. His *Journal to Stella* is a series of intimate letters (1710–13), in which he described his life in London. From about 1738 his mind began to fail.

SWILLY, LOUGH

Inlet in County Donegal. It enters from the Atlantic between Fanad Point and Dunaff Head (6 km/4 mi in width) and extends inland for 40 km/25 mi. Its shores have sandy beaches and curious rock formations. It is surrounded by mountains.

SWISS COTTAGE

Self-consciously rustic thatched cottage (cottage ornée) near Cahir, County Tipperary. It was built in 1810 for Richard Butler, 12th Lord Cahir, probably by the English architect John Nash (1752–1835). Unlike other similar buildings of this size, which were used by the nobility as fishing or shooting lodges or as tea houses, Swiss Cottage was built for Lord and Lady Cahir to live in when they were in Ireland. It was restored in the late 1980s by the Port Royal Foundation of New York, and the interior contains one of the few examples of coloured scenic wallpaper in Ireland.

SWORDS

Town in County Dublin, 20 km/12 mi north of the city of Dublin. Swords has large manufacturers of pharmaceuticals and mobile phones, and smaller chemical and light manufacturing industries.

Colum Cille (St Columba) allegedly founded a monastery here in the 6th century. Swords Castle, begun in 1200 but altered in the 13th and 15th centuries, is in the form of a pentagon.

SYNGE, J(OHN) M(ILLINGTON)
(1871–1909)

Dramatist and leading figure in the Irish literary revival of the early 20th century, born in Rathfarnham, County Dublin. His six plays, which include *In the Shadow of the Glen* (1903), *Riders to the Sea* (1904), and *The Playboy of the Western World* (1907), reflect the speech patterns of the Aran Islands and western Ireland. *The Playboy of the Western World*, Synge's best-known work, caused violent disturbances at the Abbey Theatre, Dublin, when it was first performed.

*T*here is no language like the Irish for soothing and quieting.

J M Synge *The Aran Islands* (1907).

In the Shadow of the Glen, in which a woman prefers a wandering life with a tramp over security with an old husband or even lover, contains echoes of Henrik Ibsen's *A Doll's House*. Synge's next play, *Riders to the Sea*, evokes the threats of the sea and the hardship of a family on the Aran Islands. In *The Playboy of the Western World* the protagonist, Christy Mahon, arrives in a little town in County Mayo and is received as a hero when he boasts that he has murdered his father. Synge's other plays are *The Well of the Saints* (1905), *The Tinker's Wedding* (1908), and the unfinished *Deirdre of the Sorrows*.

*h*e loves all that has edge, all that is salt in the mouth, all that is rough to the hand, all that heightens the emotions by contest, all that strings into life the strength of tragedy.

W B YEATS Poet On J M Synge in *J. M. Synge and the Ireland of his Time* (1910).

Synge's breakthrough, achieved in part through some early translations from classic Gaelic prose and poetry, was to forge a distinctive linguistic style and tragicomic vision for the Irish stage. His ambivalent representation of rural life in western Ireland proved unpalatable to audiences expecting an unproblematically positive contribution to nationalism.

Although Synge was raised in a strongly religious family, he rejected all religion early in his life. He took a degree at Trinity College, Dublin, and spent some time in France. He was fascinated by the Irish language and rural life, and spent time in Wicklow and the Aran Islands. Hodgkin's disease caused his death before he was able to finish *Deirdre of the Sorrows*.

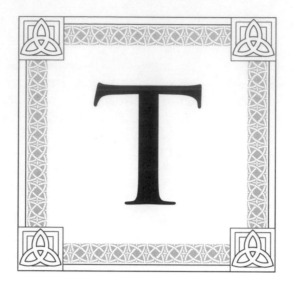

TAAFFE, PAT(RICK) (1959–1992)

National Hunt jockey, born in Rathcoole, County Dublin, who famously rode Arkle to victory in the Cheltenham Gold Cup in 1964, 1965, and 1966. With his victory on Fort Leney in 1968 he became the first jockey to win the Cheltenham Gold Cup four times. He won the Aintree Grand National twice and the Irish Grand National a record six times.

Son of the trainer Tom Taaffe, Taaffe began his racing career in 1945 as an amateur. He turned professional five years later, on being appointed first jockey to the Killsallaghan-based trainer, Tom Dreaper. On his retirement in 1970 Taaffe became a trainer, enjoying his greatest success with Captain Christy.

TAILTEANN GAMES

Early 20th-century revival of an ancient festival held at Teltown, County Meath. Originally presided over by the Uí Néill kings of Tara, the festival observed the advent of winter and was held from 632 BC until 1169. A historical and political symbol of the kingship of Tara, the festival was promoted by both ⇨Brian Bóruma and Rory ⇨O'Connor in recognition of their high kingship of Ireland. Then, having lapsed for 755 years, the festival was revived in 1924 as the 'Tailteann Games' with a gathering of international athletes at Croke Park.

Held again in 1928 and 1932 as 'Aonach Tailteann' or 'the festival of Teltown', the event consisted of several athletic competitions, with games of hurling and Gaelic football as highlights. After the suspension of the games in 1932, they resumed again in 1963 and are now staged as a festival of schools athletics each summer.

TAISCE, AN

Conservation organization, founded in 1946, that is mandated under the 1963 Planning Act to comment on planning proposals.

TALBOT, MATT (1856–1925)

Dockworker, recovered alcoholic, and Franciscan tertiary, declared Venerable in 1975 by Pope Paul VI.

Talbot was born in the Dublin docklands and worked from the age of 16 for Dublin Docks. He became an alcoholic, but took a total abstinence pledge in 1882, replacing drink with prayer in his life. He prayed daily in church and joined the Franciscan Tertiaries in 1890, following the Franciscan ideal in secular employment. Talbot was a dedicated reader of religious and nationalist literature, but avoided political activity.

TANDY, (JAMES) NAPPER (1740–1803)

Radical leader, born in Dublin, who became the first secretary of the Society of United Irishmen. He embraced political radicalism in the 1760s and in the 1770s he campaigned against British colonialism in the American War of Independence (1775–83), and led protests in favour of free trade and legislative independence. He established an armed force on the pattern of the Paris National Guard, but his movement failed and he was obliged to take refuge in the USA. In 1798 he went to Paris, and in conjunction with Wolfe ⇨Tone and others planned an invasion of Ireland, aided by the French. They landed in Ireland in September 1798, but the rising was unsuccessful.

Tandy fled to Hamburg, where he was arrested and taken to Ireland. He was convicted of treason but reprieved through the intervention of the French.

TAOISEACH (plural Taoisigh)

Irish title for the prime minister of the Republic of Ireland. The Taoiseach has broadly similar powers to the UK prime minister.

TARA HILL (or HILL OF TARA)

Ancient religious and political centre in County Meath. A national monument, and depicted in a 7th-century *Life of St Patrick* as the 'capital of the Irish', Tara Hill was the site of a palace and was the coronation place of many Irish kings. Its heyday was in the 3rd century AD, and the site was still in use in the 10th century. St ⇨Patrick, patron saint of Ireland, preached here. Some tumuli and earthworks remain, and the pillar stone, reputed to be the coronation stone, can still be seen on the summit. In 1843 it was the venue for a meeting held by the Daniel O'Connell, 'the Liberator', following the launch of his campaign for the repeal of the Act of Union (1801) in 1841.

In the 1990s Tara Hill was the subject of a literary and historical survey that aimed to survey documents in which the site was mentioned, and to construct a history of the area from AD 600 to the present.

TATE, NAHUM (1652–1715)

Poet who was born in Dublin, and educated there at Trinity College before moving to London. He wrote an adaptation of Shakespeare's *King Lear* with a happy ending, entitled *The History of King Lear* (1681). He wrote the libretto for Purcell's *Dido and Aeneas*; he also produced *A New Version of the Psalms* (1696); his hymn 'While Shepherds Watched Their Flocks by Night' appeared in the *Supplement* (1703). He became British poet laureate in 1692.

TAYLOR, JEREMY (1613–1667)

English scholarly prelate, Church of Ireland bishop of Down and Connor from 1660. He was an episcopalian who opposed the Presbyterianism of Oliver Cromwell's Commonwealth. He lectured in Lisburn, County Antrim, in 1658, partly to avoid confrontation in England. At the same time, he was vice-chancellor of Trinity College, Dublin, bishop of Down and Connor, and administrator of Dromore diocese and on the Irish Privy Council from 1661. While bishop, he wrote *Defense and Introduction to Confirmation*

(1663) and *Dissuasive Against Popery* (1664). He elevated Lisburn to cathedral status in 1662 and restored Dromore Cathedral, where he was buried.

TD

Abbreviation for Teachta Dála (Irish 'a member of the Irish parliament').

TEMPERANCE MOVEMENT

Nineteenth-century national, mainly Catholic, campaign against alcohol in Ireland. Inspired by the success of similar movements in the USA, and taking their example from Presbyterian and Quaker organizations against drinking in the 1820s, the first major temperance societies in Ireland were formed in 1829, the year of Catholic emancipation. The drinking of whiskey, especially poteen, an illegal distill, had become a major problem in Irish society over the previous decades and the movement aimed at limiting the general consumption of alcohol.

In many cases the societies were linked to religion, and the Roman Catholic Church in particular. In the 1830s the Capuchin priest Father Theobald ⇨Matthew introduced the principle of abstinence, and led a national campaign against drinking. This faded after the Great Famine (historically dated 1845–49, but now believed to have lasted until 1852), but resumed under the Pioneer Total Abstinence Association of the Sacred Heart, formed between 1898 and 1901. The temperance movement continued into the 20th century, with less success, although many of the societies are still active today.

TENANT LEAGUE

Organization formed in Dublin by Charles Gavan ⇨Duffy and the Catholic Frederick Lucas in August 1850 to campaign for Irish tenant rights. The main demand of the League was to secure 'the three Fs' – fair rents, fixity of tenure, and freedom of sale (also known as tenant right). Growing out of two different groups, one in the northeast of the country, and one in the south, the League had a large support base amongst Presbyterian ministers and Catholic clergy.

Duffy, a journalist and Young Irelander, was the main strategist of the movement, but it had little short-term success and internal divisions and fighting weakened its appeal. Although 40 members of parliament elected in 1852 supported the League, little was achieved, and the movement had its last meeting in 1892. The 'three Fs' were finally secured in 1881.

TENANT RIGHT (known as 'the Ulster custom')

Tenant right was a vague term used to describe freedom to sell land. In general, it meant that a tenant should be free to sell his occupancy to the highest bidder, subject to the landlord approving the purchaser. This allowed for the tenant to be compensated for any improvements done on the farm. It was a concern mainly of larger-scale farmers. This right was eventually granted to areas where it was customary in the 1870 Land Act, while the 1881 Land Act made it compulsory throughout Ireland.

The other key areas of tenants' rights were fair rents and fixity of tenure (with freedom of sale, known as 'the three Fs'). The first was very important to smaller farmers, while the second was more of a concern for larger tenants. Both were conceded in the 1881 Land Act.

TENNENT, GILBERT (1703–1764)

Irish-born Presbyterian minister whose revivalist preaching was crucial to America's Great Awakening of the 1720s to 1740s. He was born in County Armagh, and taken to America as a child. Ordained to a largely Ulster émigré congregation in New Brunswick, New Jersey, in 1726, he was influenced by the Dutch Reformed minister Theodore Frelinghuysen (1691–*c*. 1748), the first North American revivalist. Tennent became one of the main itinerant revivalists and was recognized as such by the leading revivalist George Whitefield (1714–1770) who, on his return to his English homeland, invited Tennent to continue the revival work in Boston.

TEXTILES

Wool, linen, cotton, and silk are the traditional Irish textiles, and weaving, knitting, crochet, and embroidery have been the main techniques.

wool

Woollen cloth dating from 750 BC has been found in Ireland, and its quality indicates even earlier origins. It is thought that dyeing was first attempted in Ireland around 1500 BC. The earliest existing Irish spinning tool is a spindle (500–800 AD). Woven Irish woollen textiles have been exported from medieval times, sought for their high quality and weatherproofing. Flannel and ⇨tweed have been produced from wool for over 600 years, although in the late 17th century, taxes imposed by Britain on Irish wools severely curtailed the industry. The Irish Industries Association and the Congested Districts Board actively revived production in the late 19th century. Knitting woollen garments is also a traditional industry, the best-known products being from the Aran Islands and Donegal, usually made from báinín (homespun, undyed, oiled wool) and involving intricate plaited and cabled patterns. Aran-style knitting began in the very early 20th century, when the islanders combined influences from Scandinavia, Central Europe, and Britain.

linen

Made from flax, linen has been produced in Ireland since at least the 5th century. Principally manufactured in Northern Ireland, woven damask (figured) linen was introduced to the country by immigrant Huguenot weavers in the 17th century. As well as damasks, linen could be plain, check, striped, or printed. Mechanization in the mid-19th century boosted the industry, but since the 1950s demand for table linen has declined, and so has production. The

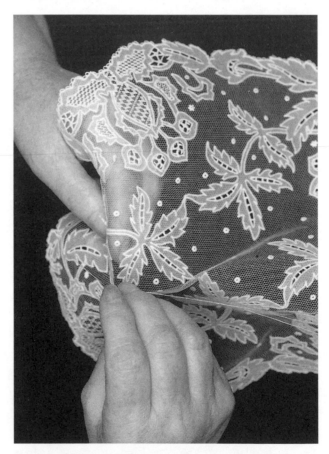

TEXTILES *The lace design is embroidered on to a net background to make this typical design from Carrickmacross, near Dundalk. In other parts of the country lace is made using crochet or needlepoint techniques*

fashion industry is now the main market for Irish linen.

cotton

Cotton production began in Belfast, in the 18th century, and rapidly became a significant industry, although it went into decline early in the 19th century. Crafts using cotton, however, such as embroidery, crochet, and lacemaking, continue. Crochet was first produced in Ireland in the 16th century, while embroidery was known as a craft in the Early Christian period, as Irish law placed special value on an embroiderer's needle. From the mid-18th century until the early 1900s, crochet was taught, often through the convents, as a means of employment. In the Republic of Ireland counties Cork and Monaghan were the main centres of crochet lacemaking, while needlepoint lace was made at Kenmare and Youghal, embroidered laces in Limerick and Carrickmacross, and Mountmellick was the centre of production for white padded embroidery. Embroidery was further developed by the Dun Emer Guild at the beginning of the 20th century. Most of these crafts enjoyed modest revivals at the end of the 20th century.

silk

Silk and silk poplin (a mixture of silk and wool) were first woven in Ireland in the 17th century from imported silk, but production died out in the late 20th century.

THEATRE, 17TH–19TH CENTURY

The restoration of Charles II as king of England, Scotland, and Ireland in 1660 brought to an end the ban on stage amusements. Smock Alley Theatre (1662–1788) was the first major playhouse in the Irish capital and presented French tragedies, English drama, and, occasionally, new Irish pieces such as *Mustapha* (1665), a heroic drama by Roger Boyle (1621–1679). Originally, mainly English actors, managers, and writers helped to create Restoration drama in Ireland, but William Congreve (1670–1729) and George ⇨Farquhar marked a new era in bringing Irish dramatists to the fore on the Dublin and London stages. Congreve's successful melodrama *The Mourning Bride* (1697) held the stage until the late 19th century; Farquhar's plays on the other hand were a novelty to the theatre, with their country settings, good humour, and distinctively Irish character.

Theatre-going at the time was a full-evening experience, with afterpieces, comic sketches, or dance per-formances supplementing the main production. New theatres opened at Capel Street and Crow Street, sentimental comedies were increasingly successful, and Peg Woffington (1714–1760) became one of the greatest actresses of the century in the British Isles. Other names who put their mark on 18th-century Irish drama were Charles Macklin (*c.* 1697–1797), actor at Drury Lane and playwright; Spranger ⇨Barry, actor; Thomas Sheridan (1719–1788), actor, playwright, and theatre manager; and Isaac Bickerstaffe (1735–1812), author of musical comedies such as *Love in the Village* (1762). Oliver ⇨Goldsmith, whose dramatic triumph *She Stoops to Conquer* (1773) remained a favourite with Dublin audiences well into the 20th century, Richard Brinsley ⇨Sheridan, author of the comic social satire *School for Scandal* (1777), and John O'Keeffe, became some of Ireland's most distinguished playwrights.

None of the above theatres survived the 19th century, but the new Theatre Royal at Hawkins Street (1821) became the most prestigious institution of its time, later rivalled by the Gaiety Theatre (1871). James Sheridan Knowles (1784–1862) made his name as a playwright and actor in Dublin, London, and the USA. However, it was Dion ⇨Boucicault who had the greatest impact on the development of Irish drama. His Irish comedies *The Colleen Bawn* (1860), *Arrah-na-Pogue* (1864), and *The Shaughraun* (1974) feature the stock character of the 'stage Irishman', and were a distinct success in Ireland and the USA. The Queen's Theatre (1844), a popular playhouse, stood out at the end of the 19th century for the melodramatic and nationalist Irish pieces of its own playwright-manager, James Whitbread (1848–1916).

THEATRE, 20TH CENTURY

As the ⇨Abbey Theatre (founded in 1904), effectively Ireland's national theatre, grew in success in the 1920s and 1930s, there was a growing demand for diversity and experimentation in the performing arts. The Peacock Theatre, established in 1925 as an experimental platform for the Abbey Theatre and its school of acting, answered this need, and housed other companies such as the ⇨Gate Theatre, which acquired its own hall in 1928. This theatre, founded by Hilton Edwards and Micheál MacLiammóir, aimed to offer a wider repertoire of continental and classical drama than the Abbey. The same two actors were also responsible for the inauguration of the Irish-language theatre ⇨An Taibhdhearc in Galway (1928).

In the 1950s and 1960s the principal theatrical events occurred outside the Abbey. Samuel ⇨Beckett shocked the Paris stage with his existentialist play *Waiting for Godot/En Attendant Godot* (1953), which was to have a profound influence on drama, both in writing and performance in Ireland. The Dublin Theatre Festival (1957) was responsible for a dramatic reawakening in Ireland and launched the careers of many upcoming playwrights, including Eugene MacCabe, Brian Friel, and Thomas Kilroy (1934–), while the Pike Theatre (1953), Dublin's first 'fringe' theatre, presented experimental and original work. In Belfast the Lyric Theatre (1951), set up by Mary O'Malley, aimed to fill a gap with its emphasis on literary and poetic drama. Ria Mooney (1903–1973), the first female director of the Abbey Theatre, was involved, as well as Patrick Galvin (1927–) and Austin Clarke (1896–1974).

In the 1970s and 1980s the Abbey participated in the dramatic revival with, for example, Thomas Kilroy's *Talbot's Box* (1977), Tom Murphy's *The Gigli Concert* (1983), *The Great Hunger* (1983) by Tom MacIntyre, and *Dancing at Lughnasa* (1990) by Brian Friel.

The major change of the last decades, however, was a growing professionalism in regional theatres. Galway witnessed the formation of a successful new company, the Druid Theatre, in 1975, which produces Irish and classical masterpieces with an original, fresh approach. The Belltable Arts Centre opened in Limerick in 1981, and the Red Kettle Theatre Company in Waterford in 1985. The experimental group Rough Magic found its start on the premises of the Project Arts Centre (1966) in Dublin, the first Irish theatre to concentrate its creative energy on community arts. This is also the objective for the street parades and physical theatre of Macnas in Galway (1986). The Field Day Theatre Company (1980), with its headquarters in Londonderry, has sought to create an artistic fifth Irish province, transcending sectarian differences.

Though playwrights were possibly the strongest forces in 20th-century Irish drama, some notable actors, such as Cyril ⇨Cusack, FJ McCormack, Eileen Crowe, and Fiona Shaw, deserve recognition for their contribution to Irish theatre.

THIN LIZZY

Rock band of the 1970s led by the enigmatic singer and bass player Phil Lynott (1949–1986). After the ⇨showband era, Thin Lizzy was the first great Irish rock band and the first Irish rock group to gain an international following. Their first chart success was the uncharacteristic Irish folk song 'Whiskey in the Jar' (1972) and their major breakthrough came in 1976 with the album *Jailbreak*, which introduced their distinctive harmony guitars sound.

Despite their success, the band always maintained a capacity for self-destruction and finally split in 1982 under financial pressure and the worsening of Lynott's heroin habit which led to his premature death.

THOMPSON, WILLIAM (1785–1833)

Economic theorist. A follower of the social reformer and founder of the cooperative movement, Robert Owen, Thompson called for the redistribution of wealth and denounced unearned income and private property. His awareness of capital as the product of labour influenced Karl Marx and the Irish trade-union leader James Connolly. Thompson also actively espoused the cause of sexual equality.

Thompson was born in Rosscarbery, into a wealthy property-owning family. His major works were *An Enquiry into the Principles of the Distribution of Wealth Most Conducive to Human Happiness* (1824), and *Appeal of One Half of the Human Race, Women, against the Pretentions of the Other Half, Men, to Retain them in Political, and thence in Civil and Domestic, Slavery* (1825). He bequeathed most of his estate to the cooperative movement, but his will was challenged and overturned by his relatives after years of litigation.

THOMSON, JAMES (1822–1892)

Physicist and engineer who in 1849 discovered that the melting point of ice decreases with pressure. He was also an authority on hydrodynamics and invented the vortex waterwheel in 1850.

Thomson was born in Belfast, the elder brother of the future physicist William Thomson, Lord Kelvin. He was only 12 when he began to attend Glasgow University with his younger brother, obtaining his MA in 1839. He held a succession of engineering posts before settling in Belfast in 1851 as a civil engineer. He was professor of civil engineering at Belfast 1857–73 and at Glasgow 1873–89.

The vortex water wheel was a smaller and more efficient turbine than previous designs, and it came into wide use. Thomson continued his investigations into whirling fluids, making improvements to pumps, fans, and turbines.

Thomson's discovery about the melting point of ice led him to an understanding of the way in which glaciers flow. He also carried out detailed studies of the phase relationships of solids, liquids, and gases, and was involved in both geology and meteorology, producing scientific papers on currents and winds.

THOMSON, WILLIAM

Physicist, see Lord ⇨Kelvin.

THOOR BALLYLEE

Sixteenth-century castellated tower house near Gort, County Galway. It was owned by the poet W B Yeats from 1915 and was his matrimonial home from 1917. The Yeats had extensive alterations made to the building, which is now a museum containing Yeats memorabilia.

I, the poet William Yeats, / With old mill boards and sea-green slates, / And smithy work from the Gort forge, / Restored this tower for my wife George; / And may these characters remain / When all is ruin once again.

W B YEATS Poet 'To be Carved on a Stone at Thoor Ballylee' (1918).

THURLES

Market town in County Tipperary, on the River Suir. There are turf-workings and coal mines nearby. Thurles produces electrical goods, baby powder, and dental goods, and has food-processing industries. The Gaelic Athletic Association (GAA) was founded here in 1884.

Thurles is on the main Dublin to Cork road and rail routes. The Catholic cathedral was built in 1857 on the site of the Carmelite foundation (established in 1300 by the Butlers of Ormond). The ruins of two keeps erected by the Butlers of Ormond can be seen here.

St Patrick's Diocesan College was established here in 1837 in a Romanesque-style building. Thurles is the cathedral town of the diocese of Cashel and Emly.

TIPPERARY

County of the Republic of Ireland, in the province of Munster, divided into North and South Ridings; county town ⇨Clonmel; area 4,255 sq km/ 1,643 sq mi; population (1996) 133,500. It includes part of the Golden Vale, a fertile dairy-farming region. Agriculture is the chief industry; barley and oats are the main crops, but potatoes and turnips are also grown. Cattle are reared in large numbers, and there are flour mills and butter factories. There is also horse and greyhound breeding. Other main towns are Cahir, Carrick-on-Suir, Cashel, Templemore, Tipperary, Thurles, Nenagh, and Roscrea. Major tourist attractions in the county include the Rock of Cashel and Cahir Castle.

history

The county is one of those supposed to have been created by King John in 1210. It was granted to the Earls of Ormond in 1328, and was the last of the Irish palatine counties. In 1848 it was the scene of the Young Ireland rising, an abortive rebellion staged by a group who wanted to have repealed the Act of Union that had been introduced in January 1800 by the British prime minister William Pitt.

historical remains

There are many interesting castles and ecclesiastical buildings in various parts of the county, notably at Cashel, where there are the 12th-century ruins of a cathedral and towers; at Athassel, where there is an Augustinian priory; at Holy Cross, where there is a Cistercian abbey, founded in 1180 and now a working parish church after 400 years of dereliction; and at Fethard, where there is a Templar's Castle. Moor Abbey stands at the head of the Glen of Aherlow.

topography

Tipperary is bounded by counties Galway and Offaly in the north, Cork and Waterford to the south, Laois and Kilkenny to the east, and Clare and Limerick to the west. The border with County Clare is formed by the River ⇨Shannon. The other principal river is the Suir, which flows through the centre of the county and forms the boundary with County Waterford; other rivers include the Little Brosna and the Nenagh. Lough ⇨Derg is the county's main lake. To the north and west lies a mountainous region, the highest point of which is Slieve Kimalta, or Keeper Hill (672 m/2,205 ft); also in the north are the Silvermine Mountains (highest peak Knockaunderrig, 490 m/1,609 ft). To the south lie the Galty Mountains (highest point Mount Galtymore, 920 m/3,018 ft), and the Comeragh and Knockmealdown Mountains; further east are Slievehamon (804 m/2,368 ft) and the Slieveardagh Hills.

natural resources
Coal, copper, lead, and zinc are mined, as are slate and limestone.

TIPPERARY

Market town in County Tipperary; population (1996) 4,600. Situated at the foot of the Slievenamuck Hills, in the fertile Golden Vale plain, 6 km/4 mi from the Glen of Aherlow, it is a centre for climbing and hill-walking. Tipperary has an electronic-games manufacturer, service industries, and a creamery. The ruins of a 13th-century Augustinian friary remain in the town.

> Ít's a long, long way to Tipperary, / It's a long way to go; / It's a long way to Tipperary, / To the sweetest girl I know! / Goodbye Piccadilly, Farewell Leicester Square, / It's a long, long way to Tipperary, / But my heart lies there.
>
> JACK JUDGE Songwriter Jack Judge (1878–1938) and Harry Williams (1874–1924), 'It's a Long Way to Tipperary' (1912, popular song).

~

Erasmus Smith obtained confiscated land in Tipperary in the 17th century and founded several schools; the ruins of one of them can still be seen.

Muintir na Tíre, a movement for the development of rural life in Ireland, was founded in Tipperary in 1931. The town was the birthplace of John O'Leary (1830–1907), a leader of the Fenian movement.

Just outside the town is New Tipperary, a village built by the tenants of the Smith Barry estate in 1890 during a Land League dispute. This settlement was unsuccessful.

TITANIC

White Star passenger liner launched in Belfast in 1912 by shipbuilders Harland and Wolff. Thought to be unsinkable, it struck an iceberg on its maiden voyage and sank off the Grand Banks of Newfoundland 14–15 April 1912. Estimates of the number of lives lost, largely due to inadequate provision of lifeboats, vary between 1,503 and 1,517. In 1985 it was located by robot submarine 4 km/2.5 mi down in an ocean canyon, preserved by the cold environment. Salvage operations began in 1987, but have been unsuccessful; by 1996 the cost of the project to raise the wreck stood at $5 million/£3.3 million. It was initially thought that the iceberg inflicted a 91 m/300 ft gash in the hull, but ultrasonic scans have revealed that it only caused a series of six short slits, with a total area of about 1.1–1.2 sq m/12–13 sq ft.

TITHE

Tax levied on crops and minor agricultural produce from the 12th century for the support of the Protestant church in Ireland. It was a major source of grievance for Irish Catholic tenants up to the 19th century. Defined as one-tenth of the annual increase from the profits of lands, stock, and crafts, it became a money payment in the 17th century. Although it was intended to support the Protestant clergy, in reality much of the income was used to support the hierarchy. As Catholicism was the majority religion in Ireland, there was deep resentment of the obligation and movements like the Whiteboys and the Oakboys in the 18th century sprang from this deep-rooted anger.

The Tithe Compensation Act (1823) linked the issue with the land problem, in what was intended as a compromise. Tensions increased, however, and the issue remained controversial. It was eventually a significant factor in the Disestablishment of the Church of Ireland Act (1869) which did away with the tithe completely.

TOD, ISABELLA (1836–1886)

Women's suffragist and education campaigner. Born in Scotland, Tod spent most of her life in Belfast and advocated a feminism which encouraged active charity and political duty. She is best known for advocating equal educational opportunities for girls to enable them to earn a living. She founded the Belfast Ladies' Institute in 1867 to educate middle-class women and her political pressure helped to include girls in the Intermediate Education Act (1878). Throughout her career Tod was opposed to ⇨home rule for Ireland.

TOÍBÍN, COLM (1955–)

Writer, born in County Wexford. Toíbín became a travel writer and journalist before turning to novels. Toíbín uses a delicate minimalist style to tell stories of troubled, modern characters struggling to find love and a sense of belonging. *The Heather Blazing* (1993) is set in Ireland, but *The Story of the Night* (1996) and *The South* (1990) have protagonists wandering the world, seeking to rectify a sense of lost origins. *The South* won the 1991 *Irish Times*/Aer Lingus Award and was shortlisted for the Booker Prize.

TONE, (THEOBALD) WOLFE (1763–1798)

Nationalist and United Irishman leader, born in Dublin. Tone studied at Trinity College, Dublin, and trained as a barrister in London, but never practised. His anonymous pamphlet 'An argument on behalf of the Catholics of Ireland' (1791) was an eloquent assessment of the case for emancipation, and Tone was soon invited to become involved in the Catholic Committee. In 1792 he was appointed secretary, and visited London as part of the delegation sent by the Catholic Convention.

A founding member of the United Irishmen in 1791, he gradually changed the direction of this constitutional radical movement to a more extreme position. Disappointed with the progress of the United Irishmen through nonradical means, he started asking revolutionary France for help in arming the resistance to English rule. He accompanied Gen Hoche on an

*t*o unite the whole people of Ireland, to abolish the memory of all past dissension and to substitute the common name of Irishman in place of the denominations of Protestant, Catholic, and Dissenter.

WOLFE TONE Speaking of his aims in August 1796, quoted in *Wolfe Tone* (1989) by Marianne Elliott.

WOLFE TONE *One of the leaders of the Rebellion of 1798, Tone was captured when attempting to land with French forces, and committed suicide. Tone had been attracted to the United Irish movement from his youth, and published An Argument on Behalf of the Catholics of Ireland in 1791, at the age of 28.*

attempted landing with French forces in 1796, and when the Rebellion of 1798 broke out, tried again to land forces, but was captured by the British navy in October 1798 at Lough Swilly.

Tried and convicted of treason, Tone committed suicide in prison by cutting his own throat to avoid public hanging. He was buried at Bodenstown, County Kildare, and his grave is the site of annual commemorations by Sinn Féin and Fianna Fáil. His autobiography and journals were published posthumously by his widow, and they helped establish his reputation as a key Irish nationalist. Widely regarded as the father of Irish republicanism, Tone's death marked the apotheosis of the 1798 rebellion.

TOWNSEND, JOHN SEALY EDWARD (1868–1957)

Mathematical physicist who pioneered the study of electrical conduction in gases, and was the first researcher to take a direct measurement of the charge held by a single electron.

Born in Galway, Townsend studied at Trinity College, Dublin, and later at Trinity College, Cambridge. He carried out research in the Cavendish Laboratory under the English physicist J J Thomson, and was a student with the New Zealand-born physicist Ernest Rutherford, a pioneer of modern atomic science.

In 1900 Townsend became the first Wykeham professor of experimental physics at Cambridge where he studied the conductivity of gases ionized by the newly discovered X-rays. He later developed a way to ionize gases using electrolysis. He described ionization caused by collisions with other ions which allowed these gases to conduct electricity.

Townsend studied electron swarms and, independently of Carl Ramsauer, discovered the Ramsauer–Townsend effect which states that the mean free path of an electron depends on its energy. This work later proved important in the development of quantum theory. Townsend was knighted in 1941, the year he retired, but he remained actively involved in scientific writing.

TRALEE

County town of County ⇨Kerry, and the gateway to the Dingle Peninsula; population (1996) 19,100. It has agricultural and light industries, including food processing and the manufacture of polyester fibre, textiles, and clothing, electrical goods, and leisure goods. The town's history is associated with the Desmond clan and the Dominican order, brought to Tralee by John Desmond in 1243.

After the confiscation of the Desmond estates, the land was granted to Edward Denny. Tralee was a centre of the struggle for Irish independence from Britain (1919–22).

The Dominican church of the Holy Cross was designed by the English Gothic revival architect Augustus Pugin in the 19th century. Rathas Church, 2 km/1 mi east of Tralee, is now a national monument.

The song 'The Rose of Tralee' was composed by William Mulchinock (1820–1864). A beauty contest for those with Irish ancestors, the Rose of Tralee International Festival, is held in September.

TRAMORE (Irish *Trá Mhór*)

Seaside resort in County Waterford, on Tramore Bay between Brownstone Head and Great Newton Head, 12 km/7 mi south of Waterford; population (1996) 5,800. Swept by the warm waters of the Gulf Stream, its 5 km/3 mi stretch of sands are backed by high dunes to the east. A sandy spit immediately to the east of Tramore separates Black Sand lagoon from the sea. Tourist facilities include a racecourse, pier, amusement park, golf courses, and surfing. The headlands are marked by pillars erected by Lloyds of London in the early 19th century after a shipwreck in the bay; Great Newtown Head also carries the Metal Man, an enormous cast-iron figure pointing towards the safety of Waterford Harbour.

Local legend maintains that girls who hop around the giant's base three times non-stop will be married within a year.

TREACY, PHILIP (1967–   )

Milliner who was born in County Galway and following graduation from the National College of Art and Design in Dublin, won a scholarship to study at the Royal College of Art, London. As well as working for private clients, he designed hats and accessories for fashion designers such as Versace, Valentino, Chanel, and Rifat Osbek.

Treacy's hats can be simple, abstract shapes, or extravagant and unconventional, for instance a dyed black feather hat in the form of a sailing ship, entitled 'The Ship' (1995).

TRENCH, RICHARD CHENEVIX

(1807–1886)

Anglican archbishop of Dublin 1864–86, during ⇨disestablishment; also a philologist and poet. Born in Dublin and educated at Harrow and Cambridge, he was ordained in 1841 and became rector of Itchenstoke, Hampshire, England, in 1845. He was professor of theology at King's College, London 1847–56, and dean of Westminster Abbey 1856–64, where he was buried.

Trench instigated what became the *Oxford English Dictionary*. He also published six volumes of poetry (1835–46) and an influential philology, *The Study of Words* (1851). His principal religious writings were *Notes on the Parables of our Lord* (1841) and *Notes on the Miracles of our Lord* (1846).

TREVOR, WILLIAM (pseudonym of WILLIAM TREVOR COX) (1928–   )

Writer who was born in Michelstown, County Cork, and studied at Trinity College, Dublin. Trevor came to prominence with his second novel, *The Old Boys* (1964), and has since published several highly acclaimed novels, including *The Children of Dynmouth* (1976), *Fools of Fortune* (1983), and *Death in*

*W*hen I think of the town now I can see it very clearly: cattle and pigs on a fair day, always a Monday; Mrs Driscoll's vegetable shop, Vickery's hardware, Phelan's the barber's, Kilmartin's the turf accountant's, the Convent and the Christian Brothers, twenty-nine public houses.

WILLIAM TREVOR *The Raising of Elvira Tremlett* (1977).

~

Summer (1998). Widely regarded as one of Ireland's finest contemporary short-story writers, he published the collections *The Day We Got Drunk On Cake* (1967) and *The News from Ireland* (1986). He has also written plays and screenplays. Frequently taking the loss of innocence as his theme, he writes perceptively about childhood and old age; his novels, stories, and plays are noted for their gentle irony, their humour, and their subtle characterization.

Trevor worked as a teacher, sculptor, and copy writer before publishing his first novel, *A Standard of Behaviour*, in 1958.

TRIM

Market town in County Meath, on the River Boyne; population (1996) 1,700. Trim has agricultural and light industries. It is one of the oldest ecclesiastical centres in Ireland, and ⇨Trim Castle is the largest Anglo-Norman fortress in the country.

St Loman was the first bishop here, in a see said to have been established by St Patrick in the 5th century. It was amalgamated in 1152 to form the diocese of Meath. A number of parliaments were held in Trim in the 15th century.

Besides Trim Castle, there are two other castles, Nangle's Castle and Talbot's Castle, built in 1415. The Yellow Steeple is a 14th-century bell tower, 38 m/125 ft high, and the ruins of St Mary's abbey also remain in the town.

At Newtown Trim, 2 km/1 mi away, are the ruins of the abbey of the Canons Regular of St Victor, founded by Bishop Simon de Rochfort in 1206.

The satirist Jonathan Swift was rector of Laracor (3 km/2 mi to the south) 1700–13, and the friend he called Stella (Esther Johnson) lived nearby.

TRIMBLE, DAVID (1944–)

Northern Irish politician, leader of the ⇨Ulster Unionist Party (UUP, or Official Unionist Party, OUP) from 1995 and Northern Ireland's first minister-elect in 1998, taking full power following devolution on 2 December 1999. Representing the Upper Bann constituency in the UK House of Commons from 1990, he won the leadership of the UUP in August 1995, when James Molyneaux retired at the age of 75. In 1998 Trimble shared the Nobel Peace Prize with John ⇨Hume in recognition of their work to find a peaceful solution to the conflict in Northern Ireland.

Trimble, originally seen as a hardliner and not likely to move easily into Molyneaux's seat, proved to be more flexible and tolerant than had been predicted. Following his election as UUP leader, he sought to give an impetus to the Northern Ireland peace process, meeting UK prime minister John Major, Irish Taoiseach John Bruton, and US president Bill Clinton. Still emphasizing the need for the Irish Republican Army (IRA) to decommission its weaponry, he nevertheless suggested a route to all-party talks through elections, although this proposal was opposed by republican spokespersons.

We are not saying that, simply because someone has a past, they can't have a future. We always acknowledge that people have to change.

DAVID TRIMBLE Accepting his election as first minister of the Northern Ireland Assembly, *Daily Telegraph*, July 1998.

He accepted the 1998 Good Friday agreement on power-sharing, which was rejected by the more extreme Democratic Unionist Party, led by Ian Paisley, and the United Kingdom Unionist Party, led by Robert McCartney. He was chosen as Northern Ireland's first minister after the newly elected Northern Ireland Assembly met in June 1998, and seemed determined to make the peace agreement work. In the first meeting between Unionist and republican leaders for several generations he met the president of Sinn Féin, Gerry Adams, at Stormont in September 1998.

Educated at Queen's University, Belfast, Trimble qualified as a barrister and lectured in law at Queen's for 22 years before fully committing himself to politics. He represents a new, less dogmatic breed of Northern Ireland politicians, willing to accept links with the Republic of Ireland.

TRIM CASTLE (also called King John's Castle)

The first and largest stone castle in Ireland, an Anglo-Norman fortress at Trim, County Meath. Completed in 1224 and covering an area of about 1 ha/3 acres, it replaced an earlier wooden castle built by the Norman baron Hugh de Lacy, who was granted the lands of Trim during the Anglo-Norman occupation. It is bounded by curtain walls and a moat. The massive,

TRINITY COLLEGE *The campanile stands in the midst of the buildings of Trinity College, Dublin. The library, right, designed by Thomas Burgh, was one of several splendid buildings added to the college during the 18th century.*

partly ruined keep is 23 m/75 ft tall, has 20 sides, and walls 3 m/11 ft thick.\

TRINITY COLLEGE, DUBLIN

Ireland's oldest university, founded by Elizabeth I in 1592 with Archbishop Adam ⇨Loftus as the first chancellor, and opened in 1594. Originally intended as a seminary to train Protestant clergy, the college rapidly became an exclusivist centre of radical Protestantism. Amidst Ireland's upheavals in the 17th century the college was occupied by troops on a number of occasions, and the provost and fellows expelled by the Catholic Jacobite forces of James II. Despite these disruptions Trinity managed to produce some outstanding scholars in its early years, including the philosopher James ⇨Ussher and the writer, scientist, and military engineer William Molyneaux. Its library houses the Book of ⇨Kells and other ancient manuscripts.

A long period of peace in the 18th century allowed for an ambitious programme of rebuilding and expansion. Trinity's great facade was designed by Keene and Saunders, and dates from 1759. The library, completed in 1732, is modelled on the library at Trinity College, Cambridge, England, designed by the English architect Christopher Wren. Although the great architectural achievements of this period were not matched equally by developments in scholarship, several of Trinity's graduates, such as the patriot politician Henry ⇨Grattan and nationalist revolutionary Wolfe ⇨Tone, were to play central roles in 18th-century Irish politics.

The 19th century witnessed substantial academic development but, despite the contribution of graduates such as the poet Thomas ⇨Davis and the journalist John ⇨Mitchel to the ⇨Young Ireland movement, the college as a whole entered a long period of introversion and conservatism which persisted beyond the foundation of the Irish Free State in 1922. By 1950 Trinity had become reconciled to the Republic of Ireland and received a substantial state grant. It is now recognized as one of the major further educational institutions in Ireland, with a distinguished reputation in research and a vastly increased student body, which at 14,000 in 1999 represented a ten-fold increase in 60 years.

TROY, JOHN THOMAS (1739–1823)

Dominican friar, born in Dublin; bishop of Ossory 1776–86 and archbishop of Dublin 1786–1823. He ruled his problem-ridden archdiocese with energy but little tact, and is remembered for political conservatism and denunciation of the ⇨United Irishmen. Like many prelates, he sternly criticized democratic aspirations, 'the French disease'. His policy was collaboration with government even when this meant public silence on repression. His pragmatism discouraged many of his priests and laity.

Troy's attitudes were more complex and have received less than full justice. His *Duties of Christian Citizens* (1793), a call 'to fear God and honour the King', dismayed many Catholics but also displeased the civil authorities. Yet he was rewarded for this work by government support of St Patrick's College, Maynooth, founded in 1795. His closing years were marked by tensions, mitigated by his auxiliary, Daniel Murray, who later succeeded him. By 1823 Troy was a spent force.

TUAM

Chief town in northern County Galway; population (1996) 3,500. Lenses, electronics, and electrical components are manufactured here. The area around Tuam has many prehistoric and historic remains, significantly ring forts, several of which have a souterrain (or underground) system.

Tuam is the seat of a Catholic archbishop and of a Protestant bishop. The Anglican cathedral of St Mary's was built in 1152 by Turlough O'Connor, King of Connacht, on the site of a monastic house founded by St Jarleth in the 6th century. Two chancels survive – one from the 12th century in the

Romanesque style and another from the 14th century. The cathedral was extended by Thomas Deane between 1861 and 1878. The Roman Catholic cathedral was erected in 1846. The Cross of Tuam in the market square has inscriptions to Turlough O'Connor and a 12th-century abbot.

Some 3 km/2 mi north of Tuam is the Georgian Bermingham House, open to the public.

TUATHA DÉ DANANN ('people of the goddess Danu')

In mythology, warriors and magicians. Aided and led by the ⇨Dagda and Lugh, they became early rulers of Ireland, but were eventually defeated by the Milesians (Celts). The kingdom was divided, the Tuatha Dé Danann ruling the invisible otherworld below ground and the Milesians ruling the world above.

The Tuatha Dé were said to have a great knowledge of supernatural lore, and were skilled in all arts. The progeny of a mother goddess, Danu, they were regarded as possessing divine natures and some of the more famous Tuatha Dé have clear links with ancient Celtic divinities.

TULLAMORE

County town of County ⇨Offaly; population (1996) 9,200. It is situated on the Grand Canal and is a market centre for a fertile agricultural district. Medical products, clothing, and electrical goods are manufactured, and there is food processing. Tullamore has a number of fine Georgian buildings.

At Durrow Abbey, 6 km/4 mi north of Tullamore, is the site of a monastery said to have been founded by St Columba (St Colum Cille) in 551, the only remains of which are a high cross and some gravestones. The Book of Durrow (Trinity College Library, Dublin) was written here in the 7th century.

Charleville estate, 3 km/2 mi southwest of Tullamore, has a baronial house designed by Francis Johnston in 1801.

TULLYNALLY CASTLE

Country house to the north of Mullingar, County Westmeath. Originally a 17th-century garrison house owned by the Pakenham family (now the Earls of Longford), the property was remodelled in the Classical style by Graham Myers about 1780. Further alterations were made from 1801 to 1806 for the 2nd Earl of Longford by Francis Johnston when he con-

structed turrets and a battlement parapet. Other Gothic-style features were added in the 1820s by James Shield, and the house was again enlarged about 1840 by Sir Richard ⇨Morrison. Further additions in 1860 make Tullynally the largest currently occupied, castellated country house in Ireland.

TWEED

Traditional textile, usually woven in speckled wool, with a rough, sturdy texture. Tweed has been woven for at least 600 years in Ireland if, as is likely, Irish woollen fabrics exported in 1357 to various European locations included tweed – the term 'tweed' was first used in the early 19th century. The main centres of tweed production are Connemara in the west and Donegal in the north.

Poverty, taxation, and famine led to a decline in tweed production in the first half of the 19th century. In the 1850s, however, sport and country activities became fashionable for the upper classes, and this created a rising demand for the warmth and waterproof quality of tweed. Donegal tweed, in particular, began to be exported in quantity to Europe and the USA. In the 20th century, demand and production waxed and waned with changing trends in international fashion. Mechanical spinning became the norm, creating a more even, but less interesting fabric. Designers have

TWEED *Donegal tweed, seen here on the loom, was highly popular in the latter part of the 19th century. Using top-grade machinery, manufacturers could produce superb quality traditional Irish fabrics for export and home use.*

influenced the type of tweed being produced: Sybil ⇨Connolly in the 1950s required lighter shades of tweed than had previously been woven. Irish tweeds continue to be produced for home and export markets.

TYNAN, KATHARINE (married name Hinkson) (1861–1931)

Poet and novelist. Born in Clondalkin, County Dublin, and educated at the Dominican Convent, Drogheda, Tynan established her reputation as a writer through journalism. A leading figure in the Irish literary revival of the late 19th century, her works are influenced by Irish patriotism, devout Catholicism, and Celtic mythology. She was a prolific writer, producing some 18 volumes of verse, over a hundred novels, and around 40 other books.

The Irish always jest even though they jest with tears.

KATHARINE TYNAN *The Wandering Years* (1922).

❦

Tynan was a friend of the nationalist leader Charles Stewart Parnell and (in London) of the literary families, the Meynells and the Rossettis. Her works include the poetry collections *Oh! What a Plague is Love* (1896), *She Walks in Beauty* (1899), and the novel *The House in the Forest* (1928). She also wrote five volumes of autobiography.

TYNDALL, JOHN (1820–1893)

Physicist who demonstrated why the sky is blue. He conducted experimental work on the scattering of light by invisibly small suspended particles, an effect now known as the Tyndall effect.

Born in Leighlin Bridge, County Carlow, Tyndall studied at Marburg, Germany. He became professor of natural philosophy at the Royal Institution in 1853 and was also a professor at the Royal School of Mines 1859–68. As superintendent of the Royal Institution from 1867 he did much to popularize science in Britain, and also in the USA were he was a visiting lecturer 1872–73. He wrote 16 books and 145 papers.

TYRCONNELL, RICHARD TALBOT (1st

Earl of Tyrconnell; Viscount Baltinglass, Baron of Talbotstown) (1630–1691)

⇨Jacobite soldier and administrator. Born into an Old English family in County Meath, he became a leading figure in the revival of the Catholic interest in Ireland under James II. A close companion of James during the Stuart exile of the 1650s and an influential courtier in the Restoration, he was created Earl of Tyrconnell on James's accession to the throne in 1685, and appointed lord lieutenant of Ireland in 1687.

Tyrconnell's radical plans to create an exclusively Catholic government and to effect a full reversal of the anti-Catholic land settlements of the 1650s and 1660s were interrupted by the deposition of James by William (III) of Orange in 1688, and the subsequent outbreak of war in Ireland. Shocked by the defeat of Jacobite forces at the Battle of the ⇨Boyne (1690), Tyrconnell briefly contemplated making peace but soon resumed his defiance of the Williamites. He died suddenly, just after the Battle of Aughrim.

TYRONE

County of Northern Ireland; population (1991) 158,500; area 3,160 sq km/1,220 sq mi. It is largely rural, with evidence of the once flourishing linen industry. Many Americans trace their family roots to Tyrone, including 11 US presidents. The chief towns are ⇨Omagh (county town), Dungannon, Strabane, and Cookstown.

physical

Lough Neagh is in the east and the Sperrin Mountains in the north. The main rivers in the county are the Derg, Blackwater, and Foyle.

features

The county contains several Neolithic graves and stone circles, notably at Beaghmore, west of Cookstown. The Ulster History Park, north of Omagh, presents history from Neolithic times, with reconstructions of typical historic buildings. Many Tyrone villages have heritage centres, describing the linen industry. The Peatlands Park east of Dungannon preserves an ancient Irish bog. The family home of the US president Woodrow Wilson is at Dergalt, near Strabane. The Ulster-American Folk Park, north of Omagh, was endowed by the Mellon banking family of Pittsburgh.

economy

The economy is based mainly on agriculture. There is also brick making, and production of linen, hosiery, and shirts.

U

U2

Rock group formed in Dublin in 1977. U2 became one of the most popular and successful rock bands of the 1980s and 1990s, managing to sustain their fan base throughout two decades by clever reinvention. The group are known for their political views, combining their music with political messages, for example in 'Sunday, Bloody Sunday' (1983) which was an expression of the band's feelings about the violence and conflict in Northern Ireland. The album *The Joshua Tree* (1987) propelled the band to super-stardom, and the band continued to release highly successful and critically acclaimed albums, including *Achtung Baby* in 1992, and *Zooropa* in 1993.

The band's members are singer Bono (born Paul Hewson, 1960–), guitarist 'The Edge' (born Dave Evans, 1961–), bassist Adam Clayton (1960–), and drummer Larry Mullen Jr (1961–).

U2's first major release was *War* in 1983, which entered the UK chart at number one. The strong political messages contained in this album helped pave the way for future charity music events, including Band Aid, an initiative which raised millions of pounds for famine victims in Ethiopia, which followed in 1984. *The Unforgettable Fire* was released in 1984, to similar success, and gave the band their first top forty US single with '(Pride) In the Name of Love'. After the release of the album and film collaboration of *Rattle and Hum* (1988), the band took a break.

The eagerly awaited release of *Achtung Baby* showed that the band had moved on, with a new style influenced by the Manchester scene in the UK, and late 1970s Bowie. The band also developed their

for U2, read Ireland: a country that, increasingly, defines itself on its own terms, whose cultural identity no longer hinges solely on its relationship with... 'the mainland'.

SEAN O'HAGAN Journalist 'Music: Pop Smart', quoted in *The Guardian*, 13 June 1997.

~

touring style, with an elaborate tour called Zoo TV which featured many innovative multimedia elements, including huge TV screens. The 1993 release *Zooropa* showed an even heavier dance and techno influence. In 1997 *Pop* was released, followed by a 'Best of' album in 1998.

UDA

See ⇨Ulster Defence Association.

ULSTER

A former kingdom and province in the north of Ireland, annexed by England in 1461. From Jacobean times it was a centre of English, and later Scottish, settlement on land confiscated from its owners; divided in 1921 into Northern Ireland (counties Antrim, Armagh, Down, Fermanagh, Derry, and Tyrone) and the Republic of Ireland (counties Cavan, Donegal, and Monaghan).

ULSTER DEFENCE ASSOCIATION (UDA)

Northern Ireland Protestant paramilitary organization responsible for a number of sectarian killings. Fanatically loyalist, it established a paramilitary wing (the Ulster Freedom Fighters) to combat the ⇨Irish Republican Army (IRA) on its own terms and by its own methods. No political party has acknowledged any links with the UDA. In 1994, following a cessation of military activities by the IRA, the UDA, along with other Protestant paramilitary organizations, declared a ceasefire.

ULSTER PLANTATION

Confiscation and resettlement, in 1609, of the Ulster counties of Armagh, Cavan, Donegal, Derry, Fermanagh, and Tyrone by the English government after the ⇨Flight of the Earls. Provided with lots of 2,000, 1,500, and 1,000 acres as determined by government surveyors, the English and Scottish undertakers (those accepting grants of land) were also burdened with unrealistically heavy obligations relating to the settlement, development, and defence of their holdings. Delays in preparing the territory for occupancy, coupled with disputes among prospective settlers and government officials, accentuated these difficulties. Harsh treatment of native freeholders whose existing rights were frequently overridden by the new grants ensured an extremely hostile reception for the newcomers.

By the mid-1620s the progress of the official plantation was inconsiderable as undertakers frequently defaulted on their obligations, particularly in regard to the matter of removing native tenants. By then, however, independent migrations from England and especially from Scotland were rapidly creating patterns of settlement far different from the intentions of the original planners. Interspersed pockets of English, Scottish, and native Irish settlements were thus emerging within the planted territories. This situation was to prove explosive by 1641 and thereafter laid the basis for the chronic sectarian problems of the province as a whole.

ULSTER REVIVAL

Protestant revival that began in 1859 in Northern Ireland, inspired by the 'Second Great Awakening' in the USA. It transformed the nature of Ulster Protestantism in general and Ulster Presbyterianism in particular. The revival itself was short-lived, but it consolidated a strong Evangelical wing within Ulster Protestantism that has remained influential to this day.

The impact of the Ulster revival was not so marked in the Church of Ireland, where the Evangelical party faced opposition from the High Church revival that Alexander ⇨Knox and Richard ⇨Mant had inspired.

Despite its effect on the Presbyterian Church, the response to the revival was not unanimous within that church. W Gibson, later Presbyterian moderator, eulogized it in *The Year of Grace* (1860), which provoked the liberal Presbyterian response in Isaac Nelson's *The Year of Delusion* (1861). Nelson was deeply critical of the 'unseemly' displays of revivalist phenomena that Gibson had praised.

ULSTER TELEVISION (UTV)

Television station that holds the licence for independent television (ITV) in Northern Ireland. UTV first went on air on Halloween night 1959 and, although run on a very tight budget, was gaining a reputation for quality local programming by the early 1960s. Its most prominent productions include the *Kelly* Friday night chat show and *UTV Live*, a nightly news programme that received much acclaim for its sensitive coverage of the Omagh bombing and its aftermath in 1998. Although UTV does not formally broadcast to the Republic of Ireland, it has gained a substantial share of the Irish television market, making it currently the third most popular channel in Ireland as a whole and the most popular in Northern Ireland itself.

ULSTER UNIONIST PARTY (UUP) (also known as the Official Unionist Party OUP)

Largest political party in ⇨Northern Ireland. Right-of-centre in orientation, it advocates equality for Northern Ireland within the UK and opposes union with the Republic of Ireland. The party has the broadest support of any Ulster party, and has consistently won a large proportion of parliamentary and local seats. Its central organization, dating from 1905, is formally called the Ulster Unionist Council. Its leader from 1995 is David ⇨Trimble. It secured 28 of the 108 seats in the new Northern Ireland Assembly, elected in June 1998, and Trimble was elected Northern Ireland's first minister at the assembly's first meeting on 1 July 1998. On 30 May 2000, the Council agreed to a motion supporting its return to the

Northern Ireland Assembly, but by a narrow margin of 53% to 47%, leaving grave doubts regarding the continuity of support for the Assembly.

The party is the main successor of the once dominant Unionist Party, which governed the province 1921–72. The first Ulster Unionist Council was set up to support continued union with Britain, and to oppose any measure of ⇨home rule. Its first prominent leader was Edward ⇨Carson. After Ireland was partitioned in 1921 and home rule was introduced in Northern Ireland, the Unionists took control of the new institutions that had been established in the province. There were six successive Unionist prime ministers 1921–72. The Unionist Party enjoyed wide support among the Protestant population and the mainstream Protestant churches, and with the powerful ⇨Orange Order. The Unionists' abolition of proportional representation helped to prevent the rise of rival pro-union groups.

1960s and 1970s

Divisions within the Unionist Party intensified during the late 1960s and the early 1970s as a result of the agitation of the Catholic minority for civil rights, and there was a revival of support for hardline Protestant groups. Following the suspension of home rule in 1972 the party split, one of the offshoots being Ian Paisley's Democratic Unionist Party (DUP). The 1973 Sunningdale agreement and the introduction of a Protestant–Catholic power-sharing executive in early 1974 led to further divisions. In 1977 the Official Ulster Unionist Party and Paisley's DUP emerged as the only major unionist contenders.

1980s and 1990s

The UUP completely rejected the Anglo-Irish agreement in 1985, and joined forces with the DUP to campaign against it. All its MPs resigned their seats in order to demonstrate the degree of unionist hostility to the agreement.

In February 1995 the Ulster Unionists rejected the British and Irish governments' published proposals on the future of Northern Ireland and threatened to withdraw their support of the government. Under Trimble's leadership, from 1995, the UUP became more accommodating in the peace negotiations and accepted the 1998 Good Friday agreement on power-sharing. The party still maintains close links with the Orange Order.

ULSTER VOLUNTEER FORCE (UVF)

Most recently a loyalist (pro-Union) paramilitary group, especially active in the 1970s, 1980s, and early 1990s. Originally a paramilitary wing of the Ulster Unionists, the first UVF was formed in 1913 to coordinate ad hoc paramilitary activity. A second UVF, active in the Anglo–Irish War, became part of the Ulster Special Constabulary. The name was revived in the 1966 for a Belfast-based group, which was legalized in 1974 but banned the following year. In 1994 the UVF was one of the signatories to a loyalist ceasefire.

UNION, ACT OF

Act of Parliament which came into effect in 1801 creating the United Kingdom of Great Britain and Ireland, passed by both British and Irish parliaments in 1800.

In May 1798 the British prime minister, William Pitt the Younger, finally became convinced that union between the Irish and British parliaments was imperative. Pitt believed that the Irish parliament's 'legislative independence', gained in 1782, led to instability in Anglo-Irish relations. He also felt that the Irish government's initial failure to contain the ⇨Rebellion of 1798 showed the danger of divided authority and that imperial resources, including Ireland's, must be consolidated if Britain was to win the ongoing war with France, declared by the revolutionary government there in 1793. The new Irish viceroy Charles ⇨Cornwallis and his chief secretary, Viscount Castlereagh, were instructed to negotiate the terms for a union. In January 1799 they failed to get a majority in the Irish parliament. After this initial defeat they embarked on a two-pronged campaign to create a majority by employing government patronage to the utmost and appealing to public opinion by distributing pamphlets and orchestrating petitions. Opposition to union was motivated partly by patriotism, partly by self-interest, and partly by fear, as Pitt and Cornwallis wanted Catholic emancipation to follow union. Anti-unionists also engaged in petitions and pamphleteering but could not match the government's power and manipulation of patronage. Opponents, such as John Parnell (1744–1801), chancellor of the exchequor, an uncompromising opponent to union and Catholic political rights, were stripped of office. In 1800 both British and Irish parliaments voted in favour of union, and the Act of Union came into force on 1 January 1801.

Under the Act of Union, Ireland's political representation at Westminster was set at 100 members (there were 300 in the Irish parliament), 64 of whom represented counties, 35 represented boroughs, and one represented Trinity College, Dublin. In the House of Lords, Ireland was represented by 4 bishops and 28 representative peers, elected for life by their fellow peers. The Anglican churches of Ireland and England were unified, as were the respective military and customs establishments. Each country kept its financial system temporarily, with Ireland's contribution to the national revenue set at two-seventeenths of the total. In 1817 the two exchequers and the currencies were amalgamated.

The refusal of George III to allow ⇨Catholic emancipation to follow union led to Catholics, who had initially supported union, feeling aggrieved. Conversely Protestant anti-unionists, who included many of the ⇨Orange Order and the ⇨Irish Yeomanry, were soon reconciled. Opposition to the union in the 19th century was strongest among Catholics, while support for its maintenance was most evident among Protestants, particularly in the northeast which, unlike the rest of Ireland, had benefited economically from Britain's industrialization. After the 1921 Anglo-Irish Treaty set up the ⇨Irish Free State, only Northern Ireland sent representatives to Westminster.

UNITED IRISHMEN

Society formed in Belfast in 1791 by Wolfe ⇨Tone, Thomas ⇨Russell, and others to campaign for parliamentary reform in Ireland. It later became a secret revolutionary group.

The idea of a brotherhood of Irishmen of all religions dedicated to political reform originated with William Drennan (1754–1820), a Belfast physician and poet. Following the foundation of the first United Irishmen society in Belfast, similar societies soon appeared in Dublin and parts of Ulster. These societies campaigned legally for parliamentary reform and Catholic emancipation. However, the United Irishmen supported the ideas of the French Revolution and from 1795, after their reform campaign had failed, they began to reorganize as an underground revolutionary movement. They established an alliance with the Catholic ⇨Defenders, and sought French military aid for a rebellion intended to overthrow British rule in Ireland. In December 1796 a large French fleet, with Wolfe Tone on board, was only prevented from landing at Bantry Bay by storms. Government advisors, particularly the lord chancellor John Fitzgibbon, 1st Earl of Clare (1749–1802), advocated a campaign of severe repression against the United Irishmen. This resulted in arms seizures and arrests of leaders which diminished the chances of a successful insurrection. Though badly damaged, the United Irish movement survived the ⇨Rebellion of 1798. Some new leaders, such as Robert ⇨Emmet and Thomas Russell, tried unsuccessfully to organize a new rebellion in 1803.

USSHER, JAMES (1581–1656)

Protestant cleric and ecclesiastical historian, who calculated the creation of the world as 23 October 4004 BC. Born in Dublin and one of the first students at Trinity College, Dublin, Ussher became bishop of Meath in 1621 and archbishop of Armagh in 1635. His published complete works runs to 17 volumes and his vast collection of books and Irish manuscripts made a significant contribution to modern Irish libraries. Works by Ussher include *A Discourse on the Religion Anciently Professed by the Irish and the British* (1631) and *Veterum Epistolarum Hibernicarum Sylloge* (1632).

V

VALENTIA (or VALENCIA)

Small rocky island off the coast of County Kerry, Republic of Ireland; area 11 km/7 mi by 3 km/2 mi; population (1996) 700. Geokaun Mountain (268 m/880 ft) and Bray Head (241 m/792 ft) are the largest hills on the island. There were formerly several cable and signalling stations here, a small harbour, and a meteorological observatory.

Valentia Island was a terminal station for the first transatlantic cable. There are several ruined medieval churches, beehive-shaped cells, and stones inscribed with ogham characters on the island.

VALERA, ÉAMON DE

Politician; see ⇨de Valera.

VALLANCEY, CHARLES (1721–1812)

English-born general and Irish antiquarian. Born in Windsor, Vallancey was posted to Ireland with the British army in 1762. He started an antiquarian journal, *Collectanea de Rebus Hibernicis*, in 1770 and his 1773 *Grammar of the Hiberno-Celtic or Irish Lan-guage* characterized Gaelic as a complex, 'masculine' language capable of great subtlety, akin to Persian and Chinese. He was a forceful initiator of many scholarly projects such as the study of ogham, an Irish alphabet based on 25 characters.

In 1779 Vallancey set up the Hibernian Antiquarian Society, and he became a founder member of the ⇨Royal Irish Academy (RIA), Dublin, in 1782.

VAN MORRISON *Morrison weaves together strands from blues, soul, folk, and rock to produce memorable songs in his own very distinctive style. His distinguished musical career, spanning more than 30 years, was recognised with a Brit Award in 1994.*

VAN MORRISON (stage name of GEORGE IVAN MORRISON) (1945–)

Singer, songwriter, and saxophonist. His jazz-inflected Celtic soul style was already in evidence on *Astral Weeks* (1968) and has been highly influential. Among other albums are *Tupelo Honey* (1971), *Veedon Fleece* (1974), and *Avalon Sunset* (1989). He continued to release albums throughout the 1990s, with a consistently retrospective tone, one of the finest being *Hymns to the Silence* (1991). In 1994 he was awarded a Brit award for his outstanding contribution to music.

Morrison started out in the beat-music era and

THE VIKINGS AND NORMANS INVADE

by Sean Duffy

The Vikings, seafaring adventurers from Scandinavia, were the first people to invade Ireland in the historic era. Using technically advanced warships, they began raiding Ireland in 795 when they assaulted several island monasteries off the east coast. Attacks at first rarely penetrated far inland, the raiders simply making off with moveable goods from churches located within easy access of the coast. However, raids intensified in the mid-9th century when the Vikings began attacking further inland. Large Viking fleets were recorded on the rivers Liffey, Boyne, Shannon, and Erne in the 830s and, from 841, instead of returning to their homelands, they began to over-winter in Ireland, building longphorts (defended ship-camps); a number of these harbour sites developed into Ireland's first towns, including Dublin (established in 841), Wexford, Waterford, Cork, and Limerick.

a diminishing threat

Settlement meant that, in time, the Vikings became part of the political landscape of Ireland, being involved in the endemic inter-provincial wars, and allying themselves with one Irish king in opposition to another. Divisions within the Viking ranks further limited their capacity to dominate. Therefore, although plundering activity was renewed during a second wave of Viking incursions from 914 to around 950, the Viking threat gradually diminished. Instead, the port towns of the Ostmen, as they called themselves, became centres of commerce and a lasting legacy. When, by the mid-10th century, they began to convert to Christianity, there were few overt differences between the Hiberno-Norse and their Irish neighbours who, however, continued to regard them as Gaill, 'foreigners'. Although the Battle of Clontarf (1014) was traditionally lauded as the final suppression of the Viking Gaill in their struggle for the sovereignty of Ireland, the victory of forces led by Brian Bóruma, king of Munster, over an alliance of Leinster and Viking forces near Dublin, is now considered a significant event in the struggle for provincial dominance between Leinster and Munster. The defeat of the Vikings heralded the end of their independent control of Dublin, completed around 1054 when Diarmait mac Máel na mBó, King of Leinster, made his son Murchad king of Dublin, but the Hiberno-Norse presence continued.

Other Gaill, described as Saxain (English) in contemporary records, invaded the country in the 12th century. These new arrivals, descendants of the Norman conquerors of England, first began to appear in Ireland in 1167 as mercenaries of the dispossessed king of Leinster, Dermot MacMurrough (Diarmaid Mac Murchadha Uí); MacMurrough had sought help from Henry II, king of England, and received permission to recruit aid amongst his nobles. The main invasion began, however, with the arrival of Robert fitz Stephen, Maurice fitz Gerald, and others in 1169, Anglo-Norman adventurers intent not merely on reinstating MacMurrough but on acquiring land for themselves. Most of these early invaders hailed from south Wales, as did their figurehead, Richard de Clare, known as 'Strongbow', who landed in Waterford in 1170. He certainly envisaged a future in Ireland as he married MacMurrough's daughter and succeeded him as ruler of Leinster in 1171.

the start of colonization

Henry II, who had looked covetously on Ireland in the past, and been given papal permission to invade and reform the Irish church in 1155, now responded with alacrity to the possible development of an independent Norman power on his western shore. In 1171 he came to Ireland, the first English king to do so, and assumed control over his barons, at the same time receiving the submission of a number of Irish kings. The earlier haphazard invasion soon became an ordered process of conquest accompanied by an extensive programme of colonization; this included the large-scale immigration into Ireland of people at every level of the social ladder, and the transference to Ireland of the system of government developed by the Normans in England.

Substantial tracts of the country were taken, primarily on the eastern seaboard from about Carrickfergus to Cork, and a westerly expansion of the colony continued throughout the 13th century. However strong Irish resistance to encroachment, rivalries among the colonists themselves, and the extinction of some of the leading baronial families led to the conquest losing impetus. The failure of Anglo-Norman landholders to reside on their Irish property, became a problem, as did cultural assimilation as the colonial community intermingled ever-increasingly with the Irish. The result was a decline in the strength of the colony, and increased lawlessness which, by the 14th century, the impoverished Dublin-based government was unable to combat; by the end of the Middle Ages the attempted conquest of Ireland by the English crown remained incomplete.

formed the group Them (1964–66), which had two hits, 'Here Comes the Night' and 'Gloria'; the latter became a standard.

VIGNOLES, CHARLES BLACKER

(1793–1875)

Railway engineer who was involved in building the first railway line in Ireland from Dublin to Kingstown (now Dun Laoghaire) 1823–34. He also helped to construct the four-span Nicholas suspension bridge over the River Dnieper at Kiev, Ukraine 1848–55, at the time the longest such bridge in the world.

Born in Woodbrook, County Wexford, Vignoles served in the British army before beginning his career in civil engineering under the Scottish engineer and bridge builder John Rennie. He helped the English railway engineer George Stephenson survey and build the Liverpool to Manchester railway in the late 1820s, and was involved in the construction of many other lines until the 1860s.

Work on the first Irish line, completed in 1834, involved the route from central Dublin to Dun Laoghaire, an important ferry terminal about 16 km/10 mi south of the city. His greatest work was the suspension bridge over the Dnieper. He was appointed the first professor of civil engineering at University College, London.

VIKINGS

See feature essay on the Vikings and Normans in Ireland, page 352.

VINEGAR HILL, BATTLE OF

See ⇨Rebellion of 1798.

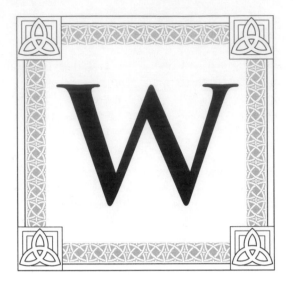

WADDING, LUKE (1588–1657)

Franciscan scholar, born in Waterford, who founded two ⇨Irish Colleges in Rome and actively supported the ⇨Confederation of Kilkenny. He entered the Franciscan order in Portugal in 1605 and trained in Lisbon and Coimbra. Ordained in 1613, he was briefly professor of theology at Salamanca, Spain (1617), before becoming theologian to the Spanish embassy in Rome (1618). He founded St Isidore's (Irish Franciscan) College in 1625 and the Ludovisian (Irish secular priests') College in 1628. He became the agent for the Kilkenny confederation in Rome in 1642.

Wadding also published extensively on Franciscan history and the 13th-century Scottish scholastic theologian John Duns Scotus.

WALKER, JAMES COOPER (1761–1810)

Antiquarian, born in Dublin. Walker was a founder-member of the ⇨Royal Irish Academy (RIA), Dublin, and worked with Gaelic enthusiasts such as Charlotte ⇨Brooke and Charles ⇨Vallancey. Most notable is his *Historical Memoirs of the Irish Bards* (1786), which traces Irish poetry and music from their earliest points with the benefit of contemporary scholarship. Like other members of the academy, Walker worked to establish Irish culture as a dignified and vibrant area of study.

WALL, MERVYN (EUGENE WELPLY)
(1908–)

Writer, born in Dublin. Wall was educated in Germany and at University College, Dublin. His writing is a combination of serious fiction and burlesque drama; his best-selling *The Unfortunate Fursey* (1946), a comedic satire of Catholic Ireland, stands in stylistic contrast to his *Leaves for the Burning* (1952), a meticulously crafted and strong indictment of the repression in Ireland during the 1930s and 1940s.

Wall worked as a civil servant throughout his career, rising to secretary of the Arts Council.

WALLACE, (WILLIAM) VINCENT
(1812–1865)

Composer who established himself internationally as a pianist and violinist on tours that included Europe, Australia, and North and South America. He used the musical influences from the places he visited in his own compositions, such as the highly successful opera *Maritana* (1845), with its Spanish and gypsy elements.

He studied with his father, a bandleader and bassoon player who moved to Dublin, where Wallace played the organ and violin in public as a boy. In 1831 he married Isabella Kelly, but they separated in 1835 (in New York in 1850 he met the pianist Hélène Stoepel, with whom he lived and had two sons). In 1834 he appeared in Dublin with a violin concerto of his own. He was in Australia and elsewhere abroad 1835–45, then went to London and was induced to compose *Maritana*. After a successful operatic career, including a visit to South America in 1849 and 14 years in Germany, a commission from the Paris Opéra (which he was unable to finish owing to failing eyesight), and another visit to South and North America 1850–53, his health broke down and he was ordered to the Pyrenees, where he died.

His works include: OPERA *Maritana* (1845), *Matilda of Hungary* (1847), *Lurline* (1860), *The Maid of Zürich* (unpublished), *The Ambler Witch* (1861), *Love's Triumph* (1862), *The Desert Flower* (1863), *Estrella* (unfinished); unperformed operettas *Gulnare*, *Olga*. OTHER cantata *Maypole*; violin concerto; piano music.

WALSH, MAURICE (1879–1964)

Novelist, born near Listowel, County Kerry. Walsh was educated in Ireland before working in the Scottish Highlands in the Customs and Excise service. His stories are mostly historical romances set in Ireland and Scotland, and his works include *The Key Above the Door* (1926), *Green Rushes* (1935), and *Sons of the Swordmaker* (1938). *Green Rushes* contains his most noted story 'The Quiet Man', which became the basis of John Ford's celebrated film of the same name in 1950.

WALSH, WILLIAM JOSEPH (1841–1921)

Catholic archbishop of Dublin from 1885. His independent mind was shown by his misgivings (privately expressed) on the papal condemnation of the Land League's 'Plan of Campaign' (1888) to withhold rents. He was more circumspect on Charles Stewart Parnell's relationship with Kitty O'Shea than other Irish bishops. During the rise of Sinn Féin, Walsh supported the independence movement 1919–21. Civil war was imminent as he lay dying, but he was unable to influence events. He is remembered in Ireland for patriotism and social concern.

Before his ordination in 1866, Walsh was a professor at St Patrick's College, Maynooth, published in law and economics, and was hailed as the foremost canon lawyer in the Irish church. A Dubliner, he understood the feelings of his people better than Cardinal Paul Cullen.

WALTON, ERNEST THOMAS SINTON (1903–1995)

Physicist who collaborated with English physicist John Cockcroft on investigating the structure of the atom. They developed the first particle accelerator and in 1932 succeeded in splitting the atom. In 1951 they shared the Nobel Prize for Physics for their groundbreaking work.

Walton was born in Dungarvan, County Waterford, and attended Methodist College, Belfast, then entered Trinity College, Dublin, in 1922, graduating four year's later with a double honours in experimental science and mathematics. He was a research assistant at the Cavendish Laboratory, Cambridge University 1927–34, where he and Cockcroft developed a particle accelerator which used an arrangement of condensers to produce a beam of protons, and could achieve energies of 700,000 electron volts.

In 1932 they used their accelerator to become the first to split the atom. They also used it to transform one element into another by bombarding lithium nuclei to form helium nuclei. Walton left Cambridge in 1934 to become professor of physics at Trinity College, Dublin, where he remained until his retirement in 1974. However, he continued with his research at Trinity, making regular visits until the 1990s.

WARD, TONY (ANTHONY JOSEPH PATRICK) (1954–)

Rugby union player, born in Dublin. A fly-half renowned for his goal-kicking feats, he scored 113 points in 19 internationals for Ireland between 1978 and 1987. Selected for the 1980 British and Irish Lions tour of South Africa, he set a Lions record for the highest individual score in a single international with 18 points (from five penalties and a drop goal) in the first Test at Cape Town. His most memorable performance, however, came two years earlier in 1978 when he kicked two drop goals and a conversion in Munster's famous 12–0 victory over the All Blacks.

WARDE, MOTHER MARY FRANCIS XAVIER (born Frances Teresa Warde) (1810–1884)

Religious leader, born in Mountrath. A wealthy Dubliner, she did charitable work and joined the newly formed Sisters of Mercy in 1831. In 1843 she took a group of these nuns to the USA, where she founded institutions and led religious communities in Pennsylvania, Rhode Island, New Hampshire, and elsewhere. She was also a pioneer in adult religious education.

WATERFORD

County of the Republic of Ireland, in the province of Munster; county town ⇨Waterford; area 1,840 sq km/ 710 sq mi; population (1996) 94,700. Other towns include Dungarvon, Lismore, and Tramore. The chief rivers are the Suir and the Blackwater; the Comeragh and Monavallagh mountain ranges lie in the north and centre of the county. Agriculture and dairy farming are important; wheat, barley, and vegetables are also grown. Industries include glassware, pharmaceuticals, and electronics, and there are tanneries, bacon factories, and flour mills.

features

At Lismore there is a castle, the Irish seat of the Duke of Devonshire; and at Ardmore a medieval cathedral on the site of a 7th-century monastic foundation, and St Declan's well, where pilgrims used to wash. At Cappoquin lies Mount Melleray Abbey; founded in 1831 by the Cistercians, it remains an important place of pilgrimage and retreat.

topography

Waterford is bounded on the north by Kilkenny and Tipperary, on the south by the Atlantic, to the east by Waterford Harbour and Wexford, and to the west by Cork. On the northwest border are the Knockmealdown Mountains, the highest point of which reaches 796 m/2,612 ft; in the north of the county are the Monavullagh Mountains and the Comeragh Mountains (highest point Fascoum, 792 m/2,597 ft); in the southwest lie the Drum Hills, (highest point 302 m/991 ft). The coastline is much indented, the principal inlets being Waterford Harbour, Tramore Bay, Dungarvan Harbour, Ardmore Bay, and Youghal Harbour.

natural resources

Marble, iron, and copper are found. There is salmon fishing on the River Blackwater, and sea fishing is important at Dunmore East and elsewhere.

WATERFORD

Port and county town of County ⇨Waterford on the River Suir; population (1996) 44,000. It is a major distribution centre, and container traffic is important. Industries include bacon, flour-milling, brewing, paper and board, pharmaceuticals, furniture, and electrical equipment. The factory producing handmade Waterford crystal glass (34% lead content instead of the normal 24%) was opened in 1783 and closed in 1851. It reopened in 1951, and is now the city's largest employer.

history

Danes founded Waterford in the 9th century, and much of their material culture has survived. In 1170 the city was wrested from them by Richard de Clare, Earl of Pembroke and Striguil. Henry II visited Waterford the following year. King John landed here in 1205, and again in 1211. Waterford received its first charter from him in 1205. After the Battle of the ⇨Boyne, James II sailed for France from Duncannon Fort on the Wexford side of Waterford Harbour, and William III sailed from there to England. In 1650 Waterford was taken by the English general Henry Ireton. Waterford was the second most important Anglo-Norman stronghold after Dublin, and was noted for its consistent loyalty to the English crown through to the 17th century.

features

Fragments of two portions of the old city walls remain, both from the Danish occupation and that of the Anglo-Normans, notably ⇨Reginald's Tower, traditionally dating from the 11th century, and a number of well-preserved Norman towers. There are remains of the 13th-century Greyfriars Monastery, and Blackfriars, a Dominican monastery founded in the city in 1226. The city has Protestant and Roman Catholic cathedrals: the Church of Ireland (Protestant) Christ Church Cathedral stands on the site of an earlier Danish foundation of 1050, and the present structure dates from 1773; the Catholic cathedral dates from

COUNTY WATERFORD *Close to the sea at Ardmore, east of Waterford, stand the ruins of St Declan's Church. This Romanesque relief of Adam and Eve is on the surviving western wall.*

1796. St Olaf's Church was founded by the Danes in the 11th century, and was restored during the 18th century. Other notable 18th-century buildings include the City Hall. St John's College seminary (founded 1871) contains an important collection of early manuscripts and books. A bridge connects Waterford with the suburb of Ferrybank on the north bank of the River Suir, which has an estuary in common with the River Barrow.

WELLINGTON, ARTHUR WELLESLEY

(1st Duke of Wellington) (1769–1852)

British soldier and Tory politician, born in Dublin. The third son of Garrett Wellesley, 1st Earl of Mornington, he was educated at Eton, England, and later at Pignerol's Military Academy at Angers, France. He was Irish chief secretary 1807–08 but returned to active duty soon after. He won fame as commander in the Peninsular War between the French and the British, and he expelled the French from Spain in 1814. He defeated Napoleon Bonaparte at Quatre-Bras and Waterloo in 1815, and was a member of the Congress of Vienna. He became Duke of Wellington in 1814 as a reward for his services. Entering politics, he was prime minister 1828–30, but because of Daniel O'Connell's campaign was forced to concede Roman Catholic emancipation. He held the office of commander-in-chief of the forces at various times from 1827 and for life from 1842.

WESTLIFE

See ⇨pop and rock music.

WESTMEATH

County of the Republic of Ireland, in the province of Leinster; county town ⇨Mullingar; area 1,760 sq km/ 679 sq mi; population (1996) 63,300. The rivers Brosna, Inny, and Shannon flow through the county, and its principal lakes are loughs Ree (the largest, and an extension of the River Shannon), Ennell, Owel, and Sheelin. The Royal Canal cuts through the county but is now disused. The land is low-lying, about 76 m/249 ft above sea-level, with much pasture. The main agricultural activity is cattle and dairy farming. Limestone is found, and textiles are also important. Fishing for trout is popular. Other principal towns are Athlone and Moate.

historical remains

The county contains many ancient monuments. Par-ticularly noteworthy are the ruins near Lough Derrevaragh of Multyfarnham Abbey, with its lofty towers. The abbey was founded in 1236, and is now the site of a Franciscan college.

WESTPORT

Market town and seaport in County Mayo; population (1996) 4,300. Westport is situated on Clew Bay, 20 km/12 mi southwest of Castlebar, and is a tourist centre for the Connemara region and Achill Island, and a centre for salmon and trout fishing. Clothing and pharmaceuticals are manufactured, and there is a printing industry. The town was planned by the English architect James Wyatt in 1780.

⇨Westport House, a Georgian mansion designed about 1730 with later 18th-century additions, has been restored and is open to the public.

Croagh Patrick (765 m/2,510 ft), 10 km/6 mi west of Westport, a quartzite cone-shaped mountain, is a site of pilgrimage in July. Legend has it that St Patrick fasted and prayed on the mountain for 40 days in 441.

WESTPORT HOUSE

Classical early Georgian house and a seat of the Marquess of Sligo, at Westport, County Mayo. It was designed by Richard Castle about 1730 using the existing fortified house, and alterations were made in the 18th century by Thomas Ivory and James Wyatt. The dining room contains particularly good examples of plasterwork by Wyatt.

WESTPORT HOUSE *Situated near to the ragged coastline of Clew Bay, County Mayo, the serene setting of this early Georgian mansion was enjoyed by 19th-century authors de Quincey and Thackeray, both of whom stayed here.*

WEXFORD

County of the Republic of Ireland, in the province of Leinster; county town ⇨Wexford; area 2,350 sq km/ 907 sq mi; population (1996) 104,400. Wexford is one of the most intensively cultivated areas in Ireland. The main crops are wheat, barley, beet, and potatoes. Fishing is important, the main fishing port being Kilmore Quay in the south; sheep and cattle rearing are also significant, as is dairy farming. Industries include agricultural machinery and food processing. Wexford was the first part of Ireland to be colonized from England; Normans arrived in 1169. The John F Kennedy Arboretum is one of the most popular visitor attractions in the county.

physical

The surface is hilly in the north and west, with a fertile, low-lying central plain, the highest peak being Mount Leinster (796 m/2,612 ft) in the Blackstairs Mountains. The principal rivers are the Barrow, the Nore, and the Slaney, and the principal towns Enniscorthy, Gorey, and New Ross. The county has long sandy beaches with a number of holiday resorts, including Ballymoney and Courtown, and the only inlet of importance is Wexford Harbour. Off the coast to the southeast is Tuskar Rock with a lighthouse (erected in 1815), and farther south are the Saltee Islands, the largest bird sanctuary in Ireland, beyond which there is a lightship. Waterford Harbour divides County Wexford from County Waterford.

historical remains

There are a number of ancient monuments in the county, including Donbrody Abbey, Ferns Abbey, and the castles at Ferns and Enniscorthy; the latter has now been established as a county museum. County Wexford was an important centre of conflict during the ⇨Rebellion of 1798, and has a number of memorials to this rebellion; Vinegar Hill, near Enniscorthy, is the site of the final battle between the Wexford pikemen, or insurgents, and British troops.

WEXFORD

Seaport and county town of ⇨Wexford, on the estuary of the River Slaney; population (1996) 16,000. Industries include food processing, and the manufacture of textiles, cheese, agricultural machinery, furniture, and motor vehicles. There is an annual international opera festival in October. Wexford was founded in the 9th century by Danes; it was taken by the Anglo-Normans in 1169, and besieged and devastated by Oliver Cromwell in 1649. In the ⇨Rebellion of 1798 Wexford was briefly held by Irish insurgents.

the harbour

Wexford's initial importance was mainly due to its harbour, which is formed by a bar across the mouth of the river's estuary. Since large vessels were unable to enter the harbour at low tide, Rosslare Harbour was built some 13 km/8 mi down the coast. Rosslare Harbour is connected by rail with Wexford. The Wexford Wildfowl Reserve on the northern side of the harbour is an important bird sanctuary.

history

The Danes built a wall around Wexford and remained until 1169, after which the town was settled by Normans; the 13th-century west gate tower forms part of the Norman walls, and is now a heritage centre. Wexford town received its first charter in 1318. William III garrisoned the town in 1690, and it was captured and held for a month by Irish pikemen during the rebellion of 1798. Some fragments of the old town walls survive. There are also the ruins of St Selskar's Abbey, dedicated to St Sepulchre, which are incorporated into the Protestant church of St Selskar. The first Anglo-Irish treaty was signed in St Selskar's Abbey in 1169; it was later destroyed by Cromwellian troops in 1649. Henry II is reputed to have spent the whole of Lent here in 1172 in penitence for the murder of Thomas à Becket.

WEXFORD OPERA FESTIVAL

Classical music festival, held annually in Wexford, in October. Established in 1951, the ethos of the festival has been to stage relatively unknown or forgotten operas. The festival initially focused on Italian opera, particularly the works of Bellini, Donizetti, Rossini, and the young Verdi, but has since widened its scope to other lesser-known works. Three operas are staged each year, providing a platform for young international singers to make their mark; Mirella Freni, Janet Baker, Geraint Evans, and Sergei Leiferkus are among those to have performed at Wexford. The festival also features recitals, performances, and fringe events.

WHELAN, BILL (1950–)

Composer, arranger, and keyboard player. He wrote the music for the 1994 Eurovision Song Contest interval-piece, ⇨Riverdance (1994), which developed into the phenomenally successful dance show of the same name. Born in Limerick, he was a member of ⇨Planxty 1979–81, and co-wrote their Eurovision interval piece in 1981, *Timedance*. He has composed music for films, including *Bloomfield* (1970), *Lamb* (1984), and *Some Mother's Son* (1996), and has worked with various contemporary and folk artists such as U2, Van Morrison, Kate Bush, Andy Irvine, Paul Brady, and Stockton's Wing. His compositions include *The Ó Riada Suite* (1987), *The Seville Suite* (1992).

Whelan's talent can perhaps best be described as bringing aspects of different musical traditions together to form attractive hybrids. This is most evident in *Riverdance*, which draws from Irish traditional, Spanish Flamenco, Balkan, gospel, jazz, and classical styles.

WHISKEY, IRISH

Strong alcoholic spirit distilled in wood casks from fermented grains. An inferior grade can be made from potatoes, beets, or other root vegetables. Unlike Scotch, to which it is similar, Irish whiskey does not use peat in its preparation and has a full, sweet taste.

Whiskey was originally confined to the upper classes but by the end of the 18th century it was widely consumed and had become the most popular drink in Ireland. Excise legislation introduced in 1779 put many smaller distilleries out of business or drove them underground and allowed larger southern distilleries such as Powers and Jamesons in Dublin and Cork to expand. Coffey's patent still, invented in the 1830s, powered a huge expansion in the northern industry in Belfast and Londonderry. The new process produced a lighter, cheaper whiskey that appealed to the British palate and allowed the northern distilleries to move into a dominant position by the end of the 19th century.

Southern distilleries, meanwhile, retained their traditional distilling methods. By the 1920s the northern industry had lost their British market to the Distillers Company of Scotland, who took them over and closed them down, leaving the southern distillers to

WHISKEY *Inside the distillery at Bushmills Brewery, County Antrim, the magical process is underway that transforms the peaty waters of the River Bush, plus malted or unmalted barley, into Irish whiskey.*

dominate a much reduced Irish whiskey industry once more.

WHITAKER, THOMAS KENNETH

(1916–)
Irish civil servant. He was a hugely influential secretary of the Department of Finance 1956–69 and governor of the Central Bank 1969–76. He was later chancellor of the National University of Ireland 1976–96, president of the Royal Irish Academy 1985–87, and became a member of Ireland's Council of State in 1991. Whitaker is credited with the authorship of 'Economic Development' (1958), which turned the Republic of Ireland's economic policy from one of isolationism and protection to free trade, and is regarded as one of the most influential documents in modern Irish history.

WHITE ISLAND

Island off the eastern shore of Lower Lough Erne, County Fermanagh. Seven primitive stone statues and a mask, dating from between the 7th and 10th centuries, are displayed on the ruined wall of a 12th-century Romanesque church. Some are Christian in appearance, but the majority are pagan, including a ⇨*sheela-na-gig* (a crude female figure). The mysterious carvings, discovered between 1840 and 1958, appeared to have been deliberately hidden or buried, but may have decorated an earlier monastery on the island.

WICKLOW

County of the Republic of Ireland, in the province of Leinster; county town ⇨Wicklow; area 2,030 sq km/ 784 sq mi; population (1996) 102,700. It includes the Wicklow Mountains, the rivers Slaney, Avoca, Vartry, and Liffey, and the coastal resort of Bray. Other towns include Arklow, Greystones, and Baltinglass. The village of Shillelagh gave its name to rough cudgels of oak or blackthorn made there. Agriculture is important; there is livestock rearing (in particular a special breed of mountain sheep), and dairy farming. Wheat and oats are grown, and seed potatoes and bulbs are produced. Granite is mined at Aughrim and Ballyknockan.

physical

Wicklow is bounded to the north by County Dublin, to the south by Wexford, to the east by St George's Channel, and to the west by Carlow and Kildare. The Wicklow Mountains run through the centre from north to south, the highest points being Mount Lugnaquilla (926 m/3,038 ft), the second-highest mountain in Ireland, Mount Kippure (754 m/2,474 ft), Djouce Mountain (727 m/2,385 ft), and Duff Hill (723 m/2,372 ft). The rivers Liffey and Slaney rise there; the county's other principal rivers are the Avonmore, the Dargle, and the Vartry. The two main harbours are at Arklow and Wicklow. Lakes include Loughs Bray, Dan, and the Upper and Lower loughs at Glendalough. There are artificial lakes at Roundwood, which is the Dublin reservoir, and at Pollaphuca, which forms part of the Blessington hydroelectric scheme.

features

The county is known for its scenery; there are gorges and valleys, notable among which are Glenmalure (11 km/7 mi), the Vale of Avoca, and the Croghan Valley; the coast has steep cliffs and sandy beaches. Glendalough is the site of a large and well-preserved 7th-century monastery, and a place of pilgrimage; near the village of Glencree is the Dargle ravine, which has a 91 m/300 ft-high waterfall. There are many other ecclesiastical remains and castles in the county.

WICKLOW (Danish *Wykinglo*)

Resort and county town of County ⇨Wicklow, on the River Vartry, 50 km/31 mi southeast of Dublin; population (1996) 6,400.

history

St Patrick and St Manntann landed at Wicklow in 431; from the latter is derived the Irish name Cill (Church) Manntain, after which the church in the town, St Mantan, is named. After the Viking occupation and Norman invasion, when the lands were granted to the Fitzgerald family, Wicklow was the scene of constant fighting between the O'Byrne and O'Toole clans, until the final struggle with Cromwell in 1649. There are the ruins of a friary and a castle, both built by the Fitzgerald family. The 13th-century Franciscan friary later came under the patronage of the O'Byrne clan; Black Castle was built by Maurice Fitzgerald in 1176, but not completed until the 14th century. It was held by the O'Byrnes in the early 16th century, but surrendered to the crown in 1641.

WILDE, JANE FRANCESCA (pen name SPERANZA) (born Elgee) (1826–1896)

Writer, born in Wexford. Wilde became a committed nationalist, and an influential presence in Dublin literary and political circles. From 1845 she contributed poetry and prose to *The Nation* under the pen name 'Speranza'.

In 1851 she married the eye surgeon William Wilde, and they had two sons, the younger of whom was the writer Oscar ⇨Wilde. After her husband's death in 1876, she moved to London and published several works on folklore, including *Ancient Legends of Ireland* (1887) and *Ancient Cures* (1891).

WILDE, OSCAR (FINGAL O'FLAHERTIE WILLS) (1854–1900)

Writer. With his flamboyant style and quotable conversation, he dazzled London society and, on his lecture tour in 1882, the USA. He published his only novel, *The Picture of Dorian Gray*, in 1891, followed by a series of sharp comedies, including *A Woman of No Importance* (1893) and *The Importance of Being Earnest* (1895). In 1895 he was imprisoned for two years for homosexual offences; he died in exile.

Wilde was born in Dublin and studied at Dublin and Oxford, where he became known as a supporter of the Aesthetic Movement ('art for art's sake'). He published *Poems* (1881), and also wrote fairy tales and other stories, criticism, and a long, anarchic political essay 'The Soul of Man Under Socialism' (1891). His elegant social comedies include *Lady Windermere's Fan* (1892) and *An Ideal Husband* (1895). The drama *Salomé* (1893), based on the biblical character,

If, with the literate, I am / Impelled to try an epigram, / I never seek to take the credit; / We all assume that Oscar said it.

DOROTHY PARKER US writer and wit *A Pig's Eye View of Literature* (1937).

a man cannot be too careful in the choice of his enemies.

OSCAR WILDE *The Picture of Dorian Gray.*

~

was written in French; considered scandalous by the British censor, it was first performed in Paris in 1896 with the actor Sarah Bernhardt in the title role.

Among his lovers was Lord Alfred Douglas, whose father provoked Wilde into a lawsuit that led to his social and financial ruin and imprisonment. The long poem *Ballad of Reading Gaol* (1898) and a letter published as *De Profundis* (1905) were written in jail to explain his side of the relationship. After his release from prison in 1897, he lived in France. He is buried in Père Lachaise cemetery, Paris.

I never saw a man who looked / With such a wistful eye / Upon that little tent of blue / Which prisoners call the sky.

OSCAR WILDE 'The Ballad of Reading Gaol'.

~

Wilde's fate at the hand of the establishment and the magnitude of his ruin have led to his being regarded as a martyr for gay liberation and social freedom generally. In recent years, his Irish nationalism, expressed especially in speeches that he made before Irish-American audiences in the USA, has been the object of attention. The tragedy inflicted on his wife Constance and their children has also attracted more attention than previously, while his plays continue to be revived with great success in Ireland and elsewhere.

WILDE, WILLIAM ROBERT WILLS

(1815–1876)

Eye and ear surgeon, and archaeologist. He founded an ophthalmic hospital, developed innovative surgical

*L*ife imitates Art far more than Art imitates Life.

OSCAR WILDE *Intentions* (1891)

~

OSCAR WILDE *In the preface of* The Picture of Dorian Gray, *published in 1891, Wilde wrote, 'There is no such thing as a moral or an immoral book. Books are well written or badly written. That is all.'*

procedures, and invented an ophthalmoscope. An archaeologist of considerable skill, he wrote many books on the subject and became a leading authority on the ⇨Boyne Valley burial site.

Wilde was born in Castlerea, County Roscommon, into an Irish Protestant family, and studied medicine in London, Berlin, and Vienna. He returned to Dublin to serve as medical commissioner on the Irish Census of 1841, a role he repeated in the census of 1851. His appendix to the 1851 census report became a major medical report published as *The Epidemics of Ireland* (1851).

In 1844 he founded St Mark's Ophthalmic Hospital in Dublin. He published papers and textbooks on ocular and aural surgical techniques, and had a major impact on medical procedures at the time. He was appointed eye surgeon to Queen Victoria and also attended King Oskar I of Sweden.

He was deeply involved in archaeology and his books, such as *The Beauties of the Boyne and The*

Blackwater (1849), established him as a leading authority on Irish archaeology. He also compiled a catalogue of the holdings of the Royal Irish Academy.

Wilde was a fluent speaker of the Gaelic language, unusual at the time given his Anglo-Irish background. He married the nationalist poet Jane Francesca ⇨Wilde ('Speranza') and was the father of the writer Oscar ⇨Wilde.

WILLIE CLANCY SUMMER SCHOOL

Traditional music summer school and festival held annually in the first full week of July in Miltown Malbay, County Clare. Affectionately known as the 'Willie Week', it is one of the most important traditional music festivals of the year. It features instrumental classes, lectures, céilís (dances), concerts, and informal pub sessions with the leading performers of traditional Irish music.

WOOD, CHARLES (1886–1926)

Music scholar, teacher, and composer. He taught at the Royal College of Music in London from 1883 and at Cambridge University from 1897. As a composer he is remembered for his church music.

Wood learnt music from the organist of Armagh Cathedral, where his father was a lay vicar, and studied at the Royal College of Music in London 1883–87, becoming professor there in 1888. He conducted the University Music Society at Cambridge 1888–94, and took a doctorate in music there in 1894. In 1897 he became music lecturer to the University and in 1924 succeeded Charles Stanford as professor of music.

His works include: STAGE opera *The Pickwick Papers* (after Dickens; 1922); incidental music to Euripides' *Ion* and *Iphigenia in Tauris*. ORCHESTRAL AND VOCAL *Ode to the West Wind* (1890) and *The Song of the Tempest* for solo voices, chorus, and orchestra (performed 1902); *Ode on Music* (Swinburne; 1894), *Ode on Time* (Milton; 1898), *Dirge for Two Veterans* (Whitman), *Ballad of Dundee* for chorus and orchestra (performed 1904); *Passion according to St Mark* (1921). CHAMBER eight string quartets.

WOOD, KEITH (1972–)

Rugby player, born in Killaloe, County Clare. He made his debut for Ireland in 1994 and has since been the first-choice hooker for his country. Weighing 108 kg/17 stone and standing at 1.83 m/6 ft, Wood surprisingly began playing hurling at under-age level before following in his father's footsteps and turning to rugby. His attacking play earned him a call-up for the British Lions tour to South Africa in 1997. After a spell with the English club Harlequins, Wood returned to Ireland in 1999 to play for Young Munster. Capped over 30 times at international level, Wood broke the Irish record for most tries in one game, scoring four against the American Eagles in the 1999 World Cup, a world best for a player in that position.

WOOL TRADE

Trade in wool developed substantially in Ireland as a consequence of the Anglo-Norman conquest of the country. In general, Irish wool was inferior to English wool in the Middle Ages, although a profitable trade in woollen cloaks still took place with mainland Europe. Between the 1580s and the 1640s foreign trade increased dramatically, as woollen products became cheaper and easier to produce. The Woollen Act (1699) prohibited the exportation of wool, although the large demand for the product in the domestic market maintained production levels. The introduction of mechanization in Dublin in the 1790s changed the trade irrevocably, although smaller production methods survived in rural areas for some years. Exportation resumed in the 19th century, with a small yet profitable niche for Irish wool products.

WORKHOUSES

Workhouses were established in Ireland under the Poor Law Act of 1838. Aiming to provide basic, often minimal, food and accommodation for those in poverty, their conditions were deliberately inferior so as to discourage anyone but the very needy to enter. Adults were obliged to work for their maintenance and engaged in various forms of menial labour, while children were educated in workhouse schools and given lesser tasks.

The workhouses had their greatest use during the Great Famine (historically dated 1845–49, but now believed to have lasted until 1852), but because families were separated upon entering, they were usually seen as a last resort, and deep shame and humiliation usually accompanied admittance. The workhouse system ended with Irish independence in the south, while in Northern Ireland the workhouses were gradually phased out by 1946.

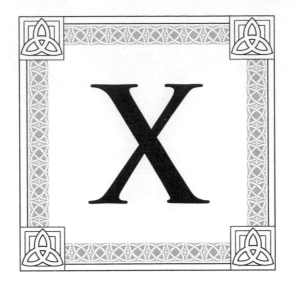

'X' CASE

Court case in the Republic of Ireland in 1992, concerning a 14-year-old girl who was being prevented by the state from leaving the country to seek an abortion, despite her suicide threats. She had been raped, and her father had enquired whether evidence from the abortion should be retained to aid charges against the accused, leading to intervention by the attorney general and an injunction on her travel for nine months. Following a supreme court ruling, which favoured the right of a woman to travel to obtain an abortion, the injunction was lifted. The case led to further referendums on abortion and strained the Labour–Fianna Fáil coalition.

The motives of the attorney general, Harry Whelehan, were questioned, but he claimed to be merely acting in his role as guardian of the 1937 constitution. Having received indication from the girl's parents that she would be seeking an abortion, the attorney general had applied to the high court to obtain an injunction, and the Garda (Irish police) were instructed to prevent the child from leaving the country. As the girl was already in England, the injunction imposed a fine or imprisonment on her parents to secure her return.

The case was referred to the supreme court, which indicated that a pro-life amendment to the constitution inserted in 1983, did allow a woman to travel to obtain an abortion, and cited the right to freedom of movement under European Union (EU) legislation. The case prompted three referendums later the same year on the right to travel, right to information, and right to abortion in the Republic of Ireland, the first two of which were passed. However, it is expected that even these amendments have not finally ended the abortion debate. The 'X' case also led to criticism of the supreme court, whose judgement seemed to change the meaning of the 1983 amendment.

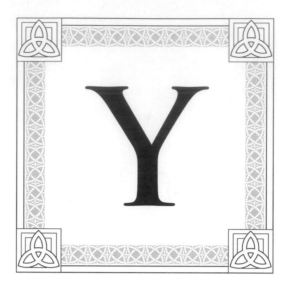

YEATS, JACK BUTLER (1871–1957)

Painter; the best-known Irish artist of the 20th century. Yeats worked first as an illustrator, then turned to oil painting, emerging as an Expressionist who depicted Irish life and landscape in a colourful and highly individualistic style. He was the brother of the poet W B Yeats.

Yeats was born in London and lived with his grandparents in Sligo from 1879 to 1887, a formative period for him as an artist. As part of the literary circle that included his brother William, he toured the west of Ireland in 1905 to illustrate the writings of J M Synge and later designed sets for Synge's *The Playboy of the Western World*. His early oil paintings, such as *Before the Start* (1915; National Gallery of Ireland, Dublin), are strongly linear in style and capture the atmosphere of Irish rural life. *The Liffey Swim* (1923; National Gallery of Ireland) with its dynamic brushwork and heightened colour is a key work in his emergence as an Expressionist. His subjects became increasingly personal as colour became the means by which he conveyed the emotions they aroused in him. To this end he developed the poetic, symbolic visual language of works such as *There is no Night* (1949; Hugh Lane Municipal Gallery of Modern Art, Dublin).

Though never politically active, Yeats identified with the republican cause in the early 1920s, in opposition to his brother. Since his death his international reputation has continued to rise. More recently he has been acknowledged as making a significant contribution to avant-garde European literature with novels such as *The Charmed Life* (1938). The largest public collection of his work is in the National Gallery of Ireland.

YEATS, W(ILLIAM) B(UTLER) (1865–1939)

Poet, dramatist, and scholar. He was a leader of the Irish literary revival and a founder of the ⇨Abbey Theatre in Dublin. His early work was romantic and lyrical, as in the poem 'The Lake Isle of Innisfree' and the plays *The Countess Cathleen* (1892) and *The Land of Heart's Desire* (1894). His later poetry, which includes *The Wild Swans at Coole* (1917) and *The Winding Stair* (1929), was also much influenced by European and Eastern thought. He was a senator of the Irish Free State 1922–28, and won the Nobel Prize for Literature in 1923.

C̲ast a cold eye / On life, on death. / Horseman pass by!

W B Yeats 'Under Ben Bulben'.

～

Yeats was born into a Protestant family in Dublin and was educated both in London and Dublin. He spent much time in England, and died in the south of France, but his most productive years were spent living in County Sligo. Following his artist father's footsteps, he first studied painting but soon turned to writing. In his early verse and poetic plays, such as *The Wind Among the Reeds* (1899), *The Wanderings of Oisin* (1889), and *Deirdre* (1907), he drew heavily on Irish legend to create allusive, sensuous imagery. Later, his work adopted a more robust, astringent style and a tighter structure, and displayed a preoccupation with public affairs, all evident in the collection *Responsibilities* (1914).

W B Yeats *An outstanding poet, with the reputation for creating a distinctive style for Irish literature written in English, Yeats was an active campaigner for Irish culture and dominated the Irish literary scene.*

Yeats was committed to the cause of Irish nationalism, but not as a political activist; rather, he saw nationalist aspirations as part of a wider spiritual revival, and felt that by finding a 'unity of being' in himself, he might help create a kind of cultural and intellectual unity among his compatriots. In this, he was greatly influenced by the renowned beauty and ardent nationalist Maude Gonne, whom he met in 1889, and to whom many of his poems were

turning and turning in the widening gyre / The falcon cannot hear the falconer; / Things fall apart; the centre cannot hold; / Mere anarchy is loosed upon the world, the blood-dimmed tide is loosed, and everywhere / the ceremony of innocence is drowned; / The best lack all conviction, while the worst / Are full of passionate intensity.

W B Yeats 'The Second Coming' (1921).

addressed. However, she refused to marry him, and in 1917 he married Georgie Hyde-Lees, whose work as a spiritual medium reinforced his leanings towards mystic symbolism, as in the prose work *A Vision* (1925 and 1937). Among his later volumes of verse are *The Tower* (1928) and *Last Poems and Two Plays* (1939). His other prose works include *Autobiographies* (1926) and *Dramatis Personae* (1936). After his death, his body was brought back from France and buried in Drumcliffe churchyard, County Sligo.

When you are old and gray and full of sleep, / And nodding by the fire, take down this book, / And slowly read, and dream of the soft look / Your eyes had once, and of their shadows deep.

W B Yeats 'When you are Old'.

Throughout his career Yeats's poetic style underwent an extraordinary process of reinvention and modernization, and shaped itself around an array of personal, mythological, and political concerns. His deep influence on both Irish literature and on poetry in English in general, and his stature as an imaginative artist, can hardly be exaggerated.

YOUGHAL

Town and seaside resort in County Cork; population (1996) 5,600. Youghal (pronounced 'Yawl') is situated on the west side of the Blackwater estuary, 48 km/30 mi east of the city of Cork. Carpets, healthcare products, and computer products are manufactured here, a type of needlepoint lace ('pointe d'Irlande') is made, and there are salmon fisheries. The town contains the ruins of Benedictine and Dominican abbeys and has medieval town walls and towers.

Youghal was founded by the Anglo-Normans in the 13th century. During the plantation of Munster in the 16th century the town and surrounding lands were granted to the adventurer Walter Raleigh.

The Clock Gate, built in the 18th century on the site of a medieval gate, was used as a jail until 1837. St Mary's Protestant church dates from the 13th century but was heavily restored in the 19th century.

The ruins of Rincrew Abbey, which was built for

the Order of St John, lie 3 km/2 mi north of Youghal. Also to the north (5 km/3 mi) are the ruins of Templemichael Castle.

YOUNG, ARTHUR (1741–1820)

English agriculturalist and writer. He visited Ireland on two occasions, in 1776 and 1777, and published the two-part work *A Tour in Ireland with General Observations on the Present State of that Kingdom* (1778), which gives an account of his experiences in Ireland (including a spell as agent on the Kingsborough estate), and also an analysis of the country's economy and society.

The chief advantage of Young's work was its wealth of statistical data, based on his meetings with the leading landed families in the country. He described mainly average, rather than advanced, farming methods in use in Ireland.

YOUNG IRELAND

Romantic nationalist organization, centred on a group of young idealists associated with the *Nation* newspaper from 1844. They sought to create a non-sectarian spirit in an independent Ireland, and promoted Irish cultural nationalism. Young Ireland initially sided with Daniel ⇨O'Connell's Repeal Association, but split over his nonviolent policies and organized a disastrous rebellion in Tipperary in 1848 led by William Smith O'Brien (1803–1864) and Thomas ⇨Meagher. Its failure destroyed Young Ireland, most of the leaders fled abroad or were transported to the penal colonies, but they left a lasting legacy in their concept of a cultural nationalism.

Notable founders of Young Ireland included Thomas ⇨Davis, Charles ⇨Duffy, John Blake Dillon (1816–1866), and Thomas D'Arcy McGee, who returned from the USA in 1845. The group was named for its similarities with other continental nationalist groups, such as the Young Italy organization.

APPENDICES

CHRONOLOGY OF IRELAND

c. **7000 BC** Hunter-gatherers of the Mesolithic (Middle Stone Age) era appear in Ulster, possibly via a land bridge from Scotland. Communities hug coastlines and river passages, avoiding the densely forested hinterlands.

c. **3500 BC** Animal and crop husbandry, weaving, and pottery introduced by Neolithic (New Stone Age) people arriving by sea, probably from Britain. Large areas of forest cleared for cultivation and permanent settlements formed (as at Lough Gur, Limerick).

c. **3000 BC** Earliest **megaliths** constructed, including Boyne Valley passage grave complexes.

c. **2000 BC** Bronze and gold metalworking and new pottery skills are introduced by Bronze Age Beaker people from Western Europe.

c. **300 BC** Iron Age Celtic-speaking people arrive, migrating from Central Europe via France and Britain. Their language, heavily influenced by pre-Celtic dialects, will develop into the Gaelic language.

c. **130–80** First account and map of Ireland (named Isamnium), drawn up by Ptolemy (*c.* 90–168), identifies physical features, kingdoms, and royal centres, and indicates the rich racial and linguistic mixture of Ireland's population; Eblana occupies present site of Dublin.

367 Major offensive on Roman Britain by Irish, Picts, and Saxons. Irish settlement in western Britain includes parts of Wales, Scotland, Cornwall, and Devon.

431 Pope Celestine I (422–32) sends Palladius as bishop to Irish Christians.

432 Traditional date of St **Patrick**'s arrival in Ireland on his mission to convert pagan Gaelic kings to Christianity.

c. **550–680** Growth of **monasteries** in Ireland, including the foundations of Iona and Derry by **Colum Cille**. Iona and Armagh become chief ecclesiastical power centres. Latin and Irish law tracts and literature reveal patriarchal society of clientship and kinship groups supported by mixed farming. Over 60,000 ringforts (farmsteads enclosed by a circular protective wall) are constructed; *raths* feature an earth rampart and ditch; *cashels* have stone walls and foundations.

c. **590** Convention of Druim Ceat regulates the activities of *files* or poets, keepers of oral law and traditions, believed to have semi-mystical powers. The bardic caste had become so numerous and demanding that they had exhausted the generosity of their patrons.

590 Colum Cille (St Columba) begins Irish mission to continental Europe.

7th–8th centuries Ireland's Golden Age: flowering of Irish literature, art, and craft including Old Irish lyric poetry and sagas, metalwork, stone sculpture, and illuminated manuscripts (Book of **Durrow**, Book of **Kells**).

8th–10th centuries Sub-kingdoms within Munster, Connacht, Meath, Leinster, and Ulster struggle for high kingship (king over kings) over their provinces or other rulers. The Uí Néill dynasty, self-styled descendants of legendary kings of Tara, dominate northwest and midland provinces; rival branches fight for overkingship of Uí Néill kingdoms; overkings attempt high kingship of all Ireland. Viking invasions and settlement from late 8th century attract retaliation, but alliances are fostered for political purposes.

c. **700–900** Eóganacht dynasty of east Munster dominate Munster, fostering close clerical connections to extend power; they claim to be the most Christian kings in Ireland.

721–42 Cathal mac Finguine, Eóganacht high king of Munster; conducts successful wars against Uí Néill.

*c.***725** Uí Briúin dynasty gain dominance in Connacht.

734 Flaithbertach mac Loingsig abdicates overkingship of the Uí Néill; his line, the Cenél Conaill, is excluded from further supremacy.

743 Clann Cholmáin, southern branch of Uí Néill, achieve overkingship of Uí Néill kingdoms.

*c.***750** Armagh under Uí Néill control.

795 First Viking raids on Iona, Rathlin, Inishmurray, and Inishbofin.

c. **800** Uí Néill dominate north Leinster.

820–47 Feidlimid MacCrimthainne, Eóganacht high king of Munster; he successfully challenges church power, plunders monasteries, and raids Uí Néill territory.

836–842 Vikings raid deep inland, and establish coastal bases. Large Viking fleets overwinter by the Boyne, Liffey, and Lough Neagh.

c. **841** Vikings conquer and establish fortified harbour at Dubh-linn, which merges with Baile Átha Cliath north of the Liffey to form Dublin.

842 First reported Viking–Irish alliance.

846–62 Reign of Máel Sechnaill I, powerful Uí Néill overking; he presses provincial high kings for recognition as king of Ireland.

866 Áed Finnliath, northern Uí Néill king, clears north coast of Viking bases.

914–50 Second wave of Viking raids begins with arrival of great fleet at Waterford. Trading centres, founded by Norse merchants and sailors, advance sailing and trading practice in Ireland, and establish Dublin as a great European trading city.

980 Máel Sechnaill II becomes Uí Néill overking.

975–1014 Brian Bóruma, of the Dál Cais of north Munster, is high king of Munster and becomes is high king of Ireland from 1002.

c. **997** Norse establish mint in Dublin.

997 Máel Sechnaill II and Brian Bóruma divide Ireland.

999 Battle of Gelenn Máma; Leinster Irish and Dublin Norse defeated by Brian Bóruma; Sitric Silkenbeard, king of Dublin, surrenders.

1002 Brian Bóruma, with Dublin Norse support, displaces Máel Sechnaill II, who submits and concedes the high kingship (domination of all Ireland achieved by 1011).

1014 Battle of **Clontarf**: large Norse contingent, with Leinster Irish allies, defeated decisively by Munster Irish. Brian Bóruma killed, having failed to consolidate kingship of Ireland as a permanent institution.

1086–1114 Reign of Muirchertach O'Brien, High King of Munster. O'Brien dominates most of Ireland, briefly banishes Connacht dynasty (1095), negotiates with king of Norway and Anglo-Normans.

12th century Church reorganized into dioceses; national church created under the primacy of Armagh (1152). New surge of monasticism begins; foreign orders take over; decline of old monastic schools destroys social, economic, and cultural base of Irish learning. Norman colonization begins.

1106–56 Turlough O'Connor, High King of Connacht, subjugates Munster to become dominant king in Ireland.

1142 Foundation of first Cisterican house and foreign order in Ireland at Mellifont.

1156 Muirchertach Mac Lochlainn, Uí Néill overking, allies with Dermot **MacMurrough**, High King of Leinster, to hold Dublin against Rory **O'Connor**, High King of Connacht.

1166–67 Dermot MacMurrough, banished by O'Connor, seeks aid from **Henry II** of England. Authorized to recruit support in Wales, he opens Ireland to expansive Norman feudalism.

1169 Norman invasion begins in south Wexford with arrival of Anglo-Norman military leaders, FitzStephen, FitzGerald, and others. Dermot MacMurrough restored to kingship of Leinster.

1170–71 Strongbow (Richard de Clare, Earl of Pembroke) takes Waterford; Dublin falls to MacMurrough and Anglo-Norman allies. Strongbow marries MacMurrough's daughter and succeeds MacMurrough as king of Leinster. The threatened establishment of an independent Norman power on his western shore prompts Henry II belatedly to withdraw his consent to the invasion force.

1171–72 Henry II lands large army at Waterford to take control; receives submission of Anglo-Norman leaders, Irish bishops, and most Irish kings.

1175 Treaty of Windsor recognizes Rory O'Connor as high king of all Ireland outside Leinster, Meath, and the environs of Waterford, ruling as a vassal of Henry II.

1177 Henry II's son Prince John made lord of Ireland (first visit 1185).

13th century Anglo-Norman lords colonize profitable sites and reserve large personal demesnes. Planned towns created. Immigrants arrive from England, Wales, France, and Flanders. Remaining Irish nobles generally confined to inferior tracts; some Irish landowners reduced to serfdom. Irish kings refused security of succession. Increasing militarization occurs in Gaelic territories; all sides hire any roving mercenary bands (whether Irish, Anglo-Norman, or Scots) and adopt military contracts with native chiefs.

*c.***1200–1600** Classical Irish period in literature; *Book of Ballymote* (*c.*1384), *Book of Lismore* (1500) produced.

1210 John, king of England, makes his second visit to Ireland. Lordship of Meath, earldom of Ulster, and honor of Limerick (former kingdom of Thomond) confiscated by English crown, stalling the growing power of Anglo-Norman (Anglo-Irish) nobility.

1224 Cathal Croibhdearg O'Connor, last independent king of Connacht dies. Dominicans become first mendicant friars in Ireland, followed in same year by Franciscans.

1226 Leading Anglo-Irish baron Richard de Burgh (d.1243) begins invasion of Connacht, granted to his father William de Burgh (d. 1205) by English king John in about 1195; conquest completed 1235.

1257–1262 Widespread revolt in Irish kingdoms. Godfrey O'Donnell, King of Tír Conaill, devastates Norman Sligo; Conor O'Brien and his son Tadhg defeat Normans of Thomond.

1260 Battle of Down: crown justiciar defeats O'Connor and O'Neill kings; death of Brian O'Neill, self-proclaimed 'King of the kings of Ireland'.

1261 Battle of Callan: Finghin McCarthy (Mac Carthaig) victorious over crown justiciar and Norman lords in Kerry, but is defeated himself (1262).

1264 Earldom of Ulster bestowed on Walter de Burgh, lord of Connacht.

14th century Gaelic resurgence occurs. Every native ruler is legally tenant of an Anglo-Norman magnate or the crown, but in practice enjoys great liberty and the allegiance of numerous minor chieftains. By 1327 almost half the colonized lands are held by absentee landowners; resident Anglo-Irish complain of decaying defences and administrative incompetence.

1315 Edward **Bruce** invades Ireland; in 1316 he is proclaimed king of Ireland by Irish allies.

1318 Battle of Faughart: Edward Bruce killed by Anglo-Irish forces.

1333 Murder of William de Burgh, 'Brown Earl' of Ulster. Crown loses control of Connacht and Irish chiefs in Ulster.

1348–49 Black Death spreads from east coast ports; depopulation and depression cause marginal lands to be abandoned; colonists of all classes migrate back to England; landlords increasingly dependent on Irish tenants.

1366 Statutes of Kilkenny ban the adoption of Irish language by English settlers and prohibit marriage between the settlers and the Irish.

1394–95 Richard II's expedition to Ireland defeats Leinster Irish; nearly all Irish and rebel Anglo-Irish leaders submit to his authority.

15th century Area under royal administration (English Pale) shrinks to the eastern counties of Louth, Meath, Dublin, and Kildare. The Pale, a fortified earthern rampart, protects the eastern half of each county. Growth in cultural uniformity; Anglo-Irish leaders offer patronage to Irish bards and historians to stress their Irish roots; Irish literature favours adaptations of English and European texts.

1414–47 Protracted feud between factions of John **Talbot**, Earl of Shrewsbury, and James Butler, 4th Earl of Ormond, for control of royal government.

1423 Observant movement opens first priory in Connacht with mission of spiritual renewal; their friars' influence spreads rapidly in Gaelic areas.

1449 Richard of York, heir to Meath, Ulster, and Connacht lands, arrives as king's lieutenant.

1460 Parliament at Drogheda upholds Richard of York's authority against Henry VI and reaffirms supremacy of Irish parliament. Richard of York killed in Wars of the Roses.

1479–1513 Gerald Mór Fitzgerald, 8th Earl of Kildare, preferred candidate of the Anglo-Irish, is appointed lord deputy of Ireland (the king's representative in Ireland).

1494 Kildare dismissed by Henry VII following Anglo-Irish support for Lambert Simnel (1478) and Perkin Warbeck (1492), pretenders to the English throne (Kildare reappointed 1496). Lord deputy Edward Poynings establishes **Poynings's Law**, making all English parliamentary legislation applicable to Ireland.

16th century Prolonged delegation of royal authority in Ireland to Anglo-Irish aristocrats leads to formation of political factions and increasing militarization as rival Irish and Anglo-Irish vie for control. Ulster makes increasing use of Scots mercenaries. Henry VIII and Tudor successors consolidate their hold over the Pale, anxious to prevent Ireland being used as a base for Spanish or French attacks. Reformation in Ireland takes place; Old English Catholics refuse to comply spiritually but most continue to support crown in temporal matters. Tudor **plantations** begin.

1504 Battle of Knocktoe: Kildare defeats Burke of Clanricard, and O'Brien, completing his dominance over the Irish and Anglo-Irish.

1513 Gerald **Fitzgerald**, 9th Earl of Kildare, made lord deputy.

1534–36 Fitzgerald summoned to England, leaving his son Lord Offaly (Silken Thomas) as vice-deputy. His death in the Tower of London sparks a rebellion against English rule by his son, who is arrested with his five uncles (all executed 1537).

1536–37 Meeting of Irish Reformation parliament: **Church of Ireland** established; supremacy of English king Henry VIII and suppression of monasteries proposed. Observant Friars lead opposition to changes in the church; Old English Catholics send their sons abroad for education and refuse to attend the state church.

1539 Dissolution of monasteries within the Pale begins. Geraldine League formed by northern and southern Anglo-Irish to protect Kildare child heir.

1541 Kingdom of Ireland officially enacted under

English sovereignty; Henry VIII declared king of Ireland by Dublin parliament. Integration of Gaelic lordships proceeds with the **surrender and regrant** programme, whereby Irish lords revoke their Gaelic title, assume an English one, and gain a royal grant of their lands. Land confiscated from dissolved monasteries and rebel lords redistributed by Anthony St Leger (lord deputy 1540–48) to establish crown patronage outside Old English Catholic factions.

1542 First Jesuit mission to Ireland contributes to the Catholic revival.

1547–53 Edward VI begins establishment of doctrinal reformation in Ireland. Introduction of Protestant liturgy and bishops provokes hostile reaction amongst previously conformist clergy and laity. Inauguration of garrison policy to fortify the Pale.

1553 Accession of Mary Tudor who pursues untroubled restoration of Catholicism.

1557 Military plantation in Laois and Offaly, renamed Queen's and King's counties.

1560 Reformation parliament following accession of Elizabeth I (1558); Act of Supremacy and Act of Uniformity re-establishes Anglican church. English monarch declared supreme governor of Church of Ireland; all citizens to attend parish church on Sunday and worship using Book of Common Prayer. English-born Protestants begin to fill government posts.

1562–67 Shane O'Neill, lord of Tyrone, at war with crown in Ulster over title to the earldom.

1566–67 Henry Sidney appointed lord deputy of Ireland; crown campaigns in Ulster; Tyrone killed at Cushendun by MacDonalds. Sidney attempts to control Munster by arresting the Earl of Desmond.

1569–73 First Desmond revolt. Following imprisonment of the Earl of Desmond, his captain general, James Fitzmaurice Fitzgerald, raises rebellion against the crown assisted by other Old English Catholic dissidents; they offer allegiance to Philip II of Spain. Release of Earl of Desmond ends revolt.

1571 William FitzWilliam appointed governor of Ireland. First book in Irish printed: *Aibidil Gaoidheilge & Caiticiosma*, a Gaelic alphabet and catechism by J Kearney.

1573–76 Private colonization continues in Ulster; Earl of Essex is among the venturers. Sidney (reappointed 1576) launches conciliatory policy, halting any further private colonization. James Fitzmaurice Fitzgerald (in exile from 1575) seeks French and Spanish aid to liberate Ireland.

1579–83 Second Desmond revolt in Munster, aided by

Catholic forces (papal and Spanish) under James Fitzmaurice Fitzgerald. Separate rebellion occurs in Leinster, led by James Eustace, Viscount Baltinglas, and Feagh Mac Hugh **O'Byrne**, and supported by discontented Palesmen. Lord deputy Arthur Lord Grey de Wilton appointed to put down revolts; suffers defeat at Glenmalure, Wicklow, but ousts the continental force at Smerwick; Earl of Desmond killed (1583).

1585 Munster property forfeited by Desmond and his supporters. **Composition** of Connacht devised by the president of Connacht.

1586 Plantation of **Munster** by English and Scottish settlers.

1592 Hugh O'Donnell, Earl of Tyrconnell, seeks to expel English officials from the lordship of Tyrconnell. O'Donnell and Hugh Maguire, lord of Fermanagh, oppose imposition of composition on their territories. **Trinity College**, first Irish university, established in Dublin.

1595 Rebellion of Hugh O'Neill, Earl of Tyrone, and the Northern Confederacy. Rebellion in Leinster and Connacht by dissatisfied lords.

1598–1600 Tyrone annihilates crown forces at Yellow Ford, Ulster. Plantation of Munster is overthrown. Charles Blount, Baron **Mountjoy**, made governor.

17th century Large-scale confiscation of lands and plantations of Protestant Scottish and English settlers take place from the mid-17th century. Irish and Old English Catholics are relocated to less prosperous regions, and anti-Catholic penal codes enacted.

1601 Spanish fleet at Kinsale joined by rebel army from Ulster under Tyrone and O'Donnell; alliance is defeated by Mountjoy.

1603 Tyrone surrenders; general amnesty follows Treaty of Mellifont. Accession of James I leads to enforcement of English law in Ireland, especially Ulster.

1605 Arthur **Chichester** made lord deputy. Jesuits and seminary priests are expelled and Dublin merchants pressed to conform in religion.

1607 Flight of the Earls: following government judicial investigation of Ulster lordships, Tyrone and Tyrconnell flee to Spain with 90 other Irish chiefs; their lands are forfeited.

1608–10 Ulster plantation prepared; six confiscated counties surveyed. Plantation of Derry and Coleraine County agreed by City of London.

1613 Irish parliament endorses plantation scheme in Ulster, and provides increased representation for settlers. Derry is incorporated as Londonderry.

1621 Smaller private plantations begin in Leinster (Longford and Wexford).

1626–28 Charles I offers Graces (tacit toleration of Catholicism) in return for Irish subsidy. Native Irish are permitted as tenants in plantation settlements.

1633–40 Thomas **Wentworth**, Earl of Strafford, lord deputy; intends to proceed with plantation of Connacht and disregard Graces.

1641 Strafford executed in England on a charge of treason. Ulster rising begins; Catholic–Gaelic rebels kill Protestant settlers.

1642 English parliament passes Adventurers Act to facilitate Irish suppression. Robert Munro's Scottish Covenanter army lands in Ulster; Owen Roe **O'Neill** lands in Donegal to form an Ulster Catholic army. English Civil War begins. The Catholic **Confederation of Kilkenny**, an independent parliament, forms.

1643 Marquis of Ormond, appointed lord lieutenant by Charles I, negotiates truce with confederates.

1645–46 Papal envoy Archbishop Rinuccini at Kilkenny aims to re-establish Catholicism as the state religion; confederates encouraged to reject peace. O'Neill's confederates defeat Monro at Benburb, County Tyrone.

1647 Parliamentary forces under Michael Jones land near Dublin; Ormond surrenders Dublin and confederates are defeated in County Meath.

1649 Execution of Charles I. Oliver **Cromwell** arrives in Ireland, and takes Drogheda, Wexford, and New Ross.

1650–51 Henry Ireton appointed lord deputy and Cromwellian conquest proceeds; Limerick besieged.

1652–55 Implementation of Cromwellian plantations. Down Survey maps lands for soldiers; transplantation of old English and Gaelic Irish to Connacht and Clare.

1660 Restoration of Charles II following death of Cromwell (1658). Cromwellian conquest upheld, but declares land will be restored to 'innocent papists'.

1662 Marquis of Ormond reappointed lord lieutenant. Act of Settlement (1662) commission hears claims for Irish lands.

1665 Act of Explanation: Cromwellian settlers to surrender one third of their holdings to restored Catholics.

1666 Act of Uniformity: schoolmasters to be licensed by the Established Church.

1673 Test Act: officeholders required to take Anglican sacrament; Catholic clergy to be banished; religious houses and schools closed.

1678–81 Titus Oates's 'popish' plot in England precipitates measures against public Catholic worship in Ireland. Irish Jesuit and primate of Ireland Oliver **Plunkett** executed in London.

1685 Accession of James II. Publication of *Dublin News-letter*, first Irish newspaper.

1687–91 Richard **Talbot**, Earl of Tyrconnell and Jacobite lord deputy, replaces Protestant officials with Catholics.

1688 William (III) of Orange invited to accept English throne; James II flees to France.

1689 Arrival of James II; unsuccessful siege of Londonderry; James II's Catholic parliament in Dublin revokes anti-Catholic laws.

1690 French force enters Cork. William III joins Danish force near Belfast, and defeats James II at the Battle of the **Boyne**, securing the Protestant succession; James II escapes to France. William takes Dublin, but sieges of Athlone and Limerick fail.

1691 Baron van Ginkel, Dutch commander of the Williamite forces, takes Athlone, and defeats Jacobite force at Aughrim. His suppression of Galway and Limerick leads to the Treaty of **Limerick**. Land confiscations follow, and Catholics are excluded from Irish parliament and office.

1692–1700 Williamite land settlement completes dispossession of Catholic landholders.

1695 Anti-Catholic penal legislation begins, restricting rights in education and armsbearing; Catholic clergy banished. Catholics hold less than 15% of Irish land (by 1778 barely 5%). Illegal 'hedge schools' continue to teach Irish language and culture.

1696–1700 Linen manufacture is encouraged by duty-free access to England and subsidies. Acts concerning the export of Irish woollens impose prohibitive import duties on trade to England, and ban Irish woollen exports elsewhere to protect English wool market.

18th century Dublin ranked Europe's fifth largest city. Laws passed in the Protestant-only parliament still need approval from England; and pressure begins from the Protestant ascendancy (ruling class) to gain independence. Outbreak of French Revolution (1789) and Franco-Irish republican alliances and rebellions cause ruling classes to reaffirm connection to Britain, leading to the Act of **Union**.

1704 Test Act restricts presence of Catholics and Protestant dissenters in landholding and public offices.

1718 First large-scale **emigration** from Ulster to American colonies (second 1729). First charitable infirmary in British Isles built in Dublin.

1719 Toleration Act exempts Protestant Dissenters from Test Act.

1720 'Sixth of George I': Declaratory Act asserting British parliament's right to legislate for Ireland.

1726 Publication of Jonathan **Swift**'s *Gulliver's Travels*.

1728 Act removing franchise (right to vote) from Catholics.

1740–41 Famine mortality estimated at 20,000–40,000.

1741 Handel's *Messiah* first performed in Dublin.

1759 Removal of restrictions on importing Irish cattle into Britain. Arthur **Guinness** leases brewery in Dublin; first brew of dark stout 1799.

1760 **Catholic Committee** formed by John Curry and Charles O'Connor in Dublin.

1761 Beginnings of Whiteboy movement (secret agrarian associations) in Munster; property damaged in night raids.

1766 Execution of Father Nicholas **Sheehy**; Tumultuous Risings Act against Whiteboyism.

1772 Relief Act allows Catholics to lease boglands.

1775 Rise to prominence of Henry **Grattan** leader of (Protestant) Patriot Party for reform of the Irish parliament.

1778 First Volunteer force forms in Belfast to guard against invasion and preserve law and order, while regular troops are posted to the American Revolution; other Volunteer detachments are established in a variety of locations. A mainly Protestant middle-class movement, they rapidly evolve into a political force and campaign against colonial restrictions on Irish trade. Relief Act allows Catholics leaseholding and inheritance rights.

1779 Volunteers parade in Dublin and agitate for free trade; trade restrictions are repealed. Belfast cotton industry begins as poor-relief measure.

1780 British restrictions on Irish trade removed. Sacramental Test Act for dissenters abolished.

1782 Convention of Volunteers at Dungannon; Irish parliament's legislative independence conceded by British parliament, completed in the **Renunciation Act** (1783). Relief Acts allow Catholics to own freeholds outside parliamentary boroughs and have access to educational rights.

1791 Protestant republican Wolfe **Tone** publishes his 'Argument on behalf of the Catholics of Ireland'; foundation of Society of **United Irishmen** in Belfast and Dublin. First convicts transported from Ireland arrive in New South Wales, Australia.

1792 Relief Act allows Catholics to practise law.

1793 Volunteers suppressed in Ulster; Convention Act prohibits assemblies and an Irish militia established. Relief Act admits Catholics to parliamentary franchise.

1794 Publication of the United Irishmen's plan for parliamentary reform leads to their suppression in Dublin.

1795 Protestant **Orange Order** established in County Armagh. **Fitzwilliam episode**.

1796 Insurrection Act imposes death penalty on people administering illegal oaths; special measures permitted in 'disturbed areas' include curfews, the suspension of trial by jury, and sweeping powers of search and detention. Tone accompanies a French invasion fleet in Bantry Bay.

1797 Gen Gerard Lake, commander of the government forces in Ulster, conducts policy of repression to disarm the province, severely weakening the organization of the radical **United Irishmen**. Election of last Irish parliament.

1798 Gen Lake suppresses United Irishmen in the counties around Dublin. **Rebellion of 1798**; United Irishmen rise in Leinster and Ulster, and French force under Jean-Joseph-Amable Humbert campaign in Connacht. French squadron suffers defeat off Lough Swilly; Tone captured in November and commits suicide.

19th century Catholic–Gaelic revival follows the scourge of the Great **Famine** (historically 1845–49, now considered to have lasted until 1852) with increasing emancipation, successful agitation to secure tenant rights, and movement to home rule. Protestant northeast unites to protect its status and privilege.

1800 Public opposition to union from Daniel **O'Connell**, and Orange lodges. Act for legislative union passed by British and Irish parliaments.

1801 Act of **Union** joins Ireland to Great Britain, creating the United Kingdom of Great Britain and Ireland; transference of Ireland's government to Westminster marks the end of independent Irish parliament.

1803 Rising of Irish nationalist leader Robert **Emmet** in Dublin followed by his trial and execution.

1811 Beginning of sustained agricultural depression.

1821 First population census (6,801,827).

1822 Irish Constabulary Act; country police forces and salaried magistracy established.

1823 Catholic Association founded by O'Connell to campaign for Catholic political rights.

1828 O'Connell's election as MP for County Clare forces granting of Catholic right to sit in parliament.

1829 Catholic Emancipation Act permits Catholics to hold senior government office, to sit on the Privy Council, to be a judge, king's counsel, or county sheriff, and to be a member of parliament; raises freehold franchises from 40 shillings to 10 pounds.

1831 Tithe war begins: sporadic violent resistance to church tithes occurs.

1838 Tithe Act (abolishing payment) removes a major source of discontent. Foundation of **temperance movement** inspired by Theobald **Matthew** in Cork; an estimated 5 million Irish pledge total abstinence by 1842.

1840–44 O'Connell's Repeal Association founded; 'monster meetings' held for repeal of union. Radical **Young Ireland** movement formed.

1845 Potato blight in 11 counties. Beginning of the the Great **Famine** and consequent mass emigration, mainly to North America; population reduced by 20%. Cereal harvests remain excellent (Ireland continues to export), but prices too high for the poor. Irish-Americans provide major financial support towards later nationalist struggles.

1846 Public Works Act to relieve distress and Corn Laws repealed. First deaths from starvation reported in October.

1847 Worst year of famine; malnutrition-related disease rife. Government soup kitchens instituted February–September; the burden of further relief is placed on inadequate local workhouses.

1848 Abortive rebellion by Young Ireland movement in Munster. Encumbered Estates Acts facilitates sale of land; evictions from agricultural holdings begin.

1849 Historic date for the end of the Great Famine.

1850 Tenant League formed in Dublin to champion tenants' rights. Irish Franchise Act extends voters from 61,000 to 165,000.

1852 General election: 40 MPs promise support for tenant-right questions. Tenant League in Dublin adopts policy of independent opposition in parliament. Great Famine actually ends.

1853 Foundation of the Catholic University of Ireland in Dublin.

1857 Sectarian rioting in Belfast.

1858 James **Stephens** founds the **Irish Republican Brotherhood**.

1859 Fenian movement, sister organization of the Irish Republican Brotherhood, founded in the USA.

1866 Fenian raids in Canada. Archbishop Paul Cullen becomes the first Irish cardinal.

1867 Fenian risings (Kerry, Dublin, Cork, Limerick, Tipperary, and Clare) fail to establish independent republic.

1869 Disestablishment of the Church of Ireland by British prime minister William Gladstone.

1870 First of Gladstone's three Irish **Land Acts** recognizes tenant rights but fails to halt agrarian disorder. Home Government Association (Home Rule League) founded by Isaac **Butt** initiates idea of Irish **home rule**.

1874 General election; Home Rule League wins 59 seats and adopts policy of obstruction; Butt's home rule motion defeated.

1875 Charles Stewart **Parnell** elected MP for County Meath.

1876 Irish Republican Brotherhood withdraws support for home rule. Society for the Preservation of the Irish Language formed.

1877 Parnell elected president of the Home Rule Confederation of Great Britain.

1879 Irish National **Land League** founded by Michael Davitt to support peasants' rights of tenancy.

1879–82 Land war: tenants defy their landlords en masse for the first time. Land agents and tenants of evicted properties suffer 'boycott' (after land agent Charles **Boycott**); widespread evictions and disorders in Mayo and west Cork.

1880 Parnell chairman of Irish Parliamentary Party (Irish nationalists), dominated by Catholic groups. Boycotts against landlords unwilling to agree fair rents.

1881 Second Land Act restricts rents and grants tenants security of tenure; greeted with hostility. Parnell and other nationalist leaders imprisoned but issue 'No Rent Manifesto'. Land League proclaimed unlawful.

1882 Kilmainham Treaty between Liberal government and Parnell agrees conciliation, but cooperation is threatened by the **Phoenix Park murders** of chief secretary Cavendish and under-secretary Burke.

1884 First woman graduate in Ireland at Royal University.

1885 Franchise reform gives Home Rulers 85 seats in new parliament and balance between Liberals and Tories.

1886 Ulster Loyalist Anti-Repeal Committee organizes demonstrations against home rule; Gladstone's Home Rule Bill defeated.

1889 Parnell cited in a divorce case, though liaison with Katharine O'Shea, (court hearing 1890), and suffers political ruin; home rule movement splits.

1892 Ulster Convention opposes home rule. Irish Education Act abolishes fees; school compulsory for ages 6–14. Belfast Labour Party formed (first in Ireland).

1893 Gaelic League founded by Douglas **Hyde** to revive Irish literature and language. Gladstone's second Home Rule Bill defeated in the House of Lords.

1897 First Oireachtas and Feis Ceoil (Irish literary and music festivals) held.

1898 United Irish League founded, a radical agrarian organization. Women granted limited municipal franchise.

1899 Foundation of **Irish Literary Theatre**, and first issue of *An Claidheamh Soluis*, the Gaelic League's official newsletter.

20th century Establishment of Independent Irish state; partition; separation of the six counties of Northern Ireland. The political role of the Catholic Church at first dominates then diminishes in the Republic.

1900–18 John **Redmond** made leader of the Irish Parliamentary Party and United Irish League; 82 MPs elected; reunited nationalists press for home rule.

1903 St Patrick's Day declared a bank holiday.

1904 Abbey Theatre established in Dublin to promote works by new Irish writers; a major catalyst in early 20th-century nationalist literary revival.

1905 Ulster Unionist Council formed, basis of **Ulster Unionist Party**. Redmond secures promise of home rule from Liberal leader Campbell-Bannerman. **Sinn Féin** political party founded by Arthur **Griffith**; aims to create united republican Ireland.

1906 Bill for devolution of power to Ireland rejected by nationalists.

1909 Health Resorts and Watering-Places Act, first legislation related to tourism.

1910 General election; Irish nationalists hold balance. Edward **Carson** made leader of Irish Unionist Party; aims to mobilize resistance to home rule in Ulster.

1912 Passage of third Home Rule Bill through the House of Commons prompts northern Protestant protests; Catholic workers expelled from Belfast shipyards. Over 200,000 Protestant men and women sign the Ulster covenants, pledging opposition to home rule by all means necessary.

1913 Formation of (Protestant) Ulster Volunteers, and the southern (Catholic) **Irish Volunteers** and Irish Citizen Army. Home Rule Bill defeated twice in House of Lords. Ulster Unionist Council sets up mechanism for provisional government of Ulster. Importation of arms forbidden by royal proclamation.

1914 Curragh 'Mutiny' casts doubt on reliability of British troops against Ulster unionists. Illegal importation of arms by Ulster Volunteers and Irish Volunteers. Buckingham Palace conference fails to resolve Irish problem. Enactment and suspension of home rule following outbreak of World War I. Ulster Volunteers form the 36th (Ulster) Division. Irish nationalist movement splits as the Irish Republican Brotherhood considers insurrection during war, while Redmond calls on Irish Volunteers to serve the allies. Roger **Casement** seeks German support for Irish independence.

1915 Irish Republican Brotherhood reorganized and military council formed, joined by Patrick **Pearse**.

1916 Easter Rising: Irish Republic proclaimed by Irish Republican Brotherhood and Sinn Féin leaders in Dublin and martial law declared. Pearse orders surrender to British forces, and 15 rebels are executed. Ulster Division decimated at the Battle of Somme. Lloyd George fails in his proposal to implement home rule, with temporary exclusion of six Ulster counties. Anti-Partition League formed in Londonderry. Irish Convention established by Lloyd George to improvise a settlement; boycotted by Sinn Féin and opposed by Ulster unionists, its proceedings were ineffectual. Éamon **de Valera** is elected leader of Sinn Féin and Irish Volunteers.

1918 Men over 18 and women over 30 gain vote; electorate rises from 700,000 in 1910 to just under 2 million.

1919 Sinn Féin forms the **Dáil Éireann**, an unofficial national assembly, and declares independence; de Valera is elected president. Michael **Collins** reorganizes Irish Volunteers into the **Irish Republican Army** (IRA), as the militant wing of Sinn Féin, and the **Anglo–Irish War** begins.

1920 Royal Irish Constabulary recruit **Black and Tans** (British soldiers). The Government of Ireland Act introduces partition between two home rule states, provoking riots in Derry and Belfast; expulsion of Catholic workers from Belfast shipyards; and republican boycott of Belfast. Violent confrontations with British forces include Dublin's **Bloody Sunday**

when government forces opened fire on spectators at a Gaelic football match, following the IRA's assassination of British secret agents; 12 civilians are killed.

1921 Anglo–Irish War ends. Creation of **Irish Free State**: **Anglo-Irish Treaty** (December) gives southern Ireland dominion status within the Commonwealth; six Ulster counties (those with minority Catholic populations) receive limited self-government within the UK as Northern Ireland (NI). George V opens NI parliament in Belfast; James **Craig** prime minister. Truce with IRA called.

1922 Irish Free State general election produces pro-treaty majority; de Valera supports the anti-treaty IRA faction, now known as the Irregulars. Irish Civil War begins; IRA Irregulars in Dublin are destroyed by national army forces. Irish Free State Constitution Act approved without NI; Cosgrave elected president of Dáil Éireann, and Timothy **Healy** first governor-general. Irish language to be taught daily in national schools. NI police receive special powers and inaugurate the **Royal Ulster Constabulary** (RUC). James **Joyce**'s *Ulysses* published in Paris, banned for obscenity in the UK and USA.

1923 Civil war ends; de Valera orders IRA to dump arms. Cosgrave founds **Cumann na nGaedheal**. Free State admitted to League of Nations. W B **Yeats** receives Nobel Prize for Literature. Women aged 21–30 gain vote in Irish Free State; in 1928 women over 21 gain vote in Northern Ireland.

1924 Free State army reorganization and cutbacks lead to mutiny.

1925 Partition confirmed by tripartite agreement between the UK government, Northern Ireland parliament, and Irish Free State; border remains as set out under the terms of the Anglo-Irish Treaty.

1926 De Valera founds **Fianna Fáil**. George Bernard **Shaw** receives Nobel Prize for Literature.

1927 General election: Fianna Fáil largest opposition party. Separate Free State currency created.

1929 Proportional representation abolished in NI.

1930 Irish Labour Party separates from Trades Union Congress.

1931 Free State bans IRA. Statute of Westminster extends autonomy of Free State.

1932 General election won by Fianna Fáil; de Valera president. De Valera chairs League of Nations assembly at Geneva. **Stormont** parliament buildings officially opened in NI.

1933 National Guard (**Blueshirts**) formed. Eoin **O'Duffy**, leader of the Blueshirts, forms the United Ireland Party (**Fine Gael**) with William **Cosgrave** as president.

1935 Importation and sale of contraceptives forbidden in Free State.

1936 Free State declares IRA illegal following atrocities. Passing of External Relations and Constitutional Amendment Acts in Free State further weakens links with crown.

1937 Constitution of **Éire** replaces Irish Free State.

1938 Douglas **Hyde** appointed first president of Éire. Anglo-Irish Agreement settles trade disputes, treaty ports restored to Éire. UK agrees to subsidize NI social welfare payments.

1939–45 Éire neutral in World War II; NI excluded from conscription. IRA bombing campaign in England from 1939 (ends March 1940).

1940 Death of IRA hunger strikers in Éire. Anglo-Irish military consultations followed by the imposition of economic sanctions. De Valera rejects Winston Churchill's offer to recognize principle of united Ireland in return for Éire's entry into the war.

1941 Intensive German air raids on Belfast and Dublin.

1942 Stationing of US troops in NI condemned by de Valera; naval base established in Derry.

1945 Congress of Irish Unions formed. De Valera declares Éire a republic.

1946 NI Elections and Franchise Act increases business vote in local elections. NI National Insurance brought in line with Britain.

1948 General election in Éire; Fianna Fáil defeated; coalition government formed under John **Costello** (Fine Gael). National Health Service introduced in NI. Costello repeals External Relations Act, removing Ireland from the British Commonwealth. Interparty government passes Republic of Ireland Act, declaring the **Republic of Ireland**, with Dublin as capital.

1949 Ireland Act passed by the British government reaffirms partition; citizens of the Republic granted special status in the UK and colonies, and the Republic will not be treated as a foreign country in trade and citizenship.

1951 Catholic bishops' opposition to Noel **Browne**'s mother-and-child healthcare scheme, amidst concerns over the possible provision of moral instruction and birth control, leads to resignation of Costello's government; de Valera returns to office. Ernest **Walton** shares Nobel Prize for Physics.

1952 Irish Tourist Board formed.

1953 Health Act provides free mother-and-child care in Republic.

1954 IRA attacks on Armagh military bases.

1955 Republic admitted to United Nations.

1957 Republic general election: de Valera made **Taoiseach** (prime minister), Seamus **O'Kelly** president. Catholics boycott Protestants during an interfaith marriage dispute in County Wexford.

1956–62 Border campaign initiated by IRA.

1958 First Programme for Economic Expansion in Republic of Ireland (others 1963–64, and 1969).

1959 De Valera president of the Republic; Seán **Lemass** Taoiseach. Irish Congress of Trade Unions formed.

1961 Republic's application for EEC membership denied. Republic joins UNESCO.

1963 Terence **O'Neill** prime minister of NI.

1964 Lemass–O'Neill talks held on reconciliation. **Nationalist party** accepts role of official opposition at Stormont.

1966 Jack Lynch succeeds Lemass as Taoiseach. Ratification of Anglo-Irish trade agreement signals Ireland's departure from protectionist economic policies (favoured since the 17th century, and vigorously pursued from 1932); UK and Ireland agree to establish a joint free-trade area by the mid-1970s.

1967 Northern Ireland Civil Rights Association (NICRA) founded.

1968 First **civil rights movement** march clashes with police in Londonderry. Opposition to O'Neill's proposals for eliminating discrimination against Catholics in local government, housing, and franchise.

1969 People's Democracy march from Belfast to Derry attacked by militant Protestants; British troops brought in to aid police following severe rioting in Belfast and Derry. Chichester-Clark becomes prime minister of Stormont parliament, and Bernadette Devlin (Unity MP for Mid-Ulster) elected to Westminster. Samuel **Beckett** awarded Nobel Prize for Literature.

1970 Breakaway divisions form within IRA and Sinn Féin; IRA splits into Official and **Provisional** wings. Ian **Paisley** takes seat at Stormont. New NI bodies include the **Alliance Party of Northern Ireland**; Ulster Defence Regiment; and the **Social Democratic and Labour Party** (SDLP), formed from moderate nationalist groups.

1971 Mary **Robinson**'s bill to liberalize law on contraceptives rejected by senate (Seanad Éireann) of Republic. In NI Brian **Faulkner** becomes prime minister at Stormont, internment is reintroduced, and Ian Paisley founds the **Democratic Unionist Party**.

1972 **Direct rule** imposed in NI under British Conservative secretary of state William Whitelaw, following Derry's **Bloody Sunday** (13 civilian marchers killed by soldiers from the British army) and bombing of Aldershot barracks. Belfast IRA's Bloody Friday explosions kill 11. Republic expunges 'special position' of Catholic church from its constitution.

1973 Republic of Ireland and UK join EEC. Republic general election results in Fine Gael–Labour coalition. Referendum in NI, boycotted by SDLP, produces majority for continuance of partition. NI consitutional acts introduce a 78-member assembly elected by proportional representation and a power-sharing executive appointed by the British secretary of state. Sunningdale agreement signed; UK, Republic, and NI executive affirm rights; framework established for cross-border cooperation.

1974 NI executive condemned by United Ulster Unionist Council (UUUC), who take the majority of NI seats under the new Labour government; Merlyn Rees appointed secretary of state for NI. NI executive resigns following a general strike enforced by the Ulster Workers Council; direct rule is reimposed. Bombing in Dublin, and Guildford and Birmingham pubs. Seán **MacBride** shares Nobel Peace Prize.

1975 Secret talks between NI officials and Provisional Sinn Féin. NI hold elections for new Convention, and internment is suspended.

1976 NI Convention collapses over power-sharing disagreements. British ambassador in Dublin murdered. Peace People formed in Belfast after death of three children in terrorist incident. European Commission of Human Rights finds UK guilty of torture of republican prisoners. Anne Dickson becomes leader of Unionist Party of Northern Ireland and first woman party leader in NI.

1977 UUUC parliamentary coalition dissolved. Republic general election returns a record majority for Fianna Fáil. Peace People founders awarded Nobel Peace Prize.

1978 European Court of Human Rights declares 1971 internees suffered inhuman and degrading treatment, not torture. Rioting occurs in Derry during anniversary celebrations of civil rights marchers; most injuries perpetrated by loyalists on police.

1979 John **Hume** made leader of SDLP. Bomb explosions kill 18 British soldiers at Warrenpoint, and Earl Mountbatten and relations off Sligo. The Republic relaxes its ban on contraceptives. Pope John

Paul II visits Ireland.

1980 Stormont's constitutional conference fails, and NI devolution plan rejected by Unionists and SDLP. Withdrawal of 'special category' status to terrorist prisoners provokes an immediate 'dirty' protest. Thatcher meets with Taoiseach Charles **Haughey** in Dublin.

1981 Paisley holds rallies against Anglo-Irish talks. H-block hunger strikes begin in March; deaths of ten republican hunger-strikers, including Bobby **Sands** elected Sinn Féin Westminster MP, prompt nationalist riots; strikes end in October. IRA bombs British military targets in Europe.

1982 Republic general elections: Fianna Fáil returned in February with minor party support; Fine Gael–Labour coalition succeed in November. Failure of Rolling Devolution proposals from secretary of state James Prior. SDLP refuse to take seats won in the assembly elections. Multiple killings of soldiers at Knightsbridge and Ballykelly, County Derry.

1983 Alliance and Unionist parties reject New Ireland forum set up by the Republic. Unionists hold majority of NI seats in the UK general election; Provisional Sinn Féin take West Belfast. Referendum confirms ban on abortion in Republic, but adds a clause to the constitution asserting the mother's and the foetus's equal right to life.

1984 NI assembly bans extension of 1967 Abortion Act (permitting abortion on medical and psychological grounds) to NI. First extradition of terrorist leader charged with murder to NI. Provisional IRA bombs Conservatives' Brighton conference.

1985 Anglo-Irish agreement at Hillsborough (increase in cross-border cooperation between security forces; Republic given a greater voice in NI's affairs), precipitates massive loyalist protests.

1986 Unionists resign seats over Anglo-Irish Agreement. NI assembly dissolved. Republic referendum confirms ban on divorce.

1987 Republic general election returns minority government. Unionist leaders end boycott of government ministers. IRA bomb kills 11 civilians at Enniskillen's Remembrance Day service.

1988 SDLP–Sinn Féin talks break down. Direct statements by paramilitary representatives banned on UK radio and TV.

1989 Republic general election: Fianna Fáil form their first coalition government with Progressive Democrats; Charles **Haughey** rejected as Taoiseach in favour of Garret **FitzGerald** (Fine Gael). Restrictions on Sinn Féin lifted in NI council elections; widespread calls to suspend Anglo-Irish Agreement after Gerry **Adams** supports IRA right to pursue armed struggle.

1990 Dublin Supreme Court rejects extraditions to the UK. Abolition of capital punishment in Republic proposed. Haughey regains Taoiseach; Mary Robinson elected 7th president of Republic, the first woman to hold the office. Ireland reaches quarter-finals of soccer World Cup in Italy, led by Jack **Charlton**.

1991 Dublin named European City of Culture.

1992 Albert **Reynolds** succeeds Haughey in Fianna Fáil and as Taoiseach. In the **X case**, the Republic's Supreme Court lifts High Court ban on the overseas travel of a pregnant 14-year-old seeking an abortion. Maastricht treaty on European union endorsed by Republic. Ulster Defence Association banned in NI; 3,000th victim of sectarian violence, since Troubles began in 1969, dies.

1993 Fianna Fáil–Labour coalition established under Reynolds; Mary Harney becomes leader of the Progressive Democrats, first woman party leader in Republic. Condoms declassified as contraceptives in measures against AIDS. Downing Street Declaration begins **Northern Ireland peace process**; affirms constitutional change would require majority agreement of population in NI and the Republic.

1994 IRA and loyalist paramilitary groups announce ceasefire; broadcasting ban on Sinn Féin and paramilitary organizations lifted. John **Bruton** becomes Taoiseach over a Fine Gael–Labour–Democratic Left cabinet.

1995 Anglo-Irish 'Framework Document' for all-party peace negotiations; David **Trimble** elected leader of Ulster Unionists. US president Bill Clinton permits Adams to raise funds in USA and later visits NI and Dublin. US senator George Mitchell chairs three-person commission to examine decommissioning of paramilitary groups and all-party talks. Republic approves right to freedom of information on abortion outside the state; a referendum permits civil divorce and remarriage.

1996 End of IRA ceasefire marked by London Docklands bombing. Sinn Féin barred from all-party talks at Stormont because of IRA activities; SDLP leader John **Hume** and Gerry Adams meet IRA leaders. Loyalist terrorists break ceasefire in Belfast.

1997 British Labour MP Mo (Marjorie) **Mowlam** appointed first woman secretary of state for Northern Ireland. Mary McAleese succeeds Mary Robinson as president of Republic. Sinn Féin invited to all-party talks following IRA's resumption of ceasefire. Republic general election leads to a Fianna Fáil–Progressive Democrat coalition under Bertie **Ahern**.

1998 Good Friday agreement (Belfast agreement): Ireland, Britain, and the political parties of NI reach accord over the devolution of a wide range of executive and legislative powers to a NI Assembly; Trimble and Hume share Nobel Peace Prize for their part in the accord. Sinn Féin and Ulster Unionist leaders meet for the first time since 1922. Violence continues as Orange Orders march to celebrate 308th anniversary of the Battle of the Boyne, despite pressure to desist following deaths of three Catholic children in an arson attack. A car bomb kills 28 civilians in Omagh: IRA splinter group, the Real IRA, admit responsibility and announce complete ceasefire; loyalist terrorists admit the random murder of a Catholic man.

1999 Bilateral talks on decommissioning of IRA weapons between Ulster Unionists and Sinn Féin are unsuccessful. Deadline for creation of NI executive pushed back from 10 to 29 March to allow resolution of decommissioning dispute; suspension of NI peace talks until 13 April follows. NI Equality Commission includes 13-year target to end employment imbalance favouring Protestants, and an EU commission considers the future of the RUC. Former US senator Mitchell conducts a review of the Good Friday agreement to facilitate establishment of NI executive. Patten report recommends far-reaching changes to Royal Ulster Constabulary (RUC), including recruitment policies, name, and insignia, plus introduction of a measure of local democratic control. NI Assembly becomes fully operational on 2 December.

2000 NI Assembly suspended on 11 February but reconvened on 30 May following stalemate on the IRA's decommissioning of weapons.

WEB SITES

ABBEY THEATRE
http://www.abbeytheatre.ie/
Official Web site of the National Theatre Society of Ireland, which comprises both the Abbey and Peacock Theatres in Dublin. Featured here are listings of current and future events, a detailed history of the Abbey Theatre, and a selection of links to related theatres and festivals.

ACHILL ISLAND
http://www.achill-island.com/home_nt.htm
Informative guide to Achill Island, County Mayo, that includes information on accommodation, restaurants, and sports facilities. There is also an illustrated history of the island, together with detailed information on cultural attractions and festivals.

ADARE MANOR
http://www.adaremanor.ie/hotel1.html
Features a detailed history of Adare Manor, County Limerick, as well as photographs, a guide to nearby places of interest, and information on the commercial side of the manor.

AHERN, BERTIE
http://www.irlgov.ie/taoiseach/blogs/frmain.htm
Detailed information on the political career of politician Bertie Ahern, the Taoiseach (Irish prime minister) from 1997 and leader of Fianna Fáil from 1994.

ALEXANDER, CECIL FRANCES
http://hymnuts.luthersem.edu/hcompan/writers/alexande.htm
Features a brief biography of the poet and hymn writer, as well as information about a selection of the hymns that she translated.

ALTAN – THE OFFICIAL WEBSITE
http://www.altan.ie
Comprehensive guide to the traditional music band Altan. A detailed biography and discography are featured here, as well as a photo gallery and information on forthcoming live appearances. Fans of the band can leave their messages on the site's guestbook and can e-mail Altan.

AMERICAN CONFERENCE FOR IRISH STUDIES
http://www.acisweb.com
Founded in 1960, this non-profit organization runs conferences, not just for academics, in all aspects of Irish Studies. The site provides extensive links to sites about Ireland.

ANCIENT IRELAND, A–Z OF
http://www.atlanticisland.ie/atlanticisland/arts/flatoz.html
A–Z listing of the features of ancient Irish history and mythology. This site is comprehensive in its descriptions of the people, places, things, and events that make up legends and history. However, the site is not big on multimedia content.

ANTRIM CASTLE GARDENS
http://www.clubi.ie/garden-club/gardens/antrim_castle.html
Includes an illustrated description of the gardens, as well as information on opening times and admission prices.

ANTRIM, COUNTY
http://www.interknowledge.com/northern-ireland/ukiant00.htm
Official Web site of the Northern Ireland tourist office on County Antrim. The Web site describes the history and major attractions of this county; photographs of several of these attractions are illustrated on this page.

ARAN ISLANDS – IRELAND FOR VISITORS
http://goireland.about.com/travel/goireland/library/weekly/aa101799.htm?iam=mt&terms=%2Baran+%2Bislands
Informative guide to the Aran Islands, complete with photographs and links to related Web sites. Also included are articles on the individual islands and places of interest.

ARCHITECTURAL DUBLIN
http://www.archeire.com/archdublin/
Very aesthetically pleasing site on the architectural variety of Dublin. It contains hyperlinked, illustrated sections on buildings from 17th to 20th century, as well as information on major architectural figures, city planning, derivation of street names, and endangered buildings in Ireland's capital.

ARMAGH, COUNTY
http://www.interknowledge.com/northern-ireland/ukiarm00.htm
Official Web site of the Northern Ireland tourist office on County Armagh. The Web site briefly describes the history and major attractions of the county, and photographs of several of these attractions are included on the page.

ARMAGH OBSERVATORY HOME PAGE
http://star.arm.ac.uk/home.html
Historical astronomical observatory in Armagh. Founded in 1790, the observatory was at the forefront of astronomy for over a hundred years, and still remains a highly active educational institution today.

ASHFORD CASTLE
http://www.historic.irishcastles.com/ashford.htm
Features a detailed history of Ashford Castle, County Mayo, together with numerous photographs and a video. Also included are links to related Web sites.

BACON, FRANCIS
http://www.oir.ucf.edu/wm/paint/auth/bacon/
Site at the WebMuseum, Paris, devoted to Francis Bacon, providing biographical details and photographs of his work, including *Head VI* and *Man with Dog*.

BALLYCASTLE, CO ANTRIM, NORTHERN IRELAND
http://www.altananam.freeserve.co.uk/
Personal tribute to the town of Ballycastle in County Antrim. The site includes a map of the area, together with an illustrated guide to the places of interest in the town.

BECKETT, SAMUEL END PAGE
http://beckett.english.ucsb.edu/
Features a biography, chronology, and bibliography of the writer. This site also includes a list of Beckett's contemporaries, the home of the official Samuel Beckett Society and general information on the Theatre of the Absurd.

BELFAST CASTLE
http://www.belfastcastle.co.uk/
Illustrated history of Belfast Castle from Belfast City Council. Featured on this site is information on the castle's gardens, its location, and also its commercial enterprises.

BERKELEY, GEORGE
http://www.knuten.liu.se/%7Ebjoch509/philosophers/ber.html
Devoted to the life and works of the philosopher George Berkeley. The biography includes an extensive appreciation by the 18th-century writer Joseph Stock. There are also links to his works including *Treaties Concerning the Principles of Human Knowledge*, *Three Dialogues*, and *The Analyst*. In addition, there are images and a link to another Berkeley site.

BINCHY, MAEVE
http://www.readireland.ie/aotm/Binchy.html
Detailed biography of the writer. There is also an analysis and description of some of her writing.

BLARNEY CASTLE
http://www.historic.irishcastles.com/blarney.htm
Describes the history of Blarney Castle and the Blarney Stone, together with numerous photographs and a video. Also included are links to related Web sites.

BLOODY SUNDAY
http://cain.ulst.ac.uk/events/bsunday/sum.htm
Dignified but moving account of the events that took place in Derry, on 30 January 1972, which came to be known as Bloody Sunday. Part of the Conflict Archive on the Internet (CAIN) Web site, this page contains quotations from some of the protagonists and those involved in subsequent inquiries into the deaths that occurred.

BRANAGH, KENNETH
http://www.geocities.com/~realbillie/ken.html
Profile of the dynamic actor and director. There is a listing of the television, stage, and film productions in which Branagh has been involved. A 'Frequently Asked Questions' provides biographical details. There is also regularly updated news of Branagh's latest projects, plus links to other related sites, and photos.

BUNRATTY CASTLE
http://www.historic.irishcastles.com/bunratty.htm
Features a history of Bunratty Castle, County Clare, together with a selection of photographs. Also included are links to related Web sites.

BURREN
http://www.hooked.net/~comber/
Guide to the Burren, a region in County Clare. The site features articles on the Burren's main attractions, such as the Cliffs of Moher, Leamaneh Castle, and its wild flowers. A bibliography is also included.

CAHIR CASTLE
http://www.historic.irishcastles.com/cahir.htm
Features a history of Cahir Castle, together with a selection of photographs. Also included are links to related sites.

CAMOGIE
http://www.gaa.ie/sports/camogie/index.html
Detailed guide to the sport camogie, including a history of the game. The site also features information on forthcoming fixtures.

CASTLE RACKRENT
http://mockingbird.creighton.edu/english/micsun/IrishResources/CastleRackrent/rackcont.htm
Includes the complete text of novelist Maria Edgeworth's *Castle Rackrent*, first published in 1800.

CATHOLIC EMANCIPATION
http://dspace.dial.pipex.com/mbloy/peel/emancip.htm
Page devoted to the Catholic emancipation movement, which brought an end to legislation barring Roman Catholics from holding public office or voting in elections. The text outlines the significance of the movement to the career of Robert Peel, Chief Secretary for Ireland, the subject of the larger site from which this page is taken, and to the awakening consciousness of Irish nationalism.

CHIEFTAINS, THE
http://www.bmgclassics.com/irish/chieftains/tearsoftone/index.html
Official site of the band, offering an illustrated biography, discography, and numerous press reviews. There are also several audio and video files, as well as details of forthcoming live appearances.

CLARE IRELAND
http://www.clareireland.com/
Informative and well-designed guide to County Clare. Aimed at both locals and tourists, this site features information on accommodation, sight-seeing, and cultural attractions. It also offers a map of the area.

CLONMEL, VIRTUAL TOUR OF
http://ireland.iol.ie/tip/clontour.htm
Guide to Clonmel, the largest inland town in the Republic of Ireland. The site offers descriptions of a number of

Clonmel's attractions, and even suggests several walks through the town, though it lacks photographs.

COLLEGIANS, THE
http://mockingbird.creighton.edu/english/micsun/IrishResources/Collegians/collcont.htm
Complete text of novelist and dramatist Gerald Griffin's book *The Collegians*, first published in 1829 and later adapted by Dion Boucicault as the hugely successful play, *The Colleen Bawn*.

COLLINS, MICHAEL
http://www2.cruzio.com/~sbarrett/mcollins.htm
Full details of the turbulent life of the Irish nationalist hero. It traces his childhood and role in the Easter Rising, the Anglo–Irish War, and civil war. There is a poem in tribute of 'the Big Fella'.

COMPLETE GUIDE TO IRELAND
http://members.tripod.com/~AndrewGallagher/ireland/
Guide to the geography, history, and politics of Ireland. The site can be viewed with or without frames and also includes sections on sport, tourism, culture, and the Celts.

CONFIRMATION SUIT, THE
http://www.ireland-information.com/confirmationsuit.htm
Features a brief biography of writer and dramatist Brendan Behan, as well as the complete text of his short story *The Confirmation Suit*.

CONNEMARA, IRELAND
http://www.connemara-ireland.com/
Large source of well-presented information on this western region. The site includes information on landscape, history, accommodation, restaurants, tourist attractions, business information, and genealogy. There is also a map and descriptions of a large number of towns.

CONQUEST OF IRELAND
http://www.fordham.edu/halsall/source/geraldwales1.html
Excerpt from Giraldus Cambrensis's 12th-century account of the Norman conquest of Ireland, taken from the Internet Medieval Library.

CORK FILM FESTIVAL
http://www.corkfilmfest.org/
Official Web site of the Cork International Film Festival, established in 1956. Featured here are the latest news on the festival, the complete programme listing, as well as background information about the event.

CORK GUIDE ONLINE
http://www.cork-guide.ie/corkcity.htm
Good source of information on Ireland's third-largest city. A description of the city, its heritage, and attractions is accompanied by some fine photographs. There is also information on accommodation, entertainment, transport, and restaurants.

CORN LAWS, CAMPAIGN FOR THE REPEAL OF THE
http://dialspace.dial.pipex.com/town/terrace/adw03/peel/c-laws2.htm
Information on the campaign for repeal of the Corn Laws, focussing on the Anti-Corn Law League. This page, part of a larger site on politics in the time of Robert Peel, gives a concise analysis of the Corn Law crisis and its effect on the Peel administration, its significance in the wider sphere of political reform, and the impact of the famine on the cause of repeal.

CROMWELLIAN CONQUEST OF IRELAND, THE
http://www.thehistorynet.com/MilitaryHistory/articles/1999/10992_cover.htm
Article reprinted from *Military History* magazine on Oliver Cromwell's ruthless suppression of the rebellion of the 1640s. The page contains an abstract as well as the lengthy and detailed full text version, and links to a profile of Cromwell and an editorial on leadership.

CURRAGH RACECOURSE, WELCOME TO THE
http://www.curragh.ie/
Site of Ireland's premier racecourse. There is a good history of the Curragh and descriptions of facilities for punters. This site also includes information on the Irish Derby and other events, and a link to the Irish National Stud.

DARK LADY OF THE SONNETS, THE
http://www.clubi.ie/qualitycompany/ss/darklady.txt
Includes the complete text of dramatist George Bernard Shaw's *The Dark Lady of the Sonnets*.

DERRY, CITY OF
http://www.interknowledge.com/northern-ireland/ukidcr00.htm
Official Web site of the Northern Ireland tourist office on the city of Derry/Londonderry. The Web site briefly describes the history and major attractions of the city; photographs of several of these attractions are included on the page. The surrounding area is also described on this Web site, including the Sperrin Mountains and County Derry.

DEVENISH ISLAND
http://www.cassidyclan.org/devinish.htm
Detailed and well-illustrated history of Devenish Island, County Fermanagh. The site pays particular attention to the island's religious significance, but also includes practical information on its attractions and how it can be reached. Also featured are links to related subjects.

DONEGAL
http://www.infowing.ie/donegal/
Informative guide to County Donegal, with sections for tourists, residents, and businesses. The site covers accommodation and restaurants, as well as forthcoming events and cultural activities.

DOWN, COUNTY
http://www.interknowledge.com/northern-
ireland/ukidwn00.htm
Official Web site of the Northern Ireland tourist office on
County Down. The Web site briefly describes the history
and major attractions of the county, and photographs of
several of these attractions are included on the page. The
Web site also features further pages of information on the
county, such as descriptions of St Patrick's Grave and the
Mountains of Mourne.

DOWN DISTRICT COUNCIL
http://www.downdc.gov.uk/
Official guide to County Down. Services provided by local
government, the functioning of local democracy, and business opportunities are well described. There is a list of
tourist attractions in the county and a brief history. However, there isn't that much practical information for visitors
here.

DRUID THEATRE
http://www.library.nuigalway.ie/druid/
Includes the history of the Druid Theatre in Galway, as well
as contact details and an overview of past performances.

ENYA
http://www.repriserec.com/enya/
From the Reprise record label, this site features numerous
sound and video files from the singer, musician, and composer Enya. Also included are links to related sites.

FAMINE, COMMEMORATION OF THE GREAT
http://www.toad.net/~sticker/nosurrender/PotatCo
m.html
Comprehensive account of the potato famine and its consequences for Ireland. The disaster is traced through examination of contemporary accounts as well as through historical
articles placing the famine within the broader history of Ireland. There are a large number of photos. This well-written
site is of interest to anybody studying the history of Ireland.

FAMINE, VIEWS OF THE
http://vassun.vassar.edu/~sttaylor/FAMINE/
Using contemporary accounts from both Irish and English
sources, this site attempts to portray the horrors of the
Great Famine. It includes a selection of illustrations and
paintings related to the period.

FERMANAGH DISTRICT COUNCIL
http://www.fermanagh.gov.uk/
Official guide to the county. A useful and expandable map is
offered on the home page. There are also some details of its
history, amenities, local government functions, and business
opportunities.

FIRST CONFESSION, THE
http://www.ireland-information.com/
firstconfession.htm
Complete text of writer Frank O'Connor's short story *The
First Confession*.

FRIEL, BRIAN
http://www.eng.umu.se/lughnasa/brian.htm
Dedicated to the playwright Brian Friel, this site includes a
biography, guide to his work, and suggestions for possible
interpretations of his plays. Also featured is a guide to further study.

GAELIC AND GAELIC CULTURE
http://sunsite.unc.edu/gaelic/gaelic.html
Dedicated to the Gaelic and Celtic culture and language.
This site includes information on the three Gaelic languages: Irish, Manx, and Scottish, along with audioclips
giving examples of each.

GAELIC ATHLETIC ASSOCIATION
http://www.gaa.ie/
Official site of the Gaelic Athletic Association that includes
news, a history of the organization, and information on its
structure. There are also details of forthcoming competitions and a selection of video clips.

GAELIC FOOTBALL
http://www.gaa.ie/sports/football/index.html
Detailed guide to Gaelic football, including a diagram illustrating the players' positions. The site also features the rules
for the game, as well as information on forthcoming fixtures.

GALWAY, COMPLETE GUIDE TO
http://www.wombat.ie/galwayguide/
Thorough and well-arranged source of information on this
western county. The needs of residents, tourists, and
investors are fully met with sections on attractions, transport, entertainment, accommodation, things to do with
children, community groups, and local government services. In addition to a good summary of Galway's history,
there are online versions of several detailed history books of
the county.

GARVAGHY ROAD RESIDENTS' COALITION
http://members.aol.com/garvaghy/index.html
The Drumcree stand-off explained from the point of view of
the organization representing the mainly nationalist residents of the Garvaghy Road. The polarity of the two points
of view, the would-be marchers and those refusing to be
marched upon, is a good illustration of the divisions within
Irish society.

GELDOF, BOB HOME PAGE
http://www.bobgeldof.com/
Dedicated to the musician and singer Bob Geldof, this site
includes a biography and photo gallery. Also featured are a
chat room, games room, and information on the causes
Geldof supports.

GOVERNMENT OF IRELAND
http://www.irlgov.ie/gov.htm
Complete guide to all the departments of the government,
including contact details. The 'Department of the taoiseach'
includes a virtual tour of the parliament building, complete

with the history of the position of taoiseach, or prime minister.

GUINNESS GLOBAL GATEWAY
http://www.guinness.ie/
Official Guinness Web site that describes itself as 'online refreshment'. The topics covered range from 'How to pour the perfect pint' to the history of the drink itself. There are also Guinness games, a brewing guide, and screen savers.

GUINNESS JAZZ FESTIVAL CORK 2000
http://www.corkjazzfestival.com/
Complete guide to the Cork Jazz Festival. The site features the complete programme listing, as well as booking information and a history of the event, which was founded in 1977.

HAMILTON, SIR WILLIAM ROWAN
http://www-history.mcs.st-and.ac.uk/history/Mathematicians/Hamilton.html
Extensive biography of the mathematician. The site contains a description of his contribution to mathematics, and in particular his discovery of quaternions. The Web site includes a page from his notebook on which there are several examples of the multiplication of quaternions. Several literature references for further reading are also listed, and the Web site also features a portrait of Hamilton.

HEDGE SCHOOL, THE
http://mockingbird.creighton.edu/english/micsun/IrishResources/carlcont.htm
Features the complete text of novelist William Carleton's *The Hedge School*.

HURLING
http://www.gaa.ie/sports/hurling/
Detailed guide to the sport of hurling, including a diagram illustrating the players' positions. The site also includes the rules for the game, as well as information on hurling competitions.

IMPORTANCE OF BEING EARNEST, THE
http://www.clubi.ie/qualitycompany/ss/earnest.txt
Complete text of writer Oscar Wilde's play *The Importance of Being Earnest*, first published in 1895.

INTERACTIVE TRAVEL GUIDE TO THE BEST OF IRELAND
http://www.iol.ie/~discover/welcome.htm
Visit this site to find out more about Ireland. Down the righthand side of the screen there is an index of places throughout the four provinces. Across the bottom is a list of topics such as 'Accommodation', 'Pictures', 'Business', and 'What's on'.

IRELAND'S POTATO FAMINE
http://www.geocities.com/Athens/Rhodes/6477/potato.html
Concise and well-balanced page on the potato famine, notable for its attempt to look at a hugely emotive topic from both sides of the argument. The text covers the background to the famine, explaining the risks involved in over-dependence on the potato and the factors that conspired to turn an attack of blight into a national catastrophe.

IRISH FREE STATE AND CIVIL WAR
http://news1.thls.bbc.co.uk/hi/english/events/northern_ireland/history/newsid_64000/64206.stm
Useful, impartial summary of the complex and emotive events that led to the partition of Ireland. Part of a British Broadcasting Corporation (BBC) Web site on the conflict in Northern Ireland, this page contains a timeline as well as a short article on the founding of the Irish Free State and the start of the Irish Civil War. Contemporary photographs illustrate the text.

IRISH HISTORY ON THE WEB
http://wwwvms.utexas.edu/~jdana/irehist.html
Well-organized source of information about Irish history, including issues regarding home rule. There are sections on general history, the famine, timelines, key documents, suggested reading, and genealogical research links.

IRISH IN AMERICA: LONG JOURNEY HOME
http://www.pbs.org/wghh/pages/irish/
Companion to a US Public Broadcasting Service (PBS) television programme, this site chronicles the significant role that Irish immigrants have had in shaping the USA. It is divided into five sections covering genealogy, music, language, and notable Irish-Americans. Here you can learn how to trace immigrant ancestors; hear how surnames sound in the native language, hear the roots of some common US English words, and learn about the history of the language; read about the instruments and music used in the series' soundtrack; listen to an poem about the Great Famine; and read brief biographies of some of the many important Irish-Americans.

IRV THE SWERVE
http://www.geocities.com/MotorCity/7864/
Fan site devoted to Formula 1 star Eddie Irvine. The site contains a biography of the Ferrari driver, and a page of statistics on his Grand Prix career.

JAMES JOYCE WEB SITE
http://www.2street.com/joyce
Dedicated to the appreciation and analysis of the literary works of writer James Joyce. The site includes articles, e-texts, maps, links to both online and offline Joycean resources, a timeline, multimedia, and the online journal *Hypermedia Joyce Studies*.

KELLS, BOOK OF
http://www.geocities.com/Heartland/Park/6748/kells.html
Central source of information about the famous manuscript, including stunning high resolution images. There are links to research about the manuscript and further sources of

information about Celtic knotwork and other Celtic and Anglo-Saxon manuscripts.

KERRY INSIGHT
http://ireland.iol.ie/kerry-insight/
Guide to the county. This site includes sections on fishing, sports, entertainment, accommodation, places of historical interest, events and festivals, an extensive commercial directory, community organizations, guides to towns in the county, maps, and a weather report.

KILDARE, COUNTY
http://travel.lycos.com/Destinations/Europe/Ireland/County_Kildare/
Large source of information on the county. There are guides to the main towns and attractions in Kildare, a description of the county and its economy, and a map. Accommodation information and links to local media and institutions are also included.

KILKENNY, WELCOME TO COUNTY
http://www.countykilkenny.com/
Detailed guide to County Kilkenny. The site includes maps and information on accommodation, and describes the county's cultural attractions, wildlife, and restaurants. An illustrated account of the county's heritage is also included.

KILKENNY CASTLE
http://www.historic.irishcastles.com/kilkenny.htm
Features a history of Kilkenny Castle, together with a selection of photographs. Also included are links to related sites.

KILLARNEY ONLINE
http://www.killarneyonline.ie/
Good source of information on Killarney and its famous lakes. There is a profile of the city, its history, and economy. This site offers comprehensive information on accommodation, local places of interest, and a wide range of leisure activities.

LIBERATION OF IRELAND
http://homepages.iol.ie/~dluby/history.htm
Introduction to modern Irish history, from the Easter rising of 1916 to the present day. It includes biographies and pictures on important figures involved in the struggle for independence. There's a chart of all prime ministers and presidents and it even plays the national anthem if you have the correct plug-in.

LIMERICK ONLINE
http://www.limerickonline.com/
Large source of information on the county. There are descriptions of the county, Limerick, and other towns. Other sections include details of accommodation, entertainment, a weather report, and an online version of a local newspaper.

MAGH EÓ, HISTORY OF (MAYO ABBEY)
http://www.mayo-ireland.ie/Mayo/Towns/MayAbbey/HistMAbb/HistMAbb.htm
History of the abbey from which the county of Mayo takes its name. The abbey was founded in the 7th century, and this Web site explains the motives for its slightly unusual location in the centre of a plain miles from anywhere. The Web site also features a wealth of historical details about the abbey and the surrounding area from the time of its founding right up to the present day.

MALAHIDE CASTLE
http://www.historic.irishcastles.com/malahide.htm
Features an informative history of Malahide Castle, together with a selection of photographs. Also included are links to related sites.

MAYO ON THE MOVE
http://www.mayo-ireland.ie/motm.htm
Comprehensive guide to Mayo, for both residents and tourists. The site contains information on accommodation, transport, and leisure activities. It also features sections on less common topics, such as healing, farming, and genealogy.

MOORE, THOMAS, SELECTED POETRY OF (1779–1852)
http://www.library.utoronto.ca/utel/rp/authors/moore.html
Contains the text of a number of the poet's works, including 'Lalla Rookh' and 'Time I've Lost in Wooing'.

NATIONAL ANCIENT ORDER OF HIBERNIANS WEB SITE
http://www.aoh.com/
Official site of the Ancient Order of the Hibernians, the Irish-American Catholic society, in the USA. There are links to the Web sites of local divisions of the AOH, as well as a detailed history of the organization, a listing of forthcoming events, and information on becoming a member.

NEESON, LIAM
http://mrshowbiz.com/people/liamneeson/
Interesting profile of the actor. It traces his childhood interest in boxing, his training as a teacher, interest in amateur dramatics, growing experience in cinema, promotion to lead status, and fame won through the title role in *Schindler's List*. There are also sections on recent show business news and a more fullsome biography.

NIO ONLINE
http://www.nio.gov.uk/index.htm
Comprehensive information on the administration of criminal justice, security, and the police in Northern Ireland. Frequently updated, this site charts the latest developments in the search for peace and also provides a good introduction to the economy and culture of Ulster.

NORTHERN IRELAND ASSEMBLY
http://www.ni-assembly.gov.uk/index.htm
Information about the Assembly, its publications and committees, and a 'Register of members' interests'.

NORTHERN IRELAND PEACE AGREEMENT
http://www.nio.gov.uk/agreement.htm
Full transcript of the historic 1998 Good Friday agreement, which agreed on the devolution of a wide range of executive and legislative powers from the UK Parliament to a Northern Ireland Assembly.

NORTHERN IRELAND PUBLIC SERVICE WEB
http://www.nics.gov.uk/
Details of many government services, including the departments of agriculture, economic development, the environment, and health and social services for Northern Ireland.

NORTHERN IRELAND TOURIST BOARD
http://www.ni-tourism.com/index.asp
This site covers the needs of anyone planning to visit Northern Ireland, from accommodation to events and attractions. It also features a virtual tour covering history, activities, food and drink, and places to stay.

NOWLANS, THE
http://mockingbird.creighton.edu/english/micsun/IrishResources/Nowlans/nowlcont.htm
Complete text of writer John Banim's book *The Nowlans*, published in 1826.

PATRICK, ST
http://www.newadvent.org/cathen/11554a.htm
Extended account of the long life of the patron saint of Ireland from the *Catholic Encyclopedia*. It relates how his six years as a kidnap victim prepared him for his future apostolic work to convert the Irish. His many journeys in Ireland are described with the help of extracts from Irish texts. His work to build the church is described in detail, together with a summary of his *Confessio*.

PEARSE, PATRICK
http://wwwvms.utexas.edu/~jdana/pearsehist.html
All-text biography of the turn-of-the-century poet and nationalist.

PLANTATIONS OF HENRY VIII TO THE CREATION OF AN IRISH REPUBLIC
http://wwwvms.utexas.edu/~jdana/towwii.html
Concise discussion of Henry VIII's plantation of protestant settlers in Ireland, with the aim of subduing the turbulent Gaelic natives, and its disastrous consequences. The author traces a direct causal chain between the plantations, continued enthusiastically by Henry's successors, and the birth of Irish republicanism.

OLIVER PLUNKETT, BLESSED
http://www.newadvent.org/cathen/12169b.htm
Biography of the martyred Jesuit. It traces his distinguished academic studies, his ordination, his successes as Primate of Ireland, and his forbearance as he was led to execution at Tyburn. There is an account of the miracles associated with his relics.

PORTADOWN DISTRICT ORANGE LODGE NO. 1 CIVIL RIGHTS WEB SITE
http://www.orangenet.org/civilrights/content.htm
Orange Order Web site explains the Drumcree stand-off from its own point of view, painting the dispute, between the parading Orange order and the Catholic residents who refuse them access through their housing estate, as a human rights issue.

REAPING RACE, THE
http://www.ireland-information.com/thereapingrace.htm
Includes a brief biography of writer and radical Liam O'Flaherty, and also the complete text of his short story *The Reaping Race*.

RIDERS TO THE SEA
http://etext.lib.virginia.edu/etcbin/browse-mixed-new?id=SynRide&tag=public&images=images/modeng&data=/texts/english/modeng/parsed
Complete text of this play by J M Synge. This site also features a number of illustrations from the print edition of the work.

ROCK OF CASHEL
http://www.historic.irishcastles.com/rockofcashel.htm
Features a detailed history of the Rock of Cashel in the Republic of Ireland, together with a selection of photographs and video footage. Also included are links to related sites.

SINN FÉIN
http://sinnfeln.ie/index.html
Against a background of a green and united Ireland, the oldest political party in Ireland presents its case. There are extensive links to sites supporting the republican cause in Northern Ireland. The online edition of the *An Phoblacht* newspaper provides a republican outlook on the search for a lasting peace in Northern Ireland.

SODA BREAD WISDOM
http://www.ibmpcug.co.uk/~owls/sodabred.htm
Soda bread recipes and history. If you've ever thought of making this variety of bread this would be a good place to find out how, and if you haven't, then it's a good place to find out why maybe you should.

STONES OF IRELAND
http://www.stonepages.com/Ireland/Ireland.html
Reference guide with impressive photos from a variety of stone circles, dolmens, court and passage tombs, cairns, and stone forts from around Ireland.

ST PATRICK'S DAY
http://www.st-patricks-day.com/
Comprehensive source of information on the legend of St Patrick and the history of celebrations on 17 March. The significance of the shamrock is also explained. There is also regularly updated information on St Patrick's Day celebra-

tions and St Patrick societies in Ireland and around the world.

TARA LITERARY PROJECT
http://www.iol.ie/~discovry/taralit.htm
Describes the Tara Literary and Historical project which aims to survey the documents in which Tara is mentioned and to construct the history of Tara from about AD 600 to the present century. In Irish mythology Tara is the seat of the high kings of Ireland.

THIN LIZZY WORLD WIDE WEB PAGE
http://www2.uncg.edu/~edpoole/
Comprehensive guide to the rock band Thin Lizzy. Featured here are a biography and timeline of the band, as well as numerous lyrics and images. Also included are links to related sites.

TONE, BIOGRAPHY OF THEOBALD WOLFE
http://www.esatclear.ie/~ei5em/tone.html
Clear and well-balanced biography of the revolutionary leader, attached to a personal home page. The page contains excerpts from Tone's speeches as well as an analysis of his significance to the history of Irish nationalism.

TOP FORTY IRISH FAMILY NAMES
http://www.genealogy.ie/categories/familynames/index.htm
Listing of the most popular family names, together with a description of the name's derivation. This page is part of a larger site on genealogy.

TRIM CASTLE
http://www.historic.irishcastles.com/trim.htm
Features an informative history of Trim Castle in the Republic of Ireland, together with a selection of photographs. Also included are links to related sites.

TYRONE, COUNTY
http://www.interknowledge.com/northern-ireland/ukityr00.htm
Official Web site of the Northern Ireland tourist office on County Tyrone. The Web site briefly describes the history and major attractions of the county, and photographs of several of these attractions are included on the page.

U2 ZONE
http://www.theu2zone.com/
Well-designed tribute to the rock band U2 that features a discography, complete with numerous sound clips and lyrics for many of their songs. There are also several video clips and screen savers, as well as an illustrated history of the band.

ULSTER UNIONIST PARTY
http://www.uup.org/
Union Jack-filled site of Ulster's main political party. This well-organized site has comprehensive information on the party, its officers and party conferences. The constantly updated current affairs section presents a detailed exposition of mainstream Unionist views on the difficult search for a lasting peace.

UNIVERSITY OF DUBLIN – TRINITY COLLEGE
http://www.tcd.ie/
Features information on Trinity College's courses, faculties, and attractions. Also included here are sections on the history of the college, its library, and forthcoming events.

VAN MORRISON HOME PAGE
http://www.harbour.sfu.ca/~hayward/van/
Lots of information about Van Morrison and his music. There's even a glossary of terms and references, from barmbrack to Wagon Wheel biscuits, found in his lyrics.

WATERFORD CITY
http://goireland.miningco.com/library/weekly/aa092297.htm
Guide to the city. There is a description of the prosperous modern town and an outline of its history. Details are provided about monuments and other sites in the town, together with practical information on food, accommodation, and entertainment.

WATERFORD, IRELAND
http://www.cs.ncl.ac.uk/genuki/irl/Waterford/
Good source of information on the southeastern county. Profiles of the main communities may be accessed through the interactive map on the home page. There is a good description of Waterford's distinctive geology and landscape, and a summary of the county's rich history.

WELCOME TO COUNTY WICKLOW – THE GARDEN OF IRELAND
http://www.wicklow.ie/
Well-arranged guide to this eastern county from the local Enterprise Board. An interesting virtual tour of the county can be accessed via a 'clickable' map. In addition to details of the county's history and heritage, there is a wealth of practical information for both visitors and residents alike.

WEXFORD FESTIVAL OPERA
http://www.wexfordopera.com/
Comprehensive guide to the Wexford Festival Opera, in County Wexford, including information on concerts, events, and artists. Also featured is a history of the festival, a photo gallery, and information on travelling to the event.

YEATS, W B
http://www.lit.kobe-u.ac.jp/~hishika/yeats.htm
Appreciation of the life and work of the poet as well as links to more than 300 poems, class notes for teaching on the poet, newsletters, and Yeats fan clubs.

PICTURE CREDITS